2017 Annual Competitiveness Analysis and Impact of Exchange Rates on Foreign Direct Investment Inflows to Sub-National Economies of Indonesia

NUS National University of Singapore

LKY Lee Kuan Yew School of Public Policy
ASIA COMPETITIVENESS INSTITUTE

In 2016 and 2017, ACI was ranked 13th globally, 2nd in Asia and 1st in Singapore amongst 90 think tanks worldwide under the "Best University Affiliated Think Tank" category by the Think Tanks and Civil Societies Program at the University of Pennsylvania, USA.

About ACI

The Asia Competitiveness Institute (ACI) was established in August 2006 as a research centre at the Lee Kuan Yew School of Public Policy (LKYSPP), National University of Singapore (NUS). It aims to build the intellectual leadership and network for understanding and developing competitiveness in the Asia region. ACI seeks to contribute to the enhancement of inclusive growth, living standards and institutional governance through competitiveness research on sub-national economies in Asia. It identifies mitigating issues and challenges for potential public policy interventions through close collaboration with regional governments, business corporations, policy think-tanks and academics. ACI's three key research pillars include (i) sub-national economies level competitiveness analysis and city-level liveability analysis, (ii) firm-level competitiveness analysis in 16 Asia economies, and (iii) Singapore's long-term growth strategies and public policy analysis.

ACI's value propositions may be encapsulated in its acronym:
Analytical inputs to initiate policies for policy-makers and business leaders in Asia
Capacity building to enable others through improvement in productivity and efficiency
Intellectual leadership to create pragmatic models of competitiveness and inclusive growth

The institute's core research competencies can also be encapsulated in this acronym describing our evidence-based assessments conducted on public policies for **A**SEAN in the context of the rise of **C**hina and **I**ndia.

Vision and Mission

- ACI's over-arching vision is to build up its research credibility with policy impact, contributing as a professional, world-class think-tank.
- ACI's mission is to establish our niche as a leading policy think-tank by identifying competitiveness trends, opportunities and challenges, as well as promoting competition and synergising complementarities amongst Asian economies and business corporations.
- ACI endeavours to articulate sound recommendations, entice discourse, and shape agenda in the arena of public policy amongst Asian governments.
- ACI undertakes evidence-based analysis of public policy issues and decisions, in order to provide assessment of their effectiveness as well as economic and societal impact.

Research Initiatives and Collaborations

I. Identify trends of competitiveness and policy analysis on trade and investment of ASEAN, within the regional context of competition and complementarities with China and India.
II. Identify competitive strengths and conduct policy analysis on Singapore within the context of regional economies with international benchmarking.
III. We are regularly releasing three indices on liveability ranking including 64 Global Cities, 100 Greater China Cities and 17 Shandong Cities.
IV. We have established an Ease of Doing Business Index on Attractiveness to Investors, Business Friendliness and Competitive Policies for 21 sub-national economies of India and 33 sub-national economies of Indonesia.
V. We have signed Memoranda of Understanding with The World Bank (2015), SPRING Singapore (2014) and European Central Bank (2014). The Memorandum of Understanding between The World Bank and National University of Singapore, coordinated through ACI, was signed in 2016.

VI. We have signed Memoranda of Understanding with various institutions in Greater China economies, including Shanghai Academy of Social Sciences (2016), Shandong Academy of Social Sciences (2015), Chongqing Municipal People's Government (2015), China Institute for Reform and Development, Haikou (2015), Counsellors' Office of the People's Government of Guangdong Province (LOI, 2014) and Chung-Hua Institution for Economic Research, Taiwan (2015).

VII. We have signed Memoranda of Understanding with six Chief Ministers' Offices in Andhra Pradesh (2015 & 2017), Bihar (2015), Chhattisgarh (2015), Madhya Pradesh (2015), Odisha (2015) and Punjab (2015).

VIII. We have signed Memoranda of Understanding with Committee for Acceleration of Priority Infrastructure Delivery at Coordinating Ministry for Economic Affairs, Indonesia (2016), Indonesia Investment Coordinating Board (2014), Indonesian Agency for Agricultural Research and Development at Ministry of Agriculture (2014), Indonesian President's Delivery Unit for Developing Monitoring and Oversight (2013) and Employer's Association of Indonesia (2013).

IX. We have signed Memoranda of Understanding with ASEAN think-tanks and institutions, including Vietnam Chamber of Commerce and Industry (2016), Centre for Strategic and International Studies, Indonesia (2015), Institute of Strategic & International Studies, Malaysia (2015), Philippine Institute for Development Studies (2015), Thailand Development Research Institute (2015) and Central Institute for Economic Management, Vietnam (2015).

About ACI's Research Pillars

ACI has consciously engaged in economic research that has significant relevance to Singapore and the Asian region. Over the years, ACI has focused on our expertise in quantitative competitiveness analysis and simulation, spinning off volumes of research output in the applications of our methodology and regional insight. At this stage, ACI has identified three core research pillars that will guide and define its research efforts moving forward. The three research pillars are as follows:

Pillar I. Sub-national Economies Competitiveness Analysis

ACI engages in systematic and methodical competitiveness analyses of the *sub-national economies* by using an evidence-based, empirical approach involving a comprehensive list of relevant indicators, which are categorised under multiple layers called the 'environments'. A number of our projects, including competitiveness analyses of Greater China, ASEAN-10, India, and Indonesia, as well as other thematic research projects, were conducted by adopting this common methodology, with potential variations in the specific environments and indicators. ACI's competitiveness analysis of Asian economies goes beyond the usual ranking to offer constructive policy recommendations on how individual member states can improve their rankings vis-à-vis their sub-national or regional peers through the application of the 'what-if' simulation, which provides the projected improvements of each state's ranking whereby the bottom one-fifth of its indicators are enhanced.

Pillar II. Micro-based Firm Level Competitiveness Analysis

Micro-based firm level competitiveness analysis is ACI's second research pillar that has been developed in view of the intrinsic importance of firm-level competitiveness in terms of productivity, efficiency, and governance. In the context of globalisation, mobility of economic activities, and blurring of borders, an understanding of the determinants and dynamics of firm-level competitiveness is paramount, in order for policy makers to make adjustments and prepare their industries for an increasingly competitive economic landscape. To this end, ACI has partnered with the European Central Bank to carry out research in this area, possessing a solid foundation in firm-level productivity research in the form of European Competitiveness Network database and methodology. ACI envisaged the expansion of CompNet into Asia, thereby pioneering the Asia CompNet research network encompassing 16 economies in Asia.

Pillar III. Singapore's Long-term Economic Growth Strategies and Public Policies Analysis

The third and imminent research pillar focuses on Singapore's long-term economic growth strategies in the context of changing circumstances, future trends, and emerging opportunities for Singapore in the decades ahead. In particular, ACI will take on the task of critically examining Singapore's public policy strengths and areas of improvement by assessing policy successes of the past, identifying new issues to address and the current policy gaps, through a systematic and evidence-based research inquiry using quantitative methodology and empirical data, leveraging on our network of policy experts.

Founding Patron and International Advisory Panel

Founding Patron

Mr George Yeo
Visiting Scholar, Lee Kuan Yew School of Public Policy, National University of Singapore & Former Minister of Foreign Affairs, Singapore

International Advisory Panel

Co-Chairs:

Professor Michael Porter (2006-2010)
Bishop William Lawrence University Professor

Ms Marjorie Yang (2006-2012)
Chairman, Esquel Group

Members:

Professor Kishore Mahbubani
Dean, Lee Kuan Yew School of Public Policy, National University of Singapore

Dr Kuntoro Mangkusubroto
Head, President's Delivery Unit for Developing Monitoring and Oversight (UKP4), Indonesia

Mr Narayana Murthy
Chairman, Infosys Technologies Limited

Mr Philip Yeo
Chairman, SPRING Singapore

Mr Loh Khum Yean
Permanent Secretary, Ministry of Trade and Industry

Ms Yong Ying-I
Permanent Secretary, Public Service Division

Professor Chan Kam Leung Alan
Dean, College of Humanities, Arts and Social Sciences, Nanyang Technological University

Asia Competitiveness Institute

Co-Directors:

Associate Professor Tan Khee Giap (2011 till now)
Professor Tan Kong Yam (2011 till now)

Asia Competitiveness Institute - World Scientific Series

(ISSN: 2424-9912)

Series Editor: Tan Khee Giap (*Lee Kuan Yew School of Public Policy, NUS, Singapore*)

In the tradition of the Asia Competitiveness Institute (ACI) at the Lee Kuan Yew School of Public Policy, National University of Singapore (NUS), our research publications make a distinctive contribution to the understanding of economic development in Asia. These books, first published in 2013, in the Asia Competitiveness Institute - World Scientific Series evaluate and track competitiveness for the sub-national economies of China, India, Indonesia and ASEAN annually through combining leading-edge methodologies with an extensive dataset. The study covers four environments of competitiveness: (1) Macroeconomic Stability, (2) Government and Institutional Setting, (3) Financial, Businesses and Manpower Conditions, and (4) Quality of Life and Infrastructure Development. It also conducts "what-if" policy simulations to propose policy suggestions.

2017

2017 Annual Competitiveness Analysis and Impact of Exchange Rates on Foreign Direct Investment Inflows to ASEAN Economies
by Tan Khee Giap, Luu Nguyen Trieu Duong, Chuah Hui Yin & Nguyen Duy (Lee Kuan Yew School of Public Policy, NUS, Singapore)

Balanced, Sustainable and Competitiveness Enhancement Study for Vietnam: A Critical Evaluation with Development Potentials
by Vu Tien Loc (Vietnam Chamber of Commerce and Industry, Vietnam), Tan Khee Giap, Luu Nguyen Trieu Duong & Nguyen Duy (Lee Kuan Yew School of Public Policy, NUS, Singapore)

2017 Impact Estimation of Exchange Rate on Foreign Direct Investment Inflows and Annual Update of Competitiveness Analysis for 34 Greater China Economies
by Tan Khee Giap, Zhang Xuyao, Leong Puey Ei & Tan Yang En Isaac (Lee Kuan Yew School of Public Policy, NUS, Singapore)

2017 Annual Competitiveness Analysis and Impact of Exchange Rates on Foreign Direct Investment Inflows to Sub-National Economies of India
by Tan Khee Giap, Sasidaran Gopalan, Jigyasa Sharma & Leong Puey Ei (Lee Kuan Yew School of Public Policy, NUS, Singapore)

2017 Annual Competitiveness Analysis and Impact of Exchange Rates on Foreign Direct Investment Inflows to Sub-National Economies of Indonesia
by Tan Khee Giap, Mulya Amri, Nursyahida Ahmad & Diamanta Vania Lavi (Lee Kuan Yew School of Public Policy, NUS, Singapore)

2016

2016 Annual Competitiveness Analysis and Growth Slowdown Analysis for ASEAN-10
by Tan Khee Giap, Nguyen Le Phuong Anh & Luu Nguyen Trieu Duong (Lee Kuan Yew School of Public Policy, NUS, Singapore)

*More information on this series can also be found at http://www.worldscientific.com/series/aciwss

(Continued at end of book)

2017 Annual Competitiveness Analysis and Impact of Exchange Rates on Foreign Direct Investment Inflows to Sub-National Economies of Indonesia

Tan Khee Giap

Co-Director, Asia Competitiveness Institute
Lee Kuan Yew School of Public Policy, National University of Singapore

Mulya Amri

Research Fellow & Deputy Director (Research), Asia Competitiveness Institute
Lee Kuan Yew School of Public Policy, National University of Singapore

Nursyahida Ahmad

Research Assistant, Asia Competitiveness Institute
Lee Kuan Yew School of Public Policy, National University of Singapore

Diamanta Vania Lavi

Research Assistant, Asia Competitiveness Institute
Lee Kuan Yew School of Public Policy, National University of Singapore

Special Remarks

Bambang Brodjonegoro

Minister for National Development Planning Agency, Republic of Indonesia

Reviewers

Balthasar Kambuaya
Chairman, University Senate, Cenderawasih University and Former Minister for Environment (2011–2014), Republic of Indonesia

Darius Tirtosuharto
Economist, Economic and Monetary Policy Department, Macroeconomic Division, Bank of Indonesia, Republic of Indonesia

Sin Chor-Yiu
Professor, Department of Economics, College of Technology Management, National Tsing Hua University, Taiwan, Republic of China

APINDO

Lee Kuan Yew School of Public Policy
Asia Competitiveness Institute

NUS National University of Singapore

World Scientific

Published by

World Scientific Publishing Co. Pte. Ltd.
5 Toh Tuck Link, Singapore 596224
USA office: 27 Warren Street, Suite 401-402, Hackensack, NJ 07601
UK office: 57 Shelton Street, Covent Garden, London WC2H 9HE

British Library Cataloguing-in-Publication Data
A catalogue record for this book is available from the British Library.

Asia Competitiveness Institute – World Scientific Series
2017 ANNUAL COMPETITIVENESS ANALYSIS AND IMPACT OF EXCHANGE RATES ON FOREIGN DIRECT INVESTMENT INFLOWS TO SUB-NATIONAL ECONOMIES OF INDONESIA

ISBN 978-981-3272-27-9

Desk Editor: Jiang Yulin

Typeset by Stallion Press
Email: enquiries@stallionpress.com

Printed in Singapore

Contents

*Based on the speech "Indonesia's Development Strategies and Priorities in 2017" by Dr Bambang Brodjonegoro, Minister for National Development Planning Agency of Republic of Indonesia, during the Ministerial Forum at the 2017 The World Bank Group–Asia Competitiveness Institute Annual Conference on 23 November 2017 in Singapore.

Foreword

The year 2017 marks the fifth year of collaboration between the Indonesian Employers Association (APINDO) and the Asia Competitiveness Institute (ACI). Every year since 2012, APINDO has supported one of ACI's flagship research projects on the annual study of Indonesia's sub-national competitiveness. Such localised study requires empirical data from the ground, which is gathered through field trips that allow the ACI research team to meet with local stakeholders across the 33 provinces of Indonesia. With provincial chapters across all provinces, APINDO is proud to have once again collaborated with ACI by providing coordination support, allowing the research team to interact with local business owners and operators who are APINDO members in all 33 provinces.

Given the expansiveness of Indonesia, economic conditions in one province greatly differ from another. The ACI competitiveness study helps to shed light on these differences as well as the strengths and weaknesses of each province. More importantly, the ACI study benchmarks these provinces to one another, thus promoting desirable healthy competition which will not only boost an individual province's competitiveness but also Indonesia's competitiveness as a whole.

With this in mind, APINDO greatly welcomes the timely release of *2017 Annual Competitiveness Analysis and Impact of Exchange Rates on Foreign Direct Investment Inflows to Sub-National Economies of Indonesia*. In this book, I see two important value additions compared to the analysis done in the past years. First, ACI has applied a novel approach based on Shapley values for the assignment of indicator weights that incorporates an element of objectivity. The findings using the Shapley values remain consistent with that using the equal weights method; this validates the robustness of results obtained from the ACI competitiveness index over the past years.

The second value addition of this year's book is the thematic chapter on foreign direct investment (FDI) inflows into Indonesia's sub-national economies. It is in our interest as businessowners to have more FDI inflows into Indonesia. FDI would contribute to trigger more of the much-needed infrastructure building, absorb Indonesia's labour force and make the country more productive. Despite regional efforts to improve the ease of investing, FDI is also dependent on national-level policies such as that on exchange rates. The research finding on the impact of exchange rate fluctuations on FDI in Indonesia's subnational economies is an important and beneficial one, not just for academics and policymakers but also for business owners to understand how national-level policy might impact their businesses.

To sum up, ACI's attempts to improve its competitiveness index and its thematic research are a testament to the institute's dedication in producing rigorous and meaningful research. It is my hope that the ACI continues to work together with APINDO in conducting such research on Indonesia.

Hariyadi Sukamdani
Chairman
Indonesian Employers' Association (APINDO)

Preface

The Asia Competitiveness Institute (ACI) aims to contribute to a better understanding of the economic development in Asia by conducting empirical analyses on Singapore and its surrounding regions, such as China, India and the countries of ASEAN-10, which includes Indonesia as a rising middle power. Comprising more than 17,500 islands and situated across 34 provinces, Indonesia's diversity is beyond question. To make sense of the potentials and challenges facing this large nation, a more detailed view of the country's sub-national economies is thus needed.

Indonesia's economy has undergone various reforms in the past two decades. Under the administration of President Joko Widodo, the country has sought several measures to increase its attractiveness to investors by placing greater spending priority on public infrastructure and easing business regulations. To some extent, these efforts are coming to fruition as growth has picked up, although Indonesia is still performing below its full capacity. Amidst a more modest growth outlook, Indonesia is facing pertinent risks, such as the growing political exploitation of religious sentiments, environmental pollution and strained provisions of public services, particularly in its growth region of Java. Careful management of these risks is thus necessary to raise the speed and sustainability of economic growth in Indonesia.

With such dynamism observed in the country, it is vital to keep abreast of the developments at the sub-national levels. Hence, ACI's annual competitiveness analyses of Indonesia's provinces and sub-national regions are constantly being updated and complemented with relevant research topics. Currently in its fifth iteration, ACI has also included results of its latest study on the impacts of real effective exchange rate on the foreign direct investment inflows to the provinces of Indonesia. This study emerges in a timely manner as Indonesia is currently seeking to increase investment inflows throughout the regions. To further deepen the understanding of sub-national economies, this book also features local commentaries on the recent economic, social and political developments of all provinces in Indonesia.

In short, ACI's assessment of sub-national economic development provides important insights to help policymakers raise governance standards and improve regional competitiveness in a more sustainable way. I hope this study serves as a useful contribution to the ongoing policy discussion on Indonesia's quest to achieve a healthy, stable and broad-based economic growth.

Ramkishen S. Rajan
Vice Dean (Research) and Professor
Lee Kuan Yew School of Public Policy
National University of Singapore

Acknowledgements

The *2017 Annual Competitiveness Analysis and Impact of Exchange Rates on Foreign Direct Investment Inflows to Sub-National Economies of Indonesia* provides an update to our previous studies on provincial and regional competitiveness in Indonesia with the latest available data. Our comprehensive approach to measuring competitiveness takes into account different factors that collectively shape the ability of a nation or region to achieve substantial and inclusive economic development over a sustained period of time. In this latest instalment, we introduce a novel approach of weights assignment in the form of Shapley values as a robustness test to our findings. Furthermore, we analyse the impact of exchange rates on foreign direct investment inflows to the provinces of Indonesia. This book also includes a novel addition of commentaries on recent developments in the 34 Indonesian provinces, co-written by our academic partners in Indonesia.

The research that we conducted benefited immensely from the feedback and comments given for our preliminary findings during our annual flagship events in Singapore, namely: (i) the 2016 ACI–World Bank Greater China–India Economic Forum held on 2 September 2016; (ii) the 2016 Annual Asia Competitiveness Institute Conference on "Competitiveness Ranking of Sub-National Economies and Public Policy Studies in Greater China, India, Indonesia and ASEAN" held on 24 and 25 November 2016; as well as (iii) the 2017 Asia Economic Forum on "The One-Belt One-Road Initiative: Impact and Implications" held on 29 August 2017. For these constructive feedback and comments, we would like to thank the following experts and reviewers, whose welcome notes are reproduced in this book:

- Professor Balthasar Kambuaya
  Chairman, University Senate Cenderawasih University; former Minister for Environment (2011–2014), Republic of Indonesia
- Dr Darius Tirtosuharto
  Economist, Economic and Monetary Policy Department
  Macroeconomic Division, Bank of Indonesia
- Professor Sin Chor-Yiu
  Department of Economics,
  College of Technology Management, National Tsing Hua University
  Taiwan, Republic of China

We also would like to extend our deepest appreciation for the support and encouragement we received from the following Indonesian leaders:

- Dr Bambang Brodjonegoro, Minister for National Development Planning Agency (Bappenas), Republic of Indonesia — for delivering a speech on development strategies and priorities of Indonesia's economy during our 2017 The World Bank Group–Asia Competitiveness Institute Annual Conference on 23 November 2017 in Singapore. Dr Bambang's speech is reproduced in Chapter 1 of this book.
- Dr Luky Eko Wuryanto, Vice President and Chief Administration Officer, Asian Infrastructure Investment Bank and former Deputy Minister for Infrastructure and Regional Development, Coordinating Ministry for Economic Affairs, Republic of Indonesia — for being a distinguished dinner speaker at the ACI 2017 Annual Conference.

This report is the result of a strong partnership between ACI and the business sector, government, and academics in various Indonesian provinces. We are grateful for the continued strong partnership with the Indonesian Employers' Association (APINDO) in coordinating the business perception surveys across Indonesian provinces in 2016. We would also like to extend our gratitude to various provincial government institutions and universities throughout Indonesia for their cooperation in hosting discussion in their premises and participating in our surveys.

The coordination and execution of field trips would not have been possible without an able and dedicated administrative team at ACI including Yap Xin Yi, Cai Jiao Tracy, Nurliyana Binte Yusoff, Qian Yuwei, Dewi Jelina Ayu Binte Johari, Yip Fung Yi Estelle, Shanty Citra Eka Vebriani Yusup (ACI survey coordinator in Jakarta) as well as National University of Singapore (NUS) students/research assistants Dedy Permadi, Divya Chandran, Faizal Rianto, Leoneto Elizario, Jenn Beh Yeong Wei, Lia Wulandari, Marlis Herni Afridah, Nirwansyah, Yayat Budianto and Yeni Imaniar Hamzah who conducted the surveys in 2016.

We would also like to note with great appreciation the high team spirit and contributions from ACI research staff including Professor Tan Kong Yam, Sasidaran Gopalan, Zhang Xuyao, Luu Nguyen Trieu Duong, Jigyasa Sharma and Nguyen Duy.

Importantly, we acknowledge the important research contribution in the form of commentaries on recent developments in the 34 Indonesian Provinces by our local academic partners in Indonesia and several of our NUS students/research assistants, which are included in Chapter 5.

Finally, we are immensely grateful for the continued guidance and support from Acting Dean Danny Quah, Vice Dean of Research Professor Ramkishen Rajan, Associate Dean of Research and Executive Education Mr Donald Low as well as other colleagues from the Lee Kuan Yew School of Public Policy for making this effort possible. Ultimately, a generous research funding from the Singapore Ministry of Trade and Industry enables this great effort, without which such an extensive book would not have been possible.

Tan Khee Giap, Mulya Amri, Nursyahida Ahmad and Diamanta Vania Lavi
Asia Competitiveness Institute
Lee Kuan Yew School of Public Policy
National University of Singapore

About the Authors

Tan Khee Giap is a Co-Director of the Asia Competitiveness Institute (ACI) and Associate Professor at the Lee Kuan Yew School of Public Policy, National University of Singapore. He is also the Chairman of the Singapore National Committee for Pacific Economic Cooperation. Upon graduating with a PhD from University of East Anglia, England, in 1987 under the Overseas Research Scheme awarded by the Committee of Vice-Chancellors and Principals of the Universities of the United Kingdom, he joined the banking sector as a treasury manager and served as secretary to the Assets and Liabilities Committee for three years, thereafter he taught at the Department of Economics and Statistics, National University of Singapore, 1990–1993. Dr Tan joined Nanyang Technological University in 1993 and was Associate Dean, Graduate Studies Office, 2007–2009.

Dr Tan has consulted extensively with the various government ministries, statutory boards and government-linked companies of Singapore government including Ministry of Finance, Ministry of Trade & Industry, Ministry of Manpower, Housing & Development Board, Civil Aviation Authority of Singapore, Singapore Tourism Board, Trade Development Board, Maritime Port Authority, Ministry of Information, Culture & Arts, Economic Development Board, Ministry of National Development, Media Development Authority, Ministry of Environment and Water Resources, Singapore Design Council, Ministry of Community Development, Youth & Sports, Singapore Press Holdings, Yayasan Mendaki, StarHub, CapitaLand and Great Eastern Life. He has also served as a consultant to international agencies such as the Asian Development Bank, Asian Development Bank Institute, United Nations Industrial Development Group, World Bank Group, World Gold Council, ASEAN Secretariat, Central Policy Unit of Hong Kong, Kerzner International, Las Vegas Sands and Marina Bay Sands.

Dr Tan is the lead author for more than 20 books, serving as journals editor and published widely in international refereed journals. He is the associate editor of the journal *Review of Pacific Basin Financial Markets and Policies* (US) and is on the editorial advisory board of the journal *Competitiveness Review* (UK). His current research interests include Cost of Living and Purchasing Power Index for World's 105 Cities, Global Liveable Cities Index, Ease of Doing Business Index and competitiveness analysis on sub-national economies of China, India, Indonesia and Association of South East Asian Nations.

Dr Tan was Deputy President of the Singapore Economic Society, 2004. He served in the 2002 Economic Review Committee (ERC), served as Chairman of the Task Force on Portable Medical Benefits (PMB), served as the Deputy Chairman of the IPS Forum for Economic Restructuring (IFER) in 2003 and served as a member of the Resource Panel of the Government Parliamentary Committee for Transport, Government Parliamentary Committee for Finance and Trade & Industry and Government Parliamentary Committee for Defence and Foreign Affairs since 2007. Dr Tan is currently an Independent Director of the publicly listed BreadTalk Group, Boustead Projects, TEE Land and Chengdu Rural Commercial Bank.

Mulya Amri is a Research Fellow and Deputy Director (Research) at the Asia Competitiveness Institute, Lee Kuan Yew School of Public Policy, National University of Singapore. He has held a key role in ACI's research on Indonesian sub-national competitiveness since 2011. He is also closely involved in ACI's research on city liveability and competitiveness, and has written widely on the topic of urban development and city-level governance. Mulya has 15 years of working experience in the private, public, and non-profit sectors. Upon moving to Singapore in 2008, he worked with HOK (a global planning and architecture consultancy firm) on city planning projects throughout Asia, and with Jurong Consultants (the consultancy arm of Singapore's JTC Corporation) on the planning of industrial zones in the Middle East. Prior to that, Mulya worked with international development agencies such as the World Bank, UNDP, and UN-HABITAT on projects related to urban and housing development, local governance, as well as community-driven development in various Indonesian regions. He is also a co-founder and sits on the advisory board of COMBINE Resource Institution, a non-profit organization based in Yogyakarta, Indonesia. Mulya has a PhD degree in Public Policy from the National University of Singapore. Prior to that, he graduated with a bachelor's degree from Institut Teknologi Bandung, Indonesia, and was awarded the Fulbright scholarship to study for a Master's degree in Urban Planning at the University of California, Los Angeles, and a Chevening award to study at the London School of Economics and Political Science.

Nursyahida Ahmad is a Research Assistant at Asia Competitiveness Institute (ACI) at the Lee Kuan Yew School of Public Policy, National University of Singapore. Nursyahida graduated from Nanyang Technological University, with a Bachelor of Arts (Honours) in Economics. At ACI, Nursyahida is actively involved in Indonesia's competitiveness analysis at the provincial and regional level, as well as other thematic studies such as the impact of real effective exchange rates on trade and investment. For her research involvement on Indonesia, Nursyahida has co-authored several of ACI publications on Indonesia's provincial development and policy options. She is also heavily involved in a research on firm productivity and efficiency. Her research interests include development economics and socioeconomic studies.

Diamanta Vania Lavi is a Research Assistant at Asia Competitiveness Institute (ACI) at the Lee Kuan Yew School of Public Policy, National University of Singapore (NUS). She graduated as the inaugural class of Yale-NUS College with a Bachelor of Arts (Hons) degree, and scored perfect GPA during her semester-long study at Columbia University in the City of New York. At ACI, she is the project co-coordinator for Liveability Ranking and Simulation Studies on the World's Major Cities Indices. Additionally, she is part of the Indonesia Competitiveness team, leading research fieldwork coordination and assisting with data analysis, as well as the ASEAN cluster studying the impact of real exchange rate volatility on trade in value added. Her research interests span the fields of urban competitiveness, developmental studies, policy mobility as well as the translation of research into public policy.

List of Abbreviations

ACI	Asia Competitiveness Institute
ADB	Asian Development Bank
AFC	Asian Financial Crisis
AFI	Attractiveness to Foreign Investors
Altaka	Alor, Lembata and Larantuka
APBD	Regional Development Budget (*Anggaran Pendapatan dan Belanja Daerah*)
APBN	State Budget (*Anggaran Pendapatan dan Belanja Negara*)
APBN-P	Revised State Budget (*Anggaran Pendapatan dan Belanja Negara-Perubahan*)
APINDO	Indonesian Employers' Association (*Asosiasi Pengusaha Indonesia*)
ASEAN	Association of Southeast Asian Nations
Bappeda	Regional Development Planning Agency (*Badan Perencanaan Pembangunan Daerah*)
Bappenas	National Development Planning Agency (*Badan Perencanaan Pembangunan Nasional*)
BI	Bank of Indonesia (*Bank Indonesia*)
BIS	Bank for International Settlements
BKPM	Investment Coordinating Board (*Badan Koordinasi Penanaman Modal*)
BKSAUA	Inter-Religious Cooperation Body (*Badan Kerjasama Antar Umat Beragama*)
BLK	Vocational and Skills Training Centres (*Balai Latihan Kerja*)
BLT	Direct Cash Transfer (*Bantuan Langsung Tunai*)
BOP	Balance of Payments
BOS	School Operational Assistance (*Bantuan Operasional Sekolah*)
BPK	Audit Board of Indonesia (*Badan Pemeriksa Keuangan*)
BPS	Central Statistical Agency (*Badan Pusat Statistik*)
BPTSP	One-Stop Integrated Service Agency (*Badan Pelayanan Terpadu Satu Pintu*)
BRICS	Brazil, Russia, India, China and South Africa
BUMD	Regional State-Owned Enterprise (*Badan Usaha Milik Daerah*)
BUMN	National State-Owned Enterprise (*Badan Usaha Milik Negara*)
CAGR	Cumulative Annual Growth Rate
CLMV	Cambodia, Lao PDR, Myanmar and Vietnam
CPI	Consumer Price Index
CPO	Crude Palm Oil

CRRL	Competition, Regulatory Standards and Rule of Law
CSR	Corporate Social Responsibility
CV	Coefficient of Variation
Dana Otsus	Special Autonomy Funds (*Dana Otonomi Khusus*)
DAU	General Allocation Fund (*Dana Alokasi Umum*)
DDI	Domestic Direct Investments
DI	Special Region (*Daerah Istimewa*)
DKI	Special Capital Region (*Daerah Khusus Ibukota*)
DPMPTSP	Investment and One-Stop Integrated Service Agency (*Dinas Penanaman Modal dan Pelayanan Terpadu Satu Pintu*)
DPRD	Regional People's Representative Council (*Dewan Perwakilan Rakyat Daerah*)
EDB Index ABC	Ease of Doing Business Index on Attractiveness to Investors, Business Friendliness and Competitive Policies
EMDEs	Emerging Markets and Developing Economies
FBMC	Financial, Businesses and Manpower Conditions
FDBE	Financial Deepening and Business Efficiency
FDI	Foreign Direct Investments
FE	Fixed Effects
FRAND	Fair, Reasonable and Non-Discriminatory
FRED	Federal Reserve Economic Data
FXR	Foreign Exchange Reserves
GAM	Free Aceh Movement (*Gerakan Aceh Merdeka*)
GARCH	Generalised Autoregressive Conditional Heteroskedasticity
GDP	Gross Domestic Product
Gerindra	Great Indonesia Movement Party (*Partai Gerakan Indonesia Raya*)
GFC	Global Financial Crisis
GFCF	Gross Fixed Capital Formation
GIS	Government and Institutional Setting
GNI	Gross National Income
Golkar	Party of the Functional Group (*Partai Golongan Karya*)
GPFS	Government Policies and Fiscal Sustainability
GRDP	Gross Regional Domestic Product
GSDP	Gross State Domestic Product
Ha	Hectare
Hanura	People's Conscience Party (*Partai Hati Nurani Rakyat*)
HDI	Human Development Index
HPAE	High Performing Asian Economies
ICT	Information, Communications and Technology
IGL	Institutions, Governance and Leadership
IHP	International Hub Port
IMD	International Institute for Management Development
IMF	International Monetary Fund

INDO-DAPOER	Indonesia Database for Policy and Economic Research
ITK	Consumer Confidence Index (*Indeks Tendensi Konsumen*)
Jamkesmas	National Health Insurance for the Poor and Near Poor (*Jaminan Kesehatan Masyarakat*)
JICA	Japan International Cooperation Agency
KIPI	Industrial Estate and International Port (*Kawasan Industri dan Pelabuhan Internasional*)
KPK	Corruption Eradication Commission (*Komisi Pemberantasan Korupsi*)
KPPOD	Regional Autonomy Watch (*Komite Pemantauan Pelaksanaan Otonomi Daerah*)
KSPSI	Confederation of All Indonesian Workers' Union (*Konfederasi Serikat Pekerja Seluruh Indonesia*)
LKPD	Provincial Government Financial Report (*Laporan Keuangan Pemerintah Daerah*)
LKPP	Central Government Financial Report (*Laporan Keuangan Pemerintah Pusat*)
LKYSPP	Lee Kuan Yew School of Public Policy
LLC	Limited Liability Company
LMF	Labour Market Flexibility
LPD	Village Finance Institution (*Lembaga Perkreditan Desa*)
LPJK	Construction Service Development Board (*Lembaga Pengembangan Jasa Konstruksi*)
LRT	Light Rail Transit
MASD	Moving Average Standard Deviation
MINT	Mexico, Indonesia, Nigeria and Turkey
MK	Constitutional Court (*Mahkamah Konstitusi*)
MME	Metal Goods, Machinery and Electronics
MNC	Multinational Corporation
MP3EI	Master Plan for Acceleration and Expansion of Indonesia's Economic Development (*Master Plan Percepatan dan Perluasan Pembangunan Indonesia*)
MRT	Mass Rapid Transit
MS	Macroeconomic Stability
MSH	Developing A Great North Sulawesi (*Membangun Sulut Hebat*)
MSME	Micro, Small and Medium Enterprise
MW	Megawatt
Nasdem	National Democrat Party (*Nasional Demokrat*)
NNT	Newmont Nusa Tenggara
NRI-ULI	Natural Resource Intensive and Unskilled Labour Intensive
NUS	National University of Singapore
OECD	Organisation for Economic Co-Operation and Development
OLS	Ordinary Least Squares
OTS	Openness to Trade and Services
p.a.	Per Annum

PAD	Own-Source Revenue (*Pendapatan Asli Daerah*)
PAN	National Mandate Party (*Partai Amanat Nasional*)
PBB	Crescent Star Party (*Partai Bulan Bintang*)
PBIUSE	Developments in Key Social and Economic Indicators (*Perkembangan Beberapa Indikator Utama Sosial Ekonomi*)
PCI-HCI-TI	Physical Capital Intensive, Human Capital Intensive and Technology Intensive
PDA	Aceh Region Party (*Partai Daerah Aceh*)
PDIP	Indonesian Democratic Party of Struggle (*Partai Demokrasi Indonesia-Perjuangan*)
PDR	People's Democratic Republic
Pemilu	General Elections (*Pemilihan Umum*)
Peparnas	National Paralympic Week (*Pekan Paralimpiade Nasional*)
Perda	Provincial Regulation (*Peraturan Daerah*)
Perdasus	Special Regional Regulation (*Peraturan Daerah Khusus*)
Pergub	Governor Regulation (*Peraturan Gubernur*)
Perindo	Indonesian Unity Party (*Partai Persatuan Indonesia*)
Perpres	Presidential Regulation (*Peraturan Presiden*)
PI	Physical Infrastructure
PIJAR	Cattle, Corn and Seaweed (*Sapi, Jagung dan Rumput Laut*)
Pilkada	Local Elections (*Pemilihan Kepala Daerah*)
PKB	National Awakening Party (*Partai Kebangkitan Bangsa*)
PKBL	Partnership and Environment Development Programme (*Program Kemitraan dan Bina Lingkungan*)
PKH	Conditional Cash Transfer Programme (*Program Keluarga Harapan*)
PKPI	Indonesian Justice and Unity Party (*Partai Keadilan dan Persatuan Indonesia*)
PKS	Prosperous Justice Party (*Partai Keadilan Sejahtera*)
PLB	Bonded Logistic Park (*Pusat Logistik Berikat*)
PLBN	Cross-Border Post (*Pos Lintas Batas Negara*)
PLN	State Electricity Company (*Perusahaan Listrik Negara*)
PLTA	Hydroelectric Power Plant (*Pembangkit Listrik Tenaga Air*)
PLTU	Electric Steam Power Plant (*Pembangkit Listrik Tenaga Uap*)
PMA	Foreign Investors (*Penanam Modal Asing*)
PNA	Nanggroe Aceh Party (*Partai Nanggroe Aceh*)
PNMP	Nationwide Community Programme (*Program Nasional Pemberdayaan Mandiri*)
PON	National Sports Week (*Pekan Olahraga Nasional*)
PP	Government Regulation (*Peraturan Pemerintah*)
PP	Productivity Performance
PPKD	Provincial Credit Guarantee Company (*Perusahaan Penjamin Kredit Daerah*)
PPP	The United Development Party (*Partai Persatuan Pembangunan*)

PSN	National Strategic Projects
PTSP	One-Stop Integrated Service Agency (*Pelayanan Terpadu Satu Pintu*)
Pusdatin	Data and Information Centre (*Pusat Data dan Informasi*)
Puskesmas	Community Health Centre (*Pusat Kesehatan Masyarakat*)
QLID	Quality of Life and Infrastructure Development
Rakor	Coordination Meeting (*Rapat Koordinasi*)
Raskin	Rice Subsidy Programme (*Beras Miskin*)
REER	Real Effective Exchange Rates
REV	Regional Economic Vibrancy
RPJMD	Regional Medium Term Development Planning (*Rencana Pembangunan Jangka Menengah Daerah*)
RPJMN	National Medium Term Development Plan (*Rencana Pembangunan Jangka Menengah Nasional*)
RPJPD	Regional Long Term Development Planning (*Rencana Pembangunan Jangka Panjang Daerah*)
RPZWP3K	Proposed Regulation on the Zoning of Coastal Area and Small Islands (*Rancangan Peraturdan Daerah Zonasi Wilayah Pesisir dan Pulau-Pulau Kecil*)
RTRWN	National Spatial Plan (*Rencana Tata Ruang Wilayah Nasional*)
RTRWP	Provincial Spatial Plan (*Rencana Tata Ruang Wilayah Provinsi*)
SAR	Special Administrative Region
SARA	Ethnicities, Religion, Race and Inter-Group Relations (*Suku, Agama, Ras dan Antargolongan*)
SD	Standard Deviation
SEZ	Special Economic Zone
SLESS	Standard of Living, Education and Social Stability
SME	Small and Medium-Sized Enterprise
SMK	Vocational High School (*Sekolah Menengah Kejuruan*)
SOE	State-Owned Enterprise
S&P	Standard and Poor's
TI	Technological Infrastructure
UIP	Uncovered Interest Parity
UK	United Kingdom
UMP	Provincial Minimum Wage (*Upah Minimum Provinsi*)
UNCTAD	United Nations Conference on Trade and Development
UP4PB	Unit for the Acceleration of Development in Papua and West Papua (*Unit Percepatan Pembangunan Papua dan Papua Barat*)
US	United States
WEF	World Economic Forum
WIR	World Investment Report
WTP	Normal without Exception (*Wajar Tanpa Pengecualian*)
y-o-y	year-on-year

List of Provinces

	Name of Province in English	Name of Province in Bahasa	Region
1	Aceh	Aceh	Sumatra
2	Bali	Bali	Bali-Nusa Tenggara
3	Bangka Belitung Islands	Kepulauan Bangka Belitung	Sumatra
4	Banten	Banten	Java
5	Bengkulu	Bengkulu	Sumatra
6	Central Java	Jawa Tengah	Java
7	Central Kalimantan	Kalimantan Tengah	Kalimantan
8	Central Sulawesi	Sulawesi Tengah	Sulawesi
9	DI Yogyakarta	DI Yogyakarta	Java
10	DKI Jakarta	DKI Jakarta	Java
11	East Java	Jawa Timur	Java
12	East Kalimantan	Kalimantan Timur	Kalimantan
13	East Nusa Tenggara	Nusa Tenggara Timur	Bali-Nusa Tenggara
14	Gorontalo	Gorontalo	Sulawesi
15	Jambi	Jambi	Sumatra
16	Lampung	Lampung	Sumatra
17	Maluku	Maluku	Maluku-Papua
18	North Kalimantan	Kalimantan Utara	Kalimantan
19	North Maluku	Maluku Utara	Maluku-Papua
20	North Sulawesi	Sulawesi Utara	Sulawesi
21	North Sumatra	Sumatera Utara	Sumatra
22	Papua	Papua	Maluku-Papua
23	Riau	Riau	Sumatra
24	Riau Islands	Kepulauan Riau	Sumatra
25	South Kalimantan	Kalimantan Selatan	Kalimantan
26	South Sulawesi	Sulawesi Selatan	Sulawesi

(*Continued*)

(*Continued*)

	Name of Province in English	Name of Province in Bahasa	Region
27	South Sumatra	Sumatera Selatan	Sumatra
28	Southeast Sulawesi	Sulawesi Tenggara	Sulawesi
29	West Java	Jawa Barat	Java
30	West Kalimantan	Kalimantan Barat	Kalimantan
31	West Nusa Tenggara	Nusa Tenggara Barat	Bali-Nusa Tenggara
32	West Papua	Papua Barat	Maluku-Papua
33	West Sulawesi	Sulawesi Barat	Sulawesi
34	West Sumatra	Sumatera Barat	Sumatra

List of Tables and Figures

Chapter 1

Chapter 2

Chapter 3

Chapter 4

Chapter 6

Chapter 1
Introduction

1.1 Why This Book and for Whom

The Asia Competitiveness Institute (ACI) at the Lee Kuan Yew School of Public Policy (LKYSPP), National University of Singapore (NUS) has been conducting sub-national level competitiveness studies of the economies in Asia. Among them, the provinces of Indonesia and China, along with the states of India are especially notable. The most populous sub-national economies in India (Uttar Pradesh), China (Guangdong) and Indonesia (West Java) have a population of over 200 million, 104.30 million and 43.05 million respectively in 2010. If each of these sub-national economies were to be compared against the world's countries, they would rank among the most populous. Although we agree that national-level policies and institutions matter, we also believe that economic activities are not always tied down to country-level contexts. We also argue that each of these sub-national economies deserves to be analysed on its own.

Among the economies that make up the Association of Southeast Asian Nations (ASEAN), Indonesia deserves special attention. As a region, ASEAN's population (638 million in 2013) is larger than that of the European Union (511 million). With a population of over 250 million, Indonesia is the world's fourth most populous country after China, India and the United States (US). The size of Indonesia's middle class is fast rising; it is indeed a substantial market and potentially an important producer of goods and talent.

Despite the important role that Indonesia plays, relatively little is known about the country especially at the sub-national level. The country has 34 provinces in total with a great diversity among them, ranging from the richest (DKI Jakarta, with a Gross Domestic Product or GDP per capita of Rp211.9 million in 2016) to the poorest (East Nusa Tenggara, Rp16.2 million). ACI has contributed to the development of knowledge on Indonesia since the late 2000s. In 2013, ACI published the inaugural annual competitiveness ranking of Indonesia's provinces (Tan et al. 2013) where each province was presented as a chapter. The competitiveness analysis continued on an annual basis and topical research projects were conducted every year based on sub-national data. These include, among others, a Geweke causality analysis on the determinants of economic growth in selected provinces (Tan et al. 2015), an analysis of agricultural total factor productivity at the provincial level (Tan et al. 2017b) as well as the ease of doing business and the probability of growth slowdown at the sub-national level (Tan et al. 2017a).

The objectives of this book, in particular, are (i) to analyse and track the competitiveness landscape across Indonesia's provinces and regions, (ii) to highlight specific potentials and challenges of certain provinces and regions that require special attention, (iii) to spur intellectual debate among key stakeholders to lift Indonesia's competitiveness at the national and sub-national levels as well as (iv) to further attract collaboration with strategic partners and to strengthen efforts to raise Indonesia's competitiveness through more outward-oriented policies (trade, foreign direct investment or FDI, technology transfer, etc.). This book is written for policymakers and business owners, who together with academics and non-governmental organisations make up the target audience.

To facilitate dialogue among the relevant stakeholders, ACI holds review seminars prior to the book publication. In 2016, ACI's Annual Conference was conducted in collaboration with the World Bank on 24–25 November, where findings of our research were presented and reviewed in front of an audience of about 500 people. In the following year, two review seminars were conducted at the LKYSPP: one on the economies of ASEAN-10 on 28 August and another on Greater China and India on 29 August. Also in 2017, ACI's researchers travelled to all 34 provinces of Indonesia to present the draft findings of this year's competitiveness analysis to our provincial stakeholders (academics, business owners and provincial government) for their review. Overall, there were a total of 102 seminars (three per province) that were conducted throughout Indonesia (for more details, see Chapter 2). These provided us with inputs on both the research methodology as well as the narrative behind the data.

This chapter provides an introduction to ACI's annual competitiveness analysis of Indonesian provinces in 2017. The rest of the chapter is organised as follows: first, Section 1.2 provides a brief overview of Indonesia's recent economic development in 2016 and 2017 as a context for this publication, highlighting major developments that contribute to competitiveness at the aggregate (country) level. Subsequently, Section 1.3 outlines the structure of the book and provides a brief summary of each chapter as a roadmap for the reader when navigating this book. Aside from presenting our annual competitiveness analysis of Indonesia's provinces and regions, which are updated on a yearly basis, this year we also include findings of our research on the impact of real effective exchange rates on FDI inflows at the provincial level.

1.2 Overview of Indonesia's Recent Economic Developments

This section provides an overview to the recent economic developments in Indonesia. Sections 1.2.1–1.2.4 describe the trends in various aspects of the nation's economy, while Section 1.2.5 outlines the Indonesian government's development priorities and strategies in 2017.

1.2.1 Economic Growth Trends

Indonesia promises much potential in terms of economic development, but it often disappoints in delivering that promise. The country was considered as one of the eight "East Asian miracles" due to its consistently high growth rate in the 1980s and 1990s (Birdsall et al. 1993) until the Asian Financial Crisis brought economic and political turmoil that triggered reforms. In the 2000s after rebounding from the crisis, again Indonesia brought hope and excitement due to its healthy growth rate that lasted for about a decade. The country was not included in the up-and-rising Brazil, Russia, India, China and South Africa (BRICS) bloc back in 2001. In 2013, however, it was named as part of a new bloc for investment destination: MINT, which stands for Mexico, Indonesia, Nigeria and Turkey (O'Neill 2013). A report argued that keeping an annual growth rate of 7.0 percent would bring Indonesia to be the seventh largest economy in the world by 2030 (Oberman et al. 2012). Much expectation was placed on Indonesia, but it was not met.

The global commodity price bust exposed Indonesia to the fact that a large aspect of its economy still depends on the market for raw materials. Efforts to diversify exports beyond oil and gas have brought progress, but still almost half of the country's export basket in 2015 was made of mineral products (25.0 percent) and vegetable products (15.0 percent), according to the Organisation for Economic Co-operation and Development (OECD) (2017). The global growth slowdown led to a weaker demand for such products and Indonesia's GDP growth declined from 6.2 percent in 2011 to 4.8 percent in 2015. Such decline eventually levelled off in 2015 when the country's growth rate crawled up slowly to 5.0 percent in 2016 and 5.1 percent in 2017, according to Bank Indonesia (Kompas 2018). This was lower than the rate initially targeted in the state budget (APBN) of 5.2 percent.

In a wider perspective, the decline in Indonesia's growth was not as troubling as the situation in several other developing countries. The once-mighty BRICS economies (shown in solid lines in Figure 1.1) have slowed substantially, with only China's and India's growth remaining above par — registering a rate of 6.7 percent and 7.1 percent in 2016 respectively — keeping in mind

Figure 1.1: GDP Growth Rate for Indonesia, BRICS Countries and MINT Countries, 2012–2016

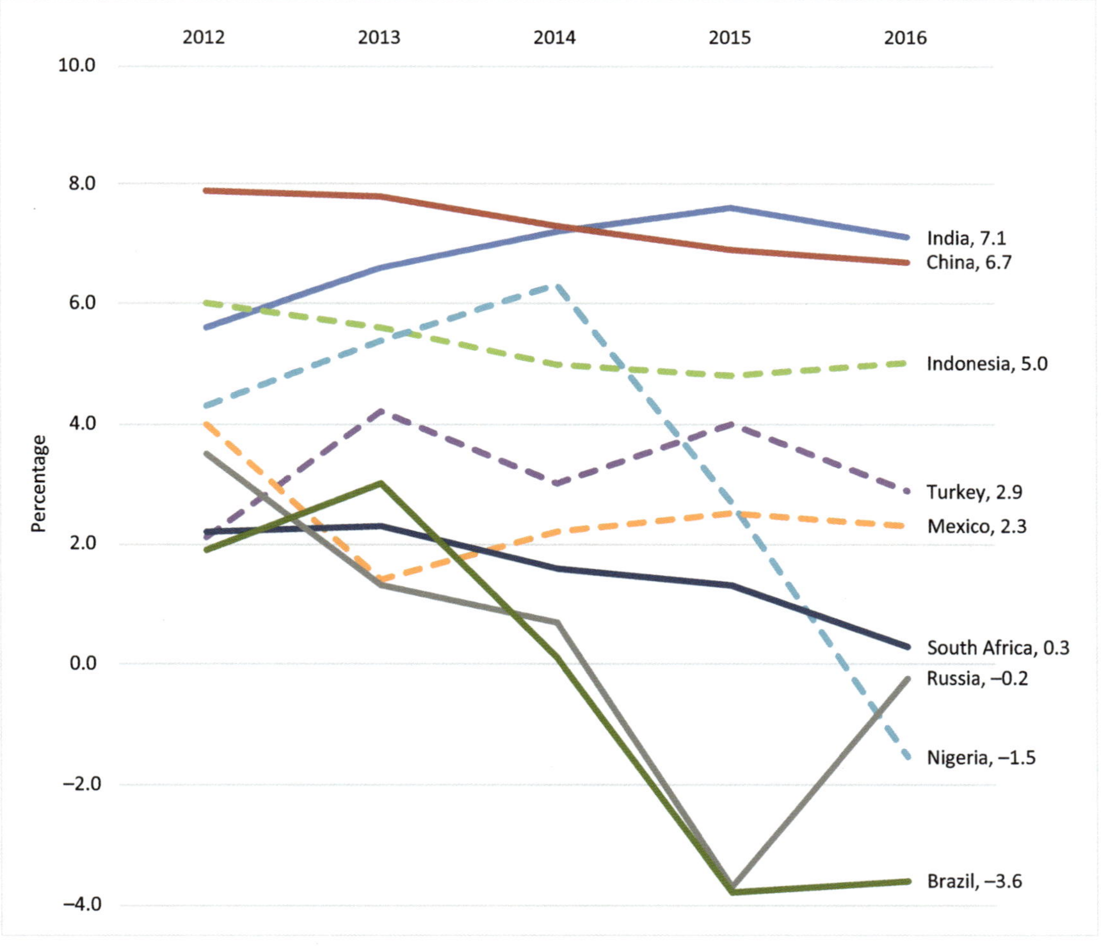

Note: Figures after country name indicate growth rates in 2016. Dashed lines represent MINT countries.
Source: ACI based on World Development Indicators data.

Figure 1.2: GDP Growth Rate for Indonesia and ASEAN-10 Countries, 2012–2016

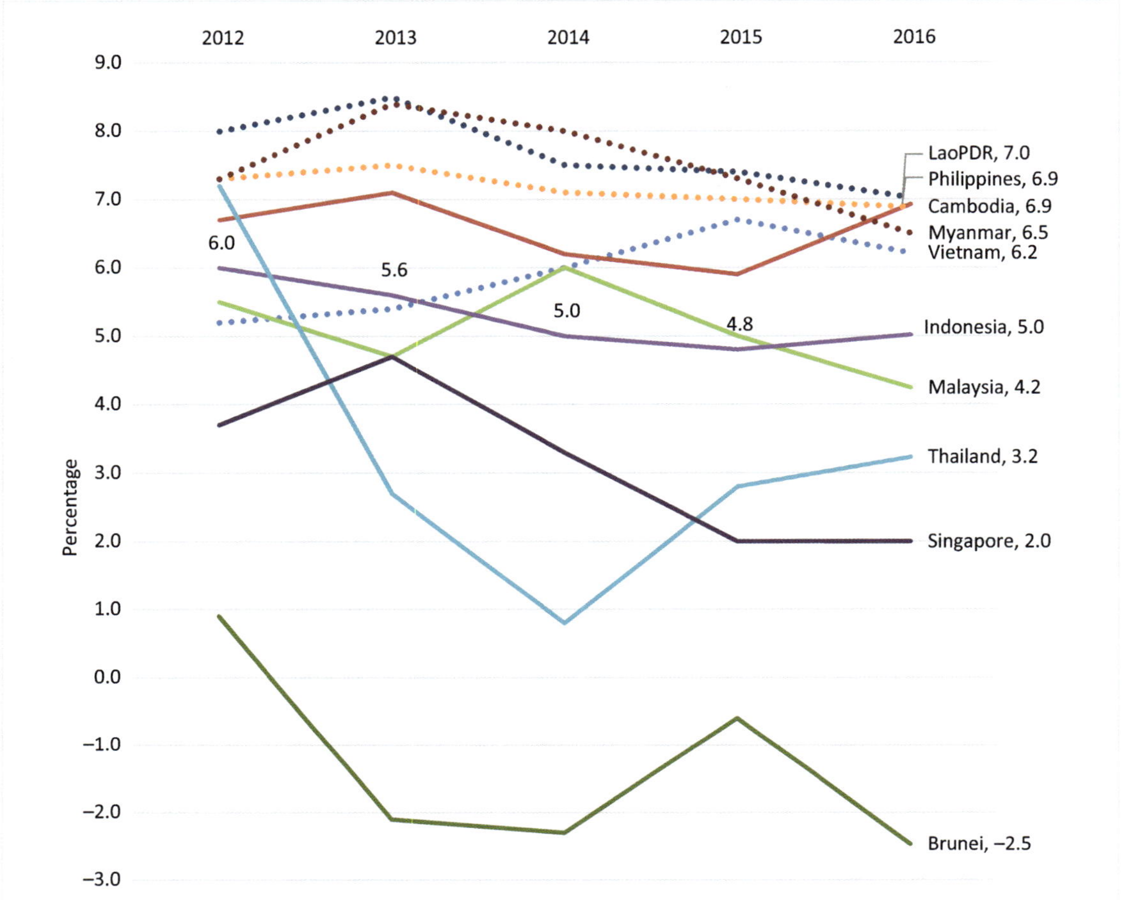

Note: Figures after country name indicate GDP growth rate in 2016. Dotted lines represent CLMV countries.
Source: ACI based on World Development Indicators data.

that China's growth was in the double-digit territory for most of the 1990s and 2000s. Meanwhile, the remainder of the MINT economies registered even more disappointing growth rates (shown in dashed lines in Figure 1.1).

Among the member countries of ASEAN-10, Indonesia still registered a marginally higher growth rate compared to the unweighted average of the 10-country bloc, which was 4.6 percent for 2016. Within this bloc, the CLMV countries of Cambodia, Lao People's Democratic Republic (PDR), Myanmar and Vietnam (shown in dotted lines in Figure 1.2) were quickly catching up and had among the highest growth rates for the past five years. It should be noted that the Philippines also had enjoyed consistent and robust growth for the past five years, registering a 6.9 percent growth rate in 2016. This was substantially higher than Indonesia's and proved that a middle-income country can still achieve strong growth despite the global slowdown.

In 2016–2017, Indonesia's GDP growth rate resumed albeit slowly, and the fundamental characteristics of Indonesia's macroeconomy seem to have improved and were relatively stable. However, the country is yet to fulfil its promise as the next economic powerhouse. Investments and tangible

Figure 1.3: GDP Growth Rate for Top-Six Largest Industries, Indonesia, 2014–2016

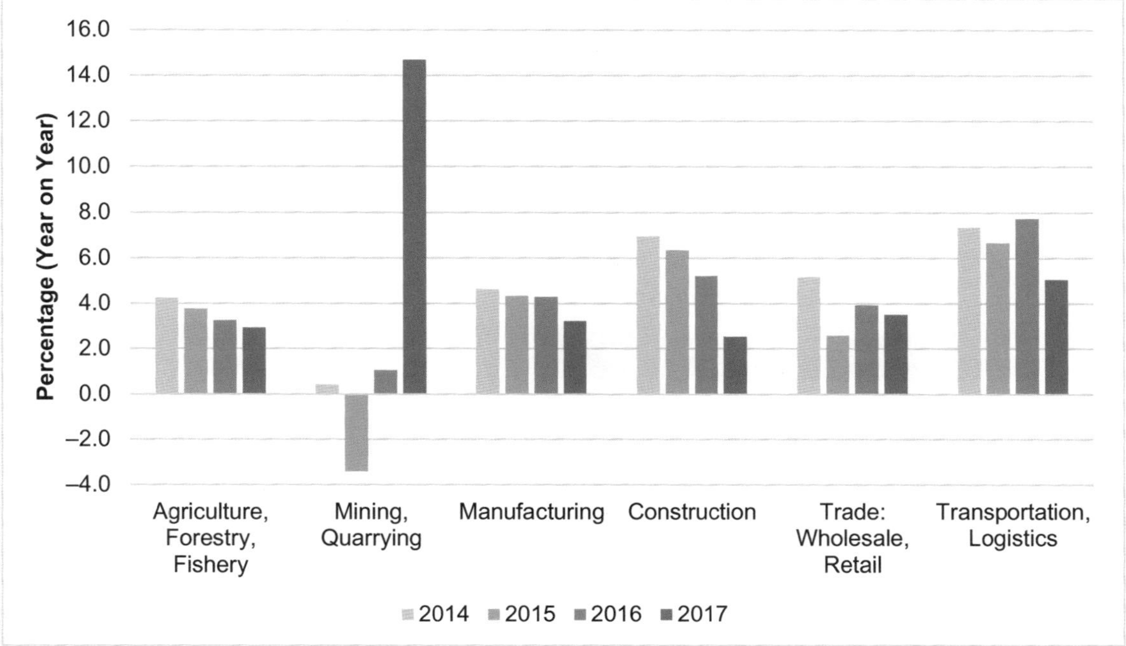

Note: Figures for 2017 are based on preliminary data.
Source: ACI based on BPS data.

results in the economy remained elusive for many parts of the country. To understand the drivers of Indonesia's growth in recent years, it is useful to review the breakdown of its GDP components.

An analysis of the annual growth rates of Indonesia's five largest industrial sectors pointed to a major uptick in the mining and quarrying sector (see Figure 1.3). In 2017, the sector grew at a remarkable rate of 14.7 percent year-on-year. This was perhaps related to the sector's challenges in the preceding years, where it contracted by 3.4 percent in 2015 and only grew by 1.1 percent in 2016. Mining and quarrying makes up 7.6 percent of Indonesia's GDP in 2017 and is the fifth largest sector after manufacturing (20.2 percent), agriculture, forestry, and fishery (13.1 percent), wholesale and retail trade (13.0 percent) and construction (10.4 percent) according the Indonesia's Central Bureau of Statistics (BPS). The largest driver of growth — simply due to its sheer size — remained to be manufacturing, although its growth rate decreased from 4.3 percent in 2016 to 3.3 percent in 2017.

Further analysis of Indonesia's growth rates by expenditure identified a major pickup in exports and imports, which had previously contracted from the fourth quarter of 2014 to the third quarter of 2016 (see Figure 1.4). Indonesia regained its exports growth starting from the fourth quarter of 2016, when it registered a 4.2 percent growth rate, and peaked in the third quarter of 2017, where it grew at a rate of 17.0 percent year-on-year. Since then, the growth rate for exports has slowed to 8.5 percent in the second quarter of 2017. Similarly, import growth rates have followed the trend of exports. Other than that, there was also a pickup in gross fixed capital formation, reaching a growth rate of 7.3 percent in the fourth quarter of 2017. Government consumption also regained its usual growth rate of around 3.5 percent starting from the first quarter of 2017, after contracting for two quarters previously in the third and fourth quarters of 2016. This contraction was more likely to be a relative contraction, considering the major push for infrastructure development in the third and fourth quarters of 2015.

Figure 1.4: GDP Growth Rate by Expenditure, Indonesia (First Quarter of 2015 to Fourth Quarter of 2017)

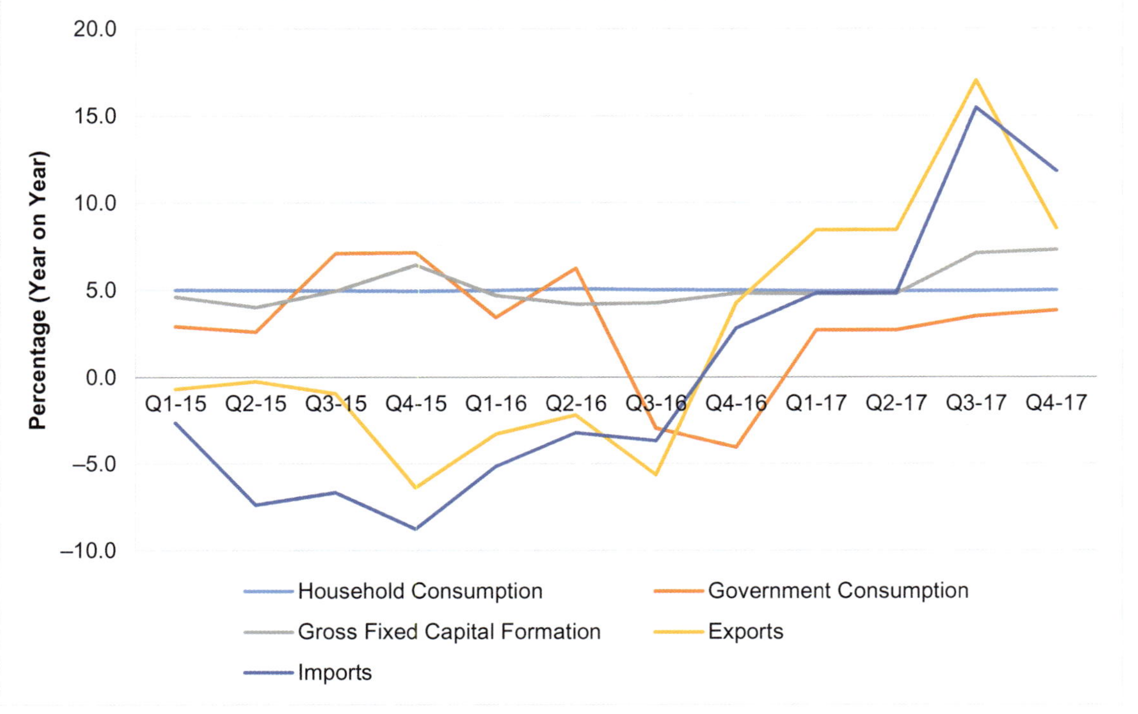

Note: Figure for fourth quarter of 2017 is based on preliminary data.
Source: ACI based on BPS data.

1.2.2 International Trade Performance

With a more favourable environment for international trade, Indonesia's exports of goods grew by 16.9 percent and that for imports grew by 16.2 percent in 2017. Meanwhile, exports and imports of services grew by a more modest rate of 2.1 percent and 6.2 percent respectively. Figure 1.5 shows that Indonesia is a net exporter of goods and a net importer of services. The largest growth in exported goods came from a combination of manufactured products (i.e. textiles, footwear and electronics) as well as raw commodities (most notably coal) and processed commodities (i.e. palm oil, rubber and base metals). Meanwhile, most of the growth in imported goods was due to an inflow of raw materials net of fuel. Indonesia's exports to China and the US grew most prominently at 50.0 percent and 20.0 percent respectively, indicating a trend of recovery in global demand (The World Bank 2017b). Overall, Indonesia's current account balance in 2017 stayed in the negative territory, amounting to a deficit of about US$17.3 trillion in 2017, equivalent to approximately 1.8 percent of the GDP.

Looking more closely into the destinations of Indonesia's merchandise exports, we see that Asian countries made up the largest share (70.0 percent) of Indonesia's market in 2017 (see Figure 1.6). Almost a quarter (23.4 percent) of Indonesia's exports went to fellow ASEAN-10 countries, while almost a third (32.2 percent) went to China, Japan, and India. Meanwhile, in terms of types of commodities, manufacturing products made up the bulk (72.3 percent) of

Figure 1.5: Current Account Components of Indonesia, 2013–2017

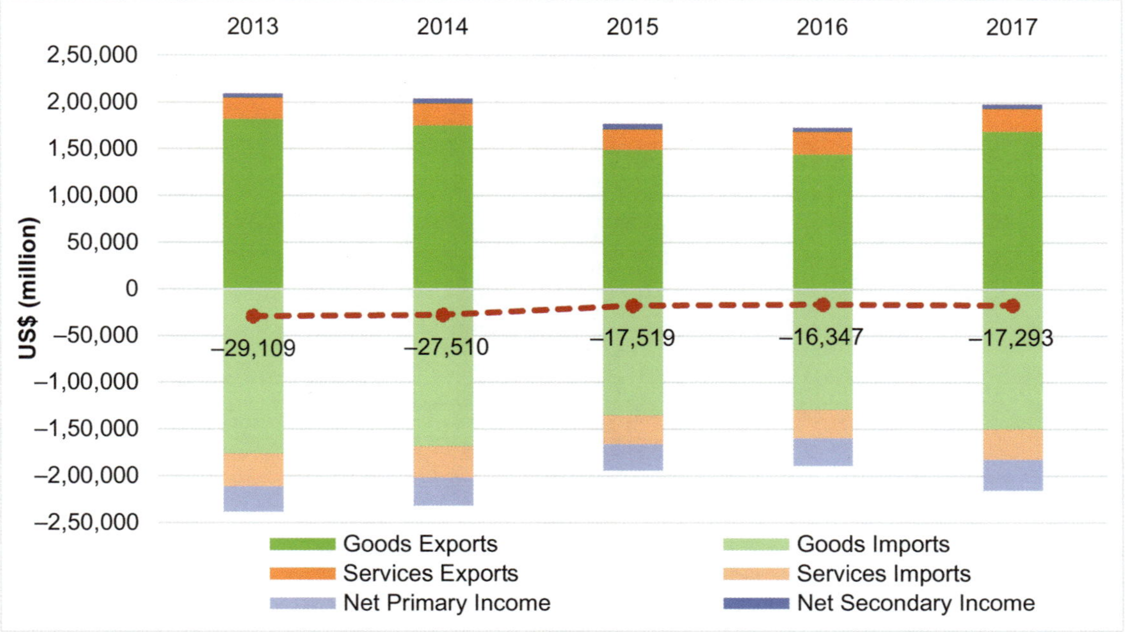

Note: Figures are in current prices. Figure for 2017 is based on preliminary data.
Source: ACI based on Bank Indonesia data.

Figure 1.6: Value of Goods Exports by Destination, 2013–2017

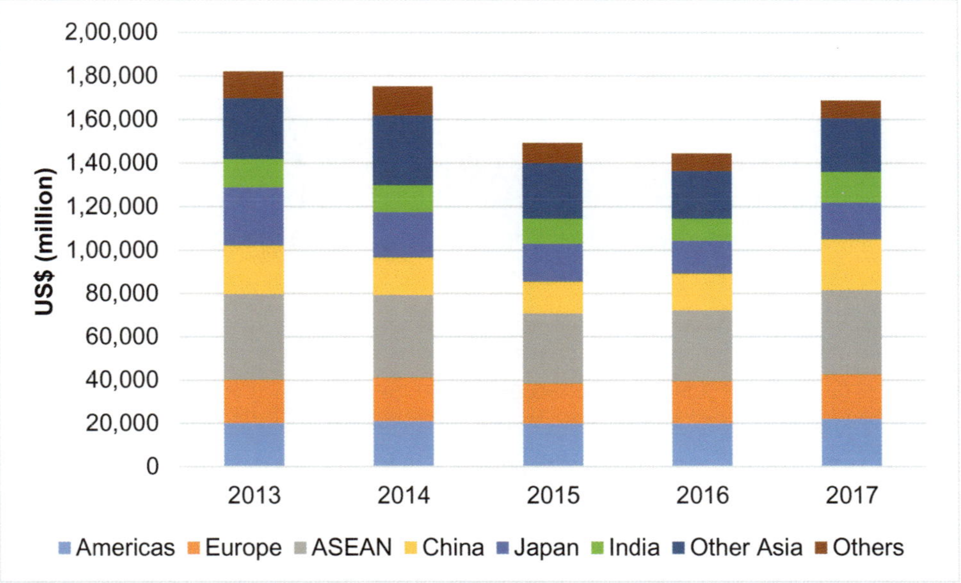

Note: Figures are in current prices. Data for October, November and December of 2017 are preliminary figures.
Source: ACI based on Bank Indonesia data.

Figure 1.7: Value of Goods Exports by Commodity Type, 2013–2017

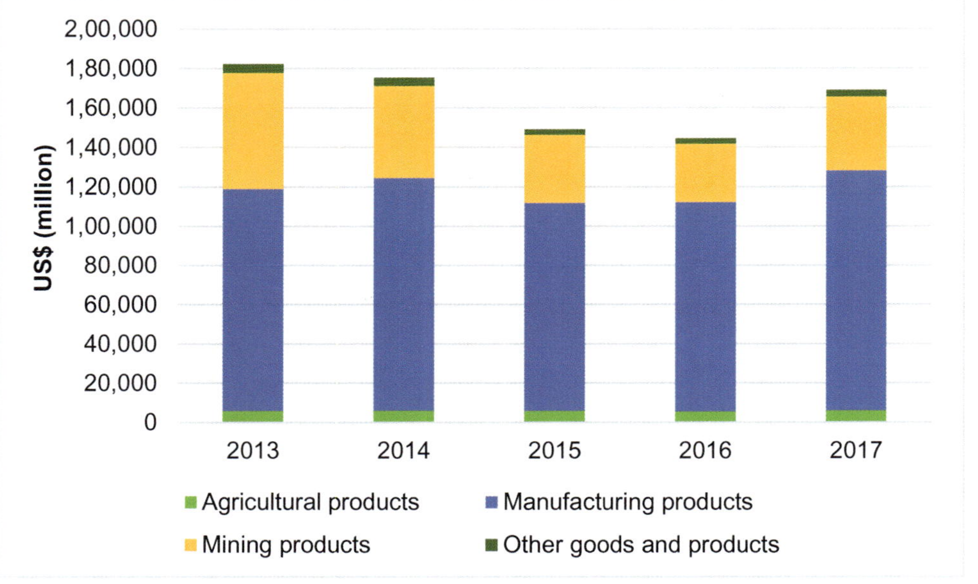

Note: Figures are in current prices. Data for October, November and December of 2017 are preliminary figures.
Source: ACI based on Bank Indonesia data.

Indonesia's products, although these included palm oils, base metals and processed rubber. Mining products contributed to 22.3 percent of the export value, and these included coal, which made up more than half of the value of these mining products (see Figure 1.7 for more details).

1.2.3 Fiscal and Monetary Trends

With an increasingly more stable and favourable external environment, the central government of Indonesia tried to improve the quality of its public spending. Figure 1.8 shows the components of government spending by expenditure types in 2014–2017. The largely mistargeted and inefficient energy subsidies were drastically cut in 2015 and continued to be tapered off in 2016 and 2017. This provided the fiscal space for other types of expenditure, such as personnel, goods and capital as well as more productive subsidies, such as education and healthcare (see Figure 1.8). There was a slight reduction of expenditure on goods and capital in 2017 in favour of more allocation for non-energy subsidies and interest payments.

In terms of expenditure function, the central government spent substantially more for housing and infrastructure and less on general public services compared to the previous years. A record amount of Rp390.7 trillion was spent on infrastructure in 2017 — a ten-fold increase compared to the figure in 2016, which was Rp34.3 billion (see Figure 1.9). Meanwhile, spending on general public services (government administration) was reduced in 2016–2017 and the money was reallocated for spending on economic affairs, education, health, social protection, public order and defence.

Government expenditure figures also reflected a trend to delegate spending towards the sub-national level. Transfers to sub-national regions as a percentage of overall government budget

Figure 1.8: Components of Actual Government Expenditure by Type, 2014–2017

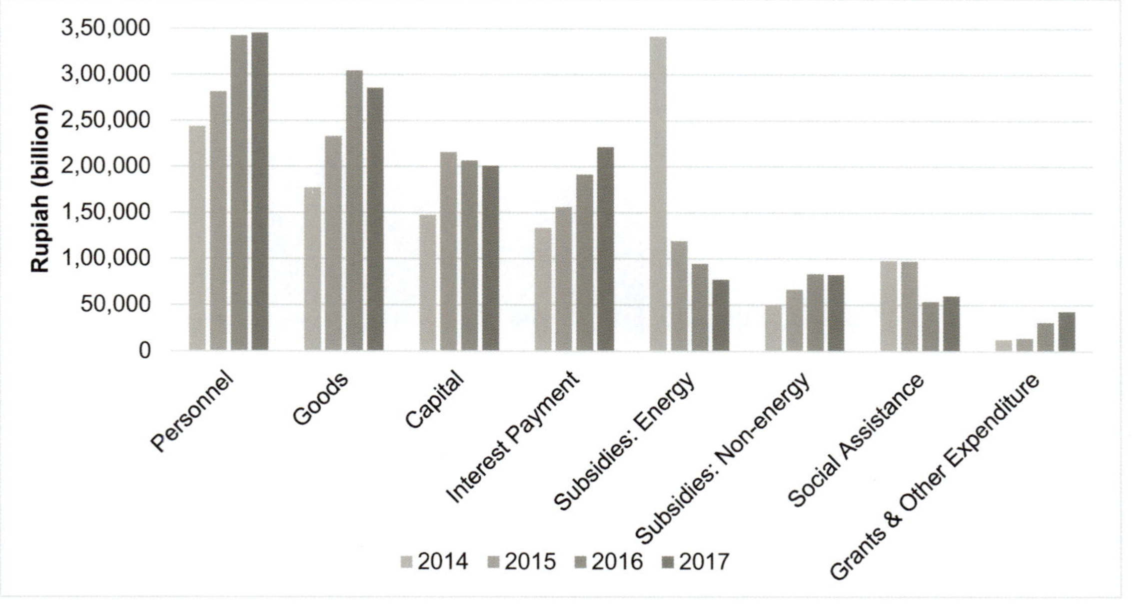

Note: Figures are in current prices. Data for 2014 and 2015 are based on Central Government Financial Report (LKPP). Data for 2016 are based on Revised State Budget (APBN-P). Data for 2017 are based on State Budget (APBN).
Source: ACI based on BPS data.

Figure 1.9: Components of Actual Government Expenditure by Function, 2014–2017

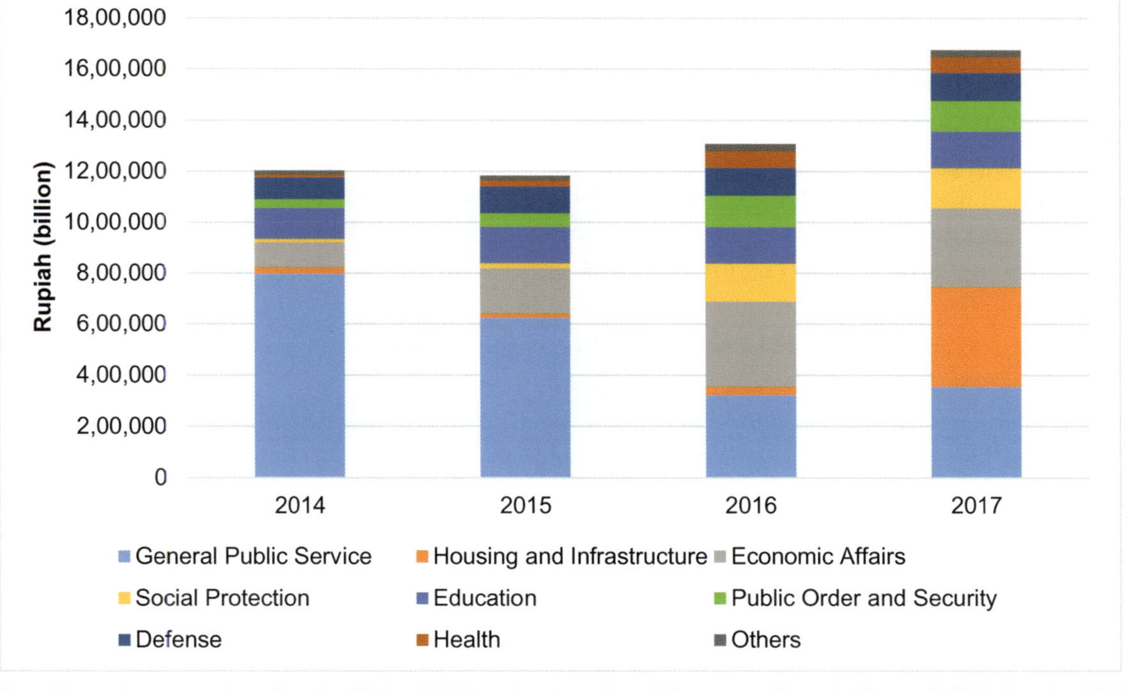

Note: Figures in current prices. Data for 2014 and 2015 are based on Central Government Financial Report (LKPP). Data for 2016 are based on Revised State Budget (APBN-P). Data for 2017 are based on State Budget (APBN).
Source: ACI based on BPS data.

Figure 1.10: Sources of Actual Government Revenue, 2014–2017

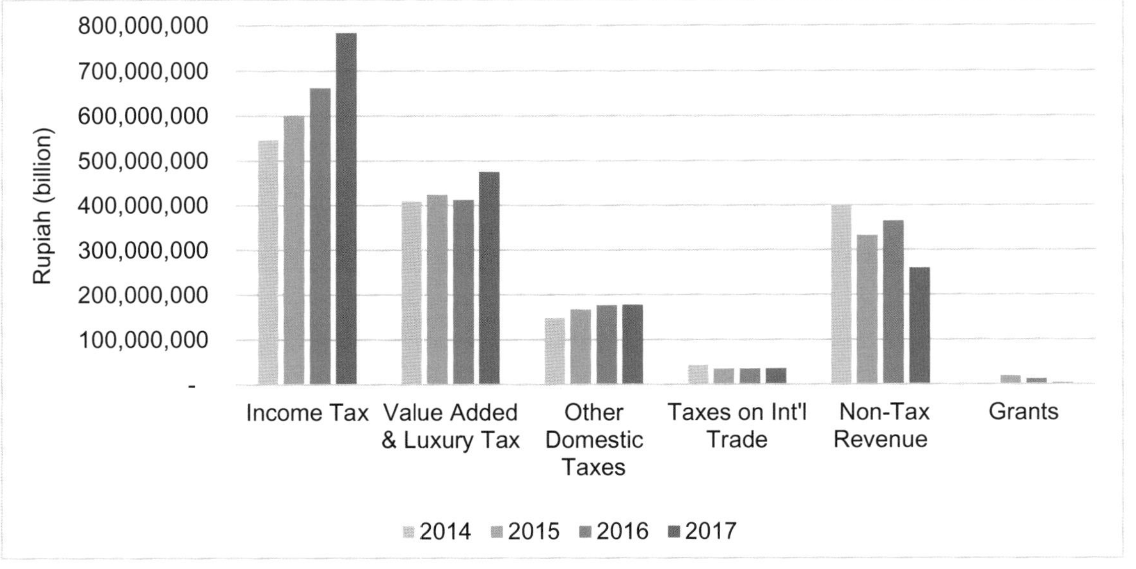

Note: Figures in current prices. Data for 2014 and 2015 are based on Central Government Financial Report (LKPP). Data for 2016 are based on Revised State Budget (APBN-P). Data for 2017 are based on State Budget (APBN).
Source: ACI based on Indonesia's Ministry of Finance data.

grew steadily from 31.1 percent in 2013 to 36.8 percent in 2017, according to data from the Ministry of Finance. This reflected more trust in the process of decentralisation and the growing role of sub-national governments. However, the principles and practices of fiscal decentralisation in Indonesia were still very much a decentralisation of expenditure as opposed to a decentralisation of revenue (Bird and Vaillancourt 2008).

In terms of revenue sources, there was an increasing trend to rely more on taxes (most notably income taxes) rather than non-tax revenues (mostly from profit-sharing of natural resources). Figure 1.10 shows this trend. The tax amnesty program, initially geared to mobilise repatriation of funds parked abroad, may not have achieved all its ambitious targets (Tempo 2017; Kompas 2017; The Jakarta Post 2017). However, it did nonetheless increase the government's revenue from tax collections. As shown in Figure 1.10, Indonesia's tax revenue alone increased from Rp546.2 quadrillion to Rp784.0 quadrillion between 2014 and 2017. These represented 35.3 percent and 45.2 percent, respectively, of the total revenue.

In 2017, Indonesia also managed to keep its inflation at a low rate of 3.61 percent in a run, which had kept inflation unusually and consistently low since late 2015 (see Figure 1.11). These were in line with the Bank of Indonesia's (BI) target of keeping a three to five percent inflation rate throughout 2016–2017.[1] Inflation reached a high of slightly over four percent during May–June of 2017 (during the festive Ramadan and Eid periods), but otherwise stayed well below four percent. This allowed BI to further adopt a more progressive monetary stance and slash the policy rate by 50.0 basis points from 4.75 percent to 4.25 percent between July and September in 2017, with the hope of generating more investments.

[1] Inflation targets for 2016, 2017 and 2018 were laid out in Minister of Finance Regulation No. 93/PMK.011/2014.

Figure 1.11: Inflation and Central Bank Policy Rate, 2015–2017

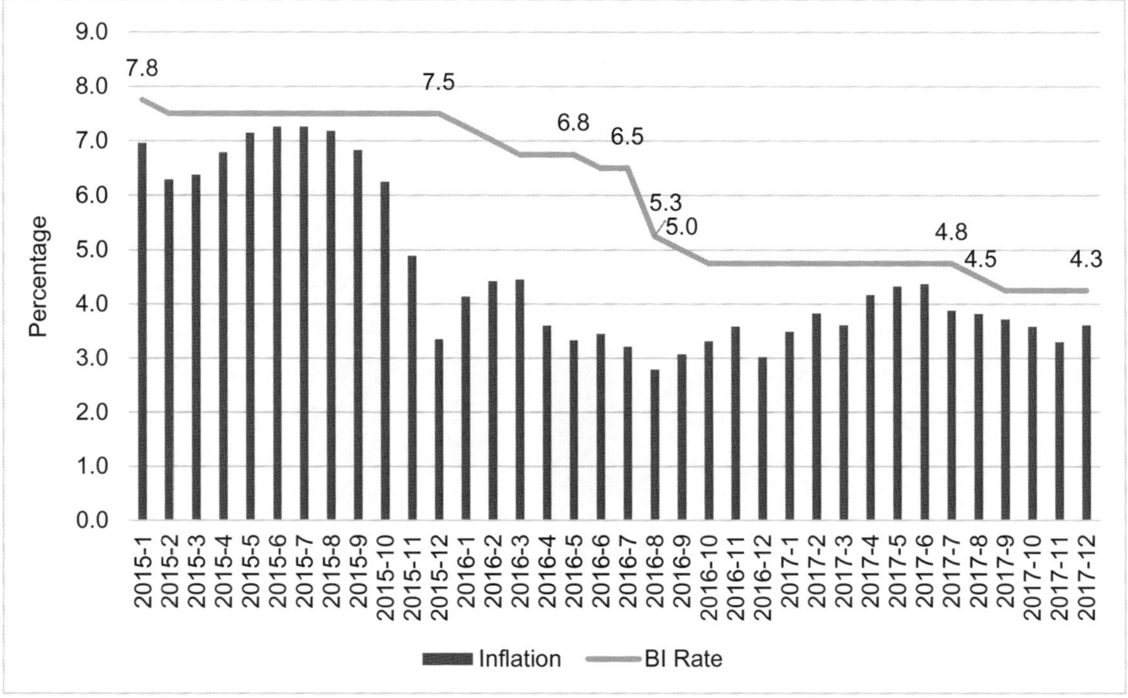

Source: ACI based on Bank Indonesia data.

Indonesia has been making strides in improving its macroeconomic policy through more prudent public spending (i.e. reducing ineffective energy subsidies in favour of infrastructure development and social services), generating more accountable revenue sources (i.e. boosting income tax receipts), keeping inflation low and reducing the central bank's policy rate. This has led the country to achieve better investment grade ratings from the major credit rating agencies (Bank Indonesia n.d.). Moody's had given a Baa3 rating for Indonesia since 2012, but had recently revised its outlook from stable to positive in February 2017.

Similarly, Fitch revised the outlook of its BBB– rating for Indonesia from stable to positive in December 2016 and eventually upgraded the rating even further to BBB in December 2017. In 2017, Standard & Poor's (S&P) finally upgraded Indonesia's rating from BB+ (one notch below investment grade, which had stood since 2011) to BBB– in May 2017.

1.2.4 Investment Trends and Outlook

FDI inflows to Indonesia rebounded strongly in 2017 following a substantial pull-out of foreign investments in fourth quarter of 2016, right after the election of Donald Trump as president of the United States (see Figure 1.12). The negative inflow was mostly related to investments in the financial intermediation sector, which was siphoned to an African offshore financial centre. Indonesia still obtained a net inflow of US$3.9 billion in 2016, but that was a decline by 84 percent year-on-year. The country gained a total net inflow of US$23.0 billion in 2017. Much of this went into retail and wholesale trade (up from US$2.0 billion to US$5.3 billion between 2016

Figure 1.12: FDI into Indonesia by Industry, 2013–2017

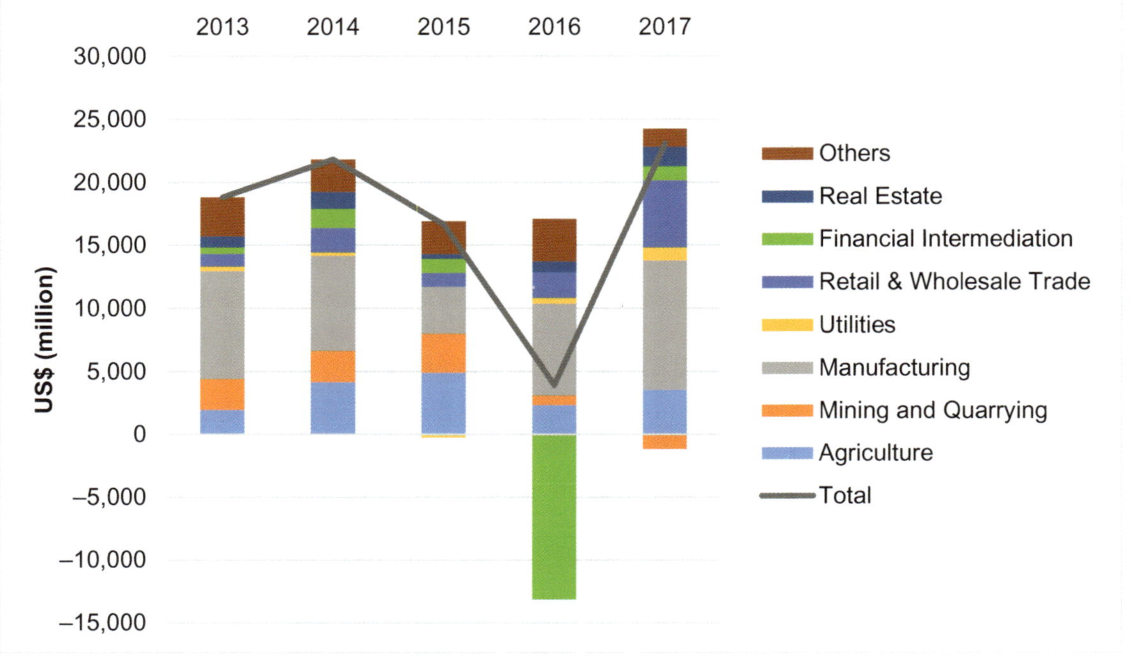

Note: Figures are in current prices. Figures for 2017 are based on preliminary data.
Source: ACI based on Bank Indonesia data.

and 2017), manufacturing (from US$7.3 billion to US$10.2 billion), agriculture (from US$2.3 billion to US$3.5 billion), utilities (from US$438 million to US$1.0 billion) and real estate (from US$870 million to US$1.5 trillion). These reflected the increasing attractiveness of Indonesia both as a producer and a market economy. However, there was also a continued waning of FDI into the mining and quarrying sector between 2015 and 2017.

In terms of FDI sources, Singapore remained strong as one of Indonesia's largest investors (see Figure 1.13). There was an increase of FDI originating from Singapore from US$8.4 billion to US$10.7 billion between 2016 and 2017. These represent 57.0 percent and 41.9 percent, respectively, of the total FDI inflows into Indonesia. The drop in relative portion of Singapore-originated investments in 2017 was due to the increase of FDI from other countries. For example, there was a substantial uptick of inflows from the Netherlands and Japan (each contributing to 15.6 percent and 15.8 percent of FDI inflows into Indonesia in 2017), China (7.2 percent) and Malaysia (5.3 percent). It was also interesting to note that FDI from Japan rebounded in 2017 after a continuous decline since 2013.

Meanwhile, in its quest to reform the business environment, Indonesia has improved substantially in the Doing Business rankings conducted annually by the World Bank (see Figure 1.14). Over a period of five years, Indonesia's ranking gradually climbed from 120th out of 189 economies in 2014 to 72nd out of 190 economies in 2018 (The World Bank 2013, 2017a). There were 10 business processes measured by the Doing Business rankings. Indonesia improved the most in terms of Resolving Insolvency (whose rank jumped from144th to 38th between 2014

Figure 1.13: FDI into Indonesia by Originating Country/Region, 2013–2017

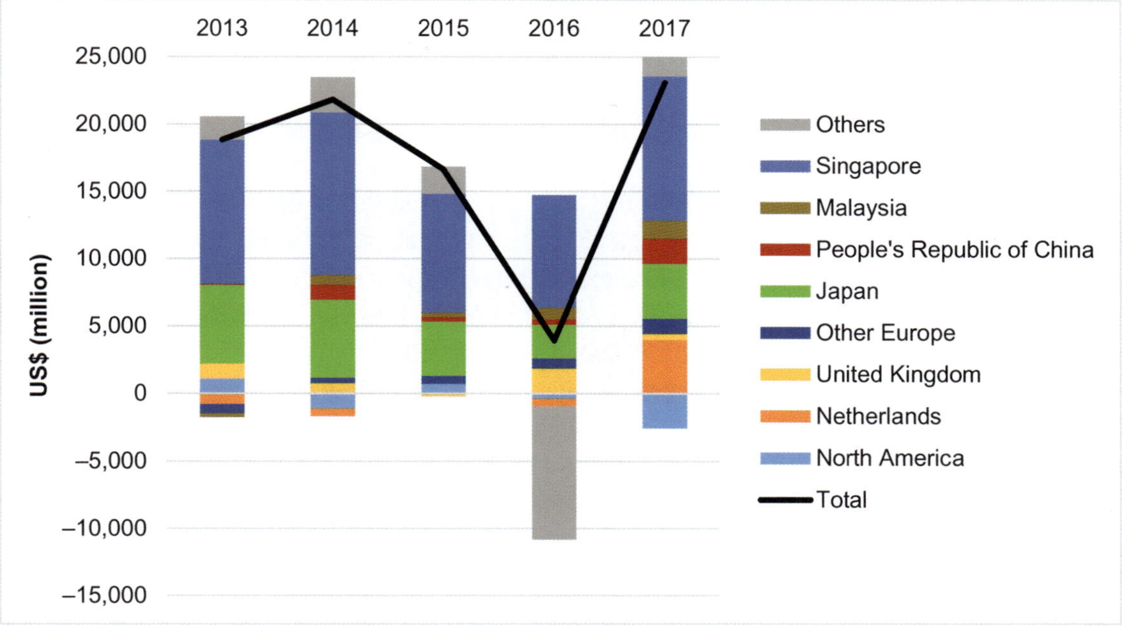

Note: Figures are in current prices. Figures for 2017 are based on preliminary data.
Source: ACI based on Bank Indonesia data.

Figure 1.14: Doing Business Rankings for China, India and Selected ASEAN Countries, 2014–2018

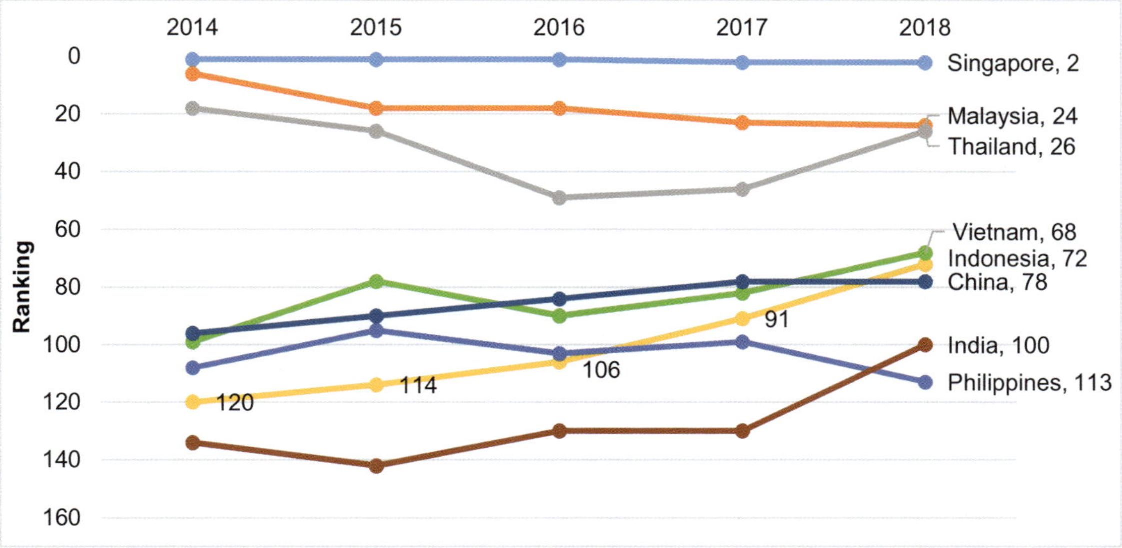

Note: *Y*-axis is reversed. Lower rank indicates better performance.
Source: ACI based on the World Bank data.

and 2018) and Getting Electricity (from 121st to 38th during the same period). On the contrary, Indonesia's rankings worsened from 54th to 112th for Trading across Borders and remained stagnant among the bottom for Enforcing Contracts and Starting a Business (The World Bank 2013, 2017a). A more comprehensive analysis of these reform efforts as well as a more thorough analysis on the ease of doing business in 33 Indonesian provinces was also conducted by ACI (Tan et al. 2017a).

While improvements at the policy level are helpful, Indonesia needs to do more on the ground and in the sub-national regions. To ensure a more robust yet stable economic development, the government must take into account the actual experience and perceptions of foreign and domestic business owners across the country. This would help identify the real issues in generating more FDI as well as boosting exports and imports.

Although FDI and exports are improving for Indonesia, a view from the international perspective argues that Indonesia is not doing enough relative to its peers. Compared to neighbouring countries in Southeast Asia with robust growth rates, Indonesia's trade and investment are still relatively miniscule. For example, Indonesia's openness to trade according to World Development Indicators was 37 percent in 2016, much lower than the Philippines (65 percent), Thailand (123 percent), Malaysia (129 percent), and Vietnam (185 percent). Also, FDI as a proportion of Indonesia's GDP stood at 2.3 percent in 2015. Again, this was much lower than the proportion for Malaysia (4.6 percent) and Vietnam (6.1 percent).

Ultimately, Indonesia's ability to maintain economic growth that is high yet inclusive is dependent on political will, institutional capacity as well as targeted efforts of its government. It is thus useful at this juncture to reflect on the current strategies and priorities that have been undertaken by the Indonesian government in recent times. They are presented in Section 1.2.5 based on the speech delivered by the Minister for National Development Planning Agency of Republic of Indonesia (Bappenas), Dr Bambang Brodjonegoro.

In his speech titled "Indonesia's Development Strategies and Priorities in 2017", Dr Brodjonegoro summed up the priorities of Indonesia's development along with the government's strategies to achieve its goals. He also identified parts of Indonesia which are potential growth engines and other parts which need to be further strengthened. In closing, Dr Brodjonegoro outlined key approaches that the government has undertaken in order to achieve a more broad-based and sustainable development. Section 1.3 will then provide the overall roadmap for the rest of the book.

1.2.5 Development Strategies and Priorities[2]

Indonesia today is still a big market with the 15th largest GDP in the world and is among the top five emerging markets with the best middle-class potential. It is also the fourth most populous country in the world, with a consumption rate that has been growing quite steadily at around five

[2]This section is adapted with permission from the speech by Dr Bambang Brodjonegoro, Minister for National Development Planning Agency of Republic of Indonesia, which was delivered during the Ministerial Forum at the 2017 The World Bank Group–Asia Competitiveness Institute Annual Conference on 23 November 2017 in Singapore.

percent. Aside from consumption growth, Indonesia's GDP per capita currently stands at around US$3,600. However, it is projected that if Indonesia can keep growing at five percent annually until 2045 — which will mark the country's century of independence — then its GDP per capita would increase to US$19,000. In that case, Indonesia will have passed the benchmark of US$15,000 per capita to become a high-income country. Of course, this will require steady policies and determination to ensure that a five percent growth rate is achievable.

1.2.5.1 *Prioritising Infrastructure Development*

To support that ambition, as well as our hope for a more prosperous Indonesia, infrastructure development is a must. There are a lot of discussions on why the current government has placed focus on infrastructure. The current government has learned that many countries which are now categorised as advanced, developed or close-to-developed have been able to attain these statuses because they already have their infrastructure intact. If we look around the world, we can see that every country needs to always improve its infrastructure.

I was in Malaysia a few days ago, attending the World Islamic Economic Forum. I read in the news that Malaysia is going to build two big seaports: one in the west at Port Klang, where it will expand the existing facilities that service the Straits of Malacca; the other one in Kuantan, at the east of the peninsula. This means that despite the fact that Malaysia is not an archipelagic country, its government understands the importance of having relatively large seaports. Of course, Malaysia already has a very large seaport at Tanjung Pelepas, which is located fairly close to Singapore.

Yesterday, I was in Istanbul, Turkey. If you are in Istanbul, you will realise that Turkey's growth has been made possible because of their infrastructure and their entrepreneurial spirit. We know that the Turkish are very entrepreneurial. More than that, however, Turkey already has infrastructure in place that is ready to support investment activities. Istanbul is currently building what will in the future be the biggest airport in the world. With five runways, it will replace the current Ataturk International Airport. Turkey has to build the new airport because Turkish Airlines is one of the biggest airlines in the world.

Again, it is very clear that Indonesia needs to build infrastructure. Since infrastructure development takes time, Indonesia will need not just one or two, but many years to build all these necessary infrastructure. Since Indonesia needs to start building infrastructure at some point, the current government is willing to do that, knowing that the positive impact and benefits will primarily be enjoyed by the subsequent governments.

This was my introduction. I would like to again express my appreciation for the participation of the Indonesian governors as well as the representatives from the various Indonesian provinces in the 2017 Asia Competitiveness Institute Annual Conference.

1.2.5.2 *Maximising Human Resource and Middle Class Potential*

Today we are talking about competitiveness, and competitiveness is not just about building infrastructure. At the end of the day, human resources will still be key. Unfortunately, Indonesia does not have enough infrastructure to build enough human resource capability. While Indonesia's population will grow, the rate of such growth will slow in the future. Indonesia's status as the world's fourth largest country by population will thus be gone by 2030, when another country — either Nigeria or Pakistan — overtakes us. By 2045, Indonesia will probably only be at number six. Indonesia is currently experiencing a demographic bonus which will last until between 2025 and 2030. However, sometime between 2038 and 2045, Indonesia will experience an ageing population, which means that the ratio of dependents is higher than the ratio of productive working people.

Indonesia thus needs to be ready. The rule of thumb in being an advanced or developed country is that a country needs to achieve that status before experiencing an ageing population. Thus, Indonesia does not have much time. It still has 20 years, but that is a relatively short period of time to turn Indonesia into a developed country.

A recent observation we have derived from Indonesia's economic data is that we have had growth of around 5.06 percent in the third quarter of 2017. However, our consumption growth in the third quarter was only 4.93 percent. If we look at consumption in terms of individual items, growth in Food and Beverages is still healthy at above five percent. However, if we pay attention to the statistics for health, education, transportation, communications as well restaurants and hotels, we can see a shift from the consumption of goods to the consumption of services. This is partly because people value leisure more, but this also means that Indonesia's middle class is growing. When a given person reaches the middle class status, they usually cut down on their consumption of basic goods and begin to consume things like high-quality education, healthcare, leisure, tourism, transportation and communications at a much greater rate. This is thus a good sign.

1.2.5.3 *Supporting Start-Ups to Adapt to the Digital Economy*

With regards to the current state of the world, Indonesia certainly needs to adapt to the digital economy, as does Singapore. We know that the digital economy is unavoidable and that some sectors will be seriously affected. This is the reason why there are so many retail shops — not only in Indonesia but also in developed countries like the United States — which have been forced out of business because they cannot compete with e-commerce businesses. They could not adapt to the digital economy. For instance, there are no more major bookstores in the United States right now because they could not compete with Amazon. Hypermarkets are also going out of business because people do not want to have to physically go to one to find things that they need when they can do it from home on their computers and have everything delivered to their front doors in two or three hours.

Indonesia is trying to help start-up companies, some of which have done very well. One industry in which Indonesia has gained international recognition for competitiveness — which was also specifically mentioned by Malaysian Prime Minister Najib Razak during our discussion in Malaysia — is bike-sharing. These start-ups are not only helping people to gain access to transportation but also help to create jobs, since bike-sharing services like GO-JEK create job opportunities that can address unemployment.

1.2.5.4 *Aiming for Sustainable and Evenly Distributed Development*

When we talk about sustainable development today, the primary objective is of course to meet the Sustainable Development Goals. This applies not only to Indonesia, Malaysia and Singapore, but every country in the world. There are 17 goals to meet. Let me just mention a few for illustrations.

For the first goal, the fulfilment of basic needs ties into the elimination of poverty. We believe that by meeting basic needs, Indonesia is able to reduce poverty quite significantly. For goal number eight of improving economic growth, we feel that this can be brought about through supporting Indonesia's leading sectors of agriculture, manufacturing and tourism. Furthermore, Indonesia also anticipates the fact that it is becoming a highly urbanised country. As mentioned previously, 80 percent of Indonesia's population will be living in urban areas by 2045, with the urbanisation rate for Java Island being even higher at 90 percent. This means that Java will not just be an island — it will be an urban island. All this will happen by 2045.

Indonesia has to anticipate this by building modern transport systems, encouraging sustainability and building smart cities. Since there are governors or representatives from all 34 provinces, the strategy of the government is one that will ensure development is not only focused on Java. Java will still dominate, given that it is still contributing 58 percent to Indonesia's GDP. However, the central government realises that it needs do more in order to disperse growth. The government seeks to do this by creating what is called the "growth centres". These "growth centres" could take the form of industrial areas, industrial estates and industrial parks, hubs and ports, or even Special Economic Zones (SEZ) and tourism areas.

There are many different types of new development areas located all around Indonesia, mostly outside of Java. Some are located in North Sumatra, like the tourist area of Lake Toba and the industrial park and SEZ at Sei Mangkei. In Kalimantan, there is SEZ in Maloy Batuta, East Kalimantan and an industrial park at Ketapang, West Kalimantan. In Sulawesi, there will be a seaport hub at Bitung, North Sulawesi as well as an industrial park at Morowali, Central Sulawesi. In North Maluku, there is Morotai while in Papua, there is Bintuni as well as Sorong. In Nusa Tenggara, we have the tourist areas of Mandalika in the west and Labuan Bajo in the east. In Java, there is the tourist area of Borobudur, DI Yogyakarta. The Indonesia government is trying to make regional development more equal by creating more growth centres outside of Java.

Of course, sustainability is not just in terms of economics but also environmental. Indonesia has launched the so-called low-carbon development strategies, which will be implemented starting with a five-year-plan that will be put in place between 2020 and 2024. This is done because Indonesia has a global commitment: by 2020, it needs to reduce emissions by 26 percent. Currently, Indonesia has been able to reduce emissions by only 13.5 percent, which means that there is still a long way to go. Nevertheless, by working on issues pertaining to land use, preventing deforestation, having productive agriculture, supporting renewable energy and transportation, promoting environmentally-friendly manufacturing as well as being mindful of waste management, Indonesia is moving towards having a low-carbon development strategy. We hope that Indonesia's economic growth after 2020 will be greener than what it is now.

Of course, after economic and environmental sustainability, Indonesia also needs to be socially sustainable. We must keep improving Indonesia's social protection system which includes social security and social assistance. This may involve working on the smart cards for health insurance, education and conditional cash transfers. It also involves continuously improving basic infrastructure such as water, sanitation, housing, arterial roads and irrigation, as well as basic services which mostly pertain to health and education as well as legal statuses.

Indonesia must of course ensure sustainable livelihoods for the poor and vulnerable. We need to empower communities and build our villages. This is the purpose of the Village Funds, which are direct transfers from the central government to around 74,000 villages all around Indonesia. The government hopes that every rupiah in the fund will have a significant impact on improving life at the village level, as long as it is managed wisely and is under good supervision. The government also hopes to reduce Indonesia's poverty rate to around seven or eight percent, and our Gini Ratio to 0.36 in 2019. Part of our efforts to reduce the Gini Ratio will be reducing inequality through effective fiscal policy, which includes ensuring that people who are supposed to pay taxes at the correct amounts do so — something I believe to be one of the biggest sources of inequality. Of course, the central government also needs to intervene in order to address regional disparities using transfer instruments. It also needs to keep providing productive job opportunities, which in this case refers to jobs which pay the minimum wage and which are part of the formal job market.

1.3 Structure and Content of the Book

This book presents the results of ACI's most updated series of research projects on Indonesia's sub-national economies. Aside from the annual competitiveness analysis and simulation studies on Indonesia's provinces and regions, in this edition, we also present results of a new thematic research project on FDI and real effective exchange rate as well as an overview of the latest developments in 34 Indonesian provinces in 2015–2017.

The book comprises six chapters, inclusive of this introductory chapter as the roadmap for readers. The chapter has also included a section on Indonesia's development strategies and priorities in 2017, which was adapted from the speech delivered by Dr Bambang Brodjonegoro, Minister of National Development Planning Agency (Bappenas) of the Republic of Indonesia, during the 2017 World Bank Group–Asia Competitiveness Institute Annual Conference on 23 November 2017 in Singapore. Next, Chapter 2 presents the 2017 annual update on provincial competitiveness ranking and simulation for Indonesian provinces. Chapter 3 features the application of a consistent analytical framework on competitiveness applied to six Indonesian regions (geographic aggregation of the provinces). Chapter 4 offers insights into the impact of exchange rate movements and fluctuations at the national level on FDI inflows at the provincial level. Chapter 5 presents the latest update on development conditions in each of Indonesia's 34 provinces, covering economic and social conditions, provincial government policies as well as local political scenes. Finally, Chapter 6 provides a summary, concluding remarks and a brief overview of ACI's future research agenda for Indonesia.

Chapter 2

The 2017 annual update of Indonesia's provincial competitiveness analysis (Chapter 2) provides the latest iteration for one of ACI's flagship research projects. We measure competitiveness as a

Table 1.1: Highlights of ACI's 2017 Overall Competitiveness Ranking of Indonesian Provinces (Top-Five and Bottom-Five Provinces)

2017 Overall Competitiveness		Province	Region
Rank	Std. Scores		
1	3.459	DKI Jakarta	Java
2	1.723	East Java	Java
3	1.303	East Kalimantan	Kalimantan
4	1.035	Central Java	Java
5	0.946	West Java	Java
...	...	...	...
29	–0.712	Maluku	Maluku-Papua
30	–1.238	East Nusa Tenggara	Bali-Nusa Tenggara
31	–1.304	North Maluku	Maluku-Papua
32	–1.706	Papua	Maluku-Papua
33	–1.891	West Papua	Maluku-Papua

Source: ACI.

composite of four environments, spanning (i) Macroeconomic Stability, (ii) Government and Institutional Setting, (iii) Financial, Businesses and Manpower Conditions as well as (iv) Quality of Life and Infrastructure Development.

As can be seen in Table 1.1, the special capital region (DKI) Jakarta occupies first place in terms of Overall Competitiveness, as it has been for the past five years since the annual analysis was first published in 2013, while East Java remains as the second-most competitive after Jakarta.[3] Overall, we can see that provinces in the Java region tend to occupy the top-end of the table, with four out of the top-five provinces coming from the Java region. Meanwhile, provinces in the Maluku-Papua region tend to occupy the bottom-end, with all four of the provinces therein occupying the bottom section. The performance of provinces in the Kalimantan, Sulawesi, Sumatra as well as Bali and Nusa Tenggara regions tends to be mixed.

Chapter 3

The 2017 update on competitiveness analysis of Indonesian regions (Chapter 3) applies the same framework used in Chapter 2 on six regions of Indonesia, wherein each region is an aggregation of several provinces based on their major island groupings. Consistent with the findings at the provincial level presented in Chapter 2, we see that the Java region tops the performance on competitiveness, while the Maluku and Papua region holds the last place, as has been the case in the past years. While the top- and bottom-performing regions are of no surprise, the dynamics of performance among the Kalimantan, Sulawesi and Sumatra regions are interesting to follow. Sumatra deserves special attention as conventional wisdom argues that it is a competitive region

[3] See Tan and Amri (2016) for causality analysis of output growth in East Java.

which does not hold ground empirically. Instead, we see Kalimantan and Sulawesi regions surging ahead.

This chapter is immediately followed by a discussant note by Professor Balthasar Kambuaya, who is the Chairman of the University Senate in Cenderawasih University, Papua as well as Former Minister of Environment in Indonesia, which was originally delivered during the Asia Economic Forum organised by ACI on 28 August 2017 in Singapore.

Chapter 4

This chapter presents ACI's analysis on the relationship between the Indonesian rupiah's real effective exchange rates (REER) and FDI inflows to 33 Indonesian provinces. We have discussed earlier the dynamics of FDI inflows to Indonesia as a whole. Considering the role that FDI plays in supplementing domestic capital, technology and skills (Barro 1997; Borensztein, De Gregorio, and Lee 1998; Alfaro et al. 2004), it is critical to look at FDI inflows at the sub-national level.

The research used a panel fixed effect regression on annual FDI inflows in 33 provinces from 2000 to 2014. The key independent variables were (i) annual average REER level in year *t*, and (ii) the standard deviation of monthly REER in year *t*, as a measure of REER volatility. Other province-specific control variables were drawn from Blonigen (2005), such as gross regional domestic product (GRDP) per capita, population, minimum wages, education level, outstanding bank loans, etc. We also tested an augmented model which included foreign exchange reserves.

Empirical results found that both REER levels and REER volatility (national-level variables) had a negative and significant correlation with FDI inflows at the sub-national level. This implies that FDI into Indonesia is mostly export-oriented. Other significant variables with consistent signs were GRDP per capita (positive), population (positive), mean years of schooling (negative) and outstanding bank loans (positive). This chapter is immediately followed by discussant notes by Dr Darius Tirtosuharto, Economist at the Bank of Indonesia, and Professor Sin Chor-Yiu from the Department of Economics, National Tsing Hua University, Taiwan.

Chapter 5

Next, Chapter 5 provides short updates of recent developments in all 34 provinces of Indonesia. The chapter is co-written with representatives of ACI's academic partners in the provinces, who have for the past five years collaborated with us to conduct the annual provincial competitiveness surveys. A wealth of knowledge on the Indonesian provinces resides with these academics. Starting this year, we have expanded the collaboration and have them contribute to this flagship publication.

Each province is featured as a two-page Section, while each Section consists of concise descriptions on the economic conditions, social conditions and development, provincial government policies as well as the local political scenes in 2015–2017. These descriptions would complement the data used in the construction of the competitiveness index as presented in Chapter 2, where the competitiveness index used hard data from the year 2014 combined with survey data from the year 2016.

Chapter 6

The final chapter of this book recapitulates the key findings of our research on Indonesia in 2017 and presents a concluding remark on the risks that Indonesia faces in further developing its economy. The book closes with a note on ACI's future research agenda, which would be to review the relationship between REER at the national level and exports at the sub-national level.

In light of Indonesia's drive to regain a healthy growth rate while keeping solid macroeconomic principles, it is critical that we review its development progress more comprehensively at the sub-national level. ACI's contribution is to support policymakers, academics as well as business owners and managers to make sense of Indonesia's vast potentials and challenges from an economic perspective. In the process, we aim to contribute to the growing knowledge base on Indonesia, provide insights for better decision-making and trigger sustainable and inclusive development that would provide stability for the wider ASEAN and Asian regions.

References

Alfaro, Laura, Areendam Chanda, Sebnem Kalemli-Ozcan, and Selin Sayek. 2004. "FDI and Economic Growth: The Role of Local Financial Markets." *Journal of International Economics* 64 (1): 89–112.

Bank Indonesia. n.d. "Indonesian Sovereign Rating — Bank Sentral Republik Indonesia." Bank Indonesia Website. Accessed March 6, 2018. http://www.bi.go.id/en/iru/market-data/indonesian-sovereign-rating/Default.aspx.

Barro, Robert J. 1997. *Determinants of Economic Growth: A Cross-Country Empirical Study*. Singapore: The MIT Press.

Bird, Richard M., and François Vaillancourt. 2008. *Fiscal Decentralization in Developing Countries*. Cambridge University Press.

Birdsall, Nancy M., Jose Edgardo L. Campos, Chang-Shik Kim, and W. Max Corden. 1993. "The East Asian Miracle: Economic Growth and Public Policy." 12351. Washington, D.C. http://documents.worldbank.org/curated/en/975081468244550798/Main-report.

Blonigen, Bruce A. 2005. "A Review of the Empirical Literature on FDI Determinants." *Atlantic Economic Journal*, no. 33: 383–403.

Borensztein, Eduardo, Jose De Gregorio, and Jong-Wha Lee. 1998. "How Does Foreign Direct Investment Affect Economic Growth? 1." *Journal of International Economics* 45 (1): 115–35.

Kompas. 2017. "Target 'Tax Amnesty' Tak Tercapai, Ditjen Pajak Siap Beri Penjelasan." KOMPAS.com. April 1, 2017. https://bisniskeuangan.kompas.com/read/2017/04/01/103700526/target.tax.amnesty.tak.tercapai.ditjen.pajak.siap.beri.penjelasan.

———. 2018. "BI: Pertumbuhan Ekonomi Indonesia 5,1 Persen Di Tahun 2017." *Kompas*, February 2, 2018.

Oberman, Raoul, Richard Dobbs, Arief Budiman, Fraser Thompson, and Morten Rosse. 2012. "The Archipelago Economy: Unleashing Indonesia's Potential." McKinsey Global Institute. http://www.mckinsey.com/global-themes/asia-pacific/the-archipelago-economy.

O'Neill, Jim. 2013. "Who You Calling a BRIC?" *Bloomberg View*, November 12, 2013. https://www.bloombergview.com/articles/2013-11-12/who-you-calling-a-bric-.

Tan, Khee Giap, Mulya Amri, Nursyahida Ahmad, and Kong Yam Tan. 2017a. *2016 Growth Slowdown Analysis, Ease of Doing Business Index, and Annual Competitiveness Studies of Indonesia's Sub-National Economies*. Asia Competitiveness Institute — World Scientific Series. Singapore: World Scientific. http://www.worldscientific.com/worldscibooks/10.1142/10621.

Tan, Khee Giap, Mulya Amri, Linda Low, and Kong Yam Tan. 2013. *Competitiveness Analysis and Development Strategies for 33 Indonesian Provinces*. World Scientific.

Tan, Khee Giap, Nurina Merdikawati, Mulya Amri, and Kong Yam Tan. 2015. *2014 Provincial and Inaugural Regional Competitiveness Analysis: Safeguarding Indonesia's Growth Momentum*. World Scientific.

Tan, Khee Giap, Nurina Merdikawati, Mulya Amri, and Kong Yam Tan. 2017b. *2015 Agricultural Productivity, Decentralisation, and Competitiveness Analysis for Provinces and Regions of Indonesia*. Asia Competitiveness Institute - World Scientific Series. Singapore: World Scientific. http://www.worldscientific.com/worldscibooks/10.1142/10245.

Tempo. 2017. "Beberapa Penyebab Target Tax Amnesty Tak Tercapai." Tempo. April 2, 2017. https://bisnis.tempo.co/read/861850/beberapa-penyebab-target-tax-amnesty-tak-tercapai.

The Jakarta Post. 2017. "Tax Amnesty Achieves 75 Percent of Target: Tax Office." The Jakarta Post. April 17, 2017. http://www.thejakartapost.com/news/2017/04/17/tax-amnesty-achieves-75-percent-of-target-tax-office.html.

The World Bank. 2013. "Doing Business 2014 — Understanding Regulations for Small and Medium-Size Enterprises." Washington, D.C.: The World Bank. http://www.doingbusiness.org/reports/global-reports/doing-business-2014.

———. 2017a. "Doing Business 2018 - Reforming to Create Jobs." Washington DC: The World Bank. http://www.doingbusiness.org/reports/global-reports/doing-business-2018.

———. 2017b. "Indonesia Economic Quarterly, December 2017: Decentralization That Delivers." The World Bank.

Chapter 2

2017 Annual Update on Competitiveness Analysis of Indonesian Provinces

2.1 Introductory Notes

Indonesia's overall competitiveness is contingent upon the central and local governments' ability to see bureaucratic reforms through and ensure that growth is broad-based across the different regions. With the threat of fluctuating oil and commodity prices affecting many provinces in most recent times, Indonesia can no longer afford to rely on resource-based growth without giving precedence to diversifying its sources of growth to other prospects such as manufacturing or service-based economic activities. As decentralisation figures in this diversification, sustainable economic growth is only possible if each province in Indonesia upholds its role in improving its own competitiveness — from macroeconomic management, governance, financial, businesses and labour conditions, to infrastructure development.

In line with the above objective, Asia Competitiveness Institute (ACI) has been tracking the competitiveness of Indonesia's provinces across the years, enabling policymakers to assess the competitiveness profile of each province in Indonesia vis-à-vis their peers (Tan et al. 2013; 2015b; 2017; Tan, Amri, and Ahmad 2017). This chapter contains the fifth iteration of ACI's annual competitiveness ranking of Indonesian provinces, making it the most consistent among other similar measurements at the country's sub-national level in recent years.

This chapter is organised as follows. Section 2.1 provides a snapshot of Indonesia's recent economic development and competitiveness. Section 2.2 outlines the methodology comprising a broad sweep of competitiveness review, ACI's competitiveness framework, indicators, data sources, standardised score, *What-if* competitiveness simulation as well as the inaugural use of an alternative computation known as Shapley weight that serves as a robustness check. Section 2.3 discusses the empirical findings and Section 2.4 concludes by drawing some policy implications.

2.1.1 Broad Sweep of Competitiveness Review

Initially, the term "competitiveness" was closely associated with firms' performance (Porter 1980) based on a notion that it was primarily firms that competed with each other. Over time, the discourse expanded into the national level (Porter 1990; Berger and Bristow 2009), as also shown by the establishment of "Council on Competitiveness" or similar institutions in various advanced industrialised countries. After all, the performances of those firms depend on various factors that are embedded in the firms' location that include, but not limited to, quality of labour and infrastructure, governance, costs of doing business as well as the performance of competing and complementary firms around the area (Bristow 2009; Camagni 2002; Kitson, Martin, and Tyler 2004).

A more common approach to measure a country's competitiveness is by constructing a benchmarking index, as adopted by the two most highly cited cross-country competitiveness studies: (i) Global Competitiveness Report published by the World Economic Forum (WEF) and (ii) World Competitiveness Yearbook by the International Institute for Management Development (IMD). The benchmarking index is effective at summarising complex and multi-dimensional factors in a user-friendly and easily digestible platform. Information from the ranking, score and progress over time can facilitate discussion with the general public to promote key reforms that often require efforts from multiple stakeholders.

Beyond country-level competitiveness, there are more studies delving into the sub-national level, either at state/provincial level or district/city level. For instance, the Beacon Hill Institute at Suffolk University has been publishing the annual competitiveness report for 50 states in the United States since 2002. As previously mentioned in Chapter 1, the ACI has been analysing the sub-national competitiveness not only in Indonesia but also in India (Tan, Gopalan, and Tandon 2017, 2016; Tan et al. 2015a) and China (Tan, Wang, and Xie 2017; Tan, Yuan, and Xie 2016; Tan, Yuan, and Yoong 2015). Conducting a competitiveness study at a smaller scale of analysis allows us to suggest development strategies which are relevant to the specific sub-national economy (provinces) in order to stimulate productive discussion among key stakeholders at this level in the first instance before engaging them at the national level.

2.1.2 Competitiveness Analyses on Indonesia

The competitiveness of Indonesia as a country is analysed regularly by a number of institutions, including the WEF, IMD and ACI.

Figure 2.1: ACI Competitiveness Rankings for ASEAN-10 Countries, 2000–2014

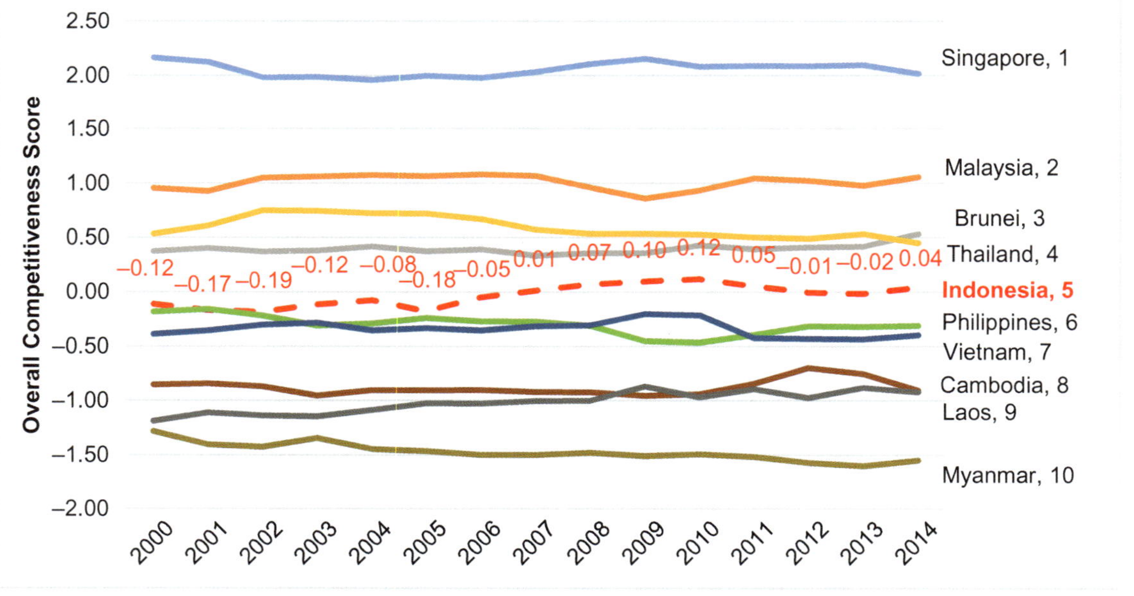

Source: ACI.

Figure 2.2: World Economic Forum Global Competitiveness Rankings, 2012–2017 (Selected Countries)

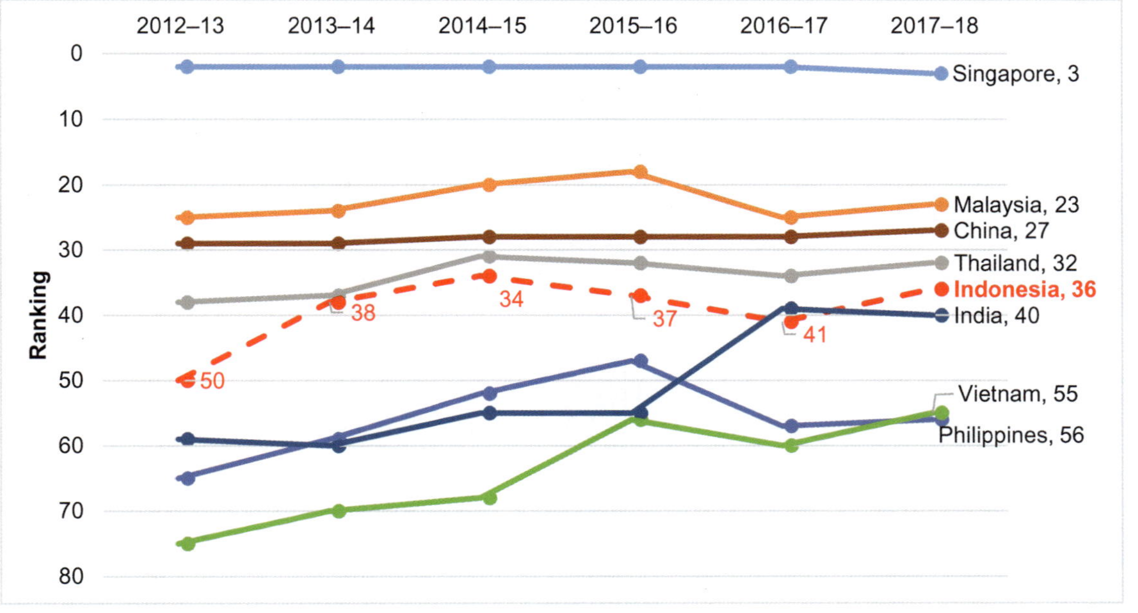

Note: *Y*-axis is reversed. Lower rank indicates better performance.
Source: WEF data, compiled by ACI.

Figure 2.3: International Institute for Management Development World Competitiveness Rankings, 2012–2017 (Selected Countries)

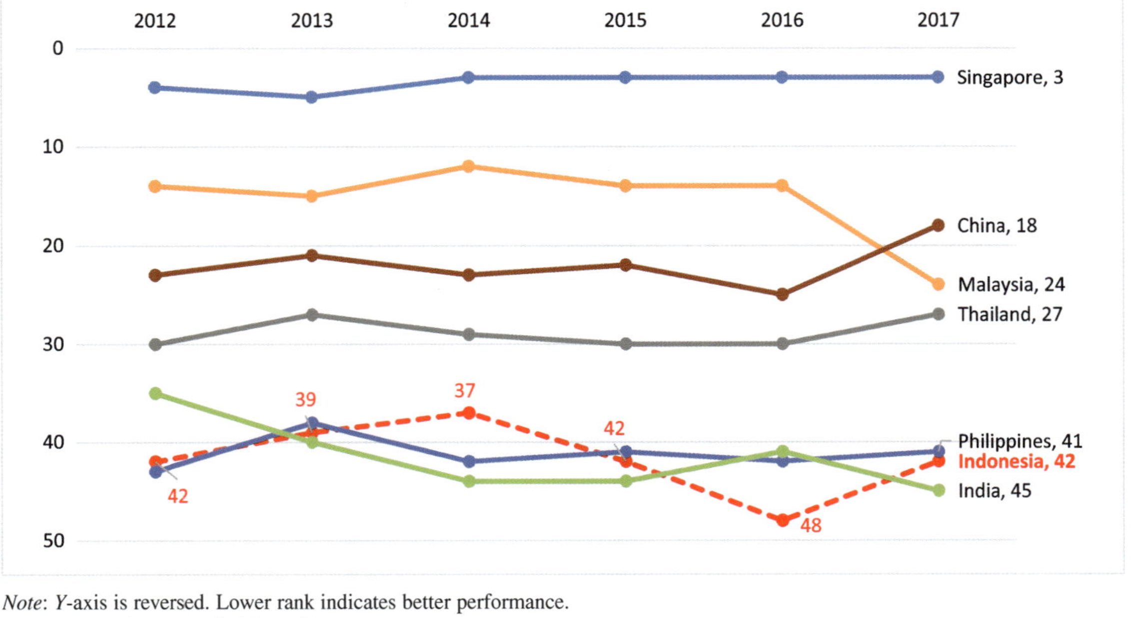

Note: *Y*-axis is reversed. Lower rank indicates better performance.
Source: IMD data, compiled by ACI.

In Figure 2.1, ACI's annual competitiveness analysis of the 10 member countries of Association of Southeast Asian Nations (ASEAN) finds Indonesia at the fifth position since 2002, behind Singapore, Malaysia, Brunei and Thailand (Tan, Nguyen, and Nguyen 2017; Tan et al. 2016, 2015c). Indonesia competed closely with the Philippines for this fifth position in 2000–2002 as well as 2005, but surged ahead and maintained its position from 2006 onwards. The country's standardised scores for Overall Competitiveness peaked in 2010 at 0.115, but declined steadily to –0.014 in 2012 and 2013, in line with the negative impact of global growth slowdown and commodity price bust. However, Indonesia's competitiveness improved again in 2014, mostly due to the stabilising global macroeconomic conditions and the relatively declining performance of Thailand and Cambodia.

In a similar light, WEF's Global Competitiveness Report shows an improvement in Indonesia's global competitiveness ranking from 2012–2013 to 2014–2015, rising from 50th to 34th ranking (Schwab and Sala-i-Martín 2014). Since then, however, Indonesia slipped to 41st place in 2016–2017 (Schwab and Sala-i-Martín 2016), although in the latest year, it has begun to show signs of improvement by rising to 36th place in 2017–2018 (see Figure 2.2), driven largely by its sizeable market and fairly robust macroeconomic conditions (Schwab and Sala-i-Martín 2017). IMD's World Competitiveness Yearbook also finds that Indonesia's competitiveness rose from 42nd in 2012 to 37th in 2014. It declined to the 48th position in 2016, but lately picked up momentum again to reach 42nd in 2017 (see Figure 2.3) (IMD 2017).

At the sub-national level, there remains a dearth of research that is specific to Indonesian provinces. One study by the Bank of Indonesia and University of Padjadjaran measured the competitiveness of provinces, cities and regencies using an input–output framework to identify the productivity of each sub-national entity (PPSK Bank Indonesia and LP3E FE-UNPAD 2008). The Indonesia Governance Index for all provinces was published subsequently, with economic governance as one of the four main sub-indices or "arena" being analysed (Partnership for Governance Reform 2013). Additionally, a ranking of economic governance for 243 cities and regencies in Indonesia was also conducted, first in 2006 and later in 2011 (KPPOD and The Asia Foundation 2007, 2011). In 2016, the same team also conducted a ranking of economic governance in 32 provincial capitals of Indonesia (KPPOD 2017).

All these are, in one form or another, an effort to measure the competitiveness of Indonesia's sub-national entities which should be welcomed. However, these studies are not conducted on a regular basis and at a frequent enough interval to enable more timely policy decision-making. The lack of regular analysis on the competitiveness of Indonesia's sub-national entities also makes it difficult to track progress.

ACI intends to fill this gap in knowledge on the economic profile of Indonesian provinces. In this sense, we choose to explore competitiveness at the provincial level as opposed to the city or regency level because provinces are typically sizeable enough to function as an economy whereas cities and regencies may not. As an illustration, the most populous province of West Java is home to about 46 million people, and the least populous, West Papua, accommodates 871,000 people as per population projections for 2015.

The following sections present the methodology, empirical findings and policy implications of the latest iteration of ACI's annual competitiveness analysis of Indonesian provinces.

2.2 Research Methodology

2.2.1 ACI's Competitiveness Framework

ACI's approach to competitiveness is a holistic one, encompassing 100 different indicators that collectively shape the ability of an economy to achieve substantial and inclusive economic development over a sustained period of time. In line with this comprehensive approach, the ACI defines competitiveness through four different environments and 12 sub-environments as follows:

1. **Macroeconomic Stability**
   This environment encompasses aggregated economic conditions that underline the comparative and competitive advantage of each province based on classical macroeconomic indicators.

   (a) Regional Economic Vibrancy
   This sub-environment captures the size of each province's economy and its growth trajectory according to the different characteristics in their economic structure. Beyond gross regional domestic product (GRDP), this sub-environment also takes into account inflation rate as well as capital formation.
   (b) Openness to Trade and Services
   This sub-environment measures the degree of openness to international trade for each province. All indicators related to exports, imports and the ratio of openness are included.
   (c) Attractiveness to Foreign Investors
   This sub-environment measures to what extent each province manages to attract both foreign and direct investments. Considering that investments may fluctuate on a yearly basis, we use the average value of the last three years of investments for each province.

2. **Government and Institutional Setting**
   This environment covers the efficacy of government institutions as well as expectations of progress in the public sector.

   (a) Government Policies and Fiscal Sustainability
   This sub-environment captures the financial capacity of each provincial government to ensure fiscal sustainability to undertake various policies under their jurisdiction. All fiscal-related indicators, such as provincial government's revenue, tax collection, expenditure and fiscal balance, are included.
   (b) Institutions, Governance, and Leadership
   This sub-environment covers the broad spectrum of governance quality ranging from the prevalence of corruption practices to how well the provincial government coordinates among the different layers of local governments.

(c) Competition, Regulatory Standards and Rule of Law

This sub-environment covers to what extent each province is able to create and enforce a consistent rule of law and regulation that allow for competition and ease of doing business to thrive.

3. **Financial, Businesses and Manpower Conditions**

This environment encompasses the performance and potential of firms as well as the conditions that managers face in running their companies.

(a) Financial Deepening and Business Efficiency

This sub-environment captures the availability of a sound financial system to support the growing firms. Additionally, wide-ranging assessments on firms' performance, strategy, human resource and equipment capacity, application of information technology as well as innovation are included.

(b) Labour Market Flexibility

This sub-environment covers the size of each province's labour force, employment and unemployment rate as well as the stickiness of labour market as measured by the minimum monthly wage, ease of recruiting managerial and technical workers as well as relationship between labour unions and management.

(c) Productivity Performance

This sub-environment covers all indicators related to productivity as measured by the output per worker, both in general term and some that are specific to each economic structure.

4. **Quality of Life and Infrastructure Development**

This environment covers wide-ranging indicators related to physical and technological infrastructure as well as provision of basic social services.

(a) Physical Infrastructure

This sub-environment not only captures market size as measured by population and urbanisation rate but also physical infrastructure including, air, sea and land connectivity as well as access to water and electricity services.

(b) Technological Infrastructure

This sub-environment captures the rate of information, communications and technology (ICT) adoption in each province. Indicators related to telephone, hand phone, desktop, and laptop ownership as well as internet access at various location points are included.

(c) Standard of Living, Education and Social Stability

This sub-environment encompasses access to education and healthcare as well as a broader set of measurements for quality of life, such as equality of income distribution, environmental sustainability and accessibility of goods and services.

As visualised in Figure 2.4, each environment contributes the same weight (25 percent) to the Overall Competitiveness Index. ACI's competitiveness framework further drills down to a nested approach, wherein each of the four environments is further divided into three sub-environments. Therefore, there are 12 sub-environments in total, with each sub-environment contributing the same weight (33.3 percent) towards its respective environment's index.

Figure 2.4: ACI's Competitiveness Framework

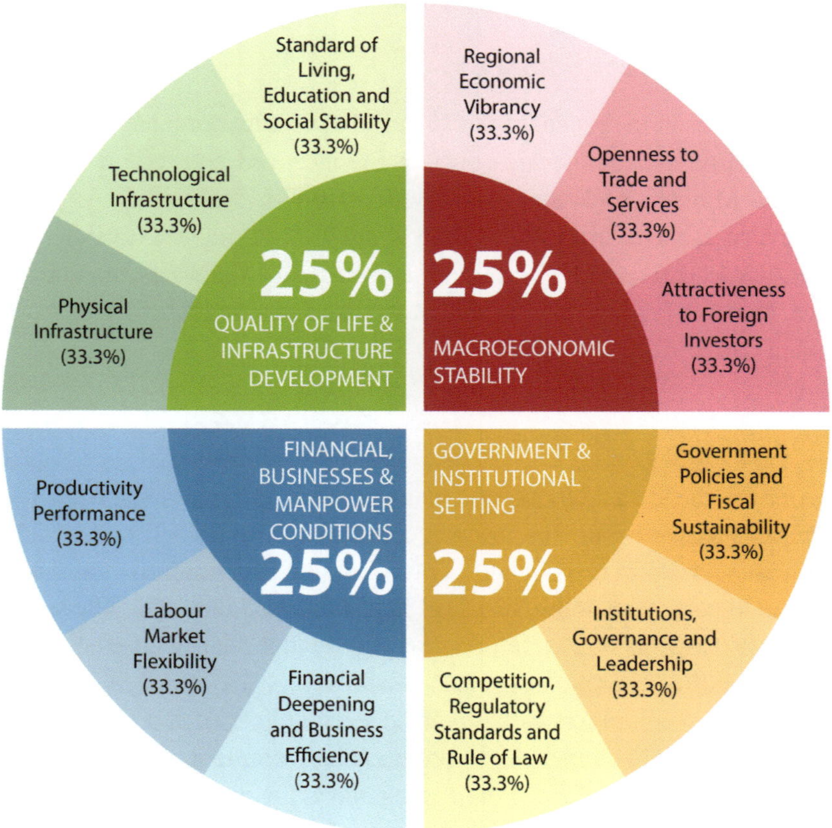

Source: ACI.

In aggregating the sub-environments into environments, and the environments into the overall ranking, ACI uses a simple averaging mechanism with equal weights. While assigning different weights for different indicators with varying levels of importance may seem appropriate, the implementations are as controversial. Thus, to achieve a balanced view towards the different factors that make up an overall notion of competitiveness, we use equal weights across all indicators. Going forward, in order to verify the robustness of our results from the subjective assumption on equal weight, we introduce an objective weighting method, namely the Shapley weight, which will be discussed in detail in Section 2.2.5.

2.2.2 Indicators and Data Sources

The ACI 2017 Competitiveness Index for Indonesia's provinces[1] uses a combination of secondary and primary data with a total of 100 indicators. Although the weights assigned to the four environments and 12 sub-environments are equal, some sub-environments have more indicators than others due to data availability. See Appendix 1 for the complete list of indicators.

2.2.2.1 *Formal Government Statistics*

Most of the indicators used in this analysis (76 out of 100 indicators) are formal secondary data drawn from various government agencies, such as Indonesia's Central Statistical Agency (BPS), Bank of Indonesia, Ministry of Trade, Ministry of Health as well as Ministry of Environment and Forestry. We also use data from World Bank's Indonesia Database for Policy and Economic Research (INDO-DAPOER) and CEIC Indonesia Premium Database which cited BPS as their original sources. Due to a lag in data availability, the latest available data at the time of collection in mid-2016 were data for the year 2014.

2.2.2.2 *Surveys in Each Province*

A smaller portion of the data (24 out of 100 indicators) is based on primary data obtained through perception surveys conducted in each province in the second half of 2016, where we obtained responses from 2,335 respondents. This allows us to capture the more recent dynamics of competitiveness to complement the time-lags from the secondary data. The surveys also allow us to understand some aspects of competitiveness that are not readily measured by formal statistical data but reside in the perception of local stakeholders.

Three categories of stakeholders were involved separately in each province as survey participants: (i) business owners and operators, (ii) provincial government officials and (iii) academics. Responses from the three stakeholders were aggregated at the provincial level, with the intention that one stakeholder group provides a balancing view for the others.

The survey relied on purposive sampling method, where ACI collaborated with local partners representing the three stakeholders.

(i) For business owners and operators, surveys were done in collaboration with the Indonesian Employers' Association (APINDO), which has chapters in each province and invited their members to participate.
(ii) For the provincial governments, surveys were supported by the Coordinating Ministry for Economic Affairs, which provided reference letters to the governors. The provincial government, in turn, invited representatives from various departments to participate.

---

[1] There are currently 34 provinces in Indonesia. North Kalimantan, as Indonesia's newest province (carved out of East Kalimantan in 2012) is not yet analysed on its own due to lack of disaggregated data. North Kalimantan is therefore still analysed as part of East Kalimantan.

(iii) For academics, the ACI collaborated with universities in each province, most often with the faculty of economics and business. The university then invited their lecturers, researchers and graduate students to participate.

Figure 2.5 illustrates the characteristics of our survey respondents in 2016. Close to one-fifth (15.2 percent) of our academic respondents were senior lecturers with more than 20 years of teaching experience. This proportion more than doubled for respondents from the provincial government, with more than one-third (37.6 percent) having over 20 years of experience in public service. More details on the characteristics of the firms will be discussed in Section 2.2.2.3.

The surveys were conducted using an electronic response system, where questions were presented on a computer projector, and participants keyed in their answers using keypads. Facilitators from ACI were present at each survey to read the questions and give clarifications when needed.

A total of 2,335 respondents participated in the surveys. Of these, 802 were business owners and operators (34.3 percent), 776 were academics, largely from the faculty of economics and business (32.4 percent), and 757 were provincial government officials from various departments (33.2 percent). The average number of respondents per province was about 71 (2,335 respondents divided by 33 provinces). Out of the 71 respondents, typically 24 were business owners and operators, 24 were academics and 22 were provincial government officials. This further shows that the sample of respondents had a balanced representation of all three stakeholders.

Within each stakeholder group, we also have a balanced representation of experience. Specifically among the academics, about 20.1 percent had less than 10 years of teaching experience, 17.1 percent had between 10 and 20 years of teaching experience while 15.2 percent had more than 20 years of teaching experience. The remainder (47.6 percent) of academic respondents were graduate students. As for government officials, 29.7 percent had less than 10 years of working experience, 32.6 percent had between 10 and 20 years of experience and 37.6 percent had more than 20 years of experience. A more detailed review of respondents from the business sectors is presented next in Section 2.2.2.3.

Figure 2.5: Characteristics of Provincial Government and Academic Respondents of ACI's 2016 Survey

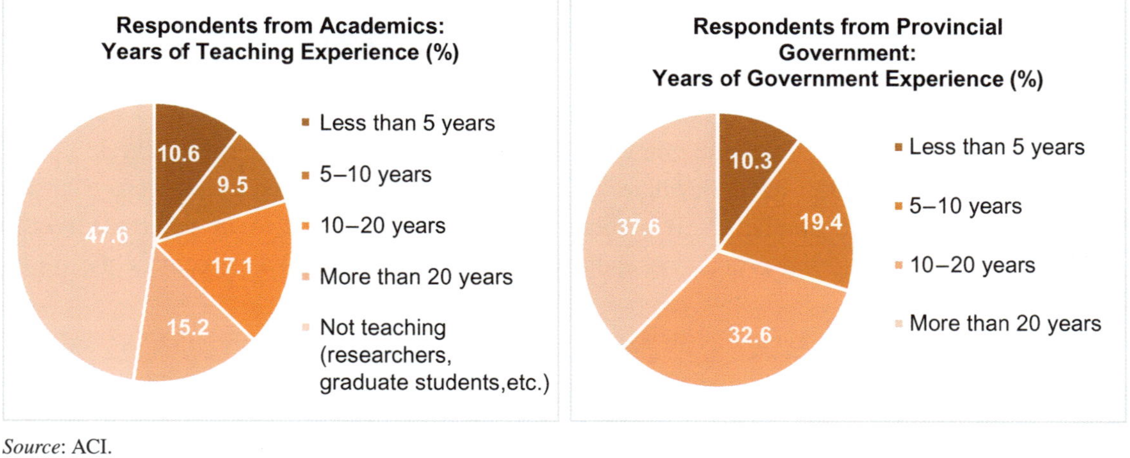

Source: ACI.

2.2.2.3 *Firm Demographics*

As mentioned earlier, a total of 802 business owners and operators had participated in the survey. Two classifications were adopted to identify firm size. The first is based on the annual turnover following Indonesia's Law No. 20 of 2008 on Micro, Small and Medium-sized Businesses which states that the annual turnover is up to Rp300 million for a micro business, between Rp300 million and Rp2.5 billion for a small business, between Rp2.5 billion and Rp50 billion for a medium-sized business while firms with a turnover of more than Rp50 billion are no longer classified as either micro, small or medium-sized (i.e. large). Based on this classification, about one-third (32.8 percent) of our business respondents in 2016 were micro, 27.8 percent were small, 21.9 percent were medium and 17.6 percent were large enterprises (see Figure 2.6).

The second classification of firm size is based on the number of employees as defined by BPS, which states that (manufacturing) enterprises with fewer than five employees are categorised as a household industry, those with between five and 19 employees are a small industry, those between 20 and 99 employees are a medium-sized industry while those with 100 or more employees are considered as a large industry (BPS 2018). Based on this classification, it can be observed that about one-fifth (19.2 percent) of our business respondents in 2016 were operating with fewer than five employees. Meanwhile, some 23.1 percent of the businesses were very large corporations which employed more than 500 employees. In general, there was a balanced representation of firms of different sizes, with each taking up about one-fifth of the sample.

Figure 2.6 also provides details on several characteristics of the businesses. It can be observed that the sample consisted of a good mix of start-ups and newly established firms as well as those which had been around longer in the market. More than one-third (36.3 percent) of the businesses had been operating for more than 20 years. This means that they had experience conducting business even in periods prior to the decentralisation in 1999, which saw fundamental changes to the political and economic autonomy in Indonesia. Thus, these firms would be the most well informed about the changing landscape of business environment in their provinces.

Zooming in on the industry type, it can be seen that a large proportion (37.8 percent) of the businesses were in the services sector. Meanwhile, some 23.2 percent of businesses were involved in trade while another 22.7 percent of the sample belonged to the processing industry. These proportions fairly correspond with the recent national statistics[2] covering businesses in Indonesia (BPS 2017), which identified that the trade (along with repair of vehicles), processing and services industries are the three largest types of businesses found in the country.

It is also worth noting that firms categorised under these industries were also the largest groups to make up the micro (revenue between 0 and Rp300 million) and large businesses (with revenue of more than Rp50 billion). Some 44.2 percent of the micro businesses were from the services industry, while another 30.0 percent of them were businesses in the trade sector. Understandably, firms in the processing industry added up to only 10.4 percent of the micro

[2]The Economic Census 2016 is carried out once every 10 years with the main goal of obtaining a complete data collection of all business units registered within the boundaries of Indonesia. It however excluded businesses that are categorized under the agricultural industry (BPS 2017).

Figure 2.6: Demographics of Firms in ACI's 2016 Survey

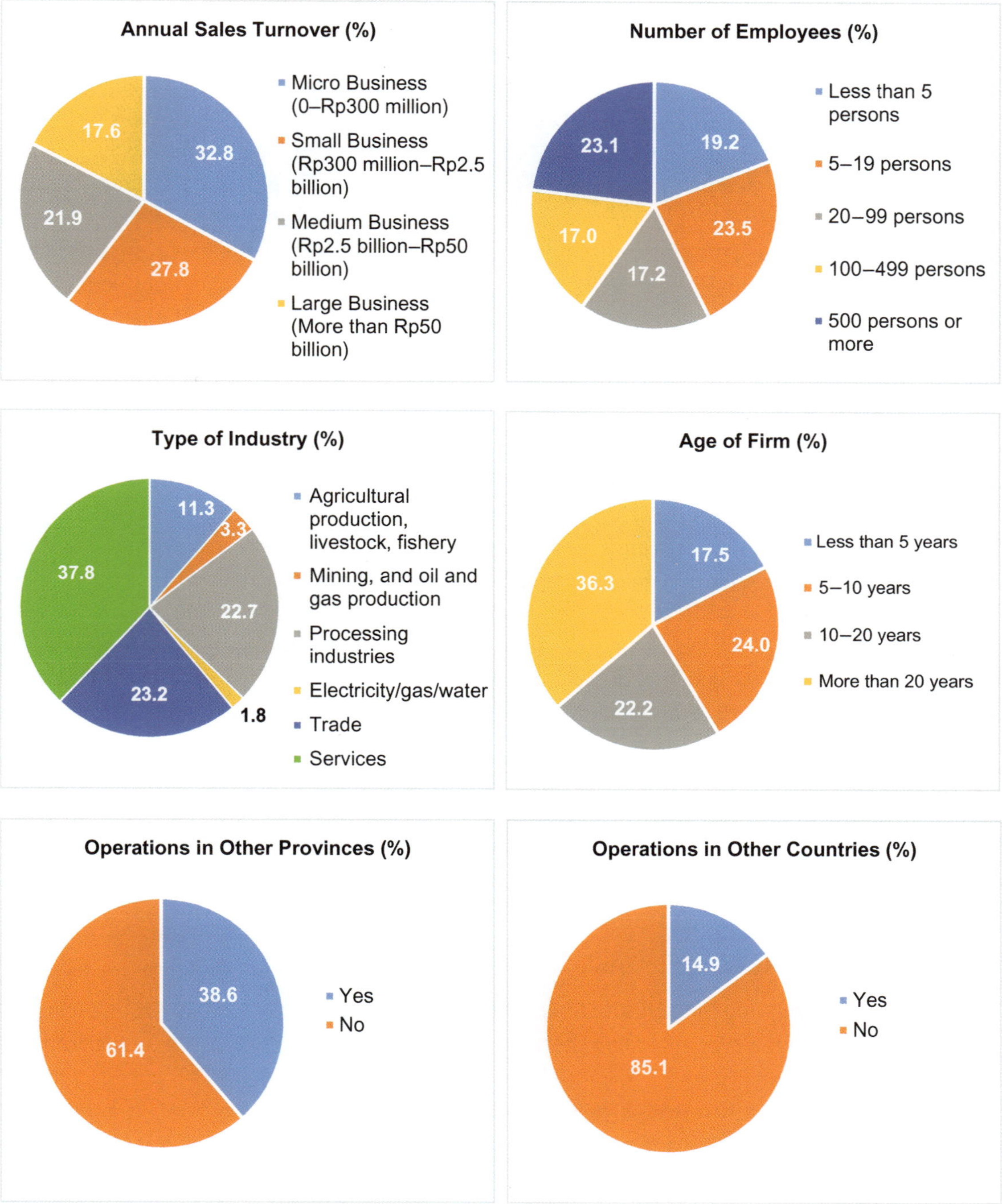

Source: ACI.

businesses, but constituted 47.1 percent of the large businesses. Meanwhile, some 22.1 percent and 10.7 percent of the large businesses belonged to the trade and services sectors respectively.

In terms of business expansion, about 38.6 percent of the businesses had operations in other provinces. To a smaller extent, however, 14.9 percent of the businesses had internationalised (i.e. had operations in other countries). Businesses which operated in both other provinces and other countries made up only 12 percent of the sample. This further shows that most businesses had mainly kept their operations to their province and would be conversant with the province's business climate, including regulations pertaining to business, manpower or financial conditions.

Taken together, these findings ultimately suggest that the businesses make up a dynamic group of respondents with diverse backgrounds, and that their perceptions would certainly be relevant and would add value to the assessment of both provincial and regional competitiveness in Indonesia.

2.2.3 The Standardised Score

After data collection, we aggregated the different types of data into a coherent dataset where the value of one indicator is comparable to the value of another. The issue, however, is that each indicator is measured in different units. For example, Government Revenue is measured in thousands of rupiah, while Cargo at International Seaport is measured in tonnes. To resolve these differences, we use the statistical method of 'standardised score'.

The standardised score has no unit of measurement because it simply measures how well a certain province performs in comparison to the average province. In statistical terms, it measures how many standard deviations away each province is from the average province. See Appendix 2 for a detailed, technical explanation.

If a province has a standardised score of zero, it is basically an average performer for that particular indicator. Having a negative score means that the province performs below average, while having a positive score means an above-average performance. The further away the score is from zero, the further away is the performance of the said province from the national average.

2.2.4 *What-if* Simulation Analysis

A competitiveness ranking in itself identifies which provinces are doing well and which ones are facing challenges. However, it stops short of giving constructive advice on improving the rankings.

ACI's *What-if* competitiveness simulation allows us to answer the question: "if a particular province improves its weakest indicators while assuming that other provinces remain constant, how would that province's ranking improve?" It is conducted based on the improvement of each province's top-20 percent weakest indicators and a recalculation of the standardised score based on such improvement.

To conduct the simulation, (1) we sorted the different indicators for each province based on their standardised scores. This allows us to identify the top-20 percent weakest indicators for each province. (2) Next, we raised the values of these indicators to the corresponding average values of all provinces. This improvement was conducted only for indicators with standardised scores that were previously negative. If the standardised scores were already zero or positive (i.e. value was average or above average), no changes were made. (3) Once the values had been raised, we re-calculated the ranking with the assumption that the values of other provinces remained constant. Therefore, this policy simulation was done individually for each province.

2.2.5 Shapley Value: A Novel Approach to the Assignment of Weights

As mentioned earlier, this year's analysis incorporates an inaugural objective weighting method, called the Shapley weight, which is aimed at verifying the robustness of ACI's standard equal weight computation. The Shapley weight is derived from the Shapley value, which is the most commonly used solution concept in cooperative game theory. Formally, a coalition game (N, v) in cooperative game theory is defined by a set of players N and a characteristic function $v(S)$: $2^N \rightarrow$ R, where it maps coalition S (or subset of players) to a real number. The function describes the expected payoffs that S players can obtain by cooperation. The Shapley value of the coalition game is an n-vector, denoted by $\Phi(v)$, satisfying a set of axioms, i.e. Individual Rationality, Efficiency, Symmetry, Additivity and Null Player.

The i-th component of $\Phi(v)$ can be determined by

$$\Phi(v) = \sum_{S \subseteq N \setminus \{i\}} \frac{|S|!(N - |S| - 1)!}{N!}(v(S \cup i) - v(S)).$$

In our context, the players will be the indicators used for the construction of the index, while the coalition will be the sub-environments and environments which the indicators belong to. The desirable properties, i.e. the axioms, are meaningful for general index ranking. Individual Rationality ensures that each indicator has a positive contribution to the index score. An indicator must satisfy the Null Player axiom[3], so that it is economically meaningful for that indicator to be considered relevant to the index. Symmetry guarantees that if two indicators carry the same value, they are equally important in the index scoring. Efficiency and Additivity are also important mathematical properties for the construction of an index.

The application of the Shapley value has been well studied in various strands of literature. The concept has been used to solve the taxation and redistribution problem as described by Aumann and Kurz (1977). It is also used in the voting for public goods problems. Aumann and Myerson (1988), for instance, studied the link or coalition formation among players using the Shapley value. Moulin (1992) studied the application of the Shapley value in fair division of unproduced goods under monetary transfer and quasi-linear utilities. Petrosjan and Zaccour (2003) studied the Shapley value cost allocation in a pollution reduction setting. More recently, Leth Hougaard, Ko, and Zhang (2017) applied the Shapley value concept to licensing under Fair, Reasonable and Non-Discriminatory (FRAND) terms. However, the Shapley value has not, to our knowledge, been previously applied to an index ranking analysis before.

[3] Null player exists when its contribution is zero, for which in this case, the weight assigned to it is zero.

As a robustness check to the equal weightage approach, we propose an objective weighting method based on the Shapley value — the "Bottom-Up" Approach.

2.2.5.1 *Shapley Weightage — The "Bottom-Up" Approach*

We first compute the Shapley value of each indicator based on the standardised score of the indicator for every province. By our definition, it measures the aggregate dispersion of the indicator, thus reflecting the disparity among the provinces. More weights are assigned to those indicators with higher Shapley values. The weights of the sub-environments are computed based on both the absolute performance (standardised scores) and the relative performance (weights) of indicators under that particular sub-environment. The weights of environments are computed in a similar way by considering the relevant absolute performance and the relative performance of the sub-environments. The detailed description of the methodology can be found in Appendix 3.

2.2.5.2 *Comparison between the Shapley Method and the Entropy Method*

Another objective weight assignment method commonly applied in the area of decision science is the entropy method (Zeleny 1982). The entropy for an indicator i is defined as

$$Entropy_i = -\frac{1}{\ln(\mathrm{E})}\sum_{e=1}^{E} p_{ei}\ln(p_{ei}),$$

where E is the number of economies, $p_{ei} = \frac{v_{ei}}{\sum_{e=1}^{E} v_{ei}}$ and v_{ei} is the characteristic of the raw data x_{ei}. The weightage of indicator i is then defined by

$$W_i = 1 - Entropy_i.$$

The interpretation of the entropy of an indicator concerns the information that the particular indicator transmits. The higher the entropy, the less the information carried, thus implying a lower weight assigned to that indicator. While this method appears to be an improvement over a subjective weighting scheme, one of the important reasons why it cannot be applied to our analysis is its inability to handle negative values due to its use of logarithm operator. Thus, an alternative standardisation method other than *z-score* is required.

A report titled "Assessing Provincial Development under the Five Development Concept" (Institute of Applied Economics Shanghai Academy of Social Sciences 2016) has applied the entropy method to assign weights to its indicators. To avoid negative values, they deploy the *max–min standardisation* method, where

$$v_{ei} = \frac{x_{ei} - \min(x_i)}{\max(x_i) - \min(x_i)}.$$

However, there is an important drawback to the max–min standardisation. If an economy performs the worst under an indicator, i.e. $x_{ei} = \min(x_i)$, then $v_{ei} = 0$, which cannot be computed by natural log either. Additional assumptions must thus be made in the computation, i.e. ln(0) must be assigned to 0.

Another reason that the entropy method is less appropriate than the Shapley method is that when applied to the field of index construction, the former method is very sensitive to indicators containing outliers.

Consider the following example. There are 11 economies and three indicators with different measurement units. Indicator 1 contains an outlier. All the economies perform equally in Indicator 2. There is a clear divergence of performance among all the economies in Indicator 3. We will use *z-score* standardisation for the Shapley method and the max–min standardisation for the entropy method.

Economy	Indicator 1	Indicator 2	Indicator 3
A	10	2	1
B	1	3	2
C	1	2	3
D	1	2	4
E	1	2	5
F	1	2	6
G	1	2	7
H	1	1	8
I	1	2	9
J	1	2	10
K	1	2	11

Under the entropy method, the weights of indicators are

$$w_1^{Entropy} = 0.866,\ w_2^{Entropy} = 0.045,\ w_3^{Entropy} = 0.089.$$

Due to the presence of an outlier under Indicator 1, i.e. Economy A, the entropy method predicts that Indicator 1 carries the most information, thus assigning it a much higher weight relative to the rest.

Under the Shapley method, the weights of indicators are

$$w_1^{Shapley} = 0.308,\ w_2^{Shapley} = 0.229,\ w_3^{Shapley} = 0.463.$$

As observed, similar to the entropy method, the Shapley weights assign a relatively higher weight to Indicator 1 than Indicator 2 because of the presence of the outlier. However, the highest weight is assigned to Indicator 3 because of the dispersion observed, overcoming the bias that the entropy method generates due to its inability to handle outliers.

To summarise the abovementioned discussion, the derivation of the final index score must be done with the help of an aggregation of all relevant information, implying that all the indicators are the determinants. Importance should be given to indicators which show that the economies are unequally developed (e.g. Indicator 3). However, as noted earlier, the entropy method fails to capture this feature due to the fact that such indicators convey less information than those with an outlier (e.g. Indicator 1). The Shapley method, on the other hand, offers a better alternative as it captures both the facts that economies are most unequally developed under Indicator 3 as well as the existence of the outlier in Indicator 1.

2.3 Competitiveness Analysis Results

Using the methodology introduced in Sections 2.2.1 and 2.2.3, competitiveness rankings are derived by sorting the standardised scores of each province as shown in Tables 2.1–2.5. Additionally, the rankings are illustrated on maps to gain insights on the geographical spread of performance across provinces.

2.3.1 Ranking and Scores for Overall Competitiveness

From Table 2.1, it is observed that the standardised scores of the provinces range from 3.459 (scored by top-ranked DKI Jakarta) to −1.891 (obtained by bottom-ranked West Papua). As the nation's capital, DKI Jakarta remains far more competitive than the rest of Indonesia, with a standardised score which is more than double that of the second-ranked East Java (std. score: 1.723). East Kalimantan regains its third ranking (std. score: 1.303) after falling to fifth place in 2016. Meanwhile, Central Java, West Java, and Banten occupy the fourth, fifth, and sixth rankings respectively in this latest 2017 publication. Most of the country's top-performing provinces remain among the top-10, with minimal changes to the ranking when compared to previous year's results in 2016. Two of the provinces have dropped out of the top-10, namely South Kalimantan (from eighth to 11th) and North Sulawesi (from ninth to 17th). Replacing these provinces are Banten and Riau Islands, which have improved from 11th to sixth and from 12th to 10th places respectively.

The score gaps amongst provinces are the least prominent for provinces in the middle-13, thereby indicating much possibility for provinces to surpass one another in competitiveness. For instance, both the provinces of Jambi (rank: 18th; std. score: –0.296) and Gorontalo (rank: 19th; std. score: –0.298) have a score difference of only 0.002, indicating a fairly similar level of competitiveness.

At the lower-end of the table, North Maluku (std. score: −1.304), Papua (std. score: −1.706) and West Papua (std. score: −1.891), occupy the bottom-three ranking. Similar to the top-10 group, most provinces in the bottom-10 remain as the least competitive when compared to previous year's results. These include Aceh (25th), Bengkulu (27th), West Sulawesi (28th) and Maluku (29th). Meanwhile, two of the provinces have improved to middle-13 rank, namely Jambi (from 28th to 18th) and North Sumatra (from 24th to 20th). Replacing these provinces in the bottom-10 are South Sumatra and West Nusa Tenggara, which have retrogressed from 22nd to 24th and 19th to 26th place respectively.

Table 2.1: 2017 Overall Competitiveness Ranking and Standardised Scores and Three-Year Ranking, 2015–2017

Rank 2015	Rank 2016	Rank 2017	Province	Region	Std. Score 2017
1	1	1	DKI Jakarta	Java	3.459
2	2	2	East Java	Java	1.723
3	5	3	East Kalimantan	Kalimantan	1.303
5	3	4	Central Java	Java	1.035
4	4	5	West Java	Java	0.946
9	11	6	Banten	Java	0.741
12	7	7	Bali	Bali-Nusa Tenggara	0.687
10	6	8	South Sulawesi	Sulawesi	0.557
6	10	9	DI Yogyakarta	Java	0.423
7	12	10	Riau Islands	Sumatra	0.399
8	8	11	South Kalimantan	Kalimantan	0.318
20	14	12	Central Sulawesi	Sulawesi	0.270
13	13	13	Central Kalimantan	Kalimantan	0.090
25	18	14	Lampung	Sumatra	0.061
22	23	15	West Sumatra	Sumatra	–0.018
16	15	16	Riau	Sumatra	–0.093
11	9	17	North Sulawesi	Sulawesi	–0.270
14	28	18	Jambi	Sumatra	–0.296
27	21	19	Gorontalo	Sulawesi	–0.298
15	24	20	North Sumatra	Sumatra	–0.304
19	17	21	West Kalimantan	Kalimantan	–0.308
30	20	22	Bangka Belitung Islands	Sumatra	–0.403
21	16	23	Southeast Sulawesi	Sulawesi	–0.412
17	22	24	South Sumatra	Sumatra	–0.460
24	26	25	Aceh	Sumatra	–0.526
26	19	26	West Nusa Tenggara	Bali-Nusa Tenggara	–0.582
23	25	27	Bengkulu	Sumatra	–0.595
18	30	28	West Sulawesi	Sulawesi	–0.597
29	29	29	Maluku	Maluku-Papua	–0.712
32	32	30	East Nusa Tenggara	Bali-Nusa Tenggara	–1.238
31	31	31	North Maluku	Maluku-Papua	–1.304
33	33	32	Papua	Maluku-Papua	–1.706
28	27	33	West Papua	Maluku-Papua	–1.891

Source: ACI.

Figure 2.7: 2017 Map of Overall Competitiveness Ranking

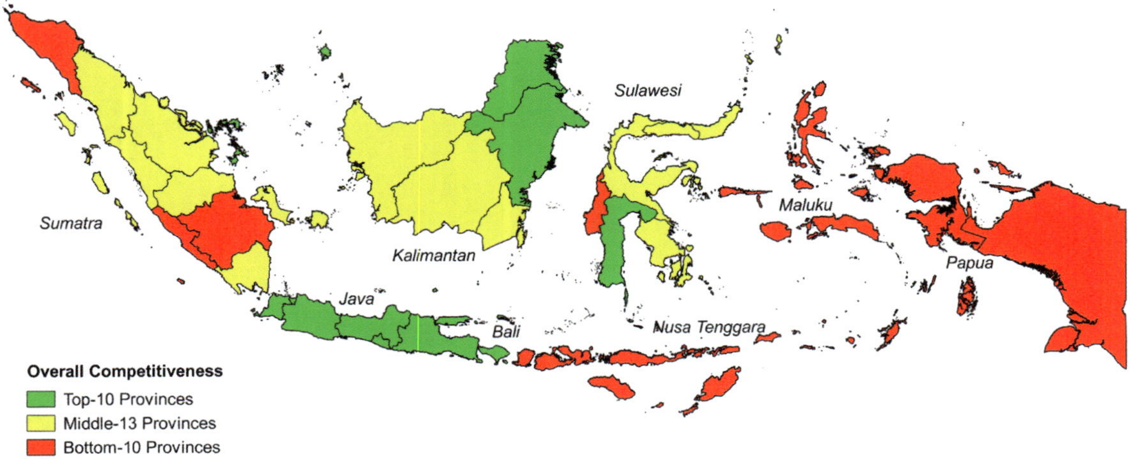

Source: ACI.

DKI Jakarta's high score (std. score: 3.459) skews the score distribution of the 33 provinces upwards. This means that an average-performing province with a standardised score of zero is positioned higher than the median province between the 14th and 15th positions. Meanwhile, the median province occupying the 17th position, North Sulawesi, has a score of –0.270. This implies that at least half of the provinces in Indonesia have obtained negative scores and have performed below average. In fact, only 14 out of 33 provinces score above average in Overall Competitiveness.

The Overall Competitiveness ranking can also be viewed on a map of Indonesian provinces, as seen in Figure 2.7. On the map, provinces are colour-coded based on three groups: top-10 positions (green), bottom-10 positions (red) and middle-13 positions (yellow). The map shows a noticeable geographic concentration of provinces with high, mediocre and low levels of competitiveness. All of the six provinces in Java rank in the top-10, while the remaining four provinces are found in the regions of Kalimantan (East Kalimantan), Bali and Nusa Tenggara (Bali), Sulawesi (South Sulawesi) and Sumatra (Riau Islands). The bottom-10 provinces are mostly part of the eastern regions of Maluku-Papua and Nusa Tenggara, highlighting the continued disparity between the eastern region vis-à-vis the rest of Indonesia. Several provinces in western Indonesia also occupy the bottom-10 positions and have fairly remained so, as demonstrated in previous findings (Tan et al. 2013; 2015b; 2017; Tan, Amri, and Ahmad 2017).

As our past findings have also suggested, provinces in the country's western area (Sumatra) are not as competitive as what conventional wisdom holds. The low-performing provinces from western Indonesia are South Sumatra (24th), Aceh (25th) and Bengkulu (27th). Meanwhile, the remaining Sumatran provinces and about half of Sulawesi and Kalimantan provinces belong to the middle-13 group. From this, we can infer that for Overall Competitiveness, (i) provinces in Java are highly competitive; (ii) provinces in Kalimantan are either competitive or mediocre; (iii) provinces in Sulawesi are either highly competitive, mediocre or low in levels of competitiveness; and thus, (iv) provinces that have mediocre and low levels of competitiveness are mostly found in the (1) Sumatra and (2) Bali and Nusa Tenggara regions, while (iv) provinces in the eastern region of Indonesia, Maluku-Papua, tend to perform poorly in Overall Competitiveness more generally.

The changing economic landscapes and advancements in Indonesia warrant a deeper analysis into the dynamics of competitiveness (or lack thereof) of these provinces. Table 2.1 also shows a trend in the competitiveness ranking of the 33 provinces between 2015 and 2017. Within the three years, several provinces have shown consistent improvements in their rankings. For instance, Lampung has improved by 11 positions, moving up from 25th in 2015 to 18th in 2016 before increasing further to 14th in 2017. A similar set of improvements is observed in two provinces in the Sulawesi region, Central Sulawesi and Gorontalo, for which both have improved by eight positions. Central Sulawesi's rank has climbed up from 20th in 2015 to 12th in 2017, while Gorontalo's has increased from 27th to 19th place in the same period. Beyond these provinces, others have also improved considerably — albeit not annually — over the three-year period. For instance, Bangka Belitung Islands and West Sumatra have increased by eight and seven positions to rank 22nd and 15th respectively.

Conversely, there are also provinces that have had consistent deterioration in rankings from 2015 to 2017. South Sumatra, for instance, has fallen by seven positions from 17th in 2015 to 22nd in 2016 and down to 24th in 2017. Similarly, Bengkulu's ranking has also declined by two positions annually, from 23rd in 2015 to 27th in 2017. Beyond these Sumatran provinces, other provinces have also had considerable net decline in ranking over the three years. For instance, West Sulawesi's rank has retrogressed by 10 positions from 18th in 2015 to 28th in 2017.

There are also provinces that have remained stable in their rankings for three consecutive years. DKI Jakarta (first) and East Java (second) have consistently been named as the two most competitive provinces in Indonesia, thereby further cementing their positions as the economic powerhouses in the country. Meanwhile, all provinces in the regions of Maluku-Papua and East Nusa Tenggara have remained as the five least competitive provinces in Indonesia.

The aforementioned observations highlight several conclusions. Firstly, it is worth reiterating that the assessment of a province's competitiveness is not merely an evaluation of the individual progress made by that particular province; rather, it is a relative assessment that compares a province's performance to those of other provinces. Thus, the rank improvements and deteriorations just within the three years (2015–2017) indicate that boosting competitiveness of a province is an ongoing process that ought to be constantly undertaken by each province in order to stay competitive and ahead of their peers. Secondly, there are provinces which have developed well beyond other provinces. For instance, provinces like DKI Jakarta and East Java each has strengths in certain aspects of competitiveness which give them a competitive edge over other provinces. Likewise, provinces in the eastern part of Indonesia have remained at the bottom for several years, indicating persistent weaknesses in certain aspects of competitiveness which have prevented them to develop in the same pace as the rest of Indonesia.

These strengths and weaknesses can be gleaned further in the following sections, which will discuss competitiveness performance by the four different environments.

2.3.2 Ranking and Scores by Four Environments

2.3.2.1 *Macroeconomic Stability*

DKI Jakarta (std. score: 4.055) tops the Macroeconomic Stability ranking, further strengthening its position as the epicentre of Indonesia's economic growth (see Table 2.2). It is worth noting that seven provinces have remained as the top-seven when compared to the previous year. Two provinces have dropped out of the top-10, namely South Kalimantan (from eighth to 12th) and Riau (from 10th to 11th). Replacing these provinces are North Sumatra and South Sumatra, which have improved from 12th to ninth and 13th to 10th respectively.

Meanwhile, North Maluku (std. score: −1.132) ranks at the bottom of 33 provinces in terms of Macroeconomic Stability. Similar to the top-10 group, most provinces in the bottom-10 have remained as such when compared to previous year's results. Three provinces, namely West Sulawesi (26th), Jambi (25th) and West Nusa Tenggara (23rd), have improved in rankings and are replaced by DI Yogyakarta (24th), Gorontalo (25th) and West Papua (27th), which have deteriorated to rank among the bottom-10 provinces.

The performances of DKI Jakarta and East Java (std. score: 2.496) skew the score distribution upward, rendering an average province to be positioned between the 11th and 12th places, while the median Papua at the 17th place has a standardised score of –0.341. In fact, only 11 out of the 33 provinces have performed above average in this environment, which is the lowest number of provinces to have scored positively in a given environment.

By delving into the sub-environment scores, we can identify the underlying driver(s) behind each province's performance in Macroeconomic Stability. Most provinces at the top-10 excel in all three sub-environments, although several fall short in either (i) Openness to Trade or (ii) Attractiveness to Foreign Investors. For instance, despite scoring well in the overall Macroeconomic Stability environment, West Java (third) falls short in terms of Openness to Trade and Services, while Riau Islands (sixth) struggles in the Attractiveness to Foreign Investors sub-environment. These are interesting developments as West Java used to be one of Indonesia's prime manufacturing centres geared for exports while Riau Islands used to be an attractive place for foreign investors.

On the other hand, the bottom-10 provinces tend to underperform in all three sub-environments. For instance, the bottom-performing province North Maluku scores the lowest among all provinces in both (i) Regional Economic Vibrancy and (ii) Attractiveness to Foreign Investors. It is also worth noting that of the 33 provinces in Indonesia, only five provinces have performed above average in all sub-environments of Macroeconomic Stability. These provinces are DKI Jakarta (first), East Java (second), East Kalimantan (fourth), Central Java (fifth) and Banten (seventh). Meanwhile, all other provinces have performed below average in at least one of the sub-environments.

Table 2.2: 2017 Macroeconomic Stability Ranking and Standardised Scores and Three-Year Ranking, 2015–2017

Rank			Province	Std. Score	Sub-Environment Std. Scores		
2015	2016	2017		2017	REV	OTS	AFI
1	1	1	DKI Jakarta	4.055	3.868	4.822	2.208
2	2	2	East Java	2.496	2.469	1.209	3.033
3	3	3	West Java	1.370	1.787	–0.399	2.294
4	4	4	East Kalimantan	0.830	0.356	0.777	1.099
7	5	5	Central Java	0.678	1.096	0.197	0.531
5	6	6	Riau Islands	0.596	0.691	1.730	–0.818
6	7	7	Banten	0.456	0.127	0.054	1.044
8	9	8	South Sulawesi	0.128	0.176	–0.379	0.546
10	12	9	North Sumatra	0.090	0.358	0.221	–0.337
12	13	10	South Sumatra	0.067	0.063	–0.311	0.429
9	10	11	Riau	0.019	–0.078	0.050	0.078
11	8	12	South Kalimantan	–0.012	–0.368	0.564	–0.228
13	14	13	North Sulawesi	–0.189	–0.172	–0.343	0.008
18	17	14	Bali	–0.243	–0.040	–0.487	–0.127
17	26	15	West Sulawesi	–0.263	–0.381	–0.494	0.169
25	22	16	Lampung	–0.274	–0.298	–0.100	–0.339
22	15	17	Papua	–0.341	–0.715	–0.060	–0.141
16	11	18	Central Sulawesi	–0.348	–0.735	–0.495	0.293
14	16	19	Central Kalimantan	–0.349	–0.275	–0.466	–0.197
15	20	20	Southeast Sulawesi	–0.358	–0.271	–0.432	–0.259
21	25	21	Jambi	–0.429	–0.308	–0.397	–0.448
23	18	22	West Kalimantan	–0.431	–0.649	–0.429	–0.080
27	24	23	West Nusa Tenggara	–0.443	–0.779	–0.486	0.074
20	19	24	DI Yogyakarta	–0.461	–0.498	–0.540	–0.201
30	21	25	Gorontalo	–0.523	–0.485	–0.521	–0.401
24	30	26	West Sumatra	–0.547	–0.495	–0.284	–0.690
19	23	27	West Papua	–0.628	–0.113	–0.348	–1.228
31	31	28	Bangka Belitung Islands	–0.649	–0.491	–0.177	–1.078
28	27	29	Maluku	–0.673	–0.560	–0.397	–0.853
26	28	30	Aceh	–0.754	–0.768	–0.498	–0.760
33	32	31	East Nusa Tenggara	–0.865	–0.692	–0.535	–1.098
32	33	32	Bengkulu	–0.874	–0.826	–0.520	–1.004
29	29	33	North Maluku	–1.132	–0.995	–0.528	–1.521

Notes: REV: Regional Economic Vibrancy; OTS: Openness to Trade and Services; AFI: Attractiveness to Foreign Investors.
Source: ACI.

Figure 2.8: 2017 Map of Macroeconomic Stability Ranking

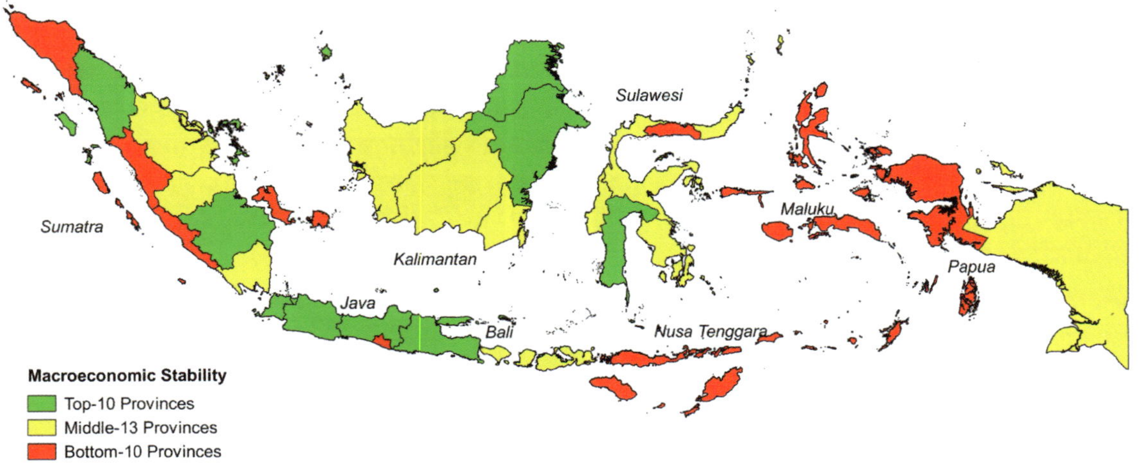

Source: ACI.

The map for Macroeconomic Stability (Figure 2.8) shows less apparent geographic concentration among provinces with high, mediocre and low levels of competitiveness. Although half of the top-10 provinces are from Java, the remaining five are scattered across Sumatra (Riau Islands at sixth, North Sumatra at ninth and South Sumatra at 10th), Kalimantan (East Kalimantan at fourth) and Sulawesi (South Sulawesi at eighth). The middle-13 and bottom-10 provinces are even more spread out. Kalimantan is the only region wherein none of its provinces fall under the bottom-10 category. Both the Sumatra and Sulawesi regions have provinces in all three groups, while provinces in the Bali-Nusa Tenggara and Maluku-Papua regions belong to either the middle-13 or bottom-10 category. Meanwhile, all provinces in the Java region are in the top-10 except DI Yogyakarta.

We can infer that for Macroeconomic Stability, (i) with the exception of DI Yogyakarta at 24th, provinces in Java are highly competitive; (ii) provinces in Kalimantan are either competitive or mediocre; (iii) provinces in Sumatra and Sulawesi show mixed performance as they host a range of provinces with high, mediocre and low levels of competitiveness; and (iv) provinces in the Bali-Nusa Tenggara and Maluku-Papua regions exhibit either low or mediocre performance.

Within the three years (2015–2017), several provinces have shown consistent improvements in their rankings for Macroeconomic Stability (see Table 2.2). The largest improvement is achieved by Lampung which has improved by nine positions, increasing from 25th in 2015 to 22nd in 2016 and 16th in 2017. Such annual, consistent improvement is also observed in Bali (from 18th to 14th), West Nusa Tenggara (from 27th to 23rd) and East Nusa Tenggara (from 33rd to 31st). Beyond these provinces, other provinces have also made considerable progress between 2015 and 2017 including Papua (currently 17th) and Gorontalo (currently 25th), which have increased their ranks by five positions each.

Conversely, there are also provinces which have had consistent deterioration in rankings from 2015 to 2017. West Papua, for instance, has decreased by eight positions from 19th in 2015 to 23rd in 2016 and down to 27th in 2017. A similar decline is also observed for Riau (from ninth to 11th), Central Kalimantan (from 14th to 19th) and Aceh (from 26th to 30th), albeit to a smaller extent.

There are also provinces which have remained stable in their rankings for three consecutive years. DKI Jakarta (first), East Java (second), West Java (third) and East Kalimantan (fourth) have consistently remained as the top-four most competitive provinces in terms of Macroeconomic Stability.

2.3.2.2 *Government and Institutional Setting*

For the Government and Institutional Setting environment, the top-10 provinces are relatively more diverse, with six of them belonging to regions other than Java (see Table 2.3). DKI Jakarta (std. score: 2.680) tops the environment while West Papua (–2.788) ranks at the bottom. Four provinces have shown marked improvements and emerge among the top-10 provinces this year: East Kalimantan (from 18th to fifth), Banten (from 15th to sixth), West Sulawesi (from 21st to ninth) and Lampung (from 19th to 10th).

With the exception of Aceh and West Nusa Tenggara — which were ranked among the middle-13 provinces last year — all other provinces in the bottom-10 have remained among the least competitive in this year's ranking for Government and Institutional Setting. Replacing these two provinces in the middle-13 are West Sumatra and Jambi, which have improved from 26th to 18th and 24th to 20th respectively.

The spread of the scores between the top- and bottom-performing provinces is more symmetrical compared to the other environments (see Tables 2.2, 2.4 and 2.5 for comparison), with the average province positioned just below the median province between 18th and 19th. It is also worth noting that compared to Macroeconomic Stability, there are more provinces (18 out of 33) which have scored above average in Government and Institutional Setting.

Analysing the performance in greater detail reveals that the top-10 provinces tend to perform well across the three sub-environments. However, Central Sulawesi (second), West Sulawesi (ninth) and Lampung (10th) fare below average in the Government Policies and Fiscal Sustainability sub-environment. In fact, only 10 provinces have scored above average in this sub-environment, thereby suggesting that fiscal sustainability may be an issue for many provinces. As the top-ranked province, DKI Jakarta scores disproportionately high in this environment due to its large budget. Meanwhile, Central Sulawesi scores the highest for the remaining two sub-environments.

Provinces in the bottom-10 perform poorly in all three sub-environments, except for North Sumatra which scores above average in Government Policies and Fiscal Sustainability. Most of these provinces appear to perform the worst either in (i) Institutions, Governance and Leadership or (ii) Competition, Regulatory Standards and Rule of Law. Bottom-ranked West Papua, for instance, scores the lowest amongst all provinces in both of the aforementioned sub-environments.

Table 2.3: 2017 Government and Institutional Setting Ranking and Standardised Scores and Three-Year Ranking, 2015–2017

Rank			Province	Std. Score	Sub-Environment Std. Scores		
2015	2016	2017		2017	GPFS	IGL	CRRL
1	1	1	DKI Jakarta	2.680	4.522	1.109	0.603
15	9	2	Central Sulawesi	1.395	−0.535	1.545	2.235
13	2	3	South Sulawesi	1.066	0.023	1.346	1.112
19	8	4	Bali	0.885	0.098	0.561	1.400
2	18	5	East Kalimantan	0.844	0.340	0.662	0.960
16	15	6	Banten	0.745	0.541	0.875	0.317
12	6	7	West Java	0.730	1.823	0.035	−0.161
4	3	8	Central Java	0.700	0.945	0.571	0.114
9	21	9	West Sulawesi	0.649	−0.742	1.211	1.041
28	19	10	Lampung	0.606	−0.149	0.698	0.859
5	5	11	East Java	0.506	1.488	0.428	−0.738
6	4	12	North Sulawesi	0.431	−0.407	1.199	0.210
22	11	13	Gorontalo	0.404	−0.687	0.152	1.475
7	7	14	South Kalimantan	0.298	−0.033	0.479	0.247
3	10	15	DI Yogyakarta	0.246	−0.242	0.224	0.591
14	12	16	West Kalimantan	0.178	−0.293	0.327	0.379
8	16	17	Central Kalimantan	0.164	−0.370	0.346	0.405
24	26	18	West Sumatra	0.129	−0.282	0.288	0.294
10	17	19	Southeast Sulawesi	−0.062	−0.616	−0.033	0.506
11	24	20	Jambi	−0.153	−0.415	−0.221	0.280
26	14	21	Maluku	−0.167	−0.692	0.459	−0.157
30	22	22	Riau	−0.174	0.256	−0.309	−0.351
32	20	23	Bangka Belitung Islands	−0.426	−0.526	0.353	−0.817
29	23	24	Aceh	−0.541	−0.364	−0.416	−0.480
23	25	25	Bengkulu	−0.672	−0.583	−0.432	−0.548
20	13	26	West Nusa Tenggara	−0.676	−0.397	−0.453	−0.724
17	27	27	South Sumatra	−0.849	−0.072	−0.987	−0.915
21	29	28	East Nusa Tenggara	−0.941	−0.604	−0.646	−0.938
25	28	29	Papua	−0.956	−0.352	−1.102	−0.770
27	33	30	North Sumatra	−1.019	0.234	−1.881	−0.723
33	31	31	North Maluku	−1.510	−0.818	−1.514	−1.181
18	32	32	Riau Islands	−1.722	−0.416	−2.141	−1.449
31	30	33	West Papua	−2.788	−0.676	−2.734	−3.076

Notes: GPFS: Government Policies and Fiscal Sustainability; IGL: Institutions, Governance and Leadership; CRRL: Competition, Regulatory Standards and Rule of Law.
Source: ACI.

Figure 2.9: 2017 Map of Government and Institutional Setting Ranking

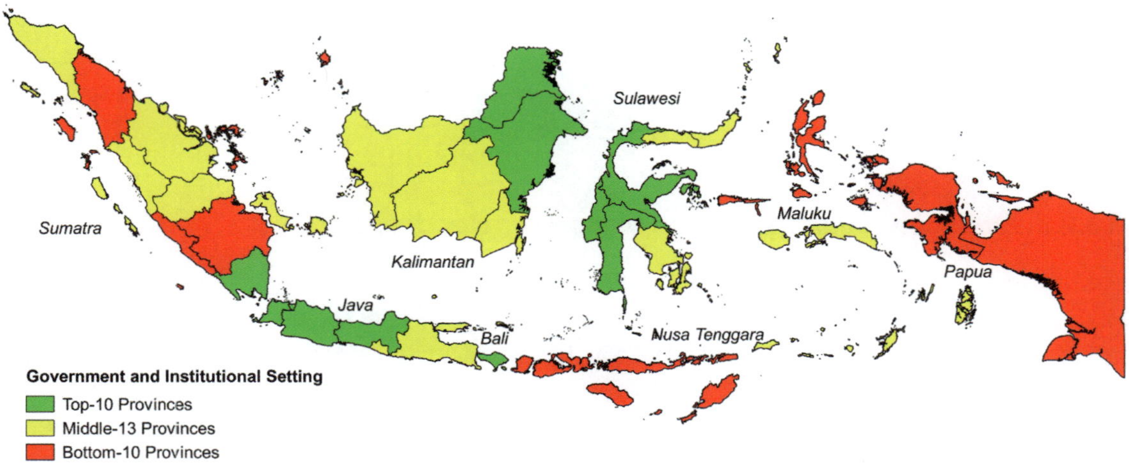

Source: ACI.

The map in Figure 2.9 shows a noticeable geographical concentration of provinces with high and low levels of competitiveness in terms of Government and Institutional Setting. There are four provinces from Java, three from Sulawesi and one each from the Kalimantan, Sumatra and Bali-Nusa Tenggara regions. In fact, it is only in this environment that we can see six representations of non-Java provinces in the top-10. The Sulawesi and Kalimantan regions deserve a special mention as about half of their provinces are ranked among the top-10 while none are in the bottom-10. On the other hand, mediocre- and low-performing provinces tend to be found in the Maluku-Papua and Sumatra regions.

We can infer that for Government and Institutional Setting, (i) provinces in the Java, Kalimantan and Sulawesi regions are either competitive or mediocre; (ii) provinces in Sumatra show mixed performance as the region hosts provinces with a range of high, mediocre, and low competitiveness scores; and (iii) with the exception of Bali which ranks fourth, provinces in the Bali-Nusa Tenggara and Maluku-Papua regions exhibit either low or mediocre performance.

Between 2015 and 2017, several provinces have shown consistent improvements in their rankings for Government and Institutional Setting (see Table 2.3). Similar to the previous rankings, Lampung achieves the largest improvement of 18 positions. Its rank has increased from 28th in 2015 to 19th in 2016 and 10th in 2017. Other provinces with consistent improvements are Bali (by 15 positions), Central Sulawesi (by 13 positions) as well as South Sulawesi and Banten (by 10 positions each).

Conversely, there are also provinces which have had consistent decline in rankings from 2015 to 2017. DI Yogyakarta, for instance, has fallen by 12 positions from third in 2015 to 10th in 2016 and 15th in 2017. A similar decline is also observed for Central Kalimantan as well as Southeast Sulawesi (by nine positions each) and, to a much lesser extent, Papua (by four positions).

With the exception of DKI Jakarta, which remains as the top province for three consecutive years, all other provinces have had changes to their rankings. Many of these provinces have also experienced substantial ranking differences unlike in Macroeconomic Stability, thereby suggesting that the Government and Institutional Setting environment may be a more prominent factor in determining changes to the overall competitiveness.

2.3.2.3 *Financial, Businesses and Manpower Conditions*

Similar to the previous environment, in the Financial, Businesses and Manpower Conditions environment, DKI Jakarta (std. score: 3.375) and West Papua (std. score: −1.295) are ranked first and last respectively (see Table 2.4). The top-10 provinces largely consist of incumbents with only three new entrants: Central Kalimantan (from 12th to eighth), West Kalimantan (from 11th to ninth) and DI Yogyakarta (from 14th to 10th). They have replaced South Sulawesi (from eight to 13th), South Kalimantan (from 10th to 19th) and resource-dependent West Papua (from sixth to 33rd), whose economy and resulting business sentiments may have been affected by the fluctuation of global oil prices.

West Papua, together with Southeast Sulawesi (24th) and North Sulawesi (30th), have declined in performance and are ranked among the bottom-10 provinces. This coincides with major improvements by Jambi (by nine positions), Central Sulawesi and East Nusa Tenggara (by eight positions each), which currently rank among the middle-13 provinces. The distribution is skewed upwards, with the average province placed between 13th and 14th positions. This also means that only 13 out of 33 provinces score above average in this environment.

All of the top-10 provinces fare below average in at least one of the sub-environments. Provinces located in Java tend to excel in Labour Market Flexibility, owing to a large pool of workforce. DKI Jakarta, however, is behind in this sub-environment as its unemployment rate and minimum wage remain among the highest in the country. All the provinces that excel in this environment and provinces that rely heavily on labour-intensive sectors, including those in Java (but not DKI Jakarta), tend to perform poorly in Productivity Performance, which is partly determined by value-added per worker. Those with high scores in Productivity Performance tend to be very productive relative to the other provinces in Indonesia, either in the service industries (DKI Jakarta, ranked first), manufacturing (Riau Islands, ranked fourth) or primary resources (East Kalimantan, ranked seventh). Interestingly, for both the aforementioned sub-environments, only fewer than 10 provinces have obtained positive scores. This suggests that employment and productivity remain as some of the key issues facing many provinces which ought to be tackled.

The bottom-10 provinces have mostly scored negative in all sub-environments, except West Papua (33rd) and Papua (32nd). Despite scoring the lowest in Financial Deepening and Business Efficiency, West Papua fares well in Productivity Performance due to its economic activity in primary resources, while its neighbour Papua scores just above average in Labour Market Flexibility.

Table 2.4: 2017 Financial, Businesses and Manpower Conditions Ranking and Standardised Scores and Three-Year Ranking, 2015–2017

Rank			Province	Std. Score	Sub-Environment Std. Scores		
2015	2016	2017		2017	FDBE	LMF	PP
1	1	1	DKI Jakarta	3.375	3.029	–0.330	3.851
2	2	2	East Java	1.998	0.926	3.142	–0.190
3	3	3	Central Java	1.665	0.926	2.935	–0.630
6	9	4	Riau Islands	1.463	0.945	–0.845	2.739
5	4	5	West Java	0.887	–0.306	2.471	–0.444
8	7	6	Bali	0.635	1.125	0.542	–0.436
4	5	7	East Kalimantan	0.575	–0.623	–0.490	2.229
11	12	8	Central Kalimantan	0.560	1.207	–0.146	0.026
12	11	9	West Kalimantan	0.332	0.782	–0.024	–0.114
9	14	10	DI Yogyakarta	0.270	0.467	0.679	–0.622
21	16	11	Lampung	0.100	0.401	0.405	–0.612
17	18	12	Banten	0.057	0.187	–0.111	0.036
14	8	13	South Sulawesi	0.014	0.182	–0.012	–0.142
28	13	14	Bangka Belitung Islands	–0.032	0.735	–0.727	–0.069
13	15	15	North Sumatra	–0.039	0.083	–0.122	–0.036
24	21	16	West Sumatra	–0.068	0.474	–0.370	–0.236
22	25	17	Central Sulawesi	–0.091	0.048	0.061	–0.286
20	27	18	Jambi	–0.161	0.154	–0.142	–0.324
15	10	19	South Kalimantan	–0.310	–0.262	–0.022	–0.319
25	17	20	South Sumatra	–0.315	–0.312	–0.061	–0.238
19	22	21	Bengkulu	–0.346	–0.028	–0.089	–0.556
10	23	22	Riau	–0.364	–0.502	–0.640	0.434
31	31	23	East Nusa Tenggara	–0.522	0.239	–0.445	–0.808
30	19	24	Southeast Sulawesi	–0.706	–0.665	–0.396	–0.308
32	24	25	West Nusa Tenggara	–0.720	–0.591	–0.002	–0.805
26	30	26	Aceh	–0.731	–0.054	–0.995	–0.369
27	26	27	Gorontalo	–0.755	–0.423	–0.303	–0.741
23	33	28	North Maluku	–0.807	–0.293	–0.956	–0.318
33	32	29	Maluku	–1.083	–0.543	–1.118	–0.441
18	20	30	North Sulawesi	–1.134	–1.120	–1.028	–0.054
16	29	31	West Sulawesi	–1.209	–1.620	–0.126	–0.600
29	28	32	Papua	–1.241	–2.204	0.028	–0.233
7	6	33	West Papua	–1.295	–2.365	–0.766	0.617

Notes: FDBE: Financial Deepening and Business Efficiency; LMF: Labour Market Flexibility; PP: Productivity Performance.
Source: ACI.

Figure 2.10: 2017 Map of Financial, Businesses and Manpower Conditions Ranking

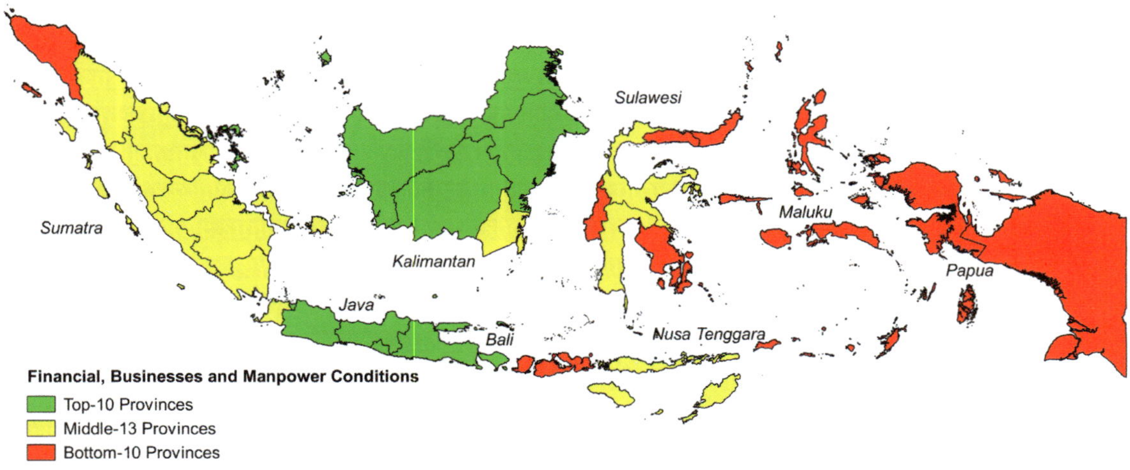

Source: ACI.

Based on the geographic concentration, the top-10 provinces for Financial, Businesses and Manpower Conditions are mostly in labour-intensive Java and resource-rich Kalimantan (see Figure 2.10). In fact, these are the only regions with provinces that are largely competitive in this aspect. The Sumatra and Bali-Nusa Tenggara regions have provinces with a diverse range of competitiveness, with the most competitive provinces being Riau Islands (fourth) and Bali (sixth). Both provinces are known for their business opportunities and income generation in the manufacturing and tourism sectors respectively. Meanwhile, the Sulawesi region has provinces that are mediocre or low-performing, while provinces in Maluku-Papua remain low-performing.

In general, it can be observed that (i) provinces in Java and Kalimantan tend to be competitive, except for Banten and South Kalimantan which are mediocre; (ii) provinces in the Sumatra and Bali-Nusa Tenggara regions show mixed performance; (iii) provinces in Sulawesi are either mediocre- or low-performing; and (iv) all provinces in the Maluku-Papua region have low levels of competitiveness.

Several provinces have shown consistent rank improvements in this environment (see Table 2.4). Lampung, in particular, has improved by 10 positions from 21st in 2015 to 16th in 2016 and 11th in 2017. Other provinces with improvements, albeit to smaller extent, are West Sumatra (by eight positions), West Kalimantan (by three positions) and Bali (by two positions). It is also encouraging to observe improvements in certain eastern provinces, such as East Nusa Tenggara (by eight positions) and Maluku (by four positions), as well as the archipelagic Sumatran province of Bangka Belitung Islands (by 14 positions).

On the other hand, provinces with a consistent deterioration in rankings include West Sulawesi (by 15 positions), North Sulawesi (by 12 positions) and, to a smaller extent, East Kalimantan (by three positions). It is also worth highlighting that Riau (22nd) and the last-ranked West Papua have also declined substantially by 12 and 26 positions respectively.

Meanwhile, with a strong presence of financial and labour market, the top-three provinces of DKI Jakarta, East Java and Central Java have continued to maintain their competitiveness for the past three years.

2.3.2.4 *Quality of Life and Infrastructure Development*

While DKI Jakarta tops the ranking in the aforementioned environments, Quality of Life and Infrastructure Development continues to be a strength of East Kalimantan (std. score: 2.068), as observed in the province's first position for several years (see Table 2.5). Likewise, the bottom-ranked province at 33rd place has been Papua (std. score: –3.111). In general, there are minimal changes to the composition of provinces occupying the top-10, middle-13 and bottom-10 groups, thereby suggesting that it takes time to observe the impacts of policy reforms on living standards. The new entrant to the top-10 provinces is West Sumatra (currently ranks 10th, up from 13th last year), which replaces Central Java (from ninth to current rank of 11th). Meanwhile, Southeast Sulawesi drops its rank to 25th (from 17th previously), replacing Gorontalo (21st) to be among the bottom-10 provinces.

In general, the standardised scores tend to be distributed more evenly albeit with a large gap observed between the scores of bottom-ranked Papua (std. score: –3.111) and second-to-bottom East Nusa Tenggara (std. score: –1.773). In contrast to the situation in previous environments (compare against Tables 2.2–2.4), the score distribution tends to be skewed downwards towards Papua's extremely low score.

As the top-ranked province, East Kalimantan fares well in all sub-environments of Quality of Life and Infrastructure Development. Its scores, however, are not the highest in any sub-environment. In fact, the top-scoring provinces in each sub-environment are attained by three different provinces: DI Yogyakarta in Standard of Living, Education and Social Stability, DKI Jakarta in Technological Infrastructure and Banten in Physical Infrastructure. This also suggests that having strengths in one aspect does not necessarily translate into positive impacts in other aspects. In this regard, despite being among the top-10, some provinces still score below or just slightly above average in the sub-environment of Standard of Living, Education and Social Stability. These include provinces with dense population where public services are highly strained, such as DKI Jakarta (third), Banten (fourth) and East Java (eighth). Interestingly, several provinces in the bottom-10 have favourable scores for this sub-environment, such as Jambi (24th), Southeast Sulawesi (25th) and Maluku (27th).

Papua's position as the bottom-performing province for three consecutive years is a concern. Papua scores the lowest in all sub-environments and is particularly far behind the rest of Indonesia in Standard of Living, Education and Social Stability (–3.693). Despite the Special Autonomy Law which have accrued substantial resources for Papua to improve living standards and President Joko Widodo's quest for accelerated development in the province, the pace of progress in Papua has not been quick enough to match the developments of the rest of Indonesia.

Table 2.5: 2017 Quality of Life and Infrastructure Development Ranking and Standardised Scores and Three-Year Ranking, 2015–2017

Rank			Province	Std. Score	Sub-Environment Std. Scores		
2015	2016	2017		2017	PI	TI	SLESS
1	1	1	East Kalimantan	2.068	1.810	1.509	1.405
2	4	2	DI Yogyakarta	1.347	–0.323	1.579	1.821
3	3	3	DKI Jakarta	1.347	–0.398	3.482	–0.008
6	10	4	Banten	1.197	2.625	1.095	–0.984
8	6	5	South Kalimantan	1.076	2.138	0.114	0.206
7	5	6	Bali	0.999	0.717	0.905	0.659
4	8	7	Riau Islands	0.986	0.378	1.581	0.293
5	2	8	East Java	0.706	1.596	0.136	–0.120
11	7	9	South Sulawesi	0.637	0.647	0.191	0.616
12	13	10	West Sumatra	0.427	–0.359	0.279	1.055
14	9	11	Central Java	0.383	1.214	0.146	–0.484
15	15	12	Aceh	0.284	–0.272	–0.597	1.517
16	16	13	Riau	0.213	–0.230	0.233	0.484
9	12	14	West Java	0.146	1.142	0.507	–1.316
13	11	15	North Sulawesi	–0.001	–0.656	0.097	0.558
10	20	16	North Sumatra	–0.040	0.370	–0.252	–0.210
21	18	17	Central Sulawesi	–0.061	–0.161	–0.592	0.613
18	14	18	Central Kalimantan	–0.076	–0.302	–0.180	0.309
19	21	19	Bengkulu	–0.079	–0.542	–0.067	0.428
22	19	20	West Nusa Tenggara	–0.089	0.159	–0.759	0.397
26	26	21	Gorontalo	–0.111	–0.034	–0.290	0.069
24	23	22	Lampung	–0.228	–0.434	–0.453	0.366
25	22	23	Bangka Belitung Islands	–0.229	–0.045	–0.197	–0.280
17	25	24	Jambi	–0.239	–0.694	–0.271	0.420
23	17	25	Southeast Sulawesi	–0.240	–0.260	–0.525	0.237
20	24	26	South Sumatra	–0.427	–0.319	–0.321	–0.336
27	29	27	Maluku	–0.435	–0.567	–0.758	0.331
28	28	28	North Maluku	–0.870	–0.691	–0.995	–0.301
29	27	29	West Kalimantan	–1.100	–1.084	–0.466	–0.963
30	30	30	West Sulawesi	–1.155	–1.192	–0.888	–0.559
32	32	31	West Papua	–1.550	–1.554	–1.002	–0.986
31	31	32	East Nusa Tenggara	–1.773	–1.113	–1.393	–1.544
33	33	33	Papua	–3.111	–1.564	–1.850	–3.693

Notes: PI = Physical Infrastructure; TI = Technological Infrastructure; SLESS = Standard of Living, Education and Social Stability.
Source: ACI.

Figure 2.11: 2017 Map of Quality of Life and Infrastructure Development Ranking

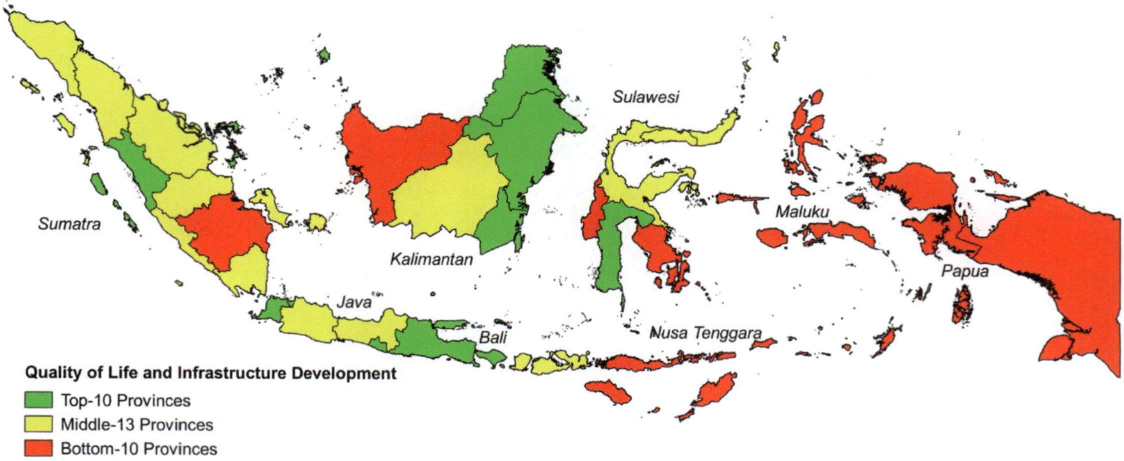

Source: ACI.

The geographical concentration of low-performing provinces is even more apparent in the map in Figure 2.11. All provinces from the easternmost region of Maluku-Papua are part of the bottom-10 group, while provinces belonging to the middle-13 group are more spread out. In general, (i) provinces in Java tend to be competitive and mediocre, (ii) provinces in Sumatra, Kalimantan, Sulawesi and Bali-Nusa Tenggara islands show mixed performance while (iii) provinces in Maluku-Papua tend show low performance.

Despite the minimal changes in ranking, several provinces have achieved consistent improvements (see Table 2.4). These provinces include Central Sulawesi (improvement by four positions) as well as Lampung and South Kalimantan (improvement by three positions each). Central Sulawesi and Lampung have favourable Standard of Living, Education and Social Stability, while geographically strategic South Kalimantan is strong in its Physical Infrastructure, scoring highest in cargo at inter-island seaport and provision of pipe water services. Others which have improved over the three years include Aceh (12th), Riau (13th) and Gorontalo (21st).

Provinces with a consistent deterioration in rankings include South Sumatra (by six positions from 20th to 26th) and West Java (by five positions from ninth to 14th). Other provinces which have larger net declines are Jambi (by seven positions from 17th to 24th) and North Sumatra (by six positions from 10th to 16th).

Demonstrating a fairly stable ranking in this environment, East Kalimantan (first) and DKI Jakarta (third) remain consistently competitive, while provinces of North Maluku (28th), West Sulawesi (30th) and Papua (33rd) have struggled to develop their infrastructure and living conditions over the years.

2.3.3 *What-if* Simulation Analysis on Overall Competitiveness

The methodology for *What-if* competitiveness simulation has been explained earlier in Section 2.2.4. The scenario is to raise each province's top-20 percent weakest indicators to the average values. Afterwards, the standardised score is recalculated based on such improvement with the assumption that all other provinces' standardised scores remain constant. Each province's top-20 percent weakest and strongest indicators can be found in the provincial profiles in Appendix 5.

The complete simulation results are shown in Tables 2.6–2.10, which compare the ranking and score of each province before and after the simulation. The simulation hopes to assist provinces in prioritising key areas which will increase their competitiveness.

For Overall Competitiveness (Table 2.6), the pattern shows that substantial changes in ranking are less likely to occur among the top-10 provinces as competition is already intense to begin with. Nevertheless, the provinces' standardised scores have increased after the policy stimulation, indicating that there are still various aspects to be improved for each province and that even low-hanging fruits exist for the top performers.

After the simulation, some provinces end up improving their ranking to a position that is similar to what other provinces would have attained. For instance, there are three provinces which eventually sit at the 13th position after the simulation, namely North Sulawesi, North Sumatra and Bangka Belitung Islands. The *What-if* competitiveness simulation assumes *ceteris paribus* assumption, i.e. when simulation is conducted for one province, other provinces are held as constant. As a result, provinces may share the same ranking after the simulation exercise. This is also more commonly observed for provinces currently positioned at the middle-13, wherein their rankings after simulation range from 11th to 15th positions.

Some provinces have emerged with considerably higher rankings, demonstrating their potential to improve competitiveness. These provinces are largely in the bottom-10. For instance, the largest increase in rank can be achieved by West Sulawesi and Maluku, which have both increased their rankings by 12 positions in the simulation (to 16th and 17th respectively). Bottom-performing West Papua also records the largest increase in standardised score from −1.891 to −0.592 after the simulation. Despite their extensive score improvements, the rankings of the bottom-four provinces in the simulation have improved to a much lesser extent compared to the other provinces. This suggests that the disparity among these provinces and others are substantially large to the extent that inasmuch as there is potential for these provinces to grow, their levels of competitiveness post simulation are still comparably lower than many other provinces.

Regardless of large or small rank improvements, the potential progress for each province shown in this exercise should serve as an impetus for provinces to expedite their development and growth. Section 2.3.4 discusses in greater detail the improvements that can be achieved in each environment of competitiveness.

Table 2.6: 2017 *What-if* Simulation on Overall Competitiveness

Province (in alphabetical order)	Rank		Std. Score	
	Before	After	Before	After
Aceh	25	**16**	–0.526	**–0.051**
Bali	7	**5**	0.687	**0.969**
Bangka Belitung Islands	22	**13**	–0.403	**0.117**
Banten	6	**4**	0.741	**1.115**
Bengkulu	27	**17**	–0.595	**–0.159**
Central Java	4	**3**	1.035	**1.409**
Central Kalimantan	13	**11**	0.090	**0.347**
Central Sulawesi	12	**8**	0.270	**0.569**
DI Yogyakarta	9	**6**	0.423	**0.769**
DKI Jakarta	1	**1**	3.459	**3.900**
East Java	2	**2**	1.723	**2.099**
East Kalimantan	3	**3**	1.303	**1.640**
East Nusa Tenggara	30	**26**	–1.238	**–0.586**
Gorontalo	19	**14**	–0.298	**0.077**
Jambi	18	**15**	–0.296	**–0.018**
Lampung	14	**9**	0.061	**0.457**
Maluku	29	**17**	–0.712	**–0.235**
North Maluku	31	**25**	–1.304	**–0.492**
North Sulawesi	17	**13**	–0.270	**0.210**
North Sumatra	20	**13**	–0.304	**0.260**
Papua	32	**28**	–1.706	**–0.725**
Riau	16	**11**	–0.093	**0.368**
Riau Islands	10	**4**	0.399	**1.042**
South Kalimantan	11	**9**	0.318	**0.532**
South Sulawesi	8	**6**	0.557	**0.786**
South Sumatra	24	**16**	–0.460	**–0.082**
Southeast Sulawesi	23	**15**	–0.412	**0.027**
West Java	5	**3**	0.946	**1.440**
West Kalimantan	21	**15**	–0.308	**0.019**
West Nusa Tenggara	26	**17**	–0.582	**–0.193**
West Papua	33	**25**	–1.891	**–0.592**
West Sulawesi	28	**16**	–0.597	**–0.104**
West Sumatra	15	**12**	–0.018	**0.281**

Source: ACI.

2.3.4 *What-if* Simulation Analysis on Four Environments

The *What-if* simulation is also conducted for each of the four environments, allowing us to focus on the improvements that each province could attain in more specific areas. In Table 2.7, which shows the simulation on Macroeconomic Stability, minimal changes to ranking are common, highlighting that most of the provinces' top-20 percent weakest indicators are not from the Macroeconomic Stability environment. The biggest improvements are mostly found among the bottom-10 provinces, such as Bengkulu (from 33rd to 16th), West Sumatra (from 26th to 13th) and DI Yogyakarta (from 24th to 13th), which see their rankings increase by 16, 13 and 11 positions respectively.

Interestingly, other provinces in the bottom-10 only improved by a smaller margin after the simulation. For example, East Nusa Tenggara increases its rank by only three positions from 32nd to 30th and Gorontalo by four positions from 25th to 21st. There are also provinces which do not register any improvements, as none of their top-20 percent weakest indicators belong to the Macroeconomic Stability environment. These provinces include East Java (second), West Sulawesi (15th), Papua (17th) and West Papua (27th). This suggests that the provinces have done comparably better in macroeconomic aspects insofar as their scores for these aspects do not fall under the lowest 20 percent amongst the scores of all indicators used in the assessment.

Table 2.8 on the *What-if* simulation on Government and Institutional Setting, on the other hand, shows plenty of opportunities for provinces to increase their competitiveness by prioritising governance reforms. This is observed particularly in the bottom-four provinces, North Sumatra (from 30th to 19th), North Maluku (from 31st to 21st), Riau Islands (from 32nd to 20th) and West Papua (from 33rd to 23rd), which see their rankings increase by 10 to 11 positions. With the exception of Southeast Sulawesi, most of the provinces which perform below average before simulation have yet to reach the average score post simulation. Similar to the simulation in Macroeconomic Stability, there are provinces which do not register any improvements in this particular environment, namely Bali (fourth), Banten (sixth), Lampung (10th), West Kalimantan (16th) and Central Kalimantan (17th).

Table 2.7: 2017 *What-if* Simulation on Macroeconomic Stability

Province (in alphabetical order)	Rank		Std. Score	
	Before	After	Before	After
Aceh	30	**21**	–0.754	**–0.407**
Bali	14	**13**	–0.243	**–0.039**
Bangka Belitung Islands	28	**21**	–0.649	**–0.396**
Banten	7	**6**	0.456	**0.618**
Bengkulu	32	**16**	–0.874	**–0.288**
Central Java	5	**5**	0.678	**0.702**
Central Kalimantan	19	**13**	–0.349	**–0.187**
Central Sulawesi	18	**13**	–0.348	**–0.028**
DI Yogyakarta	24	**13**	–0.461	**–0.053**
DKI Jakarta	1	**1**	4.055	**4.084**
East Java	2	**2**	2.496	**2.496**
East Kalimantan	4	**4**	0.830	**1.025**
East Nusa Tenggara	31	**28**	–0.865	**–0.663**
Gorontalo	25	**21**	–0.523	**–0.387**
Jambi	21	**14**	–0.429	**–0.235**
Lampung	16	**13**	–0.274	**–0.158**
Maluku	29	**23**	–0.673	**–0.448**
North Maluku	33	**27**	–1.132	**–0.633**
North Sulawesi	13	**11**	–0.189	**0.017**
North Sumatra	9	**8**	0.090	**0.198**
Papua	17	**17**	–0.341	**–0.341**
Riau	11	**8**	0.019	**0.207**
Riau Islands	6	**5**	0.596	**0.757**
South Kalimantan	12	**8**	–0.012	**0.194**
South Sulawesi	8	**8**	0.128	**0.307**
South Sumatra	10	**9**	0.067	**0.094**
Southeast Sulawesi	20	**16**	–0.358	**–0.270**
West Java	3	**3**	1.370	**1.420**
West Kalimantan	22	**17**	–0.431	**–0.304**
West Nusa Tenggara	23	**21**	–0.443	**–0.367**
West Papua	27	**27**	–0.628	**–0.628**
West Sulawesi	15	**15**	–0.263	**–0.263**
West Sumatra	26	**13**	–0.547	**–0.141**

Source: ACI.

Table 2.8: 2017 *What-if* Simulation on Government and Institutional Setting

Province (in alphabetical order)	Rank		Std. Score	
	Before	After	Before	After
Aceh	24	**23**	−0.541	**−0.240**
Bali	4	**4**	0.885	**0.885**
Bangka Belitung Islands	23	**17**	−0.426	**0.149**
Banten	6	**6**	0.745	**0.745**
Bengkulu	25	**23**	−0.672	**−0.194**
Central Java	8	**5**	0.700	**0.865**
Central Kalimantan	17	**17**	0.164	**0.164**
Central Sulawesi	2	**2**	1.395	**1.586**
DI Yogyakarta	15	**15**	0.246	**0.290**
DKI Jakarta	1	**1**	2.680	**2.709**
East Java	11	**4**	0.506	**0.974**
East Kalimantan	5	**4**	0.844	**0.950**
East Nusa Tenggara	28	**24**	−0.941	**−0.504**
Gorontalo	13	**9**	0.404	**0.674**
Jambi	20	**19**	−0.153	**−0.015**
Lampung	10	**10**	0.606	**0.606**
Maluku	21	**19**	−0.167	**0.092**
North Maluku	31	**21**	−1.510	**−0.207**
North Sulawesi	12	**10**	0.431	**0.613**
North Sumatra	30	**19**	−1.019	**0.034**
Papua	29	**25**	−0.956	**−0.606**
Riau	22	**14**	−0.174	**0.332**
Riau Islands	32	**20**	−1.722	**−0.198**
South Kalimantan	14	**14**	0.298	**0.339**
South Sulawesi	3	**3**	1.066	**1.126**
South Sumatra	27	**23**	−0.849	**−0.205**
Southeast Sulawesi	19	**14**	−0.062	**0.296**
West Java	7	**6**	0.730	**0.818**
West Kalimantan	16	**16**	0.178	**0.178**
West Nusa Tenggara	26	**24**	−0.676	**−0.438**
West Papua	33	**23**	−2.788	**−0.436**
West Sulawesi	9	**6**	0.649	**0.751**
West Sumatra	18	**14**	0.129	**0.362**

Source: ACI.

Table 2.9 on the *What-if* simulation on Financial, Businesses and Manpower Conditions shows that provinces in the bottom-half of the rank largely register more increases in rankings. The largest improvements are obtained by North Sulawesi (from 30th to 19th) and Riau (from 22nd to 11th) — both of which have increased their rankings by 11 positions.

Again, we see some variations in the potential for improvements. The competitiveness ranking table on Financial, Businesses and Manpower Conditions places West Papua at the 33rd place below North Maluku (28th) and West Sulawesi (31st). However, after the simulation, West Papua manages to improve by 14 places to attain the 19th rank, while North Maluku and West Sulawesi only improve by four and seven spots respectively to rank 24th. There is also an opportunity for five provinces to share the same position at 11th after the simulation. These provinces are South Sulawesi, North Sumatra, West Sumatra, Jambi and Riau.

Meanwhile, in Table 2.10 on the *What-if* simulation on Quality of Life and Infrastructure Development), most provinces in the middle-13 and bottom-10 groupings register large increases, indicating that there are ample opportunities for improvements in all provinces, above and beyond those in the bottom-10 group. Lampung, Southeast Sulawesi and Maluku obtain the biggest leap of 12 positions. Lampung, in particular, manages to improve from the middle-13 to the top-10 group post simulation. Joining Lampung at 10th place are West Sumatra, Aceh, Riau, North Sumatra and West Nusa Tenggara.

Exceptions are, however, found in the bottom-three provinces — West Papua, East Nusa Tenggara and Papua — which see improvements in rankings to a smaller extent, causing them to remain within the bottom-10 group. Papua, in particular, only improves by five spots (from 33rd to 28th) after the simulation. This further highlights the need for attention on Papua, especially in terms of its Quality of Life and Infrastructure Development.

This is also the only environment where it is feasible — after simulation — to have two provinces (East Kalimantan and DKI Jakarta) achieve the first rank while four other provinces amongst the top-10 occupy the second position. This implies that these provinces have similar improvement gaps to overcome in this particular environment.

It is also worth noting that generally, provinces experience more movements in their rankings and scores before and after simulation in this environment. For instance, 11 out of 19 of the provinces which perform below average manage to score above average after the simulation. This suggests that for many provinces, their top-20 percent weakest indicators generally pertain to aspects of Quality of Life and Infrastructure Development.

Table 2.9: 2017 *What-if* Simulation on Financial, Businesses and Manpower Conditions

Province (in alphabetical order)	Rank		Std. Score	
	Before	After	Before	After
Aceh	26	**18**	–0.731	**–0.138**
Bali	6	**5**	0.635	**0.932**
Bangka Belitung Islands	14	**10**	–0.032	**0.301**
Banten	12	**9**	0.057	**0.500**
Bengkulu	21	**17**	–0.346	**–0.096**
Central Java	3	**2**	1.665	**2.084**
Central Kalimantan	8	**6**	0.560	**0.819**
Central Sulawesi	17	**16**	–0.091	**–0.043**
DI Yogyakarta	10	**9**	0.270	**0.538**
DKI Jakarta	1	**1**	3.375	**3.954**
East Java	2	**2**	1.998	**2.280**
East Kalimantan	7	**5**	0.575	**1.309**
East Nusa Tenggara	23	**19**	–0.522	**–0.289**
Gorontalo	27	**21**	–0.755	**–0.350**
Jambi	18	**11**	–0.161	**0.106**
Lampung	11	**7**	0.100	**0.586**
Maluku	29	**23**	–1.083	**–0.416**
North Maluku	28	**24**	–0.807	**–0.563**
North Sulawesi	30	**19**	–1.134	**–0.193**
North Sumatra	15	**11**	–0.039	**0.214**
Papua	32	**23**	–1.241	**–0.484**
Riau	22	**11**	–0.364	**0.142**
Riau Islands	4	**4**	1.463	**1.581**
South Kalimantan	19	**18**	–0.310	**–0.103**
South Sulawesi	13	**11**	0.014	**0.215**
South Sumatra	20	**14**	–0.315	**–0.027**
Southeast Sulawesi	24	**19**	–0.706	**0.194**
West Java	5	**3**	0.887	**1.592**
West Kalimantan	9	**9**	0.332	**0.432**
West Nusa Tenggara	25	**21**	–0.720	**–0.333**
West Papua	33	**19**	–1.295	**–0.284**
West Sulawesi	31	**24**	–1.209	**–0.623**
West Sumatra	16	**11**	–0.068	**0.101**

Source: ACI.

Table 2.10: 2017 *What-if* Simulation on Quality of Life and Infrastructure Development

Province (in alphabetical order)	Rank		Std. Score	
	Before	After	Before	After
Aceh	12	**10**	0.284	**0.616**
Bali	6	**2**	0.999	**1.437**
Bangka Belitung Islands	23	**12**	−0.229	**0.334**
Banten	4	**2**	1.197	**1.830**
Bengkulu	19	**15**	−0.079	**0.050**
Central Java	11	**6**	0.383	**1.022**
Central Kalimantan	18	**12**	−0.076	**0.354**
Central Sulawesi	17	**11**	−0.061	**0.373**
DI Yogyakarta	2	**2**	1.347	**1.776**
DKI Jakarta	3	**1**	1.347	**2.540**
East Java	8	**4**	0.706	**1.285**
East Kalimantan	1	**1**	2.068	**2.184**
East Nusa Tenggara	32	**26**	−1.773	**−0.478**
Gorontalo	21	**12**	−0.111	**0.317**
Jambi	24	**15**	−0.239	**0.084**
Lampung	22	**10**	−0.228	**0.481**
Maluku	27	**15**	−0.435	**−0.006**
North Maluku	28	**22**	−0.870	**−0.217**
North Sulawesi	15	**13**	−0.001	**0.261**
North Sumatra	16	**10**	−0.040	**0.418**
Papua	33	**28**	−3.111	**−0.962**
Riau	13	**10**	0.213	**0.538**
Riau Islands	7	**2**	0.986	**1.374**
South Kalimantan	5	**3**	1.076	**−1.331**
South Sulawesi	9	**8**	0.637	**0.959**
South Sumatra	26	**22**	−0.427	**0.133**
Southeast Sulawesi	25	**13**	−0.240	**0.256**
West Java	14	**6**	0.146	**0.962**
West Kalimantan	29	**22**	−1.100	**−0.243**
West Nusa Tenggara	20	**10**	−0.089	**0.501**
West Papua	31	**28**	−1.550	**−0.581**
West Sulawesi	30	**22**	−1.155	**−0.210**
West Sumatra	10	**10**	0.427	**0.609**

Source: ACI.

2.3.5 Median and Maximum Competitiveness Web Analysis

The median competitiveness web analysis in Figure 2.12 plots the attained scores across the 12 sub-environments of DKI Jakarta (ranked first) and West Papua (ranked last), along with the median scores of the 33 provinces of Indonesia. Generally, the median scores in eight out of the 12 sub-environments are negative, suggesting that at least half of these provinces are performing below the national average in many aspects of competitiveness.

DKI Jakarta fares far above the median scores in nine sub-environments, with the largest difference found in (i) Openness to Trade and Services and (ii) Government Policies and Fiscal Sustainability. The province, however, scores below the median in (i) Labour Market Flexibility, (ii) Physical Infrastructure and (iii) Standard of Living, Education and Social Sustainability. It scores the lowest amongst all provinces in indicators, such as (i) Minimum Wage per Month, (ii) Environmental Quality Index as well as population-dependent factors like (iii) Population per Health Facility.

West Papua, on the other hand, scores below the median in nine sub-environments, particularly in (i) Institutions, Governance and Leadership as well as (ii) Competition, Regulatory Standards and Rule of Law. It scores above the median in (i) Regional Economic Vibrancy, (ii) Openness to Trade and Services as well as (iii) Productivity Performance, albeit with marginal differences. The province has scored the lowest amongst all provinces in one-fifth (21 out of 100) of the indicators assessed, which include (i) Employment and (ii) Tax Revenue per Government Revenue.

Figure 2.12: 2017 Median Competitiveness Web Analysis: Top- and Bottom-Performing Provinces

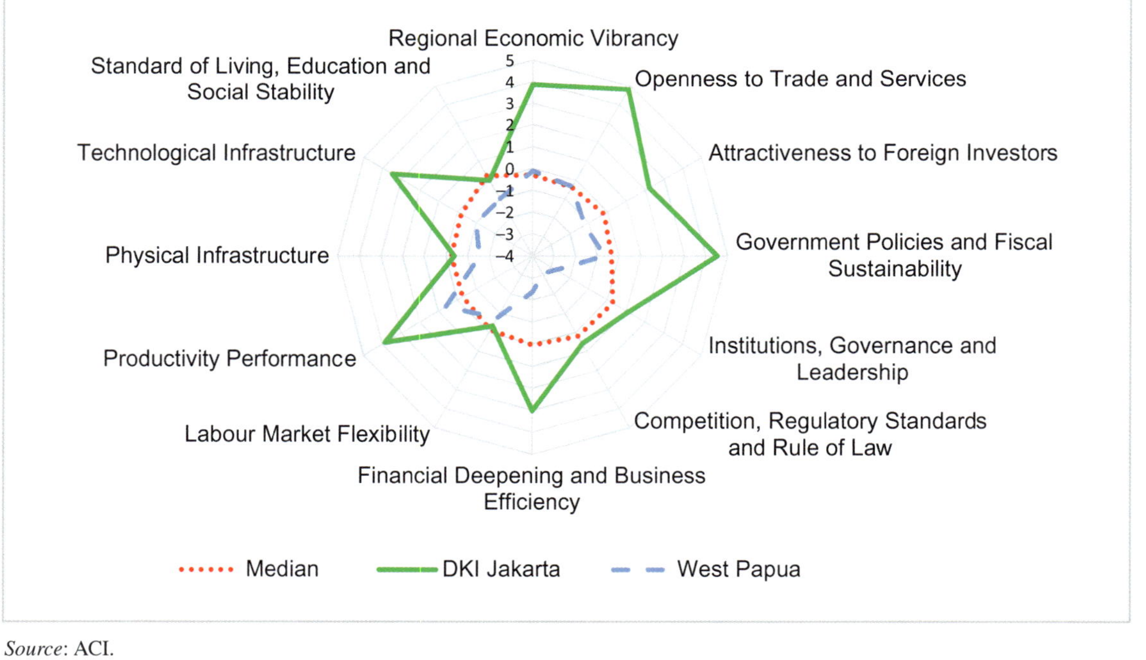

Source: ACI.

In Figure 2.13, the scores for DKI Jakarta and West Papua are also plotted along with the maximum scores among the 33 provinces of Indonesia. As the number one province, DKI Jakarta sets the maximum scores in six out of 12 sub-environments. The province becomes the nation's highest benchmark in (i) Regional Economic Vibrancy, (ii) Openness to Trade and Services, (iii) Government Policies and Fiscal Sustainability, (iv) Financial Deepening and Business Efficiency, (v) Productivity Performance as well as (vi) Technological Infrastructure. In contrast, Papua's scores are quite distant from the maximum scores. The widest gaps — with more than five standard deviations apart — are found in (i) Financial Deepening and Business Efficiency, (ii) Competition, Regulatory Standards and Rule of Law, (iii) Government Policies and Fiscal Sustainability as well as (iv) Openness to Trade and Services.

It is also worth noting that despite DKI Jakarta's dominance, there are other provinces which perform better in certain sub-environments. For instance, East Java achieves the maximum scores in (i) Attractiveness to Foreign Investors and (ii) Labour Market Flexibility. Meanwhile, Central Sulawesi tops in governance, particularly in (i) Institutions, Governance and Leadership and (ii) Competition, Regulatory Standards and Rule of Law. Banten, which houses international and domestic airports in Tangerang, understandably scores highest in Physical Infrastructure, while DI Yogyakarta tops in Standard of Living, Education and Social Stability. This highlights that DKI Jakarta's competitiveness is not all-encompassing and, more importantly, that good standards of competitiveness can be exemplified from other provinces with best practices.

Figure 2.13: 2017 Maximum Competitiveness Web Analysis: Top- and Bottom-Performing Provinces

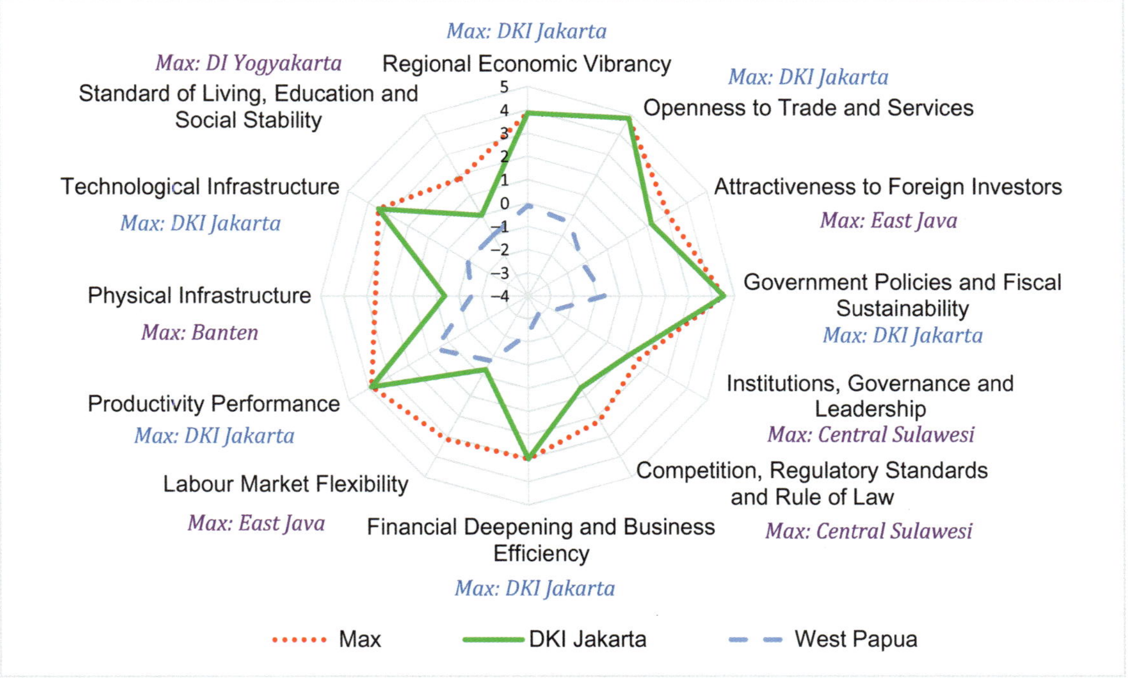

Source: ACI.

2.3.6 Shapley Value: Comparing Competitiveness Results based on Equal and Shapley Weightage

In this section, the competitiveness results which are derived based on the equal weight method are compared with results that are computed based on the alternative weight assignment by the Shapley method. Figure 2.14 shows the weights of each environment under both equal (left) and Shapley (right) methods. Unlike the equal weight method where each environment is assigned with 25 percent weightage (or 1/4), the Shapley weight method shows a diverse distribution of weights of the environments. Some 22.8 percent of the total weightage is associated with Macroeconomic Stability, 26.9 percent is assigned to Government and Institutional Setting, while Financial, Businesses and Manpower Conditions and Quality of Life and Infrastructure Development have weights of 25.6 percent and 24.7 percent respectively.

In Section 2.2.5, we have introduced that the Shapley weight of an environment measures the unequal performance among all the 33 provinces of Indonesia. Consequently, a greater divergence in the performance of provinces within a given environment would render a higher associated Shapley weight for that specific environment. Thus, the weightage of an environment represents its relative importance (compared to the other environments) in contributing to the overall competitiveness. A province will thus receive a higher score if it performs well in an environment in which there is higher disparity across all assessed provinces (i.e. higher weightage). Unequal development across different provinces is thus accounted for and captured by this Shapley weightage approach.

Figure 2.14: Comparison of Weights for Each Competitiveness Environment, 2017

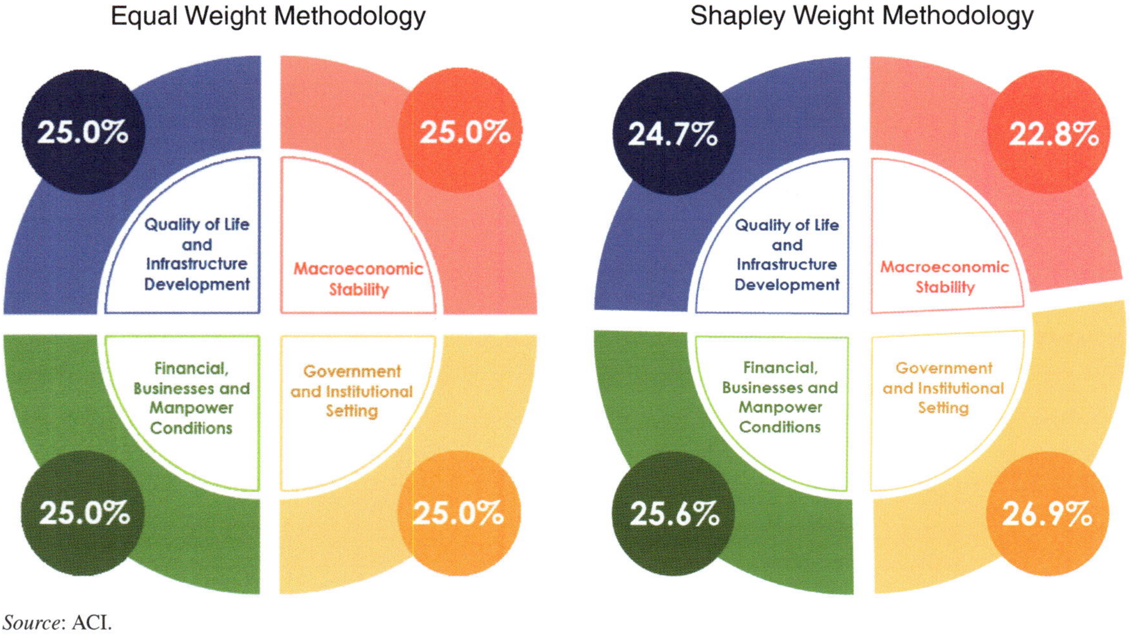

Source: ACI.

The relatively higher weightage for the environment Government and Institutional Setting (weighted at 26.9 percent) reflects the unequal development of governance amongst provinces of Indonesia. Correspondingly, the environment with the least divergence of provincial performance can be found in Macroeconomic Stability, as denoted by its relatively low weight of 22.8 percent.

Despite the different weights, the Shapley weight of each environment does not substantially deviate from the equal weightage assignment of 25 percent per environment. Mathematically, there are two plausible scenarios that could account for this phenomenon. Firstly, the minimal deviations could mean that every province is equally developed in all aspects, across all indicators, sub-environments and the corresponding environments. This is, however, highly unlikely, given that performance disparities across provinces and regions in Indonesia still largely persist. The other more plausible explanation is that the aggregate dispersion, i.e. the Shapley values of each indicator, sub-environment and corresponding environment for all provinces, has been equalised. To put simply, in most aspects of competitiveness, the strong-performing provinces continue to excel while the weak-performing provinces remain lacking behind others.

2.3.6.1 *Results for Overall Competitiveness based on Equal Weight and Shapley Weight Methods*

Table 2.11 shows the Overall Competitiveness ranking and standardised scores computed under both the equal weight and Shapley weight methods. There are no substantial ranking and score differences between these two methods, thereby indicating the robustness of the equal weight approach. This can also be observed in Figure 2.15, which shows minimal deviation of the Shapley-weighted ranking (solid line) from the equal-weighted ranking (dotted line). Even though equal weight is assigned on account of a subjective assumption, its results remain consistent with those obtained from the objective Shapley approach.

Nonetheless, under the Shapley method, certain provinces have obtained a fairly different ranking from the standard equal weight method. Provinces like West Kalimantan, Central Sulawesi and Gorontalo have higher rankings by two or three positions. To the same extent, provinces like Riau Islands and North Sulawesi have obtained lower ranks.

There are two possible explanations that can account for these differences. A province with a lower rank under the Shapley method could have performed better in indicators that are associated with less weights. These indicators are associated with less weights because under these specific aspects, all other provinces have also performed similarly or just as well as the province. Secondly, the same province with a lower rank could have performed poorly in indicators with higher weights (i.e. there is a more diverse range of achievements amongst provinces), and the province happens to be among the lower-performing economies. The antithesis of both situations would also explain the rationale behind why provinces obtain a higher rank under the Shapley method.

Table 2.11: 2017 Comparing Results based on Equal Weight and Shapley Weight Methods: Overall Competitiveness

Province (in ascending order of rank by equal weight)	Rank		Std. Score	
	Equal Weight	Shapley Weight	Equal Weight	Shapley Weight
DKI Jakarta	1	**1**	3.459	**3.253**
East Java	2	**2**	1.723	**1.667**
East Kalimantan	3	**3**	1.303	**1.268**
Central Java	4	**4**	1.035	**1.123**
West Java	5	**5**	0.946	**0.893**
Banten	6	**7**	0.741	**0.704**
Bali	7	**6**	0.687	**0.788**
South Sulawesi	8	**8**	0.557	**0.664**
DI Yogyakarta	9	**9**	0.423	**0.521**
Riau Islands	10	**12**	0.399	**0.331**
South Kalimantan	11	**11**	0.318	**0.335**
Central Sulawesi	12	**10**	0.270	**0.407**
Central Kalimantan	13	**13**	0.090	**0.181**
Lampung	14	**14**	0.061	**0.145**
West Sumatra	15	**15**	−0.018	**−0.002**
Riau	16	**16**	−0.093	**−0.152**
North Sulawesi	17	**20**	−0.270	**−0.275**
Jambi	18	**19**	−0.296	**−0.274**
Gorontalo	19	**17**	−0.298	**−0.217**
North Sumatra	20	**21**	−0.304	**−0.378**
West Kalimantan	21	**18**	−0.308	**−0.255**
Bangka Belitung Islands	22	**22**	−0.403	**−0.392**
Southeast Sulawesi	23	**23**	−0.412	**−0.397**
South Sumatra	24	**24**	−0.460	**−0.468**
Aceh	25	**26**	−0.526	**−0.562**
West Nusa Tenggara	26	**25**	−0.582	**−0.540**
Bengkulu	27	**28**	−0.595	**−0.587**
West Sulawesi	28	**27**	−0.597	**−0.563**
Maluku	29	**29**	−0.712	**−0.733**
East Nusa Tenggara	30	**30**	−1.238	**−1.255**
North Maluku	31	**31**	−1.304	**−1.387**
Papua	32	**32**	−1.706	**−1.753**
West Papua	33	**33**	−1.891	**−2.090**

Source: ACI.

Figure 2.15: Summary of Differences in Overall Competitiveness Ranking based on Equal Weight and Shapley Weight Methods

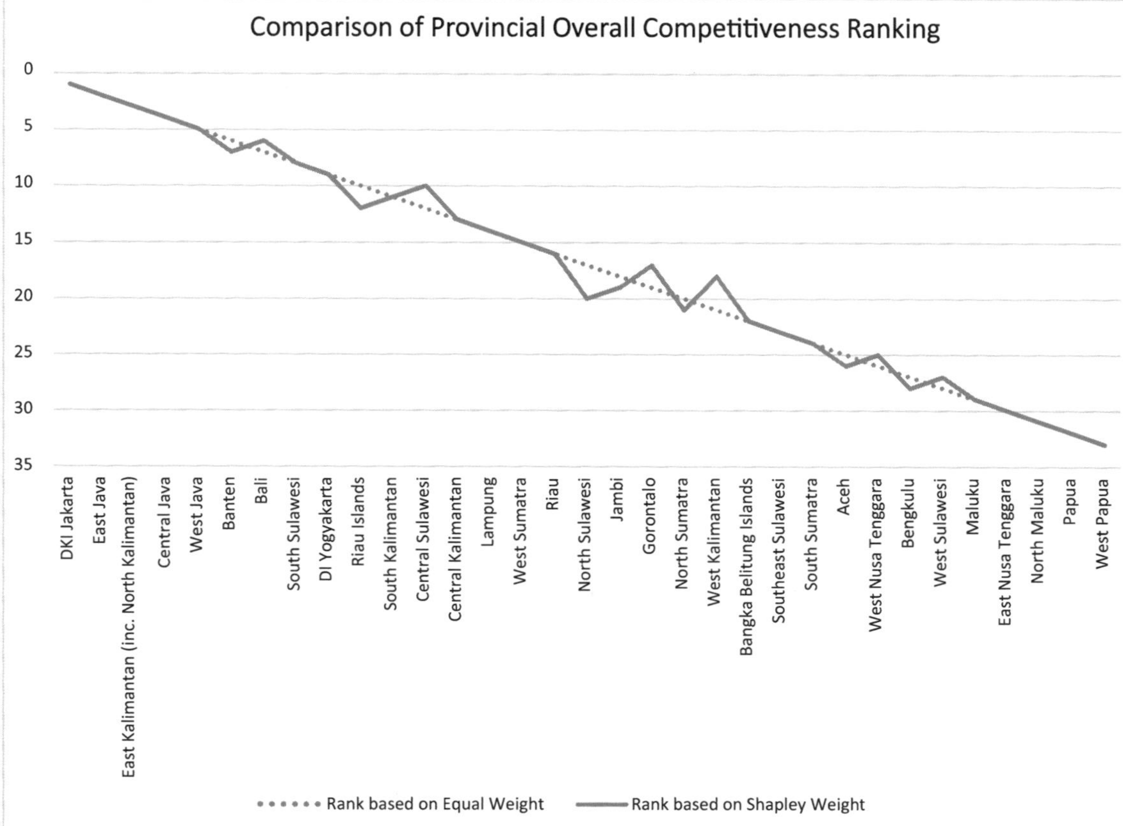

Source: ACI.

2.3.6.2 *Results for Four Environments based on Equal Weight and Shapley Weight Methods*

A comparison of the results of the two methods are also obtained for the four environments (see Tables 2.12–2.15). Generally, there are minimal changes to the ranking and score between them.

Under Macroeconomic Stability (see Table 2.12), 19 out of 33 provinces have obtained the same rank using both the equal weight and Shapley weight methods. For the remaining provinces with changes to their ranking, differences are minimal. Those with large differences of two or more positions are Papua, Southeast Sulawesi, West Kalimantan and West Nusa Tenggara (by two positions each). For Government and Institutional Setting (see Table 2.13), 27 out of 33 provinces have attained the same rank under both the equal and Shapley weight methods. The remaining provinces experience minimal rank changes. Those with large differences of two or more positions are West Sulawesi and East Java (by two positions each) as well as West Java (by three positions).

Of the 33 provinces, 17 provinces obtained the same rank (in both equal and Shapley weights) for Financial, Businesses and Manpower Conditions (see Table 2.14). Those with large

Table 2.12: 2017 Comparing Results based on Equal Weight and Shapley Weight Methods: Macroeconomic Stability

Province (in ascending order of rank by equal weight)	Rank		Std. Score	
	Equal Weight	Shapley Weight	Equal Weight	Shapley Weight
DKI Jakarta	1	**1**	4.055	**3.875**
East Java	2	**2**	2.496	**2.577**
West Java	3	**3**	1.370	**1.450**
East Kalimantan	4	**4**	0.830	**0.870**
Central Java	5	**5**	0.678	**0.721**
Riau Islands	6	**6**	0.596	**0.506**
Banten	7	**7**	0.456	**0.459**
South Sulawesi	8	**8**	0.128	**0.229**
North Sumatra	9	**10**	0.090	**0.063**
South Sumatra	10	**9**	0.067	**0.152**
Riau	11	**11**	0.019	**0.014**
South Kalimantan	12	**12**	–0.012	**–0.001**
North Sulawesi	13	**13**	–0.189	**–0.118**
Bali	14	**15**	–0.243	**–0.213**
West Sulawesi	15	**14**	–0.263	**–0.180**
Lampung	16	**16**	–0.274	**–0.252**
Papua	17	**19**	–0.341	**–0.340**
Central Sulawesi	18	**17**	–0.348	**–0.313**
Central Kalimantan	19	**20**	–0.349	**–0.344**
Southeast Sulawesi	20	**18**	–0.358	**–0.318**
Jambi	21	**22**	–0.429	**–0.425**
West Kalimantan	22	**24**	–0.431	**–0.449**
West Nusa Tenggara	23	**21**	–0.443	**–0.401**
DI Yogyakarta	24	**23**	–0.461	**–0.428**
Gorontalo	25	**25**	–0.523	**–0.496**
West Sumatra	26	**26**	–0.547	**–0.588**
West Papua	27	**27**	–0.628	**–0.680**
Bangka Belitung Islands	28	**29**	–0.649	**–0.708**
Maluku	29	**28**	–0.673	**–0.701**
Aceh	30	**30**	–0.754	**–0.805**
East Nusa Tenggara	31	**31**	–0.865	**–0.922**
Bengkulu	32	**32**	–0.874	**–0.948**
North Maluku	33	**33**	–1.132	**–1.287**

Source: ACI.

Table 2.13: 2017 Comparing Results based on Equal Weight and Shapley Weight Methods: Government and Institutional Setting

Province (in ascending order of rank by equal weight)	Rank		Std. Score	
	Equal Weight	Shapley Weight	Equal Weight	Shapley Weight
DKI Jakarta	1	**1**	2.680	**2.371**
Central Sulawesi	2	**2**	1.395	**1.495**
South Sulawesi	3	**3**	1.066	**1.141**
Bali	4	**4**	0.885	**0.945**
East Kalimantan	5	**5**	0.844	**0.864**
Banten	6	**6**	0.745	**0.770**
West Java	7	**10**	0.730	**0.637**
Central Java	8	**8**	0.700	**0.693**
West Sulawesi	9	**7**	0.649	**0.717**
Lampung	10	**9**	0.606	**0.662**
East Java	11	**13**	0.506	**0.429**
North Sulawesi	12	**11**	0.431	**0.473**
Gorontalo	13	**12**	0.404	**0.453**
South Kalimantan	14	**14**	0.298	**0.339**
DI Yogyakarta	15	**15**	0.246	**0.293**
West Kalimantan	16	**16**	0.178	**0.215**
Central Kalimantan	17	**17**	0.164	**0.210**
West Sumatra	18	**18**	0.129	**0.156**
Southeast Sulawesi	19	**19**	–0.062	**–0.034**
Jambi	20	**20**	–0.153	**–0.136**
Maluku	21	**21**	–0.167	**–0.151**
Riau	22	**22**	–0.174	**–0.246**
Bangka Belitung Islands	23	**23**	–0.426	**–0.394**
Aceh	24	**24**	–0.541	**–0.554**
Bengkulu	25	**25**	–0.672	**–0.661**
West Nusa Tenggara	26	**26**	–0.676	**–0.668**
South Sumatra	27	**27**	–0.849	**–0.882**
East Nusa Tenggara	28	**28**	–0.941	**–0.937**
Papua	29	**29**	–0.956	**–0.997**
North Sumatra	30	**30**	–1.019	**–1.054**
North Maluku	31	**31**	–1.510	**–1.532**
Riau Islands	32	**32**	–1.722	**–1.747**
West Papua	33	**33**	–2.788	**–2.870**

Source: ACI.

Table 2.14: 2017 Comparing Results based on Equal Weight and Shapley Weight Methods: Financial, Businesses and Manpower Conditions

Province (in ascending order of rank by equal weight)	Rank		Std. Score	
	Equal Weight	Shapley Weight	Equal Weight	Shapley Weight
DKI Jakarta	1	**1**	3.375	**3.087**
East Java	2	**2**	1.998	**1.962**
Central Java	3	**3**	1.665	**1.727**
Riau Islands	4	**4**	1.463	**1.507**
West Java	5	**7**	0.887	**0.720**
Bali	6	**5**	0.635	**0.818**
East Kalimantan	7	**8**	0.575	**0.500**
Central Kalimantan	8	**6**	0.560	**0.721**
West Kalimantan	9	**9**	0.332	**0.454**
DI Yogyakarta	10	**10**	0.270	**0.449**
Lampung	11	**11**	0.100	**0.223**
Banten	12	**13**	0.057	**0.029**
South Sulawesi	13	**12**	0.014	**0.053**
Bangka Belitung Islands	14	**16**	–0.032	**–0.054**
North Sumatra	15	**17**	–0.039	**–0.108**
West Sumatra	16	**15**	–0.068	**–0.021**
Central Sulawesi	17	**14**	–0.091	**–0.002**
Jambi	18	**18**	–0.161	**–0.115**
South Kalimantan	19	**20**	–0.310	**–0.270**
South Sumatra	20	**21**	–0.315	**–0.305**
Bengkulu	21	**19**	–0.346	**–0.254**
Riau	22	**22**	–0.364	**–0.417**
East Nusa Tenggara	23	**23**	–0.522	**–0.457**
Southeast Sulawesi	24	**26**	–0.706	**–0.739**
West Nusa Tenggara	25	**24**	–0.720	**–0.694**
Aceh	26	**27**	–0.731	**–0.785**
Gorontalo	27	**25**	–0.755	**–0.703**
North Maluku	28	**28**	–0.807	**–0.841**
Maluku	29	**29**	–1.083	**–1.154**
North Sulawesi	30	**30**	–1.134	**–1.245**
West Sulawesi	31	**31**	–1.209	**–1.269**
Papua	32	**32**	–1.241	**–1.339**
West Papua	33	**33**	–1.295	**–1.476**

Source: ACI.

Table 2.15: 2017 Comparing Results based on Equal Weight and Shapley Weight Methods: Quality of Life and Infrastructure Development

Province (in ascending order of rank by equal weight)	Rank		Std. Score	
	Equal Weight	Shapley Weight	Equal Weight	Shapley Weight
East Kalimantan	1	**1**	2.068	**1.964**
DI Yogyakarta	2	**3**	1.347	**1.350**
DKI Jakarta	3	**2**	1.347	**1.474**
Banten	4	**4**	1.197	**1.054**
South Kalimantan	5	**5**	1.076	**1.031**
Bali	6	**7**	0.999	**0.945**
Riau Islands	7	**6**	0.986	**0.977**
East Java	8	**9**	0.706	**0.670**
South Sulawesi	9	**8**	0.637	**0.705**
West Sumatra	10	**11**	0.427	**0.388**
Central Java	11	**10**	0.383	**0.528**
Aceh	12	**12**	0.284	**0.291**
Riau	13	**14**	0.213	**0.182**
West Java	14	**13**	0.146	**0.195**
North Sulawesi	15	**17**	−0.001	**−0.030**
North Sumatra	16	**20**	−0.040	**−0.059**
Central Sulawesi	17	**15**	−0.061	**−0.020**
Central Kalimantan	18	**19**	−0.076	**−0.057**
Bengkulu	19	**21**	−0.079	**−0.096**
West Nusa Tenggara	20	**16**	−0.089	**−0.019**
Gorontalo	21	**18**	−0.111	**−0.030**
Lampung	22	**24**	−0.228	**−0.237**
Bangka Belitung Islands	23	**22**	−0.229	**−0.165**
Jambi	24	**25**	−0.239	**−0.253**
Southeast Sulawesi	25	**23**	−0.240	**−0.225**
South Sumatra	26	**26**	−0.427	**−0.425**
Maluku	27	**27**	−0.435	**−0.433**
North Maluku	28	**28**	−0.870	**−0.891**
West Kalimantan	29	**29**	−1.100	**−1.141**
West Sulawesi	30	**30**	−1.155	**−1.176**
West Papua	31	**31**	−1.550	**−1.679**
East Nusa Tenggara	32	**32**	−1.773	**−1.837**
Papua	33	**33**	−3.111	**−3.056**

Source: ACI.

differences of two or more positions are West Java, Central Kalimantan, Bangka Belitung Islands, North Sumatra, Bengkulu, Southeast Sulawesi and Gorontalo (by two positions each) as well as Central Sulawesi (by three positions). For Quality of Life and Infrastructure Development (see Table 2.15), only 12 out of 33 provinces remained in the same positions in both methods. Those with large differences of two or more positions include North Sulawesi, Central Sulawesi, Bengkulu, Lampung and Southeast Sulawesi (by two positions each), Gorontalo (by three positions), and North Sumatra as well as West Nusa Tenggara (by four positions each).

2.4. Concluding Notes and Policy Implications

The results from our 2017 competitiveness analysis still highlight the high competitiveness of six provinces in Java Island. DKI Jakarta tops in most environments, though the province still struggles to ensure improvements in the quality of life beyond progress of technological infrastructure. East Java, Central Java and West Java should also take caution as these provinces have experienced a decline in rankings for Quality of Life and Infrastructure Development. Being economically competitive and attractive should not deter a province from providing adequate living standards for its population. Provinces should ensure that progress and development are accelerated not at the expense of a sustainable living condition. Meanwhile, DI Yogyakarta and Banten are showing signs of improved competitiveness after their decline in the previous year. However, DI Yogyakarta still struggles with governance and macroeconomic conditions, which warrants more attention and improvement particularly in trade and investments as well as fiscal sustainability.

The performances of resource-rich provinces remain varied, indicating differing capabilities in optimising the benefits of having natural resources. Being the only province after DKI Jakarta to rank among the top-10 in all aspects of competitiveness (see Table 2.16) and having maintained its lead in Quality of Life and Infrastructure Development, East Kalimantan has shown that with proper developments and careful investments, the province is able to optimise the use of its natural resources to the advantage of its people and economy.

Several other resource-rich provinces like West Papua, Papua and South Sumatra are less successful in turning natural wealth into sustained economic growth and better living standards. These provinces have persisted with subpar scores and low or declining rankings in most of the environments, despite having relatively more favourable macroeconomic conditions. Business efficiency and productivity in West Papua have declined considerably in particular, possibly due to the effects of the declining commodity prices.

It is perhaps worth noting, however, that the full impact of falling commodity prices have yet to take place this year,[4] and would thus create a dampening effect on the performance of commodity-dependent provinces in future assessments. This further highlights the need for these provinces to diversify their sources of growth in order to place less reliance on commodity-based development.

---

[4] Most of the indicators in this analysis are based on 2014 secondary data, although the primary data are based on 2016 perception surveys.

Table 2.16: 2017 Overall Competitiveness and by Four Environments: Summary of Ranking and Standardised Scores

Province		Overall Competitiveness	By Four Environments			
			MS	GIS	FBMC	QLID
DKI Jakarta	Rank	1	1	1	1	3
	Std. Score	3.459	4.055	2.680	3.375	1.347
East Java	Rank	2	2	11	2	8
	Std. Score	1.723	2.496	0.506	1.998	0.706
East Kalimantan	Rank	3	4	5	7	1
	Std. Score	1.303	0.830	0.844	0.575	2.068
Central Java	Rank	4	5	8	3	11
	Std. Score	1.035	0.678	0.700	1.665	0.383
West Java	Rank	5	3	7	5	14
	Std. Score	0.946	1.370	0.730	0.887	0.146
Banten	Rank	6	7	6	12	4
	Std. Score	0.741	0.456	0.745	0.057	1.197
Bali	Rank	7	14	4	6	6
	Std. Score	0.687	–0.243	0.885	0.635	0.999
South Sulawesi	Rank	8	8	3	13	9
	Std. Score	0.557	0.128	1.066	0.014	0.637
DI Yogyakarta	Rank	9	24	15	10	2
	Std. Score	0.423	–0.461	0.246	0.270	1.347
Riau Islands	Rank	10	6	32	4	7
	Std. Score	0.399	0.596	–1.722	1.463	0.986
South Kalimantan	Rank	11	12	14	19	5
	Std. Score	0.318	–0.012	0.298	–0.310	1.076
Central Sulawesi	Rank	12	18	2	17	17
	Std. Score	0.270	–0.348	1.395	–0.091	–0.061
Central Kalimantan	Rank	13	19	17	8	18
	Std. Score	0.090	–0.349	0.164	0.560	–0.076
Lampung	Rank	14	16	10	11	22
	Std. Score	0.061	–0.274	0.606	0.100	–0.228
West Sumatra	Rank	15	26	18	16	10
	Std. Score	–0.018	–0.547	0.129	–0.068	0.427
Riau	Rank	16	11	22	22	13
	Std. Score	–0.093	0.019	–0.174	–0.364	0.213
North Sulawesi	Rank	17	13	12	30	15
	Std. Score	–0.270	–0.189	0.431	–1.134	–0.001

(Continued)

Table 2.16: (*Continued*)

Province		Overall Competitiveness	By Four Environments			
			MS	GIS	FBMC	QLID
Jambi	Rank	18	21	20	18	24
	Std. Score	−0.296	−0.429	−0.153	−0.161	−0.239
Gorontalo	Rank	19	25	13	27	21
	Std. Score	−0.298	−0.523	0.404	−0.755	−0.111
North Sumatra	Rank	20	9	30	15	16
	Std. Score	−0.304	0.090	−1.019	−0.039	−0.040
West Kalimantan	Rank	21	22	16	9	29
	Std. Score	−0.308	−0.431	0.178	0.332	−1.100
Bangka Belitung Islands	Rank	22	28	23	14	23
	Std. Score	−0.403	−0.649	−0.426	−0.032	−0.229
Southeast Sulawesi	Rank	23	20	19	24	25
	Std. Score	−0.412	−0.358	−0.062	−0.706	−0.240
South Sumatra	Rank	24	10	27	20	26
	Std. Score	−0.460	0.067	−0.849	−0.315	−0.427
Aceh	Rank	25	30	24	26	12
	Std. Score	−0.526	−0.754	−0.541	−0.731	0.284
West Nusa Tenggara	Rank	26	23	26	25	20
	Std. Score	−0.582	−0.443	−0.676	−0.720	−0.089
Bengkulu	Rank	27	32	25	21	19
	Std. Score	−0.595	−0.874	−0.672	−0.346	−0.079
West Sulawesi	Rank	28	15	9	31	30
	Std. Score	−0.597	−0.263	0.649	−1.209	−1.155
Maluku	Rank	29	29	21	29	27
	Std. Score	−0.712	−0.673	−0.167	−1.083	−0.435
East Nusa Tenggara	Rank	30	31	28	23	32
	Std. Score	−1.238	−0.865	−0.941	−0.522	−1.773
North Maluku	Rank	31	33	31	28	28
	Std. Score	−1.304	−1.132	−1.510	−0.807	−0.870
Papua	Rank	32	17	29	32	33
	Std. Score	−1.706	−0.341	−0.956	−1.241	−3.111
West Papua	Rank	33	27	33	33	31
	Std. Score	−1.891	−0.628	−2.788	−1.295	−1.550

Notes: MS: Macroeconomic Stability; GIS: Government & Institutional Setting; FBMC: Financial, Businesses & Manpower Conditions; QLID: Quality of Life & Infrastructure Development.
Source: ACI.

Against this backdrop, our findings capture notable observations: the prevailing disparity between the easternmost provinces and rest of Indonesia and the increasingly lagging competitiveness of provinces in the Sumatra region against their neighbouring islands.

West Papua and Papua remain among the bottom provinces in Overall Competitiveness for three consecutive years. Other provinces in the eastern part of Indonesia, especially archipelagic provinces, such as East Nusa Tenggara, North Maluku, Maluku and West Nusa Tenggara, also perform poorly, i.e. score below average in all aspects of competitiveness (see Table 2.16).

Meanwhile, provinces in Sumatra, such as Bengkulu, Bangka Belitung Islands and South Sumatra, continue to decline in Overall Competitiveness. Despite having relative proximity to the Java region, provinces in Sumatra have yet to benefit from spillover effects. Nevertheless, there are also several provinces that have come to speed with proper progress and developments. Lampung, in particular, has demonstrated consistent improvements in Overall Competitiveness as well as in all four environments. With its priority programmes such as improving city connectivity and developing the industry and tourism well underway (Lampung Province 2016), Lampung has the potential to inch its way further in competitiveness.

Table 2.16 also shows that all provinces have their own sets of strengths and weaknesses, wherein they rank highly in certain environments but perform poorly in others. For instance, Riau Islands may be among the top-10 in Overall Competitiveness. However, it ranks second to last in governance. Likewise, South Sumatra may be among the bottom-10 in Overall Competitiveness. However, its macroeconomic conditions still remain among the best (ranked 10th) across all provinces. Such varying successes and failures of provinces to maintain competitiveness suggest that there are plenty of opportunities for peer learning to identify the areas that can be adopted from the experience of high-performing provinces, as well as learn from the less successful policies (or the lack thereof) of provinces which are relatively worse off.

Benefits attained from neighbouring economies through the trade of goods, manpower and market could happen if intra- and inter-regional connectivity is established. Hence, further efforts to strengthen connectivity not only within the provinces but also across provinces are the way forward to revitalise Indonesia's competitiveness as a whole.

Beyond improving connectivity, it is necessary that provinces continue to improve their own competitiveness (as is the case of Lampung), tapping and optimising their own resources while finding solutions in others.

To sum up, ACI's competitiveness analysis provides insights into the competitiveness profile of each province. This year, the findings, which are based on equal-weighted assessment, have been validated with the introduction of the objective-based Shapley weight. The results computed from the latter generally conform to our main findings, thereby attesting to the robustness of ACI's past and current analyses of using equal-weighted method. The mapping of the potential, strengths and weaknesses of the provinces continues to provide a roadmap for central and local government officials to review their past policies, fine-tune their ongoing policies and plan their future policies in advance. The competitiveness framework should not be viewed as merely promoting competition with one another, but more as a platform to track each province's performance that offers a fresh perspective to learn from one another's success story.

References

Aumann, Robert J., and Mordecai Kurz. 1977. "Power and Taxes." *Econometrica* 45 (5): 1137–61. https://doi.org/10.2307/1914063.

Aumann, Robert J., and Roger Myerson. 1988. "Endogenous Formation of Links between Players and Coalitions: An Application of the Shapley Value." *The Shapley Value*, 175–91.

Berger, Thomas, and Gillian Bristow. 2009. "Competitiveness and the Benchmarking of Nations — A Critical Reflection." *International Advances in Economic Research* 15 (4): 378. https://doi.org/10.1007/s11294-009-9231-x.

BPS. 2017. "Result of Establishment Listing of Economic Census 2016." 06130.1721. BPS-Statistics Indonesia.

———. 2018. "Large and Medium Manufacturing." 2018. https://www.bps.go.id/subject/9/industri-besar-dan-sedang.html.

Bristow, Gillian. 2009. *Critical Reflections on Regional Competitiveness: Theory, Policy and Practice*. Vol. 31.;31; Book, Whole. Abingdon, Oxon; New York, NY; Routledge.

Camagni, Roberto. 2002. "On the Concept of Territorial Competitiveness: Sound or Misleading?" *Urban Studies* 39 (13): 2395–2411. https://doi.org/10.1080/0042098022000027022.

IMD. 2017. *IMD World Competitiveness Yearbook 2017*. Switzerland: IMD: Institute for Management Development.

Institute of Applied Economics Shanghai Academy of Social Sciences. 2016. "五大发展理念指标体系及省级区域评估报告 Assessing Provincial Development under the Five Development Concepts (in Chinese)". Shanghai Academy of Social Sciences.

Kitson, Michael, Ron Martin, and Peter Tyler. 2004. "Regional Competitiveness: An Elusive yet Key Concept?" *Regional Studies* 38 (9): 991–99. https://doi.org/10.1080/0034340042000320816.

KPPOD. 2017. *Regional Economic Governance 2016*. Jakarta, Indonesia: KPPOD, supported by Knowledge Sector Initiative (KSI) and Australian Department of Foreign Affairs and Trade (DFAT).

KPPOD, and The Asia Foundation. 2007. "Local Economic Governance: A Survey of Business Operators in 243 Districts/Municipalities in Indonesia, 2007." Jakarta, Indonesia: KPPOD, The Asia Foundation, supported by USAID.

———. 2011. "Local Economic Governance: A Survey of Business Operators in 245 Districts/Municipalities in Indonesia, 2011." Jakarta, Indonesia: KPPOD, The Asia Foundation, supported by Australian AID.

Lampung Province. 2016. "Program Prioritas Pembangunan Provinsi Lampung Tahun 2017." March 28, 2016. http://lampungprov.go.id/berita/program-prioritas-pembangunan-provinsi-lampung-tahun-2017.html.

Leth Hougaard, Jens, Chiu Yu Ko, and Xuyao Zhang. 2017. "A Welfare Economic Interpretation of FRAND." SSRN Scholarly Paper ID 2958212. Rochester, NY: Social Science Research Network. https://papers.ssrn.com/abstract=2958212.

Moulin, Herve. 1992. "An Application of the Shapley Value to Fair Division with Money." *Econometrica* 60 (6): 1331–49.

Partnership for Governance Reform. 2013. *Indonesia Governance Index 2012*. Jakarta: Partnership for Governance Reform and Australian Agency for International Development.

Petrosjan, Leon, and Georges Zaccour. 2003. "Time-Consistent Shapley Value Allocation of Pollution Cost Reduction." *Journal of Economic Dynamics and Control* 27 (3): 381–98.

Porter, Michael E. 1980. *Competitive Strategy: Techniques for Analyzing Industries and Competitors*. Book, Whole. New York: Free Press.

———. 1990. *The Competitive Advantage of Nations*. Book, Whole. New York: Free Press.

PPSK Bank Indonesia, and LP3E FE-UNPAD. 2008. *Profil Dan Pemetaan Daya Saing Ekonomi Daerah Kabupaten/Kota Di Indonesia*. Jakarta: Rajawali Pers.

Schwab, Klaus, and Xavier Sala-i-Martín. 2014. "The Global Competitiveness Report 2014–2015." Geneva: World Economic Forum.

———. 2016. "The Global Competitiveness Report 2016–2017." Geneva: World Economic Forum.

———. 2017. "The Global Competitiveness Report 2017–2018." Geneva: World Economic Forum.

Tan, Khee Giap, Mulya Amri, and Nursyahida Ahmad. 2017. *2016 Annual Competitiveness Analysis and Development Strategies for Indonesian Provinces*. Singapore: World Scientific. http://www.worldscientific.com/worldscibooks/10.1142/10622.

Tan, Khee Giap, Mulya Amri, Linda Low, and Kong Yam Tan. 2013. *Competitiveness Analysis and Development Strategies for 33 Indonesian Provinces*. World Scientific.

Tan, Khee Giap, Mulya Amri, Nurina Merdikawati and Nursyahida Ahmad. 2017. *2015 Annual Competitiveness Analysis and Development Strategies for Indonesian Provinces*. Asia Competitiveness Institute — World Scientific Series. Singapore: World Scientific. http://www.worldscientific.com/worldscibooks/10.1142/10246.

Tan, Khee Giap, Sasidaran Gopalan, and Anuja Tandon. 2016. *2015 Agricultural Total Factor Productivity and Competitiveness Analysis for States and Federal Territories and Five Regions of India*. Singapore: World Scientific. http://www.worldscientific.com/worldscibooks/10.1142/10231.

———. 2017. *2016 Annual Competitiveness and Growth Slowdown Analysis for Sub-National Economies of India*. World Scientific.

Tan, Khee Giap, Linda Low, Kartik Rao, and Kong Yam Tan. 2015a. *2014 Regional Competitiveness Analysis and a Master Plan on Regional Development Strategies for India: Annual Competitiveness Update and Evidence on Economic Development Model for Selected States of India*. Book, Whole. Singapore: World Scientific Publishing Co. Pte. Ltd.

Tan, Khee Giap, Nurina Merdikawati, Mulya Amri, and Blake Harley Berger. 2015b. *2014 Annual Competitiveness Analysis and Development Strategies for Indonesian Provinces*. World Scientific.

Tan, Khee Giap, Le Phuong Anh Nguyen, Sasidaran Gopalan, and Nguyen Trieu Duong Luu. 2016. *2015 Annual Competitiveness Analysis, Agricultural Productivity and Development Vision for ASEAN-10*. Singapore: World Scientific. http://www.worldscientific.com/worldscibooks/10.1142/10219.

Tan, Khee Giap, Le Phuong Anh Nguyen, and Trieu Duong Luu Nguyen. 2017. *2016 Annual Competitiveness Analysis and Growth Slowdown Analysis For Asean-10*. World Scientific. https://www.bookdepository.com/2016-Annual-Competitiveness-Analysis-Growth-Slowdown-Analysis-For-Asean-10-Khee-Giap-Tan/9789813226753.

Tan, Khee Giap, Peng Wang, and Teleixi Xie. 2017. *2016 Growth Slowdown Analysis By Income Thresholds And Annual Update Of Competitiveness Analysis For 34 Greater China Economies*. World Scientific.

Tan, Khee Giap, Sangiita Wei Cher Yoong Yoong, Sasidaran Gopalan, and Le Phuong Anh Nguyen. 2015c. *2014 Annual Competitiveness Ranking and Simulation Study for ASEAN-10 and Development Strategies to Enhance Asia Economic Connectivity*. Singapore: World Scientific. http://www.worldscientific.com/worldscibooks/10.1142/10004.

Tan, Khee Giap, Randong Yuan, and Teleixi Xie. 2016. *2015 Estimation of Agricultural Productivity and Annual Update of Competitiveness Analysis for Greater China*. Singapore: World Scientific. http://www.worldscientific.com/worldscibooks/10.1142/10244.

Tan, Khee Giap, Randong Yuan, and Sangiita Wei Cher Yoong. 2015. *2014 Annual Provincial and Regional Competitiveness Analysis for Greater China Economies: Development Strategies under the New Normal*. Book, Whole. Singapore: World Scientific.

Zeleny, Milan. 1982. *Multiple Criteria Decision Making*. New York: McGraw-Hill. https://www.amazon.com/Multiple-Criteria-McGraw-Hill-quantitative-management/dp/0070727953.

Chapter 3
2017 Annual Update on Competitiveness Analysis of Six Indonesian Regions

3.1 Introductory Notes

Indonesia is made up of over 17,500 islands spanning five major island groups: Sumatra, Java, Kalimantan, Sulawesi and Papua. As an archipelagic country, about two-thirds of Indonesia's territory is made up of water, while the remaining one-third is split across islands of various sizes. In 2015, the overall population was estimated to be 255.5 million. However, its geographical distribution is highly uneven; more than half of the nation's population reside in Java, despite the fact that the island only makes up seven percent of the nation's landmass.

With this urban agglomeration, Java has been the epicentre of the Indonesian archipelago's economy for many hundreds of years. When comprehensive regional data finally became available in 1976, it showed that then, Java already contributed to more than 50 percent of Indonesia's Gross Domestic Product (GDP). Additionally, development in the Soeharto regime — also known as the New Order (1966–1998) — was highly centralist (Hill 2014). Java's status as the epicentre of Indonesia's economy thus became even more pronounced in the years that followed. In 2000 — just two years after the end of the New Order and the Asian Financial Crisis — Java's contribution to Indonesia's economy had increased to 59 percent. In contrast, the Maluku-Papua region's contribution to Indonesia's GDP since 1976 has only hovered at around two percent.

While the end of the New Order was marked by political and economic turmoil, it also signified Indonesia's turn to democracy and decentralisation. Governed under Law 22/1999 on Local Government and Law 25/1999 on Intergovernmental Fiscal Relationship, the devolution of power from central to regional governments officially commenced in 2001. With decentralisation, regional governments have more autonomy and power to manage their resources, and cities and regencies were favoured over provinces in receiving these devolved power and responsibilities, especially during the early phases of decentralisation (Malley 2009). Decentralisation also appeases local governments, which had previously grown increasingly discontent with how local natural resources were utilised by the central government with little returns to their own regions.[1] It was hoped, therefore, that decentralisation could spread out development in Indonesia.

Two provinces in the New Guinea islands — Papua and West Papua — were granted special autonomy under Law 21/2001, which gave the provincial governments more authority in making decisions regarding most sectors of governance (Resosudarmo et al., 2014). This special autonomy also allowed the two provinces to receive a substantially higher share (70–80 percent) of

[1] For a more comprehensive discussion on how decentralisation has affected economic development in Indonesia, please refer to Chapter 4 of Tan et al. (2017b).

revenue originating from the region's forestry, fishery and mining as well as oil and gas sectors. Unlike other provinces, the region was given additional special autonomy funds from the central government on top of the existing financial transfers, which amounted to two percent of the general allocation fund (DAU) ceiling.

To further address the pressing poverty, education and health issues in the Papua region, the Susilo Bambang Yudhoyono administration (2004–2014) also launched the Unit for the Acceleration of Development in Papua and West Papua (UP4B) in 2011. In the same year, the Masterplan for Acceleration and Expansion of Indonesia's Economic Development 2011–2025 (MP3EI), aimed at achieving "high, balanced, fair and sustainable economic growth", was unveiled (Coordinating Ministry for Economic Affairs and Ministry of National Planning and Development/National Development Planning Agency 2011). More specifically, the masterplan was envisioned to accelerate Indonesia's development program — particularly in the sectors of infrastructure development, energy supply, human resources and sciences and technology — that is evenly distributed across all regions in Indonesia. To achieve this, six economic corridors were identified as growth centres to facilitate the eight programs and 22 economic activities that were outlined in the masterplan: Sumatra, Java, Kalimantan, Sulawesi, Bali-Nusa Tenggara and Maluku-Papua (see Figure 3.1).

Although the MP3EI gained less traction after President Joko Widodo in 2014 favoured a more maritime-based development strategy that is based on connecting various islands through seaports rather than developing each island grouping through land-based connectivity, there has presently been no revised or alternative document that describes how the sub-national but supra-provincial regions are to be grouped. Therefore, for the purpose of regional analysis, the Asia Competitiveness Institute (ACI) has kept to the six economic corridors as identified by the MP3EI while being cognisant and supportive of the current national policy to improve various types of connectivity among the regions. It is also acknowledged that an alternative way of grouping the regions is to combine Bali with the Java provinces, rather than with the Nusa Tenggara provinces. However, again, for the sake of consistency, the ACI has stuck to the existing formal delineation of regions.

Figure 3.1: Map of the Six Economic Corridors

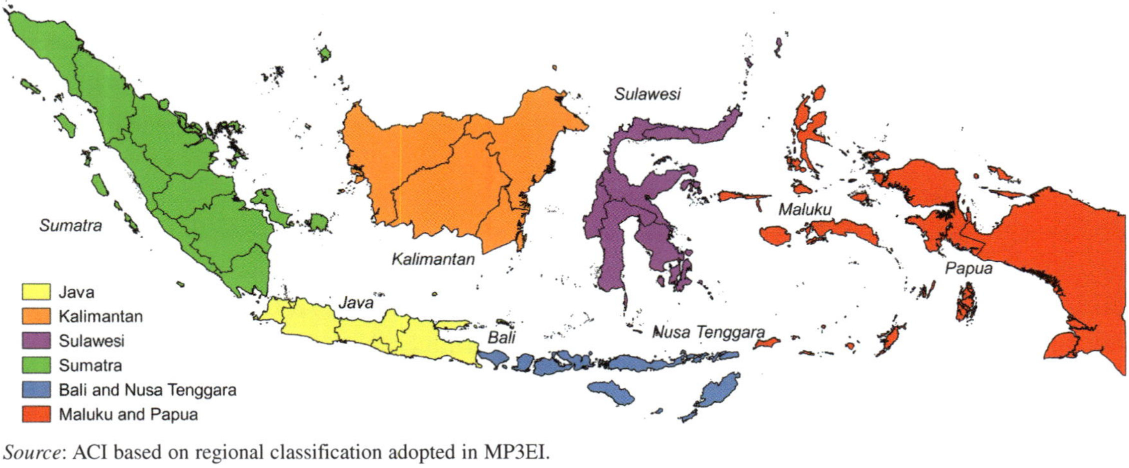

Source: ACI based on regional classification adopted in MP3EI.

Figure 3.2: Regional Share of GDP, FDI, Population and Land Area

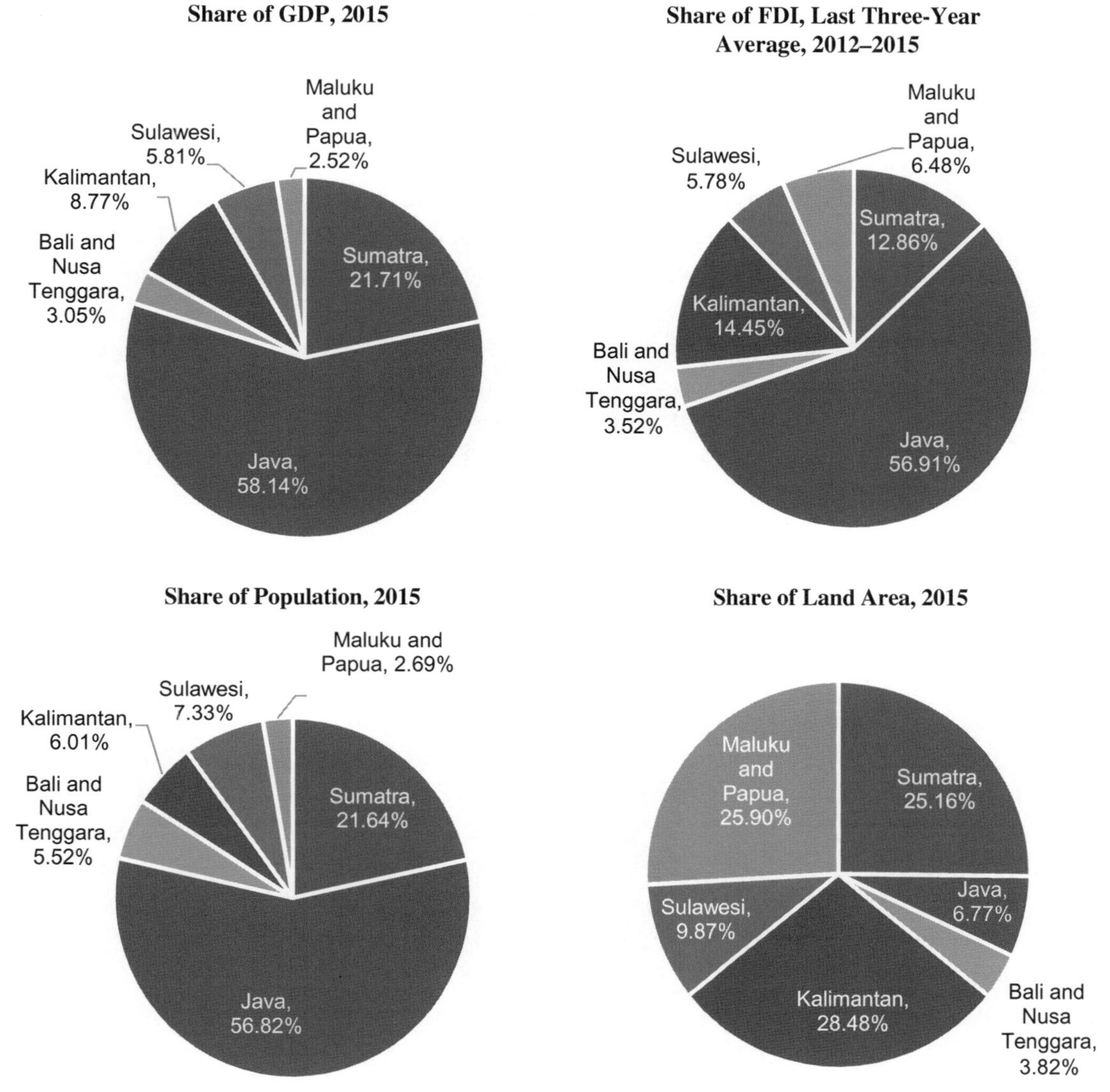

Source: Indonesia's Central Bureau of Statistics (BPS), compiled by ACI.

Despite various efforts to spread economic development across space, it appears that development in Indonesia continues to be unevenly distributed. In 2015, Java's GDP continued to dominate Indonesia's economy at around 58 percent (see Figure 3.2). The primacy of the region still persisted; despite the nation's transmigration programme being one of the largest resettlement programmes in the world, Java's population was still more than double the population in the second-most inhabited region of Sumatra in 2015. In the same year, Java was also the recipient of more than half of the foreign direct investments (FDI) that entered Indonesia.

Indeed, decentralisation does not necessarily always lead to a development that is evenly distributed. In fact, research has shown that in some cases, particularly in poorer countries, fiscal decentralisation may instead result in wider regional disparities (Rordíguez-Pose and Ezcurra 2011; Lessmann 2012).

Moreover, despite the considerable time and efforts that had been invested into developing and promulgating MP3EI, the implementation of the masterplan was met with several key challenges which had ultimately placed limits on its success (Vuljanovic 2017; Ray and Yan 2016). In general, there was a lack of coherent strategy in planning and implementing programs under MP3EI. More specifically, human capital, private sector financing as well as the institutional capacity to forge meaningful Public–Private Partnerships were severely lacking (Negara 2016). MP3EI also placed too much emphasis on the development of ground transportation when land acquisition proved to be a difficult task to undertake.

When Joko Widodo — more popularly known as Jokowi — became Indonesia's seventh president in 2014, infrastructure became a key priority. Between 2014 and 2015, spending on infrastructure as a percentage of GDP rose by 0.9 percent to reach 2.7 percent. To give some context, previous infrastructure spending in the Susilo Bambang Yudhoyono era never surpassed the two percent benchmark (Ray and Yan 2016; Negara 2016). This increase was made possible through what could be considered the most significant economic reform in Indonesia in the past decade: fuel subsidies cut.

Unlike MP3EI which primarily placed emphasis on land connectivity, Jokowi has a vision to transform Indonesia — as it is the largest archipelago in the world — into a global maritime fulcrum. His focus is thus firmly placed on developing Indonesia's maritime infrastructure which would improve connectivity of major islands across Indonesia through major projects such as the maritime highways (*tol laut*). With better connectivity, it is hoped that there would be more traffic between various regions of Indonesia, leading to more efficient logistical costs of transporting people and goods, which would in turn allow the fruits of development in Indonesia to be more evenly spread.

Additionally, Jokowi also aims to increase infrastructure spending in rural areas through the "village fund": direct fiscal transfers from the central government to villages in Indonesia. This village fund further emphasises Jokowi's commitment to develop what used to be considered the peripheries of Indonesia.

Given the dynamic nature of regional policies in Indonesia, the ACI aims to contribute to the discourse by tracking regional disparity and development, specifically through the lens of economic competitiveness — a forte of ACI.[2] It is hoped that the result and analysis from this study would be able to spur key stakeholders to balance out regional developments, thus increasing Indonesia's competitiveness as a whole. The regional classification that ACI has adopted in undertaking this study follows the six economic corridors that had been outlined by the MP3EI report (see Figure 3.1).

This section provides a brief historical overview of Indonesia's regional development and efforts that have been undertaken to balance out the disparity. The remainder of this chapter is organised as follows. Section 3.2 outlines the methodology that has been used to aggregate data from provincial to regional level. Section 3.3 discusses the empirical findings of regional

[2] See previous ACI publications on Indonesia's competitiveness in Tan et al. (2013; 2015a; 2015b; 2016a; 2016b; 2017a; 2017b).

competitiveness, both in terms of Overall Competitiveness as well as the four environments and 12 sub-environments of competitiveness. Section 3.4 provides a conclusion for the chapter.

3.2 Research Methodology: A Note on Regional Data Aggregation

The methodology used to analyse regional competitiveness is based on the competitiveness framework as applied to provinces in Chapter 2, but with aggregation of data done at the regional level.[3] The 2017 result is based on 2014 secondary data collected from official sources as well as 2016 primary data which were obtained from the ACI perception survey.

The primary issue in extending competitiveness ranking and analysis from the provincial to the regional level is that of data aggregation, given that each region consists of several provinces. The ACI has adopted three approaches to data aggregation, the use of which depends on the type of data at hand.

In the first approach, the indicator value for the region is obtained by summing up the values of all the constituent provinces in that region. This approach is useful for indicators that are based on absolute quantities, such as 1.1.01 Gross Regional Domestic Product (GRDP) and 4.1.01 Population. In these contexts, regional value can be obtained through simple summation, i.e. the addition of data across all provinces within the region.

Approach 1: Simple Sum

Example: Indicator 1.1.01 GRDP (Unit: Million rupiah, 2000 Constant Prices)
For Region A with n provinces at time t,

$$GRDP_{\mathrm{A},t} = \sum_{i=1}^{n} \text{Real } GRDP_{i,t}$$

The second approach deals with indicators that are defined as ratios or proportions. In this case, aggregation can be computed directly according to the definition of a particular indicator. We first sum up the absolute quantities of the individual components of the indicator before calculating the final regional value based on the definition of that particular indicator. For instance, indicator 2.1.03 Tax Revenue/Government Revenue is defined as the ratio between tax revenue and government revenue for a particular region. Since both the numerator and denominator are absolute quantities, the two components are aggregated separately across all provinces within the region. The final regional value is obtained by dividing the numerator with the denominator.

Approach 2: Sum of Proportions

Example: Indicator 2.1.03 Tax Revenue/Government Revenue (Unit: Ratio)

[3] For the provincial analysis, the ACI uses a total of 100 indicators that cover 33 provinces. North Kalimantan, the newly created province being carved out of East Kalimantan in 2012, is not yet included pending availability of data.

For Region A with n provinces at time t,

$$Tax\ Revenue/Government\ Revenue_{A,t} = \frac{\sum_{i=1}^{n} Tax\ Revenue_{i,t}}{\sum_{i=1}^{n} Government\ Revenue_{i,t}}$$

The third approach is that of average-weighting an indicator by the population of the province. This approach is adopted for indicators collected through the ACI surveys as well as indicators that reflect proportions/percentages. An example of this is indicator 4.2.01 Telephone Ownership, which reflects the percentage of households that owns a telephone at the original province.

Approach 3: Sum of Percentages

Example: Indicator 4.2.01 Telephone Ownership (Unit: Percentage of Households)
For Region A with n provinces at time t,

$$TelephoneOwnership_{A,t} = \sum_{i=1}^{n} \left(TelephoneOwnership_{i,t} \times \frac{Population_{i,t}}{\sum_{i=1}^{n} Population_{i,t}} \right)$$

For a complete list of indicators that are used for the regional competitiveness analysis (which have also been used for the provincial analysis in Chapter 2), please refer to Appendix 1. A more comprehensive explanatory note on how to derive regional indicator data from provincial data can also be found in Appendix 4. The computation of regional competitiveness after aggregation follows that used in Chapter 2. The technical explanation of the algorithm is also provided in Appendix 2.

3.3 Competitiveness Analysis Results

3.3.1 Ranking and Scores for Overall Competitiveness

As a region, Java continues to occupy the first position in terms of Overall Competitiveness, while the Maluku and Papua region remains at the bottom (see Table 3.1). While the spread of the standardised scores across the six regions is relatively symmetrical, the gap between Java and the second-ranked region Kalimantan is exceptionally wide. This demonstrates just how far more competitive Java is relative to the other regions of Indonesia. Similarly, the gap between the last-ranked region of Maluku-Papua and the second-last region of Bali-Nusa Tenggara is also relatively wide, suggesting that the former lags behind the latter quite significantly. On the other hand, there is an opportunity for Sumatra to overtake the Sulawesi region, given that the standardised scores of the two regions are relatively close to each other.

Even though the rankings of both the Java and Maluku-Papua regions have not changed, Java's standardised score dropped between 2016 and 2017, while that of Maluku-Papua remained

Table 3.1: 2017 Overall Competitiveness: Ranking and Scores

2016 Rank	2017 Rank	Region	2017 Std. Score
1	1	Java	1.629
2	2	Kalimantan	0.534
3	3	Sulawesi	0.190
4	4	Sumatra	–0.114
5	5	Bali and Nusa Tenggara	–0.615
6	6	Maluku and Papua	–1.623

Source: ACI.

Figure 3.3: 2016 and 2017 Overall Competitiveness: Comparison of Standardised Scores

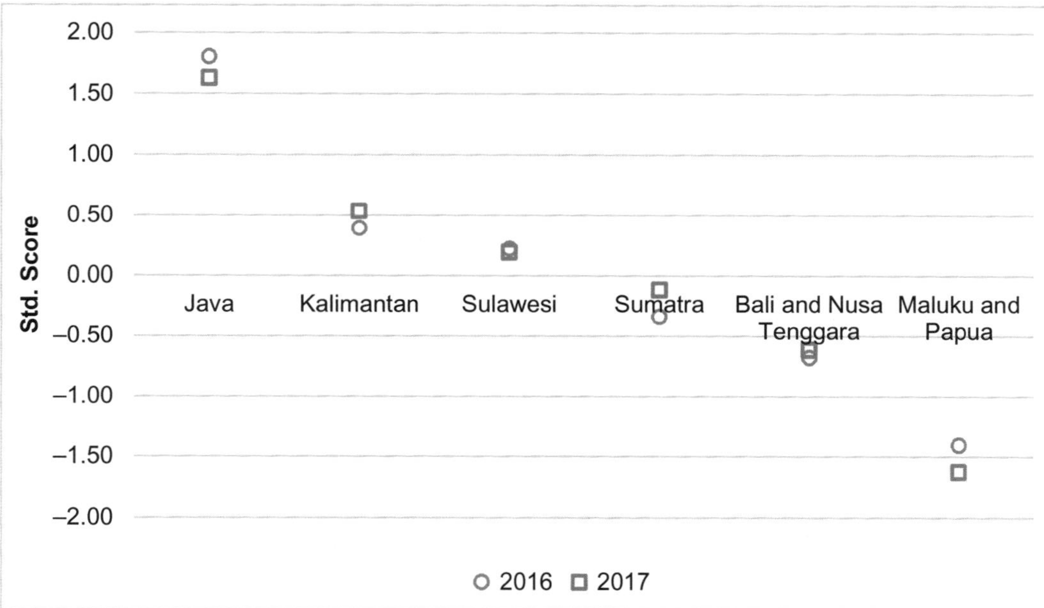

Source: ACI.

around the same value during the same period (see Figure 3.3). On the other hand, the standardised scores of the Kalimantan and Sumatra regions have experienced improvements. This means that the development gaps between these two regions and Java have decreased.

Figure 3.4 showcases the geographical spread of Overall Competitiveness rankings in the six regions of Indonesia. The darker the shade of the region, the more competitive it is and vice versa. From the map, it can be observed that the more competitive regions are mostly found in the western Java and Kalimantan regions, followed by the central region of Sulawesi. On the other hand, the less competitive regions are primarily concentrated in the eastern parts of Indonesia.

It is important to note, however, that there are still disparities within the regions themselves. Figure 3.5 illustrates the ranking of the top- and bottom-performing provinces in each region, as

Figure 3.4: 2017 Overall Competitiveness: Geographical Spread

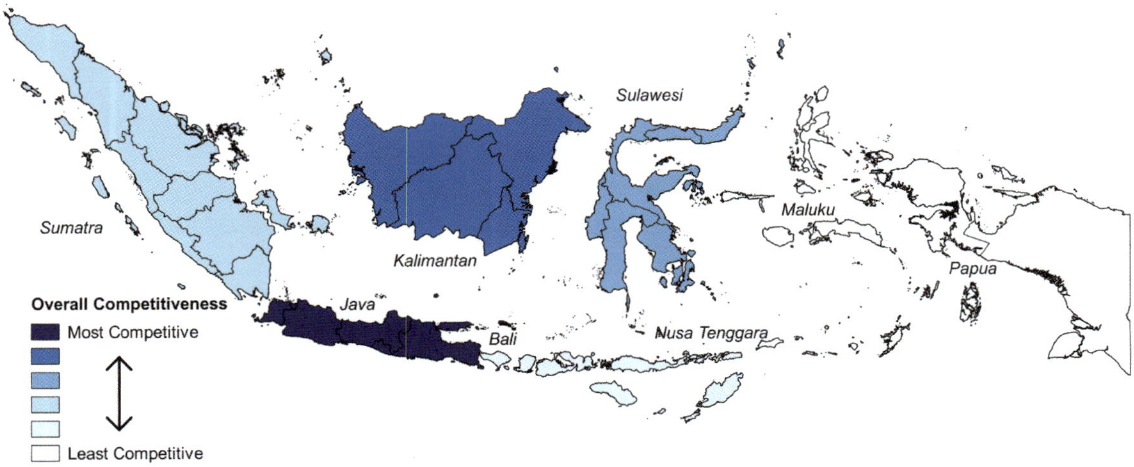

Source: ACI.

Figure 3.5: 2017 Overall Competitiveness: Top- and Bottom-Performing Provinces in Each Region

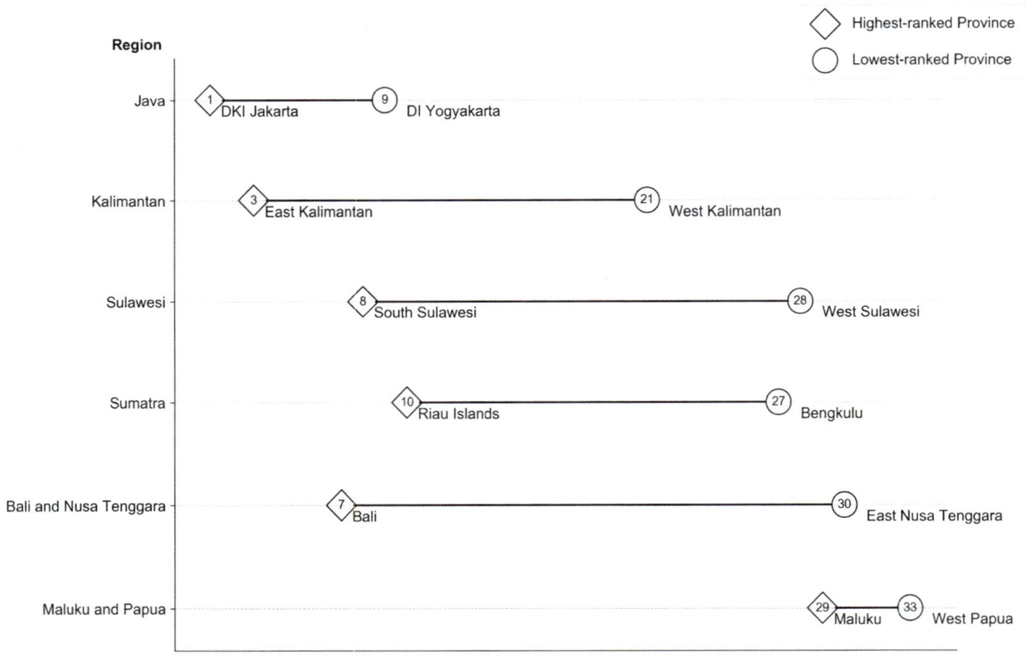

Source: ACI.

indicated by the number inside the two shapes: diamonds and circles. A diamond denotes the top-ranked province in the region, while a circle denotes the bottom-ranked province. The region on the vertical axis has been arranged in the order of their overall regional competitiveness.

From Figure 3.5, it can be gleaned that there is a large disparity in the ranking of provinces within the Bali and Nusa Tenggara region, with the top-ranked province of Bali being placed 23 rankings ahead of the bottom-ranked province of East Nusa Tenggara. This stark difference could be attributed to Bali's strong and internationally recognised tourism industry, which helps to boost its economy ahead of its peers in the region. On the other hand, the small disparity among provinces in the Maluku and Papua region only further reinforces just how uniformly far behind this region as a whole is compared to the rest of Indonesia.

Similar to provincial competitiveness, analysis of regional competitiveness can also be conducted at the environment and sub-environment levels using the competitiveness framework as outlined in Chapter 2. The following sections will go into such analysis in more detail. The methodology of data aggregation as well as the data sources in this section follow the overall competitiveness framework that has also been previously outlined in Section 3.2.

3.3.2 Ranking and Scores by Four Environments

3.3.2.1 *Macroeconomic Stability*

Similar to Overall Competitiveness, Java continues to lead at first position while Maluku-Papua occupies the bottom ranking in the Macroeconomic Stability environment (see Table 3.2). In this environment, however, Sumatra has successfully taken over Kalimantan and they occupy second and third positions respectively.

Regional development in this environment is highly uneven and heavily concentrated in Java, given that the standardised score of Java is significantly higher than the second-ranked region of Sumatra. With a difference in standardised score of 1.967, Java leads ahead in this environment due to its sizeable GDP, which is heavily factored in this environment. As previously mentioned, Java's GDP alone contributed more than 58 percent of Indonesia's economy in 2015. On the other hand, the standardised score of the third-ranked region Kalimantan is negative, indicating that the region performs below the national average. This only reaffirms just how much Macroeconomic Stability competitiveness is skewed towards Java.

Nonetheless, Bali and Nusa Tenggara successfully moved up one ranking, pushing Maluku and Papua region to the last position in the environment (see Table 3.2 and Figure 3.6). While

Table 3.2: 2017 Macroeconomic Stability: Ranking and Scores

2016 Rank	2017 Rank	Region	2017 Std. Score	Sub-Environment Scores		
				REV	OTS	AFI
1	1	Java	2.084	2.077	1.932	2.006
3	2	Sumatra	0.117	0.259	0.395	–0.316
2	3	Kalimantan	–0.155	–0.504	0.126	–0.070
4	4	Sulawesi	–0.300	–0.219	–0.871	0.225
6	5	Bali and Nusa Tenggara	–0.830	–0.712	–1.000	–0.683
5	6	Maluku and Papua	–0.916	–0.901	–0.581	–1.163

Note: REV: Regional Economic Vibrancy; OTS: Openness to Trade and Services; AFI: Attractiveness to Foreign Investors.
Source: ACI.

Figure 3.6: 2016 and 2017 Macroeconomic Stability: Comparison of Standardised Scores

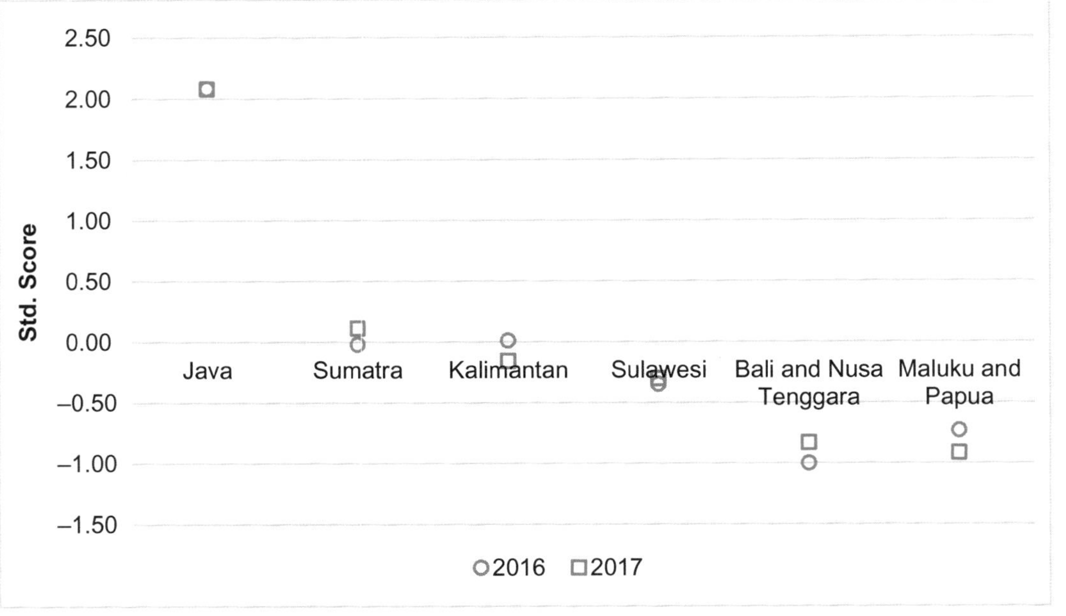

Source: ACI.

the former managed to overtake the latter, the difference in standardised scores between the two regions is relatively small (0.086). This means that Maluku-Papua still has ample opportunity to reverse the ranking, and Bali and Nusa Tenggara must not rest on its laurels. The switch in position is similarly observed between Sumatra and Kalimantan, with the regions occupying second and third places respectively in 2017. The difference in standardised scores between the two regions, however, is slightly wider at 0.272.

While ranked first, the disparity of provinces within the Java region is also among the highest in this environment. The difference between the top- and bottom-performing provinces is 23 rankings, which is slightly better than Sumatra with a difference in ranking of 26 (see Figure 3.7). Unlike its regional peers, which have relatively strong primary and secondary industries, Java's bottom-ranked province DI Yogyakarta heavily relies on its tertiary industry, which unfortunately still does not compare to the other provinces in Java. DI Yogyakarta's low rank is also a product of weak investment inflows from both foreign and domestic sources. This is also the case with Bengkulu — the bottom-ranked province in the Sumatra region. While its economy is similar to its peers in that it is mainly driven by the primary industry, Bengkulu's primary industry is simply not substantial enough to compete with the rest of the region. Similarly, Bengkulu's lack of competitiveness in this environment is further exacerbated by low foreign and domestic direct investments flowing into the province.

Regional competitiveness can also be assessed at the sub-environment level. Figure 3.8 illustrates how a region's performance in the three sub-environments of Macroeconomic Stability may greatly vary. For instance, while Sumatra scores positively in Regional Economic Vibrancy and Openness to Trade and Services, it performs poorly in the Attractiveness to Foreign Investors

Figure 3.7: 2017 Macroeconomic Stability: Top- and Bottom-Performing Provinces in Each Region

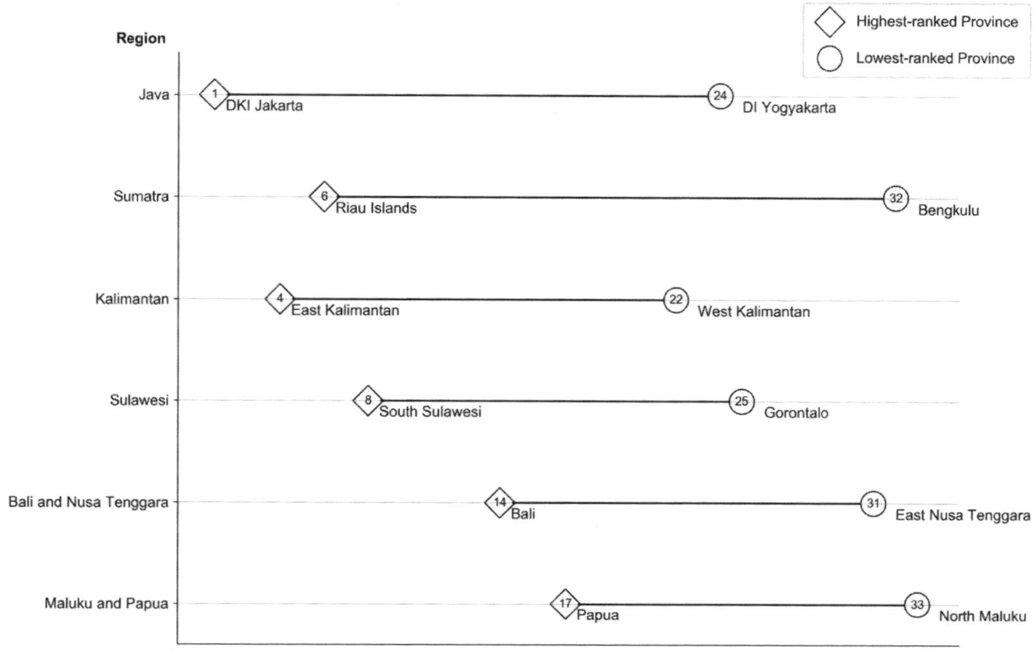

Source: ACI.

Figure 3.8: 2017 Macroeconomic Stability: Sub-Environment Spread

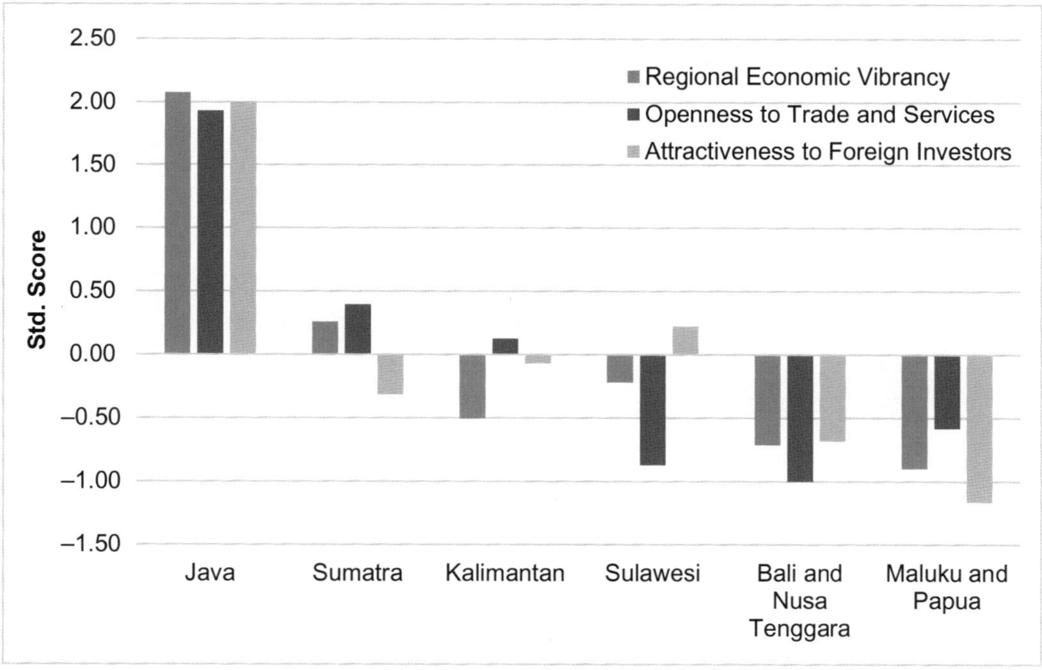

Source: ACI.

sub-environment, signifying the need for the region to revise its investment promotion policies. On the contrary, Sulawesi has been doing quite well in terms of Attractiveness to Foreign Investors although it still lags behind in Regional Economic Vibrancy and Openness to Trade and Services due to low economies of scale and limited demand for exports and imports. Despite its strong primary industry, both export and import volumes in Sulawesi have not caught up due to the lack of trading infrastructure in the region. Meanwhile, Kalimantan remains relatively open to exports and imports, but its economic vibrancy has been hit by the commodity price bust. Nonetheless, Java, Bali-Nusa Tenggara and Maluku-Papua have a more evenly distributed performance in these sub-environments.

3.3.2.2 *Government and Institutional Setting*

Regional performance in the Government and Institutional Setting environment has not differed greatly from 2016, with the only difference being the switch in ranking between Sumatra (fifth) and Maluku and Papua (sixth) (see Table 3.3). Java has remained at the top, with a standardised score that is very close to the second-ranked region Sulawesi. With a gap in standardised score of merely 0.021, there is ample opportunity for the latter to overtake the former. As it is, Sulawesi is already performing ahead of Java in two sub-environments of Institutions, Governance and Leadership as well as Competition, Regulatory Standards and Rule of Law. In order to surpass Java, Sulawesi needs to reconsider its fiscal policies and find innovative ways to increase its revenue and expenditure.

Table 3.3 also shows that the distribution of standardised score is relatively more symmetrical, which suggests that development in this particular environment is more evenly distributed.

From Figure 3.9, it can also be observed that while the standardised score of Sulawesi has remained relatively consistent between 2016 and 2017, Java's standardised score has dropped. Meanwhile, Kalimantan's standardised score has increased significantly in the same period, reaffirming its status as the more competitive region relative to Bali-Nusa Tenggara. Although Sumatra has only overtaken Maluku-Papua in 2017, the gap between the two regions has

Table 3.3: 2017 Government and Institutional Setting: Ranking and Scores

2016 Rank	2017 Rank	Region	2017 Std. Score	Sub-Environment Scores		
				GPFS	IGL	CRRL
1	1	Java	1.149	2.148	0.628	–0.122
2	2	Sulawesi	1.128	–0.538	1.510	1.632
3	3	Kalimantan	0.511	–0.291	0.620	0.851
4	4	Bali and Nusa Tenggara	–0.447	–0.503	–0.422	–0.106
6	5	Sumatra	–0.848	0.053	–1.031	–0.979
5	6	Maluku and Papua	–1.493	–0.870	–1.304	–1.275

Note: GPFS: Government Policies and Fiscal Sustainability; IGL: Institutions, Governance and Leadership; CRRL: Competition, Regulatory Standards and Rule of Law.
Source: ACI.

Figure 3.9: 2016 and 2017 Government and Institutional Setting: Comparison of Standardised Scores

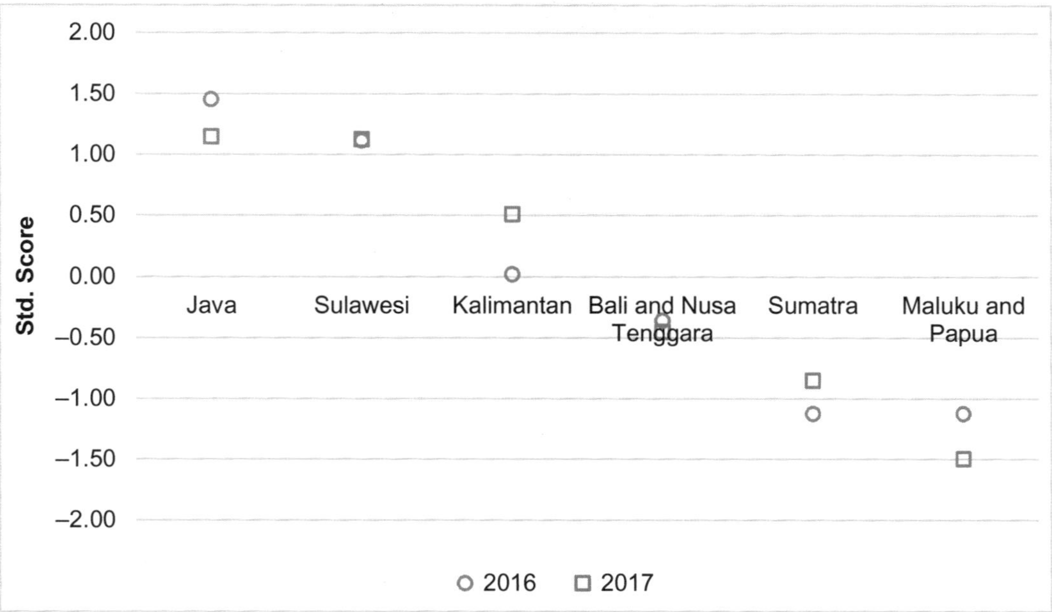

Source: ACI.

widened significantly, with the standardised score for the Maluku-Papua region dropping this year compared to the previous year. Additionally, as has been outlined in Chapter 2, three out of the four provinces in Maluku-Papua are placed among the bottom-10 provinces in this environment, which further reaffirms that governance in this region is sub-par to the rest of Indonesia.

Despite being ranked fourth, provincial disparity within the Bali-Nusa Tenggara region is the highest, with a gap of 24 positions (see Figure 3.10). In fact, while Bali is listed among the top-10 provinces in this environment, both East and West Nusa Tenggara are placed among the bottom-10. Additionally, inequality among provinces in Java has also become wider, with DI Yogyakarta falling in ranking from 10th in 2015 to 15th in 2017 as a result of a decline in Institutions, Governance and Leadership. The region with the least prominent intra-regional disparity is Kalimantan, with a gap of merely 12 positions, which indicates that relative to the other regions, Kalimantan has a more even distribution of governmental and institutional capacity.

In Government and Institutional Setting, there are also more disparities in performance at the sub-environment level (see Figure 3.11). Notably, Java is strong in Government Policies and Fiscal Sustainability because of its high fiscal budget. However, it scores below the national average in Competition, Regulatory Standards and Rule of Law — something that the region can perhaps learn from Sulawesi and Kalimantan, which excel in this sub-environment. However, both Sulawesi and Kalimantan have negative standardised scores in Government Policies and Fiscal Sustainability while scoring positively at the other two sub-environments. The Maluku-Papua region, on the other hand, has relatively poor performances across all three sub-environments, which points to plenty of room for improvement.

Figure 3.10: 2017 Government and Institutional Setting: Top- and Bottom-Performing Provinces in Each Region

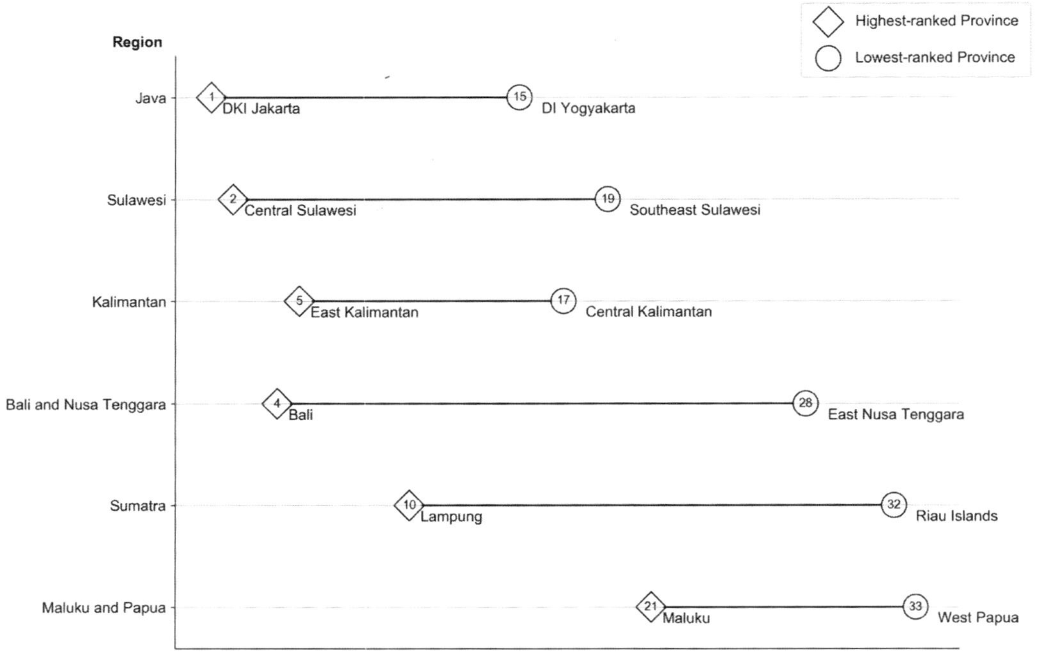

Source: ACI.

Figure 3.11: 2017 Government and Institutional Setting: Sub-Environment Spread

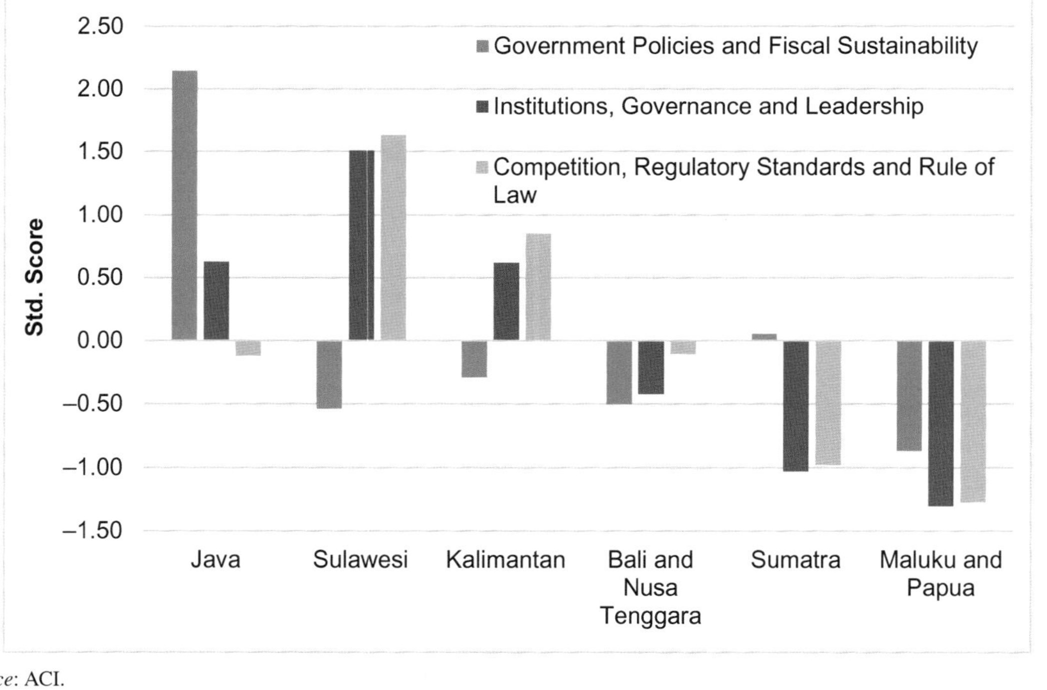

Source: ACI.

3.3.2.3 *Financial, Businesses and Manpower Conditions*

There is no change in regional ranking in the Financial, Businesses and Manpower Conditions environment between 2016 and 2017 (see Table 3.4). Similar to Government and Institutional Setting, the spread in standardised scores in this environment is also fairly symmetrical, indicating a relatively balanced distribution of performance. Nonetheless, the gap among the first three regions is rather substantial, with Java (first) leading ahead of Kalimantan (second) by 0.932 and the latter leading ahead of Sumatra (third) by 0.725. A similar gap can also be observed between the second-last and last-ranked regions of Bali-Nusa Tenggara and Maluku-Papua, with a difference in standardised score of 0.780.

Relative to 2016, the gap in standardised scores between Bali-Nusa Tenggara and Maluku-Papua has in fact widened, due to improvements in standardised score in the former combined with deteriorations in the latter (see Figure 3.12). On the other hand, the standardised scores of Sulawesi and Bali-Nusa Tenggara have become fairly close to each other; with a mere gap of 0.135, there is a possibility that the former can overtake the latter, especially if Bali-Nusa Tenggara manages to improve its weakest sub-environment, as will be discussed in the later section.

As mentioned, the standardised score of Maluku-Papua has become progressively lower between 2016 and 2017, further widening its gap relative to Bali-Nusa Tenggara. On top of this worrying trend, Figure 3.13 highlights how the spread in the ranking of provinces in the region is relatively small. There is merely a difference of five positions between the top-ranked and bottom-ranked provinces, which indicates that all the provinces in the Maluku-Papua region are among the least competitive in Indonesia in the Financial, Businesses and Manpower Conditions environment. On the other hand, provinces in the Sumatra and Sulawesi regions have the widest disparity in ranking; the gaps between the top-ranked and bottom-ranked provinces are 22 places and 18 places respectively. Although Riau Islands is among the most competitive in the environment at fourth place, the rest of the provinces in the Sumatra region are not nearly as competitive, considering that no other province is placed in the top-10. The same case applies to Sulawesi: although South Sulawesi is the most competitive province in the region at 13th, West Sulawesi is

Table 3.4: 2017 Financial, Businesses and Manpower Conditions: Ranking and Scores

2016 Rank	2017 Rank	Region	2017 Std. Score	Sub-Environment Scores		
				FDBE	LMF	PP
1	1	Java	1.693	1.132	2.176	0.585
2	2	Kalimantan	0.761	0.420	–0.281	1.609
3	3	Sumatra	0.036	0.387	–0.380	0.077
4	4	Sulawesi	–0.480	–0.330	–0.515	–0.260
5	5	Bali and Nusa Tenggara	–0.615	0.417	–0.128	–1.703
6	6	Maluku and Papua	–1.395	–2.027	–0.872	–0.308

Note: FDBE: Financial Deepening and Business Efficiency; LMF: Labour Market Flexibility; PP: Productivity Performance.
Source: ACI.

Figure 3.12: 2016 and 2017 Financial, Businesses and Manpower Conditions: Comparison of Standardised Scores

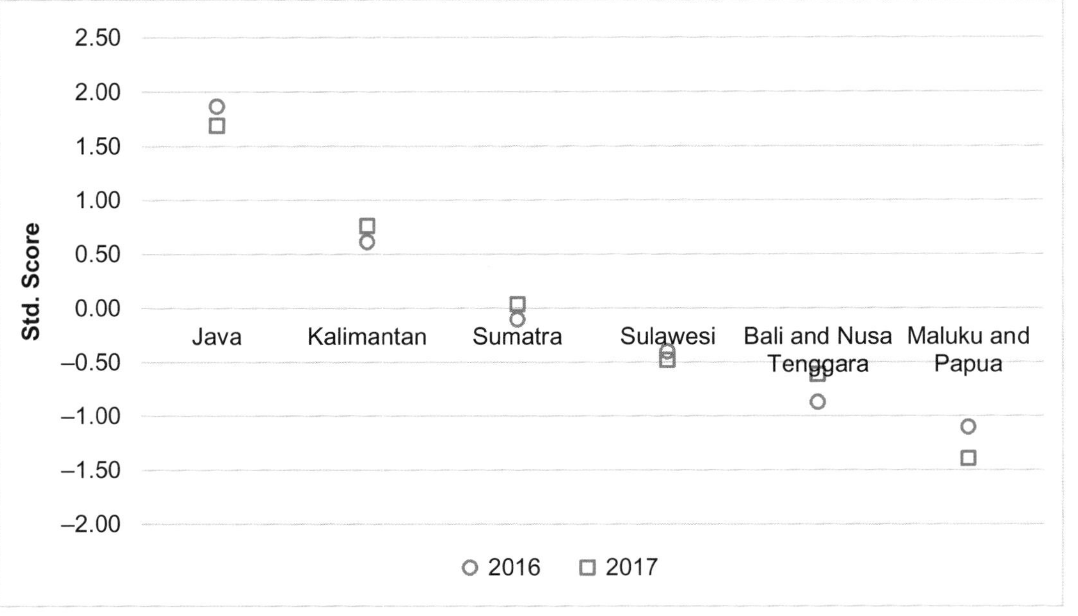

Source: ACI.

Figure 3.13: 2017 Financial, Businesses and Manpower Conditions: Top- and Bottom-Performing Provinces in Each Region

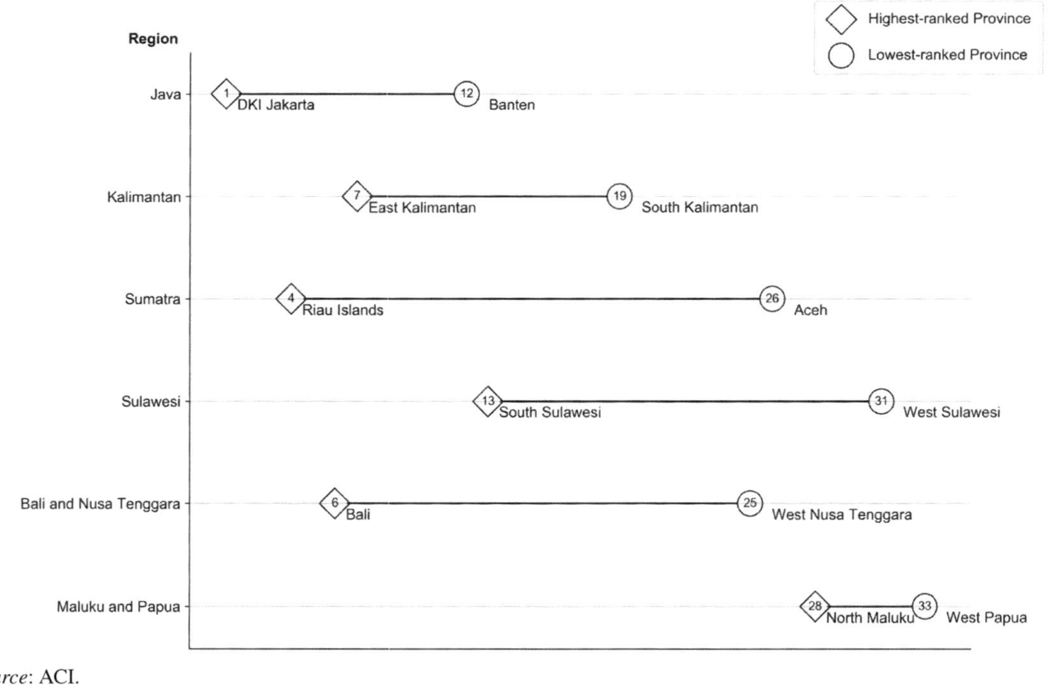

Source: ACI.

Figure 3.14: 2017 Financial, Businesses and Manpower Conditions: Sub-Environment Spread

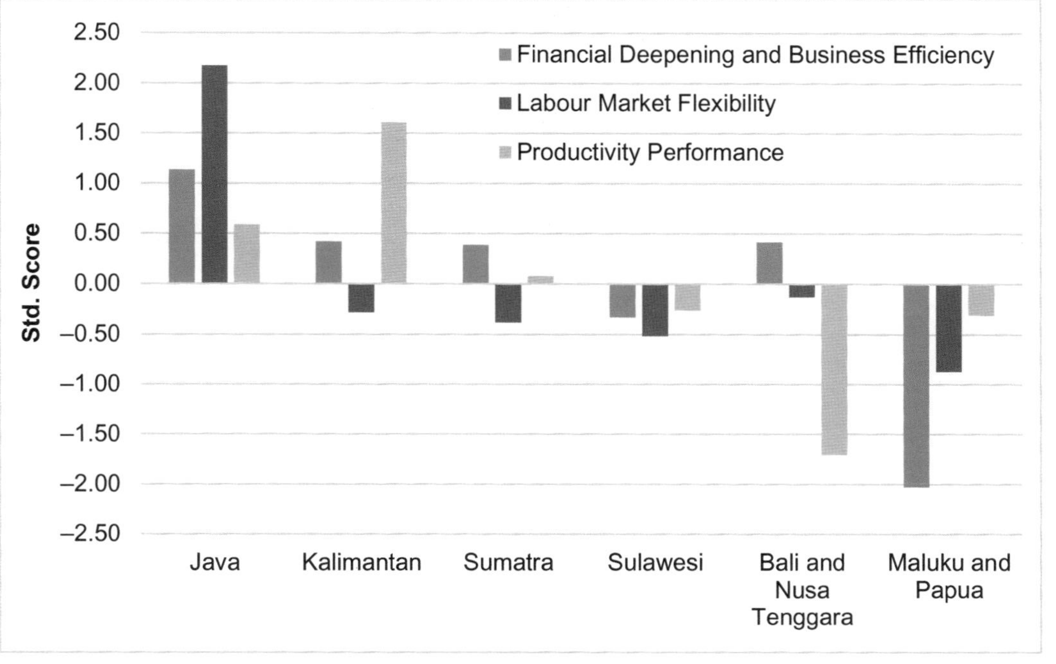

Source: ACI.

still ranked 31st or third from the bottom. The Bali-Nusa Tenggara region also showcases a similar pattern; although Bali is placed sixth, the rest of the provinces in the region still lag behind, with East Nusa Tenggara occupying 23rd and West Nusa Tenggara occupying 25th positions.

At the sub-environment level, Bali-Nusa Tenggara scores well in Financial Deepening and Business Efficiency; however, its overall performance is severely pulled down by its Productivity Performance (see Figure 3.13). Given that it already outperforms Sulawesi in the other two sub-environments, Bali-Nusa Tenggara can potentially overtake Sulawesi in the Financial, Businesses and Manpower Conditions environment if it can work towards improving its productivity across all economic sectors. The Bali-Nusa Tenggara region can perhaps learn from Kalimantan — another region which showcases an imbalance of performance across its sub-environments, but with exceptionally competitive Productivity Performance relative to the other regions. On the other hand, while Maluku-Papua's standardised scores across all sub-environments are below the national average, its performance in Financial Deepening and Business Efficiency is exceptionally poor, driven by very low bank deposits and lacking capacity in firms — be it in human resource, equipment and even innovation — which calls for comprehensive firm-level improvements in the region (see Figure 3.14).

3.3.2.4 *Quality of Life and Infrastructure Development*

Similar to the previous environment, there has been no change in regional ranking for Quality of Life and Infrastructure Development. Java still leads at first place, but Kalimantan comes at a

Table 3.5: 2017 Quality of Life and Infrastructure Development: Ranking and Scores

2016 Rank	2017 Rank	Region	2017 Std. Score	Sub-Environment Scores		
				PI	TI	SLESS
1	1	Java	0.942	1.512	1.409	–0.421
2	2	Kalimantan	0.806	0.784	0.846	0.508
3	3	Sulawesi	0.335	–0.166	0.034	1.019
4	4	Sumatra	0.282	0.024	–0.042	0.767
5	5	Bali and Nusa Tenggara	–0.323	–0.464	–0.502	0.108
6	6	Maluku and Papua	–2.041	–1.690	–1.745	–1.981

Note: PI: Physical Infrastructure; TI: Technological Infrastructure; SLESS: Standard of Living, Education and Social Stability.
Source: ACI.

close second with a mere 0.136 difference in standardised scores. The gap between Sulawesi (third) and Sumatra (fourth) is even smaller (0.053), which provides the latter with an even bigger opportunity to overtake the former. Maluku-Papua's performance in this environment, however, is perhaps the most worrying as it registers the most significant lag. Relative to the second-last region of Bali-Nusa Tenggara, Maluku-Papua's standardised score is behind by 1.718 points. Although Maluku-Papua's score skews the regional performance to the lower end, only two out of the six regions obtain negative standardised scores, which means that regional performance in Quality of Life and Infrastructure Development is relatively commendable compared to the other three environments. Maluku-Papua can therefore be considered an outlier — albeit one that all the more needs serious attention (see Table 3.5).

The gap between Maluku-Papua and the rest of Indonesia can further be visualised in Figure 3.15, which also demonstrates how the standardised scores have (or have not) changed relative to 2016. Here, it can be observed that the region's standardised scores between 2016 and 2017 have not changed even marginally. On the other hand, the Sumatra region registered the most improvement with the highest increase in standardised score by 0.238, while Bali-Nusa Tenggara's score has declined the most by 0.137.

Intra-regional disparity in this environment, however, is relatively wide. With the exception of Maluku-Papua, the gaps in ranking between the top-ranked and bottom-ranked provinces are bigger than 10. Kalimantan displays the most inequality, with East Kalimantan ranked first and West Kalimantan ranked among the lowest at 29th. This is followed by Sulawesi and Bali-Nusa Tenggara, both displaying a gap of 26 positions. In some ways, the distribution of competitive provinces in this environment does not show a clear regional concentration pattern, given that they are spread rather evenly across the different regions (see Figure 3.16).

Diversity is also observed at the sub-environment level, with the exception of Kalimantan and Maluku-Papua. For instance, while Java is ranked first and excels at Physical and Technological Infrastructure, its performance in Standard of Living, Education and Social Stability is among the worst — second only to Maluku and Papua (see Figure 3.17). While the

Figure 3.15: 2016 and 2017 Quality of Life and Infrastructure Development: Comparison of Standardised Scores

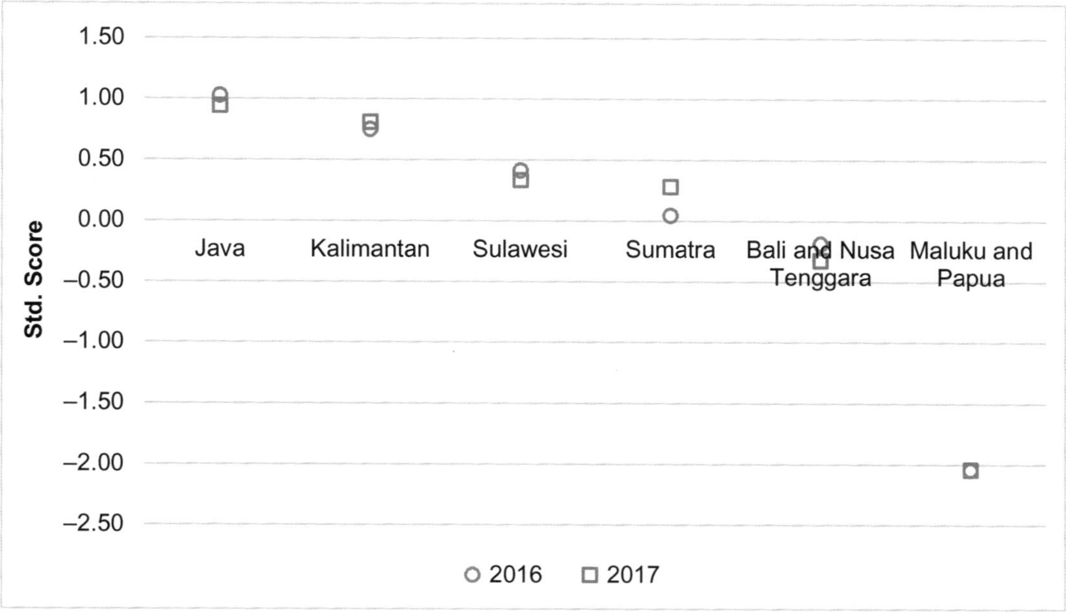

Source: ACI.

Figure 3.16: 2017 Quality of Life and Infrastructure Development: Top- and Bottom-Performing Provinces in Each Region

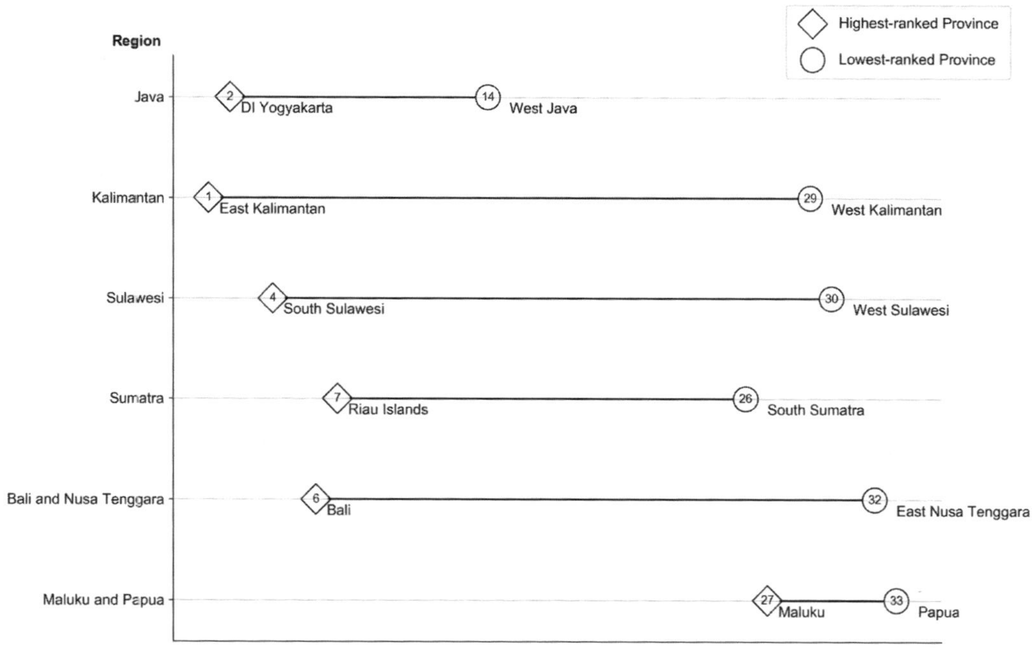

Source: ACI.

Figure 3.17: 2017 Quality of Life and Infrastructure Development: Sub-Environment Spread

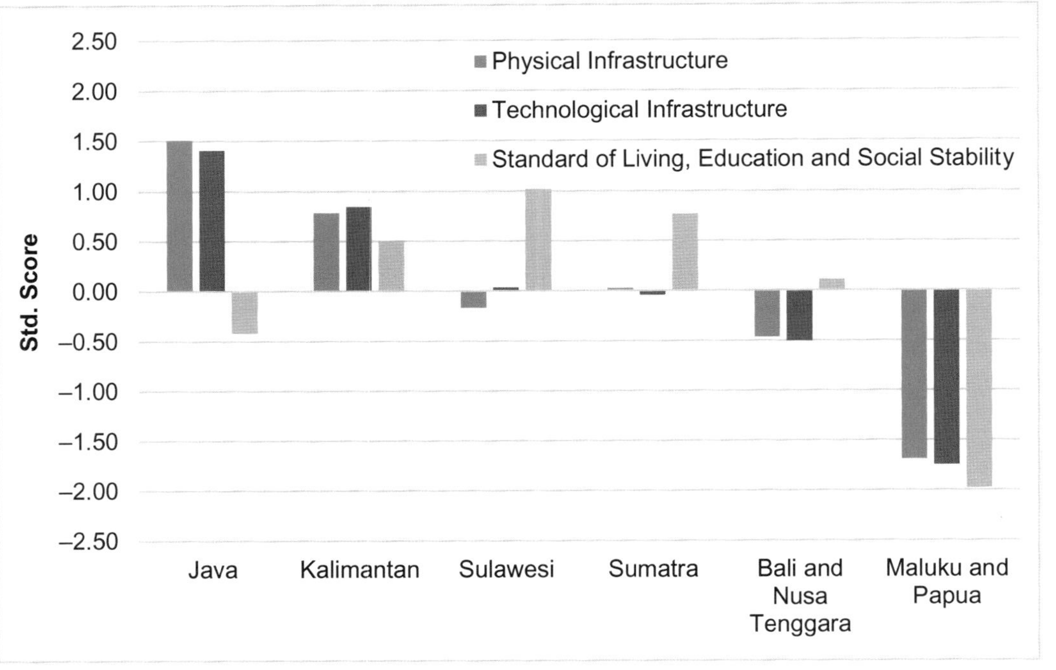

Source: ACI.

former registers the highest Human Development Index and life expectancy, public services have yet to catch up with the overpopulation in the region, resulting in the underprovision of key services, such as education and healthcare. Among Java's weakest indicators are (i) Population per Medical Worker, (ii) Environmental Quality Index, (iii) Households with Pipe Water Services, (iv) Student–Teacher Ratio and (v) Population per Health Facility. Much can perhaps be learned from Sulawesi and Sumatra — both of which have exceptionally high standardised scores in this sub-environment.

Although Maluku-Papua's scores across all three sub-environments are negative, the region displays the most worrying performance in Standard of Living, Education and Social Stability. In fact, eight out of the region's bottom-20 indicators belong to this sub-environment. In addition to working to improve its physical and technological infrastructure, the region also needs to pay special attention to providing basic services, such as education and healthcare.

3.3.3 Median and Maximum Competitiveness Web Analysis

In Section 3.3.2, competitiveness analysis at the sub-environment level — which allows for a better understanding of the performance at the environment level — has been touched upon briefly. This section will delve into such sub-environment analysis in greater detail, comparing each region's performance to the medium and maximum performance in each of the 12 sub-environments.

Figure 3.18: 2017 Median and Maximum Web Analysis: Bali and Nusa Tenggara

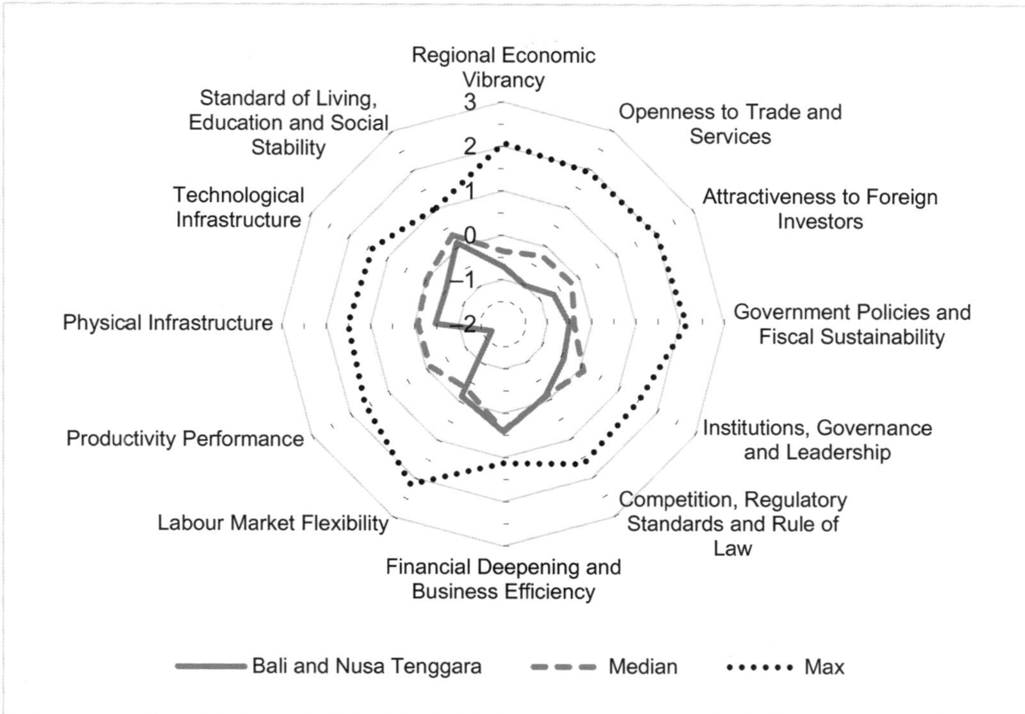

Source: ACI.

We describe the competitiveness web analysis for each region by alphabetical order. To start off, Bali and Nusa Tenggara as a region generally performs below the regional median, as shown in Figure 3.18. The only three sub-environments in which it performs better than the median is (i) Competition, Regulatory Standards and Rule of Law, (ii) Financial Deepening and Business Efficiency as well as (iii) Labour Market Flexibility. The region, however, has exceptionally worrying Productivity Performance, as showcased by the substantial gap to the regional median and maximum. Indeed, all five indicators in this sub-environment are among the region's 20-weakest indicators.

Next, we turn to Java. While Java's standardised scores in eight sub-environments are the maximum across the six regions, it has much to improve in four other sub-environments: (i) Institutions, Governance and Leadership, (ii) Competition, Regulatory Standards and Rule of Law, (iii) Productivity Performance as well as (iv) Standard of Living, Education and Social Stability (see Figure 3.19). As has been mentioned in Section 3.3.2, the inability to accommodate Java's large and dense population with adequate public services and living conditions has contributed to its poor performance in the Standard of Living, Education and Social Stability sub-environment. Its performance in this aspect is the only one that is below the median of the six regions. Java also has to look into ways to significantly increase its Productivity Performance in order to fully utilise its rich labour market, given that it already

Figure 3.19: 2017 Median and Maximum Web Analysis: Java

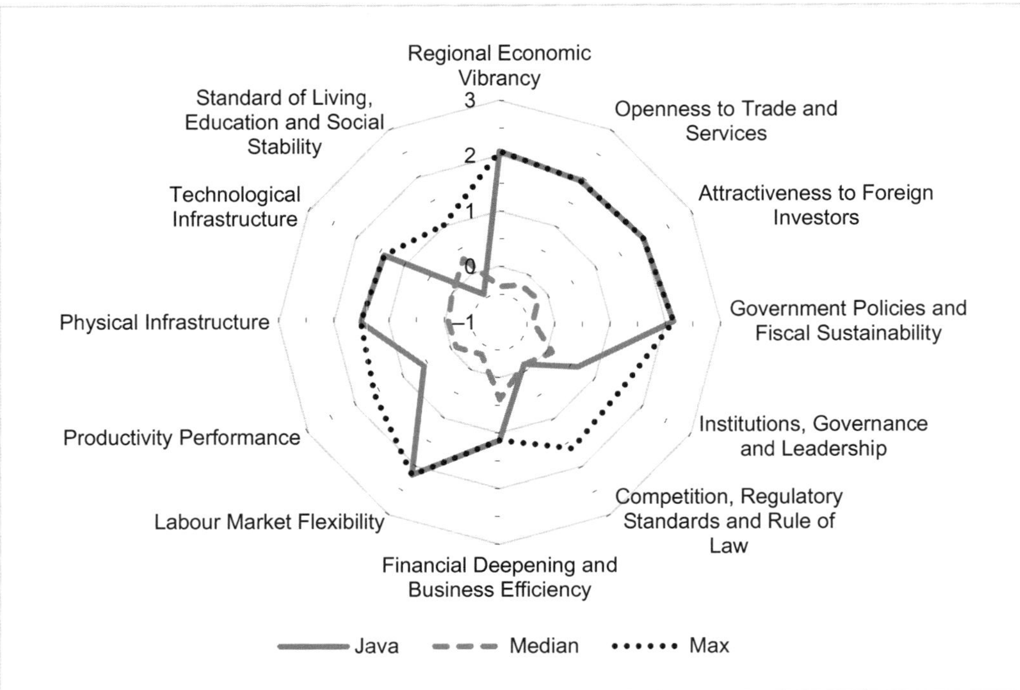

Source: ACI.

scores the highest in the sub-environment of Labour Market Flexibility. The region still relies on labour-intensive economic activities that is large on aggregate, but where the productivity of each worker is relatively small.

Next, Kalimantan on average performs better than regional median, scoring exceptionally well in Productivity Performance; in fact, its standardised score in this sub-environment is the maximum among all other regions (see Figure 3.20). The region is also performing substantially better than the median in Competition, Regulatory Standards and Rule of Law, as well as Institutions, Governance and Leadership. The only sub-environment in which its performance is slightly below the median is Regional Economic Vibrancy, caused by the region's high inflation rate and low GRDP growth which are largely due to the negative impact of commodity price bust in recent years. Meanwhile, the region's performances in the sub-environments (i) Labour Market Flexibility and (ii) Financial Deepening and Business Efficiency are very much on par with the regional medians.

In contrast, the Maluku and Papua region performs below the median for all 12 sub-environments, which further highlights the pressing need for this region to catch up. In fact, the scores for 10 out of these 12 sub-environments are the lowest across the six regions. In order to catch up with the rest, it can perhaps start by fixing its weakest aspects, namely (i) Financial Deepening and Business Efficiency, and (ii) Standard of Living, Education and Social Stability, while further capitalising on some of its strongest aspects, namely (i) Openness to Trade and Services as well as (ii) Productivity Performance (see Figure 3.21).

Figure 3.20: 2017 Median and Maximum Web Analysis: Kalimantan

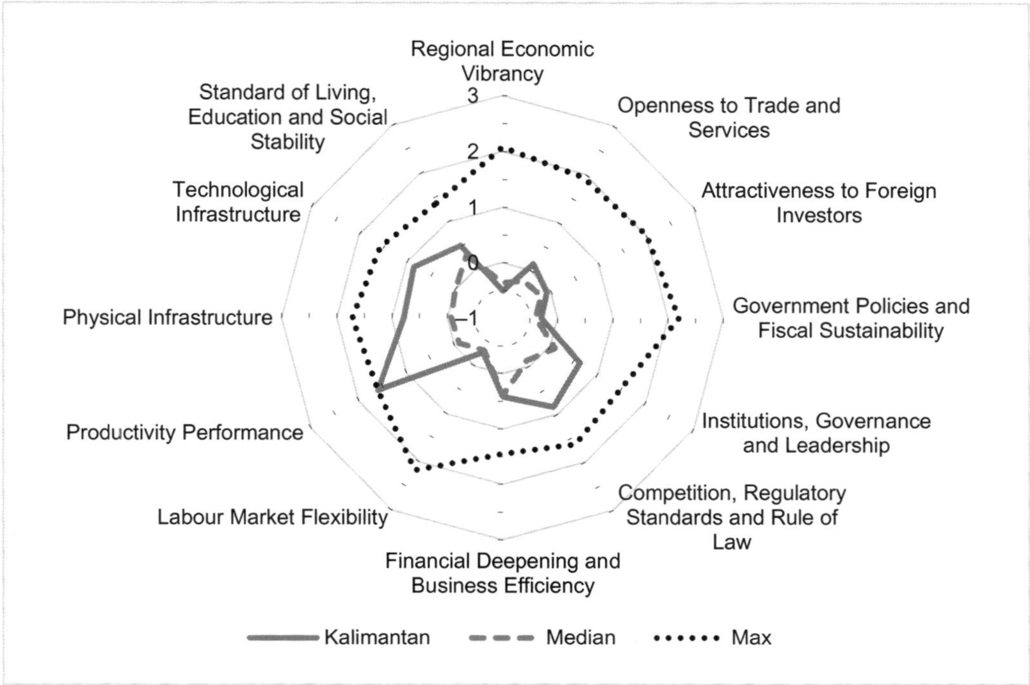

Source: ACI.

Figure 3.21: 2017 Median and Maximum Web Analysis: Maluku and Papua

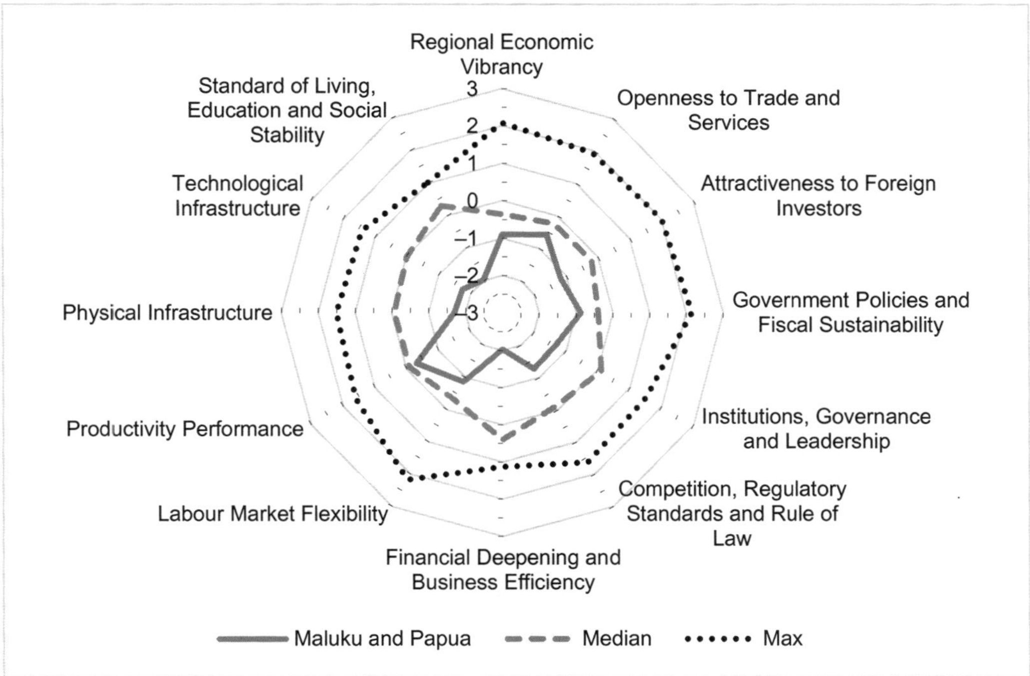

Source: ACI.

Figure 3.22: 2017 Median and Maximum Web Analysis: Sulawesi

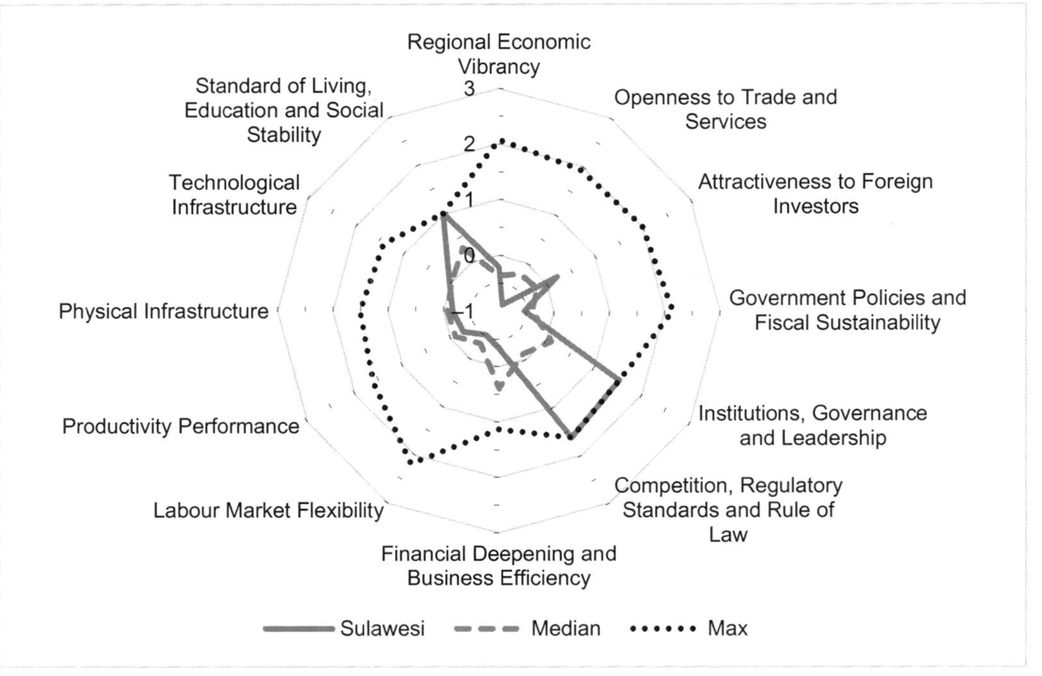

Source: ACI.

Sulawesi's performance, in contrast, is a little more diverse. Figure 3.22 showcases how the region sets the maximum scores for sub-environments (i) Institutions, Governance and Leadership, (ii) Competition, Regulatory Standards and Rule of Law as well as (iii) Standard of Living, Education and Social Stability. However, the region performs below the median in six other sub-environments, most notably in (i) Openness to Trade and Services as well as (ii) Financial Deepening and Business Efficiency. Given that the region as a whole already excels in its governance and public service, it can work towards improving policies and provision that are more geared towards the economic and financial sectors.

Finally, Sumatra's overall performance hovers around the median. Its standardised scores across the 12 sub-environments are neither the highest nor the lowest. Among its weakest sub-environments are (i) Institutions, Governance and Leadership as well as (ii) Competition, Regulatory Standards and Rule of Law. Despite weak governance, the region has relatively strong (i) Regional Economic Vibrancy, (ii) Openness to Trade and Services, and (iii) Government Policies and Fiscal Sustainability, especially in terms of the provincial budget. In fact, Sumatra's Standard of Living, Education and Social Stability is also the closest to the maximum score. This showcases that the region has potentials to improve, especially if the region focuses on improving its technological and physical infrastructure as well as strengthening its labour market and government capacity (see Figure 3.23).

Figure 3.23: 2017 Median and Maximum Web Analysis: Sumatra

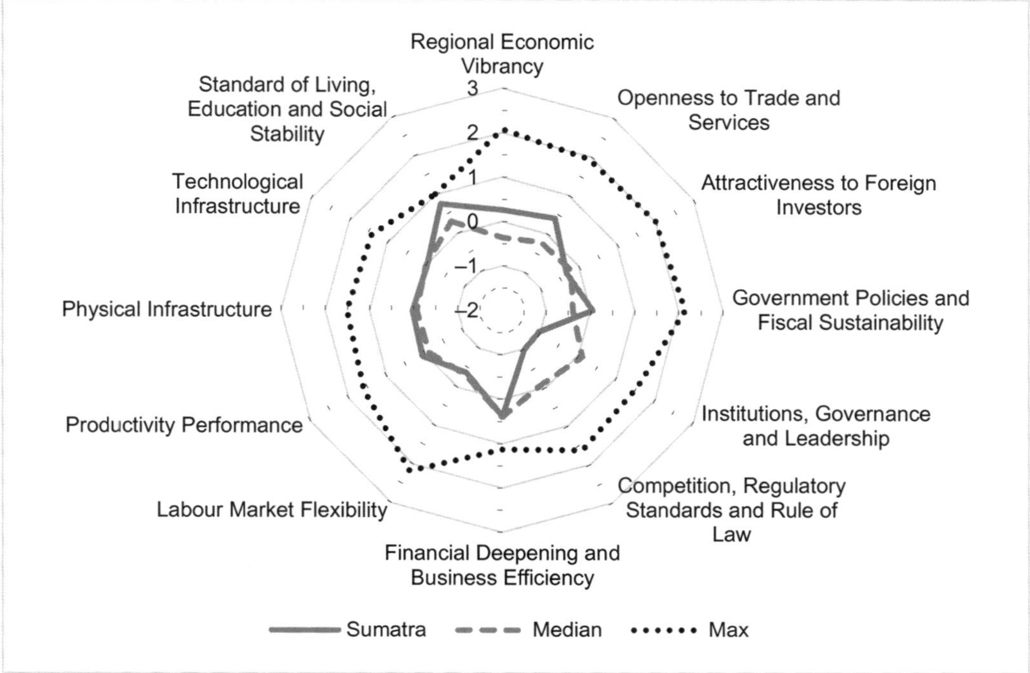

Source: ACI.

3.4 Concluding Notes and Policy Implications

The ACI has conducted regional competitiveness analysis according to the grouping of economic corridors as outlined by MP3EI. From this 2017 update of the regional competitiveness study, our research found that Java still leads ahead of the other regions in all environments of competitiveness. There has also been minimal change in ranking compared to 2016, which could perhaps be due to the time lag effect of implementation of the more recent regional policies.

Similar to 2016, Sumatra and Sulawesi continue to break the myth of a clear east–west divide in Indonesia. Sulawesi as a region emerges as a strong contender in competitiveness that is quite far ahead of Sumatra.

Additionally, competitiveness analysis conducted at both the environment and sub-environment levels allows us to look at specific factors that help boost or pull down a region's competitiveness. Such analysis thus allows us to identify a region's specific strengths and weaknesses. For instance, despite being placed third in Overall Competitiveness, Sulawesi surpasses the second-ranked region Kalimantan in all aspects of Government and Institutional Setting. Sulawesi's Standard of Living, Education and Social Stability is also ahead of both Java and Kalimantan by a significant margin. The existence of different units of analysis in which competitiveness can be evaluated also allows us to identify regions with potential best practices in specific aspects of competitiveness. It is hoped that such comparison could further push inter-regional learning, which would ultimately allow each region to maximise its fullest potentials.

Despite the relatively wide disparity among the six different regional classifications, our research has also indicated that such disparity is found within the regions themselves, although the extent differs across regions. Most notably, Riau Islands in Sumatra and Bali in Bali-Nusa Tenggara tend to perform far ahead of the other provinces in their respective regions, often with a substantial gap. The gap among oil-rich and non-oil rich provinces is also apparent; for instance, oil-rich East Kalimantan is ranked first in the Quality of Life and Infrastructure Development environment, while its immediate neighbour West Kalimantan is among the bottom-10 provinces at 29th place. In Indonesia's efforts to address inter-regional disparity, such intra-regional gap must be taken into account. However, not all resource-rich provinces could translate their natural endowments into actual competitiveness that benefits the population. For example, Riau, South Sumatra, Papua and West Papua are still wanting in this area.

Finally, the Maluku-Papua region remains the least competitive in 2017. With a low intra-regional disparity, it appears that the region as a whole does seem to be falling behind. This is especially evident in the Quality of Life and Infrastructure Development environment, which has not seen improvements across the years. Granted, such improvement may not be captured within a short period of time; however, as previously outlined in Section 3.1, Indonesia has significantly boosted its infrastructure spending and its commitment to increase connectivity and spread out development, especially to its most remote regions. Maluku-Papua's future thus seems promising, as it could stand to benefit the most from the regional policies under the Jokowi leadership.

References

Coordinating Ministry for Economic Affairs, and Ministry of National Planning and Development / National Development Planning Agency. 2011. "Masterplan — Acceleration and Expansion of Indonesia Economic Development 2011–2025." Coordinating Ministry for Economic Affairs.

Hill, Hal. 2014. "An Introduction to the Issues." In *Regional Dynamics in a Decentralized Indonesia*, edited by Hal Hill, 1–22. Singapore: ISEAS-Yusof Ishak Institute.

Lessmann, Christian. 2012. "Regional Inequality and Decentralization: An Empirical Analysis." *Environment and Planning A* 44 (6): 1363–88. https://doi.org/10.1068/a44267.

Malley, Michael S. 2009. "Decentralization and Democratic Transition in Indonesia." In *Democratic Deficits: Addressing Challenges to Sustainability and Consolidation Around the World*, edited by Gary Bland and Cynthia J. Arnson. Wilson Center Reports on the Americas 21. Princeton: Woodrow Wilson International Center for Scholars. https://www.wilsoncenter.org/publication/democratic-deficits-addressing-challenges-to-sustainability-and-consolidation-around-the.

Negara, Siwage Dharma. 2016. "Indonesia's Infrastructure Development Under the Jokowi Administration." *Southeast Asian Affairs*, 145–65.

Ray, David, and Lily Yan Ing. 2016. "Addressing Indonesia's Infrastructure Deficit." *Bulletin of Indonesian Economic Studies* 52 (1): 1–25. https://doi.org/10.1080/00074918.2016.1162266.

Resosudarmo, Ida Aju, Ngakan Putu Oka, Sofi Mardiah, and Nugroho Adi Utomo. 2014. "Governing Fragile Ecologies: A Perspective on Forest and Land-Based Development in the Regions." In *Regional Dynamics in a Decentralized Indonesia*, edited by Hal Hill, 260–84. Singapore: ISEAS-Yusof Ishak Institute.

Rodríguez-Pose, Andrés, and Roberto Ezcurra. 2011. "Is Fiscal Decentralization Harmful for Economic Growth? Evidence from the OECD Countries." *Journal of Economic Geography* 11 (4): 619–43. https://doi.org/10.1093/jeg/lbq025.

Tan, Khee Giap, Mulya Amri, and Nursyahida Ahmad. 2017. *2016 Annual Competitiveness Analysis and Development Strategies for Indonesian Provinces*. Singapore: World Scientific.

Tan, Khee Giap, Mulya Amri, Nursyahida Ahmad, and Kong Yam Tan. 2017. *2016 Growth Slowdown Analysis, Ease of Doing Business Index, and Annual Competitiveness Studies of Indonesia's Sub-National Economies*. Singapore: World Scientific.

Tan, Khee Giap, Mulya Amri, Linda Low, and Kong Yam Tan. 2013. *Competitiveness Analysis and Development Strategies for 33 Indonesian Provinces*. Singapore: World Scientific.

Tan, Khee Giap, Mulya Amri, Nurina Merdikawati, and Nursyahida Ahmad. 2016. *2015 Annual Competitiveness Analysis and Development Strategies for Indonesian Provinces*. Singapore: World Scientific.

Tan, Khee Giap, Nurina Merdikawati, Mulya Amri, and Blake Harley Berger. 2015. *2014 Annual Competitiveness Analysis and Development Strategies for Indonesian Provinces*. Singapore: World Scientific.

Tan, Khee Giap, Nurina Merdikawati, Mulya Amri, and Kong Yam Tan. 2015. *2014 Provincial and Inaugural Regional Competitiveness Analysis*. Singapore: World Scientific.

———. 2016. *2015 Annual Competitiveness Analysis and Development Strategies for Indonesian Provinces*. Singapore: World Scientific.

Vujanovic, Peter. 2017. "Decentralisation to Promote Regional Development in Indonesia." *OECD Publishing*, OECD Economics Department Working Papers, no. 1380. https://doi.org/10.1787/d9cabd0a-en.

Discussant Note 3.1

2017 Provincial and Regional Competitiveness Ranking and Simulation for Indonesia: An Annual Update[1]

Professor Balthasar Kambuaya

Chairman, University Senate, Cenderawasih University and Former Minister for Environment (2011–2014), Republic of Indonesia

Good evening, audience. I am not going to comment on the details, but I will provide an overview of my thoughts about this study. First of all, I would like to express my appreciation and thanks to the Asia Competitiveness Institute at the Lee Kuan Yew School of Public Policy, National University of Singapore (ACI-LKYSPP, NUS) for conducting this study regarding the level of competitiveness and ranking of provinces and regions in Indonesia. In my view, this indicates the consistent, high commitment and also hard work of ACI-LKYSPP, NUS as part of our responsibility towards the development of Association of Southeast Asian Nations (ASEAN), especially in our commitment to become a single economic community. We appreciate and thank ACI at NUS for this research effort.

There are a few aspects I would like to comment. Indonesia is a very unique country in terms of its demography, geography, culture, distance and infrastructure development, even in terms of the stages of development. The Java and Sumatra regions for example, are more developed than the rest of the regions, especially when compared to the eastern part of Indonesia. As such, it is hoped that the data and information raised from this study, as well as its methodology, variables, indicators, and scoring used to identify development and growth, do consider the diversity and uniqueness of the provinces and regions in Indonesia.

On that note, more analysis and details are needed on the provinces, which have high natural resources but low competitiveness and ranking.

I have a few points in mind regarding the importance of this study. Firstly, the results of the study is important as a basis for provinces and regions to develop their policies and strategic decisions, in order to improve their competitiveness ranking.

Secondly, the identification of the strengths and weaknesses of each province and region would help them develop their strategy and action to improve their competitiveness.

[1]The contents of this discussion note were delivered during the 2017 Asia Economic Forum on "The One-Belt One-Road Initiative: Impact and Implications" on 28 August 2017, in Singapore.

Finally, the implementation of the *What-if* Competitiveness Simulation provides a clear understanding of the potential for each economy to improve, its corresponding improved competitiveness scores as well as the areas of intervention that needs to be prioritised.

The study has several areas for improvements. Firstly, some provinces and regions that have high natural resources but ranked low on competitiveness, such as Papua and West Papua, require a more detailed study. As someone who comes from Papua, I am very concerned about this study. Papua and West Papua have very high natural resources, but still face a lot of problems with development. Hence, a more detailed study is needed to find out the key factors that lead to such conditions. Some possibilities of the key factors include the quantity and quality of human resource or manpower, infrastructure challenges and difficulties and the role of small and medium enterprises on economic development of the provinces.

Secondly, data findings from the study have been presented in a way wherein the provinces are grouped accordingly into categories of high, middle and low competitiveness. It would be good to do an analysis of these provinces within the groupings and find out the strengths, weaknesses and challenges faced by the province or region.

My next recommendation is for ACI to study areas such as the effectiveness of infrastructure development, the quality of human resources or manpower, the role of small and medium enterprises on provincial and regional development and economic growth as well as the role of financial institutions in promoting economic activities. As observed from the previous presentations by the representatives of banks from China, the role of banking in the market is usually very important for the economic development of the country.

For Papua and West Papua, this is a special request for ACI to help do a detailed research on Papua and West Papua provinces. These provinces have high natural resources and have implemented the Special Autonomy Law, wherein the central government has provided more money and has also given more authority to these provinces. However, as identified by this research, both provinces still have low competitiveness and ranking. This needs a critical and detailed study in order to identify the weaknesses and challenges faced by both provinces, especially in terms of capacity and capability of human resources, as well as leadership capacity of the local governments in the provinces.

Finally, as this is a very important study, I hope that the institute will hold seminars or discussions like this at the provincial or regional level. This will provide the chance for all stakeholders in the province to give their opinion and comments on the study.

Thank you, ACI and NUS. This is a very important session to prepare us towards a single market in ASEAN. Thank you very much.

Chapter 4

Impact of Real Effective Exchange Rates on Foreign Direct Investment Inflows to Indonesian Provinces

4.1 Introduction and Motivation

Foreign direct investment (FDI) inflows to developing economies play a significant role in supplementing domestic capital, technology and skills which fundamentally accelerate the economic growth of a country.[1] A growing strand of economic literature has provided evidence on the impact of FDI inflows, given the enhanced participation of countries in the global and regional value chains, which not only enhances export competitiveness but also favours trade facilitation by exercising comparative advantage in specific domains.[2] Indeed, as the production process becomes increasingly fragmented and diversified, access to more technology-intensive and high-income yielding activities requires participation in global and regional production networks. This also implies that institutions and level of competencies to attract FDI have a critical role in facilitating that process.[3]

Global FDI inflows have increased exponentially since the 1990s. Figure 4.1 plots the global FDI inflows for the period 1992–2015. Notwithstanding the dips at the onset of the 21st century and during the global financial crisis (GFC), world FDI reached a peak of over US$1.3 trillion in 2000 and hit a new high of over US$1.9 trillion before the GFC in 2007. Though the global FDI inflows have recovered after the GFC, it has not been able to reach pre-GFC levels.

Figure 4.2 plots FDI inflows to developed, developing and transition economies as a share of total world's FDI inflows. Even though the developed economies dominated the world FDI inflows for the most part of 1990s and 2000s, the importance of developing economies has increased over time. A closer look at the trends reveals that an average of 68 percent of global FDI flowed to developed economies from 1992 to 2000. Since then, it has gradually dipped to a low of over 40 percent in 2014, before rebounding to around 55 percent in 2015.

Taken together, the shares of FDI inflows to developing and transition economies had increased more than three times from about 18 percent in 2000 to over 58 percent in 2014. The share of world FDI inflows to developing economies gained prominence and was larger than that

[1] Among the early works, see Barro (1997), Borensztein, De Gregorio, and Lee (1998), Bosworth and Collins (1999), Carkovic and Levine (2002), Mencinger (2003), Alfaro et al. (2004), Razin (2004), Mody and Murshid (2005). For more recent assessments, see Herzer (2012) and Iamsiraroj (2016).

[2] See, for instance, Hill and Athukorala (1998), Hobday (2001), Ng and Yeats (2003) for some of the early literature on this phenomenon of FDI and production fragmentation. Also, see Assche and Gangnes (2010) for a relatively recent discussion.

[3] See Kaplinsky (2000) for a discussion on the proliferation of global production networks.

Figure 4.1: Global FDI Inflows (US$ Trillion), 1992–2015

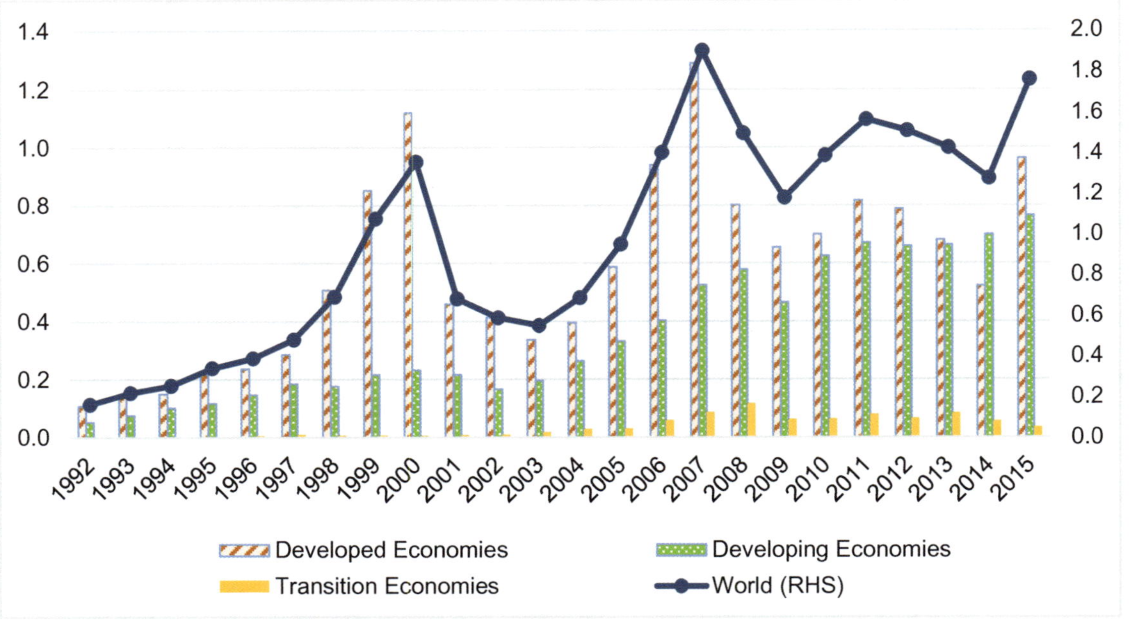

Source: Asia Competitiveness Institute (ACI) based on data from United Nations Conference on Trade and Development (UNCTAD), World Investment Report 2017 (WIR 2017).

Figure 4.2: FDI Inflows by Category (Percent of World FDI Inflows), 1992–2015

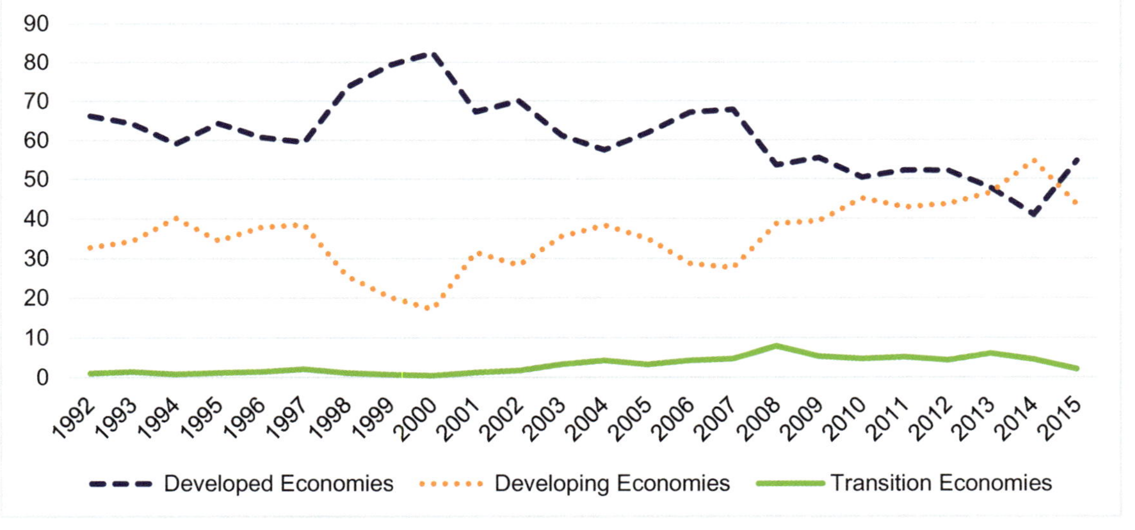

Source: ACI based on data from UNCTAD, WIR 2017.

of the developed economies in 2014, but was subsequently lower than the latter in 2015. In 2014, developing economies received the highest world FDI inflows at about 55 percent. However, it slumped to around 43 percent in 2015. The share of transition economies has remained somewhat stable and stood low at about two percent of world FDI inflows in 2014.

Figure 4.3: Top-20 Recipients of FDI Inflows in 2014 and 2015 (US$ Billion)

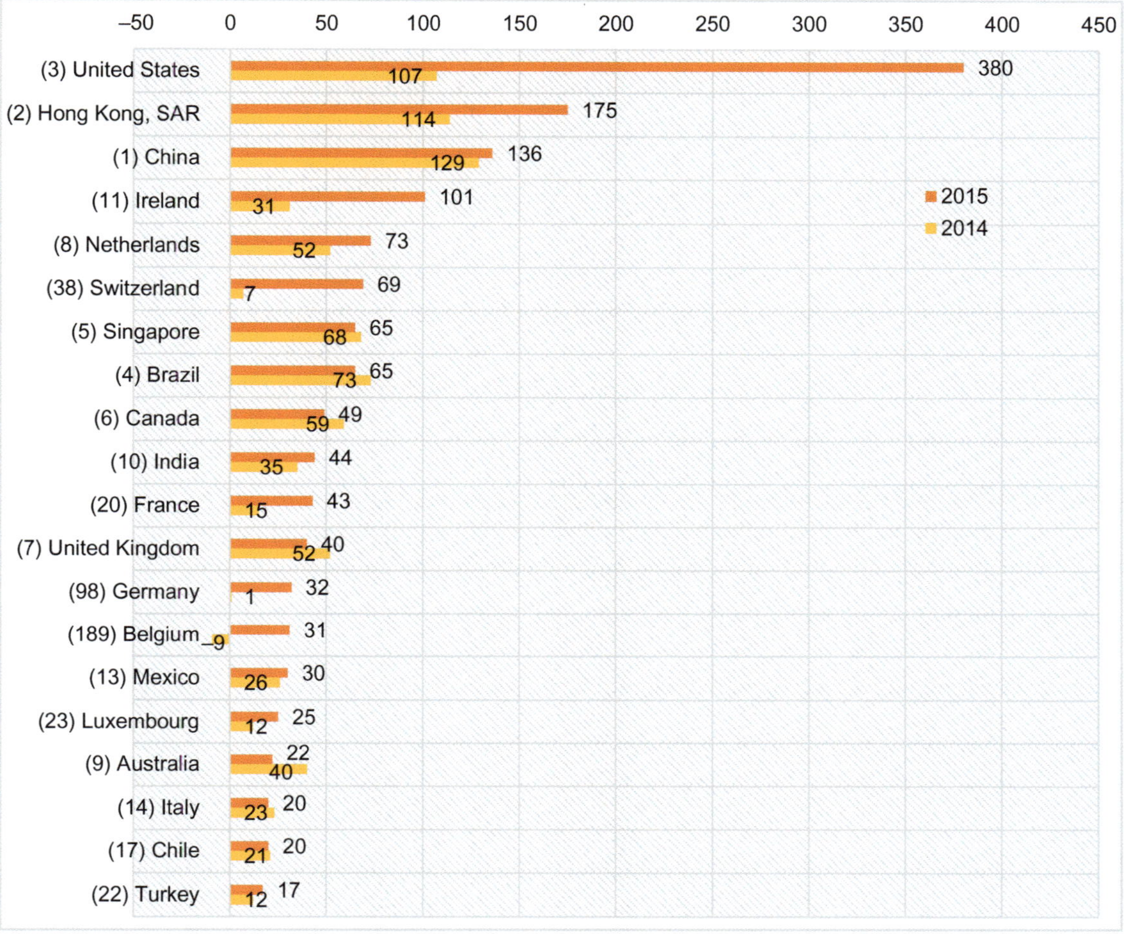

Note: Numbers in parentheses denote the ranks in 2014 of the economies.
Source: ACI based on data from UNCTAD, WIR 2017.

We further delve into the FDI inflows by countries and focus on the top-20 FDI recipients in the years 2014 and 2015 (Figure 4.3). More than half of the 20 economies have witnessed an increase in their FDI inflows in 2015 vis-à-vis 2014. Concurrently, FDI inflows to most of the developed economies have increased in 2015. It is notable that about half of the largest recipients of FDI inflows are developing and transition economies.

The United States (US) received the most FDI inflows, which had increased by nearly four times from US$107 billion in 2014 to around US$380 billion in 2015. This accounted for the highest increase (in absolute terms) in FDI inflows among the top-20 recipients. Second to the US are Hong Kong Special Administrative Region (SAR) and China, which together accounted for over US$300 billion and ranked second and third respectively. Apart from China and Hong Kong SAR, Singapore and India are the only two other Asian economies to appear in the list, ranking sixth and 10th respectively in 2015.

From our analysis above, two things are quite evident. First, there has been a slowdown in global FDI inflows and that it has not yet reached the pre-GFC levels. Second, FDI inflows to the developing and transition economies have gained prominence over the past decade, however, developed economies still continue to dominate the global FDI inflows.

Among various emerging markets and developing economies (EMDEs), FDI inflows into Indonesia have gained prominence since the early 1990s. Recognising FDI's significant contribution in pushing productivity and strengthening international trade, Indonesia has followed many other developing countries' footsteps to attract FDI inflows. Constitutionally, Indonesia opened its doors to FDI in 1967 in order to promote investments both at the provincial and sectoral levels. The government of Indonesia opened capital account transactions in 1972, allowing for the free movement of capital flows. This was followed by the establishment of a non-departmental government agency — the Investment Coordinating Board (BKPM) — to grant FDI licensing and approvals, on top of formulating policies pertaining to capital investment (Hornick and Nelson 1987). With an open economy policy framework, Indonesia undertook gradual reforms aimed at liberalising trade, investment and financial markets (Iqbal and James 2002).

Figure 4.4 shows that in absolute terms, FDI inflows into Indonesia had gradually increased since 1990s, hovering at around US$6 billion to US$8 billion between 1996 and 2005. The inflows witnessed a declining trend and amounted to around –US$4.5 billion in 2000 due to the Asian Financial Crisis (AFC). This was followed by a series of other internal instabilities. Despite experiencing negative FDI inflows from 1999 to 2001, Indonesia rebounded strongly

Figure 4.4: FDI Inflows to Indonesia (in US$ Billion and as a Percent of World FDI), 1990–2014

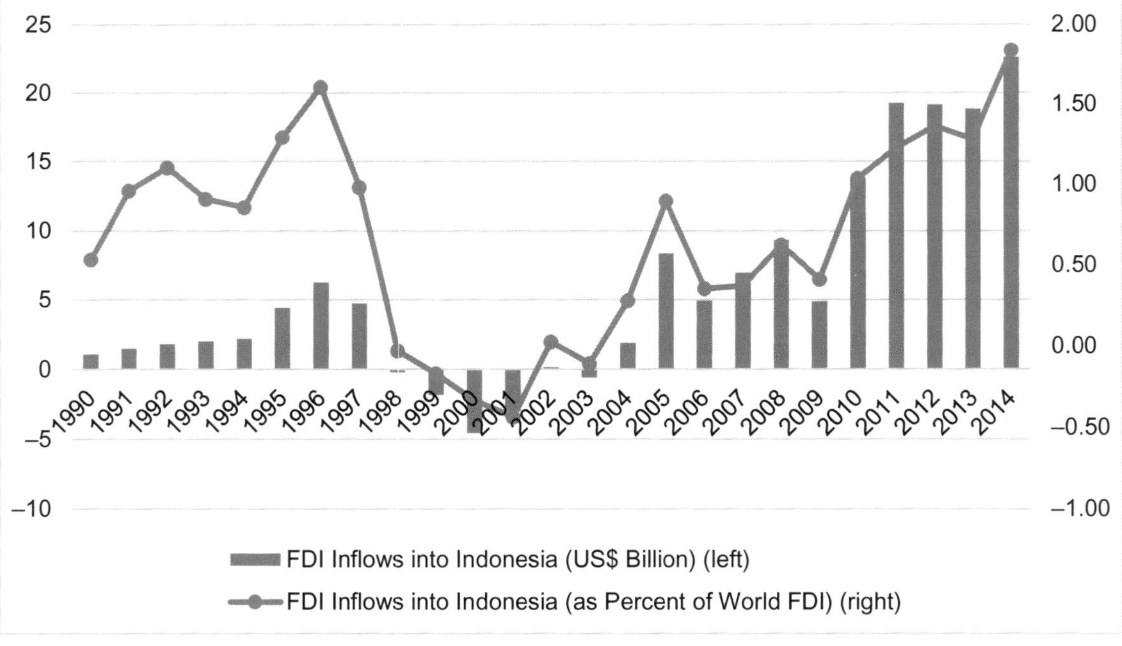

Source: ACI based on data from BKPM and UNCTAD.

and took the second position after Singapore among the Association of Southeast Asian Nations (ASEAN) member countries between 2010 and 2014. Notwithstanding the dips in 2006 and 2008 (GFC), FDI inflows to Indonesia had increased steadily, reaching a peak of approximately US$23 billion in 2014. Correspondingly, Indonesia's share of world FDI closely mapped the trends in Indonesia's FDI inflows, which had been increasing since 2009. At a global level, however, FDI inflows in Indonesia still accounted for a meagre share to the world's FDI, averaging at around 0.9 percent between 2004 and 2014, and rising to about 2.0 percent in 2014.

Blonigen (2005) provides a comprehensive review of a number of factors that determine FDI inflows, especially in emerging and developing economies. One of the many determinants of FDI concerns the movements of exchange rates both in terms of their levels and volatility. In general, a depreciation of the host country's currency enables the country to gain "locational advantage" as a result of a possible reduction in its wages and costs of production, *ceteris paribus* (Froot and Stein 1991; Klein and Rosengren 1994; Goldberg 2009), thus enhancing the attractiveness of the country as a destination for FDI. Although there are various other confounding factors, such as future expectations of exchange rates, that need to be taken into account in order to empirically determine the extent to which exchange rate movements affect FDI inflows, the broader point to note is that cost competitiveness remains one of the crucial determining variables affecting FDI inflows.

For an emerging economy like Indonesia, maintaining cost competitiveness is crucial in order to position itself as an attractive destination for global FDI inflows. Exchange rates become all the more important when we consider the recent trends in Indonesia's real effective exchange rates (REER) — a widely accepted measure of competitiveness. Despite operating as an inflation target setter, with *de facto* flexible though not fully floating exchange rate regime since the AFC in 1997–1998, the Bank of Indonesia (BI) has intervened in the foreign exchange market several times to manage volatility, especially during periods of external shocks.

Figure 4.5 provides a snapshot of historical trends in Indonesia's REER and volatility since 1995. Focusing on the last five years, we can observe that Indonesia's REER against a basket of currencies has shown clear upward pressures since 2013. For instance, the REER index clearly shows that the Indonesian rupiah has appreciated by 6.8 percent since the end of 2014. Other REER series such as the one by the Bank for International Settlements (BIS) or the Organisation for Economic Co-operation and Development (OECD) also reveal that the Indonesian rupiah has recorded an appreciation of over four percent between 2014 and 2017. The history of REER movements suggests that during the crisis periods of 1997–1999 and 2007–2009 as well as the immediate aftermath of these downturns, Indonesia's REER depreciated quite significantly. In recent years, however, concerns mostly pertained to an appreciating REER which has a significant bearing on the country's external competitiveness. Considering the fact that fluctuations in REER are observable not only in terms of levels but also in terms of volatility, systematic foreign exchange market interventions by the BI to reduce the rupiah volatility have been a regular feature of the country's exchange rate management.

In light of this background, this chapter examines the relationship between REER (both in terms of levels and volatility) and FDI inflows to 33 Indonesian provinces. While there are some

Figure 4.5: REER Levels and Volatility, 1995–2016

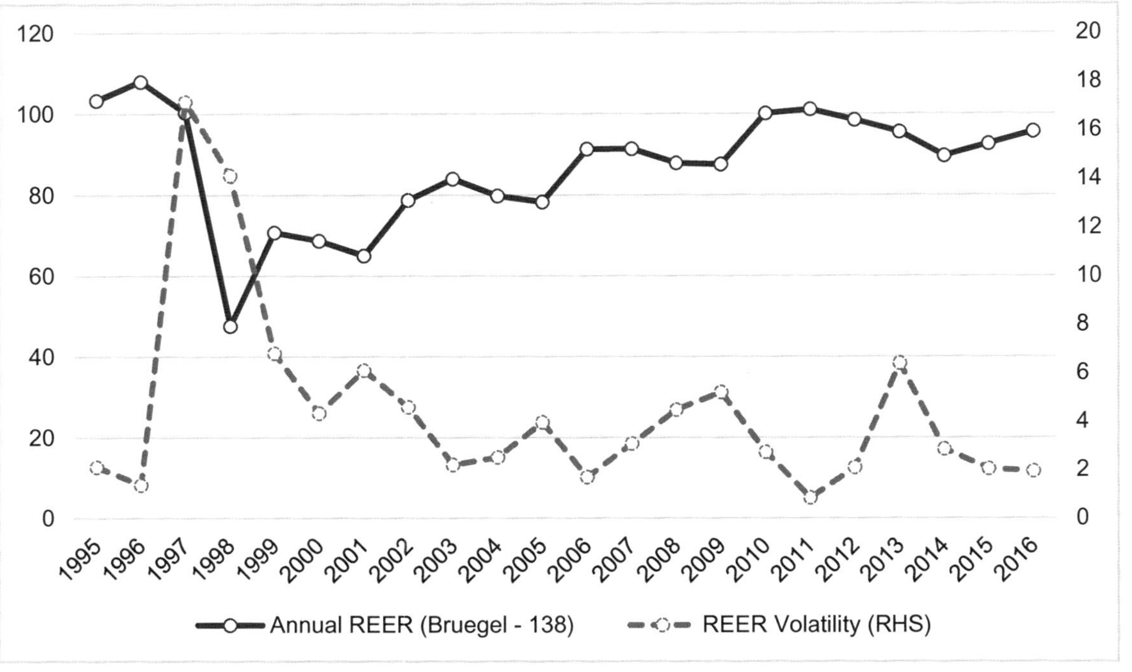

Source: ACI based on data from Bruegel.

studies that have investigated the relationship between exchange rates and FDI in the context of Indonesia, most of the literature explored this relationship at the aggregate level.

Considering the highly disproportionate distribution of Indonesia's FDI inflows only to a handful of provinces, a provincial-level analysis becomes even more important in order to understand such variations. Differences in FDI at a disaggregated level could probably arise due to wide disparities in a host of structural and institutional factors across provinces. Therefore, it is critical to undertake an analysis at the provincial level. Further, consistent with related literature that points to varying levels of competitiveness as well as structural and institutional factors observed across Indonesia's provinces, we believe that undertaking an empirical analysis at the provincial level is warranted.

The remainder of this chapter is structured as follows. In Section 4.2, we will discuss the importance of FDI as a source of external financing for Indonesia and provide an analysis of the trends and patterns of FDI inflows to Indonesia at the national and provincial levels. Section 4.3 discusses the theory of interest, drawing on the general literature on the impact of exchange rates on FDI on top of providing literature on the determinants of FDI specific to Indonesia. In Section 4.4, we provide a detailed description of the data used in our empirics, while Section 4.5 focuses on the broad analytical framework and methodology that highlight the empirical model to be tested. Finally, Sections 4.6 and 4.7 deal with the empirical results as well as analysis and robustness check respectively, while Section 4.8 summarises the research with conclusions and policy implications.

4.2 Importance of Foreign Direct Investment (FDI) Inflows as a Source of External Financing: Trends and Patterns

For much of the last one and a half decades, Indonesia's current account surpluses between 2005 and 2011 had been modest at around 1.3 percent of Gross Domestic Product (GDP) (US$5.6 billion). After 2011, however, Indonesia's current account balance took a 180 degree turn and remained at a deficit until 2014. Meanwhile, Indonesia's financial account, which records the country's net capital inflows, was generally positive at around US$26 billion (3.0 percent of GDP) between 2011 and 2014 (Gopalan, Hattari, and Rajan 2017).

From these balance of payments data, we can also conclude that FDI inflows are an important source of external non-trade financing in Indonesia. While there are other types of investment flows that make up private capital flows, the share of FDI flows relative to the others has become increasingly significant; FDI flows as a share of Indonesia's private external financing had doubled from about 30 percent in 2001 to more than 50 percent in 2016. Meanwhile, the significance of portfolio investments, which is another component of private capital flow, saw a temporary dip between 2004 and 2009 but have risen again since (Figure 4.6).

In order to delve deeper into the trends and patterns of FDI inflows to Indonesia, we have divided the section into two parts: the first will discuss these trends and patterns at the national level, while the second will provide insights at the provincial level.

Figure 4.6: Components of Private External Financing in Indonesia (US$ Billion), 2000–2016

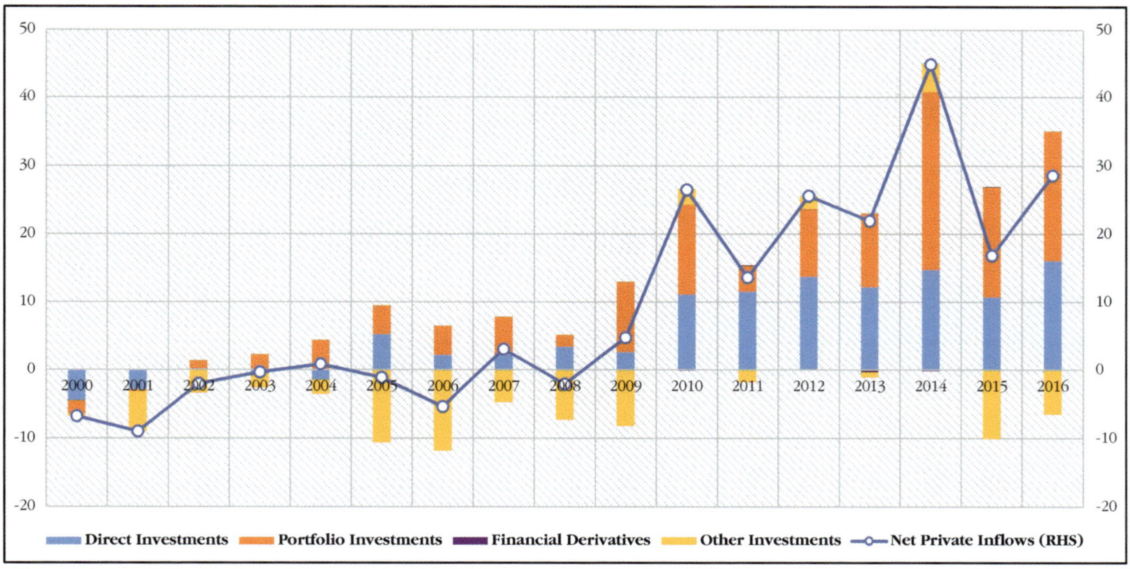

Source: ACI based on data from International Monetary Fund (IMF).

4.2.1 FDI Inflows to Indonesia at the National Level

Figure 4.7 represents FDI inflows to Indonesia as a percentage of GDP and Gross Fixed Capital Formation (GFCF). Based on UNCTAD data, Indonesia's FDI inflows averaged around 1.5

percent of GDP — about US$8.0 billion — between 1990 and 1997 as well as 2002 and 2013. It reached its peak in 2005, contributing to about three percent of the country's GDP. The GFC in 2009, however, resulted in a clear dip in the inflows of FDI to Indonesia. Although it had recovered and been on an overall rising trend since, its growth had been modest. As of 2014, FDI inflows as a percentage of Indonesia's GDP remained at just under three percent. Given Indonesia's size, this is relatively modest — lower than what would be expected from the country of its size.

In contrast, the trend of FDI as a percentage of Indonesia's GFCF has been more volatile. In 1996, its share was high at 9.3 percent; however, it plummeted to −13.9 percent post-AFC. It managed to bounce back significantly to reach its peak of 12.3 percent in 2005 but plunged again in 2009. Since then, however, the share of GFCF had been increasing relatively steadily.

This rising trend of FDI inflows suggests that the Indonesian equity market is highly institutionalised, wherein the free-float values of the equity market in Indonesia are mostly held by foreign institutions. Increasing FDI inflows is also supported by the fact that foreign investors are leveraging in order to hold up to 100 percent ownership wherever feasible.

Figure 4.7: FDI Inflows to Indonesia (Percent of GDP and GFCF), 1990–2014

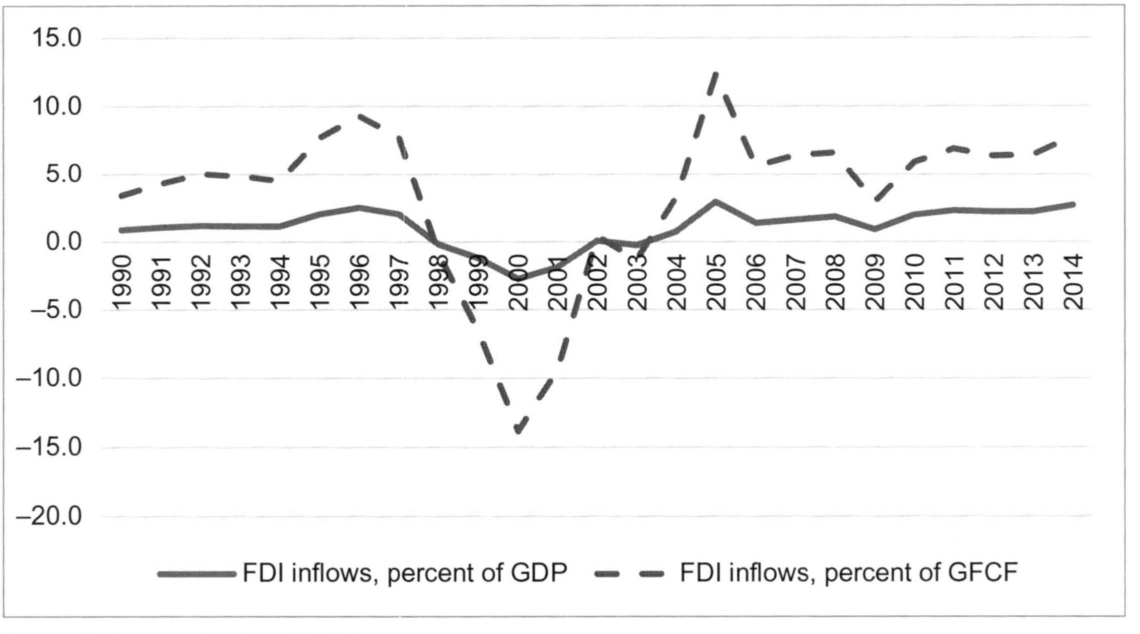

Source: ACI based on data from UNCTAD.

Between 2004 and 2009, most FDI in Indonesia originated from Singapore, contributing to 15.4 percent of overall FDI inflow (see Figure 4.8). This is followed by Japan, Netherlands and the US at about 14 percent each. The US economy's FDI into Indonesia is primarily export-oriented in nature, where firms invested in Indonesia for export purposes. Other countries that are among the top-10 contributors of FDI inflows to Indonesia — albeit to a smaller extent — are Malaysia, China, France, Australia, Germany and South Korea.

Figure 4.8: Share of Gross FDI Inflows from Top-10 Source Countries (Percent), 2004–2009

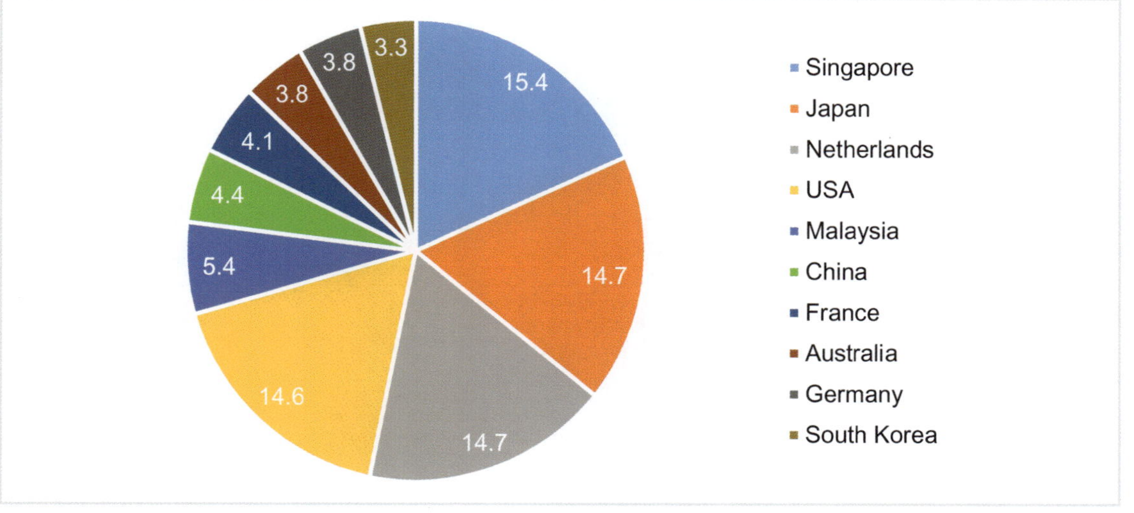

Source: ACI based on data from Bank Indonesia.

Figure 4.9: Share of Gross FDI Inflows from Top-10 Source Countries (Percent), 2010–2015

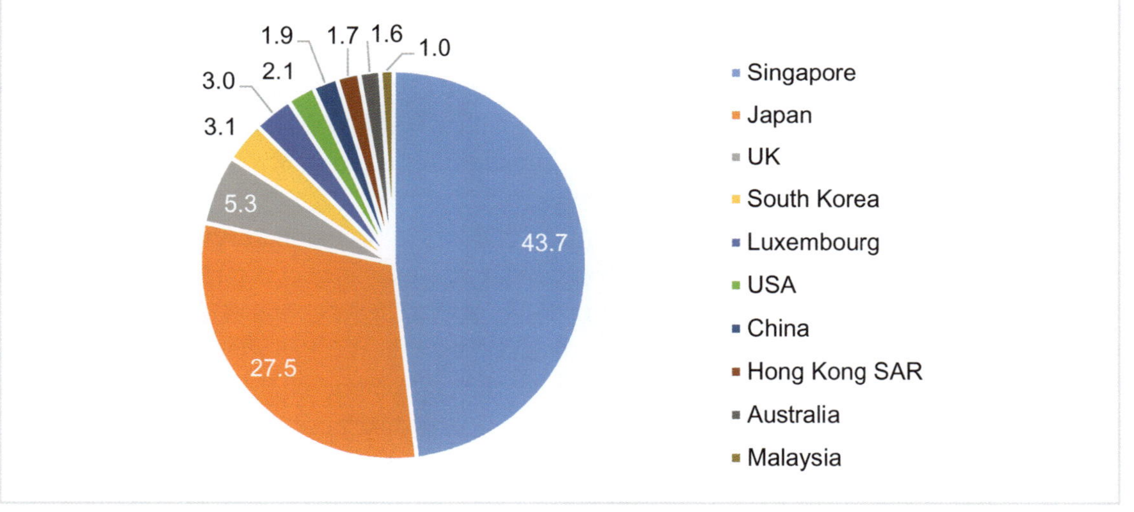

Source: ACI based on data from Bank Indonesia.

Between 2010 and 2015, Singapore's role in the total FDI inflows grew even more significantly, averaging to about 43.7 percent. Japan still the occupied the second place, although its share had almost doubled to about 27.5 percent. The United Kingdom (UK) overtook Netherlands to occupy the third place, but with a less significant average contribution at about 5.3 percent. South Korea, Malaysia, China and the US continued to be among the top-10 contributors of FDI inflows to Indonesia (see Figure 4.9).

Figure 4.10: Sectoral Distribution of FDI Inflows (Percent), 2006–2015

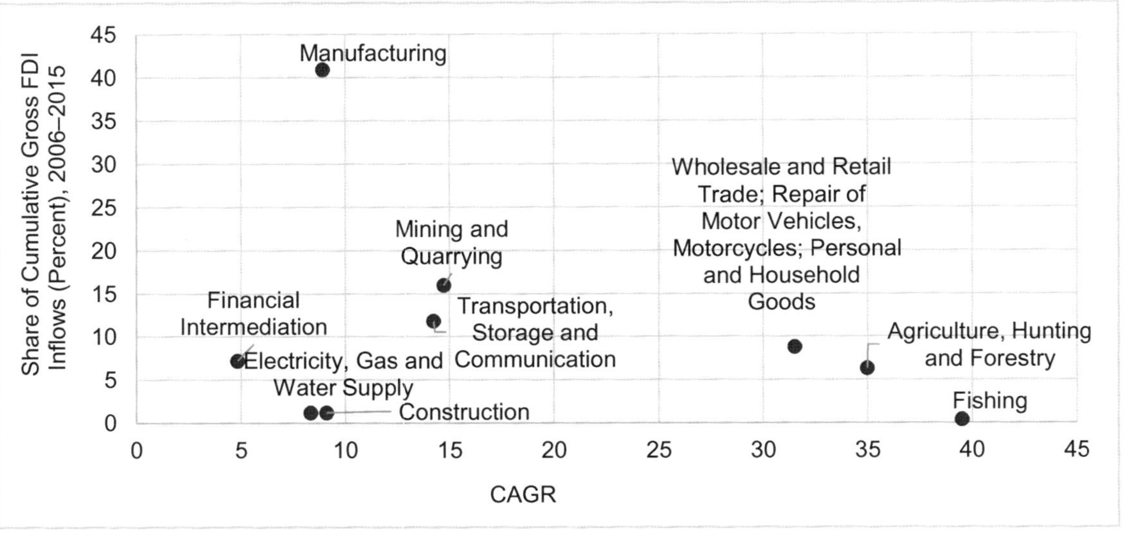

Source: ACI based on data from Bank of Indonesia.

In terms of economic sectors, an average of 68.7 percent of FDI inflows into Indonesia between 2006 and 2015 have been channelled into a combination of the manufacturing, mining and quarrying as well as transportation, storage and communication sectors (see Figure 4.10). Even though the share of the fishing sector was significantly small at about 0.4 percent, its cumulative annual growth rate (CAGR) over the corresponding period was the highest at around 40 percent. This was followed by the agriculture, hunting and forestry sector, which registered a CAGR of about 35 percent during the same period.

While our analysis of the trends and patterns of FDI inflows to Indonesia at the national level is able to give us an overview of the investment climate in the country, it is imperative to analyse such trends and patterns at the regional and provincial levels. This is because there may be variations in FDI inflows at the disaggregated level, which may arise due to a wide array of structural and institutional differences across regions and provinces. Section 4.2.2 thus undertakes such study in order to provide a more microscopic view of the distribution of FDI inflows across Indonesia. The grouping of regions has been done in accordance to that used in Chapter 3.

4.2.2 FDI Inflows to Indonesia at the Provincial Level

Between 1990 and 2015, the inflows of FDI had been heavily clustered in the Java region (see Figure 4.11). In absolute terms, it had increased rapidly from over US$0.7 billion in 1990 to over US$15.4 billion in 2015. Following Java was the Kalimantan region, which accounted for the second highest share of FDI inflows at about US$5.8 billion in 2015. The shares of other regions, namely Sumatra, Sulawesi, Bali and Nusa Tenggara as well as Papua and Maluku, remained considerably low and stable over the same period.

Figure 4.11: FDI Inflows to Indonesia by Region (US$ Billions), 1990–2015

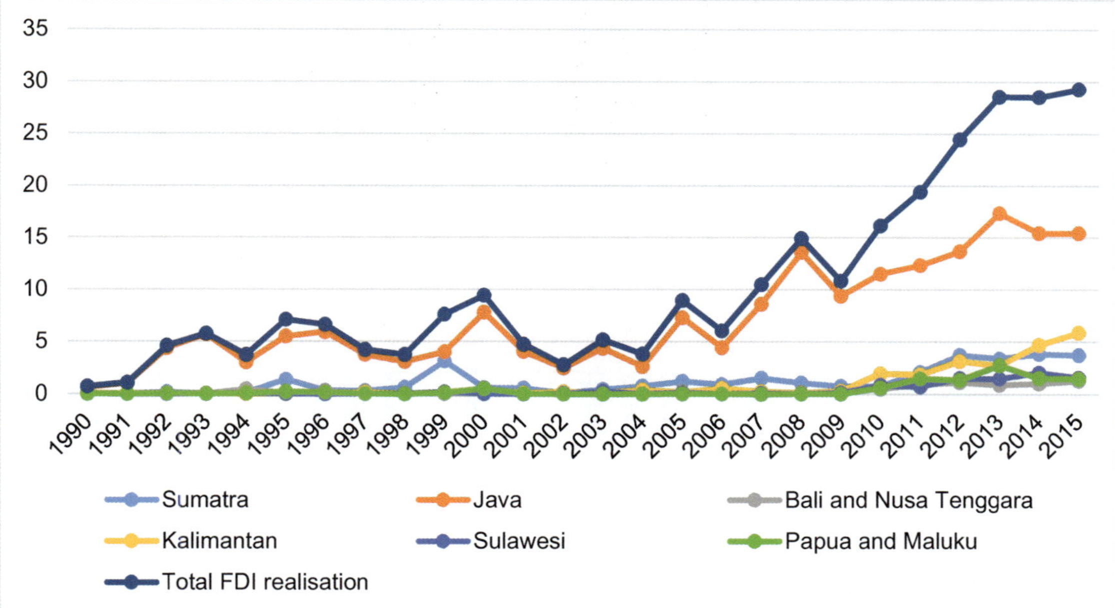

Source: ACI based on data from BKPM.

As a percentage of total FDI inflows to Indonesia, the share of the Java region had been correspondingly high, although it had dipped from over 85 percent between 1990 and 1999 to an average of 73 percent from 2000 to 2015 (see Figure 4.12). Until 2013, Sumatra's contribution was placed second at an average of over 10 percent. However, Kalimantan took over as its share grew at a faster rate, from an average of about 2.7 percent between 1990 and 2009 to over 13 percent between 2010 and 2015. During the same period, FDI shares of other regions were also on a rising trend, albeit with intermittent fluctuations. Despite the increase, the distribution of FDI inflows continues to be highly asymmetrical across Indonesian regions.

At the provincial level, FDI inflows within Java were highly concentrated in four out of six provinces — DKI Jakarta, West Java, Banten and East Java — contributing to an average of around 75 percent of total FDI inflows to Indonesia from 1990 to 2015 (see Figure 4.13). However, the share of these four provinces declined substantially from about 87 percent between 1990 and 1997 to around 63 percent between 2007 and 2015. Contemporaneously, the shares of FDI inflows to the other provinces, such as East Kalimantan, Papua, Central Sulawesi, South Sumatra and Central Kalimantan, were on a rising trend. Nonetheless, the overall distribution of FDI inflows at the provincial level has remained highly skewed, with 11 out of 33 provinces receiving more than an average of 89 percent of Indonesia's total FDI inflows from 2000 to 2014. Even within the top-11 recipients, the distribution remains concentrated in the provinces in the Java region.

Figure 4.12: Share of FDI Realisation by Region (Percent), 1990–2015

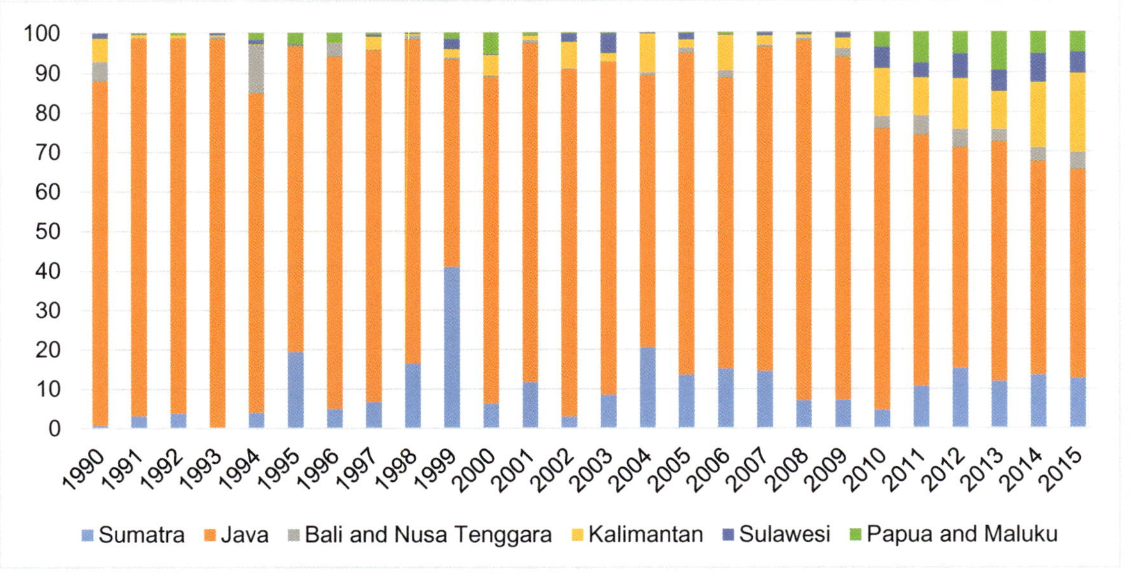

Source: ACI based on data from BKPM.

Figure 4.13: FDI Inflows to Indonesia (Percent of Indonesia's FDI) by Province, 1990–2015

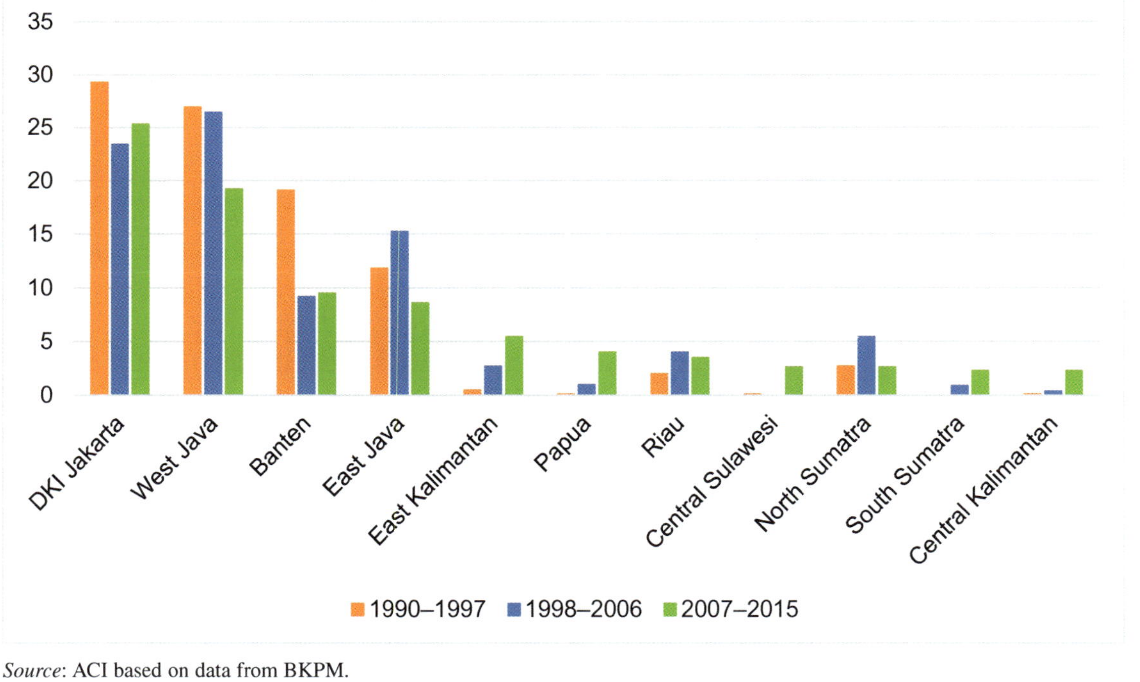

Source: ACI based on data from BKPM.

Table 4.1: Bivariate Correlation between FDI and GRDP for Select Provinces

Bivariate Correlation	DKI Jakarta	East Java	West Java	Central Java	East Kalimantan	Riau	North Sumatra
2000–2007	0.734	−0.326	0.224	0.473	0.003	0.894	0.438
2007–2014	−0.595	0.667	0.900	0.812	0.854	0.639	0.805
2000–2014	0.399	0.380	0.869	0.710	0.805	0.695	0.872

Source: ACI.

As a final exercise, we split the bivariate correlations between the FDI inflows and Gross Regional Domestic Product (GRDP) of select provinces (see Table 4.1). We classify the correlation into two phases: the pre-GFC period from 2000 to 2007 and then the post-GFC period from 2007 to 2014. It can be observed that the bivariate correlations between FDI inflows and GRDP have increased for most of the top-seven provinces, with the exception of Riau and DKI Jakarta.

There exists a strong positive correlation between GRDP and FDI in all the top-seven provinces during the post-crisis period, except for DKI Jakarta which shows a negative correlation between GRDP and FDI. For West Java, the correlation between the two variables of interest has increased substantially from about 0.2 in the pre-crisis period to around 0.9 after. West Java and North Sumatra register the highest correlation of about 0.9 during the overall period.

To sum up, our discussion on the trends and patterns shows that the distribution of FDI inflows to Indonesia is highly skewed, thus validating a provincial-level analysis. In Section 4.3, we provide a discussion on the existing theoretical and empirical literature, focusing particularly on the impact of REER on FDI inflows.

4.3 Literature Review

This section has been divided into two parts.[4] The first will offer an analytical overview of the theoretical and empirical literature, addressing the nexus between exchange rate movements and FDI inflows. The second part of the section focuses specifically on the relevant literature on Indonesia.

4.3.1 Overview of Literature

How do movements in REER, both in terms of their levels and volatility, affect FDI inflows? In answering this question, the existing theoretical and empirical literature seem ambiguous at best. However, notwithstanding the ambiguity, the literature points to some directions on what to expect from the nexus between exchange rate movements, both in terms of their levels and volatility, and FDI inflows.

Literature has posited that the exchange rate effects operate broadly through the valuation channel which can affect FDI inflows through three specific ways. At the outset, it must be

[4] This section draws heavily upon Tan *et al.* (2017).

clarified that we expect to see a positive relationship between the depreciation of the host country's currency and its FDI inflows (Froot and Stein 1991; Goldberg and Klein 1997; Blonigen 1997), which can come about in three specific ways operating through the valuation channel.

The first is through wealth effects. When there is a depreciation of the host country's currency, it makes its assets cheap which can in turn encourage FDI inflows (Chakrabarti and Scholnick 2002).

The second is what can be termed as demand effects. When there is a depreciation of the host country's currency, it makes it less attractive to repatriate profits to the home country, which in turn leads to higher reinvestment of retained earnings in the host country. Hence, a positive effect of depreciation is observed as it triggers more inflows of FDI (Goldberg and Klein 1997).

The third effect relates to cost competitiveness. There is a subtle difference observed in the literature with respect to the cost competitiveness effects of exchange rate movements on FDI inflows, which to a large extent depend on the nature of FDI inflows. In other words, if FDI inflows are export-promoting (vertical) in nature, then an REER depreciation induces FDI as firms using the host country as an export platform experience the lowering of export costs; conversely, if FDI is domestic market-oriented/commodity-seeking (horizontal), an REER depreciation induces FDI because of wealth effects. However, the caveat is that if the country is part of a supply chain and has low value-add, changes in REER levels might not have a significant effect although REER volatility might do so.

While the above effects hold in general, there are some important caveats regarding exchange rate expectations which can actually confound the positive impacts of a host country depreciation. If there are strong expectations of sustained and further depreciation in the host country's currency, it can further hold back FDI to that country. Moreover, expectations of depreciation of the host country's currency can also reduce repatriation of retained earnings. Finally, if further depreciation in the host country's currency is expected in the future, then based on the Uncovered Interest Parity (UIP), the interest rates in that country will go up, subsequently increasing the cost of credit which will lead to a reduction in FDI into that country.

Besides REER levels, the volatility of REER also matters for FDI, for which a large strand of both theoretical and empirical literature examining this relationship is available. At the risk of simplifying a complex strand of literature, there are two possible conflicting effects that the literature points to when examining the impact of exchange rate volatility on FDI inflows. Higher REER volatility can induce FDI inflows to a country if FDI is export substituting in nature. This implies that an increase in REER volatility between the firms' home country and the host country could motivate the firm to serve the host country through a local production facility rather than exports, which to a reasonable degree will insulate it against the risk of uncertainties imposed by exchange rate volatility. Empirically, some notable papers, such as Cushman (1988), Stokman and Vlaar (1996), de Ménil (1999), Pain and Van Welsum (2003), find a significantly positive relationship between REER volatility and FDI inflows in the host country.

On the other hand, a body of literature suggests that a higher exchange rate volatility can deter firms from moving to the host country because of risk aversion reasons. To be sure, a firm planning to undertake an investment in a country that is prone to greater exchange rate fluctuations might imply a riskier stream of profits. This, coupled with the sunk costs involved in the investment activity, would encourage the firm to place on hold its investment rather than undertake it (see, for instance, the discussion in Goldberg (2009) and Foad (2005)). In other words, as summarised by Goldberg (2009), considering that exchange rate volatility introduces additional risks to the return on a firm's investment, the expected values of its investment projects are reduced, which deters FDI accordingly. This hypothesis is also supported empirically by studies, such as Darby et al. (1999), Byrne and Davis (2003), Bénassy-Quéré, Fontagné, and Lahrèche-Révil (2001).

Similar to the case of movements of REER (in levels), one of the key points to be noted from the related literature is that the relationship between REER volatility and FDI inflows depends on the nature of the FDI inflows. If FDI is horizontal or domestic market-oriented in nature, an increase in REER volatility could induce FDI because the costs of exporting become high. This leads firms to serve the domestic market by establishing a base in the host country. The intuition, as alluded to earlier, is that the firm attempts to establish an early base in the country in order to avoid dealing with exchange rate risks since they already know that they are going to serve the specific host country's market. However, if the nature of FDI is vertical or export-oriented, we expect to see a negative relationship between REER volatility and FDI, viz. an increase in REER volatility is likely to deter FDI for risk aversion reasons elaborated earlier.[5]

Overall, the impact of REER both in terms of levels and volatility may have an ambiguous impact on FDI, reflecting the complex nature of the relationship governing the variables of interest.

4.3.2 Indonesia-Specific Studies

Literature focusing on the impact of REER on FDI flows often studied Indonesia within the context of ASEAN (Goldberg and Klein 1997; Xing and Wan 2006); those specifically focusing on the Indonesian context are scant. On the other hand, studies on Indonesia's FDI inflows largely examine the linkages between FDI and variables, such as growth, infrastructure and trade (Fitriandi, Kakinaka, and Kotani 2014; Khaliq and Noy 2007), while those on REER mostly examine the nexus between REER and trade (Siregar and Rajan 2004; Ginting 2013).

Most studies which included Indonesia in their sample confirm that an appreciation in the host country's currency is likely to lead to a reduction in FDI inflows. Xing and Wan (2006)

[5]The caveat to bear in mind is that if the country is part of a supply chain, firms have low value-add, implying that they will be especially sensitive to volatility because margins are thin.

studied the role of exchange rates on the relative competitiveness of recipient countries China and ASEAN-4 (Indonesia, Malaysia, the Philippines and Thailand) in their quest to receive FDI inflows from Japan. Using a panel data of Japanese FDI in the manufacturing industry to China and ASEAN-4 from 1981 to 2002, the authors used fixed effects estimation model and found that ASEAN-4 lost their competitiveness for Japanese FDI to China due to differences in exchange rate policies. Specifically, the Chinese yuan had a competitive advantage relative to the other currencies as a result of its devaluation.

Xaypanya, Rangkakulnuwat, and Paweenawat (2015), on the other hand, found that exchange rates have no significant impact on FDI inflows to ASEAN-5 economies (Indonesia, Malaysia, the Philippines, Thailand and Singapore) using panel data from 2000 to 2011.

There is hardly any literature that specifically focuses on the impact of REER volatility on FDI inflows to Indonesia. However, studies such as Kiyota and Urata (2004) and Gottschalk and Hall (2008) did analyse the impact of REER volatility on Japanese FDI inflows to a set of Southeast Asian economies and suggested that greater REER volatility will deter FDI inflows. Dhakal et al. (2010), on the other hand, conducted a time-series analysis to examine this relationship for China, Indonesia, Malaysia, the Philippines, South Korea and Thailand, and found that exchange rate volatility has a favourable impact on FDI.

There were quite a number of studies that focused on the determinants of FDI in general. Xaypanya, Rangkakulnuwat, and Paweenawat (2015) found that the effects of GDP and telephone lines on FDI supported the hypothesis that market size and infrastructure facilities are crucial in attracting FDI inflows. Meanwhile, the linkage between infrastructure development and FDI flows into Indonesia was highlighted in a study by Fitriandi, Kakinaka, and Kotani (2014) which used provinces as its unit of analysis — one of the few studies to do so, specifically on Indonesia. With panel data from 2000 to 2009 of 30 Indonesian provinces, the authors used pooled ordinary least squares (OLS) regressions, random effects and Tobit estimations, and found that infrastructure development is positively related to FDI inflows in terms of the ratio of FDI inflows to GDP and the count data of FDI projects.

Table 4.2 provides a summary of all the Indonesia-related studies on FDI and exchange rates. Clearly, no studies in the literature have explicitly focused on testing the impact of REER, both in its level and volatility, on FDI inflows to Indonesia — both at the national and even more so at the sub-national levels. Based on the growing empirical literature examining the determinants of FDI, we found that Indonesia is often studied within the context of ASEAN, which highlights the significant gap in the existing literature for Indonesia. Therefore, our study gives a significant value addition as it is the first of its kind to empirically examine the impact of both REER levels and volatility on FDI inflows at the provincial level.

Table 4.2: Overview of Literature

Citation	Topic; Unit of Analysis; Period of Study	Countries Covered	Methodology	Dependent Variable(s)	Independent Variable(s)	Findings
Azam, Muhammad, and Ling Lukman (2010). "Determinants of foreign direct investment in India, Indonesia and Pakistan: A quantitative approach." *Journal of Managerial Sciences* 4(1): 31–44	Effects of various economic factors on FDI inflows; Yearly; Country; 1970–2005	India, Indonesia, Pakistan	Log linear regression model on each country using secondary time-series data	FDI inflows into Pakistan, India and Indonesia	Market size (gross domestic product), Domestic investment, External debt, Trade openness ((X+ M)/ GDP), Infrastructure (Expenditure on electricity, gas, transport and communication), Government consumption, indirect taxes, inflation, return on Investment (1/GDP per capita)	Market size, domestic investment, external debt, trade openness, and physical infrastructure are the important economic factors determining FDI. The results for India are consistent with that of Pakistan except two factors (i.e. trade openness and government consumption). Results for Indonesia did not match those for Pakistan and India, and were statistically insignificant due to an error in data.
Athukorala, Prema Chandra, and Sarath Rajapatirana (2003). "Capital inflows and the real exchange rate: A comparative study of Asia and Latin America." *World Economy* 26(4): 613–37	Effects of capital flows on real exchange rates; Yearly; Country; 1985–1999	Asia (8 countries: China, India, Indonesia, Korea, Malaysia, the Philippines, Singapore and Thailand) & Latin America (6: Argentina, Brazil, Chile, Colombia, Mexico, Peru)	Time-series	Real exchange rate	Capital flows (including FDI)	Asian countries displayed smaller real exchange rate appreciation with capital inflows, even though several of the countries studied had higher foreign capital inflows relative to their GDP. The composition of capital flows is important in determining the impact on real exchange rate; FDI seems to have a better effect on real exchange rate. Countries in Asia also use fiscal contraction effectively to cushion their real exchange rates against pressure of appreciation in capital inflows.
Dhakal, D., R. Nag, G. Pradhan, and K.P. Upadhyaya (2010). "Exchange rate volatility and foreign direct investment: Evidence from East Asian countries." *International Business & Economics Research* 9(7): 121–128	Relationship between real exchange rate and exchange rate volatility and FDI inflows; 1974–2005 (periods vary for countries)	6 countries (China, Indonesia, Malaysia, Philippines, South Korea, Thailand)	Error Correction Model (ECM)	FDI inflow to country i	Current account balance in country i, Openness in country i (sum of export and import divided by GDP), Real exchange rate with US dollar of country i, Real exchange rate uncertainty in country i	Exchange rate volatility has a favourable effect on FDI. These countries have continued to attract considerable FDI inflows while also experiencing a great deal of volatility in exchange rates.

(Continued)

Table 4.2: *(Continued)*

Citation	Topic; Unit of Analysis; Period of Study	Countries Covered	Methodology	Dependent Variable(s)	Independent Variable(s)	Findings
Fitriandi, Primandita, and Makoto Kakinaka (2014). "Foreign direct investment and infrastructure development in Indonesia: Evidence from province-level data." *Asian Journal of Empirical Research* 4(1): 79–94	Effects of infrastructure on FDI; Provincial (30 provinces); Yearly; 2000–2009	Indonesia	Panel data, Pooled OLS, Random effects, and Tobit estimations	FDI	Infrastructure development	All infrastructure variables are positively associated to FDI inflows, for both the ratio of FDI inflows to GDP and number of FDI projects. This suggests that a province which has better infrastructure could attract more FDI inflows.
Goldberg, L.S., and M.W., Klein (1997). "Foreign direct investment, trade and real exchange rate linkages in Southeast Asia and Latin America." NBER Working Paper 6344, National Bureau of Economic Research, Cambridge.	Relationship between real bilateral exchange rates and Japanese and US FDI; 1978–1993 or 1994 (depending upon the country)	7 developing countries in Southeast Asia (Indonesia, Malaysia, Philippines, Thailand) and Latin America (Argentina, Brazil, Chile)	Fixed effects model (logarithmic form)	Real direct investment from either the United States or Japan	Real bilateral exchange rates between the host country's currency and US dollar, Real bilateral exchange rates between the host country's currency and Japanese yen, GDP of the source country, One-year lagged GDP of the source country, One-year lagged GDP of the host country, One-year lagged bilateral real exchange rates with respect to both yen and US dollar	Direct investments from Japan rise by 3% with a depreciation of the currencies of the developing country against the yen by 1%. The effect is highly statistically significant only when the movements of the currency of the developing country against the US dollar are also controlled. In general, real exchange rates have the most significant effect on FDI for Southeast Asia. A real depreciation of the currencies of the Southeast Asian countries with respect to the Japanese yen both increases FDI from Japan and decreases FDI from the US.
Gottschalk, S., and S. Hall (2008). "Foreign direct investment and exchange rate uncertainty in Southeast Asia." *International Journal of Finance and Economics* 13: 349–359	Relationship between exchange rate volatility and Japanese and US FDI; 1982–2001	4 countries (Indonesia, Malaysia, Philippines, Thailand)	Arrellano-Bond method for dynamic panel	Difference of log of real US or Japanese FDI stock in country i	Real rate of return reported by affiliates in location I, GARCH estimate of the variance of exchange rate in location I, GARCH estimate of the correlation between the exchange rate in location i and the exchange rate in	A rise in the local rate of return has a positive effect on FDI from the US and Japan. There is evidence to suggest that a rise in the volatility of bilateral dollar exchange rates would likely cause ASEAN-4 to be more attractive for outward US investment. This does not apply for Japanese outward investment.

					location j, Variance of the Japanese exchange rate, Correlation of the dollar exchange rate of location i with the yen/dollar	For estimation of US FDI, the coefficient of this variable is positive but negative for Japanese FDI, which may imply that US FDI has a longer maturity than Japanese FDI. For US FDI, only the correlation of the ASEAN-4 exchange rates with the Indonesian ringgit and with the Japanese yen matters.
Khaliq, Abdul, and Noy Ilan (2007). "Foreign direct investment and economic growth: Empirical evidence from sectoral data in Indonesia." *Journal of Economic Literature* 45(1): 313–325	Impact of FDI on economic growth in sectors; Yearly; Sectoral; 1998–2006	Indonesia	A case study (single-country) regression-based approach — data on 12 sectors	Economic growth	FDI	At the aggregate level, FDI seems to cause a positive effect on economic growth. The effects of FDI on economic growth differ across sectors, however, there are no aggregate effects. In the mining sector, FDI affects economic growth negatively. This seems to suggest that extractive FDI might not necessarily boost economic growth.
Kiyota, K., and S. Urata (2004). "Exchange rate, exchange rate volatility and foreign direct investment." *World Economy* 27(10): 1501–1536	Relationship between real exchange rate and exchange rate volatility and Japanese FDI; 1990–2000	127 countries (including 9 ASEAN countries — Brunei, Cambodia, Indonesia, Malaysia, Myanmar, Philippines, Singapore, Thailand, Vietnam)	Feasible generalized least square estimation method	Log of ratio of FDI from Japan to country I as a proportion of country i's GDP	Log of real exchange rate, Unexplained part of real exchange rate volatility (defined as the deviation of the actual value from the value explained by the failure of the law of one price), Real exchange rate volatility is the variance of the changes in the real exchange rate, Explained parts of real exchange rate volatility are fitted values obtained from a gravity equation, Time trend	A depreciation of the host country currency attracts FDI. Large volatility in exchange rates discourages FDI. Overvaluation of the currency discourages FDI. A flexible but stable exchange rate system is needed to successfully attract FDI.

(*Continued*)

Table 4.2: (*Continued*)

Citation	Topic; Unit of Analysis; Period of Study	Countries Covered	Methodology	Dependent Variable(s)	Independent Variable(s)	Findings
Rahmaddi, R., and M. Ichihashi (2013). "The role of foreign direct investment in Indonesia's manufacturing exports." *Bulletin of Indonesian Economic Studies* 49(3): 329–354	Role of direct investment on exports; Yearly; Industry; 1990–2008	Indonesia	OLS, Random effects, Fixed effects	Exports (constant)	FDI, Domestic capital investment, GDP, REER	FDI is positively and significantly correlated with manufacturing exports but the effects vary between industries. FDI has a stronger effect on physical capital, human capital and technology intensive (PCI–HCI–TI) commodities natural resource intensive and unskilled labour intensive (NRI–ULI) group but greatest effect is on the metal goods, machinery and electronics (MME) commodity. Meanwhile, a 1.00 percent REER depreciation will increase growth in manufacturing by 1.8 percent; however, REER effects on exports are industry specific.
Siregar, R., and R. S. Rajan (2004). "Impact of exchange rate volatility on Indonesia's trade performance in the 1990s." *J. Japanese Int. Economies* 18: 218–240	Impact of exchange rate volatility on trade; Quarterly; Country; 1980–1997	Indonesia	MASD and GARCH to determine REER	Total exports / imports; Capital imports; Intermediate imports; Exports and imports to Japan	REER volatility (using moving average standard deviation (MASD) and Generalised Autoregressive Conditional Heteroskedasticity (GARCH) estimations)	Total exports and exports to Japan did not increase with REER depreciation. Export-driven recovery did not happen for Indonesia post-AFC.
Ginting, A. M. (2013). "Pengaruh Nilai Tukar Terhadap Ekspor Indonesia." *Bulletin Ilmiah Litbang Perdagangan* 7(1)	Impact of exchange rate on exports; Yearly; Country; 2005–2012	Indonesia	Error correction model	Exports	Growth and exchange rate	A 1.00 percent appreciation of the exchange rate reduces exports by 1.21 percent.
Sjoholm, F. (2002). "Which Indonesian firms export? The importance of foreign networks." *Papers Reg. Sci.* 82: 333–350	Importance of foreign ownership on trade; Yearly; Firms; 1994–1997	Indonesia	Probit	Export status	Foreign ownership, Import, spillovers (share of district's output produced in foreign establishments)	Controlling for size, the results for skill, capital, research and development, age, industry, regions, foreign ownership and imports are positive and significant. Establishments with foreign networks are likely to be exporters.

						Spillovers are only significant in one estimation. A large foreign presence in the district does not seem to benefit exports. Old establishments that are founded under heavy import substitution policies may be more focused on the domestic market. At the industry level, foreign ownership increases the probability of export by seven percent to 25 percent. Accordingly, imports increase the probability of exports by two percent to 14 percent.
Xaypanya, P., P. Rangkakulnuwat, and S.W. Paweenawat (2014). "The determinants of foreign direct investment in ASEAN: The first differencing panel data analysis." *International Journal of Social Economics* 42(3): 239–250	Determinants of FDI inflows; 2000–2011	ASEAN-5 (Indonesia, Malaysia, Philippines, Singapore, Thailand) and ASEAN-3 (Cambodia, Laos, Vietnam)	First differencing pooled OLS	FDI inflows	Real exchange rate (RER), Inflation rate, GDP of host country, Number of telephone lines, Trade openness, Official development assistance (ODA) (for ASEAN-3)	For ASEAN-3: RER is negative and insignificant, inflation rate is negative and significant at 5%, GDP is positive but insignificant, telephone lines is positive and significant at 1%, trade openness is positive and significant at 1%, ODA is negative and insignificant. For ASEAN-5: RER is positive and insignificant, inflation rate is positive and significant at 5%, GDP is positive and significant at 1%, telephone lines is positive and significant at 10%, trade openness is negative and significant at 1%.
Xing, Y., and G. Wan (2006). "Exchange rates and competition for FDI in Asia." *World Economy* 29(4): 419–434	Relationship between real exchange rate and relative Japanese FDI to ASEAN-4 versus to China; 1981–2002	China and ASEAN-4 (Indonesia, Malaysia, Philippines, Thailand)	Fixed effects model (logarithmic form)	Relative Japanese FDI into one of ASEAN-4 compared to that into China (ratio of FDI flow into an ASEAN-4 country versus the FDI flow into China)	Relative yen exchange rates of the Chinese yuan and ASEAN-4's currencies, Relative market size (GDP of ASEAN-4/GDP of China), Difference in GDP growth rates, Relative trade openness between ASEAN-4 country and China	A relative 1.00 percent appreciation would reduce FDI by 1.14 percent. These imply that if a country's currency appreciates more against the yen compared to the yuan, the country obtains fewer FDI. When yuan depreciates against the yen more than the currencies of the ASEAN-4, China will obtain more FDI. This implies that a real appreciation in the currency of an FDI-recipient country against that of the FDI-source country will redirect FDI to its rival countries.

Source: ACI.

4.4 Data Description, Statistical Computation and Sources

FDI in Indonesia can be classified as assets which comprise equity capital, debt instruments and liabilities. Annual FDI inflows series for Indonesia are available from various sources, namely the Bank of Indonesia, UNCTAD and the World Bank.

Table 4.3 provides the definitions of FDI from different data sources. For instance, while the World Bank refers to FDI as the direct investment equity flows in an economy, UNCTAD defines it as a sum of equity capital, reinvested earnings and intra-company loans. BKPM, on the other hand, records FDI as the value of foreign investments that flow into Indonesia along with funds originating from foreign companies operating in the country, while the Bank of Indonesia considers FDI as non-resident investment in a company in Indonesia.

Due to differences in the definition of FDI, FDI series from different sources slightly differ from one another as shown in Figure 4.14. Since UNCTAD also sources the FDI series from the Bank of Indonesia, series from these two sources overlap with each other. However, the World Bank and the BKPM series are significantly different from the other available series; since BKPM accounts for both the value of the funds generated from foreign companies operating in Indonesia and the foreign investment that flows into Indonesia, its figures are generally higher than those reported by the Bank of Indonesia and UNCTAD.

In terms of data coverage, UNCTAD (sourced from Bank of Indonesia) provides the longest FDI series at the national level from 1970 to 2014. Additionally, the Bank of Indonesia releases a breakdown of FDI data by economic sectors and country of origin at the national level. Such data breakdown, however, is not available at the provincial level. Meanwhile, BKPM reports data by economic sectors at the regional and provincial levels for the period of 1990–2015. Since BKPM provides provincial-level FDI data, it is most suitable for our analysis.

For REER, both Bruegel and OECD (as sourced from Bluenomics) provide the longest available series. Bruegel provides two series of monthly REER, namely monthly-138 and monthly-41. REER data from Federal Reserve Economic Data (FRED) and Bank for International Settlements (BIS) overlap with each other. FRED data are originally sourced from BIS, as shown in Figure 4.15. This is also evident in Table 4.4, which displays the pairwise correlation between the different REER series. Given that the series highly correlate with one another, it is unlikely that the empirical results will be sensitive to the choice of REER series. We therefore use monthly-138 series from Bruegel Institute for our empirics as the baseline model and try other series for robustness checks in Section 4.7.

Table 4.5 summarises the definitions and data sources for all independent variables used in the empirics. Our priors for the directions of association between these variables and the FDI inflows (as discussed in detail in Section 4.5) are indicated in the first column of the table.

Table 4.6 presents summary statistics of the variables used in our analysis. The table shows that average REER index is estimated to be around 94, with no variation when measured by between standard deviation. However, the within standard deviation of REER index is found to be nearly 12.

Table 4.3: Definitions of FDI

Source	FDI Definition	Level of Aggregation	Coverage	Period & Frequency
Bank of Indonesia	Direct investment in Indonesia is non-resident investment in a company in Indonesia, which is characterised by the presence of initial transaction in ownership of equity capital of at least 10 percent. Subsequent transactions, in both assets and liabilities, between Indonesian enterprises and their direct investors as well as non-resident fellow enterprises are recorded as direct investment in Indonesia. BI uses the BOP method which records the net inflow and outflow of foreign capital fund flows that enters Indonesia from abroad.	National	BI reports FDI data at the national level by economic sectors and country of origin.	2004–2015 (Annual and quarterly)
UNCTAD	Foreign Direct Investment inflows and outflows comprise capital provided (either directly or through other related enterprises) by a foreign direct investor to a FDI enterprise, or capital received by a foreign direct investor from a FDI enterprise. FDI includes the following three components: equity capital, reinvested earnings and intra-company loans. Data on FDI flows are presented on net bases (capital transactions' credits less debits between direct investors and their foreign affiliates). Net decreases in assets or net increases in liabilities are recorded as credits (with a positive sign), while net increases in assets or net decreases in liabilities are recorded as debits (with a positive sign). Hence, FDI flows with a negative sign indicate that at least one of the three components of FDI is negative and not offset by positive amounts of the remaining components. These are called reverse investment or disinvestment.	National	UNCTAD reports data from BI and covers national level.	1970–2014 (Annual)
World Bank (World Development Indicators)	Foreign direct investment refers to direct investment equity flows in the reporting economy. It is the sum of equity capital, reinvestment of earnings and other capital. Direct investment is a category of cross-border investment associated with a resident in one economy having control or a significant degree of influence on the management of an enterprise that is resident in another economy. Ownership of 10 percent or more of the ordinary shares of voting stock is the criterion for determining the existence of a direct investment relationship. Data are in current U.S. dollars.	National	World Bank reports data from IMF BOP database, supplemented by UNCTAD and BI.	1981–2014 (Annual)
BKPM	BKPM categorises all investments made into a foreign capital investment company as FDI, even if it is a joint venture with a local partner. It records the value of the foreign investment that flows into Indonesia as well as those funds originating from foreign companies (PMA) already operating in Indonesia. For example, PMA companies that inject new capital for expansion projects coming from funds from their own operations would be captured in BKPM figures. BKPM does not include FDI from Oil and Gas, and Banking and Insurance sectors.	Regional (six regions), Provincial (34 provinces)	BKPM covers FDI at regional, provincial and regency/city levels by economic sectors and country of origin.	1990–2015 (Annual and quarterly)

Source: ACI.

Figure 4.14: FDI Inflows to Indonesia from Different Sources (US$ Billion), 1970–2014

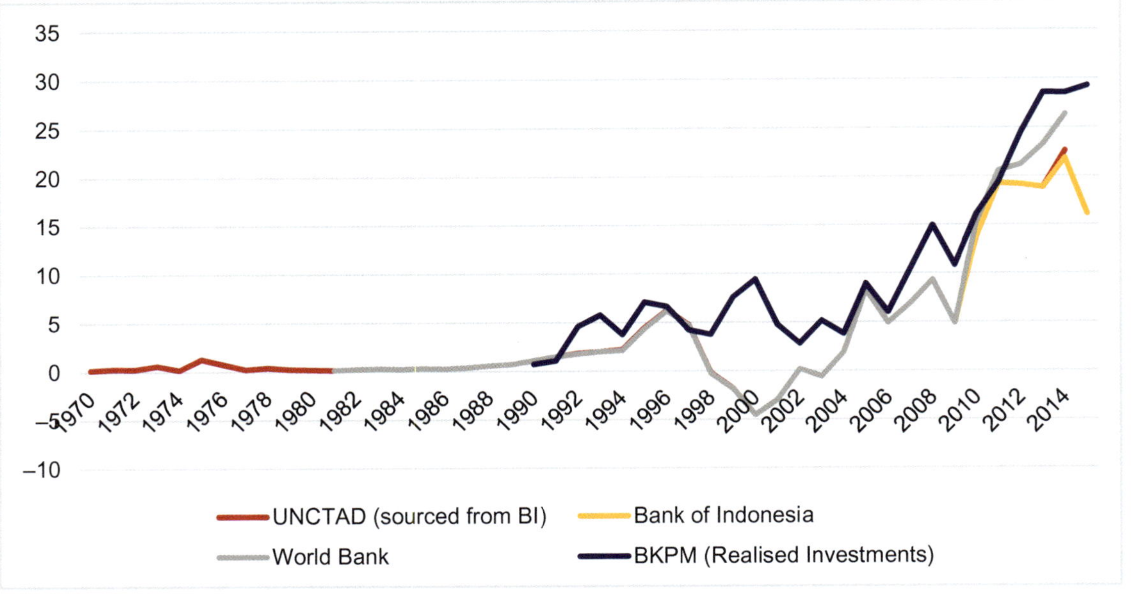

Source: ACI based on data from UNCTAD, World Bank, Bank of Indonesia and BKPM.

Figure 4.15: REER from Different Sources, 1995–2015

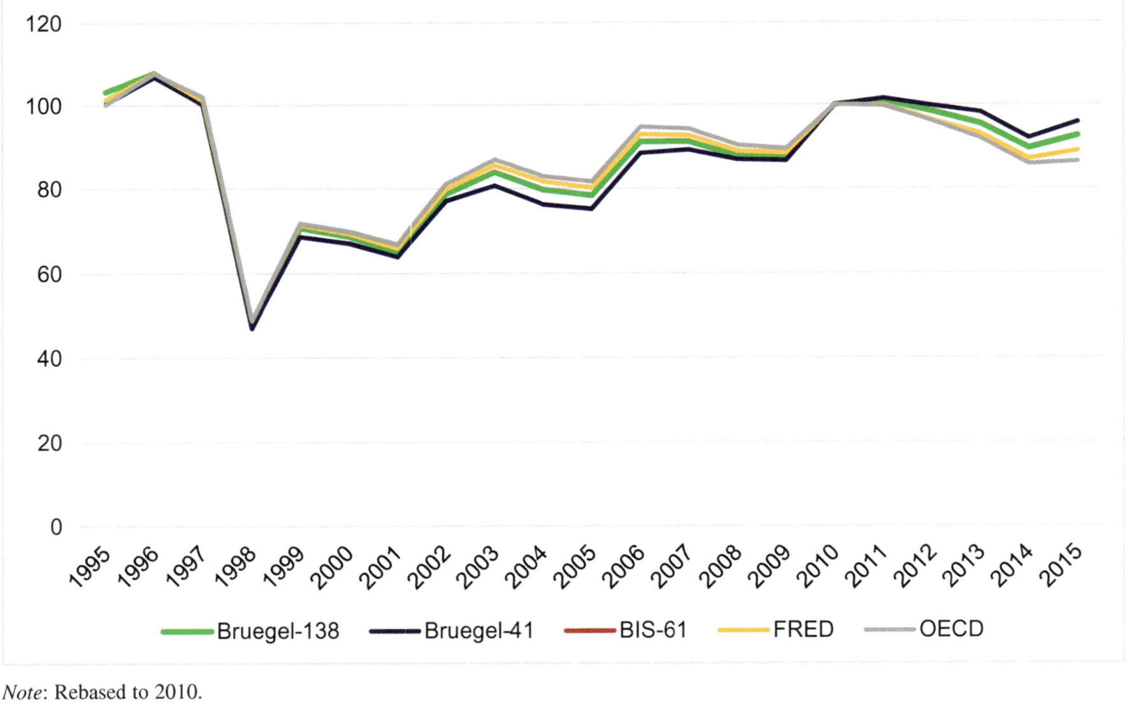

Note: Rebased to 2010.
Source: ACI based on data from Bruegel Institute, BIS, FRED and OECD.

Table 4.4: Pairwise Correlation between Different REER Series

Bruegel-138 and BIS	Bruegel-138 and OECD	BIS and OECD	Bruegel-138 and Bruegel-41	FRED and OECD
0.994	0.983	0.997	0.992	1.000

Source: ACI.

Table 4.5: Control Variables: Sources and Definitions

Variable	Unit	Definition	Source
REER (+/–)	Index	REER is calculated from nominal effective exchange rate and a measure of the relative price or cost between the country under study and its trading partners.	Bruegel Institute
REER Volatility (+/–)	Standard Deviation (SD)	Monthly standard deviation of REER.	Bruegel Institute
Foreign Exchange Reserves (+/–)	Average of Monthly Percent Change	Foreign currency deposits and bonds held by Indonesia's central bank (excluding gold holdings).	Bank of Indonesia
GRDP per Capita (+)	Rupiah, Million (Current Prices)	GRDP per capita in nominal terms is used as a proxy for provincial income levels.	BPS
Population (+)	Number of People	Population is used as a proxy for provincial market size.	BPS
Inflation (–)	Index	The consumer price index shows the changes in price against a pegged basket of goods and services at the provincial level.	BPS
Trade Openness (–)	Percent of GDP	Trade is the sum of exports and imports of goods and services measured as a share of GRDP.	Calculated based on Data and Information Centre (Pusdatin), Ministry of Trade
Education (–)	Number	Mean years of schooling from primary to tertiary or higher education is used to represent human capital development.	Developments in Key Social and Economic Indicators (*Perkembangan Beberapa Indikator Utama Sosial Ekonomi Indonesia*) Report from BPS
Domestic Credit to Private Sector (+)	Ratio	Current outstanding bank loans as a percentage of current GRDP is used to demonstrate the state of financial development in a province. Bank loans from commercial and rural banks are included.	Bank of Indonesia
Length of Paved Roads (+)	Kilometre	Total length of national, provincial and district/city roads in the province with asphalt paving at a given year.	World Bank and Transportation Statistics (*Statistik Transportasi*)
Crime Rate (–)	Number of Cases	Number of annual cases per 100,000 populations as a measure of crime rate.	Bureau of Operation Control, Indonesia National Police Headquarters and Indonesia Statistics (*Statistik Indonesia*) from BPS
Secondary Industry Productivity (+)	Ratio	GRDP for secondary industry (manufacturing, electricity, gas and water supply and construction) is divided by secondary industry workforce to derive a measure of productivity (GRDP per employed worker).	Calculated through Indonesia Statistics (*Statistik Indonesia*) from BPS
Minimum Wage (–)	Rupiah, Million (Current Prices)	Minimum wage per month per employed worker.	CEIC and Indonesia Statistics (*Statistik Indonesia*) from BPS
Natural Resource (+)	0 or 1	More than 30 percent of GRDP in natural resources = 1, otherwise = 0.	Calculated based on Indonesia Statistics (*Statistik Indonesia*) from BPS

Source: ACI.

Table 4.6: Summary Statistics

Variable	Mean	Between Std. Dev.	Within Std. Dev.	Min	Max	Observations	Number of Provinces
Ln Province FDI	13.12	1.82	1.93	0.99	18.38	420	33
Lag of Ln GRDP per Capita	2.53	0.65	0.62	0.56	5.05	462	33
Lag of Ln Population	15.13	1.03	0.09	13.26	17.63	462	33
Lag of Inflation	7.92	0.68	3.46	−1.30	20.28	462	33
Lag of Trade to GRDP	0.35	0.34	0.23	0.00	3.58	462	33
Lag of Education (Mean Years of Schooling)	7.87	0.88	1.63	5.60	38.05	363	33
Lag of Bank Loans as a Percent of GRDP	0.19	0.13	0.05	0.03	1.04	462	33
Lag of Ln Length of Paved Roads	8.57	0.69	0.34	5.75	10.48	462	33
Lag of Crime Rate	165.02	81.56	62.75	5.00	557.00	462	33
Lag of Secondary Industry Productivity	40.18	39.85	16.07	4.08	305.53	396	33
Lag of Ln Minimum Wage	13.29	0.17	0.51	12.06	14.60	462	33
Lag of Natural Resource	0.21	0.38	0.16	0.00	1.00	462	33
Lag of REER	94.42	0.00	11.81	71.16	110.63	462	33
Lag of REER Volatility (SD)	3.59	0.00	1.62	0.83	6.39	462	33
Lag of Change in Foreign Exchange Reserves (FXR) (Percent)	0.83	0.00	1.24	−0.96	3.28	462	33

Source: ACI.

Having discussed the sources, definitions, coverage and nature of data used in our analysis, we will now introduce the empirical methodology employed for our analysis in Section 4.5.

4.5 Empirical Methodology

4.5.1 Baseline Model: Panel-Fixed Effects Regression

To examine the impact of exchange rates on FDI, we compile a panel dataset for 33 Indonesian provinces,[6] covering the period from 2000 to 2014. The dependent variable of interest, FDI inflows, is sourced from BKPM which captures FDI inflows to individual provinces of Indonesia. The key independent variable is the annual REER collected at the national level from Bruegel (monthly-138 series).

[6]There are officially 34 provinces in Indonesia, including North Kalimantan which was formed in 2012. However, official sources of data for North Kalimantan are not yet available.

We employ panel-fixed effects models to explore the relationship between REER (both in terms of levels and volatility) and FDI inflows. The basic estimating equation will be to understand the impact of REER and FDI flows to Indonesian provinces, controlling for other province-specific characteristics. The baseline equation is outlined as

$$fdi_{it} = \alpha_0 + \beta_1 REER_t + \delta \boldsymbol{Y}_{it} + \gamma_i + e_t + \varepsilon_{it} \tag{1}$$

where

fdi_{it} refers to FDI inflows to a province i at time t;
$REER_t$ represents the time-varying independent variable captured by REER;
Y_{it} represents a matrix of control variables measured at time t for a province i;
γ_i captures entity-fixed effects;
e_t denotes time-fixed effects; and
ε_{it} is the idiosyncratic error term.

In equation (1), β and δ are the parameters to be estimated.

We first estimate the impact of the levels of REER on FDI before controlling for volatility in order to understand how movements in REER levels are associated with FDI inflows. Subsequently, we add monthly standard deviation of REER as a measure of volatility to the regression while using the coefficient of variation of REER series for robustness checks in Section 4.7.

Before we proceed, it is imperative to discuss some of the key econometric concerns, which will broadly be taken into consideration by establishing robustness checks during the later stages. The applicability of econometric methodologies in panel data primarily undergoes two potential concerns, resulting in biased estimates either due to simultaneity bias/reverse causality or due to endogeneity issues which might arise from omitted variable bias. Our model addresses the concern of omitted variable bias to a certain extent as we incorporate entity- and time-fixed effects in equation (1).

Our controls, informed broadly from the related literature (Blonigen 2005), cover a set of macroeconomic, financial and institutional factors specific to each province that possibly determine FDI inflows to Indonesian provinces. A brief discussion on these variables and their priors are as follows:

- **GRDP per capita**: This captures the level of development in each province; higher income level is likely to induce higher consumer demand and thus greater FDI inflows into the province. *A priori*, we expect to see a positive relationship between GRDP per capita and FDI inflows.
- **Population**: This measures market size. We expect to see a positive association between population and FDI inflows as a larger market size would enable economies of scale, thus substantially reducing per unit cost which is likely to attract FDI inflows to the province.
- **Inflation**: This is proxied by Consumer Price Index (CPI); we expect to see a negative relationship between FDI and inflation because higher inflation would imply higher investment risk, thus making FDI inflows less attractive.

- **Minimum wages**: This captures labour costs in a province; higher minimum wages imply a higher labour cost which would lead to higher production cost, thus reducing FDI inflows to the provinces. *A priori*, we expect to see a negative relationship between minimum wages and FDI inflows to Indonesian provinces.
- **Education**: This is captured by mean years of schooling and measures human capital development in a province. We expect to see a positive relationship between human capital development and FDI inflows as availability of skilled labour is likely to attract more FDI.
- **Length of paved roads**: This captures the extent of development of infrastructure in the province; a well-developed infrastructure reduces cost and thus boosts FDI inflows. *A priori*, we expect length of paved roads to have a positive impact on FDI.
- **Domestic credit to private sector**: This is used as a proxy for financial development in the province. It is likely to be positively associated with FDI inflows as a well-developed financial market in a province will help to greatly reduce investment risks.
- **Crime rate**: This is measured by the number of annual cases per 100,000 population and is likely to have an adverse effect on FDI inflows to the provinces.
- **Secondary industry productivity**: This is measured as output per unit of workforce employed, where higher productivity would reduce cost substantially, thus attracting FDI inflows to the provinces.
- **Trade openness**: This is measured as the ratio of total imports and exports to GDP. The impact of trade openness on FDI inflows will be ambiguous as it is subject to the nature of FDI. For instance, higher trade openness could deter FDI when firms prefer to export than undertake horizontal FDI. However, if one considers the case of vertical FDI, higher trade openness may induce more FDI as firms may be encouraged to move to take advantage of the greater trade engagement of the place.

Additionally, in order to capture the effects of provinces having higher natural resources endowment on FDI, we employ a dummy variable for natural resources. We expect provinces with higher endowment of natural resources to attract more FDI.

4.5.2 Augmented Model

The second part of our empirical analysis is to capture the possible effects of an exchange rate expectation on FDI inflows. Specifically, we use the accumulation of foreign exchange reserves and interact it with REER to capture expectations of sustained appreciation in the country's exchange rate. When a country intervenes in the foreign exchange market and builds foreign exchange reserves (FXR) — thereby attempting to prevent its currency from appreciating through sustained reserve accumulation — there is a likelihood of market expectations of further appreciation in the future. This is reflected in equation (2) given below:

$$fdi_{it} = \alpha_0 + \beta_1 REER_t + \beta_2 Volatility_t + \delta \mathbf{Y}_{it} + \gamma_i + \beta_3 fxr_t + \beta_4 fxr_t * REER_t + e_t + \varepsilon_{it} \quad (2)$$

If reserve changes are a good proxy for sustained REER appreciation, then *a priori*, we should observe a positive relationship between REER and FDI, implying that an REER appreciation is likely to induce domestic market-oriented FDI. On the other hand, if FDI is export-oriented, REER appreciation would deter FDI inflows.

4.6 Empirical Results

We start with our fixed effects model outlined in equation (1). Table 4.7 displays the main empirical findings for Indonesia, inclusive of Java provinces. We build our model by first taking into account only the macroeconomic, institutional and financial variables in the first column. Subsequently, we introduce REER levels and REER volatility in the second and third columns. Finally, the last column shows the augmented model, which includes average monthly percentage change in FXR and the interaction term between average monthly percent change in FXR and annual average REER.

Firstly, the key independent variable of interest, REER, is found to be insignificant and negatively associated with FDI inflows (column 2). However, it becomes weakly significant at 10 percent when we include REER volatility (column 3). Its significance improves even further to a five percent level as we augment FXR and its interaction term with REER in the model (column 4). This implies that Indonesian rupiah's appreciation as measured by an increase in REER by 1.00 percentage point will reduce the growth of FDI inflows to Indonesia's provinces by 0.09 percentage points.

Considering the impact of exchange rate volatility as measured by the standard deviation of REER, the results imply a negative and a highly significant coefficient across all specifications. The empirical results suggest that an increase in REER volatility by 1.00 percentage point will deter the growth of FDI inflows by 0.19 percentage points. As explained earlier in the paper, REER volatility will deter FDI inflows if FDI inflows are export-oriented in nature. Evidently, empirical results show that an appreciation in REER (in levels) and a higher REER volatility discourage FDI inflows, which is consistent with the fact that FDI inflows into Indonesia tend to be more export-oriented in nature.

With regard to the control variables, we find that annual GRDP per capita, population, inflation rate, trade openness, length of roads, outstanding bank loans as a share of GRDP, average years of schooling, secondary industry productivity, minimum wage and share of natural resources in GRDP are consistent across all regressions. Among these variables, however, only GRDP per capita and population consistently appear as statistically significant determinants of FDI inflows. Both enter the regressions positively, which is in accordance with the priors. A high rate of GRDP implies a strong economic performance and more profitable investment opportunities, which in turn attracts more FDI.

In the baseline model, we find highly positive and significant results for GRDP per capita, population and share of outstanding bank loans in GRDP. We find that per capita GRDP appears to be significant and positive across all regressions, implying that a higher per capita GRDP at the provincial level leads to higher FDI inflows. This suggests that the higher the income levels and market size, the higher it is likely to have FDI inflows across sectors. Second, provincial-level population is found to be positively associated with FDI inflows. This is supported by the argument that multinational corporations (MNCs) tend to invest greater in more populated

Table 4.7: Empirical Results (Including Java Provinces)

	(1)	(2)	(3)	(4)
Dependent Variable: Ln(FDI)	**Baseline**	**Augmented with REER**	**Augmented REER Volatility (SD)**	**Augmented with FXR and FXR Interaction**
Lag of Ln GRDP per Capita	**2.134*****	**2.261*****	**2.277*****	**2.569*****
	(0.754)	(0.772)	(0.788)	(0.845)
Lag of Ln Population	**9.226***	**9.199***	**9.225***	**10.582***
	(5.423)	(5.400)	(5.284)	(5.661)
Lag of Inflation	–0.024	–0.024	–0.019	–0.006
	(0.030)	(0.030)	(0.030)	(0.031)
Lag of Trade Percent of GRDP	–0.064	–0.067	–0.104	–0.163
	(0.471)	(0.475)	(0.471)	(0.479)
Lag of Mean Years of Schooling	**–0.022****	**–0.024****	**–0.023****	–0.017
	(0.010)	(0.010)	(0.010)	(0.010)
Lag of Outstanding Bank Loans/GRDP	**8.464***	8.162	8.717*	**9.715***
	(4.865)	(4.999)	(5.133)	(5.449)
Lag of Ln Length of Paved Roads	0.173	0.169	0.201	0.126
	(0.368)	(0.372)	(0.371)	(0.379)
Lag of Crime Rate	–0.000	–0.000	–0.000	–0.001
	(0.002)	(0.002)	(0.002)	(0.002)
Lag of Secondary Industry Productivity	0.005	0.005	0.005	**0.006***
	(0.003)	(0.003)	(0.003)	(0.003)
Lag of Ln Minimum Wage	–2.067	–2.013	–1.171	–0.786
	(1.392)	(1.405)	(1.451)	(1.459)
Lag of Percent GRDP from Natural Resources	–0.629 (0.822)	–0.647 (0.848)	–0.648 (0.833)	–0.758 (0.926)
Lag of REER		**–0.012**	**–0.049***	**–0.099****
		(0.018)	(0.026)	(0.044)
Lag of REER Volatility (SD)			**–0.149****	**–0.197****
			(0.068)	(0.075)
Lag of FXR				–0.525
				(0.807)
Lag of REER*FXR				0.007
				(0.008)
Observations	326	326	326	326
R-squared	0.422	0.423	0.428	0.435

Notes: (i) Robust standard errors are indicated in parentheses; (ii) *** $p<0.01$, ** $p<0.05$, *$p<0.1$; (iii) Time-Fixed Effects (FE) and Province FE incorporated.
Source: ACI.

countries, and that there exist the demand and purchasing power for products and services provided by MNCs owing to Indonesia's growing middle class population. Finally, the results for financial development, which is captured by the share of outstanding bank loans in GRDP, align with the priors; financial depth that pertains to the extent of credit availability drives potential entrepreneurship opportunities and is therefore more likely to attract FDI. However, the significance of financial development holds strong in the baseline (first column) and the augmented model (fourth column). It is also important to note that these significant results are robust to the choice of all the four specifications of the regressions as shown in Table 4.7, with an exception of average years of schooling, which becomes insignificant in the augmented model as represented in the fourth column.

In addition, cost-related factors as measured by minimum wages show negative and insignificant results. Meanwhile, results indicate that a higher inflation has an insignificant but negative impact on FDI inflows across four regression specifications, suggesting that provinces with higher inflation tend to deter FDI, which also conforms to the priors. Infrastructure development, broadly measured by the length of paved roads, is found to be positively associated with FDI inflows. However, it remains statistically insignificant. Importantly, secondary industry productivity — which is a measure of productivity (GRDP per employed worker) — as captured by the ratio of GRDP for secondary industry (manufacturing, electricity, gas and water supply, and construction) to secondary industry workforce, is found to be significant and positively associated with FDI inflows in Indonesia.

Finally, the augmented regression specification estimates the impact of expected exchange rate appreciation on FDI (column 4). It is observed that the coefficients on the average monthly percent change in FXR and its interaction term with REER are both statistically insignificant. One interpretation of these results is that market expectations of future exchange rate movements perhaps do not explain FDI inflows into Indonesia. However, the results may also point to a need for more suitable proxies for market expectation.

As a final exercise, we consider the possibility that the results might be driven by Java provinces alone, given the fact that the Java region attracts most of Indonesia's FDI inflows. We thus test our results by re-estimating our model after excluding all six Java provinces from our panel data. The results are summarised in Table 4.8.

We observe that REER loses its significance when we exclude provinces in Java. However, REER volatility continues to be significant and negatively associated with FDI, which further corroborates the fact that FDI to Indonesia is export-oriented in nature. It is observed that the coefficients of FXR and its interaction term with REER are both statistically significant. One possible interpretation of these results is that market expectations of future exchange rate movements could have a role in explaining FDI inflows to non-Java provinces.

We also observe that similar to the main empirical model, secondary industry productivity is found to be significant and positively associated with FDI inflows, thereby indicating that productivity in the secondary industry plays a key role in determining FDI across all regions beyond just Java provinces. Interestingly, minimum wage is found to be significant and positively associated with FDI inflows. A possible explanation for this is that FDI inflows outside of Java are mainly going into resource-dependent provinces which, for socio-political reasons, tend

Table 4.8: Empirical Results (Excluding Java Provinces)

	(1)	(2)	(3)	(4)
Dependent Variable: Ln(FDI)	**Baseline**	**Augmented with REER**	**Augmented with REER Volatility (SD)**	**Augmented with FXR and FXR Interaction**
Lag of Ln GRDP per Capita	−0.175	−0.000	−0.000	0.092
	(1.178)	(1.175)	(1.179)	(1.145)
Lag of Ln Population	300.437	360.743	346.855	363.578
	(750.628)	(746.394)	(751.537)	(731.975)
Lag of Inflation	−0.056	−0.052	−0.047	−0.052
	(0.038)	(0.037)	(0.038)	(0.038)
Lag of Trade Percent of GRDP	−0.154	−0.098	−0.122	−0.182
	(0.437)	(0.418)	(0.416)	(0.416)
Lag of Mean Years of Schooling	**−0.023***	−0.019	−0.018	**−0.022***
	(0.012)	(0.012)	(0.012)	(0.012)
Lag of Outstanding Bank Loans/GRDP	2.755	5.255	5.810	8.693
	(3.850)	(5.177)	(5.187)	(5.742)
Lag of Ln Length of Paved Roads	0.379	0.373	0.434	0.437
	(0.467)	(0.455)	(0.456)	(0.463)
Lag of Crime Rate	−0.000	−0.001	−0.001	−0.001
	(0.003)	(0.003)	(0.003)	(0.003)
Lag of Secondary Industry Productivity	**0.011****	**0.011****	**0.011****	**0.012*****
	(0.004)	(0.005)	(0.004)	(0.004)
Lag of Ln Minimum Wage	**2.980*****	**2.176****	**3.091****	**3.153***
	(0.594)	(0.977)	(1.218)	(1.581)
Lag of Percent GRDP from Natural Resources	−0.552 (0.904)	−0.534 (0.850)	−0.536 (0.833)	−0.477 (0.873)
Lag of REER		**0.035**	**−0.005**	**−0.028**
		(0.024)	(0.034)	(0.051)
Lag of REER Volatility (SD)			**−0.155***	**−0.158***
			(0.076)	(0.088)
Lag of FXR				**−2.564****
				(1.062)
Lag of REER*FXR				**0.025****
				(0.010)
Observations	260	260	260	260
R-squared	0.390	0.396	0.400	0.411

Notes: (i) Robust standard errors are indicated in parentheses; (ii) ***p<0.01, **p<0.05, *p<0.1; (iii) Time FE and Province FE incorporated.
Source: ACI.

to have higher minimum wages. Indeed, barring DKI Jakarta which has the highest minimum wage in Indonesia, provinces with resource-based growth like Papua, East Kalimantan, West Papua and South Sumatra have some of the highest minimum wages in Indonesia.

4.7 Robustness Checks

In order to ascertain the consistency of our findings, we undertake two types of robustness checks. First, we use coefficient of variation (CV) as an alternative measure of REER volatility. Second, we rerun our model using an alternative REER series that is sourced from BIS.

Results from the first robustness check are summarised in Table 4.9. When we use CV as a measure of volatility, we find that signs and significance levels of both REER and REER volatility are consistent with our main findings in Table 4.7. Both REER levels and volatility remain negative and highly significant, thus bolstering our main findings that increases in REER levels and REER volatility will deter FDI inflows to Indonesian provinces. Finally, the interaction term of reserves and REER remains positive and insignificant, concurring with our results in Table 4.7.

Akin to our results in Tables 4.7 and 4.8, we find that the control variables — GRDP per capita, population, outstanding bank loan per GRDP and secondary industry productivity — remain positive and significant when CV is used as a measure of REER volatility. The signs and significance levels of other variables also remain consistent with our main findings in Section 4.6.

For the second robustness check, we use an alternative REER series. As mentioned in Section 4.4, REER series are available from various sources and are computed for different sets of countries and weights. For instance, Bruegel provides two series of monthly REER, namely monthly-138 and monthly-41, computed using 138 and 41 trading partners respectively. BIS provides trade-weighted REER series covering 61 countries. In order to check if our results are sensitive to the choice of REER series, we therefore use the BIS series for the second robustness check.

Table 4.10 summarises the results from using BIS REER series. We find that both REER levels and volatility are negative and strongly significant at one percent level of significance. Interestingly, their significance increases when we use BIS REER series. It is worth noting that the signs and significance of the interaction term and the control variables are also consistent with our main findings.

Our findings from both robustness checks concur with our main empirical findings, thus validating that our fixed effects model is robust. We conduct additional robustness checks using absolute change in FXR levels and change in REER. While the coefficient of REER and REER volatility remains negative and significant when we use absolute change in FXR levels (Table 4.11), the interaction term becomes negative but remains insignificant. On the other hand, using change in REER levels results in a negative and insignificant relation between REER (level and volatility) and FDI inflows (Table 4.12). Table 4.13 provides the comparative results of the robustness checks, wherein all robustness checks remain broadly consistent with our main empirical findings in Table 4.7.

Table 4.9: Using Coefficient of Variation as an Alternative Measure of REER Volatility

	(1)	(2)	(3)	(4)
Dependent Variable: Ln(FDI)	**Baseline**	**Augmented with REER**	**Augmented REER Volatility (CV)**	**Augmented with FXR and FXR Interaction**
Lag of Ln GRDP per Capita	**2.134*** **	**2.261*** **	**2.310*** **	**2.639*** **
	(0.754)	(0.772)	(0.794)	(0.859)
Lag of Ln Population	**9.226***	**9.199***	**9.204***	**10.675***
	(5.423)	(5.400)	(5.285)	(5.667)
Lag of Inflation	−0.024	−0.024	−0.018	−0.004
	(0.030)	(0.030)	(0.030)	(0.031)
Lag of Trade Percent of GRDP	−0.064	−0.067	−0.094	−0.157
	(0.471)	(0.475)	(0.470)	(0.478)
Lag of Mean Years of Schooling	**−0.022****	**−0.024****	**−0.023****	−0.016
	(0.010)	(0.010)	(0.010)	(0.010)
Lag of Outstanding Bank Loans/GRDP	**8.464***	8.162	**8.835***	**9.999***
	(4.865)	(4.999)	(5.158)	(5.516)
Lag of Ln Length of Paved Roads	0.173	0.169	0.208	0.131
	(0.368)	(0.372)	(0.370)	(0.378)
Lag of Crime Rate	−0.000	−0.000	−0.000	−0.001
	(0.002)	(0.002)	(0.002)	(0.002)
Lag of Secondary Industry Productivity	0.005	0.005	0.005	**0.006***
	(0.003)	(0.003)	(0.003)	(0.003)
Lag of Ln Minimum Wage	−2.067	−2.013	−1.115	−0.631
	(1.392)	(1.405)	(1.438)	(1.446)
Lag of Percent GRDP from Natural Resources	−0.629 (0.822)	−0.647 (0.848)	−0.651 (0.831)	−0.772 (0.926)
Lag of REER		**−0.012**	**−0.059****	**−0.119****
		(0.018)	(0.027)	(0.048)
Lag of REER Volatility (CV)			**−17.651****	**−24.677*** **
			(7.537)	(8.785)
Lag of FXR				−0.582
				(0.818)
Lag of REER*FXR				0.007
				(0.008)
Observations	326	326	326	326
R-squared	0.422	0.423	0.428	0.437

Notes: (i) Robust standard errors are indicated in parentheses; (ii) ***$p<0.01$, **$p<0.05$, *$p<0.1$; (iii) Time FE and Province FE incorporated.
Source: ACI.

Table 4.10: Using Alternative REER Series

	(1)	(2)	(3)	(4)
Dependent Variable: Ln(FDI)	**Baseline**	**Augmented with BIS REER**	**Augmented REER Volatility (SD)**	**Augmented with FXR and FXR Interaction**
Lag of Ln GRDP per Capita	**2.134*****	**2.239*****	**2.162*****	**2.607*****
	(0.754)	(0.758)	(0.784)	(0.818)
Lag of Ln Population	**9.226***	9.124	8.813	**10.415***
	(5.423)	(5.412)	(5.316)	(5.641)
Lag of Inflation	–0.024	–0.023	–0.013	0.017
	(0.030)	(0.030)	(0.030)	(0.033)
Lag of Trade Percent of GRDP	–0.064	–0.061	–0.023	–0.021
	(0.471)	(0.476)	(0.453)	(0.441)
Lag of Mean Years of Schooling	**–0.022****	**–0.024****	**–0.019***	–0.006
	(0.010)	(0.010)	(0.010)	(0.011)
Lag of Outstanding Bank Loans/GRDP	**8.464***	8.144	**9.306***	**11.231***
	(4.865)	(4.987)	(5.290)	(5.775)
Lag of Ln Length of Paved Roads	0.173	0.171	0.226	0.131
	(0.368)	(0.372)	(0.368)	(0.380)
Lag of Crime Rate	–0.000	–0.000	0.000	–0.000
	(0.002)	(0.002)	(0.002)	(0.002)
Lag of Secondary Industry Productivity	0.005	0.005	0.005	**0.006***
	(0.003)	(0.003)	(0.003)	(0.003)
Lag of Ln Minimum Wage	–2.067	–2.021	–1.095	–0.322
	(1.392)	(1.403)	(1.474)	(1.452)
Lag of Percent GRDP from Natural Resources	–0.629	–0.642	–0.616	–0.776
	(0.822)	(0.839)	(0.793)	(0.867)
Lag of BIS REER		–0.013	**–0.064****	**–0.180*****
		(0.018)	(0.026)	(0.052)
Lag of BIS REER Volatility (SD)			**–0.200****	**–0.344*****
			(0.095)	(0.108)
Lag of (FXR)				–0.882
				(0.935)
Lag of BIS REER*FXR				0.013
				(0.010)
Observations	326	326	326	326
R-squared	0.422	0.423	0.428	0.435

Notes: (i) Robust standard errors are indicated in parentheses; (ii) *** $p<0.01$, ** $p<0.05$, * $p<0.1$; (iii) Time FE and Province FE incorporated.
Source: ACI.

Table 4.11: Using Absolute Change in FXR Levels

	(1)	(2)	(3)	(4)
Dependent Variable: Ln(FDI)	**Baseline**	**Augmented with REER**	**Augmented REER Volatility (SD)**	**Augmented with FXR and FXR Interaction**
Lag of Ln GRDP per Capita	**2.134*** **	**2.261*** **	**2.277*** **	**2.739*** **
	(0.754)	(0.772)	(0.788)	(0.890)
Lag of Ln Population	**9.226***	**9.199***	**9.225***	**10.418***
	(5.423)	(5.400)	(5.284)	(5.674)
Lag of Inflation	–0.024	–0.024	–0.019	–0.004
	(0.030)	(0.030)	(0.030)	(0.032)
Lag of Trade Percent of GRDP	–0.064	–0.067	–0.104	–0.120
	(0.471)	(0.475)	(0.471)	(0.474)
Lag of Mean Years of Schooling	**–0.022** **	**–0.024** **	**–0.023** **	–0.015
	(0.010)	(0.010)	(0.010)	(0.010)
Lag of Outstanding Bank Loans/GRDP	**8.464***	8.162	**8.717***	**9.401***
	(4.865)	(4.999)	(5.133)	(5.310)
Lag of Ln Length of Paved Roads	0.173	0.169	0.201	0.125
	(0.368)	(0.372)	(0.371)	(0.375)
Lag of Crime Rate	–0.000	–0.000	–0.000	–0.001
	(0.002)	(0.002)	(0.002)	(0.002)
Lag of Secondary Industry Productivity	0.005	0.005	0.005	0.005
	(0.003)	(0.003)	(0.003)	(0.003)
Lag of Ln Minimum Wage	–2.067	–2.013	–1.171	–0.926
	(1.392)	(1.405)	(1.451)	(1.450)
Lag of Percent GRDP from Natural Resources	–0.629 (0.822)	–0.647 (0.848)	–0.648 (0.833)	–0.791 (0.933)
Lag of REER		**–0.012**	**–0.049***	**–0.098** **
		(0.018)	(0.026)	(0.043)
Lag of REER Volatility (SD)			**–0.149** **	**–0.205** **
			(0.068)	(0.081)
Lag of FX Reserve (FXR) Levels Change				0.187
				(0.202)
Lag of REER*FXR Levels Change				–0.000
				(0.000)
Constant	–108.550	–107.987	–116.011	–133.504
	(74.775)	(74.341)	(72.720)	(79.774)
Observations	326	326	326	326
R-squared	0.422	0.423	0.428	0.435

Notes: (i) Robust standard errors are indicated in parentheses; (ii) ***p<0.01, **p<0.05, *p<0.1; (iii) Time FE and Province FE incorporated.
Source: ACI.

Table 4.12: Using Change in REER Levels

	(1)	(2)	(3)	(4)
Dependent Variable: Ln(FDI)	**Model 1a: Baseline**	**Model 1b: Augmented with dREER**	**Model 1c: Augmented REER Volatility (SD)**	**Augmented with FXR and FXR Interaction**
Lag of Ln GRDP per Capita	**2.134*****	**2.130*****	**2.030****	**1.873****
	(0.754)	(0.763)	(0.761)	(0.747)
Lag of Ln Population	9.226*	9.251	9.194	**9.743***
	(5.423)	(5.498)	(5.496)	(5.688)
Lag of Inflation	–0.024	–0.024	–0.020	0.003
	(0.030)	(0.033)	(0.033)	(0.049)
Lag of Trade Percent of GRDP	–0.064	–0.062	–0.075	–0.191
	(0.471)	(0.471)	(0.471)	(0.530)
Lag of Mean Years of Schooling	**–0.022****	**–0.022****	**–0.022****	**–0.027****
	(0.010)	(0.010)	(0.010)	(0.011)
Lag of Outstanding Bank Loans/GRDP	**8.464***	8.521	8.752	8.888
	(4.865)	(5.213)	(5.343)	(5.479)
Lag of Ln Length of Paved Roads	0.173	0.171	0.189	0.189
	(0.368)	(0.366)	(0.362)	(0.371)
Lag of Crime Rate	–0.000	–0.000	–0.000	–0.001
	(0.002)	(0.002)	(0.002)	(0.002)
Lag of Secondary Industry Productivity	0.005	0.005	0.005	**0.007***
	(0.003)	(0.003)	(0.003)	(0.003)
Lag of Ln Minimum Wage	–2.067	–2.067	–1.880	–1.816
	(1.392)	(1.396)	(1.384)	(1.367)
Lag of Percent GRDP from Natural Resources	–0.629 (0.822)	–0.630 (0.819)	–0.609 (0.804)	–0.586 (0.838)
Lag of dREER		**0.001**	**–0.002**	**–0.080**
		(0.014)	(0.014)	(0.063)
Lag of REER Volatility (SD)			**–0.041**	**–0.077**
			(0.049)	(0.055)
Lag of FX Reserve (FXR)				0.120
				(0.150)
Lag of dREER*FXR				0.026
				(0.016)
Constant	–108.550	–108.918	–110.385	–119.407
	(74.775)	(75.907)	(75.755)	(78.580)
Observations	326	326	326	326
R-squared	0.422	0.423	0.428	0.437

Notes: (i) Robust standard errors are indicated in parentheses; (ii) ***p<0.01, **p<0.05, *p<0.1; (iii) Time FE and Province FE incorporated.
Source: ACI.

Table 4.13: Summary of Robustness Checks

Variables	Baseline (Bruegel Monthly-138)	REER Volatility (CV)	BIS	Absolute Change in FXR Level	Change in REER
REER	Negative & Significant	Negative & Significant	Negative & Significant	Negative & Significant	Negative & Insignificant
REER Volatility	Negative & Significant	Negative & Significant	Negative & Significant	Negative & Significant	Negative & Insignificant
Interaction Term (FXR*REER)	Positive & Insignificant	Positive & Insignificant	Positive & Insignificant	Negative & Insignificant	Positive & Insignificant

Source: ACI.

4.8 Concluding Notes and Policy Implications

Indonesia has large potentials to attract more investment. On top of being strategically located at the heart of Southeast Asia, Indonesia is the largest market in the region with rich natural resources as well as a sizeable and growing middle class population. Despite the initial economic and political turmoil that adversely affected the country's economy following the 1997–1998 AFC, years of reforms have led to a relatively stable growth in recent years, which in turn boosted investor confidence particularly among foreign investors. The stable growth, coupled with increases in FDI that had surpassed pre-AFC level, has allowed Indonesia to gain the title of an emerging global powerhouse despite the fact that most of its growth is still primarily driven by domestic consumer spending.

In absolute terms, FDI inflows accounted for over US$22 billion in 2014 and contributed to around three percent of Indonesia's GDP in the same year. An analysis of trends and patterns of FDI inflows to Indonesia reveals that its distribution is highly skewed both at the regional and sub-national levels. Java attracts the highest share of FDI inflows, followed by Kalimantan, Sumatra and Sulawesi. At the provincial level, provinces within the Java region (Banten, Central Java, DI Yogyakarta, DKI Jakarta, East Java and West Java) account for about 80 percent of FDI inflows to Indonesia between 2000 and 2010, and 58 percent between 2010 and 2014. This is broadly driven by key indicators, such as infrastructure, labour availability, financial market depth and market size, which are more likely to be agglomerated in the Java economy. With regard to the source of FDI inflows, Singapore remains the largest source of FDI in Indonesia, broadly due to exemptions in capital gains tax on profits. Singapore and Japan together contributed to over 70 percent of Indonesia's FDI during 2010–2015. Finally, the manufacturing as well as mining and quarrying sectors received more than half of FDI inflows from 2006–2015.

While the estimates show an optimistic investment climate in Indonesia, it is important to recognise that business environment in the country, as measured by the World Bank's Doing Business rankings, is poorer than in other more developed East Asian countries. Moreover, despite small signs of improvement, corruption and poor institutions remain a problem. Indonesian institutions thus need to be improved further. On a more positive note, however, certain provinces have been able to implement good policies and improve local institutions, as shown in those that performed well in the Government and Institutional Setting environment (see Chapter 2). Instances of reforms at the national and sub-national levels provide a strong policy foundation for the continued development of Indonesia. Appropriately, the development of necessary and basic facilities such as seaports and airports as well as the improvement of human capital are also important factors to further encourage FDI inflows in the future.

Considering the heavily skewed nature of FDI inflows to large, heterogeneous countries like Indonesia, it becomes important to understand the determinants of FDI to Indonesian provinces. Exploiting the provincial-level variations in FDI inflows, we constructed a panel data for 33 Indonesian provinces, spanning the period 2000–2014 to understand the nexus between price competitiveness as captured by REER and provincial FDI.

The degree to which exchange rate movements and fluctuations affect FDI inflows is a subject of policy importance for several EMDEs like Indonesia. Our findings reveal that increases in REER levels and volatility deter FDI inflows to Indonesia's provinces. These findings imply that FDI inflows to Indonesia are export-oriented in nature. Our results remain consistent and robust for different model specifications that determine the impact of REER on FDI inflows.

References

Alfaro, Laura, Areendam Chanda, Sebnem Kalemli-Ozcan, and Selin Sayek. 2004. "FDI and Economic Growth: The Role of Local Financial Markets." *Journal of International Economics* 64 (1): 89–112.

Assche, Ari Van, and Byron Gangnes. 2010. "Electronics Production Upgrading: Is China Exceptional?" *Applied Economics Letters* 17 (5): 477–82. https://doi.org/10.1080/13504850701765101.

Barro, Robert J. 1997. *Determinants of Economic Growth*. The MIT Press. https://mitpress.mit.edu/books/determinants-economic-growth.

Bénassy-Quéré, AgnÈs, Lionel Fontagné, and Amina Lahrèche-Révil. 2001. "Exchange-Rate Strategies in the Competition for Attracting Foreign Direct Investment." *Journal of the Japanese and International Economies* 15 (2): 178–98. https://doi.org/10.1006/jjie.2001.0472.

Blonigen, Bruce A. 1997. "Firm-Specific Assets and the Link between Exchange Rates and Foreign Direct Investment." *American Economic Review* 87 (3): 447–65.

———. 2005. "A Review of the Empirical Literature on FDI Determinants." *Atlantic Economic Journal* 33 (4): 383–403. https://doi.org/10.1007/s11293-005-2868-9.

Borensztein, E., J. De Gregorio, and J.-W. Lee. 1998. "How Does Foreign Direct Investment Affect Economic Growth?" *Journal of International Economics* 45 (1): 115–35. https://doi.org/10.1016/S0022-1996(97)00033-0.

Bosworth, Barry, and Susan M. Collins. 1999. "Capital Flows to Developing Economies: Implications for Saving and Investment." *Brookings Papers on Economic Activity* 30 (1): 143–80.

Byrne, Joseph P., and E. Philip Davis. 2003. "Panel Estimation of the Impact of Exchange Rate Uncertainty on Investment in the Major Industrial Countries." *National Institute of Economic and Social Research,* no. Discussion Paper No 208.

Carkovic, Maria V., and Ross Levine. 2002. "Does Foreign Direct Investment Accelerate Economic Growth?," June. https://papers.ssrn.com/abstract=314924.

Chakrabarti, Rajesh, and Barry Scholnick. 2002. "Exchange Rate Expectations and Foreign Direct Investment Flows." *Review of World Economics* 138 (1): 1–21.

Cushman, David O. 1988. "Exchange-Rate Uncertainty and Foreign Direct Investment in the United States." *Weltwirtschaftliches Archiv* 124 (2): 322–36. https://doi.org/10.1007/BF02706782.

Darby, Julia, Andrew Hughes Hallett, Jonathan Ireland, and Laura Piscitelli. 1999. "The Impact of Exchange Rate Uncertainty on the Level of Investment." *The Economic Journal* 109 (454): 55–67. https://doi.org/10.1111/1468-0297.00416.

Dhakal, Dharmendra, Raja Nag, Gyan Pradhan, and Kamal P. Upadhyaya. 2010. "Exchange Rate Volatility and Foreign Direct Investment: Evidence From East Asian Countries." *International Business & Economics Research Journal (IBER)* 9 (7): 121–28. https://doi.org/10.19030/iber.v9i7.603.

Fitriandi, Primandita, Makoto Kakinaka, and Koji Kotani. 2014. "Foreign Direct Investment and Infrastructure Development in Indonesia: Evidence from Province Data." *Asian Journal of Empirical Research* 4 (January): 79–94.

Foad, Hisham S. 2005. "Exchange Rate Volatility and Export-Oriented FDI." *Department of Economics, San Diego State University.*, March. https://papers.ssrn.com/abstract=706524.

Froot, Kenneth, and Jeremy Stein. 1991. "Exchange Rates and Foreign Direct Investment: An Imperfect Capital Markets Approach." *Quarterly Journal of Economics* 106 (Nov.): 1191–1217.

Ginting, Ari Mulianta. 2013. "Pengaruh Nilai Tukar Terhadap Ekspor Indonesia." *Bulletin Ilmiah Litbang Perdagangan* 7 (1).

Goldberg, Linda S. 2009. "Exchange Rates and Foreign Direct Investment." *The Princeton Encyclopedia of the World Economy*. https://doi.org/10.3386/w6344.

Goldberg, Linda S., and Michael W. Klein. 1997. "Foreign Direct Investment, Trade and Real Exchange Rate Linkages in Developing Countries." *Proceedings, Federal Reserve Bank of San Francisco*, 73–100. https://doi.org/10.3386/w6344.

Gopalan, Sasidaran, Rabin Hattari, and Ramkishen S. Rajan. 2017. "Understanding Foreign Direct Investment in Indonesia." *Journal of International Trade Law and Policy* 15 (1): 28–50. https://doi.org/10.1108/JITLP-01-2016-0003.

Gottschalk, Sylvia, and Stephen Hall. 2008. "Foreign Direct Investment and Exchange Rate Uncertainty in South-East Asia." *International Journal of Finance & Economics* 13 (4): 349–59.

Herzer, Dierk. 2012. "How Does Foreign Direct Investment Really Affect Developing Countries' Growth?" *Review of International Economics* 20 (2): 396–414.

Hill, Hal, and Prema-chandra Athukorala. 1998. "Foreign Investment in East Asia: A Survey." *Asian-Pacific Economic Literature* 12 (2): 23–50.

Hobday, Mike. 2001. "The Electronics Industries of Pacific Asia: Exploiting International Production Networks for Economic Development." *Asia Pacific Economic Literature* 15 (1): 13–29.

Hornick, Robert N., and Mark A. Nelson. 1987. "Foreign Investment in Indonesia." *Asia Pacific Economic Literature* 11 (4). https://ideas.repec.org/a/bla/reviec/v20y2012i2p396-414.html.

Iamsiraroj, Sasi. 2016. "The Foreign Direct Investment-Economic Growth Nexus." *International Review of Economics and Finance* 42: 116–33.

Iqbal, Farrukh, and William E. James, eds. 2002. *Deregulation and Development in Indonesia*. Westport, Conn: Praeger.

Kaplinsky, R. 2000. "Globalisation and Unequalisation: What Can Be Learned from Value Chain Analysis?" *Journal of Development Studies* 37 (2): 117–46.

Khaliq, Abdul, and Ilan Noy. 2007. "Foreign Direct Investment and Economic Growth: Empirical Evidence from Sectoral Data in Indonesia." *Journal of Economic Literature* 45 (1): 313–25.

Kiyota, Kozo, and Shujiro Urata. 2004. "Exchange Rate, Exchange Rate Volatility and Foreign Direct Investment." *World Economy* 27 (10): 1501–36. https://doi.org/10.1111/j.1467-9701.2004.00664.x.

Klein, Michael, and Eric Rosengren. 1994. "The Real Exchange Rate and Foreign Direct Investment in the United States: Relative Wealth vs. Relative Wage Effects." *Journal of International Economics* 36 (3–4): 373–89.

Mencinger, Jože. 2003. "Does Foreign Direct Investment Always Enhance Economic Growth?" *International Review for Social Sciences* 56 (4): 491–508.

Ménil, Georges de. 1999. "Real Capital Market Integration in the EU: How Far Has It Gone? What Will the Effect of the Euro Be?" *Economic Policy* 14 (28): 167–201.

Mody, Ashoka, and Antu Panini Murshid. 2005. "Growing up with Capital Flows." *Journal of International Economics* 65 (1): 249–66.

Ng, Francis, and Alexander Yeats. 2003. "Major Trade Trends in East Asia : What Are Their Implications for Regional Cooperation and Growth." Policy Research Working Paper No. 3084. Washington, DC: The World Bank. http://documents.worldbank.org/curated/en/947081468774959058/Major-trade-trends-in-East-Asia-what-are-their-implications-for-regional-cooperation-and-growth.

Pain, Nigel, and Desirée Van Welsum. 2003. "Untying The Gordian Knot: The Multiple Links Between Exchange Rates and Foreign Direct Investment." *Journal of Common Market Studies* 41 (5): 823–46. https://doi.org/10.1111/j.1468-5965.2003.00465.x.

Razin, Assaf. 2004. "The Contribution of FDI Flows to Domestic Investment in Capacity, and Vice Versa." *National Bureau of Economic Research,* University of Chicago Press.

Siregar, Reza, and Ramkishen S. Rajan. 2004. "Impact of Exchange Rate Volatility on Indonesia's Trade Performance in the 1990s." *Journal of the Japanese and International Economies* 18 (2): 218–40. https://doi.org/10.1016/S0889-1583(03)00050-9.

Stokman, Ad C. J., and Peter J. G. Vlaar. 1996. "Volatility, International Trade and Capital Flows." *Risk Management in Volatile Financial Markets*, Financial and Monetary Policy Studies, 115–32. https://doi.org/10.1007/978-1-4613-1271-0_7.

Tan, Khee Giap, Mulya Amri, and Nursyahida Ahmad. 2017. "Determinants of Foreign Direct Investment Inflows to 33 Indonesian Provinces: What Role for Exchange Rates?" Forthcoming.

Xaypanya, Phonesavanh, Poomthan Rangkakulnuwat, and Sasiwimon Warunsiri Paweenawat. 2015. "The Determinants of Foreign Direct Investment in ASEAN: The First Differencing Panel Data Analysis." *International Journal of Social Economics* 42 (3): 239–50. https://doi.org/10.1108/IJSE-10-2013-0238.

Xing, Yuqing, and Guanghua Wan. 2006. "Exchange Rates and Competition for FDI in Asia." *World Economy* 29 (4): 419–34. https://doi.org/10.1111/j.1467-9701.2006.00791.x.

Discussant Note 4.1

Impact of Real Effective Exchange Rates on Foreign Direct Investment Inflows to ASEAN Economies and Indonesia Provinces

Dr Darius Tirtosuharto

Economist, Economic and Monetary Policy Department, Macroeconomic Division, Bank of Indonesia

What is fascinating about the Association of Southeast Asian Nations (ASEAN) economies is the fact that they remain a major recipient of foreign direct investments (FDI). ASEAN has received around 16 percent of the global FDI among developing countries. Since the 1998–1999 economic crisis, FDI has built up quite a remarkable success story in developing ASEAN countries. Globalisation has fueled the need for external financing, which in many cases has been the primary source of investments as well as a source of risk associated with exchange rate volatility and currency mis-match.

In determining the impact of the real effective exchange rate (REER) on FDI, the focus is on the transmission of currency appreciation or depreciation of trade and cost competitiveness. Both trade and cost competitiveness are considered as the primary factor that drives profits of private enterprises. An increase in REER (appreciation) implies that exports become more expensive and imports become cheaper, which may lower trade competitiveness for FDI that are export oriented and particularly that are less dependent on the import of raw materials. For this type of enterprise or investments, the key is whether lower cost of production translates to being more competitive. Nevertheless, an appreciation of REER does not always result in a higher price of exported goods due to differences in the cost structure between countries.

Inflows of FDI could also target the domestic market, particularly in a country such as Indonesia that has a large population and growing middle class consumers. In this case, REER appreciation may actually build consumer confidence to spend, as import becomes cheaper, although income from export is potentially less. Hence, without a certain incentive structure, import substitution will not take place naturally. Thus, amidst currency appreciation, the impact on FDI with domestic orientation is also no less favorable, likewise in the case of FDI with export orientation. This becomes an issue when countries are determined to depreciate their currency to gain the most economic benefits including attracting FDI, but have not considered other factors in play such as REER volatility that is relatively common in emerging market economies.

The contribution of this paper is an effort to identify the impact of cost competitiveness using REER as a proxy towards FDI, which is also consistent with the impact of REER volatility. Whereas, in the case of ASEAN countries, the findings are consistent with the hypothesis in which FDI is deterred by REER appreciation and increasing REER volatility. The paper concluded that FDI inflow to ASEAN is mostly export oriented and therefore there are incentives for policy makers to maintain REER competitiveness.[1]

In the case of Indonesia, the study shows that REER appreciation has a negative impact on FDI. Hence, volatility of the exchange rate seems to have a positive correlation with FDI. Despite this surprising result, another study also came to the same conclusion (Crowley and Lee 2003,[2] Dhakal et al. 2010).[3] Among other factors, including one argued in the paper where FDI inflow in Indonesia is more and more toward export-oriented, there are a number of factors that should be considered related to the finding that is specific to the Indonesian case. First is whether the consideration of foreign investors is merely on output growth. Thus, some degree of exchange rate volatility can still be tolerated as long as there is stability over expected growth. In other words, this is the phenomenon of risk-averse investors.

Other study highlights the importance to address the possible misperception by foreign investors. The panel data on East Asia countries (China, Indonesia, Malaysia, Philippines, South Korea and Thailand) indicates that exchange rate volatility tends to induce FDI (Dhakal et al. 2010). This finding is perceived as the possible misconception over REER volatility that is assumed to lean toward depreciation and therefore, provides an incentive to invest.

In sum, macroeconomic stability still holds the key to maintain sustainability of output growth, which is considered as the most important factor in attracting FDI. Macroeconomic stability shall also be directed to guide investors' perception towards measurable risks and opportunities. Central banks as the monetary authority are responsible to manage exchange rate volatility with the balancing over optimum exchange rate based on the economic fundamental (inflation target) and investment promotions that will generate new jobs and sustain growth,while foreign investors are assumed to be able to measure the risks associated with macroeconomic stability, market expectation and also costs competitiveness in which REER is the key indicator.[4]

---

[1] All the five ASEAN countries, initially focused on import-substitution strategy before shifted to export-oriented industrialisation (Singapore 1960s; Malaysia, Phillipine, Thailand 1970s; and Indonesia 1980s). Consequently, there are different strategies on managing exchange rate and also different motives of attracting FDI in ASEAN.

[2] Crowley, P. and J. Lee. 2003. "Exchange Rate Volatility and Foreign Investment: International Evidence," *The International Trade Journal*, Vol XVII, No. 3.

[3] Dhakal, D. et al. 2010. "Exchange Rate Volatility and Foreign Direct Investment: Evidence From East Asian Countries," *International Business & Economics Research Journal*, Vol 9, No 7.

[4] Forex reserve management or hedging is necessary to guard againts possible currency mis-match in emerging market economies.

Discussant Note 4.2

Impact of Real Effective Exchange Rates on Foreign Direct Investment Inflows to ASEAN Countries and the Sub-National Economies of Mainland China, India, and Indonesia[1]

Professor Sin Chor-Yiu

Department of Economics, College of Technology Management, National Tsing Hua University, Taiwan, Republic of China

1. Introduction

Foreign direct investment (henceforth FDI) inflows to developing economies has been a hot topic for quite a period of time. Among many reasons, this may be due to the fact that FDI arguably plays a significant role to play in supplementing not only domestic capital, but also technology, skills as well as regional value chains. Consequently, it is important to understand how FDI inflows accelerate economic growth quantitatively.

FDI inflows is different from portfolio investments and typically it is a type of capital flow which is more stable. It is documented that Asian economies, which are well-known of rapid growth in the last half-a-century or so, have been receiving FDI inflows from 25 percent of world FDI to Asia in 1995 to 40 percent in 2014.

A number of crucial determinants on FDI have been considered in the literature. For instance, there are concerns the movement of exchange rates both in terms of their levels and volatility. This is because for developing or emerging economies, cost-competitiveness is crucial to attract global FDI inflows.

More concretely, this chapter considers the impact or impacts of real effective exchange rates (henceforth REERs) on the FDI inflows. REER is used as a proxy for cost-competitiveness. The research question is how the level and volatility of the REER affect FDI inflows.

Four panel data sets are considered in this chapter. They are:

a. The Association of Southeast Asian Nations countries excluding Indonesia (henceforth ASEAN-9);

[1]The contents of this discussion note were delivered during the 2016 Annual Asia Competitiveness Institute Conference on "Competitiveness Ranking of Subnational Economies and Public Policy Studies in Greater China, India, Indonesia and ASEAN" on 24 November 2016, in Singapore.

b. The sub-national economies of Mainland China;
c. The sub-national economies of India; and
d. The sub-national economies of Indonesia.

Sub-national data are used so that heterogeneity within a country can be accounted for. Annual data are used which time span, due to the availability of data, varies with different data sets. More precisely, for ASEAN-9 and Mainland China, the time span is 1995–2014. For India, it is 2000–2013. And for Indonesia: 2000–2014.

2. Methodology and Results — A Summary

This section gives short summaries of the methodology and empirical results of the chapter. Methodologically, in the baseline model, while FDI inflows is the explained variable (for different countries/states/federal territories i and different year t),

- Apart from REER, there are a whole bunch of explanatory variables, various across the four panel data models, as controls;
- Country/state/federal territory-specific dummy;
- Time dummy.

In the augmented model, there are two more explanatory variables, namely, foreign exchange reserves (FXR), and an interaction term between FXR and REER. These two variables aim to capture the impact of the sustained appreciation (to a lesser extent, of the sustained depreciation). This major empirical findings include:

- The level of REER is significantly negative for all four panel data models.
- The volatility of REER, which is measured by its standard deviation, renders various results. More specifically, for ASEAN-9, it is insignificant. For Mainland China and Indonesia, it is significantly negative. And for India, it is significantly positive.
- The interaction term between FXR and REER is insignificant for all four panel data models.

3. Comments

Having offered an overview of the chapter, this section will focus on some specific comments, concerns and suggestions about the methodology, empirical results and some others.

In most, if not all, of the developing or emerging countries/sub-national economies, FDI is constrained by the host countries/economies. This certainly affects the demand side of direct investment. One of the authors responded that the constraints are some macroeconomic variables, which possibly affect the FDI across countries/economies.

For the supply side, if the total supply is the only concern, this kind of regulatory constraints may not be substantial. The idea of this paper is how the costs of production (or the profitability) affect the amounts of FDI. The related policy implication(s) is also discussed in this chapter. It is unclear why the REER is the major factor in determining the costs. Professor Saikat Sinha Roy commented that other factors may involve many infrastructure variables and the authors may want to take the principal components of them.

For the demand side, the factors affecting the costs may include (i) wage in terms of the host currency (or the home currency). Unfortunately, the authors do not consider any variable "wage" for ASEAN-9. For the sub-national economies, only the minimum wage is used; (ii) other costs of production; (iii) tax holiday; (iv) nominal exchange rate between the host country and the home country and those between the competitive country and the home country; and (v) the uncertainty of the nominal exchange rate or the nominal exchange rates.

All in all, the REER used in this chapter may be more relevant to trade, rather than FDI. For the FDI, the (nominal or real) exchange rate (or several choices of exchange rates) between the host economy and the home economy may be more relevant. One of the authors responded that REER is a commonly used variable in international finance.

To investigate the uncertainty of the nominal exchange rate(s), apart from the standard deviation, some other factors may be considered. They include (i) various exchange rate regimes (one of the authors responded that these can be captured in the time-specific dummies); (ii) the foreign exchange reserves, which is unfortunately only considered in the augmented model. Further, the authors may want to use the spread between the forex futures and the forex spot instead of the standard deviation of the REER.

On the other hand, for the regulatory constraints in the demand side, one may consider variables such as the competitiveness of the domestic firms, and the political power of those firms. All in all, while panel data model is used and the number of observations increases, the general principle applies: heterogeneity among the countries/economies needs to be taken care. In particular, it is unclear whether fixed-effect dummies capture all the heterogeneity. More precisely, both country/economy-specific effects and time-specific effects should be carefully accounted for. The time-specific effects seem particularly important since, just name a few pieces of fact:

- "FDI to the region has also risen in terms of its share in ASEAN's Gross Domestic Product (GDP) which increased from 3.49 percent in 1990 to 5.39 percent in 2014."
- "FDI inflows averaged around 1.5 percent of GDP between 1990 and 1997. FDI inflows were in the negative from 1998 to 2003 following AFC. Its share has remained modest post-AFC, peaking at 2.9 percent in 2005, and hovering just under three percent in 2014."
- "Mainland China–Peaks in 1995, recovers after Asian Financial Crisis (AFC) and significant turns around since 2000 up until Global Financial Crisis (GFC) and then picks up again."
- "India–Steady and gradual increase since 1990s, but marked turnaround since 2001 up until GFC and then a slow down before picking up again since 2012, reaching pre-GFC levels."

Thus, if resources permit, the authors may want to consider some other disaggregate data.

In the existing literature, the impact of the REER and that of the standard deviation are diverse. That said, the authors may want to elaborate how the current research may potentially have certain new contributions. The inclusion of the interaction term between FXR and REER is new. Unfortunately, it is insignificant for all four panel data models. One of the authors responded that there may be a better choice of variables.

The major empirical findings are not easy to interpret. The authors may want to elaborate why the impact of the standard deviation are different in the four panel data models.

Based on the empirical findings, the authors jump to a number of policy implications. On various pages of the presentation slides, the following recommendations are made:

- "ASEAN and Mainland China tend to be more export-oriented in nature." "As India positions itself as a platform for more export–oriented FDI, policy makers need to be more concerned about exchange rate competitiveness and managing REER appreciation." Judging from the empirical findings, will ASEAN and Mainland China deserve the same policy recommendation?
- "To maintain cost competitiveness, policymakers might be better off focusing on controlling domestic unit business costs." Is this a conclusion out of the empirical findings? Or is it a general comment?
- For India, "Impact of REER (levels) being weakly significant is suggestive of FDI inflows into India being relatively more domestic-oriented in nature." the results for ASEAN and Mainland China seem to be more strongly significant, though qualitatively the same. Will ASEAN and Mainland China deserve a similar policy recommendation?
- "Maintaining cost competitiveness through an exchange rate regime centred on inflation targeting, supported by disciplined fiscal policy likely to be more durable than trying to manage the currency per se." This is another strong policy recommendation. Will ASEAN and Mainland China deserve a similar policy recommendation?
- "For ASEAN countries and Mainland China: countries should aim to enhance transparency and communication in exchange rate policies and eschew short-term beggar-thy-neighbour policies." Is this a conclusion out of the empirical findings? Or is it a general comment?
- "For all countries: While managing exchange rate volatility (by the so-called "leaning against the wind") is somewhat less controversial, if too successful, might lead to moral hazard problems, i.e. agents fail to take actions in covering individual risks, which hinders the development of financial markets and instruments to hedge against FX risks." Is this recommendation also applied to ASEAN-9 and India, when the impact of the standard deviation is insignificant for the former, and it is significantly positive for the latter?

Last but not least, we would like to make the following editorial comments:

- All the references are missing.
- For a general readership, some special terms such as GSDP (gross state domestic products) and GRDP (gross regional domestic products?) should be defined at the outset.
- "weight the FDI inflows" should read "weigh the FDI inflows".

- Why Java provinces make a difference? One of the authors responded that this is to avoid the "Java effect" whose DGP accounts for 80 percent of the Indonesian GDP.
- Why change in foreign exchange reserves (FXR) is omitted.

The summaries and comments above notwithstanding, this chapter makes an important contribution to the interesting topic of the impacts of real effective exchange rates on foreign direct investment inflows.

Chapter 5
Commentary on Recent Developments in 34 Indonesian Provinces

5.1 Introductory Notes

Asia Competitiveness Institute's (ACI) study on sub-national level competitiveness in Indonesia provides a broad yet all-encompassing view of the spread of competitiveness in Indonesian provinces. While Chapter 1 has outlined recent key developments in Indonesia at the national level, it is useful to also look at province-specific information that could give contextual knowledge to the results in order to fully maximise the findings from the study. Such information can also supplement any other studies pertaining to Indonesia, for instance that of the impact of exchange rate movements and volatility on foreign investments in Indonesia, as outlined in Chapter 4. This chapter aims to provide such contextualised, province-specific information.

A novel addition to this year's update of ACI's study on Indonesia's sub-national competitiveness, this chapter features commentaries on recent developments in each of the 34 Indonesian provinces between 2015 and 2017. As far as possible, the section on each province has been contributed by ACI's respective local academic partners. Papers from these academics have been translated from Indonesian into English and, where relevant, have been summarised to fit the format of this book. In addition to supplementing our evidence-based study with the necessary background information that are context-specific to the individual provinces, this chapter is also a culmination of ACI's commitment to take the collaboration with our local academic partners to a deeper level.

Each provincial write-up consists of five sections. The first pertains to recent economic trends, which cover the province's economic growth, trade as well as investments. The second expands upon the social conditions of the province as reflected by key social indicators as well as notable incidents pertaining to social and industrial relations, if any. Key governmental policies and projects that have recently been enacted in each province are outlined in the third section, shedding light onto each provincial government's development priorities. This section also gives insight to the province's future development trajectory. The fourth section gives context to each province's political conditions by looking at the dynamics of key leaders and political parties in each province. Finally, some key economic indicators of each province are included in the last section. The data for these indicators were those from 2015 and were obtained from Indonesia's Central Bureau of Statistics (BPS). Meanwhile, all other relevant statistics, numbers and policies mentioned in the subsequent sections were obtained from various official reports and news articles that are listed in the References section.

The write-ups of all 34 provinces in this chapter have been arranged according to the province names in an alphabetical order.

5.2 Commentary on Recent Developments in Aceh, 2015–2017

By: Amri Zainal Abidin
Universitas Syiah Kuala

Province Location

Source: ACI.

5.2.1 Economic Conditions

Aceh's economy in the past two years has been growing below the national average of around five percent per annum (p.a.). Growth is largely driven by the agriculture, plantation, marine and mining sectors. Expenditure-wise, consumption appears to serve a dominant role as most consumer goods have to be imported from other provinces and countries.

As a contribution to the Gross Regional Domestic Product (GRDP), Aceh's total import and export values (including those interprovincial and abroad) currently stand at US$6.64 million and US$9.73 million respectively. Commodities exported to its major trading partners of Association of Southeast Asian Nations (ASEAN) countries are predominantly crude oil, fish and shrimps.

The prospects of both domestic direct investments (DDI) and foreign direct investments (FDI) are promising, as there has been an increase in the averages of both investments. The area of interest in investments is concentrated in the primary sector. Apart from enabling the optimal use of natural resources, it spurs the production of some consumer goods that are usually imported.

5.2.2 Social Conditions and Development

Between 2015 and 2017, indicators pertaining to the quality of life, such as Human Development Index (HDI), life expectancy and school enrolment rates in Aceh, continue to improve amid a rising unemployment rate.

These improvements can largely be attributed to the seriousness of the government in creating development in all sectors. Meanwhile, unemployment in Aceh has increased, given that the street poverty rate has not been reduced. A possible reason for this is that the Regional Development Budget (APBD) has not be "pro-poor" in that it has not prioritised the poor and that budget approvals are often delayed in the province.

Incidents pertaining to social issues are generally scarce and often limited to issues related to business competitions and misunderstandings.

Much has been done by the government in Aceh concerning the quality and condition of social relations in the province, particularly in areas pertaining to the campaigning of the governor's mission and vision to the people of Aceh.

5.2.3 Provincial Government Policies

The provincial government of Aceh has undertaken many policies, particularly on the management of the Special Autonomy Funds (Dana Otsus) as well as local regulations on the ease of doing business and investments — all of which have had impact on the province's economic growth. Likewise, many projects and activities have been launched by the government, under the administration of both the current and former governors. These include the development of infrastructure, such as Lhokseumawe-Takengon road and Kota Banda Aceh flyover, among others.

In terms of economic development, the government of Aceh has also launched the Lhokseumawe Special Economic Zone (SEZ).

All these aforementioned developments bring positive impacts as they have been proven to support economic activities of the community, which would eventually contribute to increasing their Own-Source Revenue (PAD).

Key Economic Indicators, 2015

Land Area (km²)	57,956
Population	
Total Population	5,002,000
Urban Population (%)	30.50
Poverty Rate (%)	17.11
Labour Force	2,182,824
Labour Force Participation Rate (%)	43.64
Gross Regional Domestic Products (GRDP) — 2010 prices	Rupiah (million)
GRDP	112,661,040
GRDP (non-minerals)	102,149,000
GRDP per Capita	22.52
GRDP per Capita (non-minerals)	20.42
Economic Composition	% of GRDP
Primary Sector	35.94
Secondary Sector	15.49
Tertiary Sector	48.57
Trade — 2010 prices	Rupiah (million)
Exports	1,018,257
Imports	1,274,164
Top-3 exports: mineral fuels; inorganic chemicals; coffee, tea and spices	
Top-3 imports: other engines of power; semi/wholly milled rice; petroleum bitumen	
Infrastructure	
Paved Roads (km)	11,164
Domestic Air Traffic (Passengers)	733,183
International Air Traffic (Passengers)	134,632
Domestic Cargo at Seaport (Tons)	4,590,024
International Cargo at Seaport (Tons)	1,437,427

Source: BPS Indonesia compiled by ACI.

5.2.4 Local Political Scene

Aceh province is led by Governor Irwandi Yusuf and his deputy Nova Iriansyah. The governor has been re-elected in 2017 after serving an earlier term between 2006 and 2012. The pair won the election with 270,540 votes (38.53 percent). This is followed by Muzakir Manaf–TA Khalid (30.75 percent) and Tarmizi Karim–Machsalmina Ali (16.14 percent). Other composition of the votes went to Zaini Abdullah–Nasaruddin (7.65 percent), Zakaria Saman–Alaidinsyah (5.04 percent) and Abdullah Puteh–Sayed Mustafa (1.89 percent). The win is supported by various parties including the Aceh Region Party (PDA), the National Awakening Party (PKB), the Indonesian Democratic Party of Struggle (PDIP), the Democrat Party as well as the Nanggroe Aceh Party (PNA), for which the governor is the chairman.

The governor, who was formerly an activist for the Free Aceh Movement (GAM), is affectionately known for his humorous and firm demeanour.

5.3 Commentary on Recent Developments in Bali, 2015–2017

By: I. Wayan Sukadana
Universitas Udayana

Province Location

Source: ACI.

5.3.1 Economic Conditions

Bali's economy grew by 5.68 percent in 2015, mostly contributed by the information and communications sector (9.00 percent). In 2016, there was a slight increase in growth at 5.88 percent, mostly owing to the health and social services sector (8.20 percent). Meanwhile, the first semester of 2017 saw a 5.81 percent cumulative growth, driven by the accommodation as well as food and beverages sector (8.53 percent).

Export values of goods originating from Bali have declined since 2015 to 2017. Meanwhile, Bali's exports in June 2017 has also weakened by 20.65 percent compared to the previous year. This decline is mostly a result of the slowdown in the economy of Bali's export partners, namely the United States and Europe.

Both foreign and domestic investors have continued to show interest in investing in the tourism accommodation provision sector, although this sector has been saturated and is highly competitive. According to Indonesia's Investment Coordinating Board (BKPM), investment in Bali has reached Rp13.5 trillion in 2012.

5.3.2 Social Conditions and Development

Bali's social conditions until 2017 are fairly good. Several indicators pertaining to quality of life have shown improvements. For instance, Bali's HDI reached 73.65 in 2016 and is predicted to go even higher to 73.90 in 2017. All the components of HDI have also shown improvements: life expectancy had increased from 71.00 years in 2014 to 71.41 in 2016; mean years of schooling has also reached 13.04 years in 2016. Several programs under the Mandara Bali Program — covering economic resources, health security and infrastructure — are expected to improve not only Bali's economic performance but also its social conditions.

A pertinent issue that is currently faced by the tourism industry stakeholders is the rise of online-based transportation and travel services. Although the number of tourists coming into Bali has not increased significantly, the market for service providers has been too saturated, even before the entrance of these online-based service providers. Meanwhile, moratorium policies introduced by the government have not been effective and do not apply to online-based service providers.

5.3.3 Provincial Government Policies

The latest provincial government policy pertains to the economic development of non-financial institutions, with the introduction of Provincial Regulation (Perda) No. 3/2017 on Village Finance Institution (LPD). LPD is a crediting institution that was formed in 1983 on the basis of ethnic village. The new law on LPD is hoped to strengthen the central government's policy which places the village as the epicentre of economic development.

The Presidential Regulation (Perpres) No. 15/2014 initiated a project to reclaim the Benoa bay due to Bali's saturated tourism sector. The Decree, however, was highly protested, as it might interfere with Bali's economy and might result in social conflicts. The central government has reviewed the issue through the Coordinating Ministry of Maritime and Resources, although no decision on the Decree has been made clear.

5.3.4 Local Political Scene

The political condition in Bali between 2015 and 2017 has been safe and under control. During this period, six out of nine cities/regencies elected their regional leaders: Denpasar City (I.B. Rai Dharmawijaya Mantra and I. G. N. Jayanegara, 82.14 percent), Jembrana Regency (I Putu Artha and I Made Kembang Hartawan, 60.00 percent), Tabanan Regency (Ni Putu Eka Widiastuti and I Komang Gede Sanjaya, 64.37 percent), Badung Regency (I Nyoman Giri Prasta and I Ketut Suiasa, 59.80 percent), Bangli Regency (I Made Gianyar and Sang Nyoman Sedana Yasa, 59.90 percent) and Karangasem Regency (I Gusti Ayu Mas Sumatri and I Wayan Artha Dipa, 41.76 percent).

Several notable candidates for Bali's upcoming gubernatorial election in 2018 are I Wayan Koster from the Indonesian Democratic Party of Struggle, which currently occupies 24 seats in Bali's Regional People's Representative Council (DPRD) and I Ketut Sudikerta who is backed by the Golkar Party, which currently occupies 11 seats.

Key Economic Indicators, 2015

Land Area (km²)	5,780
Population	
Total Population	4,152,800
Urban Population (%)	65.50
Poverty Rate (%)	5.25
Labour Force	2,372,015
Labour Force Participation Rate (%)	57.12
Gross Regional Domestic Products (GRDP) — 2010 prices	Rupiah (million)
GRDP	129,130,590
GRDP (non-minerals)	127,690,000
GRDP per Capita	31.09
GRDP per Capita (non-minerals)	30.75
Economic Composition	% of GRDP
Primary Sector	15.55
Secondary Sector	16.58
Tertiary Sector	67.87
Trade — 2010 prices	Rupiah (million)
Exports	2,616,488
Imports	1,353,970
Top-3 exports: fish and crustacean; jewelry and gem; non-knitted apparel	
Top-3 imports: airplane machines and appliances; mineral fuels; electrical machines and appliances	
Infrastructure	
Paved Roads (km)	7,202
Domestic Air Traffic (Passengers)	8,567,222
International Air Traffic (Passengers)	8,541,165
Domestic Cargo at Seaport (Tons)	4,391,763
International Cargo at Seaport (Tons)	80,984

Source: BPS Indonesia compiled by ACI.

5.4 Commentary on Recent Developments in Bangka Belitung Islands, 2015–2017

By: Asia Competitiveness Institute

Province Location

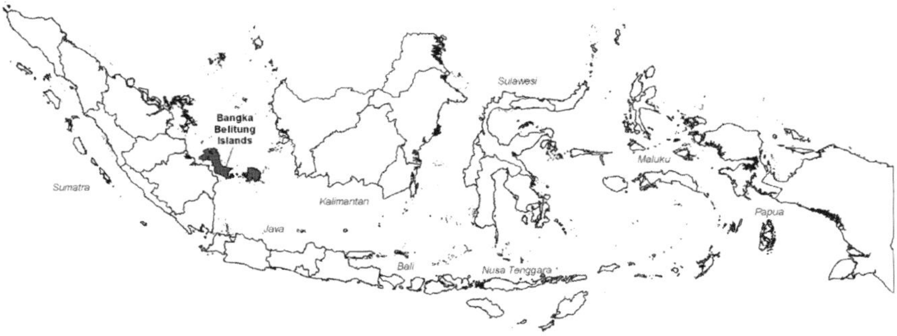

Source: ACI.

5.4.1 Economic Conditions

Bangka Belitung Islands' nominal GRDP grew by 6.74 percent in 2016 and is expected to continue growing by 7.49 percent in 2017 to reach Rp69.97 trillion. Throughout 2015–2017, the province's economic sector is dominated by the (1) agriculture, forestry and fishery, (2) processing industry as well as (3) wholesale and retail, including vehicle repairs sectors. All three sectors have also continued to increase in the same period.

The province's trade balance registered a surplus of US$1.16 billion at the end of 2016. However, there were fluctuations throughout the year driven by the volatility in exports. Exports are dominated by (i) lead, (ii) oil and gas, (iii) crude palm oil (CPO) as well as (iv) pepper. Meanwhile, Bangka Belitung's imports rose by 164.60 percent between 2015 and 2016. The oil and gas sector also dominates the province's imports, followed by (i) machinery and mechanical appliances, (ii) ships, boats and floating structures as well as (iii) electrical machinery and equipment.

As of the third quarter of 2017, Bangka Belitung province received Rp836.88 billion of investment, a majority of which was FDI (81.18 percent).

5.4.2 Social Conditions and Development

Bangka Belitung's HDI saw an improvement of 0.50 point to reach 69.55 in 2016. This places the province at the "average" category. Improvements were observed across all indicators of HDI: life expectancy improved by 0.04 years to 69.92, mean years of schooling increased by 0.16 years to reach 7.62 while Gross National Income (GNI) per capita (2012) saw an improvement of Rp179,000 to reach Rp11.96 million in 2016.

The province's y-o-y poverty rate has also improved. In 2015, it stood at 5.40 percent. This number fell to 5.22 percent and 5.20 percent in 2016 and 2017 respectively.

Industrial relations in Bangka Belitung, however, have encountered a few setbacks in the past years. Most notably, there were backlashes from the province's Confederation of All Indonesian Workers' Union (KSPSI) when the governor announced that the 2018 provincial minimum wage (UMP) would only be raised by 3.80 percent — lower than the 8.71 percent stipulated under Government Regulation (PP) No. 78/2015. After threats of mass demonstration, the governor relented and increased the UMP accordingly.

5.4.3 Provincial Government Policies

In 2016, a total of 42 Provincial Regulations (Perda) in Bangka Belitung were revoked by President Joko Widodo, as they are deemed to hinder investments and impact the community negatively. Some of these include Perda No. 2/2016 on the ban of procurement, distribution and sale of alcoholic beverages in the capital city Pangkal Pinang as well as Perda No. 14/2011 on the control and surveillance of alcoholic beverages.

Meanwhile, the Tanjung Kelayang Beach in Belitung Island has been designated as one of Indonesia's SEZs for tourism.

In 2017, the governor held a coordination meeting (Rakor) with all regents and mayors in the Bangka Belitung province, with the theme "one vision, one mission for growth and prosperity of Bangka Belitung archipelago". The meeting culminated in a total of 10 agreements, which range from the formation of a pepper/primary commodity cooperative to village aids in the form of pepper seeds and cattle.

Key Economic Indicators, 2015

Land Area (km²)	16,424
Population	
Total Population	1,372,800
Urban Population (%)	52.50
Poverty Rate (%)	4.83
Labour Force	665,842
Labour Force Participation Rate (%)	48.50
Gross Regional Domestic Products (GRDP) — 2010 prices	Rupiah (million)
GRDP	45,961,460
GRDP (non-minerals)	39,497,000
GRDP per Capita	33.48
GRDP per Capita (non-minerals)	28.77
Economic Composition	% of GRDP
Primary Sector	33.10
Secondary Sector	30.91
Tertiary Sector	35.99
Trade — 2010 prices	Rupiah (million)
Exports	13,536,315
Imports	480,770
Top-3 exports: tin and articles thereof; animal or vegetable fats and oils, miscellaneous chemical products	
Top-3 imports: mineral fuels; machinery and mechanical appliances; ships, boats and floating structures	
Infrastructure	
Paved Roads (km)	3,266
Domestic Air Traffic (Passengers)	2,350,271
International Air Traffic (Passengers)	0
Domestic Cargo at Seaport (Tons)	7,397,176
International Cargo at Seaport (Tons)	416,459

Source: BPS Indonesia compiled by ACI.

5.4.4 Local Political Scene

Bangka Belitung Islands recently held its local elections (Pilkada) in 2017. Former Governor Rustam Effendi, who led the province from 2013 to 2017, reran for election with Muhammad Irwansyah in 2017. Backed by the Indonesian Democratic Party of Struggle (PDIP), the pair lost to Erzaldi Rosman Djohan by a large margin of 16.24 percent. The latter, who was paired with Deputy Governor Abdul Fatah, won with 38.94 percent of the votes. They were backed by the Great Indonesia Movement Party (Gerindra), the National Democrat Party (Nasdem) as well as the National Awakening Party (PKB).

The Regional People's Representative Council (DPRD) of Bangka Belitung Islands consists of 45 representatives who are predominantly from PDIP (11), the Party of the Functional Group (Golkar) (7), the United Development Party (PPP) (6) as well as Gerindra (5). They were elected during the 2014 general elections (Pemilu).

5.5 Commentary on Recent Developments in Banten, 2015–2017

By: Imam Abu Hanifah and Fatah Sulaiman
Universitas Sultan Ageng Tirtayasa

Province Location

Source: ACI.

5.5.1 Economic Conditions

Banten's economic growth in the fourth quarter of 2016 grew by 5.53 percent y-o-y, which is not strong enough to boost overall economic growth. This slowdown is largely driven by global economic instability which has put pressure on several sectors in the province, particularly the processing industry, which had since relied on domestic demand. Growth in 2017 is estimated to accelerate in the range of 5.20–5.60 percent (y-o-y). The higher expected growth rate corresponds to the optimism of global and national economic recovery, which also increases potential for higher investments.

Economic conditions in major trading partners, however, were improving (International Monetary Fund–World Economic Forum 2016; 2017). As a result, foreign demand for Banten's products and services, which had initially declined, eventually increased. This is observed by the rise in exports from US$9.05 billion in 2015 to US$9.33 billion in 2016. Despite this, export performance is still expected to face limited growth as improvements to the global economy are taking place gradually.

5.5.2 Social Conditions and Development

The poverty rate in Banten, which ranged from five to seven percent, is far below the national rate of over 11 percent. Banten's Gini ratio, however, is close to the national average at around 0.40 in 2013. This implies that efforts have been made to reduce inequality to match the national standard. The drop in Banten's poverty rate is a result of efforts, such as the provision of direct cash transfer (BLT), rice subsidy programme (Raskin), and the Mandiri nationwide community programme (PNPM).

The falling poverty rate parallels the decrease in overt unemployment rate (International Monetary Fund–World Economic Forum 2016; 2017). In addition to the rise in income per capita, labour force participation rate also increased from 62.24 percent in August 2015 to 63.66 percent in August 2016. Banten's total workforce also increased by 0.26 million to 5.59 million in 2016.

There is also an increase in the percentage of population with secondary-level education, largely due to policy efforts to expand access to such education by adding new schools and classrooms as well as expanding the teaching workforce.

5.5.3 Provincial Government Policies

Several policies were proposed for the period of 2009–2016: (i) easing the approval of investment permits for labour-intensive industries in order to provide greater employment opportunities for the poor; (ii) establishing vocational and skills training centres (BLK) to reduce unemployment and poverty, especially in anticipation of the migration of workers who lack competent skills from other parts of Indonesia; (iii) requiring state-owned and private companies to establish sustainable strategic partnership with the provincial government through the corporate social responsibility (CSR) programmes, such as the partnership and environment development programme (PKBL); and (iv) resuming poverty reduction programmes, such as the National Health Insurance for the Poor and Near Poor (Jamkesmas), Raskin, the conditional cash transfer programme (PKH), scholarship for the poor as well as PNPM Mandiri in order to help and motivate the poor.

Key Economic Indicators, 2015

Land Area (km^2)	9,663
Population	
Total Population	11,955,200
Urban Population (%)	67.70
Poverty Rate (%)	5.75
Labour Force	5,334,843
Labour Force Participation Rate (%)	44.62
Gross Regional Domestic Products (GRDP) — 2010 prices	Rupiah (million)
GRDP	368,216,550
GRDP (non-minerals)	364,763,000
GRDP per Capita	30.80
GRDP per Capita (non-minerals)	30.51
Economic Composition	% of GRDP
Primary Sector	6.38
Secondary Sector	47.20
Tertiary Sector	46.42
Trade — 2010 prices	Rupiah (million)
Exports	9,466,919
Imports	96,773,021
Top-3 exports: footwear, gaiters, articles thereof; iron and steel; rubber and articles thereof	
Top-3 imports: organic chemicals; mineral fuels and oils and product of their distillation; sugar and sugar confectionery	
Infrastructure	
Paved Roads (km)	5,502
Domestic Air Traffic (Passengers)	41,889,868
International Air Traffic (Passengers)	12,401,498
Domestic Cargo at Seaport (Tons)	40,299,333
International Cargo at Seaport (Tons)	22,288,453

Source: BPS Indonesia compiled by ACI.

5.5.4 Local Political Scene

On May 2017, Banten elected Governor Wahidin Halim and Vice Governor Andika Hazrumy. Their vision for the province is a Banten that is "developed, independent, competitive, prosperous and ethical."

There are two categories of development targets for governance and reform, namely quality of public service and percentage of government institutions with good accountability.

The Provincial Democracy Index in Banten has shown an increasing trend since its decline in 2010 and 2012. Its level of democracy is evaluated as "moderate", similar to the levels obtained by provinces of DKI Jakarta, DI Yogyakarta, West Kalimantan and North Sulawesi.

In 2017, the Audit Board of Indonesia (BPK) provides the audit opinion of Normal without Exception (WTP) on the preliminary unaudited provincial government financial report (LKPD) of Banten for the fiscal year of 2016.

5.6 Commentary on Recent Developments in Bengkulu, 2015–2017

By: Lizar Alfansi and Ferry Tema Atmaja
Universitas Bengkulu

Province Location

Source: ACI.

5.6.1 Economic Conditions

The province's nominal GRDP grew from Rp45.39 trillion in 2014 to Rp55.4 trillion in 2016. However, its overall economy slowed from 5.80 percent growth rate in 2014 to 5.13 percent in 2015, before bouncing back to 5.30 percent in 2016. Growth, however, is still above the national level. Bengkulu's economic sector in 2016 was dominated by agriculture, forestry, and fishery (29.55 percent), followed by trade (14.20 percent). Despite the former's predominant share, its contribution has been decreasing since 2011.

Exports are dominated by crude oil, coal and rubber. Hence, as global commodity prices plummeted, Bengkulu's export values also dropped. In 2014, exports reached a value of US$241 million, but achieved only US$158 million in 2016. Bengkulu is expecting a better performance in 2017, with an export value that is already reaching US$124 million in May. With little reliance on imports, its import value continues to drop over the years.

The investment sector is promising, with an increase in both FDI and DDI from 2014 to 2016. In 2016, DDI reached a value of Rp949 billion, while FDI reached a value of US$56 million.

5.6.2 Social Conditions and Development

Social conditions in Bengkulu have been stable in all aspects. HDI increased from 68.06 in 2014 to 69.33 in 2016 — on track to reach the 'high' category by national standards. Life expectancy at birth increased from 68.37 years in 2014 to 68.56 years in 2016, while the mean years of schooling surged from 8.28 in 2014 to 8.37 in 2016. Poverty rate in Bengkulu has, however, fluctuated in the last three years. Between 2014 and 2015, it increased from 17.48 percent to 17.88 percent, but dropped to 17.32 percent (328,600 individuals) in 2016.

Overt unemployment rate in Bengkulu has fluctuated from 3.21 percent in 2015 to 3.84 percent and 2.81 percent in 2016 and 2017 respectively. The sharp decline in 2017 is due to an increase in employment in primary and secondary sectors. In contrast, employment in the tertiary sector has declined.

In terms of social security, local police has been facing challenges, as reflected in their case completion rate which fell from 55.00 percent in 2014 to 44.76 percent in 2015. Other than these, there are no chronic social conflicts in Bengkulu. In fact, social harmony is being maintained carefully by local leaders, the police and religious leaders.

5.6.3 Provincial Government Policies

In 2015, Bengkulu held its provincial election which was won by Ridwan Mukti and Rohidin Mersyah. They are to govern Bengkulu from 2015 to 2020. With a key campaign mandate to combat high poverty caused by inaccessibility, the two newly elected leaders had placed infrastructure building, which includes electricity, water, bridge, road and port, as their priority.

They also utilise information and technology to ease investment processes. The province supports the 'one window' policy for investment initiated by the national government. They have worked to ensure that the online platform for investors to see regulations, submit permits for businesses and log complaints remains active and responsive. As a result, investments in Bengkulu — both in terms of values and realised projects — surged from 2015 to 2016.

Other poverty-combating programmes include economic development through four superior products: agro-maritime, tourism, mining and energy. There is also potential to improve the province's natural resources potentials, such as coal, gold, iron sand and geothermal energy.

Key Economic Indicators, 2015

Land Area (km²)	19,919
Population	
Total Population	1,874,900
Urban Population (%)	31.70
Poverty Rate (%)	17.16
Labour Force	951,007
Labour Force Participation Rate (%)	50.72
Gross Regional Domestic Products (GRDP) — 2010 prices	Rupiah (million)
GRDP	38,066,010
GRDP (non-minerals)	36,607,000
GRDP per Capita	20.30
GRDP per Capita (non-minerals)	19.52
Economic Composition	% of GRDP
Primary Sector	33.25
Secondary Sector	10.99
Tertiary Sector	55.77
Trade — 2010 prices	Rupiah (million)
Exports	768,038
Imports	66,980
Top-3 exports: coal; rubber and articles of rubber; crude palm oil	
Top-3 imports: cement; asphalt; machinery and mechanical appliances	
Infrastructure	
Paved Roads (km)	5,404
Domestic Air Traffic (Passengers)	831,701
International Air Traffic (Passengers)	0
Domestic Cargo at Seaport (Tons)	1,187,198
International Cargo at Seaport (Tons)	885,106

Source: BPS Indonesia compiled by ACI.

5.6.4 Local Political Scene

The elected governors and deputy governors, Ridwan Mukti–Rohidin Mersyah, were backed by the Party of the Functional Group (Golkar) and a coalition of seven other parties. They won the election with 57.37 percent of total votes. Their competitor, Sultan Najamudin-Mujiono, were backed by the Democrat party and the Indonesian Democratic Party of Struggle (PDIP).

With a total of 45 seats, the Regional People's Representative Council (DPRD), PDIP leads with a slight margin of seven seats, followed by the Democrat party with six as well as the National Mandate Party (PAN), Golkar, and the Great Indonesia Movement Party (Gerindra), each with four seats. Other parties with even fewer seats must coalesce with bigger parties to voice their aspirations.

5.7 Commentary on Recent Developments in Central Java, 2015–2017

By: Iedo Radityo
Asia Competitiveness Institute

Province Location

Source: ACI.

5.7.1 Economic Conditions

Central Java's economy growth was at 5.47 percent in 2015 and 5.28 percent in 2016. The mining and quarrying as well as business activities sectors achieved the highest growth in 2016 at 18.73 percent and 10.62 percent respectively. However, the impact is relatively small for the entire economy as the major economic sectors are manufacturing (34.82 percent) as well as wholesale and retail, including vehicle repairs (13.39 percent).

The yarn and textile industries were the dominant export commodities in both 2015 and 2016, followed by wood, cork and straw. Meanwhile, the most imported commodities were mostly fuel oil as well as yarn and textile industries. Exports barely grew while imports contracted during the same period.

DDI in Central Java increased almost three times between 2015 and 2016, with basic chemical, chemical goods and pharmacy industry seizing the major percentage of growth. FDI, in contrast, slightly declined in the same period.

5.7.2 Social Conditions and Development

In 2016, Central Java's HDI increased by 0.49 points to 69.98, which was below the national HDI. Poverty rate also improved albeit at a slower rate from 13.58 percent in 2015 to 13.19 percent in 2016. Meanwhile, labour force participation rate went down from 67.86 percent in 2015 to 67.15 percent in 2016 while the employment rate shrank from 4.99 percent to 4.63 percent in the same period.

Additionally, education, health and social security indicators have also improved. For instance, net enrolment rates for all school levels increased from 2015 to 2016. Additional hospitals and clinics were opened, while more Central Java residents received coverage in the social security program for health.

The general development of socio-economic conditions, however, was shadowed by several controversies as the expedited infrastructure projects and key economic sites are rejected. These include the planned construction of the cement factory in Rembang, the Batang electric steam power plant (PLTU). There are also conundrums over land acquisition for these projects as well as illegal mining issues.

5.7.3 Provincial Government Policies

The landmark infrastructure project in Central Java has been the construction of the Trans-Java toll road. With the opening of the Cipali section in West Java in 2015, Jakarta and Central Java are now officially connected through toll road. Development focus has now shifted to sections in Central Java such as Pejagan-Pemalang and Semarang-Solo.

Aside from the toll road, the Ahmad Yani airport in Semarang and the Jenderal Soedirman airport in Purbalingga have been undergoing expansion. The Batang PLTU has also acquired most of the required land, and President Joko Widodo had inaugurated its construction in August 2015.

The 2013–2018 Central Java Provincial Medium-Term Development Planning (RPJMD) has acknowledged Central Java's geo-strategic position and ample human resources as its strengths, while listing demographic issues, inequality and bureaucracy as its weaknesses.

Key Economic Indicators, 2015

Land Area (km²)	32,801
Population	
Total Population	33,774,100
Urban Population (%)	48.40
Poverty Rate (%)	13.32
Labour Force	17,298,925
Labour Force Participation Rate (%)	51.22
Gross Regional Domestic Products (GRDP) — 2010 prices	Rupiah (million)
GRDP	806,775,360
GRDP (non-minerals)	741,039,000
GRDP per Capita	23.89
GRDP per Capita (non-minerals)	21.94
Economic Composition	% of GRDP
Primary Sector	16.10
Secondary Sector	45.53
Tertiary Sector	38.37
Trade — 2010 prices	Rupiah (million)
Exports	55,065,275
Imports	110,022,538
Top-3 exports: apparel and clothing accessories, not knitted or crocheted; wood and articles of wood; furniture	
Top-3 imports: mineral fuels; aircraft and parts thereof; cotton	
Infrastructure	
Paved Roads (km)	18,258
Domestic Air Traffic (Passengers)	5,018,339
International Air Traffic (Passengers)	202,082
Domestic Cargo at Seaport (Tons)	23,265,076
International Cargo at Seaport (Tons)	7,877,986

Source: BPS Indonesia compiled by ACI.

5.7.4 Local Political Scene

Central Java has continuously been the mainstay base for the Indonesian Democratic Party of Struggle (PDIP). The incumbent governor, Ganjar Pranowo, was elected in 2013 with PDIP as his sole supporting party. Yet, Ganjar Pranowo managed to seize 48.82 percent of the votes. He is paired with Heru Sudjatmoko who was previously the Regent of Purbalingga.

The dominant grip of PDIP is mirrored as well within the Regional People's Representative Council (DPRD) as it seizes 31 percent out of 100 seats, followed by the National Awakening Party (PKB) (13 percent), the Great Indonesia Movement Party (Gerindra) (11 percent), the Prosperous Justice Party (PKS) (10 percent), the Party of the Functional Group (Golkar) (10 percent), the Democrat party (nine percent), the United Development Party (PPP) (nine percent) as well as the National Mandate Party (PAN) (eight percent). The next provincial election will take place on 27 June 2018, with PDIP announcing that it is open for coalition.

5.8 Commentary on Recent Developments in Central Kalimantan, 2015–2017

By: Miar Piter
Universitas Palangka Raya

Province Location

Source: ACI.

5.8.1 Economic Conditions

Central Kalimantan's economy continues to grow at 6.36 percent and 7.01 percent in 2016 and 2017 respectively. Growth primarily comes from the mining and quarrying sector, which contributed 1.21 percent of the province's GRDP in 2016. The agricultural sector remains as the backbone of Central Kalimantan's economy, which indicates the province's reliance towards natural resources.

Most consumer goods are used mainly for physical investments (45.5 percent) and household consumption (42.06 percent). Exports hold a vital function for Central Kalimantan as 44.00 percent of all products produced within the region would eventually be exported outside the province. The province, however, heavily relies on imports as 50 percent of total products consumed by the locals are imported.

The prospects of investments in Central Kalimantan appear to be promising, with an increase of investments by 4.27 percent in 2016. Crop plants became the biggest investment target in 2016. However, there is substantial difference between FDI and DDI performance. FDI has shown a declining trend while DDI has increased by sixfold in 2016.

5.8.2 Social Conditions and Development

Social conditions in Central Kalimantan have been stable in recent years. HDI in the province continued to show positive trends between 2012 and 2016, reaching 69.30 in 2016 to attain the middle level. One of the indicators that has seen improvements is life expectancy, which reached 70 years in 2016. The province's infant mortality rate had also decreased to 34 infants per 1,000 births. Improvements in both healthcare-related indicators were made possible through the rise in the quality of service and infrastructure in the healthcare sector.

Central Kalimantan's poverty rate has also improved to reach 5.36 percent in 2016.

One pertinent problem in Central Kalimantan is the uneven distribution of the province's population, particularly in rural areas. The overall population density in Central Kalimantan is only 17.00 people per square kilometre. This is because while Central Kalimantan has a vast land area of 153,565 square kilometres, it only has a small population of 2.50 million people residing in the province.

5.8.3 Provincial Government Policies

Within the past two years, the elected governor and deputy governor have enacted changes that are in line with their vision and mission of enhancing the welfare of the people. The government has specifically put in efforts to control economic development and manage of the province's natural resources in order to increase its own-source Revenue (PDA).

One of the policies that the government has introduced pertains to the issuance of permits for plantation and mining. This programme is in line with the government's plan to create a sustainable management and utilisation of natural resources in Central Kalimantan that conforms to the provincial spatial plan (RTRWP).

The governor has requested the 2016–2010 Construction Service Development Board (LPJK) of Central Kalimantan to innovate so that the province's construction sector can become competitive at the national level.

Key Economic Indicators, 2015

Land Area (km²)	153,565
Population	
Total Population	2,495,000
Urban Population (%)	36.60
Poverty Rate (%)	5.91
Labour Force	1,272,461
Labour Force Participation Rate (%)	51.00
Gross Regional Domestic Products (GRDP) — 2010 prices	Rupiah (million)
GRDP	78,890,970
GRDP (non-minerals)	66,236,000
GRDP per Capita	31.62
GRDP per Capita (non-minerals)	26.55
Economic Composition	% of GRDP
Primary Sector	37.51
Secondary Sector	24.08
Tertiary Sector	38.41
Trade — 2010 prices	Rupiah (million)
Exports	4,577,677
Imports	701,535
Top-3 exports: fuel minerals; animal fats and vegetable oils; wood and wood products	
Top-3 imports: machinery and mechanical appliances; mineral fuels; articles of iron and steel	
Infrastructure	
Paved Roads (km)	5,840
Domestic Air Traffic (Passengers)	1,352,483
International Air Traffic (Passengers)	0
Domestic Cargo at Seaport (Tons)	10,163,253
International Cargo at Seaport (Tons)	1,691,239

Source: BPS Indonesia compiled by ACI.

5.8.4 Local Political Scene

Central Kalimantan province is led by the winner of the 2016 local election (Pilkada), Governor Sugianto Sabran and Deputy Governor Habib H Said Ismail. With 51.52 percent of total votes, the pair was backed by a coalition of parties consisting of the Great Indonesia Movement Party (Gerindra), Party of the Functional Group (Golkar), Democrat Party, National Mandate Party (PAN), National Awakening Party (PKB) and United Development Party (PPP).

The province's Regional People's Representative Council (DPRD) has a total of 45 seats. The party with the most number of seats (11), however, is not part of the coalition supporting the incumbent governor: the Indonesian Democratic Party of Struggle (PDIP). Meanwhile, Gerindra occupies six seats, while the National Democratic Party (Nasdem), Golkar, PAN and Democrat party occupy five seats each. The dynamic between the provincial government and DPRD has generally been constructive.

5.9 Commentary on Recent Developments in Central Sulawesi, 2015–2017

By: Noudhy Valdryno
Asia Competitiveness Institute

Province Location

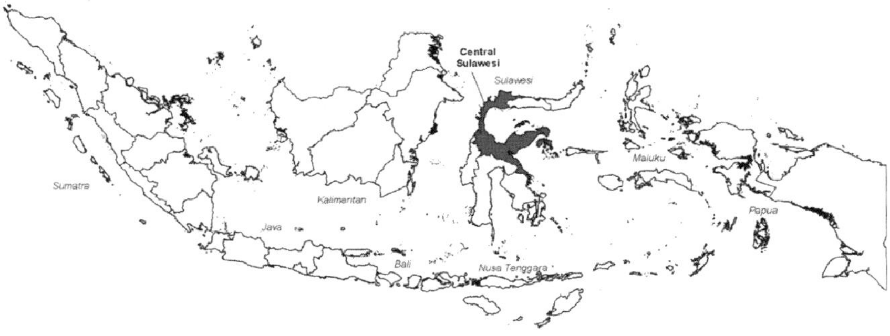

Source: ACI.

5.9.1 Economic Conditions

Central Sulawesi's economy slowed in 2017, as shown by a declining growth rate from 9.98 percent in 2016 to 7.14 percent in 2017. However, its nominal GRDP continues to grow from Rp120.33 trillion to Rp134.24 trillion in the same period. Nonetheless, Central Sulawesi is still one of the fastest growing provinces in Indonesia. The economy is dominated by three key activities, namely mining (15.18 percent), manufacturing (11.28 percent) as well as electricity and gas (9.17 percent).

Central Sulawesi's exports are dominated by mineral fuels as well as mining and animal oils, supported by an emerging fishery sector. In November 2017, exports reached US$372.91 million — an increase of 30.58 percent from the previous month, while imports reached US$118.08 million. Between January and October 2017, the province's import value was US$1.091 million.

Investment in Central Sulawesi is also promising. In 2017, realised FDI reached US$282 million with 70 ongoing projects while DDI reached US$496 million with 32 projects.

5.9.2 Social Conditions and Development

Social conditions in Central Sulawesi are improving in all aspects. HDI consistently increased from 66.43 in 2014 to 67.47 in 2016. It is on track to fall under the 'high' category by national standards. According to the latest data, Central Sulawesi's life expectancy rate is 67.31. Meanwhile, the mean years of schooling reached 8.12 years in 2016.

On the other hand, poverty rate in Central Sulawesi had experienced fluctuation in the last four years, albeit with an overall worsening trend. In 2013, there were 406,970 people living under poverty in the province, which is equivalent to 14.67 percent of the population. In 2017, this number has increased to 417,870, which is equivalent to 14.14 percent. The rise in poverty is also reflected in the increase in crime rate; in Palu city alone, there were 800 drugs cases and more than 40 robbery cases in 2017.

5.9.3 Provincial Government Policies

In 2015, Central Sulawesi held a local election (Pilkada) which was won by Longki Djanggola and Sudarto. They are to govern Central Sulawesi from 2015 to 2020. Governor Longki's campaign message was to solve social issues such as poverty, with key programmes such as infrastructure building and economic growth. This is considered successful as Central Sulawesi was able to reach 9.98 percent growth rate in 2016 — the highest in the nation.

The pair also utilised information and technology for job creation. As a result, the province's unemployment rate is way below the national rate at 3.26 percent. In 2017, Governor Longki and his administration received the Anugerah Pangripta Nusantara award, which acknowledged them for having achieved the best planning and most effective implementation of key programmes.

Key Economic Indicators, 2015

Land Area (km²)	61,841
Population	
Total Population	2,876,700
Urban Population (%)	27.20
Poverty Rate (%)	14.07
Labour Force	1,384,235
Labour Force Participation Rate (%)	48.12
Gross Regional Domestic Products (GRDP) — 2010 prices	Rupiah (million)
GRDP	82,803,200
GRDP (non-minerals)	72,330,000
GRDP per Capita	28.78
GRDP per Capita (non-minerals)	25.14
Economic Composition	% of GRDP
Primary Sector	42.90
Secondary Sector	22.84
Tertiary Sector	34.26
Trade — 2010 prices	Rupiah (million)
Exports	7,935,976
Imports	7,011,695
Top-3 exports: crude oil; iron and steel; animal and vegetable oil and fats	
Top-3 imports: machinery and mechanical appliances; electrical machinery and equipment; crude oil	
Infrastructure	
Paved Roads (km)	7,023
Domestic Air Traffic (Passengers)	1,327,555
International Air Traffic (Passengers)	0
Domestic Cargo at Seaport (Tons)	5,936,953
International Cargo at Seaport (Tons)	3,406,040

Source: BPS Indonesia compiled by ACI.

5.9.4 Local Political Scene

In the 2015 election, Governor Longki and his deputy Sudarto were supported by four parties: the Great Indonesia Movement Party (Gerindra), the Crescent Star Party (PBB), the National Awakening Party (PKB) as well as the National Mandate Party (PAN). They won with 54.50 percent of the votes, beating Rusdi Mastura–Ihwan Datu Adam who were backed by the Party of the Functional Group (Golkar), the People's Conscience Party (Hanura) and the Indonesian Justice and Unity Party (PKPI).

As for the province's Regional People's Representative Council (DPRD), the party is dominated by a party that did not contest in the 2015 Pilkada: the Indonesian Democratic Party of Struggle (PDIP), which occupies 16 out of 45 seats. The remaining seats are occupied by representatives from Golkar (7), Gerindra (6), the Democrat Party (6), PAN (3), the Prosperous Justice Party (PKS) (3) and PKB (3). The speaker of the parliament is Aminuddin Ponulele from Golkar.

5.10 Commentary on Recent Developments in DI Yogyakarta, 2015–2017

By: Vinie Puspaningrum and Poppy S. Winanti
Universitas Gadjah Mada

Province Location

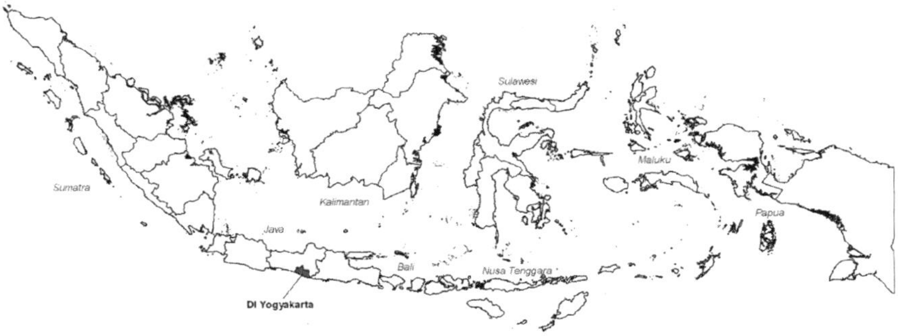

Source: ACI.

5.10.1 Economic Conditions

DI Yogyakarta's GRDP grows by 0.17 percent from 2015 to 2017, spurred by an increase in purchasing power as well as a more conducive global economy (Bank Indonesia 2017, 22). The key sector behind this growth is household consumption, which makes up 67.60 percent of GRDP in 2016 (BPS 2017, 57). However, the positive development of GRDP is not accompanied by a reduction in imports. In fact, cumulative imports in the province have increased by 54.99 percent from January to May 2017 (BPS 2017, 1).

The Central Bureau of Statistics (BPS) has reported that exports have increased by 19.90 percent (2017, 2). Three key commodities for exports in May 2017 are apparel and clothing accessories, lamps and lighting fittings as well as articles of leather (*Ibid.*). This reflects a significant rise in the demand for goods made in the province.

Investments in DI Yogyakarta have also shown a positive trend. Investment credit has grown from 12.73 percent to 19.14 percent, while construction credit from 2.01 percent to 13.77 percent. Meanwhile, demand for construction materials has increased by 11.68 percent (Bank Indonesia 2017).

5.10.2 Social Conditions and Development

While the economic condition of the province has ameliorated, it has not been supplemented with improvements in social conditions. Although life expectancy in the province is high at 74.68 years in 2017, its net enrolment rate had fallen from 2015 to 2016. It had since stagnated for those under 16 years old, although the rate increased by 1.38 percent for those above 16 years old (BPS 2017; Dinas Pendidikan, Pemuda dan Olahraga 2017). Meanwhile, unemployment in DI Yogyakarta rose significantly by 3,000 people between 2016 and 2017, which reflects that current educational qualification still has not matched existing employment opportunities (*Ibid.*).

Economic improvements have also caused environmental damages. For instance, the construction of new hotels has dried up the community's well. A study by Mongabay (2016) has identified five districts with the highest risk and which have experienced significant water deficit: Gondokusuman, Margangsan, Mantrijeron, Jetis and Umbulharjo. A moratorium introduced in 2014 was unable to control such development as 17 hotels had already received permits to operate prior to 2014.

5.10.3 Provincial Government Policies

Within the past two years, the provincial government has released several provincial regulations (Perda) to support economic development. For instance, the government enacted Perda No. 3/2015 on the planning of tourism development the Yogyakarta city to target economic development around touristic areas. The government is also in the process of proposing a regulation pertaining to the development of the creative economy of the province, particularly in four primary sectors: arts, crafts, film and fashion (Tribun Jogja 2017).

To ensure a balanced development, the government has also passed Perda No. 2/2017 on the protection of women and children who are victims of violence. This regulation provides women and children with the opportunity to grow and be protected by the government, such that development is balanced throughout all aspects.

Key Economic Indicators, 2015

Land Area (km^2)	3,133
Population	
Total Population	3,679,200
Urban Population (%)	70.50
Poverty Rate (%)	13.16
Labour Force	1,971,463
Labour Force Participation Rate (%)	53.58
Gross Regional Domestic Products (GRDP) — 2010 prices	Rupiah (million)
GRDP	83,474,440
GRDP (non-minerals)	83,003,000
GRDP per Capita	22.69
GRDP per Capita (non-minerals)	22.56
Economic Composition	% of GRDP
Primary Sector	9.75
Secondary Sector	22.44
Tertiary Sector	67.81
Trade — 2010 prices	Rupiah (million)
Exports	116,453
Imports	22,706
Top-3 exports: apparel and clothing accessories; lamp and lighting fittings; articles of leather	
Top-3 imports textile fabrics; oil seeds; printed books and other products of the printing industry	
Infrastructure	
Paved Roads (km)	3,094
Domestic Air Traffic (Passengers)	6,018,270
International Air Traffic (Passengers)	362,066
Domestic Cargo at Seaport (Tons)	0
International Cargo at Seaport (Tons)	0

Source: BPS Indonesia compiled by ACI.

5.10.4 Local Political Scene

In February 2017, Haryadi Suyuti and Heroe Poerwadi were elected as Mayor and Deputy Mayor of Yogyakarta while Hasto Wardoyo and Sutedjo were elected as Regent and Deputy Regent of Kulon Progo Regency (DPRD Kota Yogyakarta 2017; KPU 2017). The former won the election by a slight margin of 0.60 percent while the latter by a much larger margin of 71.24 percent (KPU 2017).

Prevailing issues during the election include the issue of intolerance, which has been on the rise since 2012 (Tempo 2017). In Kulon Progo, the elections supervisory committee found a minor violation of technical issues such as the inaccuracy of voter data as well as non-compliance in procedures.

Based on the general elections (Pemilu) in 2014, there are seven parties in the province's Regional People's Representative Council (DPRD). The Indonesian Democratic Party of Struggle (PDIP) dominates the seats with 34.69 percent (E-Parlemen DPRD DIY 2017). However, there is no significant political friction given the lack of strong opposition in DPRD.

5.11 Commentary on Recent Developments in DKI Jakarta, 2015–2017

By: Fathony Rahman
Universitas Prasetiya Mulya

Province Location

Source: ACI.

5.11.1 Economic Conditions

DKI Jakarta registered higher economic growth than the national level between 2015 and 2017. The high y-o-y GRDP growth rate in the second trimester of 2017 was pushed by the information and communication as well as financial services sectors (BPS 2017).

Growth primarily comes from the information and communications sector (11.81 percent), followed by other services (9.12 percent) and transportation and storage (9.09 percent), driven by improvements in internet penetration rate, social media use, e-commerce as well as online transaction. The growth in the electricity and gas provision sector, however, declined by 10.45 percent.

Both domestic and foreign investment projects increased in 2016 by 46.52 percent and 51.27 percent respectively, although their investment values declined by 21.25 percent and 6.11 percent each.

One major development projects in Jakarta is the Mass Rapid Transit (MRT) project which is hoped to solve Jakarta's traffic problem. The first phase of the project was financed by the Japan International Cooperation Agency (JICA) and was valued at around Rp20 billion.

5.11.2 Social Conditions and Development

There was a slight increase in DKI Jakarta's life expectancy from 72.43 in 2015 to 72.49 in 2016. Meanwhile, net enrolment rate has also improved across all age groups. The improvement in net enrolment rate has had a positive impact on overt unemployment rate (Mincer 1991). This is reflected in the decline in Jakarta's y-o-y overt unemployment rate between the first trimesters of 2016 and 2017 from 31.04 percent to 7.06 percent.

As a result of all the above, DKI Jakarta's HDI has continuously improved and scored above the national level between 2014 and 2016. HDI also rose from 78.39 in 2014 to 79.60 in 2016.

Despite the enhancements in these social indicators, there have been social issues surfacing in recent years that may threaten Jakarta's future development. The blasphemy case of former DKI Jakarta governor, Basuki Tjahaja Purnama "Ahok" in 2016, for instance, has caused social frictions between ethnicities and religions which have lasted until today. If left unattended, this will threaten Jakarta's future development.

5.11.3 Provincial Government Policies

One of the most beneficial government policies that has been enacted is the improvement in the bureaucracy of provincial governments through key programmes such as the One-Stop Integrated Service Agency (BPTSP) and the Smart City application. The latter increases the quality of public service as it allows citizens to report unsatisfactory experiences. The former, on the other hand, integrates all matters pertaining to permits and non-permits, thus improving the duration and flow of service.

Jakarta's primary problems are that of traffic and flooding. The provincial government has tried to improve transportation problems through the addition of new roads and by improving and adding public transportation services such as MRT and Light Rail Transit (LRT). As for flood management, the provincial government has constructed dams, normalised rivers as well as reclaimed the northern part of Jakarta.

Key Economic Indicators, 2015

Land Area (km^2)	664
Population	
Total Population	10,177,900
Urban Population (%)	100.00
Poverty Rate (%)	3.61
Labour Force	5,092,219
Labour Force Participation Rate (%)	50.03
Gross Regional Domestic Products (GRDP) — 2010 prices	Rupiah (million)
GRDP	1,454,345,820
GRDP (non-minerals)	1,451,336,000
GRDP per Capita	142.89
GRDP per Capita (non-minerals)	142.60
Economic Composition	% of GRDP
Primary Sector	0.30
Secondary Sector	26.62
Tertiary Sector	73.08
Trade — 2010 prices	Rupiah (million)
Exports	468,599,553
Imports	718,519,973
Top-3 exports: fish and crustacean; animal or vegetable fats and oil; cocoa and cocoa preparations	
Top-3 imports: machinery and mechanical appliances; electrical machinery and equipment; vehicles and accessories	
Infrastructure	
Paved Roads (km)	4,423
Domestic Air Traffic (Passengers)	2,955,332
International Air Traffic (Passengers)	103,802
Domestic Cargo at Seaport (Tons)	32,421,130
International Cargo at Seaport (Tons)	19,722,668

Source: BPS Indonesia compiled by ACI.

5.11.4 Local Political Scene

DKI Jakarta has recently concluded its provincial election in 2017. The elected leaders are Anies Baswedan and Sandiaga Uno, supported by the Great Indonesia Movement Party (Gerindra), the Prosperous Justice Party (PKS) and the National Mandate Party (PAN).

Participation level in the election was high at 77.0 percent — close to the national target of 77.5 percent. The elected pair won with 58.00 percent of the vote. Their vision and mission are heavily focused on human development through humanist and protective leaders, prioritising community participation in development.

The Regional People's Representative Council (DPRD) seats are mostly occupied by the Indonesian Democratic Party of Struggle (PDIP) with 28 seats (26.4 percent), followed by Gerindra Party with 15 seats (14.1 percent). These two parties were a coalition supporting President Joko Widodo in the previous election, but have split in the 2017 election due to differences in political views.

5.12 Commentary on Recent Developments in East Java, 2015–2017

By: Dian Agustia, Rudi Purwono, M. Khoerul Mubin and Karima Mucha
Universitas Airlangga

Province Location

Source: ACI.

5.12.1 Economic Conditions

East Java remains to be the second largest contributor to Indonesia's GDP after DKI Jakarta. Its economic growth has always been above the national level, reaching 5.55 percent in 2016. The economy is projected to grow between 5.50 percent and 5.90 percent in 2017.

Growth in household consumption is driven by relatively stable food prices and consumer confidence index (ITK). Improvements in purchasing power should continue by raising economic activities and managing inflation.

Both FDI and DDI in East Java have increased along with the province's competitiveness level, which is ranked second behind DKI Jakarta. Investments have the capacity to boost micro, small and medium enterprises (MSME) and local potentials.

Export performance is dampened by a demand slowdown from trading partners, such as China, Japan and the United States. As imported raw materials are still largely sought after by industries, maintaining stable exchange rate remains necessary. Inter-provincial trade also develops and adds value to the supply chain among provinces in Indonesia.

5.12.2 Social Conditions and Development

East Java's overt unemployment rate fell from 4.30 percent in August 2015 to 4.10 percent in February 2017. Urban areas contribute more to unemployment compared to rural areas. Large enterprises and MSMEs continue to be developed to increase manpower absorption. To support this effort, the quality of human resource, especially that of skilled workers, is also improved.

Poverty rate fell by 0.43 percent from 12.28 in 2015 to 11.85 in 2016. This is achieved through poverty prevention and alleviation measures. Managing inflation, particularly in foodstuff, has also reduced the poverty line. Meanwhile, East Java's Gini ratio has improved in both cities and villages, falling to 0.396 in March 2017 from 0.402 a year before. Encouraging the growth of start-ups (MSMEs) is critical to reduce unemployment, poverty and Gini ratio.

Progress in quality of life is also observed with HDI increasing from 68.95 in 2015 to 69.76 in 2016. Development in the quality of life can be accelerated through the distribution of income and allocation of budget that supports education and health.

5.12.3 Provincial Government Policies

To strengthen competitiveness and achieve inclusive growth, the government has implemented several reforms. Firstly, it has expanded the production base of MSMEs and big enterprises by (i) developing human resource in the form of improved vocational education, (ii) creating product standardisation, (iii) providing infrastructure, and (iv) simplifying business permits to avoid a 'high cost economy'.

Secondly, as MSMEs are always constrained by capital, the government has adopted a competitive financing model that (i) provides a larger portion of bank lending and low interest rates to MSMEs and (ii) builds the demand power through loan agreements — a new scheme developed by Governor Soekarwo, where the government and Bank Jatim work to offer low interest rate loans for the development of primary industry in rural areas such that villages can overcome the problems of inflation, poverty and urbanisation.

Thirdly, market access is widened through the expansion of national supply chain (utilising its 26 trade offices throughout Indonesia) as well as the global supply chain (via overseas trade representative offices).

Fourth, the government seeks fiscal innovation and enhanced expenditure by optimising the roles of regional state-owned enterprises (BUMD) to invest on banking and bond markets to reduce reliance on APBD.

Key Economic Indicators, 2015

Land Area (km²)	47,800
Population	
Total Population	38,847,600
Urban Population (%)	51.10
Poverty Rate (%)	12.28
Labour Force	20,274,681
Labour Force Participation Rate (%)	52.19
Gross Regional Domestic Products (GRDP) — 2010 prices	Rupiah (million)
GRDP	1,331,394,990
GRDP (non-minerals)	1,264,681,000
GRDP per Capita	34.27
GRDP per Capita (non-minerals)	32.55
Economic Composition	% of GRDP
Primary Sector	17.02
Secondary Sector	39.04
Tertiary Sector	43.94
Trade — 2010 prices	Rupiah (million)
Exports	172,265,822
Imports	194,033,429
Top-3 exports: natural, cultured pearls or precious and semi-precious stones; animal or vegetable fats and oil; wood and products	
Top-3 imports: mineral fuels; mechanical machinery and equipment; articles of iron and steel	
Infrastructure	
Paved Roads (km)	32,378
Domestic Air Traffic (Passengers)	16,199,265
International Air Traffic (Passengers)	1,687,054
Domestic Cargo at Seaport (Tons)	49,286,034
International Cargo at Seaport (Tons)	19,818,454

Source: BPS Indonesia compiled by ACI.

5.12.4 Local Political Scene

Political stability in East Java is well maintained under the leadership of Governor Soekarwo. He is assessed by many parties to have good communication skills and is able to embrace all elements in maintaining calm and order in East Java. The governor and Regional People's Representative Council (DPRD) are always in "equal partnership that is critically constructive". The governor also regularly meets with labour activists. All these guarantee investors that business and labour conditions in East Java are conducive.

5.13 Commentary on Recent Developments in East Kalimantan, 2015–2017

By: Syarifah Hudayah and Felisitas Defung
Universitas Mulawarman

Province Location

Source: ACI.

5.13.1 Economic Conditions

East Kalimantan's economy between 2015 and 2017 has slowed down due to it being prone to global economic fluctuations. As a province that is export-oriented and commodity-reliant, the fall in global demand and price of oil and gas, coal and CPO have affected the economy negatively. The province's economy had even contracted, with a negative growth rate of 1.21 percent in 2015 and 0.38 percent in 2016.

Both exports and imports of East Kalimantan had fallen between 2015 and 2017. Oil and gas exports fell significantly from US$61.41 billion to US$3.78 billion in 2016 due to declining coal exports — the province's major export commodity (54.99 percent). Imports had similarly declined by 32.60 percent in 2016.

The economic slowdown has had a negative impact on investments, which have declined during the same period. DDI fell from Rp10.42 billion to Rp6.50 billion in 2016, while FDI fell from US$2.38 billion to US$1.17 billion in the same period.

East Kalimantan's overall economic growth since 2015 has been below the national level.

5.13.2 Social Conditions and Development

The province's HDI has been increasing in the past seven years. In 2016, the province's HDI rose by 3.28 points to 74.59 relative to 2010, with improvements across all indicators. Life expectancy also improved from 72.89 to 73.68 in 2016. However, net enrolment rate has slightly declined despite the government's initiative of providing compulsory and free nine years of education.

Within the past three years, there have been several important incidents pertaining to social issues that have gained public attention. The first is related to labour lay-offs due to economic contraction in East Kalimantan. As of September 2015, it is estimated that around 10,721 workers have lost their jobs. The second involves the informal ties between civil society organisations and firms, particularly in the mining and plantation sector, which have created tension between them and the community at large. The third relates to the rejection of the operation of online transportation providers by conventional drivers. This rejection has manifested itself in violent acts such as destruction of vehicles and persecutions.

5.13.3 Provincial Government Policies

The current government has enacted provincial regulation (Perda) No. 6/2015 on incentivising and easing investments in the region. Among other things, it provides investors with legal certainty. Bureaucracy and red tapes have also been cut short with the establishment of a one-stop integrated service agency.

In order to further develop the province's economy, the government has identified certain strategic economic zones: the Kariangau-Buluminung manufacturing industry zone in Balikpapan and North Penajam Paser, the trade of goods and services zone in Samarinda, the petrochemical industry zone in Bontang-Marangkayu Kutai Kartanegara, the Maloy oleochemical industry zone in East Kutai, the agropolis in East Kutai as well as the agriculture industrial zones in Paser and North Penajam Paser, Kutai Kartanegara and West Kutai, as well as Mahakam Ulu.

Key Economic Indicators, 2015

Land Area (km²)	129,067
Population	
Total Population	3,426,600
Urban Population (%)	66.00
Poverty Rate (%)	6.1
Labour Force	1,539,491
Labour Force Participation Rate (%)	44.93
Gross Regional Domestic Products (GRDP) — 2010 prices	Rupiah (million)
GRDP	440,647,700
GRDP (non-minerals)	159,677,000
GRDP per Capita	128.59
GRDP per Capita (non-minerals)	46.60
Economic Composition	% of GRDP
Primary Sector	56.49
Secondary Sector	27.23
Tertiary Sector	16.28
Trade — 2010 prices	Rupiah (million)
Exports	169,868,135
Imports	53,499,101
Top-3 exports: mineral fuels; inorganic chemicals; wood and articles of wood	
Top-3 imports: mineral fuels; machinery and mechanical appliances; vehicles and vehicle accessories	
Infrastructure	
Paved Roads (km)	5,066
Domestic Air Traffic (Passengers)	7,921,189
International Air Traffic (Passengers)	73,229
Domestic Cargo at Seaport (Tons)	65,093,553
International Cargo at Seaport (Tons)	211,518,694

Source: BPS Indonesia compiled by ACI.

5.13.4 Local Political Scene

Local elections (Pilkada) last took place in 2013, where Awang Faroek and Mukmin Faisal won with 43.02 percent of total votes. With a mission to "build East Kalimantan for all", they aim to create a "prosperous East Kalimantan that is equal and fair, on the basis of agro-industry and eco-friendly energy". The pair was supported by a coalition of 11 political parties. Economic development was a key issue during the 2013 Pilkada.

Out of the 55 seats in the Regional People's Representative Council (DPRD), the Party of the Functional Group (Golkar) dominated with 14 seats. Not all political fractions in DPRD are pro-government; several that were known as "oppositions" include Golkar, the Indonesian Democratic Party of Struggle (PDIP), the fraction of Democrat Party, the National Mandate Party (PAN) and the Prosperous Justice Party (PKS), the Great Indonesia Movement Party (Gerindra) as well as the fraction of National Democrat Party (Nasdem) and People's Conscience Party (Hanura).

5.14 Commentary on Recent Developments in East Nusa Tenggara, 2015–2017

By: Asia Competitiveness Institute

Province Location

Source: ACI.

5.14.1 Economic Conditions

East Nusa Tenggara's economy has shown a positive trend between 2015 and 2017. Its growth rate had increased from 5.03 percent in 2015 to 5.18 percent in 2016. Nominal GRDP in 2016 stood at Rp59.78 trillion. The agriculture, forestry and fishery sector has dominated the province's economy (27.61 percent), followed by the trade and retail (11.60 percent) as well as the construction (10.95 percent) sectors.

There was a nett surplus of US$40.60 million in the province's trade balance in 2016. Exports, which were dominated by salt and sulphur as well as mineral fuels, had increased to US$55.15 million in 2016. Imports, which were dominated by mineral fuels and cereals, had similarly increased to US$15.92 million in the same year.

Realised investments in 2016 amounted to about Rp505.75billion — 99.97 percent of which was DDI. These numbers were a significant drop from 2015, where total investments were more than twofold at around Rp1.30 trillion.

5.14.2 Social Conditions and Development

HDI in the province had seen continuous improvements from 62.67 in 2015 to 63.13 in 2016. Improvements were observed in all aspects of HDI, specifically GNI per capita, which increased from 7.00 in 2015 to 7.11 in 2016, and expected years of schooling, which also improved from 12.84 to 12.97 years. Despite the improvements, the province's HDI was still ranked 32nd out of the 34 provinces in Indonesia. Although poverty rate did increase slightly in 2015, it improved by 0.57 percent to reach 22.01 in 2016.

Living conditions and quality of life in the province, on the other hand, also still leave plenty of room for improvement. As of 2017, 15.26 percent of the total households still do not have proper sanitation in their homes, while 22.64 percent of households still have not used electricity as their main source of lighting. A majority of the population — 75.25 percent — still relies on wood fire for cooking, while 23.51 percent still utilises kerosene.

5.14.3 Provincial Government Policies

In order to accelerate industrialisation in the province, three types of industries were identified as the foci of development in 2015. The first is the salt industry in five districts: Nagekeo, Ende, Kupang, East Sumba and Rote. The second is the sugar industry, focused in Southwest Sumba, Central South Timor and Rote. The third is small and medium industries producing the iconic *tenun ikat* Sumba weaving.

The provincial government had also previously implemented the provincial regulation (Perda) No. 2/2015 on the development of tourism in East Nusa Tenggara. The incumbent governor has also proposed for the Alor, Lembata and Larantuka (Altaka) region to be designated as SEZ, owing to its tourism, maritime, agriculture as well as plantation potentials.

5.14.4 Local Political Scene

East Nusa Tenggara is currently led by two-term governor, Frans Lebu Raya. First elected in 2008, he was re-elected with Benni Litelnony in 2013. Both were supported by the Indonesian Democratic Party of Struggle (PDIP) and won with 51.25 percent of the total votes. Their term will end in 2018, which is also when the next local election (Pilkada) will be held.

Four pairs of candidates have expressed their intention to run during the 2018 Pilkada. They are (i) Esthon Leyloh Foenay and Christian Rotok, (ii) Benny Kabur Harman and Benny Alexander Litelnoni, (iii) Ngada Marianus Sae and Emelia Julia Nomleni as well as (iv) Victor Bungtilu Laiskodat and Josef A. Nae Soi.

The province's Regional People's Representative Council (DPRD) consists of 65 representatives elected during the 2014 general elections (Pemilu). They are primarily from the Party of the Functional Group (Golkar) (11), PDIP (10), the Great Indonesia Movement Party (Gerindra) (8), the National Democrat Party (Nasdem) (8) as well as the Democrat Party (8).

Key Economic Indicators, 2015

Land Area (km²)	48,718
Population	
Total Population	5,120,100
Urban Population (%)	21.60
Poverty Rate (%)	22.58
Labour Force	2,307,737
Labour Force Participation Rate (%)	45.07
Gross Regional Domestic Products (GRDP) — 2010 prices	Rupiah (million)
GRDP	56,831,920
GRDP (non-minerals)	55,999,000
GRDP per Capita	11.10
GRDP per Capita (non-minerals)	10.94
Economic Composition	% of GRDP
Primary Sector	29.87
Secondary Sector	12.01
Tertiary Sector	58.12
Trade — 2010 prices	Rupiah (million)
Exports	239,002
Imports	78,603
Top-3 exports: mineral fuels; vehicles and vehicle accessories; salt, sulphur and stones	
Top-3 imports: mineral fuels; electrical machinery and equipment; machinery and mechanical appliances	
Infrastructure	
Paved Roads (km)	10,449
Domestic Air Traffic (Passengers)	2,755,369
International Air Traffic (Passengers)	16
Domestic Cargo at Seaport (Tons)	4,976,482
International Cargo at Seaport (Tons)	2,129,570

Source: BPS Indonesia compiled by ACI.

5.15 Commentary on Recent Developments in Gorontalo, 2015–2017

By: Herwin Mopangga
Universitas Negeri Gorontalo

Province Location

Source: ACI.

5.15.1 Economic Conditions

Gorontalo's economy slowed from 2012 to 2015 but bounced back to a growth rate of 6.52 percent in 2016. In the first quarter of 2017, the economy showed a promising growth of 7.27 percent. The source of growth between 2015 and 2017 has shifted from the agricultural and industrial sectors to trade and services. Consumerism, particularly in food, fashion, communication gadgets and motor vehicles, has increased owing to the rising welfare of Gorontalo's middle class.

Net exports contracted throughout 2016, with absences in export activity from October to December 2016 and March to April 2017 (BPS 2017a). Gorontalo's main exports are coconut husks and corn kernels, while its main imports are food, chemicals, transport equipment and machinery.

The ratio of public and private investment is 17:3. They both made up 28.92 percent of the province's GRDP in the first quarter of 2017 and had grown by 3.21 percent y-o-y. Realised DDI, however, had decreased from Rp1.43 trillion in 2016 to Rp82.39 billion in the first quarter of 2017. Similarly, FDI had fallen by 60.00 percent to reach US$2.10 million in the same period.

5.15.2 Social Conditions and Development

Gorontalo's poverty rate dropped from 27.35 percent in 2007 to 17.63 percent in 2016, although the latter was still way above the national standard of 11.00 percent (Bappenas 2017). Per capita income, on the other hand, had increased from US$1,902.54 in 2014 to US$2,078.33 in 2016 (BPS 2017a). The overall positive development of social conditions between 2010 and 2015 is also evident from the improvement in HDI from 62.65 to 65.86, the increase in life expectancy from 66.41 to 67.12 as well as the rise in the mean years of schooling from 11.12 to 12.70.

Certain weaknesses, however, continue to prevail and have become a major hindrance to social transformation. These include poor work ethic and weak entrepreneurial culture as well as low level of technological literacy.

Most economic activities in Gorontalo are dominated by residents of Chinese and Arabic descents, which in some cases have affected social sentiments. The government has been exerting sufficient effort to prevent social conflict and radicalism. Though crime rate has slightly increased, the government has managed to maintain the overall stable and conducive social conditions in Gorontalo.

5.15.3 Provincial Government Policies

The planning of Gorontalo's development is reflected in the province's Medium Term Development Planning (RPJMD) 2012–2017, which has mandated four key programmes, including free education and free healthcare provision, infrastructure development and enhancement of the people's economy.

In order to combat poverty, a new partnership between the central government and higher educational institutions has been forged, aimed at building new centres for economic development in the northern part of Sulawesi. The partnership was initiated in 2014 by the State University of Gorontalo through the declaration of the Strategic Zone Utara-Utara. This project involves various regencies in the provinces of Central Sulawesi, North Sulawesi and Gorontalo and covers the fields of farming, agriculture, forestry, fishing, tourism, industry, trade, education and healthcare.

National projects that have been agreed in 2017 include the revitalisation of Limboto Lake, Gorontalo Outer Ring Road, Anggrek Port and Hasri Ainun Habibie Hospital as well as the construction of a new campus for the State University of Gorontalo in Bone Bolango Regency through grants from the Islamic Development Bank.

Key Economic Indicators, 2015

Land Area (km^2)	11,257
Population	
Total Population	1,133,200
Urban Population (%)	39.00
Poverty Rate (%)	18.16
Labour Force	517,788
Labour Force Participation Rate (%)	45.69
Gross Regional Domestic Products (GRDP) — 2010 prices	Rupiah (million)
GRDP	22,068,590
GRDP (non-minerals)	21,775,000
GRDP per Capita	19.47
GRDP per Capita (non-minerals)	19.22
Economic Composition	% of GRDP
Primary Sector	37.70
Secondary Sector	16.40
Tertiary Sector	45.90
Trade — 2010 prices	Rupiah (million)
Exports	323,899
Imports	1,059,410
Top-3 exports: maize; sugars and sugar confectionery; wood and wood products	
Top-3 imports: mineral fuels; machinery and mechanical appliances; organic chemicals	
Infrastructure	
Paved Roads (km)	2,966
Domestic Air Traffic (Passengers)	487,917
International Air Traffic (Passengers)	0
Domestic Cargo at Seaport (Tons)	978,279
International Cargo at Seaport (Tons)	138,442

Source: BPS Indonesia compiled by ACI.

5.15.4 Local Political Scene

Major political parties still dominate the local political system, with the Party of the Functional Group (Golkar) occupying 27 percent of seats at the province's Regional People's Representative Council (DPRD). Other dominant parties include the National Mandate Party (PAN) (16 percent) and the Indonesian Democratic Party of Struggle (PDIP) (13 percent). The unrivalled strength of the ruling government makes most politicians unwilling to be an opposition.

In the 2017 local election (Pilkada), Rusli Habibie and Idris Rahim won 56 percent of the votes to become governor of Gorontalo with the support from Golkar, the Democrat Party and the National Awakening Party (PKB).

5.16 Commentary on Recent Developments in Jambi, 2015–2017

By: Syamsurijal Tan
Universitas Jambi

Province Location

Source: ACI.

5.16.1 Economic Conditions

Jambi province has abundant natural resources, such as rubber, CPO, coconut, coffee, oil and gas as well as coal. Yet, its economic growth rates are lower than the average national growth rates from 2015 to 2017 at 4.21 percent, 4.37 percent and 4.50 percent respectively.

The stalled economic growth is attributable to an economy that is dominated by the primary sector, which contributed to 41.03 percent and 38.40 percent of GRDP in 2015 and 2016 respectively. Specifically, the decline in exports by 3.79 percent in 2016, might be due to the low price of rubber and CPO. Imports also dropped by 16.49 percent due to lower demand in machinery, transportation and other industrial products. Jambi's economy has not yet shifted its focus to the industrial and service sectors.

Investment slightly grew by 3.37 percent in 2015 and 3.41 percent in 2017. The weak growth is caused by the declining investment in oil and gas as well as electricity projects. The sub-par quality of infrastructure in Jambi is also an impediment to the growth of investment.

5.16.2 Social Conditions and Development

In 2016, the urban population of Jambi was at 52.33 percent. Simultaneously, poverty rates also declined from 9.12 percent in 2015 to 8.47 percent in 2016. However, these numbers were still worse than the national average. The numbers were even less encouraging for Gini index, which had increased from 0.32 in 2015 to 0.36 in 2016, signalling increased inequality in the province. These numbers, however, were still lower than those at the national level.

Unemployment rate also saw an upward trend from 4.34 percent in 2015 to 4.66 percent in 2016. Although these numbers were lower than the national average, they still exceeded the target of 3.00 percent and 2.90 percent respectively. HDI, however, saw an improvement from 68.24 in 2015 to 69.01 in 2016.

Poverty, unemployment and income inequality in the province have triggered social conflicts, mainly pertaining to the presence of illegal workers in gold mines and coal-mining companies. These issues are further complicated by the society's low education level and the firms' questionable sense of social responsibility.

5.16.3 Provincial Government Policies

Between 2015 and 2017, there were no major policies that were issued by the local government. Most of the policies in this period were routine and were derived from the central government such as that of increasing the budget for infrastructure.

Nonetheless, the provincial government is constructing hydroelectric power plant to mitigate electricity deficit. Several policies were also introduced to improve the quality of bureaucracy through formal and informal education. The political promise to put qualified professionals within the local government's organisational structure, however, generally did not come to fruition as there were many officials lacking in expertise being elected.

Key Economic Indicators, 2015

Land Area (km²)	50,058
Population	
Total Population	3,402,100
Urban Population (%)	32.00
Poverty Rate (%)	9.12
Labour Force	1,620,752
Labour Force Participation Rate (%)	47.64
Gross Regional Domestic Products (GRDP) — 2010 prices	Rupiah (million)
GRDP	125,036,400
GRDP (non-minerals)	89,699,000
GRDP per Capita	36.75
GRDP per Capita (non-minerals)	26.37
Economic Composition	% of GRDP
Primary Sector	50.91
Secondary Sector	18.42
Tertiary Sector	30.68
Trade — 2010 prices	Rupiah (million)
Exports	10,897,589
Imports	1,103,936
Top-3 exports: mineral fuels; rubber and articles thereof; pulp of wood	
Top-3 imports: machinery and mechanical appliances; chemical products; industrial products	
Infrastructure	
Paved Roads (km)	8,774
Domestic Air Traffic (Passengers)	1,187,490
International Air Traffic (Passengers)	0
Domestic Cargo at Seaport (Tons)	737,723
International Cargo at Seaport (Tons)	1,131,405

Source: BPS Indonesia compiled by ACI.

5.16.4 Local Political Scene

Jambi's Governor Zumi Zola was elected through a coalition of seven political parties in 2015. With a total vote of 59.48 percent, he also obtained dominant power in the Regional People's Representative Council (DPRD). Political development in Jambi has generally been stable since every single government policy has been approved by DPRD.

Zumi Zola's high popularity was due to the fact that he was young (37 years old), handsome and a former actor. He also came from a wealthy family, being the son of Jambi's former governor. His vision was to create a Jambi 2020 that is "complete" in that it is able to complete all planned programmes and goals, such as increasing people's welfare, eradicating corruption a well as enacting pro-people economic policies. After two years of rule, however, there has been no significant progress to his promises. His actions have mostly been perceived to be an act of persona-building as opposed to real actions that can truly improve the people's wellbeing.

Jambi in 2017 secured the "normal without exception" opinion from the Audit Board of Indonesia (BPK). Nonetheless, this news was still received negatively after the arrest of four members from BPK over bribery for the review.

5.17 Commentary on Recent Developments in Lampung, 2015–2017

By: Ayi Ahadiat
Universitas Lampung

Province Location

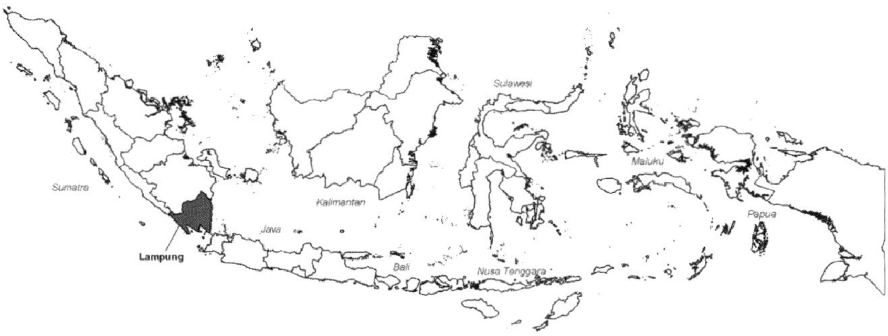

Source: ACI.

5.17.1 Economic Conditions

Lampung's economy grew at the rate of 5.15 percent in 2016 — above the national and regional growth rates. Its nominal GRDP was Rp281.11 trillion, rendering it as the fourth largest economy in Sumatra. Despite having the second highest population in Sumatra, average GRDP per capita growth rate (9.17 percent) was higher than the national average (6.39 percent). Its main economic sectors were agriculture, forestry and fisheries, processing industry as well as vehicle trade and repair.

Exports fluctuated between 2014 and 2016, but declined in 2016 largely due to the fall in global commodity prices. Exports included CPO, rubber, coal, coffee, tea and spices. Imports rose in 2016 as demand was not met by local suppliers. Imported goods included live animals, fertilisers, sugar and confectionery as well as food industry waste.

Realised investments fluctuated in 2014–2016, but values remained above the government's target. Food, electricity, gas and water as well as hotels and restaurants were the sectors receiving most FDI, while DDI were mainly found in chemical and pharmaceutical goods, services, food crops and plantation, and food industry.

5.17.2 Social Conditions and Development

Lampung's Gini ratio increased from 0.35 to 0.36 between 2014 and 2016, although it remained below the national average (0.40). Life expectancy, however, increased from 69.66 years in 2014 to 69.94 years in 2016. School enrolment rates had also increased, in line with a declining overt unemployment rate which remained below the national average. Despite the annual increases, the province's HDI in 2016 (67.75) was still below the national average (70.18) and was the lowest amongst provinces in Sumatra.

Social incidents often relate to land ownership disputes between residents and firms. Moving forward, firms will be more involved in the regional development through the provision of corporate social responsibility (CSR) programmes and participation in the ongoing coordination between government and law enforcement agencies. There have been no horizontal conflicts between ethnic and religious groups due to continuous efforts by the government as well as traditional, religious and community leaders to unite the people under Lampung's primary social philosophy of Piil Pesenggiri: "one with high moral behaviour in the community life."

5.17.3 Provincial Government Policies

The provincial government has enacted several policies aimed at easing investments which will encourage economic growth. These include (i) developing the industrial plan for Lampung Province, (ii) constructing occupational safety and health management system, (iii) protecting intellectual works in Lampung, (iv) protecting and empowering MSMEs, (v) providing incentives to ease investment, (vi) controlling forest areas and providing private health and business travel services in Lampung as well as (vii) establishing provincial credit guarantee companies (PPKD) in the province.

Since the enactment of provincial regulation (Perda) No. 23/2014 on local government, several authorities of regencies and cities have been transferred to the provincial government in order to facilitate the coordination and effectiveness of public services related to the ease of doing business. Besides deregulation, such law also serves to ensure legal certainty to businesses investing in the province.

Key Economic Indicators, 2015

Land Area (km^2)	34,624
Population	
Total Population	8,117,300
Urban Population (%)	28.30
Poverty Rate (%)	13.53
Labour Force	3,832,108
Labour Force Participation Rate (%)	47.21
Gross Regional Domestic Products (GRDP) — 2010 prices	Rupiah (million)
GRDP	199,536,100
GRDP (non-minerals)	187,441,000
GRDP per Capita	24.58
GRDP per Capita (non-minerals)	23.09
Economic Composition	% of GRDP
Primary Sector	37.99
Secondary Sector	26.97
Tertiary Sector	35.05
Trade — 2010 prices	Rupiah (million)
Exports	38,001,211
Imports	23,582,005
Top-3 exports: animal or vegetable fats and oil; meat and edible meat offal; dairy produce	
Top-3 imports: mineral fuels; sugars and sugar confectionery; livestock	
Infrastructure	
Paved Roads (km)	14,083
Domestic Air Traffic (Passengers)	1,420,443
International Air Traffic (Passengers)	0
Domestic Cargo at Seaport (Tons)	13,675,385
International Cargo at Seaport (Tons)	12,116,731

Source: BPS Indonesia compiled by ACI.

5.17.4 Local Political Scene

Governor Muhammad Ridho Ficardo and Deputy Governor Bachtiar Basri are the leaders of Lampung from 2014 to 2019. They envision Lampung as "the leading and the most advanced province in Sumatra, prosperous with a clean government, guided by the spirit of giving and service." Issues of infrastructure, agriculture, governance and poverty became the priority programme of the pair. To date, the government has helped to speed up toll road development, transform Radin Inten II into an international airport, accelerate poverty alleviation and encourage investments in industry and services.

Lampung's Regional People's Representative Council (DPRD) consists of 10 political parties, primarily the Indonesian Democratic Party of Struggle (PDIP) (20.00 percent), the Democrat Party (12.94 percent), Party of the Functional Group (Golkar) (11.76 percent) and the Great Indonesia Movement Party (Gerindra) (11.56 percent).

5.18 Commentary on Recent Developments in Maluku, 2015–2017

By: Djufri Rays Pattilouw
Universitas Pattimura

Province Location

Source: ACI.

5.18.1 Economic Conditions

Maluku's economy in the past two years continues to grow above the national average at 5.62 percent p.a. Growth primarily has come from the government administration and mandatory social security sector (1.66 percent), followed by the trading, retail and repair sector (0.94 percent). Both of these sectors have been rising. On the other hand, the agricultural, forestry and fishery sector has continued to decline while processing industry has stagnated at 0.74 percent and 0.30 percent respectively.

Most consumer goods have been imported; in fact, imports constituted 65.00 percent of the province's GRDP in 2016, of which 50.50 percent were interprovincial. Exports, on the other hand, were dominated by crude oil and fishery, and only contributed to 18.00 percent of the GRDP in the same period.

The prospects of investment in Maluku appear to be promising, with an increase in both foreign and direct investments at about 35.00 percent p.a. and a realisation rate of 160 percent in the two years. Investment is primarily concentrated in the primary sector.

5.18.2 Social Conditions and Development

Social security in Maluku has been stable in the recent years. In 2016, Maluku's HDI increased by 0.55 point to 6.70, with improvements across all aspects of HDI. Poverty rate and Gini ratio had also improved from 19.26 percent to 18.4 percent and 0.348 to 0.343 respectively between 2016 and 2017. However, instability of the workforce has driven fluctuations in unemployment figures.

There have been no notable incidents between labour and firms. Relations with the community, however, have been troubled with land and environmental issues, especially in the recently opened gold mining sites such as the Buru and Romang Islands. The government has formed an investigation team to work on the issue; however, this could have been prevented had the government been more aware and proactive in strengthening coordination. In this respect, the optimisation of the strategic role of "Badan Saniri Negeri" (an institution of the indigenous people) in bridging the communication and agreement of policies pertaining to the use of communal lands is crucial.

5.18.3 Provincial Government Policies

On 6 April 2016, President Joko Widodo officially opened the "Red and White Bridge" — now a landmark of Ambon City, capital of Maluku. The bridge has shortened the distance and time needed to travel between Pattimura Airport and education centres as well as agricultural and fishery production areas, resulting in the growth of new business centres and residence in the area. The President also announced the decision to allocate Blok Masela as an onshore oil and gas refinery, further increasing Blok Masela's expected multiplier effect and externality on the Maluku economy.

The expansion of several airports and seaports as well as construction of power plants have been ongoing between 2015 and 2017. Several agenda on "Solutions to Economic Revitalisation of Maluku 2025" have also been set, including the construction of "Trans Maluku" roads and "food estate" in Buru Island, the proposal of Banda SEZ for tourism and the optimisation of trade and investment cooperation with several countries. These efforts are expected to attract more investment to the region.

Key Economic Indicators, 2015

Land Area (km²)	46,914
Population	
Total Population	1,686,500
Urban Population (%)	38.00
Poverty Rate (%)	19.36
Labour Force	727,259
Labour Force Participation Rate (%)	43.12
Gross Regional Domestic Products (GRDP) — 2010 prices	Rupiah (million)
GRDP	24,859,060
GRDP (non-minerals)	24,048,000
GRDP per Capita	14.74
GRDP per Capita (non-minerals)	14.26
Economic Composition	% of GRDP
Primary Sector	27.03
Secondary Sector	12.85
Tertiary Sector	60.12
Trade — 2010 prices	Rupiah (million)
Exports	441,547
Imports	2,552,873
Top-3 exports: fish and crustacean; mineral fuels; ships and floating structures	
Top-3 imports: mineral fuels; ships and floating structures; articles of iron and steel	
Infrastructure	
Paved Roads (km)	4,222
Domestic Air Traffic (Passengers)	1,542,463
International Air Traffic (Passengers)	620
Domestic Cargo at Seaport (Tons)	3,923,444
International Cargo at Seaport (Tons)	0

Source: BPS Indonesia compiled by ACI.

5.18.4 Local Political Scene

Maluku province is led by the winners of 2013 regional election, Said Assagaff and Zeth Sahuburua, who have maintained political stability. In 2016, the government's financial statement was audited as normal without exception for the very first time.

The next gubernatorial election will take place on 27 June 2018. A coalition of political parties is expected, centred on those currently dominating the Regional People's Representative Council (DPRD), namely the Indonesian Democratic Party of Struggle (PDIP) (15.50 percent), Party of the Functional Group (Golkar) (13.30 percent), Democrat Party (13.30 percent), Prosperous Justice Party (PKS) (13.30 percent) and Great Indonesia Movement Party (Gerindra) (11.10 percent). Various surveys have indicated that the incumbent governor, backed by Golkar, still has the highest rate of electability.

5.19 Commentary on Recent Developments in North Kalimantan, 2015–2017

By: Pither Palungan, Syaiful Anwar and Adri Paton
Universitas Borneo Tarakan

Province Location

Source: ACI.

5.19.1 Economic Conditions

From 2015 to 2017, North Kalimantan's economy has been steadily growing, driven by improvements in the mining, agriculture, construction and trade sectors.

The province's export performance, particularly in coal and plantation, has also boosted the province's economy.

On the other hand, import performance has fluctuated. In the second quarter of 2017, the province's import activities were dominated by machineries, contributing 41.2 percent to total import value, followed by cereal (19.00 percent) and fishery (3.00 percent).

Meanwhile, investments in North Kalimantan have slowed in the second quarter of 2017 with a 3.15 percent growth rate — lower than the previous year's rate. FDI had similarly fallen by 30.71 percent from US$65.60 million in 2016 to US$45.50 million in 2017. Simultaneously, DDI plummeted from Rp151.80 billion in 2016 to Rp82.90 billion in the second quarter of 2017.

5.19.2 Social Conditions and Development

North Kalimantan's life expectancy has increased between 2015 and 2017 on an average of 0.19 percent p.a. Expected years of schooling has also increased by 0.29 percent, while mean years of schooling by 0.39 percent in the same period. GNI per capita has similarly risen by 0.83 percent p.a. The improvements across all these indicators have also resulted in the overall increase in the province's HDI from 68.76 in 2015 to 69.20 in 2016.

Despite the abovementioned improvements, overt unemployment rate in the province has worsened. In February 2016, overt unemployment in the province stood at 3.92 percent. This number rose significantly to 5.17 percent in February 2017. This is because while the economy has been growing, the business sector is unable to cope to absorb more workforce. North Kalimantan's unemployment stood at 16,774 people in February 2017.

5.19.3 Provincial Government Policies

The government has recently launched the development of the Tanah Kuning industrial estate and international port (KIPI), which is targeted to absorb 60,000 people from the workforce. This project will be supported by the development of infrastructure, such as international port, paved roads, bridges as well as airports. Electricity supply in the KIPI will be supported by the Kayan hydroelectric power plant (PLTA). This power plant, which will be constructed by the Kayan Hydro Energy limited liability company (LLC) in Bulungan Regency, is expected to hold 9,000 megawatt in capacity. A couple of investors have shown their interest to invest in Tanah Kuning KIPI. One of them is the national state-owned enterprise (BUMN) Inalum, which has signed a Memorandum of Understanding with the North Kalimantan government in June 2017.

Key Economic Indicators, 2015

Land Area (km²)	75,468
Population	
Total Population	641,900
Urban Population (%)	66.00
Poverty Rate (%)	6.32
Labour Force	283,102
Labour Force Participation Rate (%)	44.10
Gross Regional Domestic Products (GRDP) — 2010 prices	Rupiah (million)
GRDP	49,316,000
GRDP (non-minerals)	34,374,000
GRDP per Capita	76.82
GRDP per Capita (non-minerals)	53.55
Economic Composition	% of GRDP
Primary Sector	47.68
Secondary Sector	21.30
Tertiary Sector	31.02
Trade — 2010 prices	Rupiah (million)
Exports	10,058,452
Imports	319,073
Top-3 exports: mineral fuels; fish and crustaceans; wood and articles of wood	
Top-3 imports: fertilisers; mineral fuels; salt and sulphur	
Infrastructure	
Paved Roads (km)	3,266
Domestic Air Traffic (Passengers)	1,369,122
International Air Traffic (Passengers)	20,212
Domestic Cargo at Seaport (Tons)	14,059,144
International Cargo at Seaport (Tons)	10,608,958

Source: BPS Indonesia compiled by ACI.

5.19.4 Local Political Scene

In the last local election (Pilkada) in 2015, Iryanto Lamrie-Udin Hianggio won with 53.03 percent of the total votes. The pair was backed by a coalition of seven political parties: the Indonesian Democratic Party of Struggle (PDIP), the Prosperous Justice Party (PKS), the Democrat Party, the National Mandate Party (PAN), the Crescent Star Party (PBB), the Party of the Functional Group (Golkar) and the Great Indonesia Movement Party (Gerindra). Out of the 447,636 registered voters, 277,586 utilised their voting rights.

In the Regional People's Representative Council (DPRD), every party that contested in the 2014 general elections (Pemilu) managed to acquire seats. The Democrat Party, PDIP, Golkar and Gerindra led the election with over 30,000 votes. Representation by the number of seats in the DPRD is as follows: Democrat Party (5), PDIP (4), Golkar (4), Gerindra (4), People's Conscience Party (Hanura) (4), PAN (3), National Democrat Party (Nasdem) (2), PKS (2), National Awakening Party (PKB) (2), United Development Party (PPP) (2), PBB (2) and Indonesian Justice and Unity Party (PKPI) (1).

5.20 Commentary on Recent Developments in North Maluku, 2015–2017

By: Asia Competitiveness Institute

Province Location

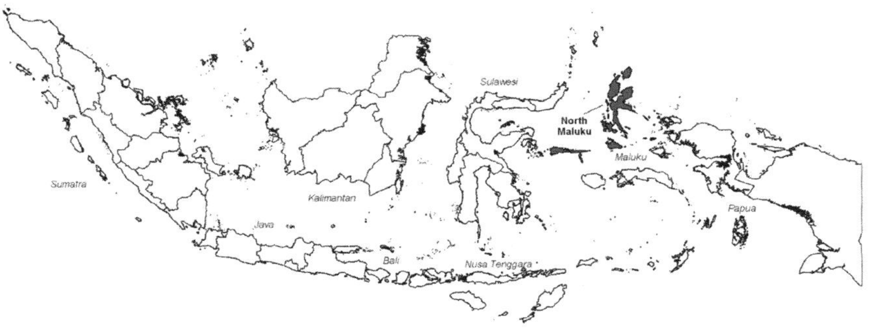

Source: ACI.

5.20.1 Economic Conditions

North Maluku's economy had fluctuated in recent years, although growth rates were still higher than the national average. Growth was 6.10 percent in 2015, 5.77 percent in 2016 and 7.67 percent in 2017 — the highest since 2011. The high growth in 2017 was driven by improvements in most sectors, particularly in the processing industry with the highest growth at 32.13 percent. Nonetheless, the economy was still largely supported by agriculture, forestry and fishing (23.95 percent of GRDP) as well as wholesale trade and automobile repairs (17.42 percent of GRDP).

In terms of expenditure, growth was mainly driven by exports, which grew sevenfold to reach US$272.09 million in 2017. Export concentration differed each year; oil seeds and oleaginous fruits were the most exported in 2015, while in 2016, they were mostly iron and steel. Meanwhile, import values dropped by 38.06 percent to reach US$149.84 million in 2017.

Investments had also fluctuated over the three years, with a total of 119 FDI and 13 DDI projects. FDI was dominated by mining while DDI was mostly in metal industry, metal goods as well as machinery and electronics.

5.20.2 Social Conditions and Development

North Maluku's standard of living had improved, with rising HDI from 65.91 in 2015 to 66.63 in 2016, caused by improvements in the respective components of HDI. North Maluku's HDI in 2016 was ranked 27th out of 34 provinces across Indonesia, indicating there is still room for improvement.

For instance, poverty rate had been on the rise, reaching 6.44 in September 2017 due to surges in consumer price index, reduction in farmer terms of trade and falling recipient rate for rice subsidy programme. The latter had remained lower than the national average.

Meanwhile, net school enrolment rates in North Maluku were 99.14 percent for ages 7–12, 96.90 percent for ages 13–15 and 75.58 percent for ages 16–18 in 2016. The rates tend to decline with increasing age. The province's average years of schooling had been gradually increasing, reaching 8.52 years in 2016.

North Maluku generally remains free from social issues. However, the province is still facing land and boundary conflicts in several regencies, such as Ternate, Sofifi and Halmahera. Interestingly, North Maluku scored the highest amongst all provinces for the Happiness Index in 2017.

5.20.3 Provincial Government Policies

Among the vision and mission of the current government is the acceleration of infrastructure development in order to support economic growth in the province. Hence, both the central and local governments have pledged to focus on connectivity development, particularly amongst the islands.

Based on Presidential Regulation (Perpres) No. 3/2016 on the acceleration of the implementation of national strategic projects, there are seven national strategic projects slated to be developed in North Maluku, including the construction of the Trans Morotai Ring Road, the revitalisation of Sultan Babullah airport and the development of Wayabula Port and Morotai Islands.

Infrastructure development in the province had been fairly slow due to factors such as insufficient allocation of funding for infrastructure projects from the province's regional development budget (APBD). The governor cited that only Rp200.00 billion out of Rp2.50 trillion had been allocated for infrastructure development. Nonetheless, the government has continued to create plans to construct airports and seaports, particularly near Morotai and Sofifi, in order to optimise the marine and fisheries sector in the province.

Key Economic Indicators, 2015

Land Area (km²)	31,983
Population	
Total Population	1,162,300
Urban Population (%)	27.80
Poverty Rate (%)	6.22
Labour Force	513,601
Labour Force Participation Rate (%)	44.19
Gross Regional Domestic Products (GRDP) — 2010 prices	Rupiah (million)
GRDP	20,381,030
GRDP (non-minerals)	18,325,000
GRDP per Capita	17.53
GRDP per Capita (non-minerals)	15.77
Economic Composition	% of GRDP
Primary Sector	33.34
Secondary Sector	12.09
Tertiary Sector	54.58
Trade — 2010 prices	Rupiah (million)
Exports	110,227
Imports	608,741
Top-3 exports: oil seeds and oleaginous fruits	
Top-3 imports: machinery and mechanical appliance; goods of iron and steel; mineral fuels	
Infrastructure	
Paved Roads (km)	3,395
Domestic Air Traffic (Passengers)	702,300
International Air Traffic (Passengers)	0
Domestic Cargo at Seaport (Tons)	2,624,075
International Cargo at Seaport (Tons)	0

Source: BPS Indonesia compiled by ACI.

5.20.4 Local Political Scene

In May 2014, North Maluku elected Abdul Ghani Kasuba as governor and Muhammad Natsir Thaib as deputy governor for the period of 2014–2019. The general elections (Pemilu) also saw the Indonesia Democratic Party of Struggle (PDIP) winning with 41 seats, followed by the Party of the Functional Group (Golkar) with 32 seats. The incumbent government had a vision of "North Maluku CINTA 2019", where CINTA stands for "intelligent, beautiful, enjoyable, full of blessings and safe." Meanwhile, North Maluku will join 16 other provinces in Indonesia to hold local elections (Pilkada) in 2018 to elect its new governor.

5.21 Commentary on Recent Developments in North Sulawesi, 2015–2017

By: Herman Karamoy, Tri Oldy Rotinsulu and Joubert Maramis
Universitas Sam Ratulangi

Province Location

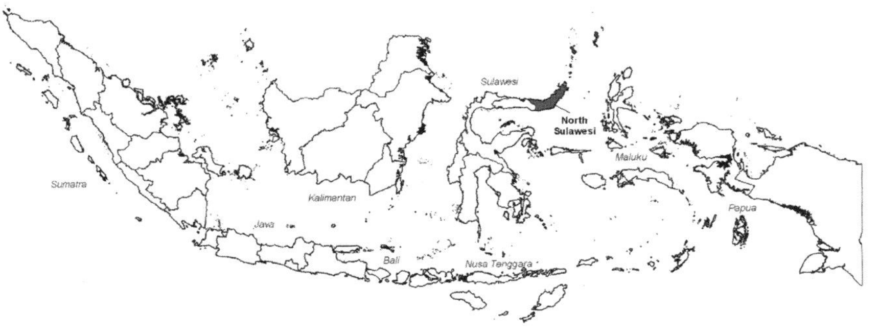

Source: ACI.

5.21.1 Economic Conditions

From 2015 to 2017, North Sulawesi's economy had grown moderately at rates that were higher than the national level but lower than the Sulawesi regional average. Its nominal GRDP amounted to Rp100.50 trillion in 2016, while GRDP per capita was higher than the regional average at Rp41.90 million. The 6.71 percent growth in 2016 was driven by substantial tourist arrivals especially from China, the relaxation of trans-shipment rules and higher agricultural production following the improved El Niño conditions. In the last five years, there has been a shift in the economic structure from the primary sector to the secondary and tertiary sectors, where growth in the latter had been high.

North Sulawesi's exports and imports had fluctuated in the last two years. Notably, there was a slowdown in non-oil and gas exports, largely caused by declining global commodity demand due to lower purchasing power. Exports were still dominated by products derived from fish and coconut.

FDI had increased with greater interest in sectors of electricity, mining and restaurants as well as hotels, with rising interest by investors from China and Korea.

5.21.2 Social Conditions and Development

Life expectancy had increased annually from 70.99 years in 2015 to 71.02 years in 2016. HDI also increased in 2016 and was the seventh highest in Indonesia. Net school enrolment rates were high in primary education, but remained low in secondary (senior high school) to higher education.

Unemployment rates had fallen each year, indicating that development had absorbed more manpower. For instance, many jobs in the trade and services sector had been absorbed in the past three years, in line with the significant growth of these sectors. Minimum monthly wage in the province in 2016 was among the third highest in Indonesia at Rp2.40 million. This, and the minimal labour conflicts in the province, caused many to migrate in search for employment.

There has been no social issues pertaining to ethnicities, religion, race and inter-group relations (SARA). North Sulawesi is famous for its high religious harmony and has an inter-religious cooperation body (i.e. BKSAUA) which monitors and anticipates such problem. The province also has a motto of *torang samua basudara* — loosely translated to "we are all brothers."

5.21.3 Provincial Government Policies

The following are some of the proposed regulations in North Sulawesi: (i) the opening of the regional state-owned enterprise (BUMD) Membangun Sulut Hebat (MSH), (ii) the zoning of coastal area and small islands (RPZWP3K) in North Sulawesi, (iii) the development of Bitung SEZ, (iv) the construction of toll roads and railways, (v) the expansion of the airport runway in Sam Ratulangi, (vi) the expansion of Bitung International Hub Port (IHP) and (vii) the expansion of the One-Stop Integrated Service Agency (PTSP) to become one of Bitung SEZ's administrative agencies.

Key Economic Indicators, 2015

Land Area (km^2)	13,852
Population	
Total Population	2,412,100
Urban Population (%)	49.80
Poverty Rate (%)	8.98
Labour Force	1,099,272
Labour Force Participation Rate (%)	45.57
Gross Regional Domestic Products (GRDP) — 2010 prices	Rupiah (million)
GRDP	70,425,140
GRDP (non-minerals)	66,919,000
GRDP per Capita	29.20
GRDP per Capita (non-minerals)	27.74
Economic Composition	% of GRDP
Primary Sector	25.72
Secondary Sector	23.76
Tertiary Sector	50.52
Trade — 2010 prices	Rupiah (million)
Exports	8,333,300
Imports	111,403
Top-3 exports: animal or vegetable fats and oil; processed meat and fish; food industry residues and wastes	
Top-3 imports: machinery and mechanical appliances; iron and steel; mineral fuels	
Infrastructure	
Paved Roads (km)	5,469
Domestic Air Traffic (Passengers)	2,124,333
International Air Traffic (Passengers)	53,416
Domestic Cargo at Seaport (Tons)	2,643,365
International Cargo at Seaport (Tons)	749,695

Source: BPS Indonesia compiled by ACI.

5.21.4 Local Political Scene

The current governor of North Sulawesi, Olly Dondokambey, and Deputy Governor Steven Kandouw were elected democratically in 2015 to govern the province from 2016 to 2021. The winning party, the Indonesian Democratic Party of Struggle (PDIP), won with a total vote of 52.27 percent.

During the election campaign, the governor advocated issues pertaining to central and local government relations, electricity provision and impoverished community. These issues were received positively by the people during the campaign period. It was thought that the harmonisation of relations between the central and local governments would ease budget allocations to the province. Meanwhile, the empowerment of the poor and the expansion of electricity supply were pressing issues during the campaign period, given the high poverty rate and problematic electricity supply in the province.

Economic self-reliance and sovereignty in governance remain a part of the governor's vision and mission for North Sulawesi. The governor aims to make the economy independent, and this necessitates good governance along with the development of infrastructure and industry as well as the increase in the quality of human resources which are in accordance with the industrial needs.

5.22 Commentary on Recent Developments in North Sumatra, 2015–2017

By: Armin Rahmansyah Nst
Universitas Negeri Medan

Province Location

Source: ACI.

5.22.1 Economic Conditions

Economic growth in North Sumatra within the past two years had been satisfactory, given that it had been above the average of five percent. In 2015, the province's growth stood at 5.10 percent, which further saw an increase in 2016 to reach 5.18 percent. It is estimated that the economic growth in 2017 will reach 5.20 percent, while that in 2018 is around 5.00 percent to 5.40 percent. The continuous and satisfactory increase in economic growth could be attributed to the positive performance in several key sectors: information and communications registered the highest growth of 7.76 percent, followed by the health services and social activities sector at 7.11 percent and the water provision and waste management sector at 6.71 percent. Consumption was the biggest contributor to the province's GRDP.

The province's growth had also been supported by satisfactory trade balance. It is projected that the province's economy — especially externally — will continue to perform positively given the increase in CPO exports.

5.22.2 Social Conditions and Development

Despite the heterogeneous population, North Sumatra has not faced major social issues and threats to security. The major ethnic groups in the province — the natives, Batak, Javanese, Minang, Chinese, Indian and Arab — have lived together in harmony and tolerance.

Social indicators in North Sumatra have generally ameliorated over the years. With improvements in health, education and economic conditions of the people, North Sumatra's HDI stood at 70.00 in 2016, placing the province at the upper middle category.

The unemployment rate of North Sumatra, however, has increased over the years. Moreover, there has been a constant problem of the Provincial Minimum Wage (UMP): labourers have been demanding for increasingly higher wages, while investors have been finding it difficult to meet the demand as they are also affected by factors at the national level. The provincial government has mediated between both parties in order to reach consensus.

5.22.3 Provincial Government Policies

Most government policies implemented by the provincial government have followed instructions from the national level. Most recently, North Sumatra — specifically Lake Toba — has been designated as one of Indonesia's major tourist destinations through the Presidential Regulation (Perpres) No. 49/2016. North Sumatra itself has set a target of one million tourist visits by 2019.

Other than designating Lake Toba as a tourist destination, the government has also turned the Silangit Airport in North Tapanuli into an international airport in order to boost overseas visitors coming from Singapore and Malaysia. The number of tourists entering North Sumatra had increased by 14 percent between 2016 and 2017.

President Joko Widodo has also officiated some parts of the Medan-Kualanamu-Tebing Tinggi highway and the Medna-Binjai highway.

Key Economic Indicators, 2015

Land Area (km²)	72,981
Population	
Total Population	13,937,800
Urban Population (%)	52.60
Poverty Rate (%)	10.79
Labour Force	6,391,098
Labour Force Participation Rate (%)	45.85
Gross Regional Domestic Products (GRDP) — 2010 prices	Rupiah (million)
GRDP	440,955,850
GRDP (non-minerals)	435,127,000
GRDP per Capita	31.64
GRDP per Capita (non-minerals)	31.22
Economic Composition	% of GRDP
Primary Sector	26.26
Secondary Sector	32.05
Tertiary Sector	41.69
Trade — 2010 prices	Rupiah (million)
Exports	77,730,955
Imports	40,025,589
Top-3 exports: animal or vegetable fats and oil; livestock; raw materials	
Top-3 imports: livestock; mineral, fuels and lubricants; chemicals	
Infrastructure	
Paved Roads (km)	22,855
Domestic Air Traffic (Passengers)	6,778,006
International Air Traffic (Passengers)	1,629,894
Domestic Cargo at Seaport (Tons)	8,340,109
International Cargo at Seaport (Tons)	7,992,125

Source: BPS Indonesia compiled by ACI.

5.22.4 Local Political Scene

Political conditions in North Sumatra since 2008 can be considered chaotic. Two elected governors (2008–2013 and 2013–2018) had been arrested by the Corruption Eradication Commission (KPK). Elected Governor Syamsul Arifin (2008–2013) was arrested and replaced by his Deputy Governor Gatot Pujo Nugroho on March 21st, 2011. The elected Governor Gatot Pujo Nugroho 2013–2018 was then also arrested and replaced by his deputy HT Erry Nuradi in May 2016.

The province will hold its gubernatorial election this coming June 2018 with three sets of candidates: Edy Rahmayadi and Musa Rajeckshah, Djarot Saiful Hidayat and Sihar Sitorus as well as Jopinus Ramli Saragih and Ance Selian.

Although social conditions in North Sumatra have generally been stable, there may be a bit of polarisation during this upcoming election owing to the effect of DKI Jakarta's religiously tinged local election (Pilkada) in 2017.

5.23 Commentary on Recent Developments in Papua, 2015–2017

By: Asia Competitiveness Institute

Province Location

Source: ACI.

5.23.1 Economic Conditions

Papua's economy between 2015 and 2017 had generally shown signs of improvements, although it slowed down closer to 2017. Its GRDP, for instance, registered an increase of 27.48 percent throughout the three-year period. Its overall growth rate, however, had fallen rather significantly from 9.21 percent in 2016 to 4.64 percent in 2017. The slowdown could be attributed to the temporary suspension of the largest mining company in Papua, Freeport. Indeed, the industry and mining sector was the largest driver of Papua's economy throughout this period, followed by the construction sector and the agriculture, forestry and fisheries sector.

Although export values had increased from US$2.00 trillion in 2015 to US$2.45 trillion in 2017, imports in the province had fallen by about 40.00 percent over the same period.

Both foreign and domestic investments also increased between 2015 and 2016; DDI rose by 28.36 percent while FDI inflows saw a significant jump of 48.59 percent just within the span of one year. In 2017, FDI in Papua reached a record high of US$1.90 trillion.

5.23.2 Social Conditions and Development

In 2016, Papua's HDI stood at 58.05 — a slight improvement from 57.25 in 2015. However, considering that the score was still below 60, Papua's HDI in 2016 still fell under the low category. Nonetheless, Papua's HDI growth rate was one of the highest nationally. This was achieved through improvements across all components of HDI, especially in the indicator expected years of schooling (2.81 percent).

Industrial relations in the province, however, faced a major setback in 2017. Amidst disruption in mining activities due to a dispute between the Indonesian government and Freeport McMoran, workers in Papua's Grasberg mine — the second largest copper mine in the world — faced uncertain employment and layoff terms. In response, 5,000 mining workers went on a strike which lasted for a few months. Freeport McMoran responded by referring to the Industrial Relations Regulation No. 3/2003 on labour, which states that any worker who is absent for five consecutive days is considered to have voluntarily resigned. This one-sided decision, coupled by the perceived lack of response from the central government, further soured industrial relations in Papua.

5.23.3 Provincial Government Policies

The Papua province has been granted special autonomy under Law No. 21/2001. Under this law, Papua gets to receive additional Special Autonomy Funds (Dana Otsus). The provincial government also has the ability to enact Special Regional Regulation (Perdasus), such as the one passed in 2016 pertaining to the management of Dana Otsus. This Perdasus No. 13/2016 was an update to an earlier Perdasus No. 25/2013 on the distribution of Dana Otsus to the province's cities, regencies and villages.

Under the Presidency of Joko Widodo, Papua's infrastructure development has become a national priority. One example is the construction of the Trans-Papua road: a network of 11 road segments that is 4,325 kilometres long, which stretches from Sorong in West Papua to Merauke in Papua. The project, which is under the purview of the Ministry of Public Works and Housing, is expected to be complete in 2018 and will help accelerate development in the province.

Key Economic Indicators, 2015

Land Area (km²)	319,036
Population	
Total Population	3,149,400
Urban Population (%)	28.40
Poverty Rate (%)	28.4
Labour Force	1,741,945
Labour Force Participation Rate (%)	55.31
Gross Regional Domestic Products (GRDP) — 2010 prices	Rupiah (million)
GRDP	130,459,910
GRDP (non-minerals)	77,512,000
GRDP per Capita	41.42
GRDP per Capita (non-minerals)	24.61
Economic Composition	% of GRDP
Primary Sector	52.32
Secondary Sector	12.94
Tertiary Sector	34.75
Trade — 2010 prices	Rupiah (million)
Exports	20,770,793
Imports	7,725,984
Top-3 exports: ores, slag and ash; wood and articles of wood; aircraft, spacecraft and parts thereof	
Top-3 imports: machinery and mechanical appliances; mineral fuels; electrical machinery and equipment	
Infrastructure	
Paved Roads (km)	11,190
Domestic Air Traffic (Passengers)	3,760,139
International Air Traffic (Passengers)	2,954
Domestic Cargo at Seaport (Tons)	8,755,203
International Cargo at Seaport (Tons)	1,773,786

Source: ACI from Statistics Indonesia Data.

5.23.4 Local Political Scene

Papua is currently led by Governor Lukas Enembe, who has been in power since 2013 and partnered with Deputy Governor Klemen Tinal. Both were previously regents of Puncak Jaya and Mimika respectively. The pair was elected with 52.00 percent of the total votes 2013, although this decision was initially challenged by the other candidates at the Indonesia Constitutional Court (MK).

Papua will be holding its next local election (Pilkada) in 2018. The incumbent has expressed interest to run together in next year's election, supported by a coalition of nine major parties.

Papua's Regional People's Representative Council (DPRD) is allowed to have 1.25 times more representatives compared to other provinces due to the province's special autonomy status. The 55-people strong committee is mostly occupied by representatives from the Democrat Party (16) and the Indonesian Democratic Party of Struggle (PDIP) (7).

5.24 Commentary on Recent Developments in Riau, 2015–2017

By: Sri Indarti and Darmayuda
Universitas Riau

Province Location

Source: ACI.

5.24.1 Economic Conditions

Despite contracting significantly in 2015 with a growth rate of 0.22 percent, Riau's economy bounced back to reach 2.23 percent in 2016 and 2.82 percent in the first quarter of 2017. This growth was driven by improvements in its three primary sectors: (i) agriculture, forestry and fishery, (ii) processing industry as well as (iii) wholesale trade and retail.

There was a decline in the mining and gas sectors due to the global fall in commodity prices, economic slowdown in China and uncertainty arising from the normalisation of United States monetary policy. While this had affected overall exports negatively with a contraction of 4.63 percent, exports without oil and gas had in fact improved in 2016 by 3.57 percent to reach US$11.22 billion. Overall imports had also declined from US$1.34 billion in 2015 to US$1.30 billion in 2016 as economic slowdown had weakened people's purchasing power.

Investment had also slowed due to the loss of confidence in global economic conditions and falling commodity prices, especially since most investments in Riau were concentrated in the primary sector.

5.24.2 Social Conditions and Development

The social conditions in Riau, as reflected by the province's HDI, had improved over the years. HDI in 2016 saw an increase of 0.36 to reach 71.20 relative to the year before. This placed the province under the "high" category by national standards. Improvements were observed across all elements of HDI, particularly in the indicator mean years of schooling which had risen from 8.49 years in 2015 to 8.59 in 2016.

Overt unemployment rate in the province, however, had shown a consistent increase over the same period due to the global commodity price bust. In 2016, overt unemployment rate stood at 7.83 percent — an increase of 1.27 percent from 2015.

Net school enrolment rates had increased across all age groups in Riau. Despite the improvements in education, there were not enough employment opportunities on the ground. For instance, despite the rise in the number of graduates from medical schools, there were not enough medical institutions to provide employment upon graduation. Graduates from vocational high schools made up the majority of those who were overtly unemployed at 8.70 percent.

5.24.3 Provincial Government Policies

The provincial government has a vision to create a Riau that is "progressive, with people who are prosperous, Malay cultured and competitive, with declining poverty, increasing employment as well as stabilising government apparatus." This is accompanied with nine missions: (i) enhance infrastructure development, (ii) increase education services, (iii) improve health services, (iv) reduce poverty, (v) increase reliability of government and strengthen political life, (vi) develop people with strong Malay culture, faith and religious beliefs, (vii) strengthen agriculture and plantation development, (viii) enhance management and conservation of the environment as well as (ix) increase the role of tourism in local development.

However, it is important to note that Riau's economy is still heavily reliant on the commodity sector. The slowdown of global commodity demand thus has great effects on the economic performance of Riau. The government thus needs to look for innovative, alternative solutions for its economy in order to maintain stability in the province.

Key Economic Indicators, 2015

Land Area (km²)	87,024
Population	
Total Population	6,344,400
Urban Population (%)	39.60
Poverty Rate (%)	8.82
Labour Force	2,771,349
Labour Force Participation Rate (%)	43.68
Gross Regional Domestic Products (GRDP) — 2010 prices	Rupiah (million)
GRDP	448,991,960
GRDP (non-minerals)	329,825,000
GRDP per Capita	70.77
GRDP per Capita (non-minerals)	51.99
Economic Composition	% of GRDP
Primary Sector	48.45
Secondary Sector	36.00
Tertiary Sector	15.56
Trade — 2010 prices	Rupiah (million)
Exports	144,203,496
Imports	13,453,467
Top-3 exports: mineral fuels; animal or vegetable fats and oil; pulp of wood	
Top-3 imports: mineral fuels; machinery and mechanical appliances; fertilisers	
Infrastructure	
Paved Roads (km)	11,203
Domestic Air Traffic (Passengers)	2,551,810
International Air Traffic (Passengers)	165,380
Domestic Cargo at Seaport (Tons)	38,449,058
International Cargo at Seaport (Tons)	13,613,534

Source: BPS Indonesia compiled by ACI.

5.24.4 Local Political Scene

The last local election (Pilkada) was held in 2013, where the pair Annas Maamun and Arsyadjuliandi Rachman (Andi Rachman), who were backed by the Party of the Functional Group (Golkar), won by 60.75 percent. In 2015, however, Annas Maamun was arrested by the Corruption Eradication Commission (KPK), resulting in Deputy Andi Rachman taking over as governor, assisted by Wan Thamrin Hasyim. The next Pilkada is slated to take place in 2018.

The province's Regional People's Representative Council (DPRD) is represented by 65 politicians, elected through the 2014 general elections (Pemilu). The party with the most number of seats is Golkar (14), followed by the Indonesian Democratic Party of Struggle (PDIP) (9), the Democrat Party (9), the Great Indonesia Movement Party (Gerindra) (7) and the National Mandate Party (PAN) (7).

5.25 Commentary on Recent Developments in Riau Islands, 2015–2017

By: Dwi Kartikasari
Politeknik Negeri Batam

Province Location

Source: ACI.

5.25.1 Economic Conditions

The economy in Riau Islands had been growing at above five percent p.a., though it had been slowing down in recent years. This was caused by the decline in trade as well as the decline in performance of the province's primary sectors of processing, mining and construction (Bank Indonesia 2017). The electronic manufacturing industry was one of the biggest contributors to GRDP. From the seven regencies/cities, Batam's contribution to the GRDP was the highest at around 60.00 percent (BPS 2017a). Riau Islands' GRDP and its per capita GRDP were considered high by national standards (BPS 2017b).

Mineral fuel was the most exported commodity, followed by electrical equipment as well as metal and steel appliances. The decline in the exports of the abovementioned was balanced by the rise in exports in the aviation industry — a growing sector in Batam and Bintan. Meanwhile, the province imported electrical appliances the most. The province's main trading partner is Singapore.

Both FDI and DDI had been fluctuating in recent years. The shipyard sector had been declining, while the aviation maintenance industry had been flourishing.

5.25.2 Social Conditions and Development

The net school enrolment rate in Riau Islands had been improving, with female participation rate that tended to be higher than male. The province's life expectancy and HDI have been improving each year as well. Nevertheless, education redistribution among the urban and rural areas is not yet optimal due to the province's archipelagic nature.

The Riau Islands province's unemployment rate is considered as relatively high by national standards. This number is on an upward trend due to regional growth slowdown.

Income inequality across the region is high, triggered by the large development gap between Batam and other regencies/cities in the province.

Every year, workers would hold protest to repudiate regulations and demand for higher wages (Bappeda Kepri 2016). As there are many firms shutting down this year, especially in the shipyard industry, there is higher risk for social problems to manifest. The government has tried to curb social turmoil by mediating between disputing parties.

5.25.3 Provincial Government Policies

One of the provincial government's policies is the redistribution of regional development through the provision of hard infrastructure, such as electricity, water, paved roads and bridges. It also aims to increase connectivity by building new airports and seaports as well as providing maiden ships to connect isolated islands. In the industrial sector, its policies align with the central government's mission to develop the fishing and marine industries. The government aims to support the growth of regions with potentials other than Batam without neglecting the growth momentum in Batam itself. In the long term, this redistribution policy is beneficial to the economy (Maryaningsih 2014). The provincial government has also launched several programmes to ease investments such as 123J and KLIK to help expedite investment realisation (Bank Indonesia 2017).

Key Economic Indicators, 2015

Land Area (km²)	8,202
Population	
Total Population	1,973,000
Urban Population (%)	83.00
Poverty Rate (%)	5.78
Labour Force	891,988
Labour Force Participation Rate (%)	45.21
Gross Regional Domestic Products (GRDP) — 2010 prices	Rupiah (million)
GRDP	155,112,880
GRDP (non-minerals)	128,072,000
GRDP per Capita	78.62
GRDP per Capita (non-minerals)	64.91
Economic Composition	% of GRDP
Primary Sector	20.05
Secondary Sector	56.71
Tertiary Sector	23.24
Trade — 2010 prices	Rupiah (million)
Exports	120,139,018
Imports	87,816,121
Top-3 exports: mineral fuels; electrical machinery and equipment; articles of iron and steel	
Top-3 imports: electrical machinery and equipment; machinery and mechanical appliances; articles of iron and steel	
Infrastructure	
Paved Roads (km)	3,507
Domestic Air Traffic (Passengers)	5,294,061
International Air Traffic (Passengers)	52,657
Domestic Cargo at Seaport (Tons)	20,223,164
International Cargo at Seaport (Tons)	6,352,248

Source: BPS Indonesia compiled by ACI.

5.25.4 Local Political Scene

The current governor of Riau Islands is Nurdin Basirun, who was initially elected as deputy governor of Riau Islands in February 2016. He was promoted to governor in April 2016 when elected Governor Muhammad Sani passed away. The deputy governor position has remained vacant since. This vacancy is argued to be the reason for Nurdin Basirun's weak leadership, which is demonstrated through his poor coordination with mayors and regents of the province (Panama 2017).

Nurdin Basirun envisioned Riau Islands as the prosperous Malay motherland that excels in the maritime sectors and that is united in its effort to redistribute development. This vision was fully supported by the Regional People's Representative Council (DPRD), although the council was dominated by representatives from his then opposition during the election — the Indonesian Democratic Party of Struggle (PDIP). Nurdin Basirun's wife is of Singapore citizenship, albeit with royal blood from Karimun. Because she refused to convert citizenship, she has been unable to assume her duty as the governor's wife (Arshad 2017).

5.26 Commentary on Recent Developments in South Kalimantan, 2015–2017

By: Arief Budiman and Ahmad Alim Bacri
Universitas Lambung Mangkurat

Province Location

Source: ACI.

5.26.1 Economic Conditions

South Kalimantan's economy had experienced growth between 2015 and 2017. In 2016, growth rate reached 5.28 percent, driven by improvements in commodity prices of coal and rubber which had previously slumped. The drop in commodity prices was triggered by weakening global demand — primarily from China due to its declining economic growth.

The most significant growth occurred in the communications and transportation sector. Despite the growth, these sectors had not contributed substantially to employment. Based on data in the third quarter of 2016, the agriculture and mining sectors experienced significant growth and contributed substantially to the province's GRDP.

Meanwhile, investments had been affected by a tightening of the province's fiscal policy. As a result, investment growth had declined from 5.43 percent in 2015 to 3.29 percent in 2016. There is a large potential for both FDI and DDI in the energy sector, such as those pertaining to power plants supplied by electricity, gas and water. The economy appears to have good prospects, given the province's stable macroeconomic and socio-political conditions, as well as good security.

5.26.2 Social Conditions and Development

Social conditions and development have been affected by the weakening labour conditions in South Kalimantan. Labour data in the fourth quarter of 2016 indicated a decline in the Employment Availability Index from 97.92 in the previous quarter to 90.83. This was caused by major layoffs in the mining sector between 2014 and 2015, which had led to a rise in unemployment figures in the formal sector.

Generally, social conditions in the province had been improving, as observed in the rising HDI between 2011 and 2016. HDI had increased at an average of 0.96 point annually between 2011 and 2014, and 0.98 point from 2015 to 2016. In 2016, HDI reached 69.05 — just below the index of 70.00, which is the benchmark for high human development status.

In addition, life expectancy in South Kalimantan had improved from 2011 to 2016, with an average annual growth of 0.31 percent. In 2016, the province's life expectancy index reached 67.92 years. This indicates that the improvements in the province's life expectancy corresponded with its improvements in HDI.

5.26.3 Provincial Government Policies

Government policies have been significant in driving and accelerating economic development. A particular focus has been given on the development of economic infrastructure, which is regarded as a prerequisite to support long-term investment programmes. Such initiatives include the transformation of the 150 hectare Syamsudin Noor Airport into an international airport and the construction of toll roads which have eased access among cities. Ports in Tanah Laut Regency have also been constructed to support the development of the largest industrial park in Indonesia that is about 6,000 hectares in size, along with the development of the 2,000 hectares industrial zone at the Tanah Bumbu Regency. The government has also encouraged the development of energy infrastructure through the construction of coal-based power plants in the industrial areas that would supplement the limited supply of electricity currently provided by the State Electricity Company (PLN).

Furthermore, various provincial regulations related to the development of ecotourism, among others, have turned the province's capital city Banjarmasin into a world-class river city.

Key Economic Indicators, 2015

Land Area (km²)	38,744
Population	
Total Population	3,989,800
Urban Population (%)	45.10
Poverty Rate (%)	4.72
Labour Force	1,987,250
Labour Force Participation Rate (%)	49.81
Gross Regional Domestic Products (GRDP) — 2010 prices	Rupiah (million)
GRDP	110,867,880
GRDP (non-minerals)	80,577,000
GRDP per Capita	27.79
GRDP per Capita (non-minerals)	20.20
Economic Composition	% of GRDP
Primary Sector	41.77
Secondary Sector	20.51
Tertiary Sector	37.72
Trade — 2010 prices	Rupiah (million)
Exports	57,204,072
Imports	14,049,029
Top-3 exports: mineral fuels; animal or vegetable fats and oil; wood and articles of wood	
Top-3 imports: mineral fuels; mechanical machinery and equipment; ships and floating structures	
Infrastructure	
Paved Roads (km)	7,827
Domestic Air Traffic (Passengers)	3,715,270
International Air Traffic (Passengers)	8,375
Domestic Cargo at Seaport (Tons)	162,703,444
International Cargo at Seaport (Tons)	81,107,605

Source: BPS Indonesia compiled by ACI.

5.26.4 Local Political Scene

The political scene in the province has been conducive and peaceful, thus enabling a promising investment climate. Under the leadership of Governor Sahbirin Noor, who is known for his humble demeanour, the Regional People's Representative Council (DPRD) provides solid support to the development of the province. There is a strong synergy between the executive and legislative councils. Sahbirin Noor's government also commits to developing the economy by leveraging on local resource excellence, particularly in the agribusiness and agro-industry sectors. The goal is to add value to the economy through ways such as employment and technology transfer, which will ultimately reduce poverty and unemployment rates as well as improve the welfare of the community.

5.27 Commentary on Recent Developments in South Sulawesi, 2015–2017

By: M. Yusri Zamhuri
Universitas Hasanuddin

Province Location

Source: ACI.

5.27.1 Economic Conditions

South Sulawesi province grew faster than the national average between 2015 and 2017. In the second quarter of 2017, it grew by 6.63 percent (y-o-y). The agricultural sector was the highest contributor of growth with 23.60 percent while the manufacturing, construction and trade sectors contribute to more than 10 percent each.

Nickel was the leading export commodity, seizing more than 50 percent of total exports. Export performance, however, slowed down in second quarter of 2017 by 13.70 percent due to the fall in global nickel price and economic slowdown in export destination countries. On the other hand, the composition of imports had changed between 2015 and 2017; while wheat was the most imported commodity in 2015, mechanical machinery took over in 2017. In general, however, y-o-y imports contracted by 1.08 percent, largely due to the fall in non-oil and gas imports.

The province still depends on multiyear projects to attract investments. Examples include large scale infrastructure projects, such as the Makassar New Port and Makassar-Parepare train line, along with the construction of smelters by mining companies.

5.27.2 Social Conditions and Development

Poverty had declined between 2015 and 2017, standing at 9.38 percent in March 2017 — the second lowest among all Sulawesi provinces. One of the supporting factors for the declining trend was the relatively controlled inflation rate, given that inflation has a significant correlation to poverty rate, particularly in rice.

South Sulawesi's Gini ratio declined from 0.43 on March 2016 to 0.41 on March 2017. Simultaneously, HDI rose from 69.20 in 2015 to 69.80 in 2016, contributed by improvements in the indicators expected years of schooling, mean years of schooling and GNI per capita. The HDI score in 2016 placed South Sulawesi at the 14th position nationally.

South Sulawesi's labour participation rate stood at 64.28 percent in February 2017. It had been increasing since August 2015 and had never fallen under 60 percent. Women made up 52.04 percent of this rate.

Overt unemployment rates in South Sulawesi were highest among those with vocational high school (SMK) and diploma certification at 6.35 percent and 9.81 percent respectively.

5.27.3 Provincial Government Policies

Large scale infrastructure development is the South Sulawesi government's mainstay. Aside from being one of the most appealing factors for investment, the projects are expected to increase productivity and improve business climate. Some of these large scale projects are the Makassar New Port, the Makassar-Parepare train line, the Jeneponto steam power plant, wind farms at Jeneponto and Sidrap, an underpass at the Mandai junction as well as various elevated roads and middle ring roads.

Additionally, there are multi-year projects that can support South Sulawei's objective of achieving food resilience, such as the Baliase dam in North Luwu Regency, Karalloe dam in Gowa Regency, Paselloreng dam in Wajo Regency as well as the Tunggu Nipa-nipa dam in Gowa and Maros Regencies.

Key Economic Indicators, 2015

Land Area (km²)	46,717
Population	
Total Population	8,520,300
Urban Population (%)	40.60
Poverty Rate (%)	10.12
Labour Force	3,706,128
Labour Force Participation Rate (%)	43.50
Gross Regional Domestic Products (GRDP) — 2010 prices	Rupiah (million)
GRDP	250,758,280
GRDP (non-minerals)	234,955,000
GRDP per Capita	29.43
GRDP per Capita (non-minerals)	27.58
Economic Composition	% of GRDP
Primary Sector	27.87
Secondary Sector	26.34
Tertiary Sector	45.79
Trade — 2010 prices	Rupiah (million)
Exports	14,445,504
Imports	9,674,160
Top-3 exports: nickel and articles thereof; cocoa and cocoa preparations; oil seeds and oleaginous fruits	
Top-3 imports: cereals, mineral fuels; machinery and mechanical appliances	
Infrastructure	
Paved Roads (km)	16,896
Domestic Air Traffic (Passengers)	9,250,045
International Air Traffic (Passengers)	115,522
Domestic Cargo at Seaport (Tons)	14,651,470
International Cargo at Seaport (Tons)	2,148,380

Source: BPS Indonesia compiled by ACI.

5.27.4 Local Political Scene

South Sulawesi is currently preparing for the 2018 local elections (Pilkada) for the governor as well as regents and mayors in 12 districts in the province. Nearing the election, the political constellation has started to indicate four potential candidates.

During the current reign of Dr Syahrul Yasin Limpo as governor, the Party of the Functional Group (Golkar) has been the most dominant. Other parties such as the Indonesian Democratic Party of Struggle (PDIP), Prosperous Justice Party (PKS) and Great Indonesia Movement Party (Gerindra) only have a small political representation in the Regional People's Representative Council (DPRD). Interestingly, PDIP is still able to garner other parties' support when it makes political decision despite its small share, which may be due to the fact that it is the majority party at the national level.

5.28 Commentary on Recent Developments in South Sumatra, 2015–2017

By: Taufiq Marwa and Mohamad Adam
Universitas Sriwijaya

Province Location

Source: ACI.

5.28.1 Economic Conditions

South Sumatra's economy between 2015 and 2017 had been improving. GRDP growth stood at 5.03 percent in 2016, while per capita GRDP increased from 4.79 percent in 2015 to 5.03 percent in 2016. In 2016, the four sectors that contributed to GRDP the most were mining (21.84 percent), processing industry (18.30 percent), agriculture, forestry and fishery (16.60 percent) as well as construction (13.24 percent).

Investments in 2015 surpassed the target of Rp18.86 trillion by about four percent. In 2016, it further increased by 9.33 percent, with FDI contributing to Rp26.30 trillion and DDI Rp1.86 trillion.

There have been massive infrastructure project developments in South Sumatra such as the construction of the 22 kilometres long Palembang-Indralaya highway, the LRT as well as the Musi IV and Musi VI bridges which will connect Palembang Ulu and Palembang Ilir. The construction of these projects is aimed at improving transportation leading to Asian Games 2018, which will be hosted in the province's capital city Palembang.

5.28.2 Social Conditions and Development

Given its large population size of 8,160,901 in 2016, South Sumatra ranked as the sixth most populated province in Indonesia. In order to support its development programmes, improvements in the quality of human resources must also be made. The province must also put in more effort into controlling population growth. Social development programs across all sectors must also be given priority so as to increase the welfare level of the people.

South Sumatra's HDI in 2015 stood at 67.46. It increased further to 68.24 in 2016. Improvements were observed in all components of HDI, particularly in the indicators GNI per capita (4.86 percent) and expected years of schooling (1.75 percent). Another improvement can also be observed in the province's poverty rate, which fell from 14.25 in 2015 to 13.54 in 2016. The urban poverty rate, however, saw a slightly more significant improvement compared to the rural poverty rate.

5.28.3 Provincial Government Policies

In order to further accelerate and support the smoothness of investments, six Provincial Regulations (Perda) were proposed for South Sumatra on (i) peace, orderliness and protection of the community, (ii) general services levy, (iii) business services levy, (iv) provincial tax, (v) industrial development for 2016–2035, and (vi) child-friendly and inclusive education provision.

The Tanjung Api-Api region has also been designated as a SEZ in order to develop industrial activities in the province. The SEZ, which is targeted to operate in June 2018, will occupy a total of 217 hectare (ha) of land. 66.13 ha of land has been successfully acquired. There have also been plans to conduct reclamation in Tanjung Carat in order to develop the area into a port. All these, along with the construction and repair works for roads connecting the ports and the city as well as the construction of highways and trains that could ease the distribution of goods and services, would hopefully increase the welfare of the people of South Sumatra.

Key Economic Indicators, 2015

Land Area (km^2)	91,592
Population	
Total Population	8,052,300
Urban Population (%)	36.50
Poverty Rate (%)	13.77
Labour Force	3,934,787
Labour Force Participation Rate (%)	48.87
Gross Regional Domestic Products (GRDP) — 2010 prices	Rupiah (million)
GRDP	254,044,880
GRDP (non-minerals)	185,801,000
GRDP per Capita	31.55
GRDP per Capita (non-minerals)	23.07
Economic Composition	% of GRDP
Primary Sector	40.79
Secondary Sector	29.91
Tertiary Sector	29.30
Trade — 2010 prices	Rupiah (million)
Exports	25,689,132
Imports	15,420,311
Top-3 exports: rubber and articles thereof; mineral fuels; animal or vegetable fats and oil	
Top-3 imports: machinery and mechanical appliances; electrical machinery and equipment; iron or steel articles	
Infrastructure	
Paved Roads (km)	10,138
Domestic Air Traffic (Passengers)	3,326,116
International Air Traffic (Passengers)	108,872
Domestic Cargo at Seaport (Tons)	4,097,266
International Cargo at Seaport (Tons)	2,226,516

Source: BPS Indonesia compiled by ACI.

5.28.4 Local Political Scene

Political scene in the province has been relatively uneventful, given that election will be held only in 2018. Some commotion may be observed in the beginning of 2018 when campaign period starts. A couple of major political parties will be involved in the upcoming election, such as the National Democrat Party (Nasdem), the Indonesian Democratic Party of Struggle (PDIP), the Party of the Functional Group (Golkar), the Democrat Party, the People's Conscience Party (Hanura), the Great Indonesia Movement Party (Gerindra), the National Mandate Party (PAN) as well as the United Development Party (PPP).

South Sumatra is currently led by Governor Alex Noerdin, who has governed the province for two terms. He was supported by Deputy Governor Edy Yusuf in his first term (2008–2013) and Ishak Mekki in his second term (2013–2018).

5.29 Commentary on Recent Developments in Southeast Sulawesi, 2015–2017

By: Muhammad Zamrun Firihu, Armid and Hasmina Tari Mokui
Universitas Halu Oleo

Province Location

Source: ACI.

5.29.1 Economic Conditions

Southeast Sulawesi's economic conditions between 2015 and 2017 had shown significant improvements. With an economy still heavily reliant on the primary sector, the three biggest contributors to the GRDP were (i) agriculture, forestry and fishery, (ii) mining as well as (iii) construction sectors.

Economic growth, however, had slightly declined from 6.88 percent in 2015 to 6.51 percent in 2016. Agriculture was still the biggest contributor in 2016 at 24.30 percent (BPS 2017). This sector also experienced the largest growth from 0.04 percent in 2015 to 7.75 percent in 2016.

In the second trimester of 2017, however, the economy showed a promising growth of 7.00 percent.

Between 2015 and 2016, Southeast Sulawesi's export values had exceeded that of imports. Despite increasing volume, there was also a decline in both export and import values in the same period.

There was also a decline in approved FDI between 2015 and 2016. However, domestic investment increased in the same period. Most investments lie in the industry sector (BPS 2017).

5.29.2 Social Conditions and Development

Southeast Sulawesi's HDI was ranked 19th out of 34 provinces in 2016, with a score that increased by 0.81 percent to 69.31 relative to 2015 (BPS 2017). In 2017, all components of HDI improved even further, most notably in the indicators life expectancy and expected years of schooling.

Investment in Southeast Sulawesi, however, has also heightened the potential of conflict between the community and conflict-prone industries such as mining. Most notably, there has been a clash between the leadership in foreign companies and local workers, which has resulted in the dissatisfaction against foreigners more generally. In December 2016, many foreigners from the People's Republic of China were found to have worked in Southeast Sulawesi using tourist visas — a revelation that only further heightened the conflict in the province. The provincial government, however, has put in place several measures to manage these conflicts.

Other than the abovementioned issues, the social conditions and developments in Southeast Sulawesi can be considered relatively conducive without any notable conflict among different ethnic and religious groups.

5.29.3 Provincial Government Policies

Under the Provincial Regulation (Perda) No. 2/2014, there are four pillars to Southeast Sulawesi's development: food, industry, sea and maritime as well as tourism. These four sectors have generally shown positive growth trends, although they recently slowed in the second trimester of 2017 due to slowdowns in both demand and supply.

Southeast Sulawesi is also geared towards being a centre for national mining industry, given that the province is rich in minerals and energy that are of high economic values such as nickel and asphalt (BPS 2017).

Although the regional government has also established Perda No. 14/2013 on environment protection and management, waste management practices on the ground still require closer supervision. A recent study, for instance, has found a significant increase in the concentration of heavy metals in the water system of Kendari Bay due to mining activities (Armid et al. 2017).

Key Economic Indicators, 2015

Land Area (km^2)	38,068
Population	
Total Population	2,499,500
Urban Population (%)	31.20
Poverty Rate (%)	13.74
Labour Force	1,138,045
Labour Force Participation Rate (%)	45.53
Gross Regional Domestic Products (GRDP) — 2010 prices	Rupiah (million)
GRDP	72,991,330
GRDP (non-minerals)	57,585,000
GRDP per Capita	29.20
GRDP per Capita (non-minerals)	23.04
Economic Composition	% of GRDP
Primary Sector	44.34
Secondary Sector	19.40
Tertiary Sector	36.26
Trade — 2010 prices	Rupiah (million)
Exports	1,395,392
Imports	4,283,219
Top-3 exports: articles of iron and steel; mineral fuels; fish and crustacean	
Top-3 imports: mineral fuels; machinery and mechanical appliances; electrical machinery and equipment	
Infrastructure	
Paved Roads (km)	3,715
Domestic Air Traffic (Passengers)	1,220,166
International Air Traffic (Passengers)	0
Domestic Cargo at Seaport (Tons)	8,420,390
International Cargo at Seaport (Tons)	70,273

Source: BPS Indonesia compiled by ACI.

5.29.4 Local Political Scene

The political scene in Southeast Sulawesi is relatively stable, although former Governor Nur Alam was recently arrested by the Corruption Eradication Commission (KPK) on 6 July 2017. Despite the arrest, local situation was not affected as Nur Alam's two-period rule has been relatively stable.

Southeast Sulawesi is currently preparing for the local election (Pikada) in 2018. Many candidates have expressed interest in running for the election, namely Lukman Abunawas (Provincial Secretary of Southeaset Sulawesi), Asrun (former Mayor of Kendari), Hugua (former Regent of Wakatobi), Rusda Mahmud (Regent of North Kolak), Syafei Kahar (former Regent of Buton), Ali Mazi (former Governor of Southeast Sulawesi 2003–2008) and Abdul Rahman Farisi (young politician). This provides the people of Southeast Sulawesi with more options to elect the best future leader.

5.30 Commentary on Recent Developments in West Java, 2015–2017

By: Maman Setiawan
Universitas Padjajaran

Province Location

Source: ACI.

5.30.1 Economic Conditions

West Java registered an economic growth of 5.67 percent in 2016. All sectors contributed to this positive growth, with the exception of the mining sector which registered a negative growth rate of 0.97 percent. On the other hand, information and communications sector registered the highest positive growth at 14.27 percent.

There was a fall in export value by 1.27 percent in 2016 driven by the declining oil and gas sector, although exports volume had increased by 8.06 percent. Meanwhile, the oil and gas sector had driven an increase in imports in the province.

Investments in West Java saw a rise of 4.59 percent between 2016 and 2015 — 52.6 percent of which came from FDI while the rest from DDI. The positive growth in investments were mainly found in the footwear industry sector, followed by rubber and plastic. Certain sectors, however, saw negative investment growth, namely the construction, housing and industrial zone, food and beverages as well as chemistry and pharmacy sectors.

West Java's investment target and realisation rates have been categorised as "excellent" in an evaluation by the Indonesia's Investment Coordinating Board (BKPM).

5.30.2 Social Conditions and Development

West Java population saw an increase of 1.4 percent to reach 47,379,390 in 2016.

Its HDI also increased by 0.80 percent in 2016 to reach 70.05. The largest contributing component was the GNI per capita indicator, which saw an increase of 2.60 percent. Life Expectancy in the province also increased by 0.03 years in the same period.

Poverty rate in West Java fell by 4.77 percent in 2016, which could be attributed to the increase in income per capita from Rp32.60 million in 2015 to Rp34.80 million in 2016.

Mean years of schooling in West Java province also increased from 7.86 years in 2015 to 7.95 years in 2016. Various educational infrastructure programmes conducted by the West Java provincial government, along with the School Operational Assistance (BOS) program by the central government, were contributing factors to this improvement.

One of the pertinent issues in West Java, especially with regard to infrastructure development, is that of land acquisition. The government has put in more effort to approach the community concerned before any infrastructure development commences.

5.30.3 Provincial Government Policies

Based on a study on ease of doing business conducted by the Regional Autonomy Watch (KPPOD) in early 2017, there were certain Provincial Regulations (Perda) considered to have hindered investment and business climate in West Java. For instance, the Perda in Social and Environmental Responsibility had caused confusion, given the fact that its implementation greatly differed from one city/regency to another.

West Java had also been aggressively building infrastructure in 2016 in four primary sectors: sports, health, education and tourism. Sports infrastructure development was driven by the National Sports Week (PON) XIX as well as the National Paralympic Week (Peparnas) XV held in West Java in 2016. In the tourism sector, development can be divided into general tourism as well as geopark-based tourism. The provincial government also aims to build 5,000 classrooms and 100 community health centres (Puskesmas) in each city/regency.

Key Economic Indicators, 2015

Land Area (km²)	35,378
Population	
Total Population	46,709,600
Urban Population (%)	72.90
Poverty Rate (%)	9.57
Labour Force	20,586,356
Labour Force Participation Rate (%)	44.07
Gross Regional Domestic Products (GRDP) — 2010 prices	Rupiah (million)
GRDP	1,207,083,410
GRDP (non-minerals)	1,156,522,000
GRDP per Capita	25.84
GRDP per Capita (non-minerals)	24.76
Economic Composition	% of GRDP
Primary Sector	9.96
Secondary Sector	52.18
Tertiary Sector	37.86
Trade — 2010 prices	Rupiah (million)
Exports	7,714,268
Imports	19,236,614
Top-3 exports: electrical machinery and equipment; machinery and mechanical appliances; apparel and clothing accessories, knitted or crocheted	
Top-3 imports: electrical machinery and equipment; machinery and mechanical appliance; plastics and articles thereof	
Infrastructure	
Paved Roads (km)	21,430
Domestic Air Traffic (Passengers)	2,499,891
International Air Traffic (Passengers)	653,046
Domestic Cargo at Seaport (Tons)	20,092,346
International Cargo at Seaport (Tons)	2,686,634

Source: BPS Indonesia compiled by ACI.

5.30.4 Local Political Scene

The political condition in West Java has been relatively stable, although it has warmed in recent months due to the upcoming local elections (Pilkada) in 2018. There is a risk of the exploitation of identity politics — as was the case in DKI Jakarta's Pilkada — which might cause tension in the community.

West Java is currently ruled by Ahmad Heryawan, who was elected for the first time in 2008 with Deputy Governor Dedi Yusuf. He was then re-elected in 2013 with Deddy Mizwar. He was represented by the Prosperous Justice Party (PKS). During his rule, West Java government's finances were audited as "normal without exception" by the Audit Board of Indonesia (BPK).

West Java's Regional People's Representative Council (DPRD) is not dominated by one single party. The party with most number of seats in the council is the Indonesian Democratic Party of Struggle (PDIP), which occupies 20 seats out of 100.

5.31 Commentary on Recent Developments in West Kalimantan, 2015–2017

By: Nurul Bariyah
Universitas Tanjungpura

Province Location

Source: ACI.

5.31.1 Economic Conditions

In the last two years, West Kalimantan's economy had outperformed Indonesia's. The agriculture, forestry and fishery sector was the main contributor to the province's GRDP, although decreasingly so. On the other hand, manufacturing industry had become more prominent in 2016 following the government's export ban on raw materials.

In line with the development of the processing industry, West Kalimantan's exports in 2016 increased by 10.15 percent, dominated by rubbers and articles of rubbers, wood and articles of wood as well as inorganic chemicals. Meanwhile, imports declined significantly from US$614,739,520 to US$351,677,706 in 2016, especially in the electrical machinery and equipment sector, driven by local regulation where 40 percent of government goods and services must come from local content.

Investment in 2015 reached Rp22.84 trillion — 73.00 percent of which was FDI. In 2016, it fell to Rp19.29 trillion. It still met its Medium Term Development Planning (RPJMD) target — commendable considering the province's lack of infrastructure, which is a prerequisite for investments.

5.31.2 Social Conditions and Development

West Kalimantan's HDI in 2016 was moderate at 65.88. The index itself had gradually increased in the last two years, although its ranking had remained constant at 29th out of 34. Improvements were primarily driven by the indicators mean years of schooling and expected years of schooling.

The rise in both investment and economic growth has not been able to solve West Kalimantan's problems. Poverty still stood at 7.88 percent, while inequality among regencies/cities was measured to be around 0.327 in 2017. Unemployment rate still remained at 4.22 percent in February 2017.

There has been jealousy among the locals over the influx of foreign workers in domestic investment projects, while locals living in the borders are working in Malaysia. Although the government had clarified that there were only 779 legal foreign workers in the province, there were many illegal ones. The government thus needs to be transparent in order to properly enforce the law. Conversely, improvements in economic and employment opportunities are also needed to address the problem of locals becoming illegal workers at the border area.

5.31.3 Provincial Government Policies

The regional government has issued Governor Regulation (Pergub) No. 13/2017, which delegates the authority to approve licenses and non-licenses to the head of the Investment and One-Stop Integrated Service Agency (DPMPTSP). This is hoped to create a conducive investment climate through fast, efficient and effective service, which is also in line with the central government's policy to boost the economy and investment in the region. Business response to the policy has generally been positive, as long as it is implemented on the ground as promised.

Infrastructure development projects which are supported by the central government in the last two years have been aimed at improving access at the borders through the construction of parallel border roads and a cross-border post (PLBN) as well as the expansion of Supadio Airport. In addition to increasing investment attractiveness, the increased access is hoped to improve the welfare of the people.

Key Economic Indicators, 2015

Land Area (km²)	147,307
Population	
Total Population	4,789,600
Urban Population (%)	33.10
Poverty Rate (%)	8.44
Labour Force	2,357,224
Labour Force Participation Rate (%)	49.22
Gross Regional Domestic Products (GRDP) — 2010 prices	Rupiah (million)
GRDP	112,324,860
GRDP (non-minerals)	107,703,000
GRDP per Capita	23.45
GRDP per Capita (non-minerals)	22.49
Economic Composition	% of GRDP
Primary Sector	26.88
Secondary Sector	28.27
Tertiary Sector	44.85
Trade — 2010 prices	Rupiah (million)
Exports	5,265,046
Imports	5,843,611
Top-3 exports: rubber and articles thereof; wood and articles of wood; animal or vegetable fats and oils	
Top-3 imports: machinery and mechanical appliances; mineral fuels; iron or steel articles	
Infrastructure	
Paved Roads (km)	7,431
Domestic Air Traffic (Passengers)	3,024,530
International Air Traffic (Passengers)	73,696
Domestic Cargo at Seaport (Tons)	4,292,980
International Cargo at Seaport (Tons)	365,288

Source: BPS Indonesia compiled by ACI.

5.31.4 Local Political Scene

There has been no fundamental change to the political landscape in West Kalimantan. In the 2012 local elections (Pilkada), the incumbent pair of Cornelis-Christiandy Sanjaya was re-elected as governor and deputy governor for 2013–2018 with a vision to "create a peaceful, healthy, intelligent, safe, cultured and prosperous West Kalimantan." The pair won with 52.13 percent of the total votes and was supported by a coalition of five major parties. The result was contested by the two other candidates at the Constitutional Court (MK), although the appeal was rejected. Cornelis has several times received awards at the national level. As President of the Dayak National Indigenous Council 2015–2020, he is also fairly popular among the Dayak community in West Kalimantan and nationally.

The Indonesian Democratic Party of Struggle (PDIP) dominated the 2014 Legislative Election (32.99 percent), followed by the Party of the Functional Group (Golkar) (14.08 percent).

5.32 Commentary on Recent Developments in West Nusa Tenggara, 2015–2017

By: M. Firmansyah
Universitas Mataram

Province Location

Source: ACI.

5.32.1 Economic Conditions

The West Nusa Tenggara province had been growing modestly in recent years, with a growth rate of 21.77 percent in 2015. The mining sector had an important role in supporting the growth, specifically through the existence of the Newmont Nusa Tenggara (NNT) Limited Liability Company (LLC) operating in the West Sumbawa Regency. Growth, however, drastically dropped in 2016 to 5.82 percent due to diminishing export quantity, given that more than 99 percent of the province's export was mining concentrates. Excluding the mining sector, however, growth in 2016 was 6.01 percent — an increase from 5.71 percent 2015. One of the major sectors was the wholesale trade and retail sector, which had been showing positive trends with the mushrooming of modern retails and malls in Mataram City.

Investment-wise, realisation until the second quarter of 2017 had been more than Rp2.25 trillion — Rp2.09 trillion of which were from DDI. Investments were concentrated at the West Sumbawa (Rp2.03 trillion from NNT LLC) and North Lombok (Rp83 billion from tourism) regencies.

5.32.2 Social Conditions and Development

West Nusa Tenggara's HDI growth in 2016 was relatively good and above the national average. In 2015, HDI was at 65.19, which further increased to 65.81 in 2016. Nevertheless, West Nusa Tenggara's HDI still hovered at the lower rank of 30 out of 34 provinces in Indonesia. The low HDI score relates to the problem of poverty, where the rate in 2017 stood at 16.07 percent. Local governments were only able to reduce the poverty rate by 1.00 percent instead of the 2.00 percent target. Income inequality was at the average level with a Gini coefficient of 0.37.

One of the main factors causing poverty other than structural and cultural issues is that of increasing inflation rate. The policies to increase the price of gasoline and electricity, along with the increased consumption during the celebration of cultural events such as the Islamic Prophet's Birth, had significantly triggered higher inflation. The overt unemployment rate as of February 2017 was at 97,220 people. There were 598,831 businesses — most of which small and medium-sized — with 1.4 million in the workforce.

5.32.3 Provincial Government Policies

Mandalika in Central Lombok has been designated as one of the SEZs for the tourism sector. However, development has not been optimal; delays were rampant due to problems with land acquisition.

In 2017, a "global hub" called the Bandar Kayangan in North Lombok Regency was finalised. The project is aimed to transform the Lombok Strait into an alternative route for extra-large ships, given the limited capacity of the Malacca Strait. It is expected to transform North Lombok into the province's growth centre.

Lobbies have also been made to redesign the National Spatial Plan (RTRWN) with changes to Government Regulation (PP) No. 26/2008 and No. 13/2017.

There are also other projects such as the construction of a sea toll line that would connect the Lombok Island to East Java.

Key Economic Indicators, 2015

Land Area (km²)	18,572
Population	
Total Population	4,835,600
Urban Population (%)	45.40
Poverty Rate (%)	16.54
Labour Force	2,255,879
Labour Force Participation Rate (%)	46.65
Gross Regional Domestic Products (GRDP) — 2010 prices	Rupiah (million)
GRDP	89,344,580
GRDP (non-minerals)	66,078,000
GRDP per Capita	18.48
GRDP per Capita (non-minerals)	13.66
Economic Composition	% of GRDP
Primary Sector	47.22
Secondary Sector	13.04
Tertiary Sector	39.73
Trade — 2010 prices	Rupiah (million)
Exports	14,427,472
Imports	1,635,998
Top-3 exports: ores, slag and ash; natural and cultured pearls, precious/semi-precious stones; fish and crustaceans	
Top-3 imports: machinery and mechanical appliances; iron or steel articles; rubber and articles thereof	
Infrastructure	
Paved Roads (km)	5,218
Domestic Air Traffic (Passengers)	3,349,727
International Air Traffic (Passengers)	248,102
Domestic Cargo at Seaport (Tons)	2,693,166
International Cargo at Seaport (Tons)	153,608

Source: BPS Indonesia compiled by ACI.

5.32.4 Local Political Scene

The two-period governor, whose development vision is PIJAR (Cattle, Corn, and Seaweed), will step down in 2018 as the local election (Pilkada) takes place. More than 80 percent of the voters will be from Lombok Island, while the rest from Sumbawa Island. This imbalance has created a turnout trend in which most of the governors in West Nusa Tenggara come from Lombok Island. This has sparked a petition from Sumbawa Island to secede and govern itself as the Sumbawa Island Province. The idea, however, was blocked as President Joko Widodo rolled out a moratorium over the creation of new provinces and regions.

Large political parties such as the Party of the Functional Group (Golkar), the Indonesian Democratic Party of Struggle (PDIP) and the Great Indonesia Movement Party (Gerindra) have dominated the political power in the province. The current Regional People's Representative Council (DPRD) is led by a Golkar politician, while the deputies hail from the Prosperous Justice Party (PKS), the Democrat Party and Gerindra.

5.33 Commentary on Recent Developments in West Papua, 2015–2017

By: Asia Competitiveness Institute

Province Location

Source: ACI.

5.33.1 Economic Conditions

West Papua's economy has fluctuated in recent years, with growth rates that were lower than the preceding years of 2013 and 2014 (7.36 percent and 5.38 percent respectively). While the rate increased from 4.15 percent in 2015 to 4.52 percent in 2016, it declined to 4.01 percent in 2017. The processing and mining industries remain dominant, although their growth rates have gradually declined. Meanwhile, growth rates in sectors such as wholesale trade and automobile repairs, construction as well as information and communications have been rising.

Export and import values have fluctuated in the last three years. Nominal foreign export values have decreased in both 2016 and 2017, while foreign import value dramatically increased in 2016. Exports, which are predominantly mineral fuels, remain as the economy's largest contributor to growth, despite its declining proportion over the years.

Likewise, FDI and DDI have also fluctuated over the three years. FDI is dominated by the mineral and non-metals industries, while DDI is predominantly made up of crops and plantation.

5.33.2 Social Conditions and Development

West Papua's quality of living has improved as observed in its rising HDI, which had increased from 61.73 in 2015 to 62.21 in 2016, resulting from improvements in health, education and life expectancy. For instance, life expectancy increased by 0.07 to 67.51 years in 2016.

While the percentage of people living under poverty had declined from 25.73 percent in 2015 to 24.88 percent in 2016, poverty gap and poverty severity indices in West Papua had been rising.

In Indonesia, education has been made compulsory for every child up until high school. In 2016, net school enrolment rates in West Papua were at 96.85 percent for ages 7–12 and 13–15 and 80.2 percent for ages 16–18 and 19–24. The lower rates among older students indicate that there is still a tendency for students to stop schooling as they get older.

West Papua remains free from various issues such as malnutrition or armed groups. However, the province is still faced with labour issues such as low minimum wage and a rising crime rate, owing to the prevalence of alcoholism (despite prohibitive laws) and high levels of unemployment.

5.33.3 Provincial Government Policies

Improving connectivity with the eastern part of Indonesia, which includes West Papua, has been President Joko Widodo's priority since the start of his administration. The central government, through a number of ministries and agencies, have agreed on 3,353 national projects in West Papua, as part of an overall objective of supporting the accelerated development programme in the province.

By 2017, many infrastructure-related projects have been carried out in the province. These include the construction of the Wariori and Oransbari dams in Manokwari Regency, which are aimed at supporting water and food security, the construction of roads in the western part of Trans Papua, which is targeted to fully open in 2017 and the opening of the first bonded logistics park (PLB) in eastern Indonesia in Sorong, aimed at strengthening business fundamentals and logistics needs.

The transportation ministry also plans to build an international port in the Seget district of Sorong Regency to facilitate the development of SEZ in Sorong and the exporting of goods from West Papua abroad.

Key Economic Indicators, 2015

Land Area (km²)	99,672
Population	
Total Population	871,500
Urban Population (%)	32.30
Poverty Rate (%)	25.73
Labour Force	413,635
Labour Force Participation Rate (%)	47.46
Gross Regional Domestic Products (GRDP) — 2010 prices	Rupiah (million)
GRDP	52,346,490
GRDP (non-minerals)	25,964,000
GRDP per Capita	60.06
GRDP per Capita (non-minerals)	29.79
Economic Composition	% of GRDP
Primary Sector	31.76
Secondary Sector	43.49
Tertiary Sector	24.75
Trade — 2010 prices	Rupiah (million)
Exports	28,489,582
Imports	372,324
Top-3 exports: mineral fuels; gem and jewellery; wood and articles of wood	
Top-3 imports: machinery and electrical appliances; machinery and aircraft mechanics; articles of iron and steel	
Infrastructure	
Paved Roads (km)	4,210
Domestic Air Traffic (Passengers)	1,460,333
International Air Traffic (Passengers)	0
Domestic Cargo at Seaport (Tons)	1,585,550
International Cargo at Seaport (Tons)	9,975

Source: BPS Indonesia compiled by ACI.

5.33.4 Local Political Scene

In the 2017 local election (Pilkada), West Papua elected Dominggus Mandacan as governor and Mohammad Lakotani as deputy governor. The pair, who won with more than 60 percent of the votes, was supported by the Indonesian Unity Party (Perindo), the Indonesian Democratic Party of Struggle (PDIP), the National Mandate Party (PAN), the Indonesian Justice and Unity Party (PKPI) and the National Democrat Party (Nasdem).

The elected leaders' mission was to create a West Papua province that is "safe, prosperous and dignified." To realise this, they have drafted various plans to create a harmonious and peaceful living condition regardless of ethnicities, religion, race and inter-group relations (SARA), improve the community's living standards by opening up employment and commit to an authoritative government administration which is free from corruption, collusion and nepotism.

5.34 Commentary on Recent Developments in West Sulawesi, 2015–2017

By: Abdul Kadir Paloloang
Universitas Sulawesi Barat

Province Location

Source: ACI.

5.34.1 Economic Conditions

A few years from its formation in 2004 as the 33rd province of Indonesia, West Sulawesi's investment development was rather slow, as reflected by its weak Gross Fixed Capital Formation (GFCF). Although the province managed to significantly increase its GFCF level to reach 11.70 percent in 2013, it fell again in 2015 to 7.40 percent. Moreover, investment had primarily been focused on a few sectors such as the processing industry and construction, with limited innovation on and diversification into other types of products.

Although only more than a decade old, West Sulawesi managed to register the highest economic growth nationally and regionally. This cocoa-producing region was able to reach 10.02 percent growth in the third quarter of 2014. This prompted even more infrastructure building in the province, from the opening of more banks as well as the expansion and addition of road infrastructure throughout the province.

5.34.2 Social Conditions and Development

West Sulawesi's HDI saw an increase in 2016 (BPS 2017). According to the Central Bureau of Statistics (BPS), this increase raised West Sulawesi's HDI standing from low to average. Between 2015 and 2016, all components of HDI also saw improvements: life expectancy in the province increased by 0.09 years to 64.31, while the expected years of schooling also rose by 0.12 years to 12.34 (Suntono 2017). Similarly, mean years of schooling — which is the number of years that the population above 25 years old have gone through education — saw improvements by 0.20 years to 7.14 years.

Meanwhile, spending per capita in West Sulawesi can be used as a proxy to estimate quality of life in the province. In 2016, West Sulawesi's adjusted spending per capita (constant 2012) also saw an increase by Rp190,000 to Rp8.50 million relative to the previous year.

5.34.3 Provincial Government Policies

Development in West Sulawesi for 2015–2017 had been guided by the Long Term Development Planning (RPJPD) 2005–2015, focusing on nine strategic issues: (i) lagging development, (ii) poverty, (iii) HDI, (iv) infrastructure, (v) human resource quality, (vi) public service, (vii) commodity, (viii) regional development and proliferation as well as (ix) regional inequality.

West Sulawesi also has 13 priority programmes on (i) regional investment climate, (ii) urban development, (iii) service and accessibility, (iv) health of mother and child, (v) accessibility and quality of education, (vi) regional infrastructure, (vii) food resilience, (viii) superior commodities and regional competitiveness, (ix) coverage and quality of clean water and sanitation, (x) renewable energy, (xi) government management bureaucratic reform, (xii) cultural and tourism destination development as well as (xiii) opening of employment opportunities and workplace.

Key Economic Indicators, 2015

Land Area (km²)	16,787
Population	
Total Population	1,282,200
Urban Population (%)	22.90
Poverty Rate (%)	11.9
Labour Force	616,549
Labour Force Participation Rate (%)	48.09
Gross Regional Domestic Products (GRDP) — 2010 prices	Rupiah (million)
GRDP	25,983,650
GRDP (non-minerals)	25,426,000
GRDP per Capita	20.27
GRDP per Capita (non-minerals)	19.83
Economic Composition	% of GRDP
Primary Sector	41.84
Secondary Sector	19.39
Tertiary Sector	38.77
Trade — 2010 prices	Rupiah (million)
Exports	0
Imports	27,350
Top-3 exports: crude palm oil; palm kernel; livestock	
Top-3 imports: cement; fertilisers; goods	
Infrastructure	
Paved Roads (km)	3,324
Domestic Air Traffic (Passengers)	82,536
International Air Traffic (Passengers)	0
Domestic Cargo at Seaport (Tons)	874,639
International Cargo at Seaport (Tons)	558,954

Source: BPS Indonesia compiled by ACI.

5.34.4 Local Political Scene

West Sulawesi's rapid growth can be attributed to the local economic development that gives a sense of security and stability, achieved through the fact that the governor and deputy governor are backed by the party majority through a large coalition.

From 2017 until 2022, West Sulawesi is led by Governor Ali Baal Masdar and Deputy Governor Enny Anggraeni Anwar, who are both supported by a coalition of seven political parties. They won over two other candidates by a slight margin of 0.65 percent with 244,763 votes (38.76 percent). Both have had prior experience in leadership, be it as a regent or as a member of Indonesia's parliament.

The Regional People's Representative Council (DPRD) is represented by 45 politicians, primarily from the following parties: Democrat Party (10), Party of the Functional Group (Golkar) (9), the Great Indonesia Movement Party (Gerindra) (6) and the National Mandate Party (PAN) (5).

5.35 Commentary on Recent Developments in West Sumatra, 2015–2017

By: Werry Darta Taifur
Universitas Andalas

Province Location

Source: ACI.

5.35.1 Economic Conditions

West Sumatra's economy in the past two years had continued to grow above the national average at 5.41 percent p.a. Growth primarily came from the accommodation, food and beverages sector (8.58 percent) as well as the Information and Communications Technology (ICT) sector (9.00 percent). This marks the change in West Sumatra's economic structure from one that was predominantly agriculture-based into a one with flourishing tourism and services sectors.

West Sumatra's exports were still dominated by the commodity sector, particularly CPO and rubber. This means that exports were highly influenced by the world's commodity price fluctuation. Other exported commodities included coffee, cocoa as well as cinnamon. Cinnamon had the least significant increase in volume and production.

The prospects of investment in West Sumatra appear to be promising, with an increase in both FDI and DDI in the past years. In 2016, FDI reached around US$70 million — a threefold increase compared to the previous year, while DDI increased by 126 percent in 2016. FDI was primarily concentrated in geothermal and water power plant, agro-industry as well as plantation.

5.35.2 Social Conditions and Development

Social conditions in West Sumatra had been stable in recent years. In 2016, West Sumatra's HDI increased by 0.75 point to 70.73 from 69.98 in 2015, with improvements across all aspects of HDI. Historically, West Sumatera's HDI had always been higher than the national HDI, although the province's life expectancy had always been below the national level. In 2016, West Sumatra's HDI was ranked ninth out of 34 provinces in Indonesia.

Overt unemployment rate of West Sumatra has hovered around six to seven percent for the past five years, with a rate higher for those with high school diplomas compared to the other groups.

Small and medium enterprises dominate the day-to-day business in West Sumatra. As such, incidents between labour and firm are relatively minimal. For large scale companies, particularly those involved in plantations and CPO processing plants, some incidents and disputes have taken place. Conflicts usually relate to the breach of negotiated agreements by firms or land disputes between firms and the locals.

5.35.3 Provincial Government Policies

The provincial government has put in numerous efforts to boost investments in order to drive economic development in West Sumatra. One of the prominent policies is the establishment of the Investment and One-Stop Integrated Service Agency (DPMPTSP) for all business permit-related matters. The government has also made revisions to certain provincial regulations (Perda) that would incentivise investors that are still respectful of the law of communal lands.

The government has also given priority to improve road and seaport infrastructure, such as through the construction of the West Sumatra-Riau highway. Several economic corridors have also been established in West Sumatra: the East Gate Economic Corridor, the Trans-Sumatra Economic Corridor as well as the West Coast Economic Corridor. All these policies would have positive impact on the province's economy as they would reduce transportation cost and generate positive externalities.

Key Economic Indicators, 2015

Land Area (km²)	42,013
Population	
Total Population	5,196,300
Urban Population (%)	44.20
Poverty Rate (%)	6.71
Labour Force	2,346,163
Labour Force Participation Rate (%)	45.15
Gross Regional Domestic Products (GRDP) — 2010 prices	Rupiah (million)
GRDP	140,704,880
GRDP (non-minerals)	134,559,000
GRDP per Capita	27.08
GRDP per Capita (non-minerals)	25.90
Economic Composition	% of GRDP
Primary Sector	28.21
Secondary Sector	19.92
Tertiary Sector	51.87
Trade — 2010 prices	Rupiah (million)
Exports	16,999,377
Imports	6,135,357
Top-3 exports: animal or vegetable fats and oil; rubber and articles thereof; coffee, tea and spices	
Top-3 imports: mineral fuels; fertilisers; cereals	
Infrastructure	
Paved Roads (km)	11,197
Domestic Air Traffic (Passengers)	6,778,006
International Air Traffic (Passengers)	231,432
Domestic Cargo at Seaport (Tons)	7,816,887
International Cargo at Seaport (Tons)	3,782,107

Source: BPS Indonesia compiled by ACI.

5.35.4 Local Political Scene

The political situation in West Sumatra has been conducive. The province is currently led by Irwan Praytino, a popular and experienced winner of the 2008 and 2015 local elections (Pilkada), whose final term will last from 2016 to 2021. His deputy, Nasrul Arbit, is formerly Regent of the Pesisir Selatan Regency for two periods. The pair, who received 58.62 percent of the votes, was supported by the Prosperous Justice Party (PKS) and the Great Indonesia Movement Party (Gerindra).

There are 65 representatives from 11 political parties in West Sumatra's Regional People's Representative Council (DPRD). No single majority party dominates the parliament, although the Party of the Functional Group (Golkar) has the most representation with nine members. There is thus a lack of "opposition" in the current legislative body.

5.36 Concluding Remarks

ACI has largely collaborated with our local academic partners to provide context-specific information for each of the 34 Indonesian provinces. Through the compilation of all these write-ups, a couple of common trends and features in the provinces across Indonesia can be observed.

Most Indonesian provinces are, first and foremost, rich in natural resources and depend on the exports of these resources as sources of growth. The government has, since 2014, put in the efforts to stop the exports of raw minerals and/or mineral concentrates out of the country in order to develop its own domestic smelters or processing facilities. With the recent commodity price bust between June 2014 and February 2015, however, the economy has slowed, causing the initial target of mineral exports ban by 2017 to be extended for another five years (Asmarini and Munthe 2017). Nonetheless, the regulation has resulted in more Indonesian provinces developing and henceforth, relying on processing industries as their sources of growth. The global commodity price bust has also generally affected the economies of most Indonesian provinces negatively. However, they have bounced back in recent years, owing to strong investment growth and robust domestic household spending. Additionally, commodity prices have strengthened in recent years.

Notwithstanding the economic slowdown, social indicators such as HDI have improved across all Indonesian provinces — albeit some faster than the others. Although indicators pertaining to education have generally seen improvements, this has not been supplemented with better employment figures. A mismatch between educational qualifications and employment opportunities thus exist in many of the Indonesian provinces, which must be addressed in order to fully maximise the province's human resource potentials.

While social relations have been stable for the most part, there are still incidences of conflict between labour and firms — sometimes even provincial governments — across Indonesian provinces. Sources of conflict include, among others, dissatisfaction over the provincial minimum wage as well as sudden layoffs. The tension in industrial relations in certain provinces is further heightened due to the purported presence of illegal foreign workers brought in by foreign companies operating in the province. Nonetheless, such conflicts have been relatively peaceful for the most part as labourers would only hold peaceful marches or protests to voice out their discontent. Provincial governments have also been quick to react by providing clarifications and mediation services.

In line with President Joko Widodo's policy to prioritise national infrastructure development connecting all regions of Indonesia, provincial governments themselves have also enacted policies to improve infrastructure within their own region. This ranges from the traditional construction of paved roads and outer ring roads to the more technologically advanced MRT and LRT. Many industrial parks and SEZs have also been slated for future development throughout the nation. Some provincial governments take it one step further to initiate their own industrial estates and offer them to the national government for possible future development. Despite these encouraging plans, the realisation on the ground has not always been smooth sailing. One of the recurring problems which has delayed infrastructure development progress across Indonesian provinces is that of land acquisition, especially in provinces with significant communal land and corresponding complex communal law.

In 2018, a total of 171 regions comprising 17 provinces, 39 cities and 115 regencies will be holding their local elections (Pilkada). Political situations in these provinces have therefore warmed up within the past few months, with respective local politicians either hinting at or publicly announcing that they will be contesting in the upcoming election.

Unfortunately, a couple of regional leaders have had to step down within the past few years due to cases of corruption. This strongly suggests that corruption no longer merely occurs at the national level; the devolution of power from the central to regional governments has also given more opportunities for the latter to engage in corrupt practices.

Finally, major political parties such as the Indonesian Democratic Party of Struggle (PDIP), Party of the Functional Group (Golkar), Great Indonesia Movement Party (Gerindra) and the Democrat Party — and to a lesser extent the National Mandate Party (PAN) and Prosperous Justice Party (PKS) — still dominate local political scenes. Increasingly, however, a coalition of many political parties, which include both the aforementioned and other smaller ones, has become a more popular option among politicians when running for election. Such coalition has unfortunately also resulted in the absence of opposition in the respective province's Regional People's Representative Council (DPRD), resulting in the corresponding lack of constructive policy debates in the province.

References

Section 5.2 Aceh:

BPS Provinsi Aceh. 2017. 'Provinsi Aceh Dalam Angka 2017'.

Section 5.3 Bali:

BPS Provinsi Bali. 2018. 'Produk Domestik Regional Bruto Provinsi Bali Menurut Lapangan Usaha 2012–2016'.

Section 5.4 Bangka Belitung Islands:

Akhlanudin. 2017. 'Rakor Gubernur Bersama Bupati/Walikota Hasilkan 10 Kesepakatan'. *AksiBabel.com*, 20 October 2017. http://www.aksibabel.com/2017/10/20/rakor-gubernur-bersama-bupatiwalikota-hasilkan-10-kesepakatan/.

BPPTPM Provinsi Kepulauan Bangka Belitung. 2017. 'Realisasi Investasi Provinsi Kepulauan Bangka Belitung Januari–September 2017'. http://bpptpm.babelprov.go.id/sites/default/files/data/REALISASI%20INVESTASI%20untuk%20website.pdf.

BPS Provinsi Kepulauan Bangka Belitung. 2017a. 'Indeks Pembangunan Manusia (IPM) Kepulauan Bangka Belitung Tahun 2016'. Berita Resmi Statistik No. 34/05/19/Th. II.

———. 2017b. 'Indikator Sosial Ekonomi Provinsi Kepulauan Bangka Belitung 2017'.

———. 2017c. 'Statistik Kesejahteraan Rakyat Provinsi Kepulauan Bangka Belitung 2017'.

———. 2018. 'Indikator Ekonomi Provinsi Kepulauan Bangka Belitung 2017'.

'KEK Pariwisata'. n.d. Dewan Nasional Kawasan Ekonomi Khusus Republik Indonesia. http://kek.go.id/kek-pariwisata.

'Pilkada Provinsi Kepulauan Bangka Belitung'. n.d. Komisi Pemilihan Umum. https://pilkada2017.kpu.go.id/hasil/t1/kepulauan_bangka_belitung.

Section 5.5 Banten:

Bappenas, and UNTIRTA. 2015. 'Evaluasi Kinerja Pembangunan Daerah Provinsi Banten 2015'.

———. 2016. 'Evaluasi Kinerja Pembangunan Daerah Provinsi Banten 2016'.

BPS Provinsi Banten. 2017a. 'Ringkasan Eksekutif Perkembangan Ekonomi Provinsi Banten Triwulan I 2017'.

———. 2017b. 'Analisis Sosial Ekonomi Provinsi Banten 2016'.

———. 2017c. 'Produk Domestik Regional Bruto Provinsi Banten Menurut Lapangan Usaha 2012–2016'.

Kantor Perwakilan Bank Indonesia Provinsi Banten. 2017. 'Kajian Ekonomi Dan Keuangan Regional Provinsi Banten Februari 2017'. Kantor Perwakilan Bank Indonesia Provinsi Banten.

Section 5.6 Bengkulu:

BKPM. 2017. 'Domestic and Foreign Direct Investment Realization in Quarter I 2017'. April 26. http://www.bkpm.go.id/en/publication/press-release/readmore/499001/25201.

BPS Provinsi Bengkulu. 2016a. 'Provinsi Bengkulu Dalam Angka 2015'.

———. 2016b. 'Provinsi Bengkulu Dalam Angka 2016'.

———. 2017a. 'Kemiskinan Provinsi Bengkulu September 2016.' Berita Resmi Statistik No.05/01/17/XI.

———. 2017b. 'Perkembangan Ekspor Dan Impor Provinsi Bengkulu Desember 2016.' Berita Resmi Statistik No.08/02/17/VIII.

———. 2017c. 'Pertumbuhan Ekonomi Provinsi Bengkulu Tahun 2016.' Berita Resmi Statistik No.10/02/17/XI.

———. 2017d. 'Keadaan Ketenagakerjaan Februari 2017.' Berita Resmi Statistik No.29/05/17/XI.

———. 2017e. 'Pertumbuhan Ekonomi Provinsi Bengkulu Triwulan I Tahun 2017.' Berita Resmi Statistik No.27/05/17/XI.

———. 2017f. 'Indeks Pembangunan Manusia Tahun 2016.' Berita Resmi Statistik No.36/06/17/II.

———. 2017g. 'Perkembangan Ekspor Dan Impor April 2016'. Berita Resmi Statistik No.33/06/17/VIII.

Section 5.7 Central Java:

BPS Provinsi Jawa Tengah. 2016a. 'Jawa Tengah Dalam Angka 2015'. https://jateng.bps.go.id/publication/2016/01/27/67d14b5ed03990ea023b7182/jawa-tengah-dalam-angka-2015.

———. 2016b. 'Jawa Tengah Dalam Angka 2016'. https://jateng.bps.go.id/publication/2016/07/15/e8273586eae1993d1adac969/provinsi-jawa-tengah-dalam-angka-2016.

———. 2018. 'Jawa Tengah Dalam Angka 2017'. https://jateng.bps.go.id/publication/2017/08/11/c7ba6078dd03a08a92893eb7/provinsi-jawa-tengah-dalam-angka-2017.

M Nur, Huda. n.d. 'Kepala Dinas ESDM Jateng: Soal Tambang, Pemprov Merasa Seperti Cuci Piring — Tribun Jateng'. *TribunJateng.Com*. http://jateng.tribunnews.com/2016/01/29/kepala-dinas-esdm-jateng-soal-tambang-pemprov-merasa-seperti-cuci-piring.

Portal PPID Provinsi Jawa Tengah, Portal. n.d. 'RPJMD Perubahan 2013-2018'. http://ppid.jatengprov.go.id/rpjmd-perubahan-2013-2018/.

Purba, David Oliver. 2017. 'Pembangunan Infrastruktur Jateng Maju Pesat Tanpa Direpoti Birokrasi'. *KOMPAS.com*, 15 October 2017. https://nasional.kompas.com/read/2017/10/15/20321481/pembangunan-infrastruktur-jateng-maju-pesat-tanpa-direpoti-birokrasi.

Saputra, Andi. 2017. 'MA Tolak PK Perusahaan Semen Rembang'. *Detiknews*, 27 September 2017. https://news.detik.com/read/2017/09/27/122412/3660190/10/ma-tolak-pk-perusahaan-semen-rembang.

Sri, Lestari. n.d. 'Masih ada masalah lahan, Presiden Jokowi resmikan PLTU Batang'. *BBC Indonesia*. http://www.bbc.com/indonesia/berita_indonesia/2015/08/150828_indonesia_pltu_batang.

Yunita, Niken Widya. 2017. 'Bandara Jenderal Sudirman Purbalingga Beroperasi Desember 2018'. *Detikfinance*, 17 November 2017. https://finance.detik.com/read/2017/11/17/152029/3731720/1772/bandara-jenderal-sudirman-purbalingga-beroperasi-desember-2018.

Section 5.8 Central Kalimantan:

BPS Provinsi Kalimantan Tengah. 2016. 'Provinsi Kalimantan Tengah Dalam Angka 2016'.

Kantor Perwakilan Bank Indonesia Provinsi Kalimantan Tengah. 2016a. 'Kajian Ekonomi Dan Keuangan Regional Provinsi Kalimantan Tengah'.

———. 2016b. 'KEKR Provinsi Kalimantan Tengah — November 2016 — Bank Sentral Republik Indonesia'.

———. 2017. 'KEKR Provinsi Kalimantan Tengah — Februari 2017 — Bank Sentral Republik Indonesia'.

Kantor Perwakilan Provinsi Kalimantan Tengah. 2016. 'Kajian Ekonomi Dan Keuangan Regional Provinsi Kalimantan Tengah Triwulan II'.

———. 2017. 'Kajian Ekonomi Dan Keuangan Regional Provinsi Kalimantan Tengah Mei 2017 — Bank Sentral Republik Indonesia'.

Section 5.9 Central Sulawesi:

AntaraSulteng. 2017. 'Golkar Sulteng Siap Buka Pendaftaran Pilkada 2018', 13 July 2017. https://sulteng.antaranews.com/berita/33418/golkar-sulteng-siap-buka-pendaftaran-pilkada-2018.

———. n.d. 'Aset Sulteng Naik Rp1,1 Triliun Pada 2015'. https://sulteng.antaranews.com/berita/25577/aset-sulteng-naik-rp11-triliun-pada-2015.

BPS Indonesia. n.d. 'Data Sulawesi Tengah 2016 (Metode Baru)'. http://ipm.bps.go.id/data/kabkot/metode/baru/7200.

BPS Provinsi Sulawesi Tengah. 2017. 'Perkembangan Ekspor Dan Impor Sulawesi Tengah, November 2017'. Berita Resmi Statistik No. 70/12/72/Th.XX.

Komisi Pemilihan Umum. n.d. 'Pilkada Provinsi Sulawesi Tengah'. https://pilkada2015.kpu.go.id/sultengprov.

Qusnulyakin, Firman. 2014. 'Wajah Baru Isi Kursi DPRD Sulawesi Tengah'. *beritasatu.com*, 3 May 2014. http://www.beritasatu.com//181764-wajah-baru-isi-kursi-dprd-sulawesi-tengah.html.

Section 5.10 DI Yogyakarta:

'Peraturan Presiden Republik Indonesia Nomor 28 Tahun 2012 Tentang Rencana Tata Ruang Pulau Jawa-Bali'. 2010. Jakarta: Departemen Hukum dan Hak Asasi Manusia.

Apriando, Tommy. 2016. 'Yogyakarta Alami Krisis Air, Mengapa?' *Mongabay Environmental News*, 24 August 2016. http://www.mongabay.co.id/2016/08/24/yogyakarta-alami-krisis-air-mengapa/.

Bank Indonesia. 2017. 'Kajian Ekonomi Dan Keuangan Regional Mei 2017'. 23 May 2017.

BPS Provinsi DI Yogyakarta. "Produk Domestik Regional Bruto Provinsi Daerah Istimewa Yogyakarta Menurut Lapangan Usaha 2012–2016," November 11, 2017.

———. "Statistik Ekspor Impor Daerah Istimewa Yogyakarta 2016," December 27, 2017.

Dinas Pendidikan, Pemuda dan Olahraga DI Yogyakarta. n.d. 'Master Data Pendidikan DIY — Dikpora. Jogjaprov.Go.Id'. Accessed 16 August 2017. http://www.pendidikan-diy.go.id/dinas_v4/?view=data-pendidikan.

DPRD Kota Yogykarta. 2017. 'Pengumuman Hasil Penetapan Pasangan Calon Walikota Dan Wakil Walikota Yogyakarta Terpilih 2017', 5 May 2017. http://dprd-jogjakota.go.id/web/berita/detail/233/pengumuman-hasil-penetapan-pasangan-calon-walikota-dan-wakil-walikota-yogyakarta-terpilih-2017.

Komisi Pilihan Umum. "Hasil Hitung TPS (Form C1) Kota Yogyakarta." Accessed August 25, 2017. https://pilkada2017.kpu.go.id/hasil/t2/daerah_istimewa_yogyakarta/kota_yogyakarta.

KOMPAS.COM. "Hotel, Mal, dan Apartemen Merenggut Yogyakarta." KOMPAS.com, 29 February 2016. https://regional.kompas.com/read/2016/02/29/15383481/.Hotel.Mal.dan.Apartemen.Merenggut.Yogyakarta.

Pemerintah Kabupaten Kulon Progo. 2012. 'Peraturan Daerah Kabupaten Kulon Progo Nomor 1 Tahun 2012 Tentang Rencana Tata Ruang Wilayah Kabupaten Kulon Progo Tahun 2012–2032'. http://www.jdih.setjen.kemendagri.go.id/files/KAB_KULON%20PROGO_1_2012.pdf.

Sleman, Sumadi. 2017. 'Peraturan Daerah Kabupaten Sleman Nomor 2 Tahun 2017 Tentang Perlindungan Perempuan Dan Anak Korban Kekerasan'.

SOLOPOS.COM. "Hotel di Jogja: Meski Ada Moratorium, Pembangunan Hotel Jalan Terus." SOLOPOS.com, October 13, 2016. http://www.solopos.com/2016/10/13/hotel-di-jogja-meski-ada-moratorium-pembangunan-hotel-jalan-terus-760225.

Tempo.com. "2 Calon Wali Kota Komentari Isu Toleransi Di Yogyakarta." Tempo, November 6, 2016. https://pilkada.tempo.co/read/818112/2-calon-wali-kota-komentari-isu-toleransi-di-yogyakarta.

Tifa Foundation. n.d. 'Terobosan-Terobosan Bupati Kulon Progo'. Http://Www.Tifafoundation.Org/Terobosan-Terobosan-Bupati-Kulon-Progo/. Accessed 25 August 2017.

TribunJogja. 2017. 'Dinilai Rawan Tsunami, LBH Yogyakarta Minta Hentikan Pembangunan Bandara Baru di Kulonprogo'. *TribunJogja.com*, 30 July 2017. http://jogja.tribunnews.com/2017/07/30/dinilai-rawan-tsunami-lbh-yogyakarta-minta-hentikan-pembangunanbandara-baru-di-kulonprogo.

TribunJogja.com. "Raperda Usaha Ekonomi Kreatif Di Yogya Perlu Segera Dirumuskan — Tribun Jogja," February 8, 2016. http://jogja.tribunnews.com/2016/02/08/raperda-usaha-ekonomi-kreatif-di-yogya-perlu-segera-dirumuskan.

Section 5.11 DKI Jakarta:

Aziza, Kurnia Sari. n.d. 'Bappenas: Kerugian akibat Macet Jakarta Rp67 Triliun Per Tahun'. *KOMPAS.com*. https://ekonomi.kompas.com/read/2017/10/06/054007626/bappenas-kerugian-akibat-macet-jakarta-rp-67-triliun-per-tahun.

BPKM Indonesia. 2016. 'Realisasi Penanaman Modal PMDN — PMA Triwulan IV Dan Januari–Desember Tahun 2015'. Badan Koordinasi Penanaman Modal Republik Indonesia, January 21.

———. 2017a. ‘Realisasi Penanaman Modal PMDN — PMA Triwulan IV Dan Januari–Desember Tahun 2016’. Badan Koordinasi Penanaman Modal Republik Indonesia, January 25.

———. 2017b. ‘Realisasi Penanaman Modal PMDN — PMA Triwulan I Tahun 2017’. Badan Koordinasi Penanaman Modal Republik Indonesia, April 26.

BPS Indonesia. 2017a. ‘Angka Partisipasi Sekolah (APS) Menurut Provinsi, 2011–2017’. 2017.

———. 2017b. ‘Indeks Pembangunan Manusia Menurut Provinsi, 2010–2016 (Metode Baru)’. 2017.

———. 2017c. ‘[Seri 2010] Laju Pertumbuhan Kumulatif Produk Domestik Bruto Menurut Lapangan Usaha (Persen), 2014–2016’. 2017.

———. 2017d. ‘Tingkat Pengangguran Terbuka (TPT) Menurut Provinsi, 1986–2017’. 15 December 2017.

BPS Provinsi DKI Jakarta. 2017a. ‘Laju Pertumbuhan PDRB Provinsi DKI Jakarta Atas Dasar Harga Konstan 2010 Menurut Lapangan Usaha (Persen), 2011–2015’. 30 January 2017.

———. 2017b. ‘Perkembangan Penanaman Modal Dalam Negeri Dan Modal Asing, 2003–2015’. 30 January 2017.

———. 2017c. ‘Pertumbuhan Ekonomi DKI Jakarta Triwulan II-2017’. Berita Resmi Statistik No. 41/08/31/Th. XIX.

Dinas Komunikasi, Informatika dan Statistik Pemprov DKI Jakarta. n.d. ‘Portal Resmi Pemerintah Provinsi DKI Jakarta’. https://jakarta.go.id.

DPRD Provinsi DKI Jakarta. n.d. ‘DPRD Provinsi DKI Jakarta’. http://www.dprd-dkijakartaprov.go.id/.

Kantor Perwakilan Bank Indonesia Provinsi DKI Jakarta. 2017. ‘Kajian Ekonomi Dan Keuangan Regional Prov. DKI Jakarta Agustus 2017’.

KPU DKI Jakarta. n.d. ‘Komisi Pemilihan Umum Provinsi DKI Jakarta’. https://kpujakarta.go.id/.

Mincer, Jacob. 1991. ‘Education and Unemployment’. Working Paper 3838. National Bureau of Economic Research. https://doi.org/10.3386/w3838.

The World Bank. 2017. ‘World Development Indicators | Data’. 2017. https://data.worldbank.org/products/wdi.

———. n.d. ‘Doing Business in Indonesia — World Bank Group’. http://www.doingbusiness.org/data/exploreeconomies/indonesia.

Section 5.12 East Java:

BPS Provinsi Jawa Timur. n.d. ‘BPS Provinsi Jawa Timur’. https://jatim.bps.go.id/.

Purwono, Rudi. n.d. ‘Berbagai Materi Presentasi Pada Tahun 2016 Dan 2017’.

Soekarwo. 2016. *Jatimnomics: Sebuah Model Indonesia Incorporated: Pemikiran, Konsep, dan Implementasi*. PT Elex Media Komputindo.

———. 2017. ‘Kegagalan Liberalisasi Dalam Mendorong Pertumbuhan Inklusif. Sambutan Rakornas Ke IV KAHMI (Non-Published)’.

Tan, Khee Giap, Nurina Merdikawati, Mulya Amri, and Kong Yam Tan. 2017. *2015 Agricultural Productivity, Decentralisation, and Competitiveness Analysis for Provinces and Regions of Indonesia*. Asia Competitiveness Institute — World Scientific Series. Singapore: World Scientific. http://www.worldscientific.com/worldscibooks/10.1142/10245.

Section 5.13 East Kalimantan:

Bappeda Provinsi Kalimantan Timur. n.d. 'Laporan Keterangan Pertanggungjawaban (LKPJ) Gubernur Kalimantan Timur Tahun 2016'.

BPS Provinsi Kalimantan Timur. 2015. 'Kalimantan Timur Dalam Angka Tahun 2015'.

———. 2016. 'Provinsi Kalimantan Timur Dalam Angka 2016'.

———. 2017a. 'Kondisi Sosial Ekonomi Dan Indikator Penting Provinsi Kalimantan Timur Triwulan IV 2016'.

———. 2017b. 'Kondisi Sosial Ekonomi Dan Indikator Penting Provinsi Kalimantan Timur Triwulan II 2017'.

———. 2018. 'Provinsi Kalimantan Timur Dalam Angka 2017'.

Section 5.14 East Nusa Tenggara:

Bifel, Hironimus, and Aloysius Lewokeda. 2017. 'KEK Altaka Jadi Prioritas'. AntaraNews NTT. 23 May 2017. https://kupang.antaranews.com/berita/3146/kek-altaka-jadi-prioritas.

BPS Provinsi Nusa Tenggara Timur. 2017a. 'Statistik Daerah Provinsi Nusa Tenggara Timur 2017'.

———. 2017b. 'Statistik Kesejahteraan Rakyat Provinsi Nusa Tenggara Timur 2017'.

———. 2018a. 'Provinsi Nusa Tenggara Timur Dalam Angka 2017'.

———. 2018b. 'Ringkasan Data Dan Informasi Kemiskinan Provinsi Nusa Tenggara Timur 2017'.

Kuwado, Fabian Januarius. 2018. 'Fakta Seputar Pilkada NTT: Perang Bintang'. *Kompas.Com*, 12 January 2018. https://nasional.kompas.com/read/2018/01/12/18261561/fakta-seputar-pilkada-ntt-perang-bintang.

Rakyat Merdeka. n.d. 'Kemenperin: Fokus Tiga Industri, Menperin Percepat Industrialisasi Di NTT'. *Kementerian Perindustrian Republik Indonesia*. http://www.kemenperin.go.id/artikel/12247/Fokus-Tiga-Industri,-Menperin-Percepat-Industrialisasi-di-NTT.

Suara Pembaruan. 2013. 'Paket Frenly Menang Pilgub NTT | Suara Pembaruan', 2 June 2013. http://sp.beritasatu.com/home/paket-frenly-menang-pilgub-ntt/36443.

Section 5.15 Gorontalo:

Biro P2E. 2016. *Indikator Ekonomi Provinsi Gorontalo 2015*. Biro Pengendalian dan Pembangunan Ekonomi.

BPS Provinsi Gorontalo. 2017a. 'Perkembangan Sosial Ekonomi Provinsi Gorontalo Tahun 2016.' presented at the Rapat Koordinasi Bidang Ekonomi Provinsi Gorontalo, Kantor Gubernur Provinsi Gorontalo, February 27.

———. 2017b. 'Pertumbuhan Ekonomi Gorontalo Triwulan I-2017'. Berita Resmi Statistik No. 26/05/75/ Th. XI.

Iryanti, Rahma. 2017. 'Prioritas Nasional Penanggulangan Kemiskinan'. presented at the Rapat Koordinasi Teknis Penanggulangan Kemiskinan, Bappenas Republik Indonesia, Gorontalo, April 6.

Section 5.16 Jambi:

BPS Provinsi Jambi. 2016. 'Provinsi Jambi Dalam Angka 2016'.

Kementerian Perhubungan Republik Indonesia. 2016. 'Direktorat Jenderal Perhubungan Udara'.

Tan, Syamsurijal. 2016. 'Perencanaan Pembangunan Daerah (Teori Dan Implementasinya Pada Pembangunan Daerah)'. *Fakultas Ekonomi Dan Bisnis Universitas Jambi.*

Section 5.17 Lampung:

BPS Provinsi Lampung. n.d. 'Badan Pusat Statistik Provinsi Lampung'. https://lampung.bps.go.id/.

Section 5.18 Maluku:

BPS Provinsi Maluku. 2017a. 'Perkembangan Data Sosial Ekonomi Provinsi Maluku Triwulan II 2017'.

———. 2017b. 'Provinsi Maluku Dalam Angka 2017'.

Section 5.19 North Kalimantan:

Kantor Perwakilan Bank Indonesia Provinsi Kalimantan Utara. 2017. 'KEKR Provinsi Kalimantan Utara Agustus 2017'.

BPS Provinsi Kalimantan Utara. 2016. 'Provinsi Kalimantan Utara Dalam Angka 2016'.

Section 5.20 North Maluku:

National Single Window for Investment (NSWi). n.d. 'Data Perkembangan Realisasi Penanaman Modal.' National Single Window for Investment (NSWi). Accessed 10 February 2018. https://nswi.bkpm.go.id/data_statistik.

BPS Provinsi Maluku Utara. Accessed 10 February 2018. https://malut.bps.go.id/.

Redaksi. 2018. 'Angka Kemiskinan di Maluku Utara Meningkat'. *Edunews.id,* 3 January 2018. Accessed 10 February 2018. https://www.edunews.id/daerah/angka-kemiskinan-di-maluku-utara-meningkat/.

LPPM. 2017. 'Kebijakan Resolusi Konflik Agraria Di Maluku Utara: Antara Harapan dan Kenyataan.' *Lembaga Penelitian, Publikasi dan Pengabdian Masyarakat,* 6 March 2017. Accessed 10 February 2018. http://lp3m.ummu.ac.id/kebijakan-resolusi-konflik-agraria-di-maluku-utara-antara-harapan-dan-kenyataan.

Kabar Timur Online. 2014. 'KPU Malut Tetapkan Hasil Pileg.' *Kabar Timur Online,* 19 May 2014. Accessed 10 February 2018. http://www.kabartimur.co.id/detail/indeks/malut/2751-kpu-malut-tetapkan-hasil-pileg.

Bappeda Provinsi Maluku Utara. 2018. 'Visi, Misi, Strategi dan Kebijakan.' *Bappeda Provinsi Maluku Utara,* n.d. Accessed 10 February 2018. http://bappeda.malutprov.go.id/statis-visi-misi-strategi-dan-kebijakan.

Investor Daily Indonesia. 2017. 'Presiden Minta Malut Optimalkan Sektor Unggulan.' *Investor Daily Indonesia,* 28 February 2017. Accessed 10 February 2018. http://id.beritasatu.com/home/presiden-minta-malut-optimalkan-sektor-unggulan/157122.

Pradana, Rio Sandy. 2017. 'Gubernur: Pembangunan Infrastruktur Maluku Utara Terkendala Dana.' *Kabar 24,* 28 February 2017. Accessed 10 February 2018. http://kabar24.bisnis.com/read/20170228/78/632554/gubernur-pembangunan-infrastruktur-maluku-utara-terkendala-dana

Section 5.21 North Sulawesi:

BPS Provinsi Sulawesi Utara. 2015. 'Sulawesi Utara Dalam Angka 2015'.

———. 2016. 'Provinsi Sulawesi Utara Dalam Angka 2016'.

———. 2017. 'Pertumbuhan Ekonomi Sulawesi Utara Triwulan IV 2016'. Berita Resmi Statistik No. 13/02/71/Th. X.

———. n.d. 'Perkembangan Ekspor — Import Sulawesi Utara Juli 2017'. Berita Resmi Statistik No. 76/8/71/Th.XI. Accessed 12 March 2018a.

———. n.d. 'Pertumbuhan Ekonomi Sulawesi Utara Tahun 2015'. Berita Resmi Statistik No. 13/02/71/ Th. X. Accessed 12 March 2018b.

Kantor Perwakilan Bank Indonesia Provinsi Sulawesi Utara. 201AD. 'Kajian Ekonomi Regional Provinsi Sulawesi Utara Triwulan II 2016'.

———. 2015. 'Kajian Ekonomi Dan Keuangan Regional Provinsi Sulawesi Utara Triwulan I 2015'.

———. 2015a. 'Kajian Ekonomi Dan Keuangan Regional Provinsi Sulawesi Utara Triwulan II 2015'.

———. 2015b. 'Kajian Ekonomi Dan Keuangan Regional Sulawesi Utara Triwulan III 2015 — Bank Sentral Republik Indonesia'.

———. 2016a. 'Kajian Ekonomi Dan Keuangan Regional Prov. Sulawesi Utara Triwulan IV 2015'.

———. 2016b. 'Kajian Ekonomi Dan Keuangan Daerah Prov. Sulawesi Utara Triwulan I 2016'.

———. 2016c. 'Kajian Ekonomi Dan Keuangan Regional Provinsi Sulawesi Utara November 2016'.

———. 2017a. 'Kajian Ekonomi Dan Keuangan Regional Provinsi Sulawesi Utara Februari 2017'.

———. 2017b. 'Kajian Ekonomi Dan Keuangan Regional Provinsi Sulawesi Utara Mei 2017'.

———. 2017c. 'KEKR Provinsi Sulawesi Utara Agustus 2017'.

Section 5.22 North Sumatra:

Bank Indonesia. 2017. 'Kajian Ekonomi Keuangan Regional Provinsi Sumatera Utara Triwulan III 2017'. https://www.bi.go.id/id/publikasi/kajian-ekonomi-regional/sumut/Pages/KEKR-Provinsi-Sumatera-Utara-Triwulan-III-2017.aspx.

BPS Provinsi Sumatera Utara. 2017. 'Provinsi Sumatera Utara Dalam Angka 2017'. https://sumut.bps.go.id/publication/2017/08/15/ae202b5bcc30b7bdcde27fd2/provinsi-sumatera-utara-dalam-angka-2017.html.

Section 5.23 Papua:

BPS Provinsi Papua. n.d. 'Badan Pusat Statistik Provinsi Papua'. https://papua.bps.go.id/.

Diah Setiawan, Sakina Rakhma. 2018. 'Lampaui Target, Realisasi Investasi RI 2017 Tembus Rp692,8 Triliun'. *KOMPAS.com*, 30 January 2018. https://ekonomi.kompas.com/read/2018/01/30/180603026/lampaui-target-realisasi-investasi-ri-2017-tembus-rp-6928-triliun.

Kementerian Kuangan Republik Indonesia. n.d. 'Kebijakan Pengalokasian, Penyaluran Dan Pelaporan Transfer Non Dana Perimbangan Serta Pinjaman Dan Hibah Daerah'. http://www.djpk.depkeu.go.id/wp-content/uploads/2017/03/Bahan-Direktur-PTNDP.pdf.

Radio New Zealand. 2017. 'Ten People Die in Papua during Mine Labour Dispute'. *Radio New Zealand*, 16 August 2017. https://www.radionz.co.nz/international/pacific-news/337286/ten-people-die-in-papua-during-mine-labour-dispute.

Reuters. 2017. 'BRIEF-Freeport, Indonesia "Highly Motivated" on Grasberg Deal', 25 October 2017. https://www.reuters.com/article/brief-freeport-indonesia-highly-motivate/brief-freeport-indonesia-highly-motivated-on-grasberg-deal-idUSL2N1N005Q.

Singgih, Viriya P. 2017. 'Workers Urge Government to Settle Dispute with Freeport'. *The Jakarta Post*, 7 March 2017. http://www.thejakartapost.com/news/2017/03/07/workers-urge-government-to-settle-dispute-with-freeport.html.

Somba, Nethy Dharma. 2017. 'Papua's Economy Slowing down Due to Freeport Saga: Bank Indonesia'. *The Jakarta Post*, 8 March 2017. http://www.thejakartapost.com/news/2017/03/08/papuas-economy-slowing-down-due-to-freeport-saga-bank-indonesia.html.

The Jakarta Post. 2017. 'Trans-Papua Road Set to Be Completed next Year — Business — The Jakarta Post'. *The Jakarta Post*, 7 March 2017. http://www.thejakartapost.com/news/2017/03/07/trans-papua-road-set-to-be-completed-next-year.html.

Utama, Abraham. 2017. 'Usai Ricuh Mogok Karyawan, Freeport "Berkeras Tak Salah Soal PHK Massal"'. *BBC Indonesia*, 21 August 2017, sec. Indonesia. http://www.bbc.com/indonesia/indonesia-41002522.

Varagur, Krithika. 2017. 'Freeport Indonesia Hentikan Operasi di Papua'. *VOA Indonesia*, 27 February 2017. https://www.voaindonesia.com/a/freeport-indonesia-hentikan-operasi-di-papua-barat/3741646.html.

Section 5.24 Riau:

Bank Indonesia. n.d. 'Bank Indonesia Official Web Site — Bank Sentral Republik Indonesia'. https://www.bi.go.id/id/Default.aspx.

BPS Provinsi Riau. n.d. 'Badan Pusat Statistik Provinsi Riau'. https://riau.bps.go.id/.

Komisi Pemilihan Umum. n.d. 'KPU Republik Indonesia'. http://kpu.go.id/.

Section 5.25 Riau Islands:

Arshad, Arlina. 2017. 'Singapore and Sambal Belacan Led Riau Governor to Love'. *The Straits Times*, 1 May 2017. http://www.straitstimes.com/asia/se-asia/spore-and-sambal-belacan-led-riau-governor-to-love-people.

Bappeda Provinsi Kepulauan Riau. 2016. 'Rancangan Akhir Rencana Pembangunan Jangka Menengah Daerah (RPJMD) Provinsi Kepulauan Riau Tahun 2016–2021'. http://bappeda.kepriprov.go.id/data/RPJMD/RPJMD_Kepri_2016.pdf.

BPS Indonesia. 2017. 'Statistik Indonesia 2017'.

BPS Provinsi Kepulauan Riau. 2017. 'Provinsi Kepulauan Riau Dalam Angka 2017'.

Kantor Perwakilan Bank Indonesia Provinsi Kepulauan Riau. 2017. 'Kajian Ekonomi Dan Keuangan Regional Provinsi Kepulauan Riau Mei 2017'.

Kartikasari, Dwi. 2017. 'The Effect of Export, Import and Investment to Economic Growth of Riau Islands Indonesia'. *International Journal of Economics and Financial Issues* 7 (4): 663–67.

Maryaningsih, Novi, Oki Hermansyah, and Myrnawati Savitri. n.d. 'Pengaruh Infrastruktur Terhadap Pertumbuhan Ekonomi Indonesia'. *Buletin Ekonomi Moneter Dan Perbankan* 17 (1): 61–98.

Panama, Riko. 2017. 'Titik Noda Setahun Nurdin Basirun Memimpin Kepri'. *AntaraNews Kepulauan Riau*, 25 May 2017. https://kepri.antaranews.com/berita/41905/titik-noda-setahun-nurdin-basirun-memimpin-kepri.

Section 5.26 South Kalimantan:

BPS Provinsi Kalimantan Selatan. 2016. 'Provinsi Kalimantan Selatan Dalam Angka 2016'.

Kantor Perwakilan Bank Indonesia Provinsi Kalimantan Selatan. 2017. 'Kajian Ekonomi Dan Keuangan Regional Provinsi Kalimantan Selatan Mei 2017'.

Section 5.27 South Sulawesi:

BPS Provinsi Sulawesi Selatan. 2015. 'Sulawesi Selatan Dalam Angka 2015'.

———. 2016. 'Provinsi Sulawesi Selatan Dalam Angka 2016'.

———. 2017. 'Provinsi Sulawesi Selatan Dalam Angka 2017'.

Kantor Perwakilan Bank Indonesia Provinsi Sulawesi Selatan. 2015. 'Kajian Ekonomi Dan Keuangan Regional Provinsi Sulawesi Selatan Triwulan II 2015'.

———. 2016. 'Kajian Ekonomi Keuangan Dan Regional Provinsi Sulawesi Selatan Periode Agustus 2016'.

———. 2017. 'Kajian Ekonomi Keuangan Dan Regional Provinsi Sulawesi Selatan Periode Agustus 2017'.

Section 5.28 South Sumatra:

BPS Provinsi Sumatera Selatan. 2015. 'Sumatera Selatan Dalam Angka 2015'.

———. 2016. 'Provinsi Sumatera Selatan Dalam Angka 2016'.

———. 2017. 'Provinsi Sumatera Selatan Dalam Angka 2017'.

Section 5.29 Southeast Sulawesi:

Armid, A., R. Shinjo, R. Ruslan, and Fahmiati. 2017. 'Distributions and Pollution Assessment of Heavy Metals Pb, Cd and Cr in the Water System of Kendari Bay, Indonesia'. *IOP Conference Series: Materials Science and Engineering* 172 (1): 012002. https://doi.org/10.1088/1757-899X/172/1/012002.

Bank Indonesia. 2017. 'Kajian Ekonomi Dan Keuangan Regional Provinsi Sulawesi Tenggara Agustus 2017'.

BPS Provinsi Sulawesi Tenggara. 2016. 'Provinsi Sulawesi Tenggara Dalam Angka 2016'.

———. 2017. 'Provinsi Sulawesi Tenggara Dalam Angka 2017'.

DetikNews. 2016. 'Jika Menemukan Pelanggaran Tenaga Kerja Asing, Harus Bagaimana?' *Detiknews*, 26 July 2016. https://news.detik.com/read/2016/07/26/000000/3259707/727/jika-menemukan-pelanggaran-tenaga-kerja-asing-harus-bagaimana.

Kiki. 2017. 'Tenaga Kerja asal China Bentrok dengan Pekerja Lokal di Kendari'. *KOMPAS.com*, 7 March 2017. https://regional.kompas.com/read/2017/03/07/21201431/tenaga.kerja.asal.china.bentrok.dengan.pekerja.lokal.di.kendari.

SultraNews. n.d. 'Gubernur Didesak Cabut Ijin Perusahaan'. *SultraNews.com*. Accessed 10 October 2017. https://www.sultranews.com/gubernur-didesak-cabut-ijin-perusahaan/.

Zona Sultra. n.d. 'Sengketa Lahan PT Sun vs Warga DPRD Bombana'. *Zona Sultra*. Accessed 10 October 2017. http://zonasultra.com/sengketa-lahan-pt-sun-vs-warga-dprd-bombana-/.

Section 5.30 West Java:

BPS Indonesia. 2017. 'Statistik Indonesia 2017'.

BPS Provinsi Jawa Barat. 2017. 'Indeks Pembangunan Manusia 2016'.

———. 2018a. 'Provinsi Jawa Barat Dalam Angka 2017'.

———. 2018b. 'Statistik Perdagangan Luar Negeri Jawa Barat 2016'.

Kantor Perwakilan Bank Indonesia Provinsi Jawa Barat. 2017. 'Kajian Ekonomi Dan Keuangan Regional Provinsi Jawa Barat Februari 2017'.

Komite Pemantauan Pelaksanaan Otonomi Daerah (KPPOD). 2017. 'Regulasi Usaha Di Daerah: Kajian Perda Pungutan Dan Perijinan'. Jakarta: KPPOD. https://www.kppod.org/backend/files/laporan_penelitian/kajian-perda-pungutan-dan-perizinan.pdf.

Puradimadja, Deny Juanda. 2014. 'Arah Kebijakan Pembangunan Provinsi Jawa Barat Tahun 2016'. presented at the Bappeda Provinsi Jawa Barat, Bandung, Jawa Barat, December 2.

Wikipedia. 2018. 'Ahmad Heryawan'. *Wikipedia bahasa Indonesia, ensiklopedia bebas*. https://id.wikipedia.org/w/index.php?title=Ahmad_Heryawan&oldid=13518292.

Section 5.31 West Kalimantan:

BPS Provinsi Kalimantan Barat. 2016. 'Provinsi Kalimantan Barat Dalam Angka 2016'.

———. n.d. 'Badan Pusat Statistik Provinsi Kalimantan Barat'. Accessed 4 October 2017. https://kalbar.bps.go.id/index.php.

DPMPTSP Provinsi Kalimantan Barat. n.d. 'Dinas Penanaman Modal Dan Pelayanan Terpadu Satu Pintu (DPMPTSP)'. Accessed 5 October 2017. http://www.bpm-ptsp.kalbarprov.go.id/berita.

JDIH KPU Provinsi Kalimantan Barat. n.d. 'Keputusan KPU Provinsi Kalbar Nomor 36/Kpts/KPU-Prov-019/2014 Tentang Penetapan Perolehan Suara Dan Kursi Partai Politik Serta Calon Terpilih Anggota Dewan Perwakilan Rakyat Daerah Provinsi Kalimantan Barat Pemilihan Umum Tahun 2014'. http://jdih.kpu.go.id/kalbar/keputusan-kpud.

JDIH Provinsi Kalimantan Barat. n.d. 'Keputusan KPU Provinsi Kalbar Nomor 68/Kpts/KPU-Prov-019/2012 Tentang Penetapan Hasil Rekapitulasi Penghitungan Suara Pemilihan Umum Gubernur Dan Wakil Kalbar Tahun 2012'. http://jdih.kpu.go.id/kalbar/keputusan-kpud.

———. n.d. 'Perubahan Atas Peraturan Gubernur Nomor 13 Tahun 2017 Tentang Pendelegasian Kewenangan Penandatanganan Penerbitan Perizinan Kepada Kepala Dinas Penanaman Modal Dan Pelayanan Terpady Satu Pintu Provinsi Kalimantan Barat | Jaringan Dokumentasi Dan Informasi Hukum Provinsi Kalimantan Barat'. http://jdih.kalbarprov.go.id/peraturan/perubahan-atas-peraturan-gubernur-nomor-13-tahun-2017-tentang-pendelegasian-kewenangan.

Mahkamah Konstitusi. 2012. 'MK Tolak Seluruh Permohonan PHPU Kalbar | Mahkamah Konstitusi Republik Indonesia', 19 October 2012. http://www.mahkamahkonstitusi.go.id/index.php?page=web.Berita&id=7659#.WqYI5JNubeR.

Section 5.32 West Nusa Tenggara:

Bank Indonesia. 2017. 'Kajian Ekonomi Dan Keuangan Regional Provinsi Nusa Tenggara Barat Mei 2017'. https://www.bi.go.id/id/publikasi/kajian-ekonomi-regional/ntb/Pages/Kajian-Ekonomi-dan-Keuangan-Regional-Provinsi-Nusa-Tenggara-Barat-Mei-2017.aspx.

BPS Provinsi Nusa Tenggara Barat. n.d. 'Badan Pusat Statistik Provinsi Nusa Tenggara Barat'. Accessed 20 July 2017. https://ntb.bps.go.id/.

Munir, B. 2017. 'Lansekap SAMOTA: Menuju Destinasi Pariwisata Dan Ekonomi Maritim Kelas Dunia'. *Regional Institute 104*.

Section 5.33 West Papua:

National Single Window for Investment (NSWi). n.d. 'Data Perkembangan Realisasi Penanaman Modal.' National Single Window for Investment (NSWi). Accessed February 10, 2018. https://nswi.bkpm.go.id/data_statistik.

Akbar, Wishnugroho. 2017. 'Pemerintah Garap 3.353 Proyek Nasional di Papua Barat.' *CNN Indonesia,* 24 March 2017. Accessed 20 February 2018. https://www.cnnindonesia.com/nasional/20170324102316-20-202453/pemerintah-garap-3353-proyek-nasional-di-papua-barat.

BPS Provinsi Papua Barat. 2018. Accessed 10 February 2018. https://papuabarat.bps.go.id.

Coordinating Ministry for Politics, Law and Security. 2017. 'Rencana Pembangunan Pelabuhan Internasional di Papua Barat.' *Berita Terkini,* 9 October 2017. Accessed 20 February 2018. https://otsus.polkam.go.id/news/detail/4.

Hanafi. 2018. 'Tingkat Kejahatan Di Kota Sorong Meningkat, Didasari Miras Dan Kurangnya Lapangan Kerja.' *Arfaknews.com,* 26 February 2018. Accessed 28 February 2018. http://arfaknews.com/read/1380/Lintas-Papua-Barat/Tingkat-Kejahatan-Di-Kota-Sorong-Meningkat-Didasari-Miras-Dan-Kurangnya-Lapangan-Kerja.

Koran SINDO. 2017. 'Pusat Logistik di Papua Barat Beroperasi, Ini Keuntungannya!' *OkezoneFinance,* 9 June 2017. Accessed 20 February 2018. https://economy.okezone.com/read/2017/06/09/320/1711701/pusat-logistik-di-papua-barat-beroperasi-ini-keuntungannya.

Papuakini.co. 2017. 'Ini Misi DOAMU Majukan Papua Barat.' *Papuakini.co,* 7 February 2017. Accessed 20 February 2018. https://www.papuakini.co/2017/02/07/ini-misi-doamu-majukan-papua-barat/.

Papuakini.co. 2018. 'Papua Barat Aman dari Kasus Gizi Buruk.' *Papuakini.co,* 10 February 2018. Accessed 20 February 2018. https://www.papuakini.co/2018/02/10/papua-barat-aman-dari-kasus-gizi-buruk/.

Sidik, Fajar. 2017. 'Pembangunan Infrastruktur Strategis di Papua Barat Dipacu.' *Bisnis.com,* 21 July 2017. Accessed 20 February 2018. http://industri.bisnis.com/read/20170721/45/673660/pembangunan-infrastruktur-strategis-di-papua-barat-dipacu.

Tim Okezone. 2017. 'Selamat! Dominggus Mandacan Menang Telak 69% dalam Pilgub Papua Barat.' *Okezone,* February 15 2017. Accessed 20 February 2018. https://news.okezone.com/read/2017/02/15/340/1619386/selamat-dominggus-mandacan-menang-telak-69-dalam-pilgub-papua-barat.

Toyyiban. 2017. 'Pangdam: Papua Barat aman dari KKB.' *Antara News,* 22 November 2017. Accessed 20 February 2018. https://www.antaranews.com/berita/666488/pangdam-papua-barat-aman-dari-kkb.

Section 5.34 West Sulawesi:

BPS Provinsi Sulawesi Barat. n.d. 'BPS Provinsi Sulawesi Barat'. Accessed 2 October 2017. https://sulbar.bps.go.id/.

Ihsannudin. 2017. 'Jokowi Apresiasi Tingginya Pertumbuhan Ekonomi Di Sulawesi Barat'. *Kompas.Com,* 2 August 2017. https://nasional.kompas.com/read/2017/08/02/16305951/jokowi-apresiasi-tingginya-pertumbuhan-ekonomi-di-sulawesi-barat.

Kantor Perwakilan Bank Indonesia Provinsi Sulawesi Barat. 2016. 'Kajian Ekonomi Dan Keuangan Regional Provinsi Sulawesi Barat Triwulan IV-2015'. https://www.bi.go.id/id/publikasi/kajian-ekonomi-regional/sulbar/Pages/Kajian-Ekonomi-dan-Keuangan-Regional-Provinsi-Sulawesi-Barat-Triwulan-IV-2015.aspx.

Komisi Pemilihan Umum. n.d. 'Visi Misi Gubernur Sulawesi Barat Periode 2017-2022'. Accessed 5 October 2017. https://pilkada2017.kpu.go.id/download/calon/2057/2057_Visi-Misi_1_.pdf/.

Section 5.35 West Sumatra:

BPHN Indonesia. n.d. 'Peraturan Daerah Provinsi Sumatera Barat, Nomor 7 Tahun 2008 Tentang Rencana Pembangunan Jangka Panjang Daerah (RPJP) Sumatera Barat Tahun 2005–2005'. Badan Pembinaan Hukum Nasional.

BPS Provinsi Sumatera Barat. 2017. 'Pertumbuhan Ekonomi,Sumatera Barat Triwulan II-2017'. Berita Resmi Statistik No. 44/08/13/ Th XX.

Repository Produk Hukum. 2017. 'Peraturan Daerah Provinsi Sumatera Barat Nomor 6 Tahun 2016 Tentang Rencana Pembangunan Jangka Menengah Daerah (RPJMD) Provinsi Sumatera Barat Tahun 2016–2021.' http://produkhukum.dprd.sumbarprov.go.id/home/produk/2/135.

Section 5.36 Concluding Remarks:

Asmarini, Winda, and Bernadette Christina Munthe. 2017. 'Indonesia Eases Export Ban on Nickel Ore, Bauxite'. Reuters, 12 January 2017. https://www.reuters.com/article/us-indonesia-mining-exports/indonesia-eases-export-ban-on-nickel-ore-bauxite-idUSKBN14W1TZ.

Chapter 6
Conclusion

6.1 Summary of Key Findings

For its flagship projects, the Asia Competitiveness Institute (ACI) has been conducting studies to evaluate competitiveness and related issues in the Association of Southeast Asian Nations (ASEAN)-10 countries as well as the economic powerhouses of China and India. Annual analyses at the sub-national level have been at the forefront of ACI's research, providing a relevant approach towards understanding the vast and diverse characteristics of Singapore's large neighbouring countries, such as Indonesia, China and India. For this, ACI has been acknowledged for its role in "contributing to building a comprehensive knowledge of economic conditions in Singapore's regional markets" (Committee on the Future Economy 2017). This book presents the results of our latest research on Indonesia, reflecting ACI's commitment to put forward evidence-based findings based on our rich sub-national database and track provincial and regional competitiveness therein.

As an overview and introduction to the book, Chapter 1 starts by providing a brief account of Indonesia's most recent macroeconomic development and ends by presenting the breakdown of the overall structure of this book. As the country strives to revive its economic growth and recover from slowdown due to low commodity prices and weak external demand, Indonesia is pushing for public spending in infrastructure development. To enable high levels of public investment, the country is boosting receipts from tax collection. It is also trying to attract more investment by enacting wide-ranging reforms to improve the ease of doing business. These strategies and reforms have been outlined in Section 1.2.5, which is adapted from the speech delivered by the Minister for National Development Planning Agency of Republic of Indonesia (Bappenas), Dr Bambang Brodjonegoro. The success of such strategies, however, very much depends on efforts conducted at both the national and sub-national levels.

Chapter 2 provides the results of ACI's 2017 annual analysis on Indonesia's provincial-level competitiveness. Provinces from the Java region remain among the most competitive, while those from the Maluku-Papua region tend to lag behind. While there are only minor changes observed in the provinces occupying the top-10 and bottom-5 ranking compared to past years' results, more dynamic changes are observed in the provinces' standardised score distributions in the last three years. Several provinces such as Lampung and Central Sulawesi have sustained improvements in their competitiveness ranking, while others such as South Sumatra and Bengkulu are consistently falling behind.

Identifying key characteristics of provinces with high and low levels of competitiveness remains a challenge. To some, a strong manufacturing sector is arguably correlated to a high level of competitiveness. However, our latest competitiveness ranking shows that some of the most industrialised provinces such as West Papua and South Sumatra — with secondary industries contributing to 43.1 percent and 31.1 percent of their respective total Gross Regional Domestic Products (GRDP) in 2014 — are ranked among the bottom-10 provinces at 33rd and 24th respectively. It is also worth noting that the secondary industries of these provinces are predominantly dependent on natural resources such as oil and gas manufacturing, thereby countering the idea that having abundant natural resources often explain the outstanding performance of provinces such as East Kalimantan (ranked third). Similarly, our latest competitiveness ranking proves this untrue, when West Papua and Riau — two provinces where oil and gas accounted for 48.00 percent and 41.00 percent of their respective GRDP in 2014 — are ranked 33rd and 16th respectively in 2017. Another theory posits that certain provinces tend to display lagging performances due to their archipelagic nature. Indeed, many archipelagic provinces do face challenges in becoming competitive, as observed by the low ranks obtained by East Nusa Tenggara (30th), North Maluku (31st) and Maluku (29th). However, exceptions are again observed in the archipelagic provinces of Riau Islands and North Sulawesi which fare relatively well at the 2017 study, occupy 10th and 17th positions respectively.

Chapter 3 provides the results of ACI's 2017 annual analysis on Indonesia's regional-level competitiveness. While the findings are generally intuitive to many policymakers' understanding of regional disparity in the country, the weak performance of Sumatra region continues to challenge the conventional belief of a clear east–west divide in Indonesia. Being located next to the Malacca Strait and closest to the Java region, Sumatra has been often been perceived as the more developed part of Indonesia. However, ACI's regional competitiveness study has, for the past three years, ranked Sumatra fourth, below Java, Kalimantan and Sulawesi. Additionally, disparities are observed not only inter-regionally, e.g. between Java and all other regions, but also intra-regionally, e.g. between Riau Islands and other provinces in Sumatra.

The empirical analysis in Chapter 4 indicates another effort to comprehend sub-national level variations by investigating the impact of real effective exchange rate (REER) on foreign direct investment (FDI) inflows to Indonesian provinces. Findings from the study suggest that the increases in REER levels, i.e. the appreciation of the Indonesian Rupiah and REER volatility deter FDI inflows to Indonesia's provinces, thereby implying that FDI inflows to Indonesia are export-oriented in nature. Other control variables such as GRDP per capita and market size as measured by provincial-level population appear to be significant determinants of FDI inflows, documenting positive relationship with FDI in the regressions.

Chapter 5 presents short commentaries on the recent developments in Indonesian provinces in the period of 2015–2017. These commentaries are mostly contributed by academics from local universities in Indonesia. The chapter supplements ACI's evidence-based research findings in the foregoing chapters by providing necessary contextual information on the economic, social and political developments in the provinces.

Apart from these chapters, we also received contributions from our reviewers. The first reviewer for Chapters 2 and 3 is Professor Balthasar Kambuaya, who is the Chairman of the University Senate at Cenderawasih University and former Minister for Environment (2011–2014) in Indonesia. Professor Kambuaya outlined key possibilities that could account for the low competitiveness of provinces with high natural resources such as Papua and West Papua.

The second reviewer for Chapter 4 is Dr Darius Tirtosuharto, an economist at the Economic and Monetary Policy Department at the Macroeconomic Division of the Bank of Indonesia. He highlighted the presence of risk-averse investors in Indonesia, who to some extent tolerate a certain degree of exchange rate volatility so long as there is stability in expected growth. He also pointed out that macroeconomic stability is key to maintaining sustainability of output growth and guides investors' perception towards measurable risks and opportunities.

The third reviewer, Professor Sin Chor-Yiu, also reviews Chapter 4. A professor in the Department of Economics at College of Technology Management, the National Tsing Hua University in Taiwan, Republic of China, Professor Sin suggested for other disaggregated data to be included in the analysis, including factors such as competitiveness and political power of domestic firms.

6.2 Concluding Remarks: Maximising Indonesia's Untapped Potentials

As the world's current 16th largest economy by Gross Domestic Product (GDP) (The World Bank n.d.), Indonesia is predicted to be the world's seventh and fourth largest economy in 2030 and 2050 respectively (Oberman et al. 2012; PwC Global 2017). These projections highlight a common theme — that Indonesia is a rising middle power and has much potential to grow. To allow Indonesia to fully maximise its untapped potential and take on its role as a rising middle power, it has to sustain its economic growth. This is achieved by enhancing its competitiveness, along with adopting a more outward-oriented approach, developing infrastructure, establishing new growth centres and managing the country's domestic risks.

6.2.1 Adopting a More Outward-Oriented Approach

One of the ways that Indonesia can boost growth is by adopting a more outward-oriented approach in aspects such as investment and trade, as previously mentioned in Chapter 1.

Many studies have identified various determinants of investments in Indonesia. One literature posits that among others, higher government investment, economic growth, credit availability and exchange rate can improve private investments in Indonesia (Suhendra and Anwar 2014). Another study found that higher economic growth, better infrastructure and stable political conditions will encourage FDI inflows to Indonesia (A. Darmawan and Azzahra 2013). The findings in Chapter 4 corroborate the aforementioned studies, in that depreciation of REER as well as higher income levels and market size do lead to higher FDI inflows to provinces in Indonesia. All these suggest that the notion of a conducive investment climate ultimately rests upon, inter alia, issues relating to macroeconomic stability, institutional policies and infrastructure. A report by the World Bank (Stern 2002) summed up these issues by defining investment climate as comprising three broad categories: (i) macroeconomic stability and openness, (ii) good governance and strong institutions as well as (iii) quality infrastructure.

For many years, however, the investment climate in Indonesia has been characterised as unfavourable and unconducive. In 2003, a firm-level survey conducted by the Asian Development Bank (ADB) and the World Bank reported that the most critical business constraints that are most often cited by firms are those related to macroeconomic instability as well as economic and regulatory policy uncertainty, followed by corruption and issues in labour, financing, taxation and infrastructure (ADB 2005). Ten years later, ACI's study on the Ease of Doing Business Index on Attractiveness to Investors, Business Friendliness and Competitive Policies (EDB Index ABC) of 33 provinces of Indonesia found only six provinces scoring far above average in the index (K. G. Tan et al. 2017). Indeed, South Sulawesi — the top-ranked province in the EDB Index ABC — has maintained the merits of an investment-friendly environment by performing well in all aspects of ACI's competitiveness framework as discussed in Chapter 2. This includes the aforementioned categories of Macroeconomic Stability as well as Government and Institutional Setting. Having a high level of competitiveness may therefore correlate to achieving a good investment climate.

Recognising the inadequacies of Indonesia's business environment, the government has regularly implemented reforms to free up complexities of business regulations and licensing procedures. Since September 2015, 16 economic packages — mostly pertaining to easing and expediting business licensing and processes — have been introduced by the national government. Its latest package on the single submission system is hoped to iron out inconsistencies and contradictions among national and regional regulations (Indonesia-Investments 2017b). Moving forward, the Indonesian government needs to continue implementing reforms in order to ensure a more stable and conducive investment climate.

Another outward-oriented stance that Indonesia can adopt is that of boosting trade, especially within the ASEAN region. A research by the World Bank has shown that trade is a major driver of growth in four High Performing Asian Economies (HPAE) in ASEAN, namely Indonesia, Malaysia, Singapore and Thailand (1993). Specifically, intra-ASEAN exports have gained more importance in recent years; as of 2011, exports among the ASEAN-8 member countries (excluding Lao People's Democratic Republic (PDR) and Myanmar) constituted the highest share of total ASEAN-8's gross exports (OECD-TiVA 2015).

The interconnectedness of the ASEAN economies means that their growth is highly dependent on the business and economic conditions of one another. For instance, as one of Indonesia's major trading partners, an increase in one percentage point in Singapore's GDP growth rate directly increases Indonesia's GDP growth rate by 0.13 percentage point; likewise, a one percentage point increase in Indonesia's GDP growth rate directly contributes to a 0.26 percentage point increase in Singapore's growth rate (K. Y. Tan, Abeysinghe, and Tan 2015). Given the importance of trade within ASEAN, Indonesia as a trade-driven HPAE can benefit from boosting trade, particularly intra-regional, as it can drive higher economic growth in the country.

6.2.2 Developing Infrastructure

Indonesia's push for better infrastructure and maritime connectivity came into force at the outset of President Joko Widodo's administration in 2015 in order to boost growth in the country. According to a report by the World Bank (The World Bank 2017a), infrastructure in Indonesia could boost productivity through the reduction in transportation and telecommunication costs, the creation of economies of scale and production scope as well as the development of investments in Indonesia's human resource. Moreover, boosting infrastructure improves the Gini ratio of the society (Seneviratne and Sun 2013) and raises the economy's growth rate. Infrastructure and maritime connectivity is expected to facilitate the movement of people and goods, which will address the problems of high logistical as well as business costs, eventually supporting the economy in broader parts of Indonesia.

The role of infrastructure development in Indonesia has never been more important than the present condition. However, Indonesia's infrastructure scene has largely been disregarded, with the country's per capita public capital stock reaching only a third of other emerging markets and developing economies (EMDEs), which equates to a gap in infrastructure assets of about US$1.5 trillion (The World Bank 2017a). The country thus suffers a large infrastructure deficit arising from its prolonged neglect.

Recognising this large infrastructure deficit, clusters of projects have since been rolled out across Indonesia; to date, there are 245 National Strategic Projects (PSN) surrounding the construction of roads, railways, airports and seaports as well as the provision of electricity, which would require a total of Rp4.20 quadrillion in financing (KPPIP n.d.). The government has increased capital expenditures, but amounts channelled are still far below the needs of the country. For instance, only Rp525 trillion (12.5 percent of total cost) of the state budget has been earmarked for the national projects. Given this shortfall, the government has turned its efforts toward boosting infrastructure through private sector investments.

Despite attempts to ramp up efforts in infrastructure development, completion progress has not been sufficiently quick. In particular, only 26 (10.6 percent) out of the 245 national projects have been completed as of 2017[1] — more than two years since their inception (Balipost 2017). Many of these projects, which are slated to be completed by 2019, are still in the planning or transaction phase. For instance, the development of the flagship 35,000-megawatt (MW) electricity procurement programme had only reached 3.8 percent completion rate as of February 2018. It is expected to miss its targeted completion date of 2019 (Singgih 2018).

6.2.3 Establishing Special Economic Zones and Industrial Parks

Indonesia is developing Special Economic Zones (SEZs) and industrial parks in various parts of the country to further boost investment and support economic growth. A total of 12 locations have been designated as SEZs, along with more than 80 existing and planned industrial parks. The government is also planning for additional 13 SEZs in places such as Merauke, Kuala Tanjung, Pulau Asam Karimun, Bangka and Nongsa, which would bring the total number of SEZs slated to operate by 2019 to 25 locations (Ministry of Industry 2017). These sites would be supported with the provision of infrastructure, facilities and incentives to ease investment, thereby allowing for concentrated investments to take place.

Similar to the infrastructure development, however, the progress of the operation of these zones and parks has remained wanting. In particular, only two out of the 12 SEZs have started commercial operations, namely Sei Mangkei in North Sumatra and Tanjung Lesung in Banten

[1] 20 projects were completed in 2016, while the remaining six were completed by 2017.

(Indonesia-Investments 2017a). Between 2015 and 2017, a total of 10 industrial parks have been constructed — seven of which are located outside of Java (Julianto 2017). Nonetheless, these new SEZs and industrial parks have proven to engender FDI as well as job creation in the area. For instance, the newly operational Kendal Industrial Park in Semarang, Central Java — which was a joint development project between Indonesian developer Jabeka and Singapore-based developer Sembcorp — has housed the operation of 39 companies and has employed more than 1,950 workers thus far (Vatvani 2018). The park is also planned to host a vocational training school for the furniture and wood processing industries. Developments stemming from partnership and collaboration with other countries are set to continue. Among others, Indonesia's trade ministry has recently offered three industrial estates to its neighbouring country Singapore for development[2] (The Straits Times 2018).

With improved conditions in the country, Indonesia has begun to observe the fruits of its labour. From an international perspective, Indonesia's investment climate and economic outlook have indeed become more promising. For instance, the country has received an upgrade in its investment grade ratings in 2017 from two of the Big Three credit rating agencies, Standard & Poor's (S&P) and Fitch Group, on the back of improvements in budget and increased resilience to external shocks. International organisations such as the United Nations Conference on Trade and Development (UNCTAD) have also recognised the increasingly conducive investment climate in Indonesia, placing it as the most promising host country among economies in the south-eastern part of Asia (UNCTAD 2017).

In statistical terms, FDI inflows to Indonesia have increased by 13.2 percent year-on-year in 2017. However, this growth is still a far cry from those observed in neighbouring counterparts such as Malaysia, the Philippines and India with growth rates of 51.0 percent, 38.0 percent and 30.0 percent respectively (Hermansyah 2018).

6.2.4 Tackling Existing and Emerging Risks

Beyond just prioritising economic growth, the government should be watchful of some of the existing and impending risks that, if left unchecked, would threaten Indonesia's future development.

6.2.4.1 *Decentralisation*

For one, decentralization — which allows provincial and local governments to manage various aspects of their sub-national entities with expanded level of autonomy (Darmawan 2008; The World Bank 2005; Bardhan and Mookherjee 2006) — has improved public services but caused variations in the governance quality across provinces. Chapter 2 recognises this; a higher disparity in the performance of provincial governments is indicated by the higher Shapley weight for the environment of Government and Institutional Setting. There have also been assessments of governance quality at the city and provincial levels conducted by the Regional Autonomy Watch Committee (KPPOD) in Indonesia. Its most recent assessment which ranks governance quality

[2] The three estates are Tanah Kuning Industrial Estate in North Kalimantan, Kuala Tanjung Industrial Estate in North Sumatra and Bitung Industrial Estate in North Sulawesi.

in the 32 provincial capitals of Indonesia found that provinces with higher income generally tend to have lower index values (i.e. lower evaluation on governance quality) (KPPOD 2017).

Unchecked decentralisation has also resulted in the persistence of investment bottlenecks due to the large number of laws and regulations passed by local governments and line ministries in addition to national-level policies (The World Bank 2017a). Not only are some of these regional policies often more restrictive than national-level regulations, a number of them are in contradiction to the latter. This discrepancy of regulations in various layers of governance indicates weak coordination between the central and regional governments, which has ultimately led to prolonged confusion in the country's investment bureaucracy.

The central government had initially tried to remove problematic local bylaws; however, this authority was recently annulled by the Indonesian constitutional court in 2017. Indonesia therefore needs to look for alternative solutions to streamline regulations and red tapes across the different layers of governance, otherwise investors would be deterred to enter the country. Greater monitoring should also be exercised by the central government on the performance and accountability of the local governments. This can be accompanied with improved incentives on the current conditional fiscal transfers that would accommodate more flexible and goal-oriented instruments of assessments (The World Bank 2017b).

6.2.4.2 *Corruption*

Some of the problems related to decentralisation also extend beyond increased bureaucracy and uncoordinated procedures to include corruption. The increased regional autonomy due to decentralisation is said to have resulted in "decentralised corruption", which is particularly rampant in the sector of public administration dealing with public procurement, licensing and budget allocation. Chapter 5 has highlighted how over the span of the three years between 2015 and 2017, many regional heads have been caught by the Corruption Eradication Commission (KPK) for corruption-related practices. Statistics from the Indonesian Home Ministry has also revealed that a total of 18 governors and 343 mayors/regents have been under investigation for corruption since Indonesia's decentralisation in 2001 (The Jakarta Post 2017). Furthermore, there have been reports by people about bribes and irregular payments made to the public servants (Pring 2017). Needless to say, these practices have caused a dent to the credibility of public services in Indonesia. Recognising this, the government has worked closely with KPK to address these issues. Among their recent policy reforms is the introduction of e-procurement programme to raise transparency in the government's procurement system.

6.2.4.3 *Political Exploitation of Religious Sentiments*

Closer to the capital, we are seeing the increasing exploitation of religious sentiments by political elites which threatens to rock the social stability of the country. This problem had intensified and was manifested right at the centre of the nation's capital DKI Jakarta, where a crowd of an estimated 200,000 Muslim protesters rallied against the province's former Governor Basuki Tjahaja Purnama (Ahok) for his alleged blasphemy against Islam. The protest was the biggest in Indonesia (Quiano and Griffiths 2016), where protesters hailing from Jakarta as well as other cities and regencies in Indonesia took to the streets for a full day march at Jakarta's main square. The crowd, which comprised students, non-governmental organisations, Islamic groups and ordinary citizens, demanded for Ahok's resignation and incarceration under the nation's blasphemy laws.

The mass demonstration not only temporarily halted economic activities in Jakarta, it also showed just how vulnerable Indonesia's growth engines are to internal risks. There have been worries that similar political exploitation of religious and ethnic sentiments may occur during the upcoming 2018 elections taking place concurrently across 171 regions involving provinces, districts and municipalities in Indonesia, as had been voiced out by the academics in Chapter 5. While observers may view this as an isolated incident, the international media has portrayed this incidence negatively. Such portrayal of a politically and socially unstable Indonesia may thus deter potential investors from entering the country.

6.2.4.4 *Strained Public Services*

Another risk that is increasingly becoming more pronounced is the strained provision of public services and infrastructure. Chapter 2 highlighted how provinces in Java such as East Java, Central Java and West Java have experienced a decline in their ranking for quality of life and infrastructure development, despite their strong performance in other areas of competitiveness. Likewise, ACI's latest study on assessing the liveability of cities around the world has ranked Jakarta 52nd out of 64 cities on the grounds of poor performance in various aspects such as environmental sustainability and socio-cultural conditions (Tan, Nie, and Baek 2017). Indeed, Jakarta and many other provinces in Java — an island that hosts about 60 percent of Indonesia's total population — have experienced problems of traffic congestions, flood hazard and water insufficiency at a high cost. Minister for National Development Planning Agency (Bappenas) of the Republic of Indonesia Bambang Brodjonegoro reported that traffic congestions have cost Indonesia about US$5.0 billion annually (Aziza 2017). Such glaring inefficiencies have also resulted in a major loss of productivity which, if left unaddressed, could affect economic activities and attractiveness to investors in the area.

At present, the country has endured all the aforementioned risks without severe implications. However, careless management of these risks could potentially cause them to intensify and escalate into larger issues. The government's vigour in accelerating growth in infrastructure and investments should thus go hand in hand with its commitment to manage and tackle these issues. The country's stability — be it economic, social or political — is contingent upon the government's ability to address the dynamics of political situations, threats to internal security as well as bureaucratic uncertainties, failing which could dampen or negate the benefits from the economic development.

6.3 Future Research Agenda: Nexus between Exchange Rates and Trade in Goods and Services

Beyond managing domestic risks, sustaining the country's growth path also involves controlling for external risks. A growing concern of late is the series of global uncertainties arising from continued threats of the 'deglobalisation' of trade and financial flows as well as protectionism, which could dampen the recovery of external demand. Thus, in addition to taking efforts towards fixing domestic structural issues, Indonesian government has an instrumental role to play in revitalising its external sector linkages with the region to ensure that growth remains diversified and broad-based, especially on the trade front.

Tapping the external growth engines of a country through sustained exports is neither new in theory nor policy practice. There is particularly a large extant of academic literature that has documented the importance of exports in order to facilitate economic growth. Exports spur competition in the domestic market, thus encouraging even the non-exporters to become competitive. Exports also enable economies of scale as well as technological spillovers. These market enhancements lead to a virtuous cycle of productivity gains, increased specialisation and optimal reallocation of resources to higher productivity export sectors.

In particular, Indonesia's exports have always played an important role in sustaining the nation's economy since the 1970s. Exports of goods to Indonesia have consistently grown, peaking at US$188.40 billion in 2014 (see Figure 6.1). Its share to Indonesia's GDP was largely stable between 1974 and 1997, fluctuating between 20 percent and 30 percent. However, the figure has been on a declining trend post-Asian Financial Crisis in 1998, ending at 15 percent in 2016 — the lowest since the beginning of Indonesia's liberalisation reforms three decades ago.

It must also be reiterated that the gradual normalisation of the US monetary policy has begun. Consequently, it has generated fears that there will be a repeat of the "taper tantrum" that battered countries like Indonesia in 2013. As a context, changes in the US monetary policies have always exerted significant spillover effects on countries like Indonesia, which are especially

Figure 6.1: Trade as a Percentage of GDP (Percent), 1960–2016

Source: World Development Indicators, World Bank compiled by ACI.

pronounced during the period following the global financial crisis. While ultra-loose monetary policies in the form of quantitative easing resulted in currency appreciations due to massive capital inflows, the tapering of the same through interest rate hikes generated massive capital outflows and the consequent currency depreciations. This impact was more severe on fragile emerging economies like Indonesia which has relatively weak macroeconomic fundamentals. The ebbs and flows of international capital flows that are sensitive to US monetary policy changes have thus generally given rise to a variety of policy challenges concerning monetary and exchange rate management in countries such as Indonesia, which in turn has a significant bearing on its overall macroeconomic and financial stability.

More generally, currency swings in Indonesia matter because of the potential macroeconomic implications they can have on its trade and foreign investments. Viewed particularly in the context of the importance of trade and foreign investments to Indonesia, one of the most significant challenges for policymakers is to understand the potential implications of exchange rate volatility on trade flows as well as on foreign investments.

Figure 6.2 shows the share of merchandise exports by Indonesia's sub-national regions from 2000 to 2015. In 2000, two regions alone — Java and Sumatra — contributed 50.5 percent and 28.3 percent of Indonesia's total exports respectively. However, there has been an increase in the share of exports originating from Sumatra and Kalimantan between 2004 and 2011, mostly generated due to the increase in raw commodity prices. This resulted in the relative decline of Java's exports in terms of proportion from 51.5 percent in 2001 to 36.2 percent in 2011. However, from 2011 onwards, there was also a decrease in the proportion of Sumatra's and Kalimantan's exports along with the global commodity price bust.

Figure 6.2: Share of Exports by Region (Percent), 2000–2015

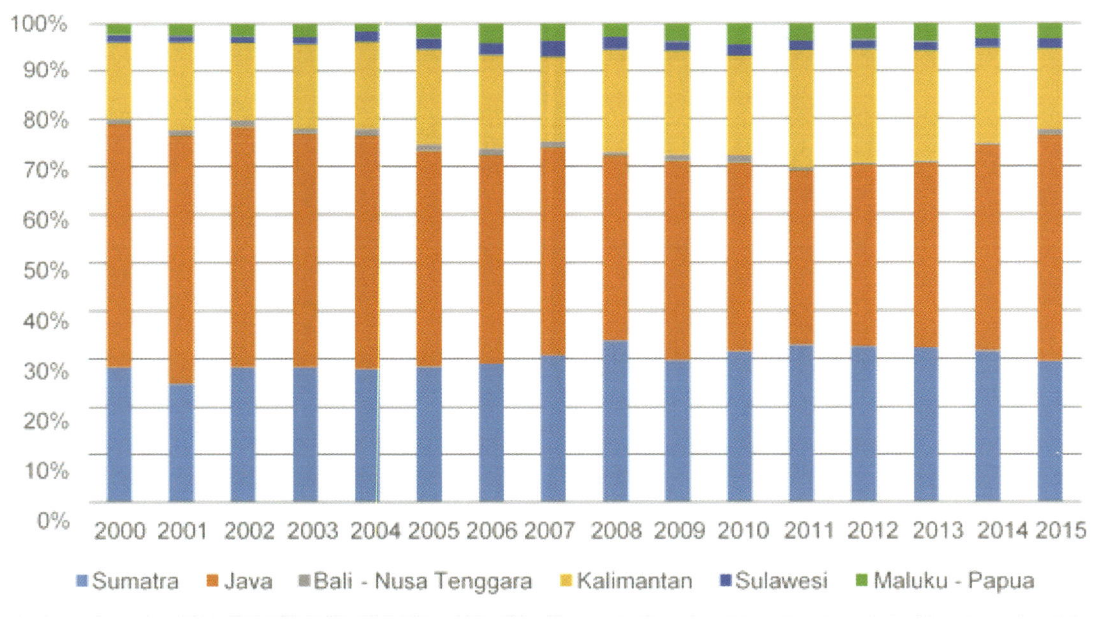

Source: Indonesia Central Bureau of Statistics (BPS), compiled by ACI.

While regional-level variations seem prominent, provincial-level disparity is even more pronounced. This is also highlighted in Chapter 2, wherein only nine out of 33 provinces score above average in the performance of openness to trade (an environment that assesses the strength of provinces' trade). These provinces are mostly in the Java region, namely DKI Jakarta, East Java, Central Java and Banten, but they also include the more peripheral provinces, such as Riau Islands, East Kalimantan, North Sumatra and Riau.

Past research have explored a number of factors that determine export performance, ranging from access to foreign markets, institutional capacity and supply conditions, to name a few (Fugazza 2004). From this list, an important factor relates to the behaviour of exchange rates and how it affects exports. Thus, one of the many determinants on exports concerns the movements of exchange rates both in terms of their levels and volatility.

How do we expect exchange rate movements to affect exports from these provinces? This is at best an empirical question. Intuitively, we can think of world demand being an influential factor in determining the magnitude of a country's exports. This is so as we would expect to see Indonesia's exports grow should there be high demand for its goods in the global market. Similarly, it is also logical to expect the supply capacity of the provinces to influence the quantum and efficiency of exports. In particular, when we have a situation where exports are concentrated in a few selected provinces, the differences in the supply capacity of each province could prove to be vital determinants of exporting patterns emanating from them.

Beyond these factors, there is an important link that comes from the relationship between exchange rates and trade flows. In fact, what receives the most attention in Indonesia and other emerging markets is the influence of relative price competitiveness captured by movements in REER. Exchange rates become all the more important when we consider the broad trends in Indonesia's REER as briefly discussed above. A persistent appreciation of Indonesia's REER could lead to a loss of export competitiveness, which could in turn affect Indonesia's economic growth moving forward, making it important for policymakers to understand the impact of movements and volatility in exchange rates.

The impact on exports could be different depending on whether we are looking at REER movements in levels or fluctuations/volatility. If we go by the conventional understanding, we would expect an REER depreciation to boost exports (and vice versa) as a weaker currency could boost price competitiveness. Similarly, higher REER volatility should deter a country's exports to the rest of the world as it increases the uncertainty of revenues from exports, which could lead to higher transaction costs.

However, these traditional relationships may not always hold true. Increasingly, in the world of global value chains, any positive impact on exports of a weaker currency could be dampened if such depreciation raises the cost of imported inputs. Similarly, negative effects of REER volatility may be moderated if, for instance, well-developed financial markets allow exporters to hedge. Also, if there are sunk costs involved, firms will be less responsive to REER volatility, thus reducing its impact on exports. Finally, while incumbent firms tend to have a "wait-and-see" attitude which make them less reactive to fluctuations in exchange rate, newer entrants tend to stay out of the market with deeper and longer fluctuations in REER. Thus, the impact of exchange rates are complicated; it is an empirical question as to what extent exchange rates influence exports.

Given this background, our future research will undertake a systematic study to empirically examine the impact of REER both in terms of levels and volatility on trade flows, using data on provinces of Indonesia. Further, given that the world has seen a proliferation of global value chains in the way that international trade transactions take place and the fact that Indonesia is plugged into this network quite densely, it naturally becomes important to understand what role exchange rate movements both in terms of levels and volatility play on the country's trade flows — a subject we deal with in our next book.

References

ADB. 2005. "Improving the Investment Climate in Indonesia." Asian Development Bank. Indonesia. https://www.adb.org/publications/improving-investment-climate-indonesia.

Aziza, Kurnia Sari. 2017. "Bappenas: Kerugian akibat Macet Jakarta Rp 67 Triliun Per Tahun." Kompas. com. October 6, 2017. https://ekonomi.kompas.com/read/2017/10/06/054007626/bappenas-kerugian-akibat-macet-jakarta-rp-67-triliun-per-tahun.

Balipost, Redaksi Portal Bali. 2017. "Rampung, 26 Proyek Bernilai Rp 46,5 Triliun." *BALIPOST.com*, December 21, 2017. //www.balipost.com/news/2017/12/21/32137/Rampung,26-Proyek-Bernilai-Rp... html.

Bardhan, Pranab K., and Mookherjee. 2006. "The Rise of Local Governments: An Overview." In *Decentralization and Local Governance in Developing Countries: A Comparative Perspective*, edited by Pranab K. Bardhan and Dilip Mookherjee. Book, Whole. Cambridge, Mass; London: MIT.

Committee on the Future Economy. 2017. "Report of the Committee on the Future Economy: Pioneers of the Next Generation."

Darmawan, Arif, and Fatimah Azzahra. 2013. "Explaining the Determinants of FDI in Indonesia: An Extended Dunning and Gravity Approach." Proceedings of International Conference on Indonesian DevelopmentICID 2013. http://www.academia.edu/12769017/Explaining_the_Determinants_of_FDI_in_Indonesia_an_Extended_Dunning_and_Gravity_Approach.

Darmawan, Rachmand Erland Danny. 2008. "The Practices of Decentralization in Indonesia and Its Implication on Local Competitiveness." Public Administration-Public Governance Study. Eschede, the Netherlands: School of Management and Government University of Twente.

Fugazza, Marco. 2004. "Export Performance and Its Determinants: Supply and Demand Constraints." UNCTAD. http://unctad.org/en/pages/PublicationArchive.aspx?publicationid=1197.

Hermansyah, Anton. 2018. "Investment Task Forces to Operate in Jakarta, Other Regions: Jokowi." *The Jakarta Post*, January 23, 2018. http://www.thejakartapost.com/news/2018/01/23/investment-task-forces-to-operate-in- jakarta-other-regions-jokowi.html.

Indonesia-Investments. 2017a. "Indonesia Seeks to Develop More Special Economic Zones." Indonesia-Investments. July 7, 2017. https://www.indonesia-investments.com/id/business/business-columns/indonesia-seeks-to-develop-more-special-economic-zones/item7962.

———. 2017b. "16th Economic Policy Package: Single Submission System." Indonesia-Investments. August 31, 2017. https://www.indonesia-investments.com/id/news/news-columns/16th-economic-policy-package-single-submission-system/item8154.

Julianto, Pramdia Arhando. 2017. "3 Tahun Jokowi-JK: 10 Kawasan Industri Dibangun." *KOMPAS.com*, October 23, 2017. https://ekonomi.kompas.com/read/2017/10/23/201745126/3-tahun-jokowi-jk-10-kawasan-industri-dibangun.

KPPOD. 2017. *Regional Economic Governance 2016*. Jakarta, Indonesia: KPPOD, supported by Knowledge Sector Initiative (KSI) and Australian Department of Foreign Affairs and Trade (DFAT).

KPPIP. n.d. "National Strategic Projects." Committee for Acceleration of Priority Infrastructure Delivery. Accessed March 7, 2018. https://kppip.go.id/en/national-strategic-projects/.

Ministry of Industry. 2017. "13 Kawasan Industri Baru Telah Beroperasi," July 19, 2017. http://www.kemenperin.go.id/artikel/17846/13-Kawasan-Industri-Baru-Telah-Beroperasi.

Oberman, Raoul, Richard Dobbs, Arief Budiman, Fraser Thompson, and Morten Rosse. 2012. "The Archipelago Economy: Unleashing Indonesia's Potential." McKinsey Global Institute. https://www.pwc.com/gx/en/issues/economy/the-world-in-2050.html.

OECD-TiVA. 2015. "Trade in Value Added (TiVA) — October 2015." 2015. https://stats.oecd.org/Index.aspx?DataSetCode=TIVA2015_C1.

Pring, Coralie. 2017. "People and Corruption: Citizens' Voices from around the World." Global Corruption Barometer. Transparency International.

PwC Global. 2017. "The Long View: How Will the Global Economic Order Change by 2050?" https://www.pwc.com/gx/en/issues/economy/the-world-in-2050.html.

Quiano, Kathy, and James Griffiths. 2016. "Indonesia: 200,000 Protest Christian Governor of Jakarta." *The Jakarta Post*, December 2, 2016.

Seneviratne, Dulani, and Yan Sun. 2013. "Infrastructure and Income Distribution in ASEAN-5: What Are the Links?" IMF Working Paper. International Monetary Fund. https://www.imf.org/external/pubs/ft/wp/2013/wp1341.pdf.

Singgih, Viriya P. 2018. "Jokowi's 35,000 MW Program Only Reaches 3.8 Percent Progress." *The Jakarta Post*, March 4, 2018. http://www.thejakartapost.com/news/2018/03/04/jokowis-35000-mw-program-only- reaches-3-8-percent-progress.html.

Stern, Nicholas. 2002. *A Strategy for Development*. Washington, DC: World Bank.

Suhendra, Indra, and Cep Jandi Anwar. 2014. "Determinants of Private Investment and The Effects on Economic Growth in Indonesia." *GSTF Journal on Business Review (GBR)* 3 (3): 1–6. https://doi.org/10.7603/s40706-014-0028-4.

Tan, Khee Giap, Mulya Amri, Nursyahida Ahmad, and Kong Yam Tan. 2017. *2016 Growth Slowdown Analysis, Ease of Doing Business Index, and Annual Competitiveness Studies of Indonesia's Sub-National Economies*. Singapore: World Scientific Publishing Co. Pte. Ltd. http://www.worldscientific.com/worldscibooks/10.1142/10621.

Tan, Khee Giap, Tongxin Nie, and Shinae Baek. 2017. *2015 Greater China Liveable Cities Index: Ranking Analysis, Simulation and Policy Evaluation.* Singapore: Whioce Publishing.

Tan, Kong Yam, Tilak Abeysinghe, and Khee Giap Tan. 2015. "Shifting Drivers of Growth: Policy Implications for ASEAN-5." *Asian Economic Papers* 14 (1): 157–73. https://doi.org/10.1162/ASEP_a_00331.

The Jakarta Post. 2017. "Indonesia's Decentralisation and Corruption: The Jakarta Post." Text. The Straits Times. September 25, 2017. http://www.straitstimes.com/asia/se- asia/indonesias-decentralisation-and-corruption-the-jakarta-post.

The Straits Times. 2018. "Indonesia Offers 3 Industrial Estates for Singapore Development." Text. The Straits Times. February 19, 2018. http://www.straitstimes.com/asia/se-asia/indonesia-offers-three-industrial-estates-for-singapore-development.

The World Bank. 1993. "The East Asian Miracle : Economic Growth and Public Policy : Main Report (English)." 12351. The World Bank. http://documents.worldbank.org/curated/en/975081468244550798/Main-report.

———. 2005. "East Asia Decentralizes: Making Local Government Work." Washington DC: The World Bank.

———. 2017a. "Indonesia Economic Quarterly Report October 2017: Closing the Gap." The World Bank. http://www.worldbank.org/en/country/indonesia/publication/indonesia-economic- quarterly-reports.

———. 2017b. "Indonesia Economic Quarterly Report December 2017: Decentralisation that Delivers." The World Bank. http://www.worldbank.org/en/country/indonesia/publication/indonesia-economic-quarterly-reports.

———. n.d. "The World Bank Database." https://data.worldbank.org/indicator/NY.GDP.MKTP.CD.

UNCTAD. 2017. "World Investment Report 2017: Investment and Digital Economy." United Nations Conference on Trade and Development.

Vatvani, Chandni. 2018. "Indonesia and Singapore to Boost Cooperation in Investment and Vocational Education." *Channel NewsAsia*, February 19, 2018. https://www.channelnewsasia.com/news/asiapacific/indonesia-and-singapore-to-boost-cooperation-in-investment-and-9972142.

Appendix 1

List of Indicators for the 2017 Competitiveness Index and Ranking for Indonesian Provinces and Regions

No.	Indicator	Unit	Source
1	**MACROECONOMIC STABILITY**		
1.1	**Regional Economic Vibrancy**		
1.1.01	Gross Regional Domestic Product (GRDP)	Rupiah (Million), 2000 Constant Prices	BPS, Statistics Indonesia
1.1.02	Gross Regional Domestic Product (GRDP), Non-oil & gas	Rupiah (Million), 2000 Constant Prices	(indicator 1.1.01) & BPS, Statistics Indonesia
1.1.03	GRDP Growth	Percentage Change Per Annum, 2000 Constant Prices	BPS, Statistics Indonesia
1.1.04	GRDP Per Capita	Rupiah (Million), 2000 Constant Prices	BPS, Statistics Indonesia, GRDP of Provinces in Indonesia by Industrial Origin
1.1.05	GRDP Per Capita, Non-oil & gas	Rupiah (Million), 2000 Constant Prices	BPS, Statistics Indonesia, GRDP of Provinces in Indonesia by Industrial Origin
1.1.06	GRDP of Primary Industry	Rupiah (Million), 2000 Constant Prices	INDO-DAPOER, World Bank Group
1.1.07	GRDP of Secondary Industry	Rupiah (Million), 2000 Constant Prices	INDO-DAPOER, World Bank Group
1.1.08	GRDP of Tertiary Industry	Rupiah (Million), 2000 Constant Prices	INDO-DAPOER, World Bank Group
1.1.09	Gross Domestic Fixed Capital Formation	Rupiah (Million), 2000 Constant Prices	BPS, Statistics Indonesia, GRDP of Provinces in Indonesia by Expenditure
1.1.10	Inflation (R)	Percentage Change Per Annum	BPS, Statistics Indonesia, Statistical Yearbook of Indonesia
1.2	**Openness to Trade and Services**		
1.2.01	Exports	Rupiah (Million), 2000 Constant Prices	PUSDATIN, Ministry of Trade
1.2.02	Exports, Non-oil & gas	Rupiah (Million), 2000 Constant Prices	PUSDATIN, Ministry of Trade
1.2.03	Imports	Rupiah (Million), 2000 Constant Prices	PUSDATIN, Ministry of Trade

(*Continued*)

(Continued)

No.	Indicator	Unit	Source
1.2.04	Imports, Non-oil & gas	Rupiah (Million), 2000 Constant Prices	PUSDATIN, Ministry of Trade
1.2.05	Openness to Trade	Ratio	(indicators 1.1.01, 1.2.01, 1.2.03)
1.3	**Attractiveness To Foreign Investors**		
1.3.01	Foreign Direct Investment, Last 3 Year Average	US Dollars (Million), Current Market Prices	BPS, Statistics Indonesia, Statistical Yearbook of Indonesia
1.3.02	Domestic Direct Investment, Last 3 Year Average	Rupiah (Billion)	BPS, Statistics Indonesia, Statistical Yearbook of Indonesia
1.3.03	Investment Promotion and Management	Index	ACI Survey, 2016
	Based on responses by business owners, academics, and government officials in each province to the following survey questions: 1. The Provincial Government has a clear strategy to attract investors; 2. The Provincial Government has done well to market the province to investors; 3. The Provincial Government channels money for appropriate development purposes/projects.		
2	**GOVERNMENT AND INSTITUTIONAL SETTING**		
2.1	**Government Policies and Fiscal Sustainability**		
2.1.01	Government Revenue	Rupiah (Thousand), 2000 Constant Prices	BPS, Statistics Indonesia, *Financial Statistics of Province Government*
2.1.02	Tax Revenue	Rupiah (Thousand), 2000 Constant Prices	BPS, Statistics Indonesia, *Financial Statistics of Province Government*
2.1.03	Tax Revenue per Government Revenue	Ratio	(indicators 2.1.01, 2.1.02)
2.1.04	Government Expenditure	Rupiah (Thousand), 2000 Constant Prices	BPS, Statistics Indonesia, *Financial Statistics of Province Government*
2.1.05	Fiscal Balance	Rupiah (Thousand), 2000 Constant Prices	(indicators 2.1.01, 2.1.04)
2.2	**Institutions, Governance and Leadership**		
2.2.01	Lack of Corruption	Index	ACI Survey, 2016
	Based on responses by business owners and academics in each province to the following survey questions: 1. Corruption is not a severe problem; 2. Corruption is not a common practice among firms in the province; 3. Public contracts are awarded based on meritocracy (not favoritism or kickbacks).		
2.2.02	Crime Rate (R)	Rate Per 100,000 population	BPS, Statistics Indonesia, Statistical Yearbook of Indonesia
2.2.03	Security	Index	ACI Survey, 2016
	Based on responses by business owners and academics in each province to the following survey questions: 1. The political condition (including ethnic and religious relations) in the province is stable; 2. Control of crimes and violence in the province is effective; 3. Businesses and citizens don't have to worry about their property rights.		

(Continued)

(*Continued*)

No.	Indicator	Unit	Source
2.2.04	Government Inclusiveness and Accountability	Index	ACI Survey, 2016
	Based on responses by business owners, academics, and government officials in each province to the following survey questions: 1. In this province, the government makes significant efforts to communicate policies and regulations to businesses and citizens; 2. In this province, the government carefully considers the voice of businesses and citizens in making their policy decisions; 3. In this province, government officials have high sense of accountability.		
2.2.05	Government Progress & Expectation	Index	ACI Survey, 2016
	Based on responses by business owners and academics in each province to the following survey questions: 1. The current government is committed to improve its performance; 2. The government in this province has improved its performance in the past 3 years; 3. The government in this province will improve its performance in the next 3 years.		
2.2.06	Government Efficiency	Index	ACI Survey, 2016
	Based on responses by business owners and academics in each province to the following survey questions: 1. Cost of dealing with permits and other public documents or matters is not burdensome; 2. Time to deal with permits and other public documents or matters is not burdensome; 3. Administrative requirement to deal with permits and other public documents or matters is not burdensome.		
2.2.07	Coordination of Local Governments	Index	ACI Survey, 2016
	Based on responses by business owners, academics, and government officials in each province to the following survey questions: 1. Laws and regulations across different local governments in the province are harmonized; 2. There is good collaboration and coordination among local governments within the province.		
2.2.08	Provincial Governing Capacity	Index	ACI Survey, 2016
	Based on responses by business owners, academics, and government officials in each province to the following survey question: 1. There is good coordination among government agencies at the provincial level.		
2.3	**Competition, Regulatory Standards and Rule of Law**		
2.3.01	Regulatory Governance	Index	ACI Survey, 2016
	Based on responses by business owners, academics, and government officials in each province to the following survey questions: 1. In this province, the government has made regulations pertaining to my business clearer (more transparent); 2. In this province, the government has made regulations pertaining to my businesses less burdensome; 3. My business receives fair treatment from regulators in this province.		
2.3.02	Rule of Law	Index	ACI Survey, 2016
	Based on responses by business owners and academics in each province to the following survey questions: 1. In the province, contracts are respected and enforced; 2. In the province, judiciary bodies are independent and fair; 3. In the province, judiciary services are readily accessible; 4. In this province, the government regulators follow closely the laws and regulations in their enforcement.		

(*Continued*)

(Continued)

No.	Indicator	Unit	Source
2.3.03	Vibrancy of Competition and Collaboration	Index	ACI Survey, 2016
	Based on responses by business owners and academics in each province to the following survey questions: 1. Competition among firms is fair; 2. My firm has close relationship with local suppliers; 3. Demand by customers in the province is strong and sophisticated; 4. Firms in the province have good platforms and incentives for collaboration.		
3	**FINANCIAL, BUSINESSES AND MANPOWER CONDITIONS**		
3.1	**Financial Deepening and Business Efficiency**		
3.1.01	Bank Deposits	Rupiah (Million), 2000 Constant Prices	Bank of Indonesia, Indonesia Banking Statistics
3.1.02	Bank Loans	Rupiah (Million), 2000 Constant Prices	Bank of Indonesia, Indonesia Banking Statistics
3.1.03	Non-Performing Loans (R)	Rupiah (Million), 2000 Constant Prices	Bank of Indonesia, Indonesia Banking Statistics
3.1.04	Non-Performing Loans per Total Bank Loans (R)	Ratio	(indicators 3.1.02, 3.1.03)
3.1.05	Number of Bank Branches or Offices	Number	Bank of Indonesia, Indonesia Banking Statistics
3.1.06	Population per Number of Bank Branches or Offices (R)	Ratio	(indicators 3.1.05, 4.1.01)
3.1.07	Ease of Dealing With Banks	Index	ACI Survey, 2016
	Based on responses by business owners in each province to the following survey questions: 1. Administrative requirement to borrow money from banks is not burdensome; 2. Interest rate for borrowing money from banks is not burdensome; 3. Banks are generally responsive to your firm's needs.		
3.1.08	Firms' Strategy	Index	ACI Survey, 2016
	Based on responses by business owners in each province to the following survey question: 1. In order to enhance your company's performance, how likely is your company to engage in each of the strategy options listed below in the next few years? 1. Cut costs, streamline business? 2. Spend more on promotion/ads? 3. Improve skills and motivation of employees? 4. Upgrade production process? 5. Introduce new products.		
3.1.09	Firms' Human Resource Capacity	Index	ACI Survey, 2016
	Based on responses by business owners, academics and government officials in each province to the following survey questions: 1. The skills of your employees are adequate for their job requirements; 2. Your firm has invested substantially in employee training programs the past 3 years; 3. Your firm will invest substantially in employee training programs the next 3 years.		
3.1.10	Firms' Equipment Capacity	Index	ACI Survey, 2016
	Based on responses by business owners in each province to the following survey questions: 1. The technology and equipment used for your firm's main production process is up-to-date; 2. Your firm is using the technology and equipment to its optimal capacity; 3. Your firm will invest in upgrading its equipment over the next five years.		

(Continued)

(*Continued*)

No.	Indicator	Unit	Source
3.1.11	Firms' Application of IT	Index	ACI Survey, 2016
	Based on responses by business owners in each province to the following questions: 1. Your firm has invested substantially in IT in the past three years; 2. Your firm will invest significantly in IT over the next three years; 3. The status of your company's internet connection; 4. The status of your company's website.		
3.1.12	Firms' Innovation	Index	ACI Survey, 2016
	Based on responses by business owners, academics and government officials in each province to the following survey questions: 1. Your firm has introduced many new products or product features over the past three years; 2. Your firm has applied many innovative methods in production process over the past three years; 3. Your firm spends substantially on Research and Development.		
3.2	**Labour Market Flexibility**		
3.2.01	Labour Force	Number	BPS, Statistics Indonesia, Statistical Yearbook of Indonesia
3.2.02	Labour Force Participation Rate	Ratio	(indicators 3.2.01, 4.1.01)
3.2.03	Employment	Number	BPS, Statistics Indonesia, Statistical Yearbook of Indonesia
3.2.04	Employment in Primary Industry	Number	BPS, Statistics Indonesia, Statistical Yearbook of Indonesia
3.2.05	Employment in Secondary Industry	Number	BPS, Statistics Indonesia, Statistical Yearbook of Indonesia
3.2.06	Employment in Tertiary Industry	Number	BPS, Statistics Indonesia, Statistical Yearbook of Indonesia
3.2.07	Unemployment Rate (R)	Percentage	(indicator 3.2.01) & BPS, Statistics Indonesia, Statistical Yearbook of Indonesia
3.2.08	Minimum Wage Per Month (R)	Rupiah, Current Market Prices	BPS, Statistics Indonesia, Statistical Yearbook of Indonesia
3.2.09	Labour Relations	Survey Data	ACI Survey, 2016
	Based on responses by business owners, academics and government officials in each province to the following survey questions: 1. It is not difficult to recruit skilled production workers; 2. It is not difficult to recruit skilled professionals and management staff; 3. Workers generally have good discipline and motivated to work; 4. There is no tension between labour unions and management.		
3.3	**Productivity Performance**		
3.3.01	Overall Labour Productivity	Rupiah (Million) per person-year, 2000 Constant Prices	(indicators 1.1.01, 3.2.03)
3.3.02	Overall Labour Productivity, Non-oil & gas	Rupiah (Million) per person-year, 2000 Constant Prices	(indicators 1.1.02, 3.2.03)

(*Continued*)

(*Continued*)

No.	Indicator	Unit	Source
3.3.03	Primary Industry Productivity	Rupiah (Million) per person-year, 2000 Constant Prices	(indicators 1.1.06, 3.2.04)
3.3.04	Secondary Industry Productivity	Rupiah (Million) per person-year, 2000 Constant Prices	(indicators 1.1.07, 3.2.05)
3.3.05	Tertiary Industry Productivity	Rupiah (Million) per person-year, 2000 Constant Prices	(indicators 1.1.08, 3.2.06)
4	**QUALITY OF LIFE AND INFRASTRUCTURE DEVELOPMENT**		
4.1	**Physical Infrastructure**		
4.1.01	Population	Persons, Year-end	INDO-DAPOER, World Bank Group
4.1.02	Population Growth	Percentage Change Per Annum	INDO-DAPOER, World Bank Group
4.1.03	Urban Population	Percentage of Total Population	ACI's estimates based on data by INDO-DAPOER, World Bank Group
4.1.04	Length of Paved Roads	Kilometres	BPS, Statistics Indonesia, *Transportation Statistics*
4.1.05	Registered Motor Vehicles per KM of Paved Road (R)	Ratio	(indicator 4.1.04) & BPS, Statistics Indonesia, *Transportation Statistics*
4.1.06	Cargo at Inter-island Seaport	Tons	BPS, Statistics Indonesia, Statistical Yearbook of Indonesia
4.1.07	Cargo at International Seaport	Tons	BPS, Statistics Indonesia, Statistical Yearbook of Indonesia
4.1.08	Passengers of Domestic Air Traffic	Number	BPS, Statistics Indonesia, *Transportation Statistics*
4.1.09	Passengers of International Air Traffic	Number	BPS, Statistics Indonesia, *Transportation Statistics*
4.1.10	Households with Pipe Water Services	Percentage of households	BPS, Statistics Indonesia, Statistical Yearbook of Indonesia
4.1.11	Households with State Electricity Services	Percentage of households	BPS, Statistics Indonesia, Statistical Yearbook of Indonesia
4.1.12	Ease of Acquiring Property	Index	ACI Survey, 2016
	Based on responses by business owners, academics and government officials in each province to the following survey questions: 1. It is not difficult to acquire land for opening or expanding business in the province; 2. The cost of renting land/ office space in the province is not burdensome.		
4.1.13	Quality of Physical Infrastructure	Index	ACI Survey, 2016
	Based on responses by business owners and academics in each province to the following survey questions: 1. Quality of Power supply ...; 2. Quality of Water supply ...; 3. Quality of Roads ...;		

(*Continued*)

(*Continued*)

No.	Indicator	Unit	Source
	4. Quality of sea port …; 5. Quality of airports …; 6. Quality of public transportation….		
4.2	**Technological Infrastructure**		
4.2.01	Telephone Ownership	Percentage of households	BPS, Statistics Indonesia, *Trends of Selected Socio-Economic Indicators of Indonesia*
4.2.02	Handphone Ownership	Percentage of households	BPS, Statistics Indonesia, *Trends of Selected Socio-Economic Indicators of Indonesia*
4.2.03	Desktop Computer Ownership	Percentage of households	BPS, Statistics Indonesia, *Trends of Selected Socio-Economic Indicators of Indonesia*
4.2.04	Laptop Computer Ownership	Percentage of households	BPS, Statistics Indonesia, *Trends of Selected Socio-Economic Indicators of Indonesia*
4.2.05	Internet Access at Home	Percentage of households	BPS, Statistics Indonesia, *Welfare Statistics*
4.2.06	Internet Access at Office	Percentage of households	BPS, Statistics Indonesia, *Welfare Statistics*
4.2.07	Internet Access at School	Percentage of households	BPS, Statistics Indonesia, *Welfare Statistics*
4.2.08	Internet Access in Handphone	Percentage of households	BPS, Statistics Indonesia, *Welfare Statistics*
4.2.09	Quality of Technological Infrastructure	Index	ACI Survey, 2016
	Based on responses by business owners and academics in each province to the following survey questions: 1. Quality of mobile phone coverage …; 2. Access/coverage of internet …; 3. Speed of internet access….		
4.3	**Standard of Living, Education and Social Stability**		
4.3.01	Adult Illiteracy Rate (R)	Percentage of Adults	INDO-DAPOER, World Bank Group
4.3.02	Mean Years of Schooling	Years	BPS, Statistics Indonesia, *Trends of Selected Socio-Economic Indicators of Indonesia*
4.3.03	School Enrolment Rate (Primary)	Percentage	INDO-DAPOER, World Bank Group
4.3.04	School Enrolment Rate (Junior High)	Percentage	INDO-DAPOER, World Bank Group
4.3.05	School Enrolment Rate (Senior High)	Percentage	INDO-DAPOER, World Bank Group
4.3.06	Student–Teacher Ratio (Primary) (R)	Ratio	BPS, Statistics Indonesia, Statistical Yearbook of Indonesia

(*Continued*)

(*Continued*)

No.	Indicator	Unit	Source
4.3.07	Student–Teacher Ratio (Junior High) (R)	Ratio	BPS, Statistics Indonesia, Statistical Yearbook of Indonesia
4.3.08	Student–Teacher Ratio (Senior High) (R)	Ratio	BPS, Statistics Indonesia, Statistical Yearbook of Indonesia
4.3.09	Human Development Index	Index	INDO-DAPOER, World Bank Group
4.3.10	Life Expectancy at Birth	Years	Ministry of Health, *Indonesia Health Profile*
4.3.11	Gini Ratio (R)	Ratio	BPS, Statistics Indonesia
4.3.12	Population per Health Facility (R)	Ratio	Ministry of Health
4.3.13	Population per Medical Worker (R)	Ratio	Ministry of Health
4.3.14	Environmental Quality Index	Index	Ministry of Environment
4.3.15	Fatalities due to Natural Disaster (R)	Number	BPS, Statistics Indonesia, Statistical Yearbook of Indonesia
4.3.16	Quality of Education	Index	ACI Survey, 2016
	Based on responses by business owners, academics and government officials in each province to the following survey questions: 1. Quality of secondary/vocational education in this province is very good compared to other provinces; 2. Quality of higher education/university in the province is very good compared to other provinces.		
4.3.17	Quality of Healthcare	Index	ACI Survey, 2016
	Based on responses by business owners, academics and government officials in each province to the following survey questions: 1. Quality of basic health services in this province is very good compared to other provinces; 2. Quality of general health services in this province is very good compared to other provinces; 3. Quality of advanced health services (specialists, etc.) in this province is very good compared to other provinces.		
4.3.18	Affordability and Accessibility of Goods	Index	ACI Survey, 2016
	Based on responses by business owners, academics and government officials in each province to the following survey questions: 1. The price of staple goods in this province is quite affordable for most people; 2. In this province, secondary/luxury goods are quite easy to find, for those who can afford them.		

Note: (R) = Reversed Indicator.
In general, survey responses range from 1 = "strongly disagree" to 9 = "strongly agree".
Source: Asia Competitiveness Institute.

Appendix 2

Algorithm for Computation of the Provincial and Regional Competitiveness Index and Ranking Using Equal Weights

A step-by-step description of the ranking process is described below for N regions (or provinces respectively), M indicators and C environments, with each environment comprising S sub-environments.

Algorithm: Ranking Methodology

(1) Compute the mean value of indicator j ($j = 1, \ldots, M$),

$$\bar{X}_j = \frac{1}{N}\sum_{i=1}^{N} X_{ij},$$

where X_{ij} represents the value that region i ($i = 1, \ldots, N$) takes for indicator j.

(2) For each indicator j ($j = 1, \ldots, M$), calculate its standard deviation (SD),

$$SD_j = \sqrt{\frac{1}{N}\sum_{i=1}^{N}\left(X_{ij} - \bar{X}_j\right)^2}.$$

(3) Compute the standardised value of indicator (SVI) that each region i ($i = 1, \ldots, N$) takes under each of the indicators j ($j = 1, \ldots, M$),

$$SVI_{ij} = \frac{X_{ij} - \bar{X}_j}{SD_j}$$

(4) Compute the 'ranked' standardised value of indicator (RSVI) that each region i ($i = 1, \ldots, N$) takes under each of the indicators j ($j = 1, \ldots, M$):

$$RSVI_{ij} = \begin{cases} SVI_{ij}, & \textit{if a higher value is better} \\ -SVI_{ij}, & \textit{if a lower value is better.} \end{cases}$$

(5) For each indicator, j ($j = 1, \ldots, M$), a ranking can be obtained for regions: regions with a higher value of RSVI for indicator j are ranked ahead of those with a lower value.

(6) For each region i ($i = 1, ..., N$), calculate the RSVI for each sub-environment k ($k = 1, ..., S$) belonging to environment l ($l = 1, ..., C$),

$$Raw\_RSVI_{i,lk} = \frac{1}{y_{lk}} \sum_{p=1}^{y_{lk}} RSVI_{i,jlk,p},$$

$$Mean\_RSVI_{lk} = \frac{1}{N} \sum_{i=1}^{N} Raw\_RSVI_{i,lk},$$

$$SD\_RSVI_{lk} = \sqrt{\frac{1}{N} \sum_{i=1}^{N} \left(Raw\_RSVI_{i,lk} - Mean\_RSVI_{lk}\right)^2},$$

$$RSVI_{i,lk} = \frac{Raw\_RSVI_{i,lk} - Mean\_RSVI_{lk}}{SD\_RSVI_{lk}},$$

where y_{ik} is the total number of indicators under sub-environment k of environment l and $(RSVI_{i,jlk,1}, \ldots, RSVI_{i,jlk,ylk})$ are the RSVIs for region i that make up sub-environment k of environment l.

(7) For each region i ($i = 1, ..., N$), calculate the RSVI for each environment l ($l = 1, ..., C$),

$$Raw\_RSVI_{i,l} = \frac{1}{S_l} \sum_{k=1}^{S_l} RSVI_{i,lk},$$

$$Mean\_RSVI_{l} = \frac{1}{N} \sum_{i=1}^{N} Raw\_RSVI_{i,l},$$

$$SD\_RSVI_{l} = \sqrt{\frac{1}{N} \sum_{i=1}^{N} \left(Raw\_RSVI_{i,l} - Mean\_RSVI_{l}\right)^2},$$

$$RSVI_{i,l} = \frac{Raw\_RSVI_{i,l} - Mean\_RSVI_{l}}{SD\_RSVI_{l}},$$

where $(RSVI_{i,l1}, ..., RSVI_{i,lS})$ are the RSVIs for the S sub-environments under each environment l.

(8) Overall rank score of region i ($i = 1, ..., N$),

$$Raw\_R_i = \frac{1}{C} \sum_{l=1}^{C} RSVI_{i,l},$$

$$Mean\_R = \frac{1}{N} \sum_{i=1}^{N} Raw\_R_i,$$

$$SD\_R = \sqrt{\frac{1}{N}\sum_{i=1}^{N}\left(Raw\_R_i - Mean\_R\right)^2},$$

$$R_i = \frac{Raw\_R_i - Mean\_R}{SD\_R}.$$

Regions with a higher R_i are ranked ahead of those with lower value of R_i, and the region with the highest R_i is the most competitive region.

Step (5) provides the ranking of each region for each individual indicator. To achieve this ranking, Step (4) adjusts the value of the SVIs so that a higher value will lead to a better ranking in terms of "competitiveness". Depending on the nature of the indicator in question, a higher or lower value may reflect a more "competitive" region. Take, for instance, the sub-indicators 'Gross Regional Domestic Product (GRDP)' and 'Unemployment Rate'. A higher GRDP but a lower "unemployment rate" suggest better economic performance, which makes a region more "competitive". In most cases, where a higher value is better (e.g. GRDP), the SVIs of regions are considered, and those with a higher SVI value will have a better ranking. However, for indicators where the inverse is true (e.g. Unemployment Rate), the "negative SVI" values are compared between regions, where a lower SVI value will lead to a better ranking. Step (4) thus seeks to make all standardised values of all indicators consistent for ranking purposes.

Step (6) determines the sub-environment rankings of each region. The average RSVI of all the indicators in the sub-environment are calculated, restandardised across all the regions and compared to the other regions. Regions with a higher average RSVI rank better in the sub-environment. Although the number of indicators varies for each sub-environment, there are three sub-environments for each of the four environments. The aggregate score for each sub-environment is given an equivalent weighting: 33.33 percent of their respective environment's score.

To arrive at the ranking for each environment, the RSVIs of the sub-environments are averaged and restandardised across all the regions as detailed by Step (7). Finally, Step (8) requires the RSVI values of each environment to be averaged and restandardised across all the regions to determine the overall ranking of the region. Regions with a higher RSVI are ranked ahead of those with a lower RSVI.

Identical weights are assigned to each environment as they represent equivalent significance to the computation of the Overall Competitiveness Index. This method is repeated and applied consistently across all the regions to ensure precision of the rankings. Mathematically, this can be illustrated as follows:

Overall Competitiveness Index:

= 25% × (Macroeconomic Stability)
+25% × (Government and Institutional Setting)
+25% × (Financial, Businesses and Manpower Conditions)
+25% × (Quality of Life and Infrastructure Development)

Appendix 3

Algorithm for Computation of the Provincial and Regional Competitiveness Index and Ranking Using Shapley Weights

A3.1 Shapley Weightage

We will present the "Bottom-up" approach in this appendix. We start with indicator level computation, then sub-environment and environment level computation, and finally the index construction.

A3.2 Indicator Level

For each indicator $i \in I$ and each region (or provinces respectively), $e \in E$, the standardised value (or z-score) is

$$SV_{ei} = \frac{X_{ei} - \overline{X_I}}{SD_i} \tag{1}$$

where X_{ei} is the data input for region e in indicator i, $\overline{X_I} = \frac{1}{E}\Sigma_{e=1}^{E} X_{ei}$ is the mean value of the indicator i, and $SD_i = \sqrt{\frac{1}{E}\Sigma_{e=1}^{E}\left(X_{ei} - \overline{X_I}\right)^2}$ is the standard deviation of the indicator i.

Now, let v^I be the characteristic function of the indicators, where v^I: $2^I \rightarrow \mathbb{R}$. Then for each indicator $i \in I$, $v^I(i)$: $\mathbb{R}^E \rightarrow \mathbb{R}$, which reflects that the value of indicator i is derived from X_{ei} for all $e \in E$. As we involve large number of indicators in our case studies, for the ease of numerical computation, we simply define that

$$v^I(i) = \sum_{e=1}^{E} \left|SV_{ei}\right|. \tag{2}$$

The absolute value is used, as (1) it guarantees the positiveness of $v(i)$ which is required by the definition of Shapley value, and (2) the simple sum of the z-scores is zero, i.e. $\Sigma_{e=1}^{E} SV_{ei} = 0$.

We further assume the Additivity of the characteristic function v^I, i.e.

$$v^I(i \cup j) = v^I(i) + v^I(j) \quad \text{for any indicator } i, j, \in I. \tag{3}$$

With all these defined, we are able to proceed with the computation of the Shapley value Φ_i^I of indicator $i \in I$.

$$\Phi_i^I = \sum_{\mathbb{I}\subseteq I\setminus\{i\}} \frac{|\mathbb{I}|!(I-|\mathbb{I}|-1)!}{I!}(v^I(\mathbb{I}\cup i)-v^I(\mathbb{I})) \quad \text{for all } i\in I. \tag{4}$$

With the assumption of Additivity, equation (4) can be simplified as

$$\begin{aligned}\Phi_i^I &= \sum_{\mathbb{I}\subseteq I\setminus\{i\}} \frac{|\mathbb{I}|!(I-|\mathbb{I}|-1)!}{I!}(v^I(\mathbb{I}\cup i)-v^I(\mathbb{I})) \\ &= \sum_{\mathbb{I}\subseteq I\setminus\{i\}} \frac{|\mathbb{I}|!(I-|\mathbb{I}|-1)!}{I!}v^I(i) = v^I(i)\cdot \end{aligned} \tag{4*}$$

Then the indicator weight w_i^I based on Shapley value is simply

$$w_i^I = \frac{\Phi_i^I}{\sum_{j=1}^I \Phi_j^I} = \frac{v^I(i)}{\sum_{j=1}^I v^I(j)}. \tag{5}$$

Economically, the Shapley value of each indicator i, Φ_i^I, measures the inequality among all the regions. The higher the Φ_i^I of an indicator i, the more divergent the performance across different regions. More weight, w_i^I, will thus be assigned to i. If a government has the aim of reducing inequality, it should implement policies to improve the indicators with more weight.

A3.3 Sub-Environment Level and Environment Level

For each region $e \in E$, the computed data of any sub-environment $s \in S$ is determined by the indicators comprised, i.e. I_s. Equation (5) has determined the weight of each indicator, and let w_i^{IS} be the weight of indicator $i \in I_s$. Thus, formally, the computed data of any sub-environment $s \in S$ for any region $e \in E$ is

$$X_{es} = \sum_{i=1}^{I_s} w_i^{Is} SV_{ei}. \tag{6}$$

Similar to the indicator level analysis, we have the standardised score for sub-environment $s \in S$ is SV_{es}.

Let $v^S : 2^S \to \mathbb{R}$ be the characteristic function for the sub-environments. Then for each sub-environment $s \in S$, $v^S(s) : \mathbb{R}^S \to \mathbb{R}$ represents that the value of sub-environment s is derived from X_{es} for all $e \in E$. We have

$$v^S(s) = \sum_{e=1}^{E} |SV_{es}|. \tag{7}$$

By the Additivity assumption, the Shapley value of each sub-environment $s \in S$ is

$$\Phi_s^S = v^S(s), \tag{8}$$

and the weight of each sub-environment is

$$w_s^S = \frac{\Phi_s^S}{\sum_{j=1}^{S} \Phi_j^S} = \frac{v^S(s)}{\sum_{j=1}^{S} v^S(j)}. \tag{9}$$

The construction of Shapley value and the weight associated with each environment is similar to the analysis above, and thus is omitted. Let $v^N : 2^N \to \mathbb{R}$ be the characteristic function for the environments. The Shapley value of each environment $n \in N$ is

$$\Phi_n^N = v^N(n), \tag{10}$$

and the weight of each environment is

$$w_n^N = \frac{\Phi_n^N}{\sum_{j=1}^{N} \Phi_j^N} = \frac{v^N(n)}{\sum_{j=1}^{N} v^N(j)}. \tag{11}$$

The economic interpretation of Φ_s^S and Φ_n^N are the same as the indicators'. They capture the inequality across all regions at the sub-environment and environment levels respectively. The higher the weight w_s^S and w_n^N, the more divergent the performance across different regions. Thus government attention should be drawn to such sub-environments and environments.

A3.4 Index Construction

In order for us to construct the final index to rank all the regions. First, we find the final computed score for each region $e \in E$, i.e.

$$F_e = \sum_{n=1}^{N} w_n^N SV_{en}, \tag{12}$$

where SV_{en} is the standardised value for region e under environment n.

Then, we standardised the final computed score,

$$R_e = \frac{F_e - \bar{F}}{SD_F}, \tag{13}$$

where $\bar{F} = \frac{1}{E}\Sigma_{e=1}^{E} F_e$ and $SD_F = \sqrt{\frac{1}{E}\Sigma_{e=1}^{E}\left(F_e - \bar{F}\right)^2}$.

All the regions, $e \in E$, will be ranked according the value R_e, which is also the index score for each region.

Appendix 4
Notes on Data Aggregation of Competitiveness Indicators from Provincial to Regional Level

No.	Indicator	Unit	Reversed Indicator	Calculated as in
1	**MACROECONOMIC STABILITY**			
1.1	Regional Economic Vibrancy			
1.1.01	Gross Regional Domestic Product (GRDP)	Rupiah (Million), 2000 Constant Prices		Approach 1
1.1.02	Gross Regional Domestic Product (GRDP), Non-oil & gas	Rupiah (Million), 2000 Constant Prices		Approach 1
1.1.03	GRDP Growth	Percentage Change Per Annum, 2000 Constant Prices		Approach 2
1.1.04	GRDP Per Capita	Rupiah (Million), 2000 Constant Prices		Approach 2
1.1.05	GRDP Per Capita, Non-oil & gas	Rupiah (Million), 2000 Constant Prices		Approach 2
1.1.06	GRDP of Primary Industry	Rupiah (Million), 2000 Constant Prices		Approach 1
1.1.07	GRDP of Secondary Industry	Rupiah (Million), 2000 Constant Prices		Approach 1
1.1.08	GRDP of Tertiary Industry	Rupiah (Million), 2000 Constant Prices		Approach 1
1.1.09	Gross Domestic Fixed Capital Formation	Rupiah (Million), 2000 Constant Prices		Approach 1
1.1.10	Inflation	Percentage Change Per Annum	R	Approach 3
1.2	Openness to Trade and Services			
1.2.01	Exports	Rupiah (Million), 2000 Constant Prices		Approach 1
1.2.02	Exports, Non-oil & gas	Rupiah (Million), 2000 Constant Prices		Approach 1
1.2.03	Imports	Rupiah (Million), 2000 Constant Prices		Approach 1
1.2.04	Imports, Non-oil & gas	Rupiah (Million), 2000 Constant Prices		Approach 1

(*Continued*)

(*Continued*)

No.	Indicator	Unit	Reversed Indicator	Calculated as in
1.2.05	Openness to Trade	Ratio		Approach 2
1.3	<u>Attractiveness to Foreign Investors</u>			
1.3.01	Foreign Direct Investment, Last 3 Year Average	US Dollars (Million), Current Market Prices		Approach 1
1.3.02	Domestic Direct Investment, Last 3 Year Average	Rupiah (Billion)		Approach 1
1.3.03	Investment Promotion and Management	Index (Survey Data)		Approach 3
2	**GOVERNMENT AND INSTITUTIONAL SETTING**			
2.1	<u>Government Policies and Fiscal Sustainability</u>			
2.1.01	Government Revenue	Rupiah (Thousand), 2000 Constant Prices		Approach 1
2.1.02	Tax Revenue	Rupiah (Thousand), 2000 Constant Prices		Approach 1
2.1.03	Tax Revenue/Government Revenue	Ratio		Approach 2
2.1.04	Government Expenditure	Rupiah (Thousand), 2000 Constant Prices		Approach 1
2.1.05	Fiscal Balance	Rupiah (Thousand), 2000 Constant Prices		Approach 1
2.2	<u>Institutions, Governance and Leadership</u>			
2.2.01	Lack of Corruption	Index (Survey Data)		Approach 3
2.2.02	Crime Rate	Rate Per 100.000 population	R	Approach 3
2.2.03	Security	Index (Survey Data)		Approach 3
2.2.04	Government Inclusiveness and Accountability	Index (Survey Data)		Approach 3
2.2.05	Government Progress & Expectation	Index (Survey Data)		Approach 3
2.2.06	Government Efficiency	Index (Survey Data)		Approach 3
2.2.07	Coordination of Local Governments	Index (Survey Data)		Approach 3
2.2.08	Provincial Governing Capacity	Index (Survey Data)		Approach 3
2.3	<u>Competition, Regulatory Standards and Rule of Law</u>			
2.3.01	Regulatory Governance	Index (Survey Data)		Approach 3
2.3.02	Rule of Law	Index (Survey Data)		Approach 3
2.3.03	Vibrancy of Competition and Collaboration	Index (Survey Data)		Approach 3

(*Continued*)

(*Continued*)

No.	Indicator	Unit	Reversed Indicator	Calculated as in
3	**FINANCIAL, BUSINESSES AND MANPOWER CONDITIONS**			
3.1	Financial Deepening and Business Efficiency			
3.1.01	Bank Deposits	Rupiah (Million), 2000 Constant Prices		Approach 1
3.1.02	Bank Loans	Rupiah (Million), 2000 Constant Prices		Approach 1
3.1.03	Non-Performing Loans	Rupiah (Million), 2000 Constant Prices	R	Approach 1
3.1.04	Non-Performing Loans per Total Bank Loans	Ratio	R	Approach 2
3.1.05	Number of Bank Branches or Offices	Number		Approach 1
3.1.06	Population per Number of Bank Branches or Offices	Ratio	R	Approach 2
3.1.07	Ease of Dealing With Banks	Index (Survey Data)		Approach 3
3.1.08	Firms' Performance	Index (Survey Data)		Approach 3
3.1.09	Firms' Human Resource Capacity	Index (Survey Data)		Approach 3
3.1.10	Firms' Equipment Capacity	Index (Survey Data)		Approach 3
3.1.11	Firms' Application of IT	Index (Survey Data)		Approach 3
3.1.12	Firms' Innovation	Index (Survey Data)		Approach 3
3.2	Labour Market Flexibility			
3.2.01	Labour Force	Number		Approach 1
3.2.02	Labour Force Participation Rate	Ratio		Approach 2
3.2.03	Employment	Number		Approach 1
3.2.04	Employment in Primary Industry	Number		Approach 1
3.2.05	Employment in Secondary Industry	Number		Approach 1
3.2.06	Employment in Tertiary Industry	Number		Approach 1
3.2.07	Unemployment Rate	Percentage	R	Approach 2
3.2.08	Minimum Wage Per Month	Rupiah, Current Market Prices	R	Approach 3
3.2.09	Labour Relations	Index (Survey Data)		Approach 3
3.3	Productivity Performance			
3.3.01	Overall Labour Productivity	Rupiah (Million) per person-year, 2000 Constant Prices		Approach 2

(*Continued*)

(*Continued*)

No.	Indicator	Unit	Reversed Indicator	Calculated as in
3.3.02	Overall Labour Productivity, Non-oil & gas	Rupiah (Million) per person-year, 2000 Constant Prices		Approach 2
3.3.03	Primary Industry Productivity	Rupiah (Million) per person-year, 2000 Constant Prices		Approach 2
3.3.04	Secondary Industry Productivity	Rupiah (Million) per person-year, 2000 Constant Prices		Approach 2
3.3.05	Tertiary Industry Productivity	Rupiah (Million) per person-year, 2000 Constant Prices		Approach 2
4	**QUALITY OF LIFE AND INFRASTRUCTURE DEVELOPMENT**			
4.1	Physical Infrastructure			
4.1.01	Population	Persons, Year-end		Approach 1
4.1.02	Population Growth	Percentage Change Per Annum		Approach 3
4.1.03	Urban Population	Percentage of Total Population		Approach 3
4.1.04	Length of Paved Roads	Kilometres		Approach 1
4.1.05	Registered Motor Vehicles per KM of Paved Road	Ratio	R	Approach 2
4.1.06	Cargo at Inter-island Seaport	Tons		Approach 1
4.1.07	Cargo at International Seaport	Tons		Approach 1
4.1.08	Passengers of Domestic Air Traffic	Number		Approach 1
4.1.09	Passengers of International Air Traffic	Number		Approach 1
4.1.10	Households with pipe water services	Percentage of households		Approach 3
4.1.11	Households with state electricity services	Percentage of households		Approach 3
4.1.12	Ease of Acquiring Property	Index (Survey Data)		Approach 3
4.1.13	Quality of Physical Infrastructure	Index (Survey Data)		Approach 3
4.2	Technological Infrastructure			
4.2.01	Telephone Ownership	Percentage of households		Approach 3
4.2.02	Handphone Ownership	Percentage of households		Approach 3
4.2.03	Desktop Computer Ownership	Percentage of households		Approach 3
4.2.04	Laptop Computer Ownership	Percentage of households		Approach 3
4.2.05	Internet Access at Home	Percentage of households		Approach 3

(*Continued*)

(*Continued*)

No.	Indicator	Unit	Reversed Indicator	Calculated as in
4.2.06	Internet Access at Office	Percentage of households		Approach 3
4.2.07	Internet Access at School	Percentage of households		Approach 3
4.2.08	Internet Access in Handphone	Percentage of households		Approach 3
4.2.09	Quality of Technological Infrastructure	Index (Survey Data)		Approach 3
4.3	Standard of Living, Education and Social Stability			
4.3.01	Adult Illiteracy Rate	Percentage of Adults	R	Approach 3
4.3.02	Mean Years of Schooling	Years		Approach 3
4.3.03	School Enrolment Rate (Primary)	Percentage		Approach 3
4.3.04	School Enrolment Rate (Junior High)	Percentage		Approach 3
4.3.05	School Enrolment Rate (Senior High)	Percentage		Approach 3
4.3.06	Student–Teacher Ratio (Primary)	Ratio	R	Approach 3
4.3.07	Student–Teacher Ratio (Junior High)	Ratio	R	Approach 3
4.3.08	Student–Teacher Ratio (Senior High)	Ratio	R	Approach 3
4.3.09	Human Development Index	Index		Approach 3
4.3.10	Life Expectancy at Birth	Years		Approach 3
4.3.11	Gini Ratio	Ratio	R	Approach 3
4.3.12	Population Per Health Facility	Ratio	R	Approach 3
4.3.13	Population Per Medical Worker	Ratio	R	Approach 3
4.3.14	Environmental Quality Index	Index		Approach 3
4.3.15	Fatalities due to Natural Disaster	Number	R	Approach 3
4.1.16	Quality of Education	Index (Survey Data)		Approach 3
4.3.17	Quality of Healthcare	Index (Survey Data)		Approach 3
4.3.18	Affordability and Accessibility of Goods	Index (Survey Data)		Approach 3

Source: Asia Competitiveness Institute.

Appendix 5

2017 Competitiveness Profile of Indonesian Provinces

Appendix 5 provides a summary of the competitiveness results for each Indonesian province, based on ACI's 2017 Annual Update on Competitiveness Analysis of Indonesian Provinces.

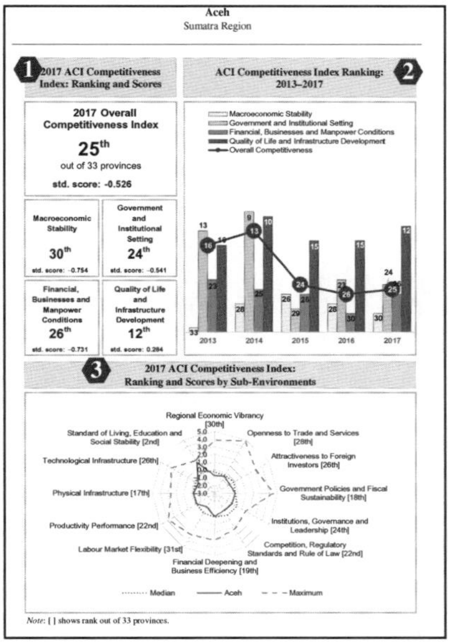

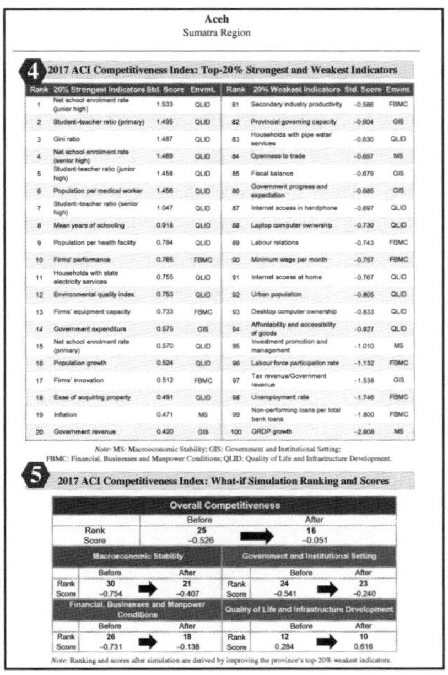

Aceh

Sumatra Region

4 2017 ACI Competitiveness Index: Top-20% Strongest and Weakest Indicators

Rank	20% Strongest Indicators	Std. Score	Envmt.	Rank	20% Weakest Indicators	Std. Score	Envmt.
1	Net school enrolment rate (junior high)	1.533	QLID	81	Secondary industry productivity	-0.586	FBMC
2	Student–teacher ratio (primary)	1.495	QLID	82	Provincial governing capacity	-0.604	GIS
3	Gini ratio	1.487	QLID	83	Households with pipe water services	-0.630	QLID
4	Net school enrolment rate (senior high)	1.469	QLID	84	Openness to trade	-0.657	MS
5	Student-teacher ratio (junior high)	1.458	QLID	85	Fiscal balance	-0.679	GIS
6	Population per medical worker	1.456	QLID	86	Government progress and expectation	-0.685	GIS
7	Student–teacher ratio (senior high)	1.047	QLID	87	Internet access in handphone	-0.697	QLID
8	Mean years of schooling	0.918	QLID	88	Laptop computer ownership	-0.739	QLID
9	Population per health facility	0.784	QLID	89	Labour relations	-0.743	FBMC
10	Firms' performance	0.765	FBMC	90	Minimum wage per month	-0.757	FBMC
11	Households with state electricity services	0.755	QLID	91	Internet access at home	-0.767	QLID
12	Environmental quality index	0.753	QLID	92	Urban population	-0.805	QLID
13	Firms' equipment capacity	0.733	FBMC	93	Desktop computer ownership	-0.833	QLID
14	Government expenditure	0.575	GIS	94	Affordability and accessibility of goods	-0.927	QLID
15	Net school enrolment rate (primary)	0.570	QLID	95	Investment promotion and management	-1.010	MS
16	Population growth	0.524	QLID	96	Labour force participation rate	-1.132	FBMC
17	Firms' innovation	0.512	FBMC	97	Tax revenue/Government revenue	-1.538	GIS
18	Ease of acquiring property	0.491	QLID	98	Unemployment rate	-1.746	FBMC
19	Inflation	0.471	MS	99	Non-performing loans per total bank loans	-1.800	FBMC
20	Government revenue	0.420	GIS	100	GRDP growth	-2.808	MS

Note: MS: Macroeconomic Stability; GIS: Government and Institutional Setting; FBMC: Financial, Businesses and Manpower Conditions; QLID: Quality of Life and Infrastructure Development.

5 2017 ACI Competitiveness Index: What-if Simulation Ranking and Scores

Overall Competitiveness	Before	After
Rank	25	16
Score	–0.526	–0.051

Macroeconomic Stability	Before	After	Government and Institutional Setting	Before	After
Rank	30	21	Rank	24	23
Score	–0.754	–0.407	Score	–0.541	–0.240

Financial, Businesses and Manpower Conditions	Before	After	Quality of Life and Infrastructure Development	Before	After
Rank	26	18	Rank	12	10
Score	–0.731	–0.138	Score	0.284	0.616

Note: Ranking and scores after simulation are derived by improving the province's top-20% weakest indicators.

Each profile consists of five sections, each presenting various components of the ACI Competitiveness Index:

1. **2017 ACI Competitiveness Index: Ranking and Scores**
   This section presents the province's ranking and standardised scores for Overall Competitiveness and the four environments of competitiveness.
2. **ACI Competitiveness Index Ranking: 2013–2017**
   The bar-line chart depicts the five-year trend of the province's Overall Competitiveness ranking (line) and the ranks of the four environments of competitiveness (bars) since the beginning of ACI's analysis in 2013.
3. **2017 ACI Competitiveness Index: Ranking and Scores by Sub-Environments**
   This web chart indicates the province's ranking and standardised scores for the 12 sub-environments of competitiveness relative to the median and maximum scores of 33 provinces of Indonesia.
4. **2017 ACI Competitiveness Index: Top-20 Percent Strongest and Weakest Indicators**
   The table on the left lists the top-20 indicators with the *highest* standardised scores while the table on the right lists the bottom-20 indicators with the *lowest* standardised scores among 100 indicators.
5. **2017 ACI Competitiveness Index: *What-if* Simulation Ranking and Scores**
   This table shows the province's competitiveness rankings and standardised scores before and after the *what-if* simulation for Overall Competitiveness and the four environments. The scores are derived by improving the province's top-20 percent weakest indicators (listed in table on the right in Section 4).

Aceh

Sumatra Region

2017 ACI Competitiveness Index: Ranking and Scores	
2017 Overall Competitiveness Index **25th** out of 33 provinces **std. score: –0.526**	
Macroeconomic Stability **30th** **std. score: –0.754**	**Government and Institutional Setting** **24th** **std. score: –0.541**
Financial, Businesses and Manpower Conditions **26th** **std. score: –0.731**	**Quality of Life and Infrastructure Development** **12th** **std. score: 0.284**

ACI Competitiveness Index Ranking: 2013–2017

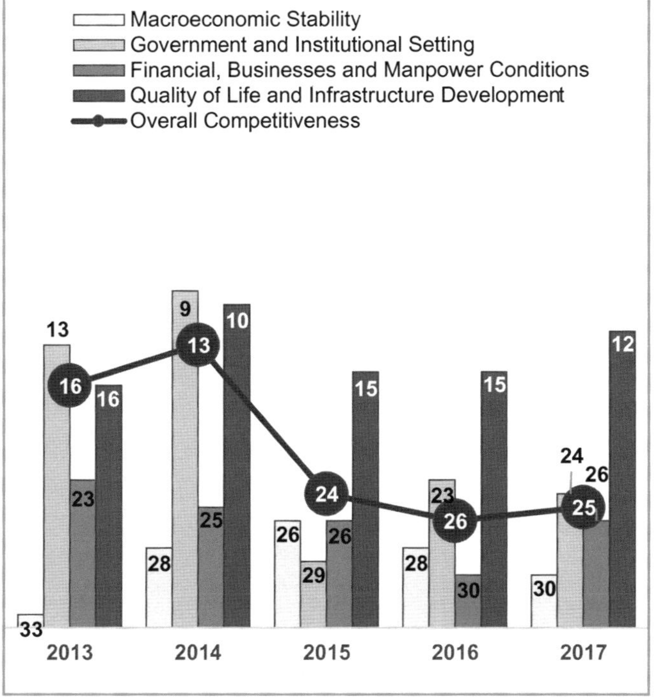

2017 ACI Competitiveness Index: Ranking and Scores by Sub-Environments

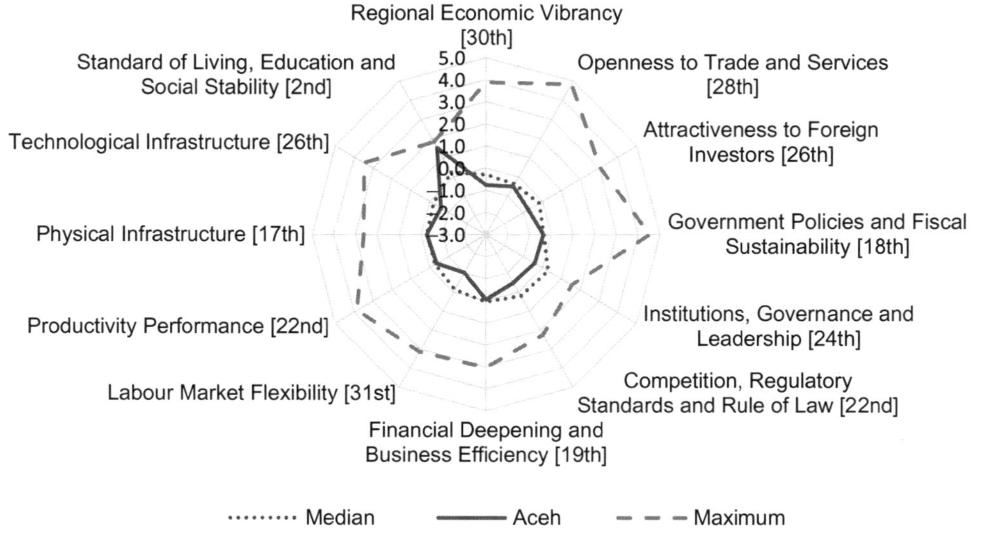

Note: [ ] shows rank out of 33 provinces.

Aceh

Sumatra Region

2017 ACI Competitiveness Index: Top-20% Strongest and Weakest Indicators

Rank	20% Strongest Indicators	Std. Score	Envmt.	Rank	20% Weakest Indicators	Std. Score	Envmt.
1	Net school enrolment rate (junior high)	1.533	QLID	81	Secondary industry productivity	–0.586	FBMC
2	Student–teacher ratio (primary)	1.495	QLID	82	Provincial governing capacity	–0.604	GIS
3	Gini ratio	1.487	QLID	83	Households with pipe water services	–0.630	QLID
4	Net school enrolment rate (senior high)	1.469	QLID	84	Openness to trade	–0.657	MS
5	Student–teacher ratio (junior high)	1.458	QLID	85	Fiscal balance	–0.679	GIS
6	Population per medical worker	1.456	QLID	86	Government progress and expectation	–0.685	GIS
7	Student–teacher ratio (senior high)	1.047	QLID	87	Internet access in handphone	–0.697	QLID
8	Mean years of schooling	0.918	QLID	88	Laptop computer ownership	–0.739	QLID
9	Population per health facility	0.784	QLID	89	Labour relations	–0.743	FBMC
10	Firms' performance	0.765	FBMC	90	Minimum wage per month	–0.757	FBMC
11	Households with state electricity services	0.755	QLID	91	Internet access at home	–0.767	QLID
12	Environmental quality index	0.753	QLID	92	Urban population	–0.805	QLID
13	Firms' equipment capacity	0.733	FBMC	93	Desktop computer ownership	–0.833	QLID
14	Government expenditure	0.575	GIS	94	Affordability and accessibility of goods	–0.927	QLID
15	Net school enrolment rate (primary)	0.570	QLID	95	Investment promotion and management	–1.010	MS
16	Population growth	0.524	QLID	96	Labour force participation rate	–1.132	FBMC
17	Firms' innovation	0.512	FBMC	97	Tax revenue/Government revenue	–1.538	GIS
18	Ease of acquiring property	0.491	QLID	98	Unemployment rate	–1.746	FBMC
19	Inflation	0.471	MS	99	Non-performing loans per total bank loans	–1.800	FBMC
20	Government revenue	0.420	GIS	100	GRDP growth	–2.608	MS

Note: MS: Macroeconomic Stability; GIS: Government and Institutional Setting; FBMC: Financial, Businesses and Manpower Conditions; QLID: Quality of Life and Infrastructure Development.

2017 ACI Competitiveness Index: *What-if* Simulation Ranking and Scores

Overall Competitiveness

	Before		After
Rank	**25**	➡	**16**
Score	–0.526		–0.051

Macroeconomic Stability	Before		After	Government and Institutional Setting	Before		After
Rank	**30**	➡	**21**	Rank	**24**	➡	**23**
Score	–0.754		–0.407	Score	–0.541		–0.240

Financial, Businesses and Manpower Conditions	Before		After	Quality of Life and Infrastructure Development	Before		After
Rank	**26**	➡	**18**	Rank	**12**	➡	**10**
Score	–0.731		–0.138	Score	0.284		0.616

Note: Ranking and scores after simulation are derived by improving the province's top-20% weakest indicators.

Bali
Bali-Nusa Tenggara Region

2017 ACI Competitiveness Index: Ranking and Scores	
2017 Overall Competitiveness Index 7th out of 33 provinces std. score: 0.687	
Macroeconomic Stability 14th std. score: –0.243	**Government and Institutional Setting** 4th std. score: 0.885
Financial, Businesses and Manpower Conditions 6th std. score: 0.635	**Quality of Life and Infrastructure Development** 6th std. score: 0.999

ACI Competitiveness Index Ranking: 2013–2017

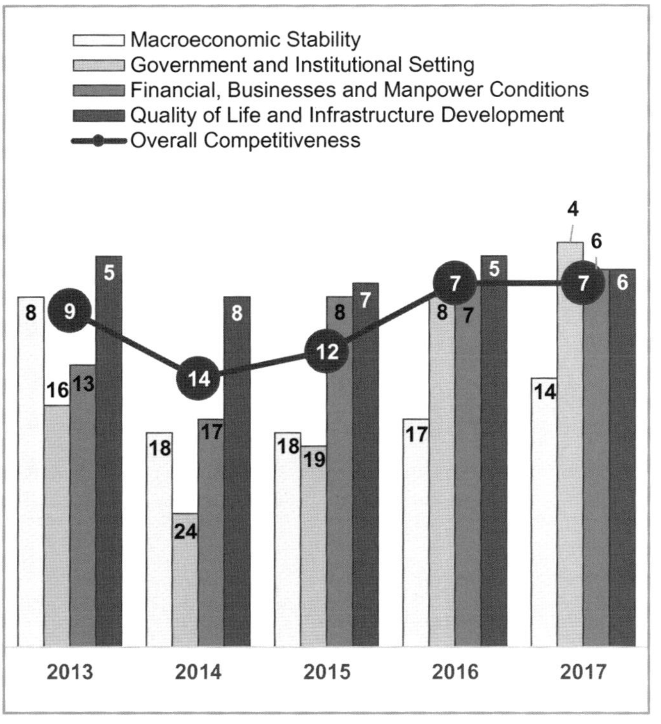

2017 ACI Competitiveness Index: Ranking and Scores by Sub-Environments

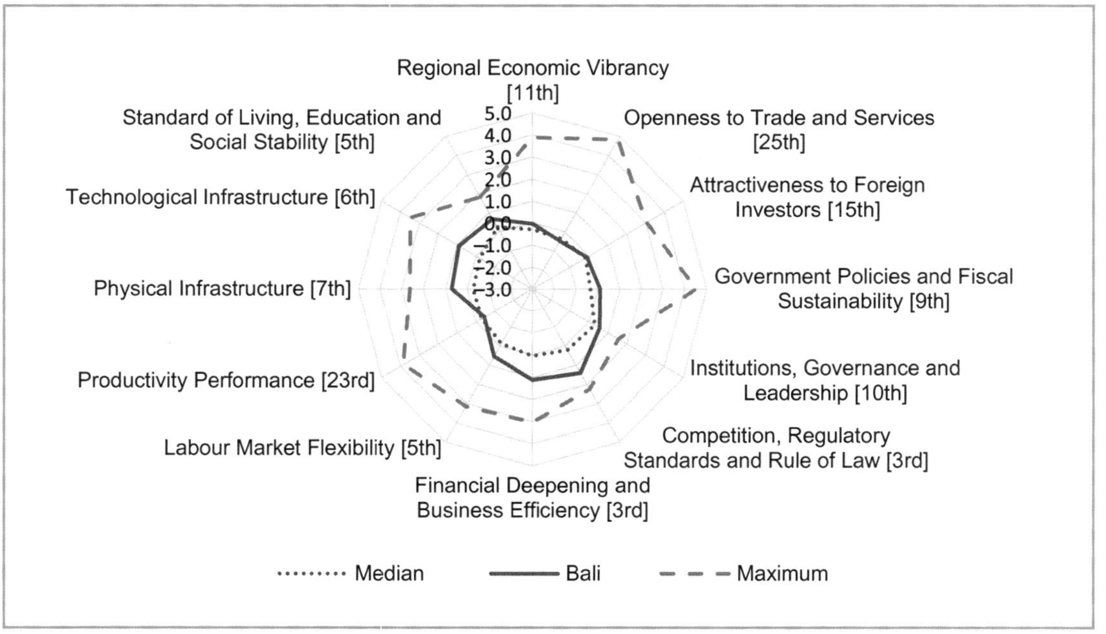

Note: [ ] shows rank out of 33 provinces.

Bali

Bali-Nusa Tenggara Region

2017 ACI Competitiveness Index: Top-20% Strongest and Weakest Indicators

Rank	20% Strongest Indicators	Std. Score	Envmt.	Rank	20% Weakest Indicators	Std. Score	Envmt.
1	Passengers of international air traffic	2.927	QLID	81	Cargo at international seaport	–0.362	QLID
2	Labour force participation rate	2.493	FBMC	82	Primary industry productivity	–0.370	FBMC
3	Firms' human resource capacity	2.027	FBMC	83	Gross Regional Domestic Product (GRDP)	–0.372	MS
4	Net school enrolment rate (senior high)	1.739	QLID	84	Overall labour productivity	–0.382	FBMC
5	Unemployment rate	1.688	FBMC	85	Cargo at inter-island seaport	–0.388	QLID
6	Telephone ownership	1.659	QLID	86	Environmental quality index	–0.441	QLID
7	Vibrancy of competition and collaboration	1.611	GIS	87	Export, non-oil and gas	–0.444	MS
8	Households with pipe water services	1.528	QLID	88	Employment in primary industry	–0.447	FBMC
9	Quality of healthcare	1.505	QLID	89	Student–teacher ratio (senior high)	–0.461	QLID
10	Non-performing loans per total bank loans	1.488	FBMC	90	GRDP of secondary industry	–0.476	MS
11	Net school enrolment rate (junior high)	1.440	QLID	91	Export	–0.496	MS
12	Laptop computer ownership	1.282	QLID	92	Adult illiteracy rate	–0.533	QLID
13	Inflation	1.278	MS	93	GRDP of primary industry	–0.584	MS
14	Ease of dealing with banks	1.209	FBMC	94	Openness to trade	–0.656	MS
15	Tax revenue/Government revenue	1.207	GIS	95	Firms' performance	–0.822	FBMC
16	Urban population	1.085	QLID	96	Population growth	–0.937	QLID
17	Human development index	1.085	QLID	97	Secondary industry productivity	–0.961	FBMC
18	Regulatory governance	1.058	GIS	98	Gini ratio	–0.966	QLID
19	Firms' innovation	0.994	FBMC	99	Student–teacher ratio (junior high)	–1.226	QLID
20	Rule of law	0.984	GIS	100	Ease of acquiring property	–1.677	QLID

Note: MS: Macroeconomic Stability; GIS: Government and Institutional Setting; FBMC: Financial, Businesses and Manpower Conditions; QLID: Quality of Life and Infrastructure Development.

2017 ACI Competitiveness Index: *What-if* Simulation Ranking and Scores

Overall Competitiveness	Before		After
Rank	7	→	5
Score	0.687		0.969

Macroeconomic Stability	Before		After	Government and Institutional Setting	Before		After
Rank	14	→	13	Rank	4	→	4
Score	–0.243		–0.039	Score	0.885		0.885

Financial, Businesses and Manpower Conditions	Before		After	Quality of Life and Infrastructure Development	Before		After
Rank	6	→	5	Rank	6	→	2
Score	0.635		0.932	Score	0.999		1.437

Note: Ranking and scores after simulation are derived by improving the province's top-20% weakest indicators.

Bangka Belitung Islands

Sumatra Region

2017 ACI Competitiveness Index: Ranking and Scores	
2017 Overall Competitiveness Index **22nd** out of 33 provinces **std. score: –0.403**	
Macroeconomic Stability **28th** std. score: –0.649	**Government and Institutional Setting** **23rd** std. score: –0.426
Financial, Businesses and Manpower Conditions **14th** std. score: –0.032	**Quality of Life and Infrastructure Development** **23rd** std. score: –0.229

ACI Competitiveness Index Ranking: 2013–2017

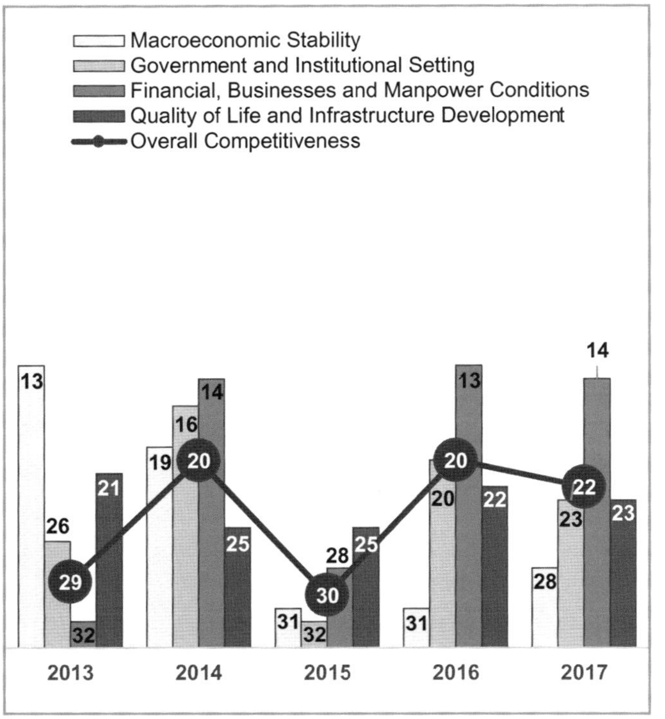

2017 ACI Competitiveness Index: Ranking and Scores by Sub-Environments

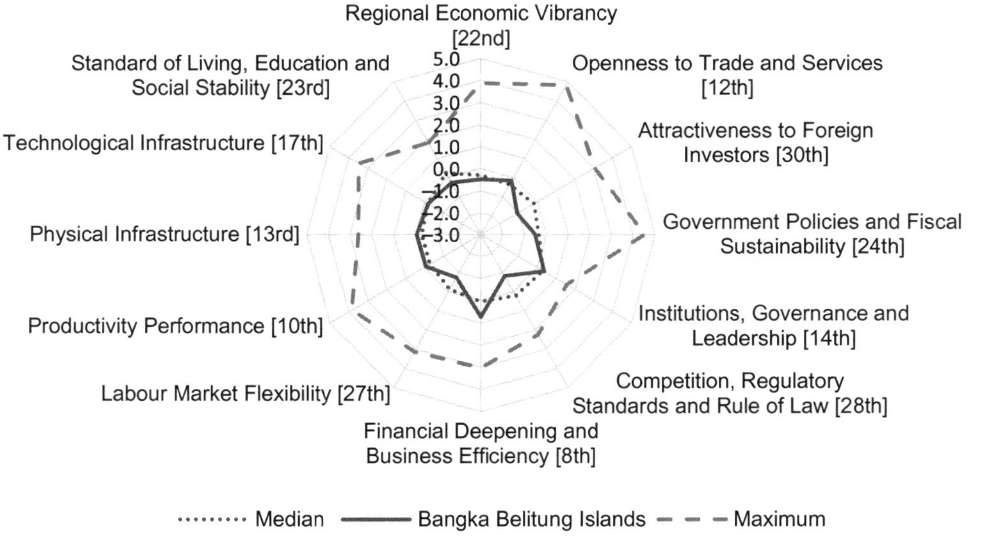

Note: [ ] shows rank out of 33 provinces.

Bangka Belitung Islands
Sumatra Region

2017 ACI Competitiveness Index: Top-20% Strongest and Weakest Indicators

Rank	20% Strongest Indicators	Std. Score	Envmt.	Rank	20% Weakest Indicators	Std. Score	Envmt.
1	Firms' application of IT	4.931	FBMC	81	Desktop computer ownership	–0.598	QLID
2	Gini ratio	2.032	QLID	82	Employment in primary industry	–0.604	FBMC
3	Ease of acquiring property	1.931	QLID	83	Student–teacher ratio (primary)	–0.608	QLID
4	Security	1.920	GIS	84	Government revenue	–0.628	GIS
5	Lack of corruption	1.842	GIS	85	Number of bank branches/offices	–0.646	FBMC
6	Quality of education	1.049	QLID	86	Government expenditure	–0.668	GIS
7	Ease of dealing with banks	0.902	FBMC	87	Length of paved roads	–0.676	QLID
8	Inflation	0.847	MS	88	GRDP of primary industry	–0.678	MS
9	Population growth	0.827	QLID	89	Provincial governing capacity	–0.688	GIS
10	Crime rate	0.654	GIS	90	Government progress and expectation	–0.703	GIS
11	Population per number of bank branches/offices	0.636	FBMC	91	Mean years of schooling	–0.772	QLID
12	Households with state electricity services	0.586	QLID	92	Quality of technological infrastructure	–1.003	QLID
13	Handphone ownership	0.526	QLID	93	Population per health facility	–1.075	QLID
14	Openness to trade	0.488	MS	94	Labour relations	–1.191	FBMC
15	Non-performing loans per total bank loans	0.460	FBMC	95	Investment promotion and management	–1.406	MS
16	Adult illiteracy rate	0.411	QLID	96	Student–teacher ratio (junior high)	–1.454	QLID
17	Urban population	0.393	QLID	97	Firms' human resource capacity	–1.483	FBMC
18	Population per medical worker	0.393	QLID	98	Affordability and accessibility of goods	–1.487	QLID
19	Firms' equipment capacity	0.382	FBMC	99	Households with pipe water services	–1.662	QLID
20	Non-performing loans	0.376	FBMC	100	Vibrancy of competition and collaboration	–2.215	GIS

Note: MS: Macroeconomic Stability; GIS: Government and Institutional Setting;
FBMC: Financial, Businesses and Manpower Conditions; QLID: Quality of Life and Infrastructure Development.

2017 ACI Competitiveness Index: *What-if* Simulation Ranking and Scores

Overall Competitiveness	Before	After
Rank	**22**	**13**
Score	–0.403	0.117

Macroeconomic Stability	Before	After	Government and Institutional Setting	Before	After
Rank	**28**	**21**	Rank	**23**	**17**
Score	–0.649	–0.396	Score	–0.426	0.149

Financial, Businesses and Manpower Conditions	Before	After	Quality of Life and Infrastructure Development	Before	After
Rank	**14**	**10**	Rank	**23**	**12**
Score	–0.032	0.301	Score	–0.229	0.334

Note: Ranking and scores after simulation are derived by improving the province's top-20% weakest indicators.

Banten

Java Region

2017 ACI Competitiveness Index: Ranking and Scores

2017 Overall Competitiveness Index

6th

out of 33 provinces

std. score: 0.741

Macroeconomic Stability	Government and Institutional Setting
7th	6th
std. score: 0.456	std. score: 0.745

Financial, Businesses and Manpower Conditions	Quality of Life and Infrastructure Development
12th	4th
std. score: 0.057	std. score: 1.197

ACI Competitiveness Index Ranking: 2013–2017

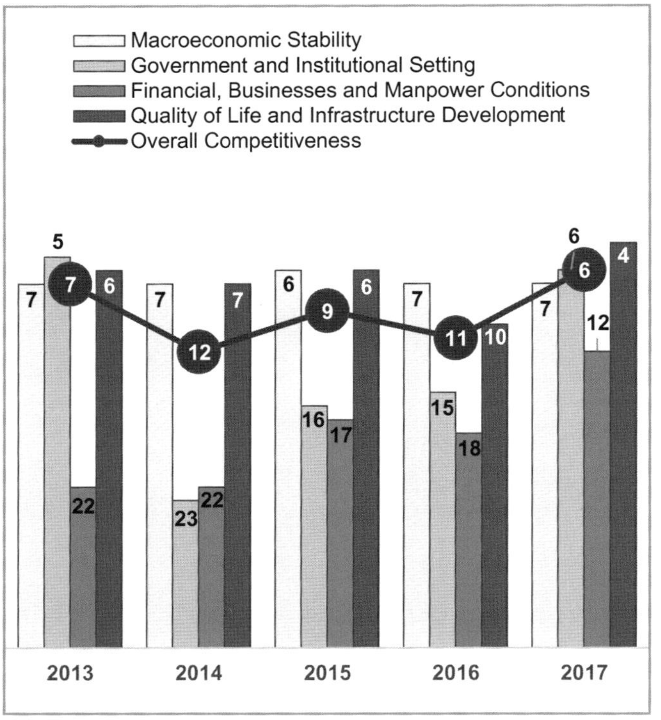

2017 ACI Competitiveness Index: Ranking and Scores by Sub-Environments

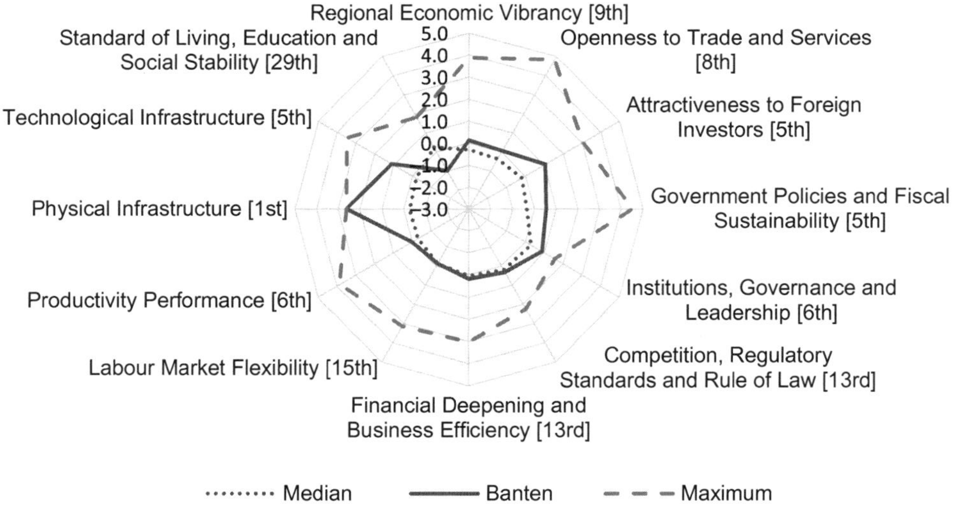

Note: [ ] shows rank out of 33 provinces.

Banten

Java Region

2017 ACI Competitiveness Index: Top-20% Strongest and Weakest Indicators

Rank	20% Strongest Indicators	Std. Score	Envmt.	Rank	20% Weakest Indicators	Std. Score	Envmt.
1	Passengers of domestic air traffic	5.114	QLID	81	Labour relations	–0.342	FBMC
2	Passengers of international air traffic	4.656	QLID	82	Employment in primary industry	–0.359	FBMC
3	Tax revenue/Government revenue	1.828	GIS	83	Export, non-oil and gas	–0.360	MS
4	Firms' performance	1.642	FBMC	84	Quality of education	–0.415	QLID
5	Foreign direct investment, last three year average	1.535	MS	85	Export	–0.416	MS
6	Desktop computer ownership	1.441	QLID	86	Gini ratio	–0.421	QLID
7	Urban population	1.256	QLID	87	GRDP of primary industry	–0.422	MS
8	Quality of technological infrastructure	1.155	QLID	88	Labour force participation rate	–0.490	FBMC
9	Internet access in handphone	1.144	QLID	89	Net school enrolment rate (senior high)	–0.569	QLID
10	Telephone ownership	1.006	QLID	90	Length of paved roads	–0.630	QLID
11	Internet access at office	0.961	QLID	91	Population per health facility	–0.670	QLID
12	Population growth	0.952	QLID	92	Households with pipe water services	–1.030	QLID
13	Households with state electricity services	0.936	QLID	93	Student–teacher ratio (senior high)	–1.359	QLID
14	Crime rate	0.924	GIS	94	Inflation	–1.469	MS
15	Internet access at home	0.862	QLID	95	Student–teacher ratio (primary)	–1.642	QLID
16	Security	0.861	GIS	96	Unemployment rate	–1.770	FBMC
17	Lack of corruption	0.815	GIS	97	Environmental quality index	–1.948	QLID
18	Internet access at school	0.807	QLID	98	Student–teacher ratio (junior high)	–1.958	QLID
19	Affordability and accessibility of goods	0.726	QLID	99	Population per medical worker	–2.182	QLID
20	GRDP of secondary industry	0.723	MS	100	Population per number of bank branches/offices	–2.199	FBMC

Note: MS: Macroeconomic Stability; GIS: Government and Institutional Setting; FBMC: Financial, Businesses and Manpower Conditions; QLID: Quality of Life and Infrastructure Development.

2017 ACI Competitiveness Index: *What-if* Simulation Ranking and Scores

Overall Competitiveness	Before		After
Rank	6	→	4
Score	0.741		1.115

Macroeconomic Stability	Before		After
Rank	7	→	6
Score	0.456		0.618

Government and Institutional Setting	Before		After
Rank	6	→	6
Score	0.745		0.745

Financial, Businesses and Manpower Conditions	Before		After
Rank	12	→	9
Score	0.057		0.500

Quality of Life and Infrastructure Development	Before		After
Rank	4	→	2
Score	1.197		1.830

Note: Ranking and scores after simulation are derived by improving the province's top-20% weakest indicators.

Bengkulu

Sumatra Region

2017 ACI Competitiveness Index: Ranking and Scores

2017 Overall Competitiveness Index

27th

out of 33 provinces

std. score: –0.595

Macroeconomic Stability	Government and Institutional Setting
32nd	**25th**
std. score: –0.874	std. score: –0.672

Financial, Businesses and Manpower Conditions	Quality of Life and Infrastructure Development
21st	**19th**
std. score: –0.346	std. score: –0.079

ACI Competitiveness Index Ranking: 2013–2017

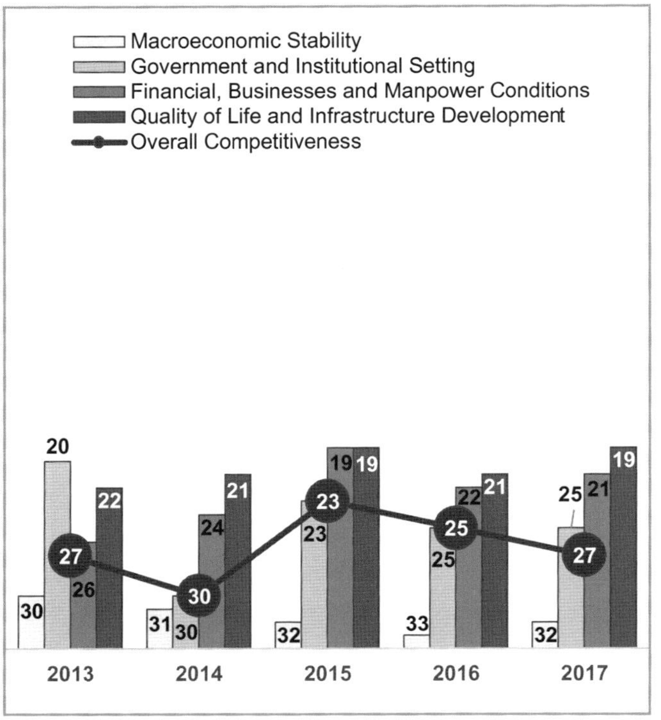

2017 ACI Competitiveness Index: Ranking and Scores by Sub-Environments

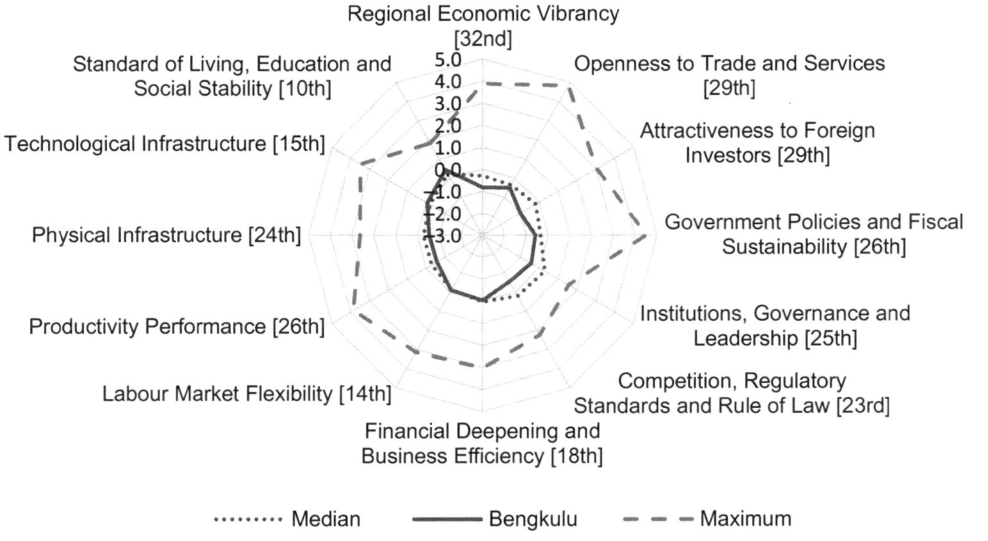

Note: [ ] shows rank out of 33 provinces.

Bengkulu
Sumatra Region

2017 ACI Competitiveness Index: Top-20% Strongest and Weakest Indicators

Rank	20% Strongest Indicators	Std. Score	Envmt.	Rank	20% Weakest Indicators	Std. Score	Envmt.
1	Ease of dealing with banks	1.302	FBMC	81	GRDP of secondary industry	–0.577	MS
2	Population per medical worker	1.048	QLID	82	Government revenue	–0.584	GIS
3	Unemployment rate	0.931	FBMC	83	Firms' innovation	–0.587	FBMC
4	Ease of acquiring property	0.815	QLID	84	Domestic direct investment, last three year average	–0.600	MS
5	Net school enrolment rate (senior high)	0.710	QLID	85	Gross Regional Domestic Product (GRDP)	–0.603	MS
6	Government efficiency	0.673	GIS	86	Number of bank branches/offices	–0.607	FBMC
7	Net school enrolment rate (primary)	0.633	QLID	87	Government expenditure	–0.612	GIS
8	Student–teacher ratio (junior high)	0.544	QLID	88	Tax revenue/Government revenue	–0.617	GIS
9	Minimum wage per month	0.485	FBMC	89	Foreign direct investment, last three year average	–0.618	MS
10	Fatalities due to natural disaster	0.457	QLID	90	Firms' human resource capacity	–0.627	FBMC
11	Households with state electricity services	0.419	QLID	91	Provincial governing capacity	–0.677	GIS
12	Gini ratio	0.396	QLID	92	GRDP of primary industry	–0.684	MS
13	Adult illiteracy rate	0.396	QLID	93	Urban population	–0.720	QLID
14	Labour force participation rate	0.387	FBMC	94	Openness to trade	–0.721	MS
15	Handphone ownership	0.367	QLID	95	Secondary industry productivity	–0.772	FBMC
16	Non-performing loans	0.362	FBMC	96	Government inclusiveness and accountability	–0.889	GIS
17	Internet access at school	0.349	QLID	97	Investment promotion and management	–1.118	MS
18	Firms' equipment capacity	0.347	FBMC	98	Vibrancy of competition and collaboration	–1.215	GIS
19	Registered motor vehicles per kilometre of paved road	0.337	QLID	99	Inflation	–1.251	MS
20	Non-performing loans per total bank loans	0.333	FBMC	100	Quality of healthcare	–1.366	QLID

Note: MS: Macroeconomic Stability; GIS: Government and Institutional Setting;
FBMC: Financial, Businesses and Manpower Conditions; QLID: Quality of Life and Infrastructure Development.

2017 ACI Competitiveness Index: *What-if* Simulation Ranking and Scores

Overall Competitiveness

	Before		After
Rank	27	→	17
Score	–0.595		–0.159

Macroeconomic Stability

	Before		After
Rank	32	→	16
Score	–0.874		–0.288

Government and Institutional Setting

	Before		After
Rank	25	→	23
Score	–0.672		–0.194

Financial, Businesses and Manpower Conditions

	Before		After
Rank	21	→	17
Score	–0.346		–0.096

Quality of Life and Infrastructure Development

	Before		After
Rank	19	→	15
Score	–0.079		0.050

Note: Ranking and scores after simulation are derived by improving the province's top-20% weakest indicators.

Central Java
Java Region

2017 ACI Competitiveness Index: Ranking and Scores

2017 Overall Competitiveness Index

4th

out of 33 provinces

std. score: 1.035

Macroeconomic Stability	Government and Institutional Setting
5th	8th
std. score: 0.678	std. score: 0.700

Financial, Businesses and Manpower Conditions	Quality of Life and Infrastructure Development
3rd	11th
std. score: 1.665	std. score: 0.383

ACI Competitiveness Index Ranking: 2013–2017

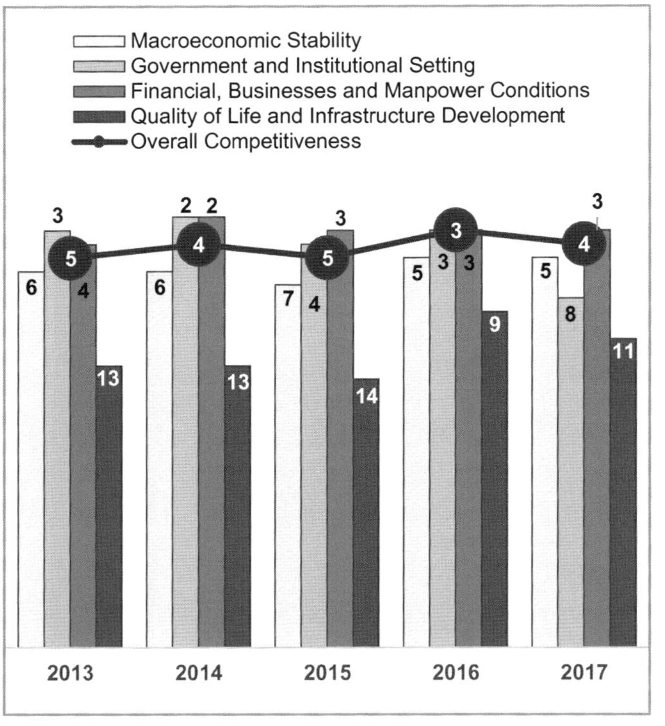

2017 ACI Competitiveness Index: Ranking and Scores by Sub-Environments

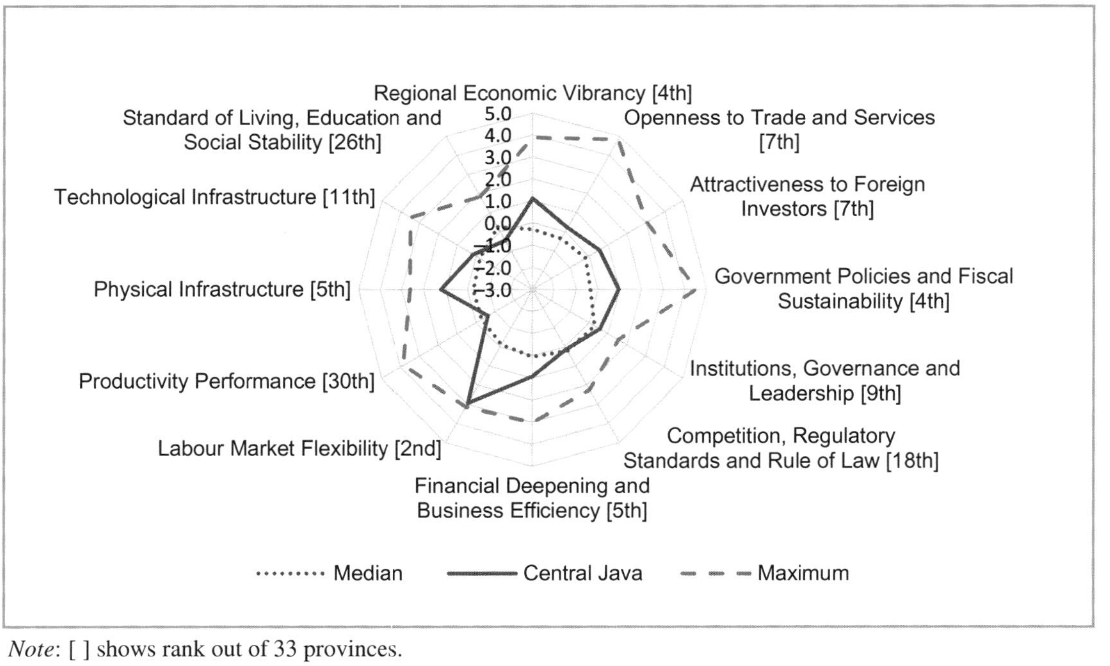

Note: [ ] shows rank out of 33 provinces.

Central Java

Java Region

2017 ACI Competitiveness Index: Top-20% Strongest and Weakest Indicators

Rank	20% Strongest Indicators	Std. Score	Envmt.	Rank	20% Weakest Indicators	Std. Score	Envmt.
1	Employment in secondary industry	2.897	FBMC	81	Regulatory governance	–0.386	GIS
2	Employment	2.665	FBMC	82	Overall labour productivity, non-oil and gas	–0.421	FBMC
3	Labour force	2.644	FBMC	83	GRDP per capita	–0.448	MS
4	Employment in primary industry	2.626	FBMC	84	Adult illiteracy rate	–0.454	QLID
5	Population	2.439	QLID	85	Vibrancy of competition and collaboration	–0.456	GIS
6	Employment in tertiary industry	2.337	FBMC	86	Government progress and expectation	–0.465	GIS
7	Length of paved roads	2.205	QLID	87	Non-performing loans	–0.488	FBMC
8	Crime rate	1.864	GIS	88	Internet access at office	–0.495	QLID
9	Life expectancy at birth	1.863	QLID	89	Overall labour productivity	–0.514	FBMC
10	Minimum wage per month	1.852	FBMC	90	Primary industry productivity	–0.520	FBMC
11	Firms' performance	1.794	FBMC	91	Student–teacher ratio (junior high)	–0.615	QLID
12	GRDP of secondary industry	1.758	MS	92	Secondary industry productivity	–0.629	FBMC
13	Number of bank branches/offices	1.723	FBMC	93	Tertiary industry productivity	–0.662	FBMC
14	Internet access at school	1.543	QLID	94	Student–teacher ratio (senior high)	–0.796	QLID
15	Quality of physical infrastructure	1.412	QLID	95	Laptop computer ownership	–0.934	QLID
16	Labour force participation rate	1.366	FBMC	96	Population per medical worker	–1.036	QLID
17	Gross Regional Domestic Product (GRDP)	1.357	MS	97	Mean years of schooling	–1.058	QLID
18	GRDP, non-oil and gas	1.313	MS	98	Population per number of bank branches/offices	–1.352	FBMC
19	Government expenditure	1.236	GIS	99	Population growth	–1.685	QLID
20	Domestic direct investment, last three year average	1.208	MS	100	Fatalities due to natural disaster	–4.551	QLID

Note: MS: Macroeconomic Stability; GIS: Government and Institutional Setting; FBMC: Financial, Businesses and Manpower Conditions; QLID: Quality of Life and Infrastructure Development.

2017 ACI Competitiveness Index: *What-if* Simulation Ranking and Scores

Overall Competitiveness	Before		After
Rank	**4**	➡	**3**
Score	1.035		1.409

Macroeconomic Stability	Before		After
Rank	**5**	➡	**5**
Score	0.678		0.702

Government and Institutional Setting	Before		After
Rank	**8**	➡	**5**
Score	0.700		0.865

Financial, Businesses and Manpower Conditions	Before		After
Rank	**3**	➡	**2**
Score	1.665		2.084

Quality of Life and Infrastructure Development	Before		After
Rank	**11**	➡	**6**
Score	0.383		1.022

Note: Ranking and scores after simulation are derived by improving the province's top-20% weakest indicators.

Central Kalimantan
Kalimantan Region

2017 ACI Competitiveness Index: Ranking and Scores

2017 Overall Competitiveness Index

13rd

out of 33 provinces

std. score: 0.090

Macroeconomic Stability	Government and Institutional Setting
19th	**17th**
std. score: –0.349	std. score: 0.164

Financial, Businesses and Manpower Conditions	Quality of Life and Infrastructure Development
8th	**18th**
std. score: 0.560	std. score: –0.076

ACI Competitiveness Index Ranking: 2013–2017

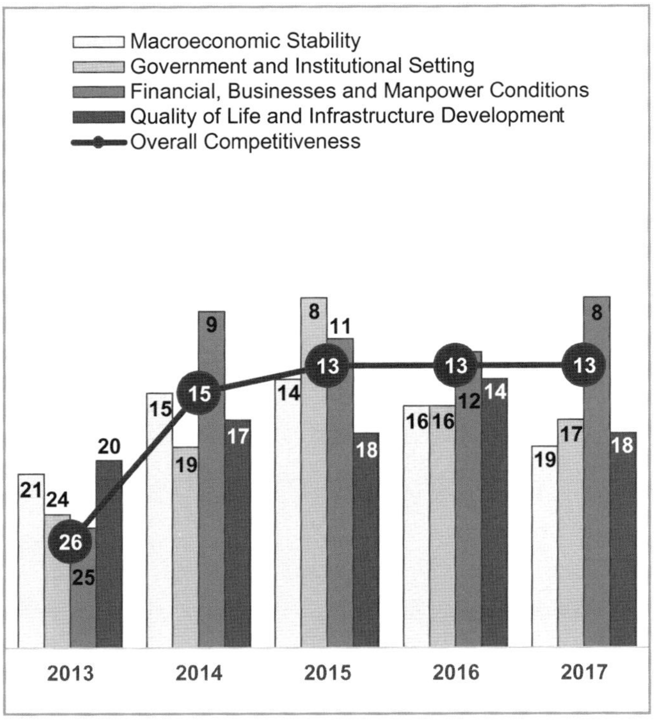

2017 ACI Competitiveness Index: Ranking and Scores by Sub-Environments

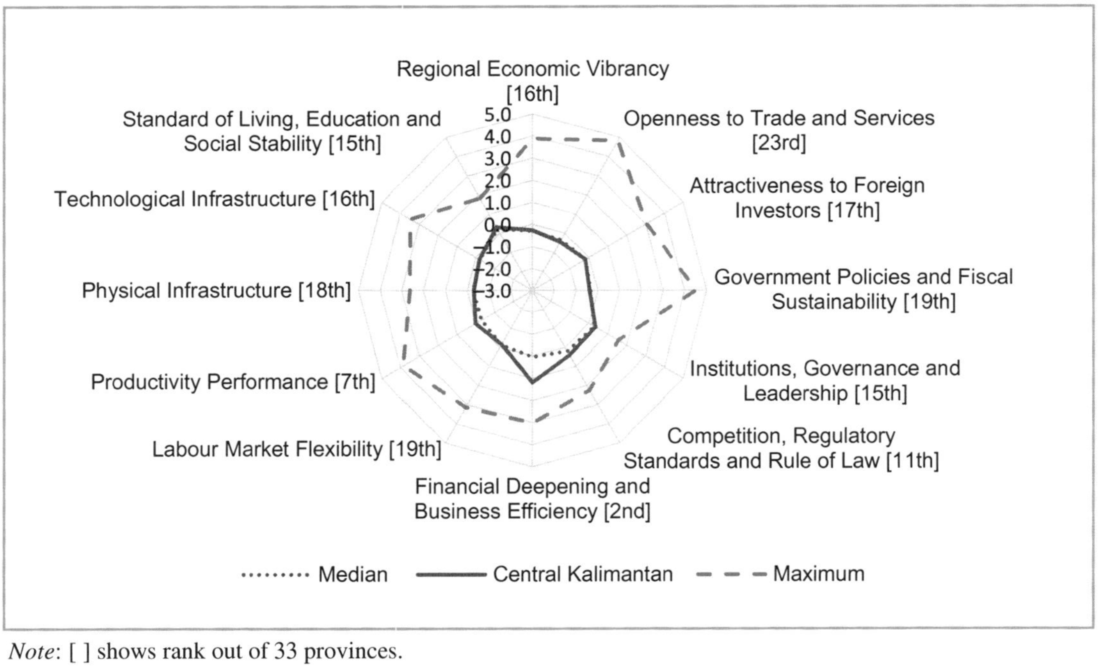

Note: [ ] shows rank out of 33 provinces.

Central Kalimantan

Kalimantan Region

2017 ACI Competitiveness Index: Top-20% Strongest and Weakest Indicators

Rank	20% Strongest Indicators	Std. Score	Envmt.	Rank	20% Weakest Indicators	Std. Score	Envmt.
1	Firms' equipment capacity	2.736	FBMC	81	Length of paved roads	–0.463	QLID
2	Ease of acquiring property	1.664	QLID	82	GRDP, non-oil and gas	–0.464	MS
3	Student–teacher ratio (senior high)	1.593	QLID	83	Employment in secondary industry	–0.468	FBMC
4	Non-performing loans per total bank loans	1.379	FBMC	84	Employment	–0.473	FBMC
5	Ease of dealing with banks	1.351	FBMC	85	Export	–0.473	MS
6	Population growth	1.095	QLID	86	Labour force	–0.477	FBMC
7	Unemployment rate	1.043	FBMC	87	Urban population	–0.477	QLID
8	Regulatory governance	0.884	GIS	88	GRDP of secondary industry	–0.480	MS
9	Firms' human resource capacity	0.860	FBMC	89	Population	–0.490	QLID
10	Crime rate	0.796	GIS	90	Gross Regional Domestic Product (GRDP)	–0.498	MS
11	Student–teacher ratio (junior high)	0.673	QLID	91	Number of bank branches/offices	–0.514	FBMC
12	Gini ratio	0.669	QLID	92	Employment in tertiary industry	–0.518	FBMC
13	Net school enrolment rate (primary)	0.668	QLID	93	Quality of healthcare	–0.550	QLID
14	Firms' application of IT	0.644	FBMC	94	Telephone ownership	–0.562	QLID
15	Labour relations	0.640	FBMC	95	Openness to trade	–0.576	MS
16	Adult illiteracy rate	0.640	QLID	96	Quality of physical infrastructure	–0.609	QLID
17	Student–teacher ratio (primary)	0.611	QLID	97	Minimum wage per month	–0.676	FBMC
18	Secondary industry productivity	0.579	FBMC	98	Households with state electricity services	–0.916	QLID
19	Handphone ownership	0.559	QLID	99	Quality of education	–1.024	QLID
20	Environmental quality index	0.544	QLID	100	Net school enrolment rate (senior high)	–1.416	QLID

Note: MS: Macroeconomic Stability; GIS: Government and Institutional Setting; FBMC: Financial, Businesses and Manpower Conditions; QLID: Quality of Life and Infrastructure Development.

2017 ACI Competitiveness Index: *What-if* Simulation Ranking and Scores

Overall Competitiveness	Before	After
Rank	**13**	**11**
Score	0.090	0.347

Macroeconomic Stability	Before	After	Government and Institutional Setting	Before	After
Rank	**19**	**13**	Rank	**17**	**17**
Score	–0.349	–0.187	Score	0.164	0.164

Financial, Businesses and Manpower Conditions	Before	After	Quality of Life and Infrastructure Development	Before	After
Rank	**8**	**6**	Rank	**18**	**12**
Score	0.560	0.819	Score	–0.076	0.354

Note: Ranking and scores after simulation are derived by improving the province's top-20% weakest indicators.

Central Sulawesi

Sulawesi Region

2017 ACI Competitiveness Index: Ranking and Scores

2017 Overall Competitiveness Index

12th

out of 33 provinces

std. score: 0.270

Macroeconomic Stability	Government and Institutional Setting
18th	**2nd**
std. score: –0.348	std. score: 1.395

Financial, Businesses and Manpower Conditions	Quality of Life and Infrastructure Development
17th	**17th**
std. score: –0.091	std. score: –0.061

ACI Competitiveness Index Ranking: 2013–2017

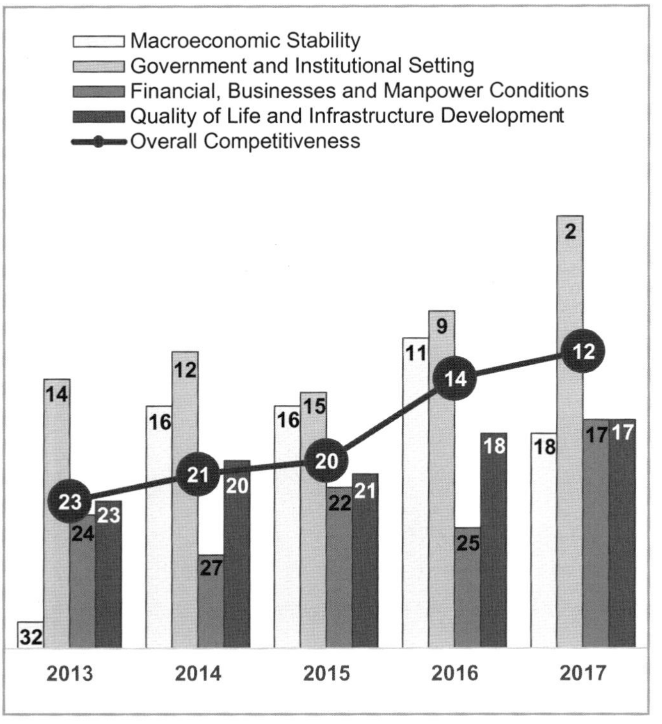

2017 ACI Competitiveness Index: Ranking and Scores by Sub-Environments

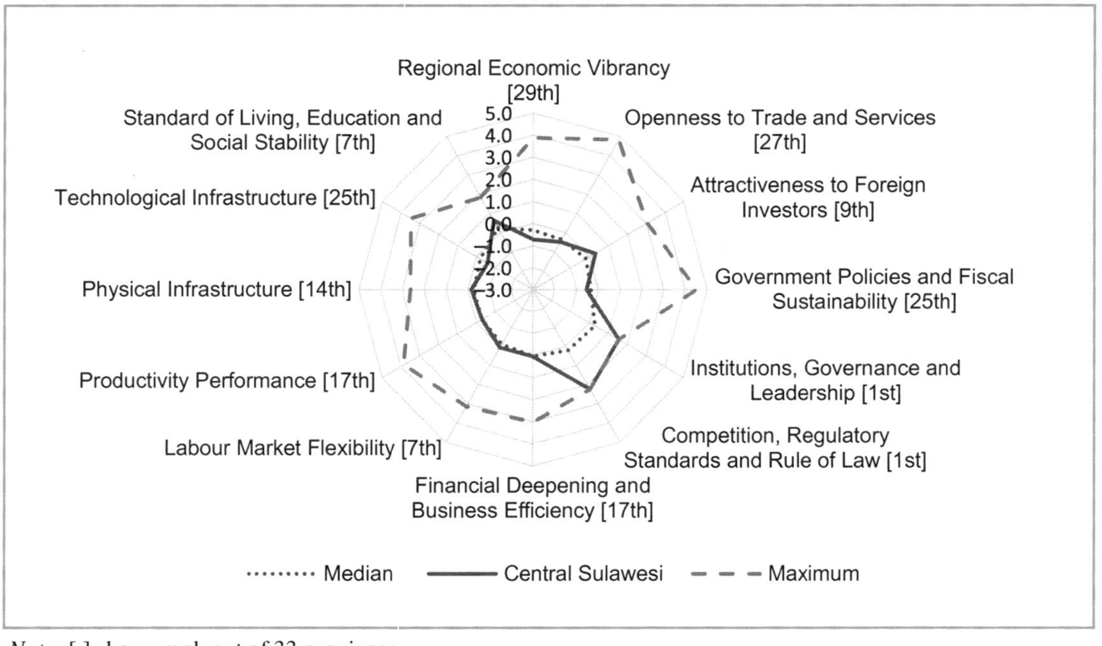

Note: [ ] shows rank out of 33 provinces.

Central Sulawesi
Sulawesi Region

2017 ACI Competitiveness Index: Top-20% Strongest and Weakest Indicators

Rank	20% Strongest Indicators	Std. Score	Envmt.	Rank	20% Weakest Indicators	Std. Score	Envmt.
1	Lack of corruption	2.919	GIS	81	Gross Regional Domestic Product (GRDP)	–0.490	MS
2	Regulatory governance	2.472	GIS	82	Handphone ownership	–0.491	QLID
3	Coordination of local governments	2.001	GIS	83	GRDP of secondary industry	–0.501	MS
4	Rule of law	1.862	GIS	84	Export	–0.506	MS
5	Ease of acquiring property	1.677	QLID	85	Number of bank branches/offices	–0.545	FBMC
6	Government inclusiveness and accountability	1.598	GIS	86	Domestic direct investment, last three year average	–0.545	MS
7	Vibrancy of competition and collaboration	1.500	GIS	87	Government revenue	–0.555	GIS
8	Government progress and expectation	1.453	GIS	88	Government expenditure	–0.572	GIS
9	Provincial governing capacity	1.311	GIS	89	Desktop computer ownership	–0.587	QLID
10	Government efficiency	1.141	GIS	90	Laptop computer ownership	–0.613	QLID
11	Investment promotion and management	1.136	MS	91	Net school enrolment rate (junior high)	–0.645	QLID
12	Environmental quality index	1.107	QLID	92	Openness to trade	–0.652	MS
13	Affordability and accessibility of goods	1.082	QLID	93	Internet access at home	–0.652	QLID
14	Quality of education	1.070	QLID	94	Life expectancy at birth	–0.713	QLID
15	Population per medical worker	1.012	QLID	95	Internet access in handphone	–0.759	QLID
16	Quality of physical infrastructure	0.925	QLID	96	Internet access at school	–0.871	QLID
17	Labour relations	0.886	FBMC	97	Urban population	–0.991	QLID
18	Unemployment rate	0.832	FBMC	98	Net school enrolment rate (primary)	–1.162	QLID
19	Minimum wage per month	0.796	FBMC	99	Crime rate	–1.439	GIS
20	Quality of healthcare	0.790	QLID	100	Inflation	–1.693	MS

Note: MS: Macroeconomic Stability; GIS: Government and Institutional Setting; FBMC: Financial, Businesses and Manpower Conditions; QLID: Quality of Life and Infrastructure Development.

2017 ACI Competitiveness Index: *What-if* Simulation Ranking and Scores

Overall Competitiveness	Before		After
Rank	**12**	→	**8**
Score	0.270		0.569

Macroeconomic Stability	Before		After	Government and Institutional Setting	Before		After
Rank	**18**	→	**13**	Rank	**2**	→	**2**
Score	–0.348		–0.028	Score	1.395		1.586

Financial, Businesses and Manpower Conditions	Before		After	Quality of Life and Infrastructure Development	Before		After
Rank	**17**	→	**16**	Rank	**17**	→	**11**
Score	–0.091		–0.043	Score	–0.061		0.373

Note: Ranking and scores after simulation are derived by improving the province's top-20% weakest indicators.

DI Yogyakarta
Java Region

2017 ACI Competitiveness Index: Ranking and Scores

2017 Overall Competitiveness Index

9th

out of 33 provinces

std. score: 0.423

Macroeconomic Stability	Government and Institutional Setting
24th	**15th**
std. score: –0.461	std. score: 0.246

Financial, Businesses and Manpower Conditions	Quality of Life and Infrastructure Development
10th	**2nd**
std. score: 0.270	std. score: 1.347

ACI Competitiveness Index Ranking: 2013–2017

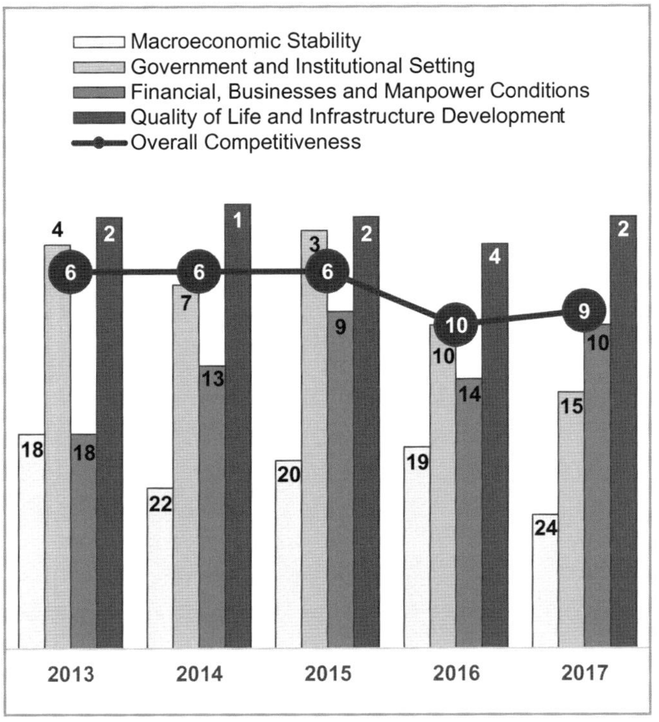

2017 ACI Competitiveness Index: Ranking and Scores by Sub-Environments

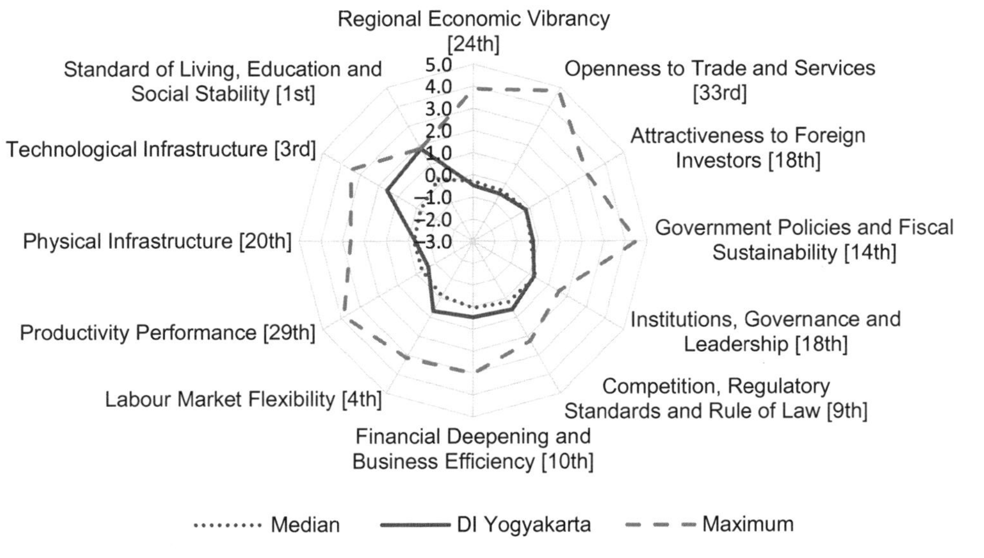

Note: [ ] shows rank out of 33 provinces.

DI Yogyakarta
Java Region

2017 ACI Competitiveness Index: Top-20% Strongest and Weakest Indicators

Rank	20% Strongest Indicators	Std. Score	Envmt.	Rank	20% Weakest Indicators	Std. Score	Envmt.
1	Internet access at school	3.460	QLID	81	Government expenditure	–0.469	GIS
2	Labour force participation rate	2.272	FBMC	82	GRDP of secondary industry	–0.473	MS
3	Laptop computer ownership	2.224	QLID	83	Export, non-oil and gas	–0.473	MS
4	Human development index	2.125	QLID	84	Gross Regional Domestic Product (GRDP)	–0.473	MS
5	Life expectancy at birth	2.102	QLID	85	Firms' equipment capacity	–0.474	FBMC
6	Desktop computer ownership	1.912	QLID	86	Cargo at inter-island seaport	–0.506	QLID
7	Internet access in handphone	1.633	QLID	87	Export	–0.524	MS
8	Minimum wage per month	1.608	FBMC	88	Domestic direct investment, last three year average	–0.540	MS
9	Student–teacher ratio (primary)	1.550	QLID	89	Overall labour productivity	–0.545	FBMC
10	Quality of education	1.406	QLID	90	Primary industry productivity	–0.575	FBMC
11	Urban population	1.373	QLID	91	Foreign direct investment, last three year average	–0.590	MS
12	Quality of healthcare	1.361	QLID	92	Ease of acquiring property	–0.714	QLID
13	Net school enrolment rate (senior high)	1.347	QLID	93	GRDP of primary industry	–0.741	MS
14	Affordability and accessibility of goods	1.283	QLID	94	Openness to trade	–0.795	MS
15	Student–teacher ratio (senior high)	1.269	QLID	95	Length of paved roads	–0.826	QLID
16	Government inclusiveness and accountability	1.229	GIS	96	Secondary industry productivity	–0.879	FBMC
17	Mean years of schooling	1.158	QLID	97	Registered motor vehicles per kilometre of paved road	–0.998	QLID
18	Quality of physical infrastructure	1.105	QLID	98	Population growth	–1.008	QLID
19	Net school enrolment rate (junior high)	1.085	QLID	99	Gini ratio	–1.239	QLID
20	Telephone ownership	1.038	QLID	100	Environmental quality index	–1.401	QLID

Note: MS: Macroeconomic Stability; GIS: Government and Institutional Setting;
FBMC: Financial, Businesses and Manpower Conditions; QLID: Quality of Life and Infrastructure Development.

2017 ACI Competitiveness Index: *What-if* Simulation Ranking and Scores

Overall Competitiveness

	Before	After
Rank	**9**	**6**
Score	0.423	0.769

Macroeconomic Stability

	Before	After
Rank	**24**	**13**
Score	–0.461	–0.053

Government and Institutional Setting

	Before	After
Rank	**15**	**15**
Score	0.246	0.290

Financial, Businesses and Manpower Conditions

	Before	After
Rank	**10**	**9**
Score	0.270	0.538

Quality of Life and Infrastructure Development

	Before	After
Rank	**2**	**2**
Score	1.347	1.776

Note: Ranking and scores after simulation are derived by improving the province's top-20% weakest indicators.

DKI Jakarta

Java Region

2017 ACI Competitiveness Index: Ranking and Scores

2017 Overall Competitiveness Index

1st

out of 33 provinces

std. score: 3.459

Macroeconomic Stability	Government and Institutional Setting
1st	1st
std. score: 4.055	std. score: 2.680

Financial, Businesses and Manpower Conditions	Quality of Life and Infrastructure Development
1st	3rd
std. score: 3.375	std. score: 1.347

ACI Competitiveness Index Ranking: 2013–2017

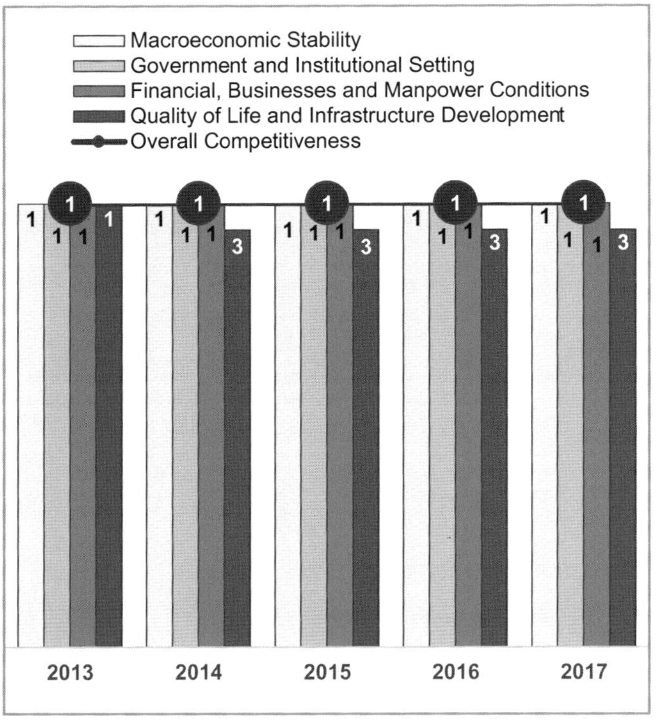

2017 ACI Competitiveness Index: Ranking and Scores by Sub-Environments

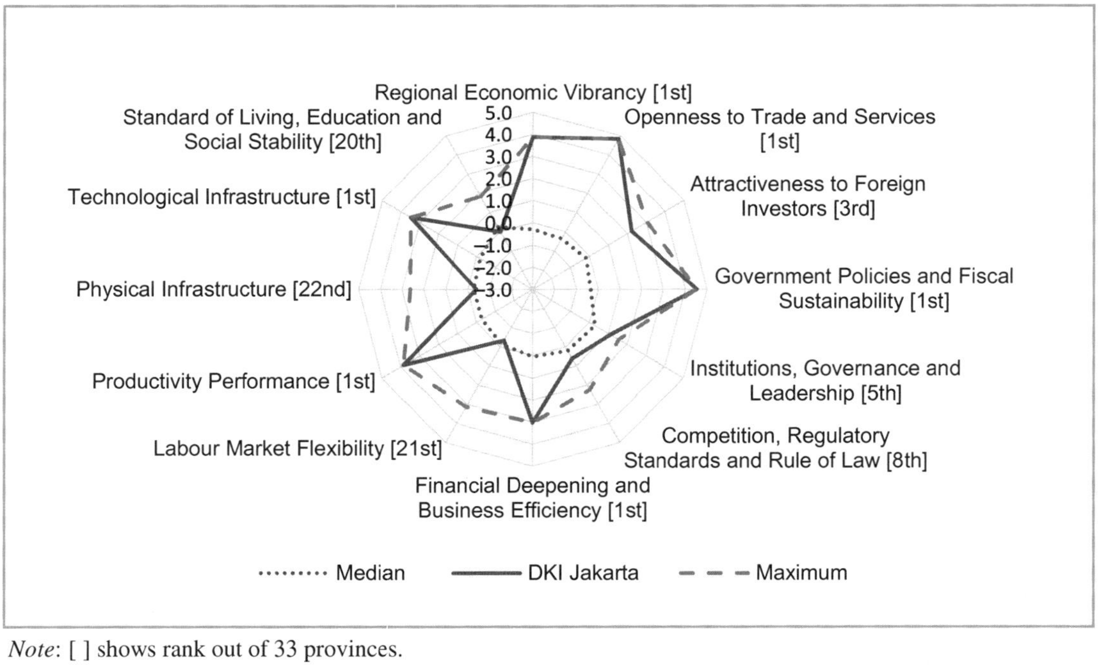

Note: [ ] shows rank out of 33 provinces.

DKI Jakarta

Java Region

2017 ACI Competitiveness Index: Top-20% Strongest and Weakest Indicators

Rank	20% Strongest Indicators	Std. Score	Envmt.	Rank	20% Weakest Indicators	Std. Score	Envmt.
1	Bank deposits	5.499	FBMC	81	Passengers of international air traffic	–0.281	QLID
2	Bank loans	5.462	FBMC	82	Fatalities due to natural disaster	–0.294	QLID
3	Import, non-oil and gas	5.427	MS	83	Inflation	–0.344	MS
4	Tertiary industry productivity	5.260	FBMC	84	Passengers of domestic air traffic	–0.379	QLID
5	Import	5.246	MS	85	Student–teacher ratio (senior high)	–0.408	QLID
6	Fiscal balance	5.087	GIS	86	Security	–0.499	GIS
7	Export, non-oil and gas	4.917	MS	87	Length of paved roads	–0.679	QLID
8	GRDP per capita, non-oil and gas	4.837	MS	88	Employment in primary industry	–0.770	FBMC
9	Overall labour productivity, non-oil and gas	4.700	FBMC	89	GRDP of primary industry	–0.820	MS
10	GRDP of tertiary industry	4.659	MS	90	Ease of acquiring property	–0.961	QLID
11	Tax revenue	4.613	GIS	91	Student–teacher ratio (primary)	–0.968	QLID
12	Government revenue	4.521	GIS	92	Population growth	–1.169	QLID
13	Export	4.512	MS	93	Student–teacher ratio (junior high)	–1.453	QLID
14	Telephone ownership	4.507	QLID	94	Unemployment rate	–1.483	FBMC
15	Internet access at office	4.388	QLID	95	Gini ratio	–1.512	QLID
16	Gross domestic fixed capital formation	4.310	MS	96	Environmental quality index	–2.581	QLID
17	Government expenditure	4.310	GIS	97	Minimum wage per month	–2.904	FBMC
18	Internet access at home	4.203	QLID	98	Population per health facility	–4.329	QLID
19	GRDP per capita	3.944	MS	99	Non-performing loans	–5.356	FBMC
20	Desktop computer ownership	3.918	QLID	100	Registered motor vehicles per kilometre of paved road	–5.406	QLID

Note: MS: Macroeconomic Stability; GIS: Government and Institutional Setting; FBMC: Financial, Businesses and Manpower Conditions; QLID: Quality of Life and Infrastructure Development.

2017 ACI Competitiveness Index: *What-if* Simulation Ranking and Scores

Overall Competitiveness	Before	After
Rank	1	1
Score	3.459	3.900

Macroeconomic Stability	Before	After	Government and Institutional Setting	Before	After
Rank	1	1	Rank	1	1
Score	4.055	4.084	Score	2.680	2.709

Financial, Businesses and Manpower Conditions	Before	After	Quality of Life and Infrastructure Development	Before	After
Rank	1	1	Rank	3	1
Score	3.375	3.954	Score	1.347	2.540

Note: Ranking and scores after simulation are derived by improving the province's top-20% weakest indicators.

East Java

Java Region

2017 ACI Competitiveness Index: Ranking and Scores

2017 Overall Competitiveness Index

2nd

out of 33 provinces

std. score: 1.723

Macroeconomic Stability	Government and Institutional Setting
2nd	**11th**
std. score: 2.496	std. score: 0.506
Financial, Businesses and Manpower Conditions	**Quality of Life and Infrastructure Development**
2nd	**8th**
std. score: 1.998	std. score: 0.706

ACI Competitiveness Index Ranking: 2013–2017

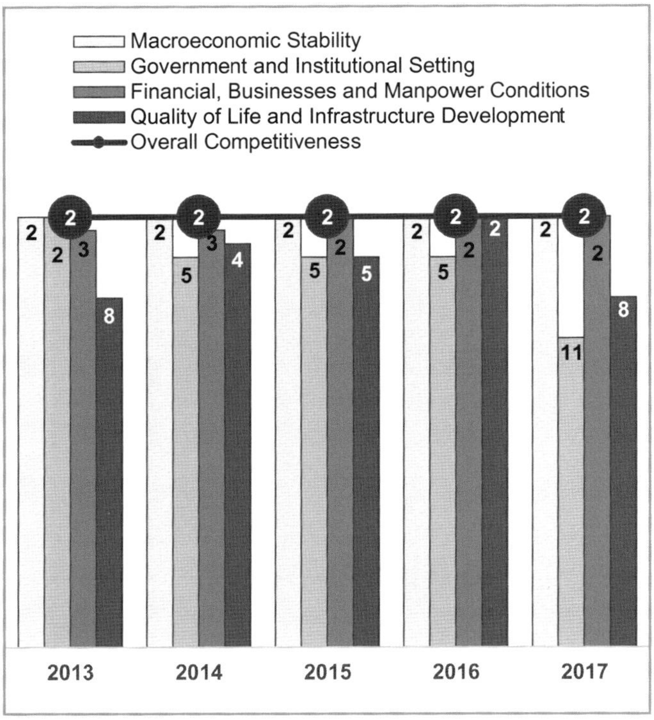

2017 ACI Competitiveness Index: Ranking and Scores by Sub-Environments

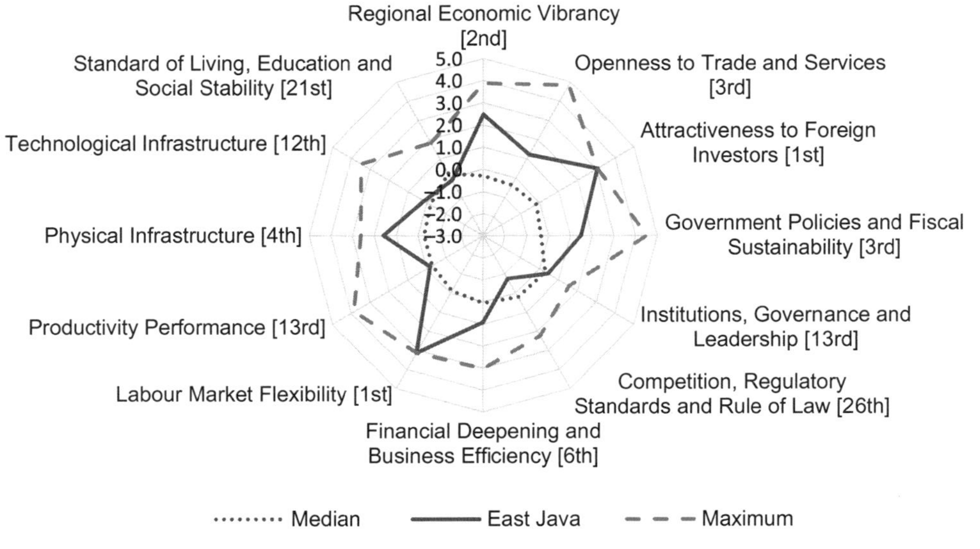

Note: [ ] shows rank out of 33 provinces.

East Java

Java Region

2017 ACI Competitiveness Index: Top-20% Strongest and Weakest Indicators

Rank	20% Strongest Indicators	Std. Score	Envmt.	Rank	20% Weakest Indicators	Std. Score	Envmt.
1	Domestic direct investment, last three year average	4.606	MS	81	Quality of education	–0.317	QLID
2	Employment in primary industry	4.020	FBMC	82	Primary industry productivity	–0.407	FBMC
3	Length of paved roads	3.515	QLID	83	Laptop computer ownership	–0.599	QLID
4	Employment	3.226	FBMC	84	Labour relations	–0.612	FBMC
5	GRDP of primary industry	3.161	MS	85	Provincial governing capacity	–0.642	GIS
6	Labour force	3.141	FBMC	86	Coordination of local governments	–0.660	GIS
7	Population	2.918	QLID	87	Vibrancy of competition and collaboration	–0.678	GIS
8	Gross Regional Domestic Product (GRDP)	2.848	MS	88	Non-performing loans	–0.688	FBMC
9	GRDP, non-oil and gas	2.805	MS	89	Environmental quality index	–0.752	QLID
10	GRDP of secondary industry	2.790	MS	90	Adult illiteracy rate	–0.758	QLID
11	Employment in tertiary industry	2.785	FBMC	91	Fatalities due to natural disaster	–0.795	QLID
12	Employment in secondary industry	2.591	FBMC	92	Student–teacher ratio (senior high)	–0.922	QLID
13	Number of bank branches/offices	2.463	FBMC	93	Population per number of bank branches/offices	–0.941	FBMC
14	Gross domestic fixed capital formation	2.186	MS	94	Mean years of schooling	–0.944	QLID
15	GRDP of tertiary industry	2.123	MS	95	Ease of dealing with banks	–1.075	FBMC
16	Crime rate	2.035	GIS	96	Ease of acquiring property	–1.091	QLID
17	Government expenditure	1.816	GIS	97	Lack of corruption	–1.130	GIS
18	Government revenue	1.661	GIS	98	Regulatory governance	–1.231	GIS
19	Tax revenue	1.582	GIS	99	Population growth	–1.917	QLID
20	Minimum wage per month	1.572	FBMC	100	Population per medical worker	–1.979	QLID

Note: MS: Macroeconomic Stability; GIS: Government and Institutional Setting; FBMC: Financial, Businesses and Manpower Conditions; QLID: Quality of Life and Infrastructure Development.

2017 ACI Competitiveness Index: *What-if* Simulation Ranking and Scores

Overall Competitiveness

	Before	After
Rank	2	2
Score	1.723	2.099

Macroeconomic Stability

	Before	After
Rank	2	2
Score	2.496	2.496

Government and Institutional Setting

	Before	After
Rank	11	4
Score	0.506	0.974

Financial, Businesses and Manpower Conditions

	Before	After
Rank	2	2
Score	1.998	2.280

Quality of Life and Infrastructure Development

	Before	After
Rank	8	4
Score	0.706	1.285

Note: Ranking and scores after simulation are derived by improving the province's top-20% weakest indicators.

East Kalimantan (inc. North Kalimantan)

Kalimantan Region

2017 ACI Competitiveness Index: Ranking and Scores

2017 Overall Competitiveness Index

3rd

out of 33 provinces

std. score: 1.303

Macroeconomic Stability	Government and Institutional Setting
4th	**5th**
std. score: 0.830	std. score: 0.844

Financial, Businesses and Manpower Conditions	Quality of Life and Infrastructure Development
7th	**1st**
std. score: 0.575	std. score: 2.068

ACI Competitiveness Index Ranking: 2013–2017

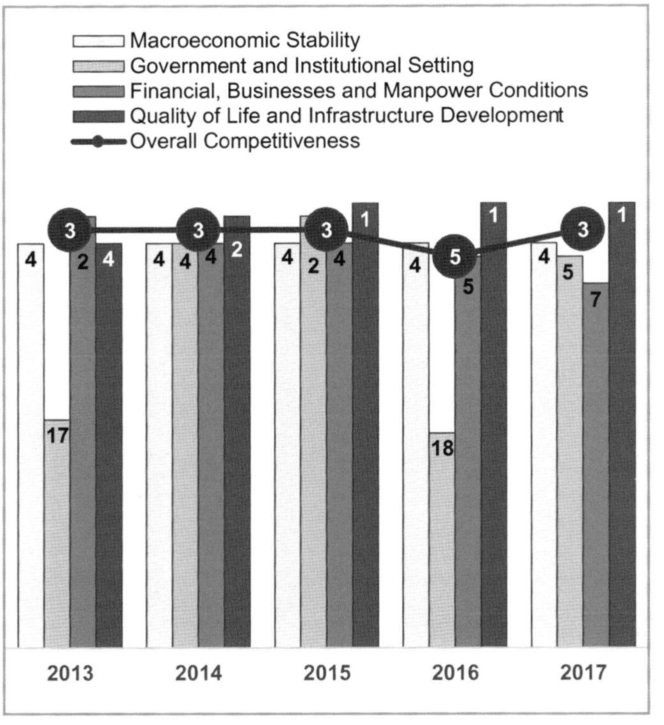

2017 ACI Competitiveness Index: Ranking and Scores by Sub-Environments

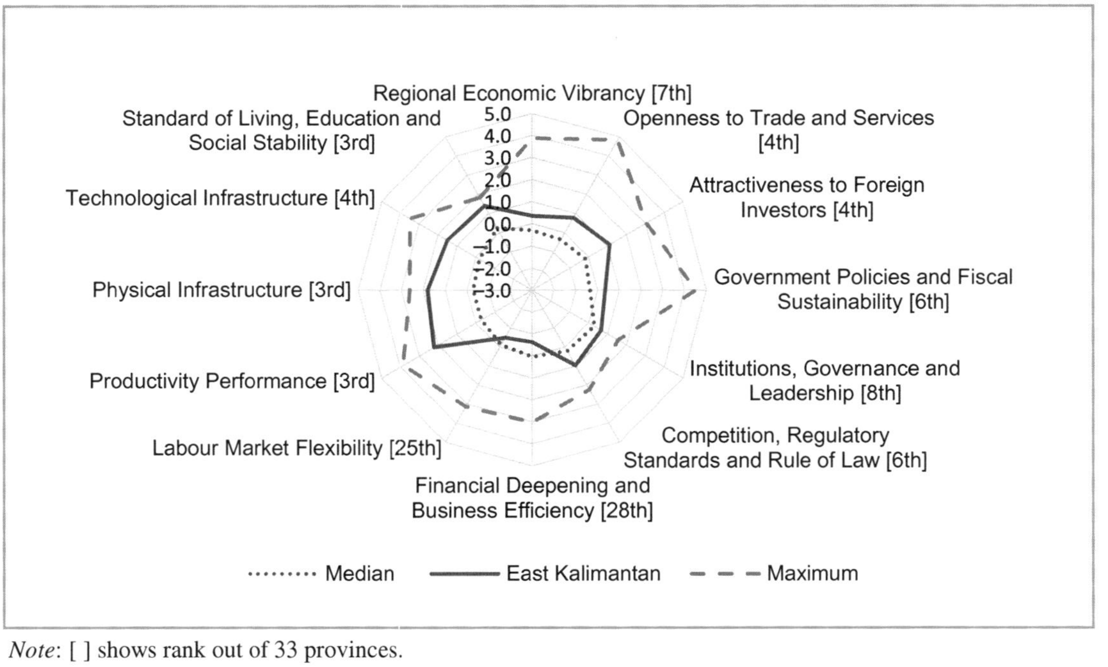

Note: [ ] shows rank out of 33 provinces.

East Kalimantan (inc. North Kalimantan)

Kalimantan Region

2017 ACI Competitiveness Index: Top-20% Strongest and Weakest Indicators

Rank	20% Strongest Indicators	Std. Score	Envmt.	Rank	20% Weakest Indicators	Std. Score	Envmt.
1	Cargo at international seaport	4.980	QLID	81	Population	–0.346	QLID
2	Primary industry productivity	3.472	FBMC	82	Labour force	–0.359	FBMC
3	GRDP of primary industry	2.769	MS	83	Employment	–0.366	FBMC
4	Secondary industry productivity	2.749	FBMC	84	Employment in secondary industry	–0.371	FBMC
5	GRDP per capita	2.579	MS	85	Employment in primary industry	–0.379	FBMC
6	Overall labour productivity	2.564	FBMC	86	Length of paved roads	–0.463	QLID
7	Laptop computer ownership	2.360	QLID	87	Firms' performance	–0.467	FBMC
8	Export	1.643	MS	88	Firms' human resource capacity	–0.475	FBMC
9	Households with pipe water services	1.590	QLID	89	Labour force participation rate	–0.484	FBMC
10	Security	1.590	GIS	90	Quality of physical infrastructure	–0.535	QLID
11	Population growth	1.558	QLID	91	Student–teacher ratio (junior high)	–0.541	QLID
12	Labour relations	1.511	FBMC	92	Firms' application of IT	–0.586	FBMC
13	Life expectancy at birth	1.461	QLID	93	Crime rate	–0.713	GIS
14	Human development index	1.407	QLID	94	Government efficiency	–0.788	GIS
15	Internet access in handphone	1.392	QLID	95	Unemployment rate	–0.955	FBMC
16	Internet access at home	1.349	QLID	96	Firms' innovation	–1.086	FBMC
17	Internet access at office	1.320	QLID	97	Inflation	–1.125	MS
18	Quality of technological infrastructure	1.312	QLID	98	Minimum wage per month	–1.181	FBMC
19	Population per number of bank branches/offices	1.270	FBMC	99	Non-performing loans per total bank loans	–2.112	FBMC
20	Quality of education	1.257	QLID	100	GRDP growth	–2.595	MS

Note: MS: Macroeconomic Stability; GIS: Government and Institutional Setting; FBMC: Financial, Businesses and Manpower Conditions; QLID: Quality of Life and Infrastructure Development.

2017 ACI Competitiveness Index: *What-if* Simulation Ranking and Scores

Overall Competitiveness	Before	After
Rank	**3**	**3**
Score	1.303	1.640

Macroeconomic Stability	Before	After
Rank	**4**	**4**
Score	0.830	1.025

Government and Institutional Setting	Before	After
Rank	**5**	**4**
Score	0.844	0.950

Financial, Businesses and Manpower Conditions	Before	After
Rank	**7**	**5**
Score	0.575	1.309

Quality of Life and Infrastructure Development	Before	After
Rank	**1**	**1**
Score	2.068	2.184

Note: Ranking and scores after simulation are derived by improving the province's top-20% weakest indicators.

East Nusa Tenggara

Bali-Nusa Tenggara Region

2017 ACI Competitiveness Index: Ranking and Scores

2017 Overall Competitiveness Index

30th

out of 33 provinces

std. score: –1.238

Macroeconomic Stability	Government and Institutional Setting
31st	**28th**
std. score: –0.865	std. score: –0.941

Financial, Businesses and Manpower Conditions	Quality of Life and Infrastructure Development
23rd	**32nd**
std. score: –0.522	std. score: –1.773

ACI Competitiveness Index Ranking: 2013–2017

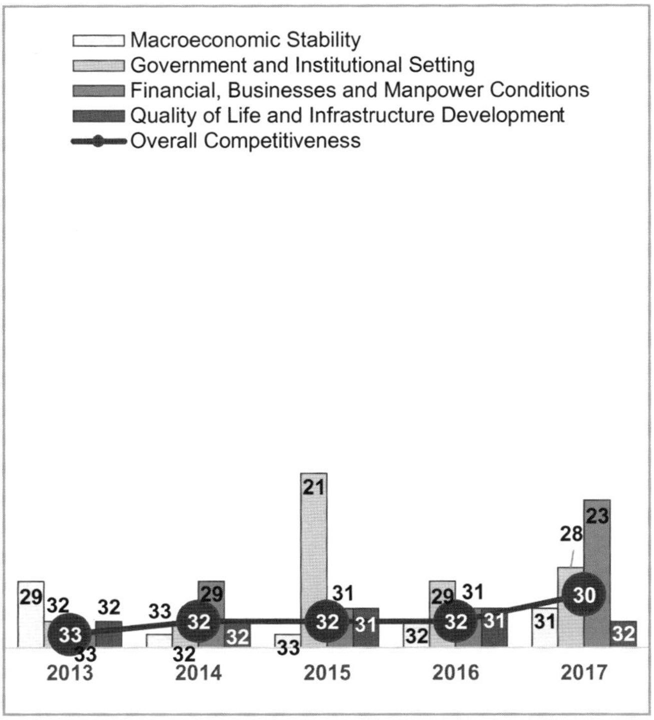

2017 ACI Competitiveness Index: Ranking and Scores by Sub-Environments

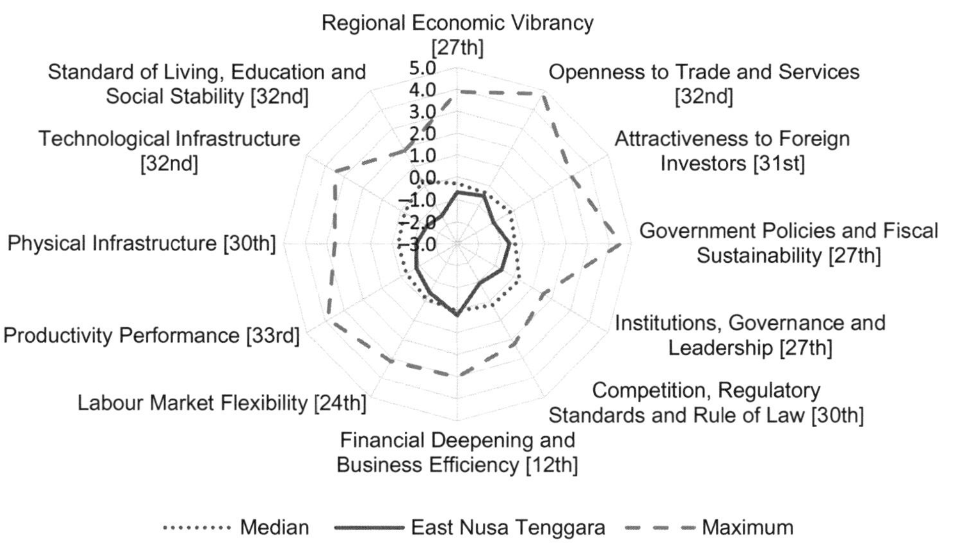

Note: [ ] shows rank out of 33 provinces.

East Nusa Tenggara
Bali-Nusa Tenggara Region

2017 ACI Competitiveness Index: Top-20% Strongest and Weakest Indicators

Rank	20% Strongest Indicators	Std. Score	Envmt.	Rank	20% Weakest Indicators	Std. Score	Envmt.
1	Ease of dealing with banks	1.837	FBMC	81	Life expectancy at birth	–1.205	QLID
2	Population per health facility	1.161	QLID	82	Regulatory governance	–1.223	GIS
3	Non-performing loans per total bank loans	1.129	FBMC	83	Mean years of schooling	–1.241	QLID
4	Minimum wage per month	1.107	FBMC	84	Internet access at school	–1.247	QLID
5	Unemployment rate	1.035	FBMC	85	Laptop computer ownership	–1.281	QLID
6	Lack of corruption	0.862	GIS	86	Urban population	–1.292	QLID
7	Crime rate	0.696	GIS	87	Internet access in handphone	–1.305	QLID
8	Fatalities due to natural disaster	0.457	QLID	88	Investment promotion and management	–1.317	MS
9	Firms' equipment capacity	0.452	FBMC	89	Net school enrolment rate (senior high)	–1.350	QLID
10	Registered motor vehicles per kilometre of paved road	0.446	QLID	90	Net school enrolment rate (junior high)	–1.355	QLID
11	Gini ratio	0.396	QLID	91	Human development index	–1.370	QLID
12	Non-performing loans	0.369	FBMC	92	Handphone ownership	–1.453	QLID
13	Inflation	0.307	MS	93	Coordination of local governments	–1.454	GIS
14	Households with pipe water services	0.288	QLID	94	Households with state electricity services	–1.510	QLID
15	Length of paved roads	0.187	QLID	95	Quality of healthcare	–1.522	QLID
16	Firms' innovation	0.138	FBMC	96	Quality of education	–1.613	QLID
17	Security	0.099	GIS	97	Government inclusiveness and accountability	–1.864	GIS
18	Employment in primary industry	0.075	FBMC	98	Quality of technological infrastructure	–1.866	QLID
19	Ease of acquiring property	–0.037	QLID	99	Quality of physical infrastructure	–2.021	QLID
20	Firms' performance	–0.066	FBMC	100	Labour relations	–2.782	FBMC

Note: MS: Macroeconomic Stability; GIS: Government and Institutional Setting; FBMC: Financial, Businesses and Manpower Conditions; QLID: Quality of Life and Infrastructure Development.

2017 ACI Competitiveness Index: *What-if* Simulation Ranking and Scores

Overall Competitiveness

	Before	After
Rank	30	26
Score	–1.238	–0.586

Macroeconomic Stability

	Before	After
Rank	31	28
Score	–0.865	–0.663

Government and Institutional Setting

	Before	After
Rank	28	24
Score	–0.941	–0.504

Financial, Businesses and Manpower Conditions

	Before	After
Rank	23	19
Score	–0.522	–0.289

Quality of Life and Infrastructure Development

	Before	After
Rank	32	26
Score	–1.773	–0.478

Note: Ranking and scores after simulation are derived by improving the province's top-20% weakest indicators.

Gorontalo
Sulawesi Region

2017 ACI Competitiveness Index: Ranking and Scores

2017 Overall Competitiveness Index

19th

out of 33 provinces

std. score: –0.298

Macroeconomic Stability	Government and Institutional Setting
25th	**13rd**
std. score: –0.523	std. score: 0.404

Financial, Businesses and Manpower Conditions	Quality of Life and Infrastructure Development
27th	**21st**
std. score: –0.755	std. score: –0.111

ACI Competitiveness Index Ranking: 2013–2017

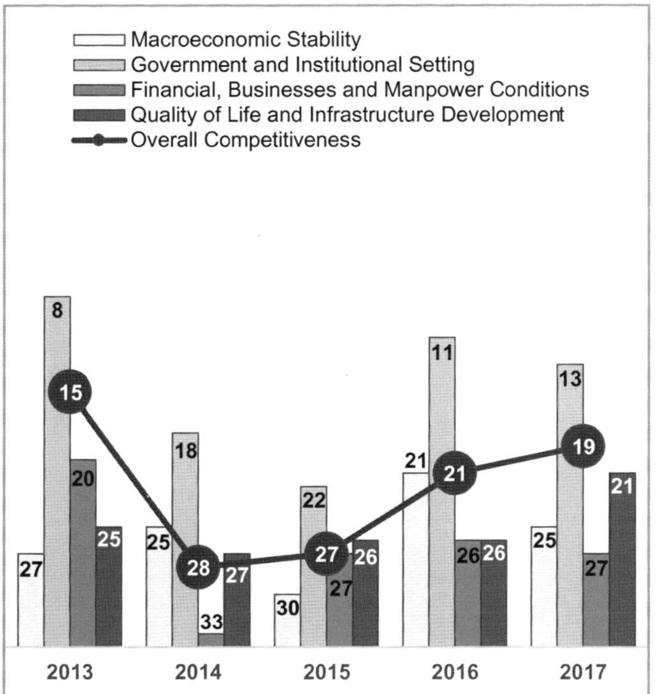

2017 ACI Competitiveness Index: Ranking and Scores by Sub-Environments

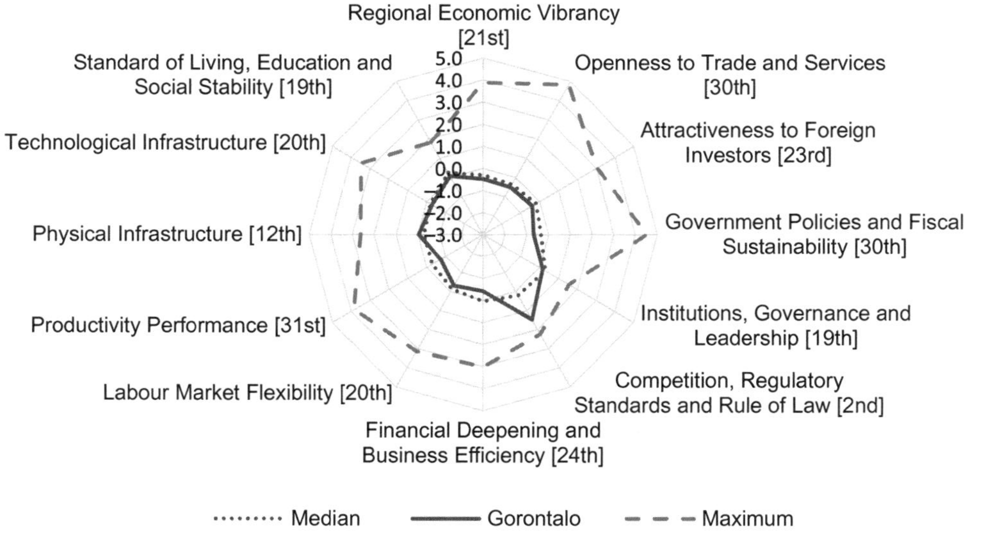

Note: [ ] shows rank out of 33 provinces.

Gorontalo
Sulawesi Region

2017 ACI Competitiveness Index: Top-20% Strongest and Weakest Indicators

Rank	20% Strongest Indicators	Std. Score	Envmt.	Rank	20% Weakest Indicators	Std. Score	Envmt.
1	Quality of education	1.796	QLID	81	GRDP per capita	–0.686	MS
2	Ease of acquiring property	1.463	QLID	82	Government expenditure	–0.692	GIS
3	Rule of law	1.431	GIS	83	Net school enrolment rate (senior high)	–0.702	QLID
4	Vibrancy of competition and collaboration	1.360	GIS	84	Labour force participation rate	–0.705	FBMC
5	GRDP growth	1.237	MS	85	Openness to trade	–0.711	MS
6	Firms' innovation	1.138	FBMC	86	Desktop computer ownership	–0.719	QLID
7	Regulatory governance	1.060	GIS	87	Number of bank branches/offices	–0.724	FBMC
8	Government inclusiveness and accountability	1.049	GIS	88	Tertiary industry productivity	–0.727	FBMC
9	Quality of physical infrastructure	1.047	QLID	89	Internet access at home	–0.759	QLID
10	Environmental quality index	1.025	QLID	90	Telephone ownership	–0.764	QLID
11	Government progress and expectation	1.021	GIS	91	Life expectancy at birth	–0.778	QLID
12	Student–teacher ratio (junior high)	0.922	QLID	92	GRDP of primary industry	–0.793	MS
13	Labour relations	0.721	FBMC	93	Tax revenue/Government revenue	–0.850	GIS
14	Coordination of local governments	0.715	GIS	94	Length of paved roads	–0.885	QLID
15	Unemployment rate	0.588	FBMC	95	Secondary industry productivity	–0.927	FBMC
16	Minimum wage per month	0.563	FBMC	96	Gini ratio	–0.966	QLID
17	Households with pipe water services	0.559	QLID	97	Mean years of schooling	–0.989	QLID
18	Affordability and accessibility of goods	0.555	QLID	98	Net school enrolment rate (junior high)	–0.992	QLID
19	Quality of technological infrastructure	0.553	QLID	99	Non-performing loans per total bank loans	–1.054	FBMC
20	Inflation	0.543	MS	100	Crime rate	–1.781	GIS

Note: MS: Macroeconomic Stability; GIS: Government and Institutional Setting; FBMC: Financial, Businesses and Manpower Conditions; QLID: Quality of Life and Infrastructure Development.

2017 ACI Competitiveness Index: *What-if* Simulation Ranking and Scores

Overall Competitiveness

	Before	After
Rank	19	14
Score	–0.298	0.077

Macroeconomic Stability

	Before	After
Rank	25	21
Score	–0.523	–0.387

Government and Institutional Setting

	Before	After
Rank	13	9
Score	0.404	0.674

Financial, Businesses and Manpower Conditions

	Before	After
Rank	27	21
Score	–0.755	–0.350

Quality of Life and Infrastructure Development

	Before	After
Rank	21	12
Score	–0.111	0.317

Note: Ranking and scores after simulation are derived by improving the province's top-20% weakest indicators.

Jambi
Sumatra Region

2017 ACI Competitiveness Index: Ranking and Scores

2017 Overall Competitiveness Index

18th

out of 33 provinces

std. score: –0.296

Macroeconomic Stability	Government and Institutional Setting
21st	**20th**
std. score: –0.429	std. score: –0.153

Financial, Businesses and Manpower Conditions	Quality of Life and Infrastructure Development
18th	**24th**
std. score: –0.161	std. score: –0.239

ACI Competitiveness Index Ranking: 2013–2017

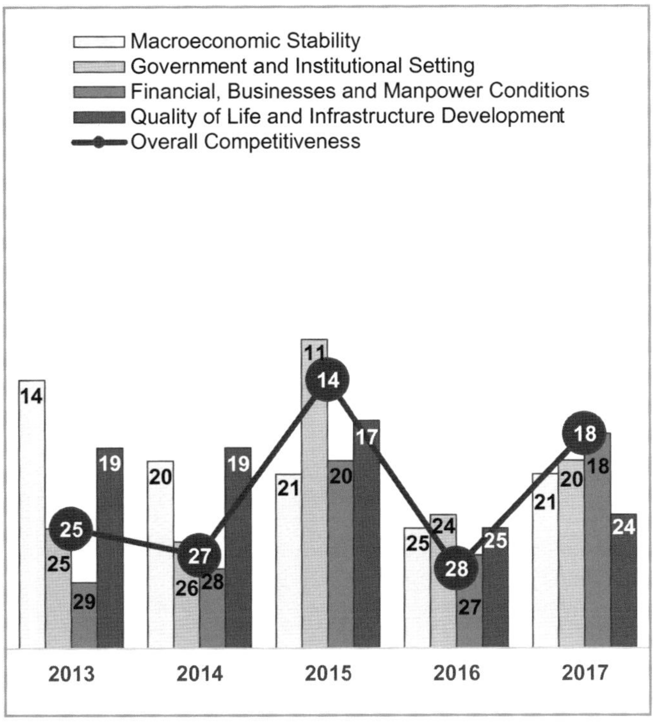

2017 ACI Competitiveness Index: Ranking and Scores by Sub-Environments

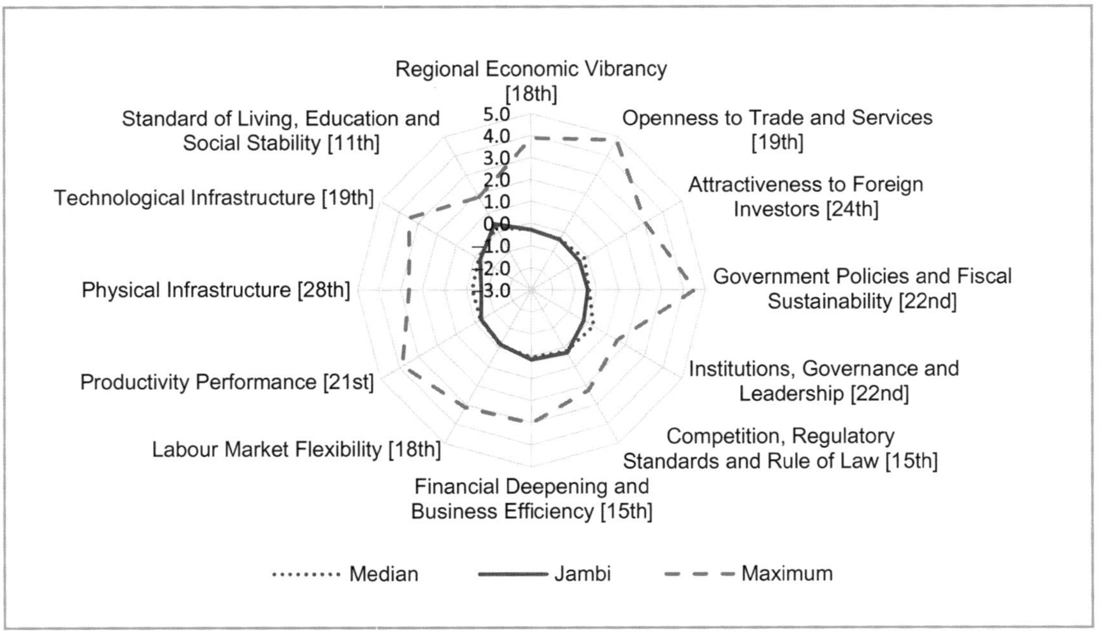

Note: [ ] shows rank out of 33 provinces.

Jambi
Sumatra Region

2017 ACI Competitiveness Index: Top-20% Strongest and Weakest Indicators

Rank	20% Strongest Indicators	Std. Score	Envmt.	Rank	20% Weakest Indicators	Std. Score	Envmt.
1	GRDP growth	1.291	MS	81	Employment in tertiary industry	–0.424	FBMC
2	Gini ratio	1.214	QLID	82	Employment in secondary industry	–0.439	FBMC
3	Vibrancy of competition and collaboration	1.206	GIS	83	Government revenue	–0.456	GIS
4	Labour relations	1.072	FBMC	84	Government expenditure	–0.457	GIS
5	Firms' human resource capacity	1.066	FBMC	85	GRDP, non-oil and gas	–0.460	MS
6	Student–teacher ratio (junior high)	0.749	QLID	86	Gross Regional Domestic Product (GRDP)	–0.471	MS
7	Firms' application of IT	0.646	FBMC	87	Tertiary industry productivity	–0.474	FBMC
8	Firms' performance	0.615	FBMC	88	Ease of dealing with banks	–0.489	FBMC
9	Handphone ownership	0.573	QLID	89	GRDP of secondary industry	–0.499	MS
10	Life expectancy at birth	0.538	QLID	90	Internet access at school	–0.507	QLID
11	Affordability and accessibility of goods	0.522	QLID	91	Gross domestic fixed capital formation	–0.507	MS
12	Student–teacher ratio (senior high)	0.516	QLID	92	Desktop computer ownership	–0.562	QLID
13	Firms' equipment capacity	0.453	FBMC	93	Foreign direct investment, last three year average	–0.578	MS
14	Adult illiteracy rate	0.443	QLID	94	Laptop computer ownership	–0.668	QLID
15	Fatalities due to natural disaster	0.426	QLID	95	Urban population	–0.710	QLID
16	Security	0.416	GIS	96	Crime rate	–0.713	GIS
17	Population per number of bank branches/offices	0.406	FBMC	97	Quality of healthcare	–0.818	QLID
18	Net school enrolment rate (primary)	0.383	QLID	98	Quality of education	–0.874	QLID
19	Net school enrolment rate (junior high)	0.359	QLID	99	Quality of physical infrastructure	–0.941	QLID
20	Population per medical worker	0.338	QLID	100	Firms' innovation	–1.089	FBMC

Note: MS: Macroeconomic Stability; GIS: Government and Institutional Setting; FBMC: Financial, Businesses and Manpower Conditions; QLID: Quality of Life and Infrastructure Development.

2017 ACI Competitiveness Index: *What-if* Simulation Ranking and Scores

Overall Competitiveness

	Before		After
Rank	**18**	→	**15**
Score	–0.296	→	–0.018

Macroeconomic Stability

	Before		After
Rank	**21**	→	**14**
Score	–0.429	→	–0.235

Government and Institutional Setting

	Before		After
Rank	**20**	→	**19**
Score	–0.153	→	–0.015

Financial, Businesses and Manpower Conditions

	Before		After
Rank	**18**	→	**11**
Score	–0.161	→	0.106

Quality of Life and Infrastructure Development

	Before		After
Rank	**24**	→	**15**
Score	–0.239	→	0.084

Note: Ranking and scores after simulation are derived by improving the province's top-20% weakest indicators.

Lampung
Sumatra Region

2017 ACI Competitiveness Index: Ranking and Scores

2017 Overall Competitiveness Index

14th

out of 33 provinces

std. score: 0.061

Macroeconomic Stability	Government and Institutional Setting
16th	**10th**
std. score: –0.274	std. score: 0.606

Financial, Businesses and Manpower Conditions	Quality of Life and Infrastructure Development
11th	**22nd**
std. score: 0.100	std. score: –0.228

ACI Competitiveness Index Ranking: 2013–2017

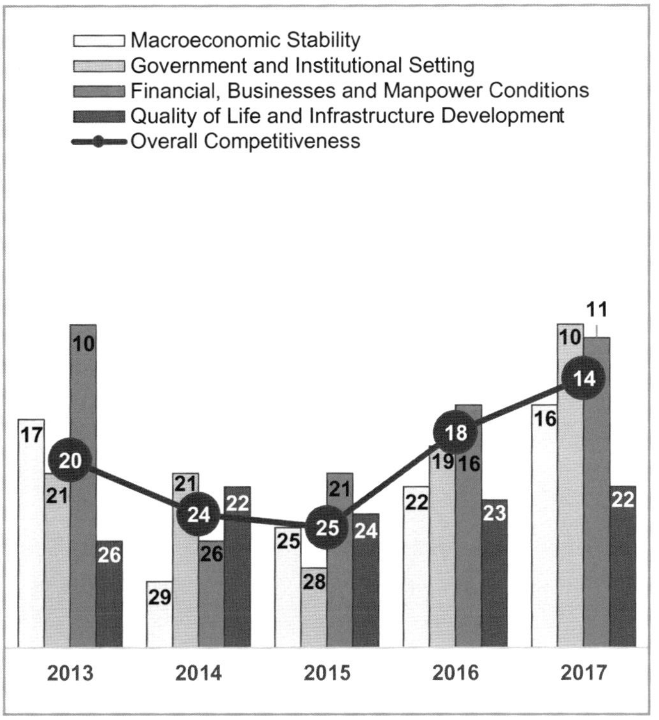

2017 ACI Competitiveness Index: Ranking and Scores by Sub-Environments

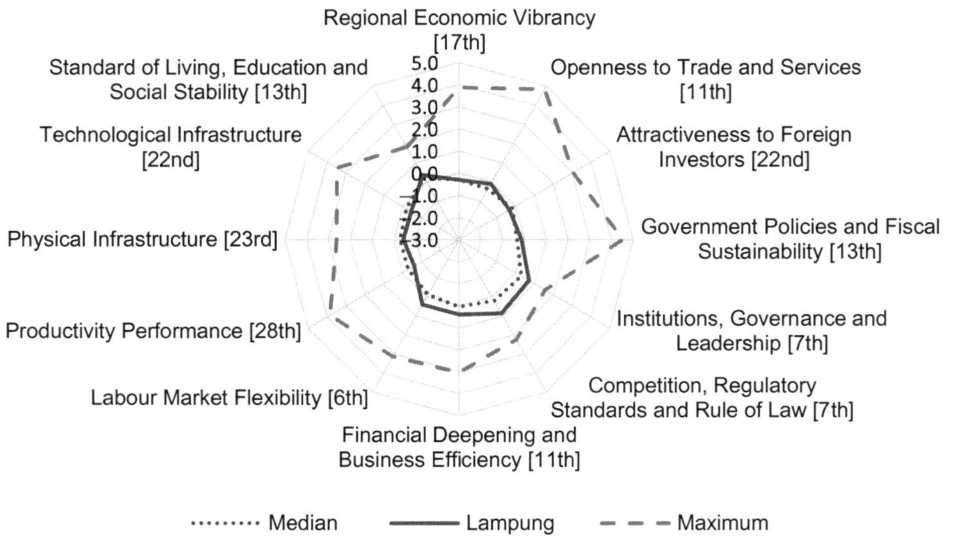

Note: [ ] shows rank out of 33 provinces.

Lampung

Sumatra Region

2017 ACI Competitiveness Index: Top-20% Strongest and Weakest Indicators

Rank	20% Strongest Indicators	Std. Score	Envmt.	Rank	20% Weakest Indicators	Std. Score	Envmt.
1	Quality of education	1.653	QLID	81	Net school enrolment rate (senior high)	–0.440	QLID
2	Government efficiency	1.646	GIS	82	Overall labour productivity, non-oil and gas	–0.461	FBMC
3	Firms' performance	1.544	FBMC	83	Internet access at home	–0.461	QLID
4	Labour relations	1.373	FBMC	84	Desktop computer ownership	–0.509	QLID
5	Ease of dealing with banks	1.201	FBMC	85	Mean years of schooling	–0.521	QLID
6	Quality of healthcare	1.163	QLID	86	Secondary industry productivity	–0.548	FBMC
7	Quality of technological infrastructure	1.153	QLID	87	GRDP per capita	–0.550	MS
8	Crime rate	1.152	GIS	88	Overall labour productivity	–0.557	FBMC
9	Regulatory governance	0.986	GIS	89	Foreign direct investment, last three year average	–0.559	MS
10	Firms' human resource capacity	0.914	FBMC	90	Student–teacher ratio (primary)	–0.566	QLID
11	Student–teacher ratio (senior high)	0.834	QLID	91	Tertiary industry productivity	–0.706	FBMC
12	Vibrancy of competition and collaboration	0.801	GIS	92	Environmental quality index	–0.758	QLID
13	Affordability and accessibility of goods	0.784	QLID	93	Internet access in handphone	–0.878	QLID
14	Gini ratio	0.669	QLID	94	Population growth	–0.901	QLID
15	Provincial governing capacity	0.649	GIS	95	Urban population	–0.928	QLID
16	Net school enrolment rate (primary)	0.622	QLID	96	Internet access at office	–0.930	QLID
17	Quality of physical infrastructure	0.592	QLID	97	Laptop computer ownership	–1.391	QLID
18	Government inclusiveness and accountability	0.554	GIS	98	Households with pipe water services	–1.393	QLID
19	Firms' equipment capacity	0.541	FBMC	99	Population per medical worker	–1.757	QLID
20	Student–teacher ratio (junior high)	0.535	QLID	100	Population per number of bank branches/offices	–2.607	FBMC

Note: MS: Macroeconomic Stability; GIS: Government and Institutional Setting; FBMC: Financial, Businesses and Manpower Conditions; QLID: Quality of Life and Infrastructure Development.

2017 ACI Competitiveness Index: *What-if* Simulation Ranking and Scores

Overall Competitiveness	Before	After
Rank	**14**	**9**
Score	0.061	0.457

Macroeconomic Stability	Before	After
Rank	**16**	**13**
Score	–0.274	–0.158

Government and Institutional Setting	Before	After
Rank	**10**	**10**
Score	0.606	0.606

Financial, Businesses and Manpower Conditions	Before	After
Rank	**11**	**7**
Score	0.100	0.586

Quality of Life and Infrastructure Development	Before	After
Rank	**22**	**10**
Score	–0.228	0.481

Note: Ranking and scores after simulation are derived by improving the province's top-20% weakest indicators.

Maluku

Maluku-Papua Region

2017 ACI Competitiveness Index: Ranking and Scores

2017 Overall Competitiveness Index

29th

out of 33 provinces

std. score: –0.712

Macroeconomic Stability	Government and Institutional Setting
29th	**21st**
std. score: –0.673	std. score: –0.167

Financial, Businesses and Manpower Conditions	Quality of Life and Infrastructure Development
29th	**27th**
std. score: –1.083	std. score: –0.435

ACI Competitiveness Index Ranking: 2013–2017

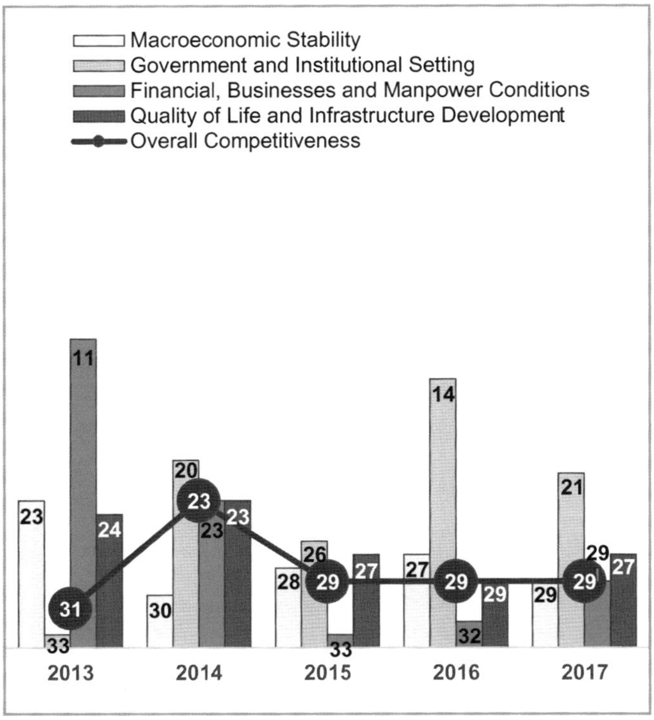

2017 ACI Competitiveness Index: Ranking and Scores by Sub-Environments

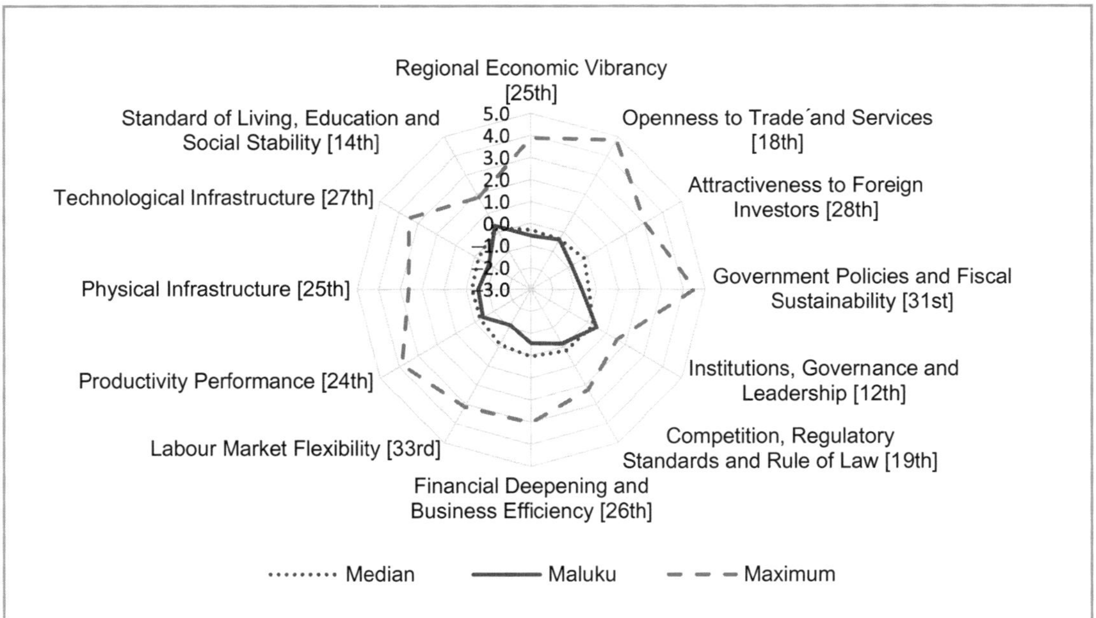

Note: [ ] shows rank out of 33 provinces.

Maluku

Maluku-Papua Region

2017 ACI Competitiveness Index: Top-20% Strongest and Weakest Indicators

Rank	20% Strongest Indicators	Std. Score	Envmt.	Rank	20% Weakest Indicators	Std. Score	Envmt.
1	Mean years of schooling	1.238	QLID	81	GRDP per capita	–0.626	MS
2	Government progress and expectation	1.094	GIS	82	Gross Regional Domestic Product (GRDP)	–0.628	MS
3	Population per medical worker	1.089	QLID	83	Length of paved roads	–0.628	QLID
4	Government efficiency	1.069	GIS	84	Internet access at home	–0.634	QLID
5	Environmental quality index	0.957	QLID	85	Internet access in handphone	–0.661	QLID
6	GRDP growth	0.793	MS	86	Firms' application of IT	–0.671	FBMC
7	Non-performing loans per total bank loans	0.779	FBMC	87	Quality of technological infrastructure	–0.692	QLID
8	Coordination of local governments	0.699	GIS	88	Investment promotion and management	–0.759	MS
9	Population per health facility	0.688	QLID	89	GRDP of primary industry	–0.767	MS
10	Provincial governing capacity	0.688	GIS	90	Handphone ownership	–0.832	QLID
11	Households with pipe water services	0.680	QLID	91	Ease of acquiring property	–0.873	QLID
12	Gini ratio	0.669	QLID	92	Lack of corruption	–0.964	GIS
13	Security	0.664	GIS	93	Internet access at school	–1.149	QLID
14	Adult illiteracy rate	0.630	QLID	94	Tax revenue/Government revenue	–1.154	GIS
15	Population per number of bank branches/offices	0.558	FBMC	95	Government inclusiveness and accountability	–1.154	GIS
16	Student–teacher ratio (primary)	0.511	QLID	96	Firms' performance	–1.195	FBMC
17	Crime rate	0.511	GIS	97	Life expectancy at birth	–1.551	QLID
18	Vibrancy of competition and collaboration	0.461	GIS	98	Ease of dealing with banks	–1.593	FBMC
19	Registered motor vehicles per kilometre of paved road	0.435	QLID	99	Labour force participation rate	–1.878	FBMC
20	Fatalities due to natural disaster	0.426	QLID	100	Unemployment rate	–2.466	FBMC

Note: MS: Macroeconomic Stability; GIS: Government and Institutional Setting; FBMC: Financial, Businesses and Manpower Conditions; QLID: Quality of Life and Infrastructure Development.

2017 ACI Competitiveness Index: *What-if* Simulation Ranking and Scores

Overall Competitiveness	Before	After
Rank	29	17
Score	–0.712	–0.235

Macroeconomic Stability	Before	After	Government and Institutional Setting	Before	After
Rank	29	23	Rank	21	19
Score	–0.673	–0.448	Score	–0.167	0.092

Financial, Businesses and Manpower Conditions	Before	After	Quality of Life and Infrastructure Development	Before	After
Rank	29	23	Rank	27	15
Score	–1.083	–0.416	Score	–0.435	–0.006

Note: Ranking and scores after simulation are derived by improving the province's top-20% weakest indicators.

North Maluku

Maluku-Papua Region

2017 ACI Competitiveness Index: Ranking and Scores

2017 Overall Competitiveness Index

31st

out of 33 provinces

std. score: –1.304

Macroeconomic Stability	Government and Institutional Setting
33rd	**31st**
std. score: –1.132	std. score: –1.510

Financial, Businesses and Manpower Conditions	Quality of Life and Infrastructure Development
28th	**28th**
std. score: –0.807	std. score: –0.870

ACI Competitiveness Index Ranking: 2013–2017

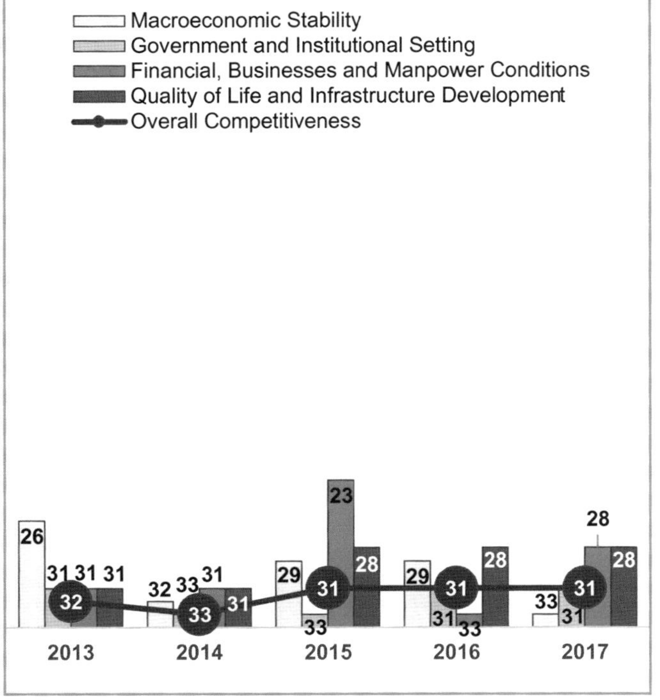

2017 ACI Competitiveness Index: Ranking and Scores by Sub-Environments

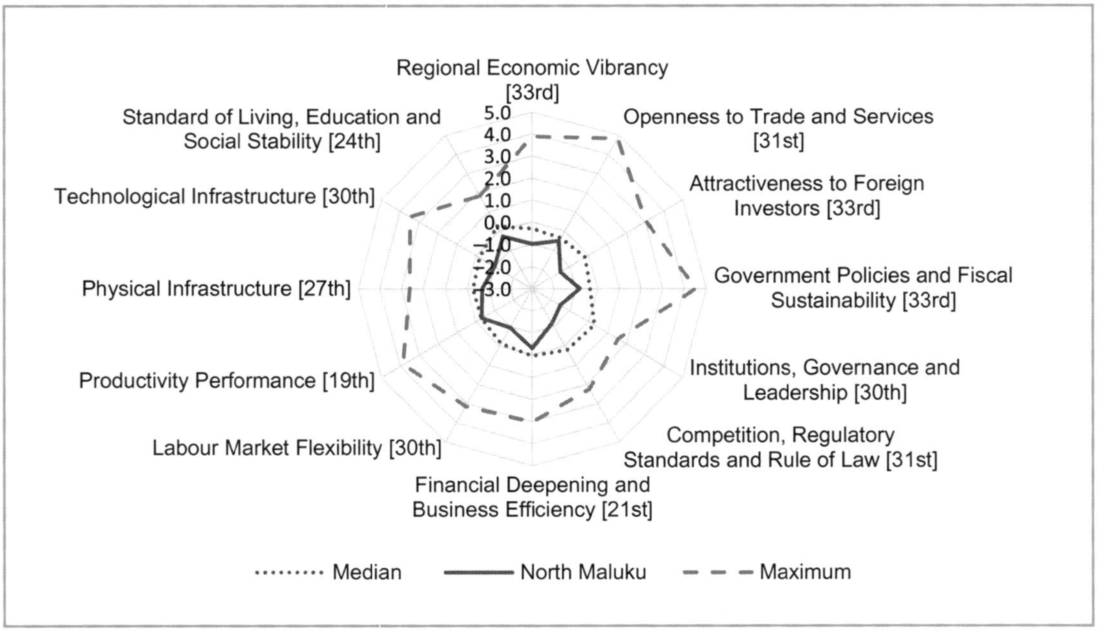

Note: [ ] shows rank out of 33 provinces.

North Maluku

Maluku-Papua Region

2017 ACI Competitiveness Index: Top-20% Strongest and Weakest Indicators

Rank	20% Strongest Indicators	Std. Score	Envmt.	Rank	20% Weakest Indicators	Std. Score	Envmt.
1	Gini ratio	1.487	QLID	81	Rule of law	–0.970	GIS
2	Environmental quality index	1.184	QLID	82	Internet access at home	–1.003	QLID
3	Crime rate	1.123	GIS	83	Vibrancy of competition and collaboration	–1.049	GIS
4	Households with pipe water services	1.101	QLID	84	Regulatory governance	–1.064	GIS
5	Population per medical worker	1.052	QLID	85	Internet access in handphone	–1.402	QLID
6	Population growth	0.792	QLID	86	Labour force participation rate	–1.404	FBMC
7	Firms' equipment capacity	0.746	FBMC	87	Tax revenue/Government revenue	–1.493	GIS
8	Population per health facility	0.743	QLID	88	Government inclusiveness and accountability	–1.503	GIS
9	Registered motor vehicles per kilometre of paved road	0.588	QLID	89	Lack of corruption	–1.511	GIS
10	Adult illiteracy rate	0.554	QLID	90	Labour relations	–1.538	FBMC
11	Fatalities due to natural disaster	0.520	QLID	91	Quality of education	–1.719	QLID
12	Population per number of bank branches/offices	0.464	FBMC	92	Quality of technological infrastructure	–1.781	QLID
13	Net school enrolment rate (senior high)	0.462	QLID	93	Coordination of local governments	–1.801	GIS
14	Mean years of schooling	0.416	QLID	94	Student–teacher ratio (primary)	–1.897	QLID
15	Non-performing loans	0.386	FBMC	95	Quality of healthcare	–2.009	QLID
16	Student–teacher ratio (senior high)	0.347	QLID	96	Provincial governing capacity	–2.118	GIS
17	Non-performing loans per total bank loans	0.289	FBMC	97	Inflation	–2.183	MS
18	Tertiary industry productivity	0.231	FBMC	98	Government progress and expectation	–2.261	GIS
19	Minimum wage per month	0.203	FBMC	99	Investment promotion and management	–2.496	MS
20	Firms' human resource capacity	0.154	FBMC	100	Affordability and accessibility of goods	–2.570	QLID

Note: MS: Macroeconomic Stability; GIS: Government and Institutional Setting; FBMC: Financial, Businesses and Manpower Conditions; QLID: Quality of Life and Infrastructure Development.

2017 ACI Competitiveness Index: *What–if* Simulation Ranking and Scores

Overall Competitiveness

	Before		After
Rank	31	→	25
Score	–1.304	→	–0.492

Macroeconomic Stability

	Before		After
Rank	33	→	27
Score	–1.132	→	–0.633

Government and Institutional Setting

	Before		After
Rank	31	→	21
Score	–1.510	→	–0.207

Financial, Businesses and Manpower Conditions

	Before		After
Rank	28	→	24
Score	–0.807	→	–0.563

Quality of Life and Infrastructure Development

	Before		After
Rank	28	→	22
Score	–0.870	→	–0.217

Note: Ranking and scores after simulation are derived by improving the province's top-20% weakest indicators.

North Sulawesi
Sulawesi Region

2017 ACI Competitiveness Index: Ranking and Scores

2017 Overall Competitiveness Index

17th

out of 33 provinces

std. score: –0.270

Macroeconomic Stability	Government and Institutional Setting
13th	**12th**
std. score: –0.189	std. score: 0.431
Financial, Businesses and Manpower Conditions	**Quality of Life and Infrastructure Development**
30th	**15th**
std. score: –1.134	std. score: –0.001

ACI Competitiveness Index Ranking: 2013–2017

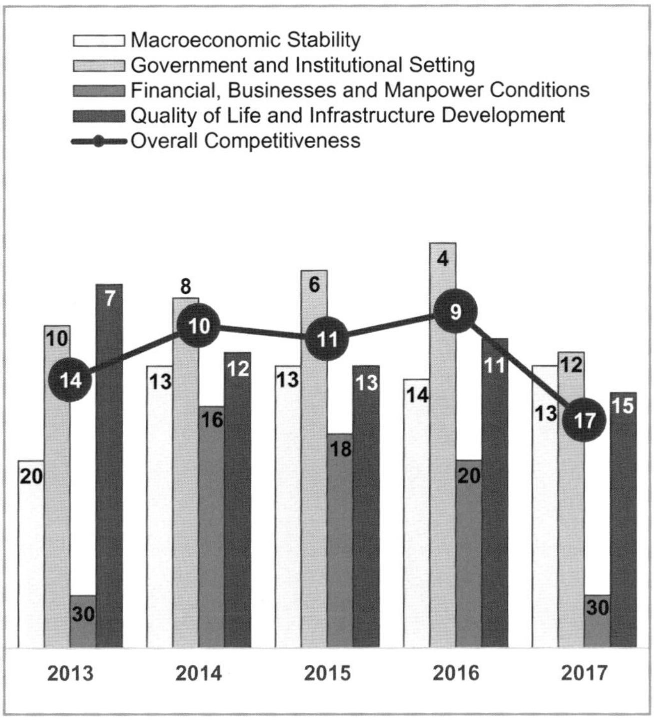

2017 ACI Competitiveness Index: Ranking and Scores by Sub-Environments

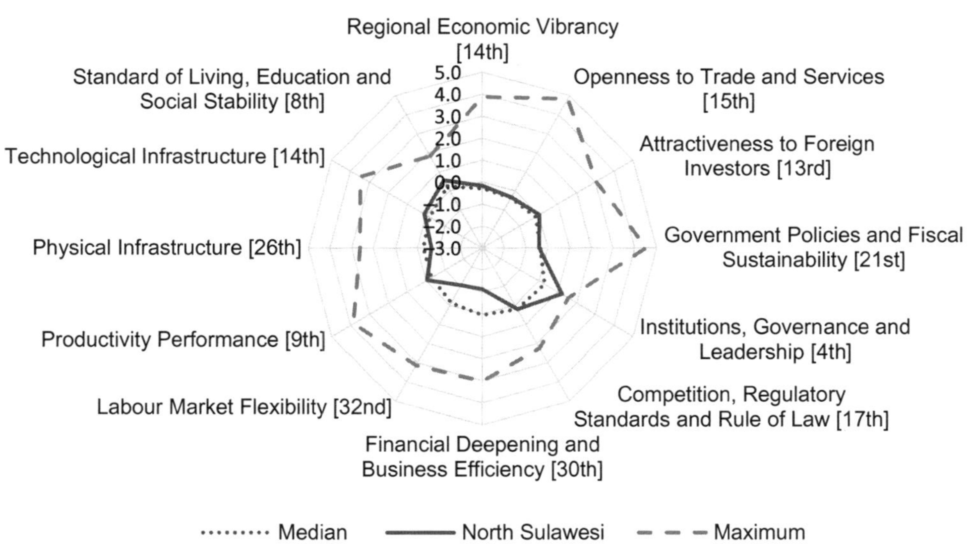

Note: [ ] shows rank out of 33 provinces.

North Sulawesi
Sulawesi Region

2017 ACI Competitiveness Index: Top-20% Strongest and Weakest Indicators

Rank	20% Strongest Indicators	Std. Score	Envmt.	Rank	20% Weakest Indicators	Std. Score	Envmt.
1	Student–teacher ratio (primary)	1.779	QLID	81	Government revenue	–0.525	GIS
2	Government progress and expectation	1.371	GIS	82	Government expenditure	–0.551	GIS
3	Coordination of local governments	1.294	GIS	83	Labour relations	–0.557	FBMC
4	Government efficiency	1.234	GIS	84	Domestic direct investment, last three year average	–0.561	MS
5	Investment promotion and management	1.159	MS	85	GRDP of primary industry	–0.562	MS
6	Inflation	1.080	MS	86	Employment in primary industry	–0.574	FBMC
7	Security	1.059	GIS	87	Foreign direct investment, last three year average	–0.579	MS
8	Government inclusiveness and accountability	1.057	GIS	88	Non-performing loans per total bank loans	–0.588	FBMC
9	Provincial governing capacity	1.033	GIS	89	Firms' innovation	–0.673	FBMC
10	Quality of education	1.028	QLID	90	Net school enrolment rate (primary)	–0.688	QLID
11	Population per number of bank branches/offices	1.022	FBMC	91	Labour force participation rate	–0.809	FBMC
12	Lack of corruption	0.940	GIS	92	Firms' application of IT	–0.917	FBMC
13	Net school enrolment rate (senior high)	0.907	QLID	93	Unemployment rate	–1.033	FBMC
14	Mean years of schooling	0.850	QLID	94	Population growth	–1.062	QLID
15	Households with state electricity services	0.820	QLID	95	Crime rate	–1.183	GIS
16	Internet access in handphone	0.779	QLID	96	Minimum wage per month	–1.223	FBMC
17	Life expectancy at birth	0.730	QLID	97	Gini ratio	–1.239	QLID
18	Population per medical worker	0.632	QLID	98	Student–teacher ratio (senior high)	–1.544	QLID
19	Quality of healthcare	0.617	QLID	99	Firms' performance	–1.863	FBMC
20	Adult illiteracy rate	0.593	QLID	100	Firms' equipment capacity	–2.585	FBMC

Note: MS: Macroeconomic Stability; GIS: Government and Institutional Setting;
FBMC: Financial, Businesses and Manpower Conditions; QLID: Quality of Life and Infrastructure Development.

2017 ACI Competitiveness Index: *What-if* Simulation Ranking and Scores

Overall Competitiveness

	Before		After
Rank	**17**	→	**13**
Score	–0.270	→	0.210

Macroeconomic Stability	Before		After	Government and Institutional Setting	Before		After
Rank	**13**	→	**11**	Rank	**12**	→	**10**
Score	–0.189	→	0.017	Score	0.431	→	0.613

Financial, Businesses and Manpower Conditions	Before		After	Quality of Life and Infrastructure Development	Before		After
Rank	**30**	→	**19**	Rank	**15**	→	**13**
Score	–1.134	→	–0.193	Score	–0.001	→	0.261

Note: Ranking and scores after simulation are derived by improving the province's top-20% weakest indicators.

North Sumatra

Sumatra Region

2017 ACI Competitiveness Index: Ranking and Scores

2017 Overall Competitiveness Index

20th

out of 33 provinces

std. score: –0.304

Macroeconomic Stability	**Government and Institutional Setting**
9th	**30th**
std. score: 0.090	std. score: –1.019

Financial, Businesses and Manpower Conditions	**Quality of Life and Infrastructure Development**
15th	**16th**
std. score: –0.039	std. score: –0.040

ACI Competitiveness Index Ranking: 2013–2017

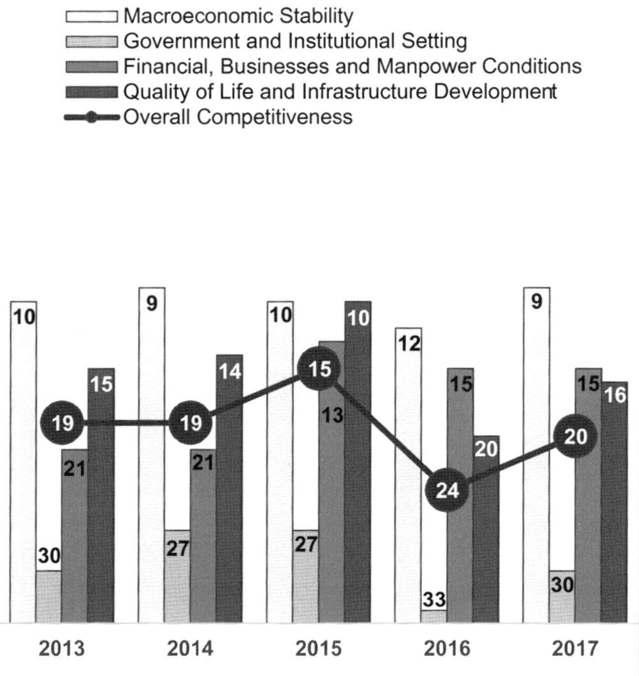

2017 ACI Competitiveness Index: Ranking and Scores by Sub-Environments

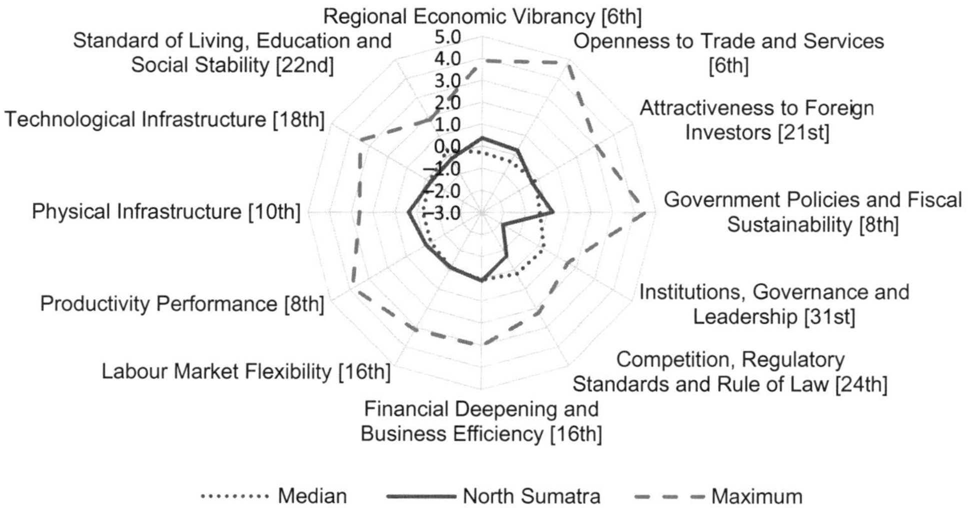

Note: [ ] shows rank out of 33 provinces.

North Sumatra
Sumatra Region

2017 ACI Competitiveness Index: Top-20% Strongest and Weakest Indicators

Rank	20% Strongest Indicators	Std. Score	Envmt.	Rank	20% Weakest Indicators	Std. Score	Envmt.
1	Length of paved roads	1.817	QLID	81	Quality of healthcare	–0.550	QLID
2	Gini ratio	1.487	QLID	82	Ease of acquiring property	–0.576	QLID
3	Firms' performance	1.262	FBMC	83	Rule of law	–0.639	GIS
4	Tax revenue/Government revenue	1.039	GIS	84	Student–teacher ratio (primary)	–0.639	QLID
5	Mean years of schooling	0.976	QLID	85	Internet access at office	–0.653	QLID
6	Employment in primary industry	0.851	FBMC	86	Security	–0.654	GIS
7	GRDP of primary industry	0.812	MS	87	Population growth	–0.670	QLID
8	Adult illiteracy rate	0.786	QLID	88	Investment promotion and management	–0.695	MS
9	Number of bank branches/offices	0.710	FBMC	89	Ease of dealing with banks	–0.761	FBMC
10	Households with pipe water services	0.601	QLID	90	Quality of education	–1.178	QLID
11	Population	0.577	QLID	91	Quality of physical infrastructure	–1.202	QLID
12	Export, non-oil and gas	0.540	MS	92	Provincial governing capacity	–1.204	GIS
13	GRDP, non-oil and gas	0.524	MS	93	Crime rate	–1.254	GIS
14	Households with state electricity services	0.509	QLID	94	Regulatory governance	–1.287	GIS
15	Labour force	0.492	FBMC	95	Coordination of local governments	–1.432	GIS
16	Employment	0.491	FBMC	96	Government inclusiveness and accountability	–1.545	GIS
17	Affordability and accessibility of goods	0.455	QLID	97	Student–teacher ratio (senior high)	–1.929	QLID
18	Gross Regional Domestic Product (GRDP)	0.450	MS	98	Government progress and expectation	–1.978	GIS
19	Export	0.422	MS	99	Government efficiency	–2.116	GIS
20	Gross domestic fixed capital formation	0.417	MS	100	Labour relations	–2.200	FBMC

Note: MS: Macroeconomic Stability; GIS: Government and Institutional Setting; FBMC: Financial, Businesses and Manpower Conditions; QLID: Quality of Life and Infrastructure Development.

2017 ACI Competitiveness Index: *What-if* Simulation Ranking and Scores

Overall Competitiveness

	Before		After
Rank	20	→	13
Score	–0.304	→	0.260

Macroeconomic Stability	Before		After	Government and Institutional Setting	Before		After
Rank	9	→	8	Rank	30	→	19
Score	0.090	→	0.198	Score	–1.019	→	0.034

Financial, Businesses and Manpower Conditions	Before		After	Quality of Life and Infrastructure Development	Before		After
Rank	15	→	11	Rank	16	→	10
Score	–0.039	→	0.214	Score	–0.040	→	0.418

Note: Ranking and scores after simulation are derived by improving the province's top-20% weakest indicators.

Papua

Maluku-Papua Region

2017 ACI Competitiveness Index: Ranking and Scores

2017 Overall Competitiveness Index

32nd

out of 33 provinces

std. score: –1.706

Macroeconomic Stability	Government and Institutional Setting
17th	**29th**
std. score: –0.341	std. score: –0.956

Financial, Businesses and Manpower Conditions	Quality of Life and Infrastructure Development
32nd	**33rd**
std. score: –1.241	std. score: –3.111

ACI Competitiveness Index Ranking: 2013–2017

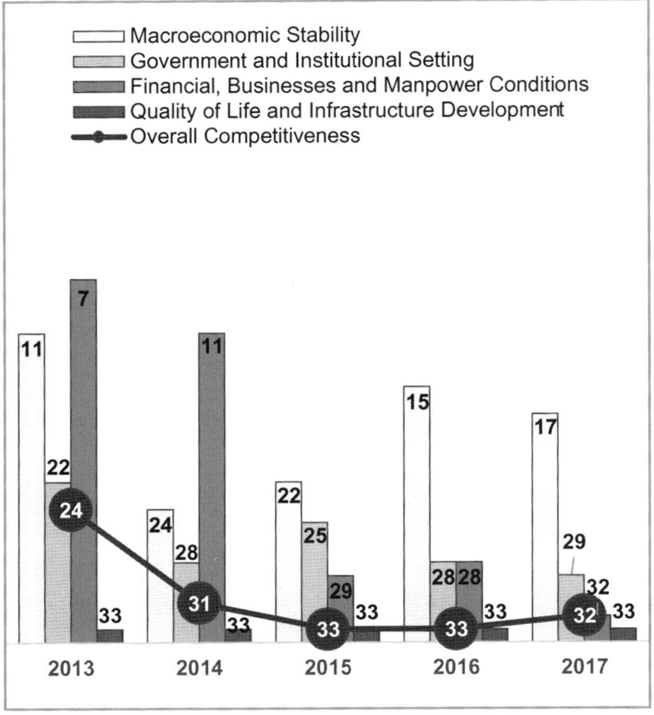

2017 ACI Competitiveness Index: Ranking and Scores by Sub-Environments

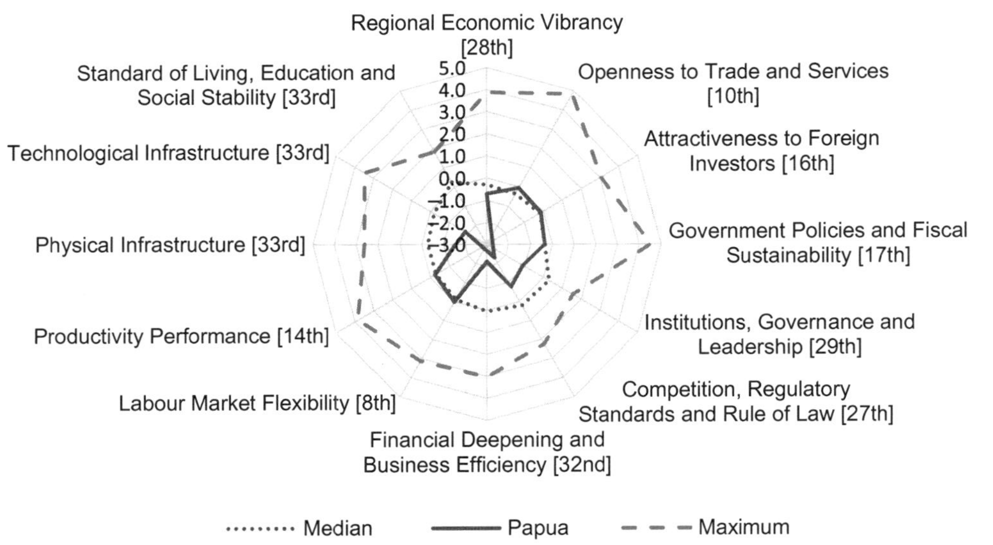

Note: [ ] shows rank out of 33 provinces.

Papua

Maluku-Papua Region

2017 ACI Competitiveness Index: Top-20% Strongest and Weakest Indicators

Rank	20% Strongest Indicators	Std. Score	Envmt.	Rank	20% Weakest Indicators	Std. Score	Envmt.
1	Labour force participation rate	1.875	FBMC	81	Internet access at school	–1.529	QLID
2	Environmental quality index	1.504	QLID	82	Life expectancy at birth	–1.613	QLID
3	Unemployment rate	0.946	FBMC	83	Firms' performance	–1.621	FBMC
4	Openness to trade	0.794	MS	84	Affordability and accessibility of goods	–1.626	QLID
5	Government efficiency	0.610	GIS	85	Internet access in handphone	–1.662	QLID
6	Population per number of bank branches/offices	0.535	FBMC	86	Firms' human resource capacity	–1.689	FBMC
7	Foreign direct investment, last three year average	0.501	MS	87	Tax revenue/Government revenue	–1.752	GIS
8	Registered motor vehicles per kilometre of paved road	0.490	QLID	88	Firms' innovation	–2.151	FBMC
9	Secondary industry productivity	0.460	FBMC	89	Student–teacher ratio (primary)	–2.348	QLID
10	Population growth	0.400	QLID	90	Student–teacher ratio (junior high)	–2.464	QLID
11	Labour relations	0.375	FBMC	91	Mean years of schooling	–2.497	QLID
12	Government expenditure	0.364	GIS	92	Security	–2.574	GIS
13	Government revenue	0.321	GIS	93	Human development index	–2.694	QLID
14	Non-performing loans	0.287	FBMC	94	Net school enrolment rate (senior high)	–2.846	QLID
15	Tertiary industry productivity	0.107	FBMC	95	Firms' equipment capacity	–3.143	FBMC
16	Regulatory governance	0.033	GIS	96	Net school enrolment rate (junior high)	–3.174	QLID
17	Population per health facility	–0.003	QLID	97	Households with state electricity services	–3.636	QLID
18	Inflation	–0.009	MS	98	Handphone ownership	–4.458	QLID
19	Fiscal balance	–0.021	GIS	99	Adult illiteracy rate	–4.616	QLID
20	Employment in primary industry	–0.041	FBMC	100	Net school enrolment rate (primary)	–5.013	QLID

Note: MS: Macroeconomic Stability; GIS: Government and Institutional Setting; FBMC: Financial, Businesses and Manpower Conditions; QLID: Quality of Life and Infrastructure Development.

2017 ACI Competitiveness Index: *What-if* Simulation Ranking and Scores

Overall Competitiveness	Before	After
Rank	32	28
Score	–1.706	–0.725

Macroeconomic Stability	Before	After
Rank	17	17
Score	–0.341	–0.341

Government and Institutional Setting	Before	After
Rank	29	25
Score	–0.956	–0.606

Financial, Businesses and Manpower Conditions	Before	After
Rank	32	23
Score	–1.241	–0.484

Quality of Life and Infrastructure Development	Before	After
Rank	33	28
Score	–3.111	–0.962

Note: Ranking and scores after simulation are derived by improving the province's top-20% weakest indicators.

Riau

Sumatra Region

2017 ACI Competitiveness Index: Ranking and Scores

2017 Overall Competitiveness Index

16th

out of 33 provinces

std. score: –0.093

Macroeconomic Stability	Government and Institutional Setting
11th	**22nd**
std. score: 0.019	std. score: –0.174

Financial, Businesses and Manpower Conditions	Quality of Life and Infrastructure Development
22nd	**13th**
std. score: –0.364	std. score: 0.213

ACI Competitiveness Index Ranking: 2013–2017

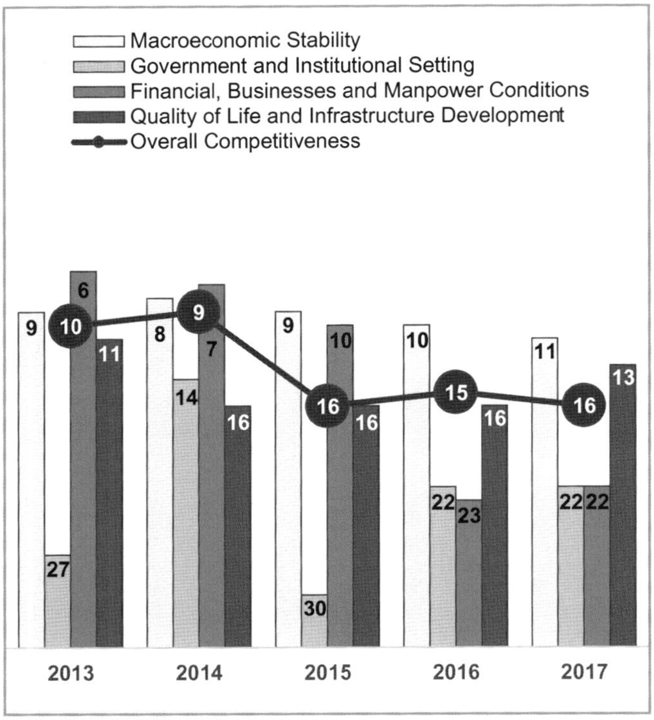

2017 ACI Competitiveness Index: Ranking and Scores by Sub-Environments

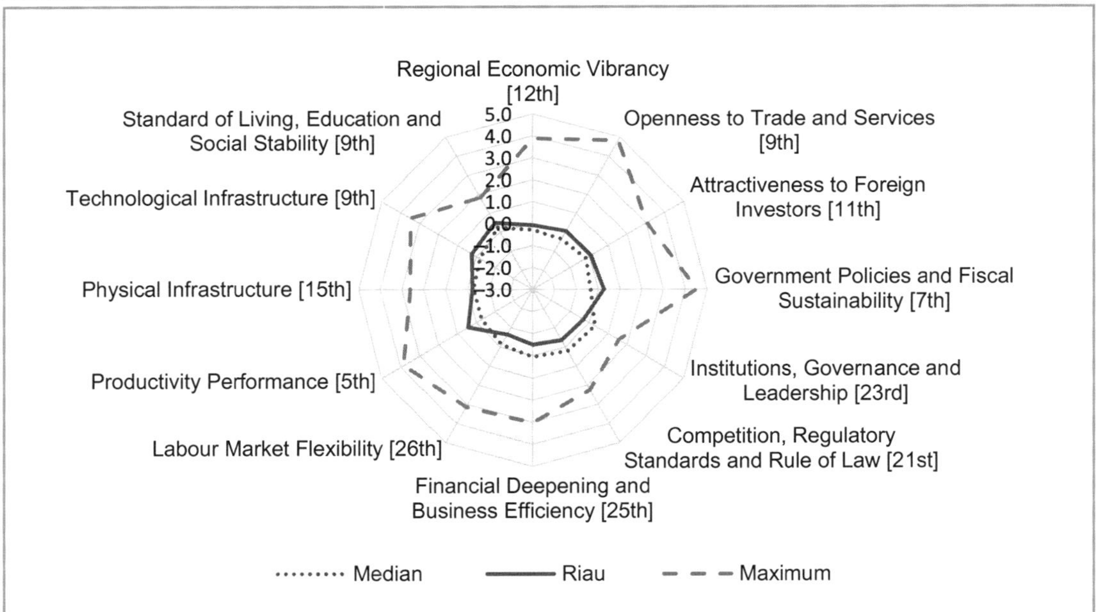

Note: [ ] shows rank out of 33 provinces.

Riau

Sumatra Region

2017 ACI Competitiveness Index: Top-20% Strongest and Weakest Indicators

Rank	20% Strongest Indicators	Std. Score	Envmt.	Rank	20% Weakest Indicators	Std. Score	Envmt.
1	GRDP of primary industry	1.993	MS	81	Population per medical worker	–0.388	QLID
2	Fiscal balance	1.651	GIS	82	Investment promotion and management	–0.391	MS
3	Population growth	1.558	QLID	83	Lack of corruption	–0.530	GIS
4	Vibrancy of competition and collaboration	1.303	GIS	84	Inflation	–0.547	MS
5	Primary industry productivity	1.050	FBMC	85	Unemployment rate	–0.558	FBMC
6	Handphone ownership	0.956	QLID	86	Minimum wage per month	–0.602	FBMC
7	Secondary industry productivity	0.884	FBMC	87	Labour relations	–0.631	FBMC
8	Affordability and accessibility of goods	0.674	QLID	88	Tertiary industry productivity	–0.741	FBMC
9	Gini ratio	0.669	QLID	89	Government progress and expectation	–0.764	GIS
10	Life expectancy at birth	0.665	QLID	90	Non-performing loans per total bank loans	–0.813	FBMC
11	Student–teacher ratio (senior high)	0.646	QLID	91	Government inclusiveness and accountability	–0.816	GIS
12	Adult illiteracy rate	0.627	QLID	92	Population per health facility	–0.817	QLID
13	Overall labour productivity	0.626	FBMC	93	Households with state electricity services	–0.863	QLID
14	Student–teacher ratio (junior high)	0.581	QLID	94	Regulatory governance	–0.920	GIS
15	Human development index	0.569	QLID	95	Labour force participation rate	–1.055	FBMC
16	Quality of technological infrastructure	0.567	QLID	96	Environmental quality index	–1.115	QLID
17	Mean years of schooling	0.484	QLID	97	Firms' innovation	–1.241	FBMC
18	Internet access in handphone	0.483	QLID	98	Rule of Law	–1.299	GIS
19	GRDP per capita	0.450	MS	99	Households with pipe water services	–1.629	QLID
20	Export	0.414	MS	100	GRDP growth	–1.835	MS

Note: MS: Macroeconomic Stability; GIS: Government and Institutional Setting; FBMC: Financial, Businesses and Manpower Conditions; QLID: Quality of Life and Infrastructure Development.

2017 ACI Competitiveness Index: *What-if* Simulation Ranking and Scores

Overall Competitiveness

	Before	After
Rank	**16**	**11**
Score	–0.093	0.368

Macroeconomic Stability	Before	After	Government and Institutional Setting	Before	After
Rank	**11**	**8**	Rank	**22**	**14**
Score	0.019	0.207	Score	–0.174	0.332

Financial, Businesses and Manpower Conditions	Before	After	Quality of Life and Infrastructure Development	Before	After
Rank	**22**	**11**	Rank	**13**	**10**
Score	–0.364	0.142	Score	0.213	0.538

Note: Ranking and scores after simulation are derived by improving the province's top-20% weakest indicators.

Riau Islands

Sumatra Region

2017 ACI Competitiveness Index: Ranking and Scores

2017 Overall Competitiveness Index

10th

out of 33 provinces

std. score: 0.399

Macroeconomic Stability	Government and Institutional Setting
6th	**32nd**
std. score: 0.596	std. score: –1.722

Financial, Businesses and Manpower Conditions	Quality of Life and Infrastructure Development
4th	**7th**
std. score: 1.463	std. score: 0.986

ACI Competitiveness Index Ranking: 2013–2017

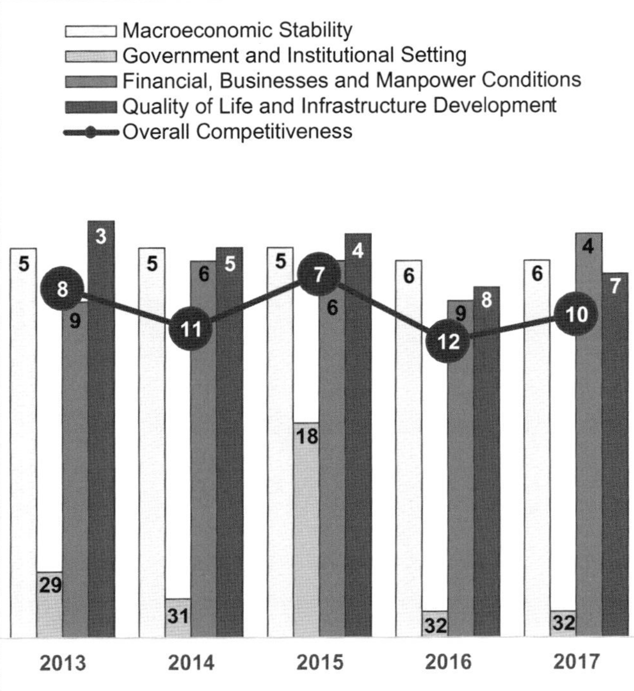

2017 ACI Competitiveness Index: Ranking and Scores by Sub-Environments

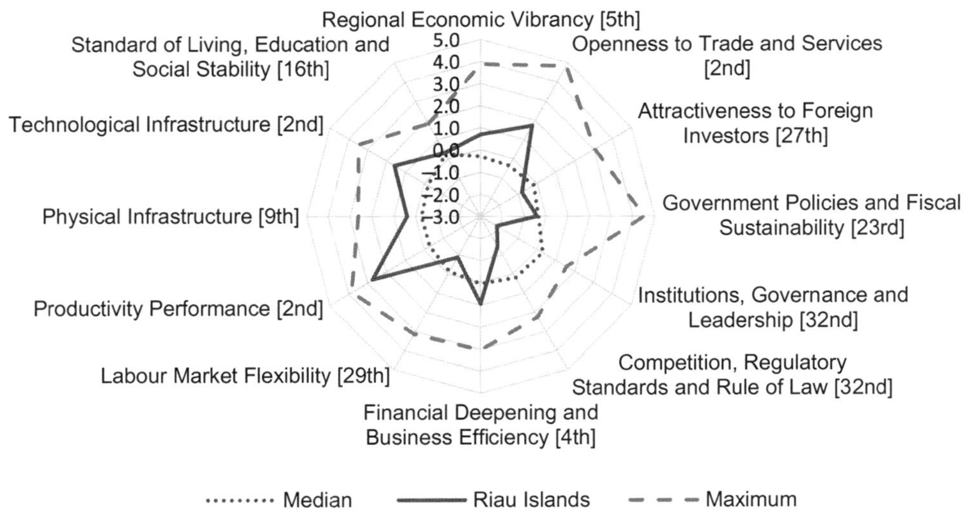

Note: [ ] shows rank out of 33 provinces.

Riau Islands

Sumatra Region

2017 ACI Competitiveness Index: Top-20% Strongest and Weakest Indicators

Rank	20% Strongest Indicators	Std. Score	Envmt.	Rank	20% Weakest Indicators	Std. Score	Envmt.
1	Openness to trade	4.136	MS	81	Government inclusiveness and accountability	–0.708	GIS
2	Primary industry productivity	3.919	FBMC	82	Fiscal balance	–0.730	GIS
3	Overall labour productivity	2.556	FBMC	83	Employment in primary industry	–0.734	FBMC
4	Overall labour productivity, non-oil and gas	2.552	FBMC	84	Households with pipe water services	–0.768	QLID
5	Population growth	2.484	QLID	85	Length of paved roads	–0.788	QLID
6	GRDP per capita	2.381	MS	86	Labour relations	–0.835	FBMC
7	GRDP per capita, non-oil and gas	2.374	MS	87	Crime rate	–0.856	GIS
8	Internet access at home	2.366	QLID	88	Quality of education	–0.868	QLID
9	Secondary industry productivity	2.164	FBMC	89	Quality of healthcare	–0.872	QLID
10	Urban population	2.102	QLID	90	Investment promotion and management	–1.066	MS
11	Internet access at office	1.911	QLID	91	Ease of acquiring property	–1.140	QLID
12	Internet access in handphone	1.835	QLID	92	Government progress and expectation	–1.415	GIS
13	Laptop computer ownership	1.796	QLID	93	Lack of corruption	–1.445	GIS
14	Net school enrolment rate (senior high)	1.689	QLID	94	Rule of law	–1.464	GIS
15	Ease of dealing with banks	1.631	FBMC	95	Security	–1.632	GIS
16	Export	1.595	MS	96	Coordination of local governments	–1.639	GIS
17	Mean years of schooling	1.524	QLID	97	Provincial governing capacity	–1.789	GIS
18	Desktop computer ownership	1.416	QLID	98	Population per health facility	–1.802	QLID
19	Firms' performance	1.352	FBMC	99	Regulatory governance	–2.093	GIS
20	Human development index	1.306	QLID	100	Government efficiency	–2.675	GIS

Note: MS: Macroeconomic Stability; GIS: Government and Institutional Setting; FBMC: Financial, Businesses and Manpower Conditions; QLID: Quality of Life and Infrastructure Development.

2017 ACI Competitiveness Index: *What-if* Simulation Ranking and Scores

Overall Competitiveness

	Before		After
Rank	**10**	→	**4**
Score	0.399	→	1.042

Macroeconomic Stability

	Before		After
Rank	**6**	→	**5**
Score	0.596	→	0.757

Government and Institutional Setting

	Before		After
Rank	**32**	→	**20**
Score	–1.722	→	–0.198

Financial, Businesses and Manpower Conditions

	Before		After
Rank	**4**	→	**4**
Score	1.463	→	1.581

Quality of Life and Infrastructure Development

	Before		After
Rank	**7**	→	**2**
Score	0.986	→	1.374

Note: Ranking and scores after simulation are derived by improving the province's top-20% weakest indicators.

South Kalimantan

Kalimantan Region

2017 ACI Competitiveness Index: Ranking and Scores

2017 Overall Competitiveness Index

11th

out of 33 provinces

std. score: 0.318

Macroeconomic Stability	Government and Institutional Setting
12th	**14th**
std. score: –0.012	std. score: 0.298

Financial, Businesses and Manpower Conditions	Quality of Life and Infrastructure Development
19th	**5th**
std. score: –0.310	std. score: 1.076

ACI Competitiveness Index Ranking: 2013–2017

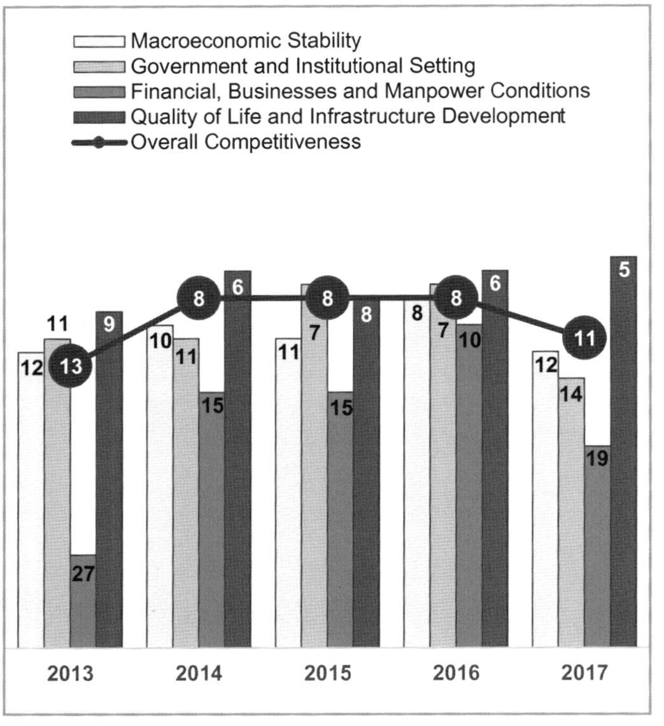

2017 ACI Competitiveness Index: Ranking and Scores by Sub-Environments

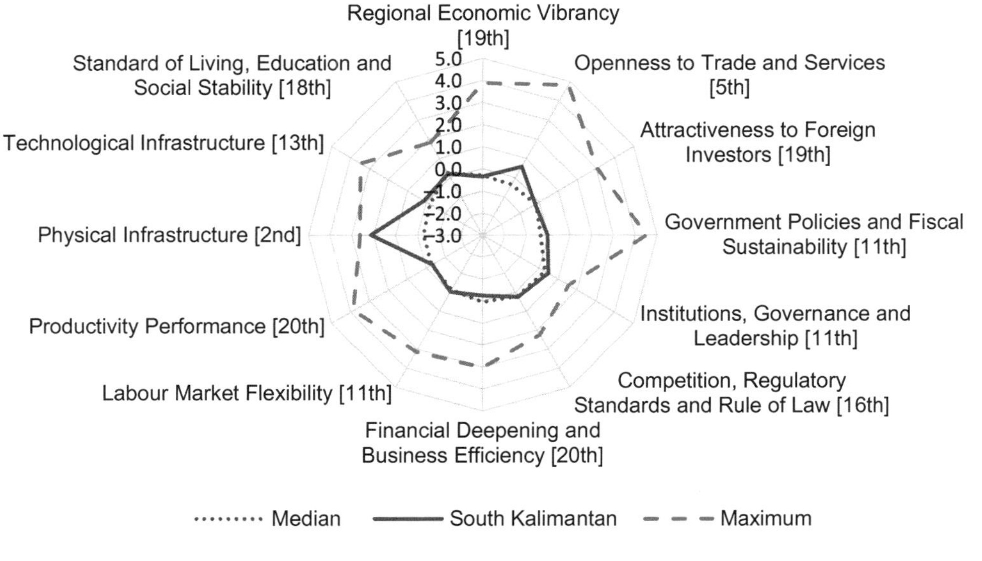

Note: [ ] shows rank out of 33 provinces.

2017 ACI Competitiveness Index: Top-20% Strongest and Weakest Indicators

Rank	20% Strongest Indicators	Std. Score	Envmt.	Rank	20% Weakest Indicators	Std. Score	Envmt.
1	Cargo at inter-island seaport	5.144	QLID	81	Population	–0.350	QLID
2	Households with pipe water services	3.125	QLID	82	Minimum wage per month	–0.353	FBMC
3	Cargo at international seaport	2.346	QLID	83	Quality of physical infrastructure	–0.360	QLID
4	Openness to trade	1.967	MS	84	Employment in secondary industry	–0.362	FBMC
5	Student–teacher ratio (primary)	1.929	QLID	85	Firms' innovation	–0.363	FBMC
6	Tax revenue/Government revenue	0.909	GIS	86	Gross Regional Domestic Product (GRDP)	–0.366	MS
7	Student–teacher ratio (senior high)	0.819	QLID	87	Foreign direct investment, last three year average	–0.369	MS
8	Student–teacher ratio (junior high)	0.799	QLID	88	GRDP growth	–0.390	MS
9	Unemployment rate	0.773	FBMC	89	Firms' human resource capacity	–0.417	FBMC
10	Inflation	0.770	MS	90	GRDP of secondary industry	–0.426	MS
11	Vibrancy of competition and collaboration	0.711	GIS	91	Gross domestic fixed capital formation	–0.440	MS
12	Ease of acquiring property	0.650	QLID	92	Fiscal balance	–0.441	GIS
13	Households with state electricity services	0.585	QLID	93	Mean years of schooling	–0.464	QLID
14	Labour force participation rate	0.579	FBMC	94	GRDP, non-oil and gas	–0.501	MS
15	Export, non-oil and gas	0.573	MS	95	Life expectancy at birth	–0.603	QLID
16	Adult illiteracy rate	0.522	QLID	96	GRDP per capita, non-oil and gas	–0.637	MS
17	Handphone ownership	0.502	QLID	97	Environmental quality index	–0.656	QLID
18	Lack of corruption	0.497	GIS	98	Overall labour productivity, non-oil and gas	–0.680	FBMC
19	Labour relations	0.484	FBMC	99	Net school enrolment rate (senior high)	–0.872	QLID
20	Population per number of bank branches/offices	0.483	FBMC	100	Net school enrolment rate (junior high)	–1.599	QLID

Note: MS: Macroeconomic Stability; GIS: Government and Institutional Setting; FBMC: Financial, Businesses and Manpower Conditions; QLID: Quality of Life and Infrastructure Development.

2017 ACI Competitiveness Index: *What-if* Simulation Ranking and Scores

Overall Competitiveness	Before	After
Rank	**11**	**9**
Score	0.318	0.532

Macroeconomic Stability	Before	After
Rank	**12**	**8**
Score	–0.012	0.194

Government and Institutional Setting	Before	After
Rank	**14**	**14**
Score	0.298	0.339

Financial, Businesses and Manpower Conditions	Before	After
Rank	**19**	**18**
Score	–0.310	–0.103

Quality of Life and Infrastructure Development	Before	After
Rank	**5**	**3**
Score	1.076	1.331

Note: Ranking and scores after simulation are derived by improving the province's top-20% weakest indicators.

South Sulawesi

Sulawesi Region

2017 ACI Competitiveness Index: Ranking and Scores

2017 Overall Competitiveness Index

8th

out of 33 provinces

std. score: 0.557

Macroeconomic Stability	Government and Institutional Setting
8th	**3rd**
std. score: 0.128	std. score: 1.066

Financial, Businesses and Manpower Conditions	Quality of Life and Infrastructure Development
13th	**9th**
std. score: 0.014	std. score: 0.637

ACI Competitiveness Index Ranking: 2013–2017

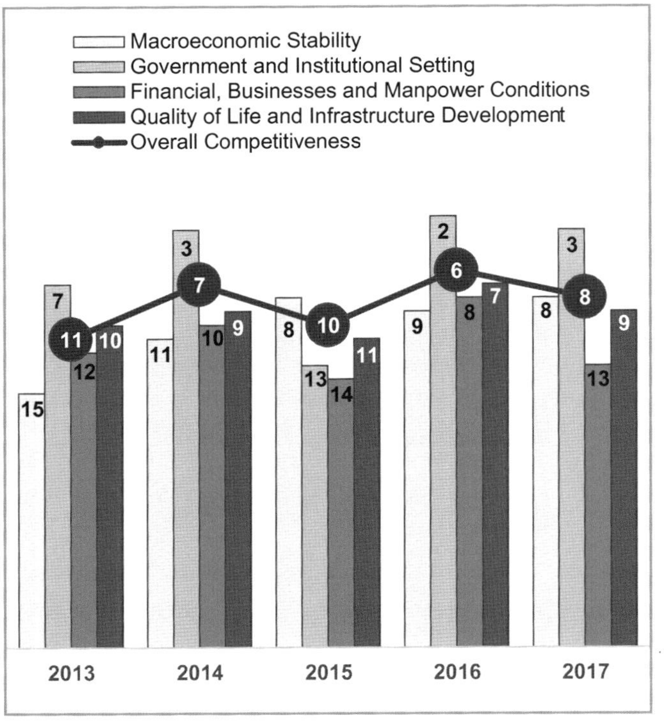

2017 ACI Competitiveness Index: Ranking and Scores by Sub-Environments

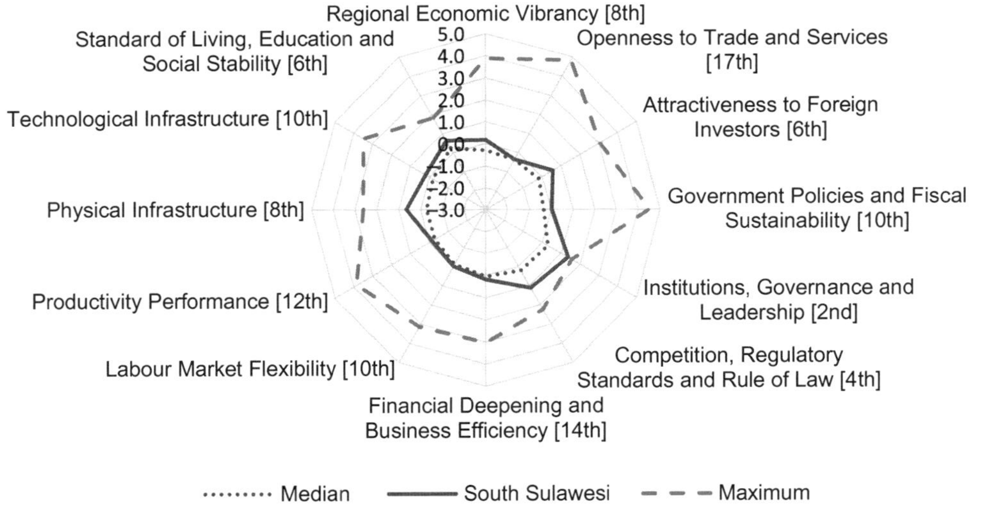

Note: [ ] shows rank out of 33 provinces.

South Sulawesi
Sulawesi Region

2017 ACI Competitiveness Index: Top-20% Strongest and Weakest Indicators

Rank	20% Strongest Indicators	Std. Score	Envmt.	Rank	20% Weakest Indicators	Std. Score	Envmt.
1	Government inclusiveness and accountability	2.150	GIS	81	Import, non-oil and gas	–0.254	MS
2	Investment promotion and management	1.708	MS	82	Net school enrolment rate (junior high)	–0.262	QLID
3	Affordability and accessibility of goods	1.630	QLID	83	Urban population	–0.267	QLID
4	Labour relations	1.591	FBMC	84	Passengers of international air traffic	–0.281	QLID
5	Provincial governing capacity	1.529	GIS	85	Foreign direct investment, last three year average	–0.283	MS
6	Quality of physical infrastructure	1.512	QLID	86	Export, non-oil and gas	–0.289	MS
7	Government progress and expectation	1.469	GIS	87	Import	–0.308	MS
8	Quality of healthcare	1.449	QLID	88	Government efficiency	–0.318	GIS
9	GRDP growth	1.419	MS	89	Cargo at international seaport	–0.321	QLID
10	Rule of law	1.277	GIS	90	Export	–0.352	MS
11	Quality of education	1.238	QLID	91	Mean years of schooling	–0.407	QLID
12	Lack of corruption	1.236	GIS	92	Fiscal balance	–0.423	GIS
13	Length of paved roads	1.111	QLID	93	Desktop computer ownership	–0.484	QLID
14	Student–teacher ratio (senior high)	1.073	QLID	94	Openness to trade	–0.511	MS
15	Ease of acquiring property	1.062	QLID	95	Non-performing loans per total bank loans	–0.534	FBMC
16	Regulatory governance	0.958	GIS	96	Adult illiteracy rate	–0.777	QLID
17	Firms' human resource capacity	0.912	FBMC	97	Minimum wage per month	–0.912	FBMC
18	Coordination of local governments	0.899	GIS	98	Labour force participation rate	–0.913	FBMC
19	Student–teacher ratio (junior high)	0.840	QLID	99	Population growth	–1.133	QLID
20	Quality of technological infrastructure	0.830	QLID	100	Gini ratio	–1.239	QLID

Note: MS: Macroeconomic Stability; GIS: Government and Institutional Setting; FBMC: Financial, Businesses and Manpower Conditions; QLID: Quality of Life and Infrastructure Development.

2017 ACI Competitiveness Index: *What-if* Simulation Ranking and Scores

Overall Competitiveness	Before		After
Rank	**8**	➡	**6**
Score	0.557		0.786

Macroeconomic Stability	Before		After	Government and Institutional Setting	Before		After
Rank	**8**	➡	**8**	Rank	**3**	➡	**3**
Score	0.128		0.307	Score	1.066		1.126

Financial, Businesses and Manpower Conditions	Before		After	Quality of Life and Infrastructure Development	Before		After
Rank	**13**	➡	**11**	Rank	**9**	➡	**8**
Score	0.014		0.215	Score	0.637		0.959

Note: Ranking and scores after simulation are derived by improving the province's top-20% weakest indicators.

South Sumatra

Sumatra Region

2017 ACI Competitiveness Index: Ranking and Scores

2017 Overall Competitiveness Index

24th

out of 33 provinces

std. score: –0.460

Macroeconomic Stability	Government and Institutional Setting
10th	**27th**
std. score: 0.067	std. score: –0.849

Financial, Businesses and Manpower Conditions	Quality of Life and Infrastructure Development
20th	**26th**
std. score: –0.315	std. score: –0.427

ACI Competitiveness Index Ranking: 2013–2017

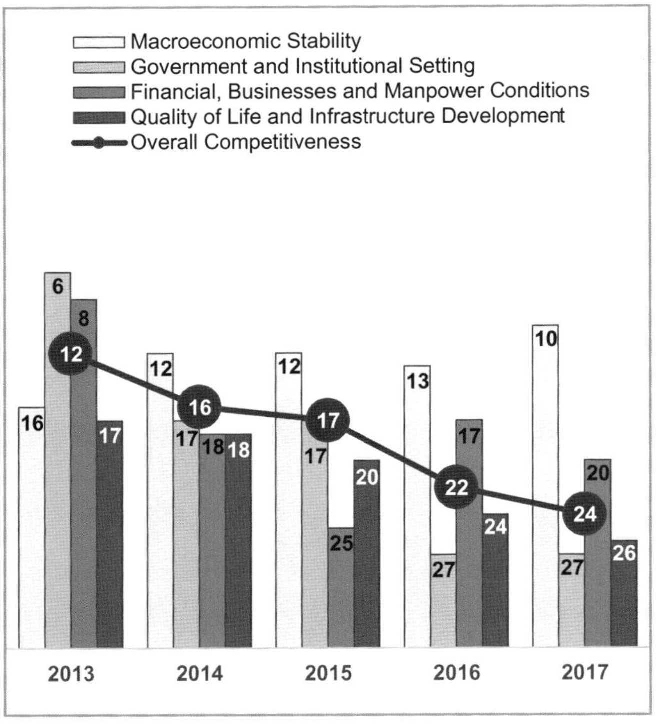

2017 ACI Competitiveness Index: Ranking and Scores by Sub-Environments

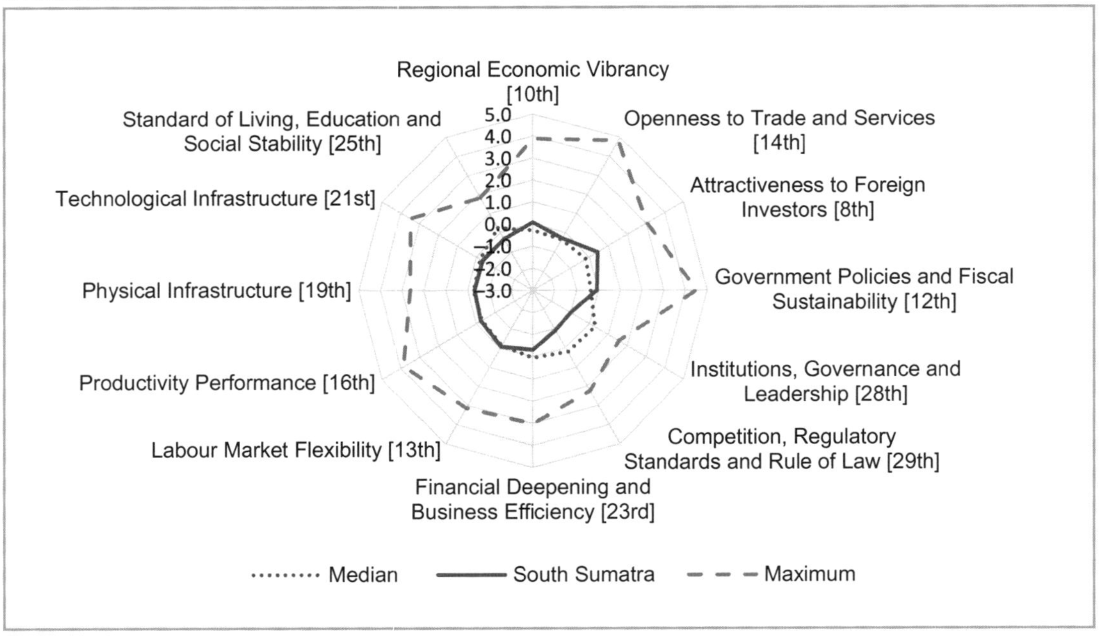

Note: [ ] shows rank out of 33 provinces.

South Sumatra

Sumatra Region

2017 ACI Competitiveness Index: Top-20% Strongest and Weakest Indicators

Rank	20% Strongest Indicators	Std. Score	Envmt.	Rank	20% Weakest Indicators	Std. Score	Envmt.
1	Inflation	1.297	MS	81	Urban population	–0.457	QLID
2	Investment promotion and management	1.013	MS	82	Firms' innovation	–0.461	FBMC
3	Households with pipe water services	0.814	QLID	83	Internet access at office	–0.470	QLID
4	GRDP of primary industry	0.687	MS	84	Population growth	–0.474	QLID
5	Adult illiteracy rate	0.512	QLID	85	GRDP growth	–0.491	MS
6	Employment in primary industry	0.510	FBMC	86	Tertiary industry productivity	–0.496	FBMC
7	Firms' performance	0.443	FBMC	87	Population per number of bank branches/offices	–0.508	FBMC
8	Labour force participation rate	0.425	FBMC	88	Laptop computer ownership	–0.611	QLID
9	Handphone ownership	0.359	QLID	89	Population per medical worker	–0.665	QLID
10	Secondary industry productivity	0.314	FBMC	90	Non-performing loans per total bank loans	–0.678	FBMC
11	Fatalities due to natural disaster	0.269	QLID	91	Gini ratio	–0.694	QLID
12	Quality of healthcare	0.251	QLID	92	Quality of technological infrastructure	–0.766	QLID
13	Unemployment rate	0.212	FBMC	93	Population per health facility	–0.792	QLID
14	Ease of dealing with banks	0.199	FBMC	94	Government efficiency	–0.831	GIS
15	Length of paved roads	0.141	QLID	95	Regulatory governance	–0.916	GIS
16	Net school enrolment rate (junior high)	0.139	QLID	96	Security	–0.943	GIS
17	Gross domestic fixed capital formation	0.137	MS	97	Minimum wage per month	–0.990	FBMC
18	Households with state electricity services	0.125	QLID	98	Rule of Law	–1.059	GIS
19	Student–teacher ratio (junior high)	0.115	QLID	99	Lack of corruption	–1.151	GIS
20	Tax revenue/Government revenue	0.098	GIS	100	Crime rate	–1.567	GIS

Note: MS: Macroeconomic Stability; GIS: Government and Institutional Setting; FBMC: Financial, Businesses and Manpower Conditions; QLID: Quality of Life and Infrastructure Development.

2017 ACI Competitiveness Index: *What-if* Simulation Ranking and Scores

Overall Competitiveness	Before	After
Rank	24	16
Score	–0.460	–0.082

Macroeconomic Stability	Before	After
Rank	10	9
Score	0.067	0.094

Government and Institutional Setting	Before	After
Rank	27	23
Score	–0.849	–0.205

Financial, Businesses and Manpower Conditions	Before	After
Rank	20	14
Score	–0.315	–0.027

Quality of Life and Infrastructure Development	Before	After
Rank	26	22
Score	–0.427	–0.133

Note: Ranking and scores after simulation are derived by improving the province's top-20% weakest indicators.

Southeast Sulawesi

Sulawesi Region

2017 ACI Competitiveness Index: Ranking and Scores

2017 Overall Competitiveness Index

23rd

out of 33 provinces

std. score: –0.412

Macroeconomic Stability	Government and Institutional Setting
20th	**19th**
std. score: –0.358	std. score: –0.062

Financial, Businesses and Manpower Conditions	Quality of Life and Infrastructure Development
24th	**25th**
std. score: –0.706	std. score: –0.240

ACI Competitiveness Index Ranking: 2013–2017

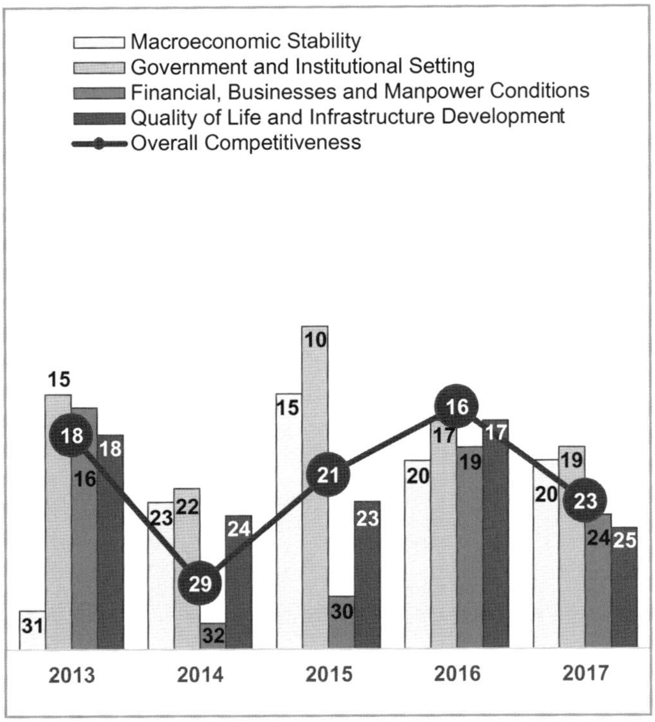

2017 ACI Competitiveness Index: Ranking and Scores by Sub-Environments

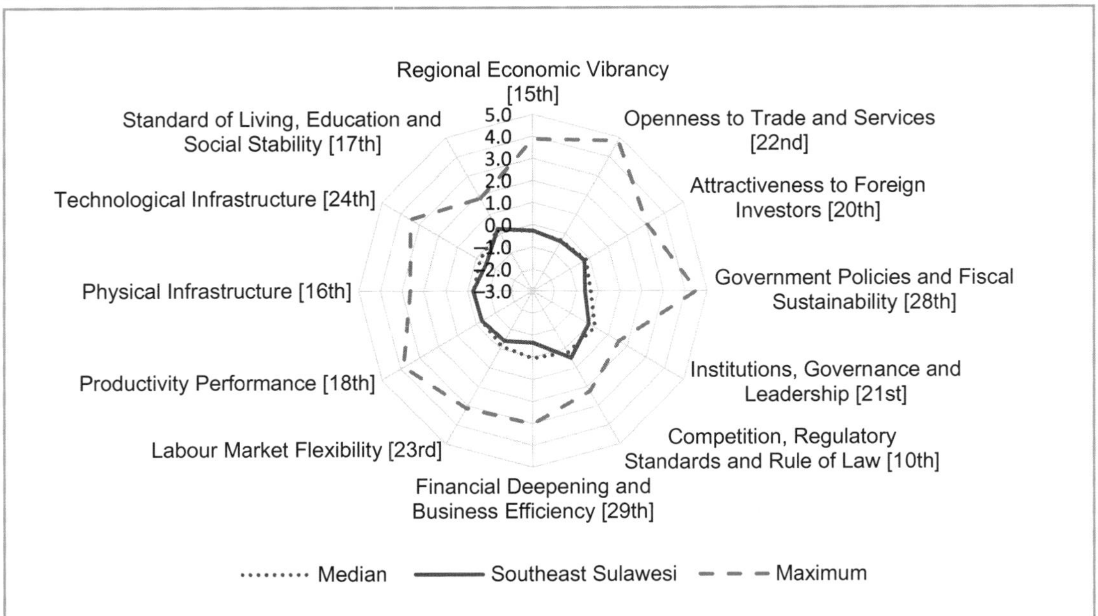

Note: [ ] shows rank out of 33 provinces.

Southeast Sulawesi
Sulawesi Region

2017 ACI Competitiveness Index: Top-20% Strongest and Weakest Indicators

Rank	20% Strongest Indicators	Std. Score	Envmt.	Rank	20% Weakest Indicators	Std. Score	Envmt.
1	Provincial governing capacity	2.224	GIS	81	Number of bank branches/offices	–0.529	FBMC
2	Ease of acquiring property	1.580	QLID	82	Foreign direct investment, last three year average	–0.567	MS
3	Inflation	1.112	MS	83	Government revenue	–0.569	GIS
4	Student–teacher ratio (senior high)	1.065	QLID	84	Length of paved roads	–0.580	QLID
5	Student–teacher ratio (junior high)	0.989	QLID	85	Government expenditure	–0.600	GIS
6	Regulatory governance	0.933	GIS	86	Crime rate	–0.628	GIS
7	Firms' equipment capacity	0.895	FBMC	87	Internet access at school	–0.768	QLID
8	Population growth	0.774	QLID	88	Urban population	–0.782	QLID
9	Environmental quality index	0.710	QLID	89	Tax revenue/Government revenue	–0.822	GIS
10	Population per health facility	0.692	QLID	90	Labour force participation rate	–0.838	FBMC
11	GRDP growth	0.558	MS	91	Government efficiency	–0.838	GIS
12	Life expectancy at birth	0.520	QLID	92	Lack of corruption	–0.894	GIS
13	Unemployment rate	0.469	FBMC	93	Gini ratio	–0.966	QLID
14	Rule of Law	0.468	GIS	94	Quality of technological infrastructure	–1.040	QLID
15	Firms' innovation	0.446	FBMC	95	Quality of physical infrastructure	–1.103	QLID
16	Population per medical worker	0.424	QLID	96	Quality of education	–1.206	QLID
17	Households with pipe water services	0.419	QLID	97	Firms' human resource capacity	–1.338	FBMC
18	Investment promotion and management	0.406	MS	98	Ease of dealing with banks	–1.429	FBMC
19	Fatalities due to natural disaster	0.363	QLID	99	Quality of healthcare	–1.529	QLID
20	Non-performing loans	0.355	FBMC	100	Firms' performance	–1.653	FBMC

Note: MS: Macroeconomic Stability; GIS: Government and Institutional Setting; FBMC: Financial, Businesses and Manpower Conditions; QLID: Quality of Life and Infrastructure Development.

2017 ACI Competitiveness Index: *What-if* Simulation Ranking and Scores

Overall Competitiveness	Before	After
Rank	**23**	**15**
Score	–0.412	0.027

Macroeconomic Stability	Before	After
Rank	**20**	**16**
Score	–0.358	–0.270

Government and Institutional Setting	Before	After
Rank	**19**	**14**
Score	–0.062	0.296

Financial, Businesses and Manpower Conditions	Before	After
Rank	**24**	**19**
Score	–0.706	–0.194

Quality of Life and Infrastructure Development	Before	After
Rank	**25**	**13**
Score	–0.240	0.256

Note: Ranking and scores after simulation are derived by improving the province's top-20% weakest indicators.

West Java
Java Region

2017 ACI Competitiveness Index: Ranking and Scores

2017 Overall Competitiveness Index

5th

out of 33 provinces

std. score: 0.946

Macroeconomic Stability	Government and Institutional Setting
3rd	7th
std. score: 1.370	std. score: 0.730

Financial, Businesses and Manpower Conditions	Quality of Life and Infrastructure Development
5th	14th
std. score: 0.887	std. score: 0.146

ACI Competitiveness Index Ranking: 2013–2017

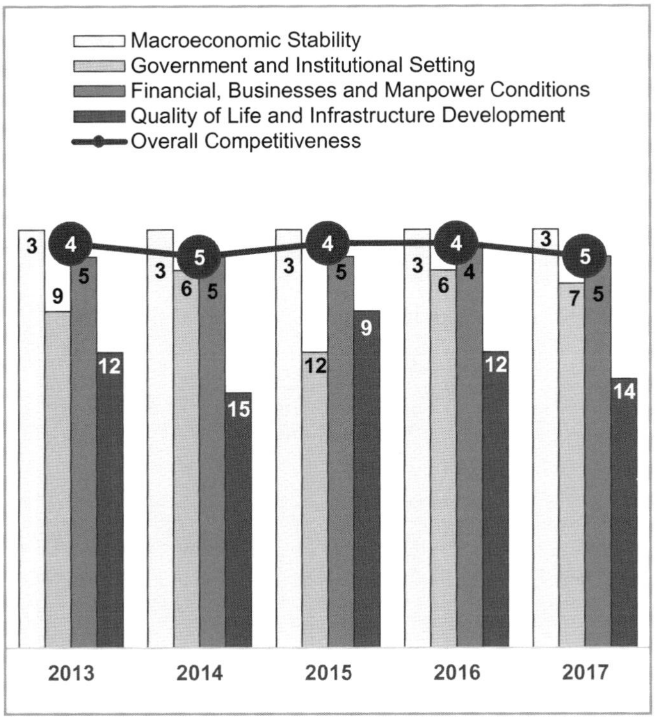

2017 ACI Competitiveness Index: Ranking and Scores by Sub-Environments

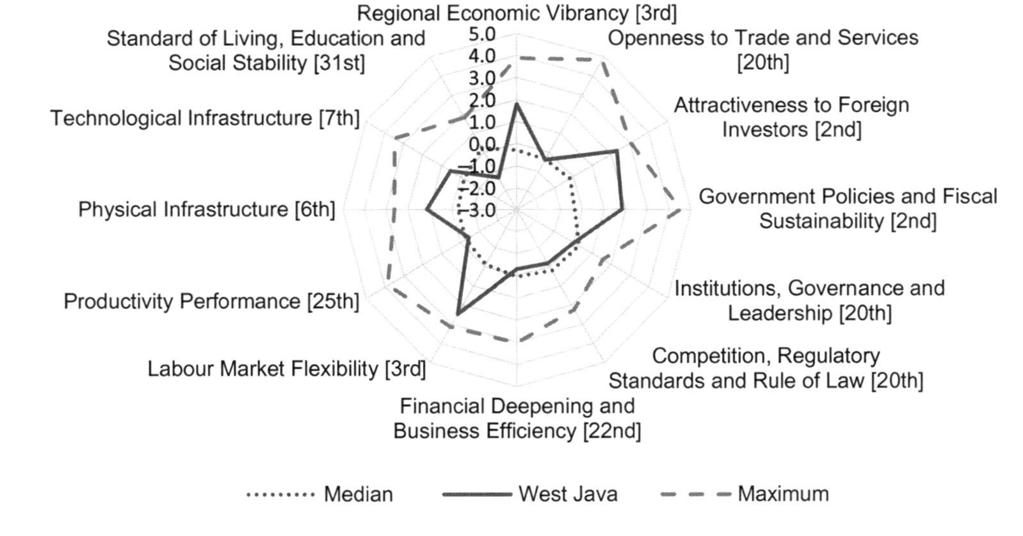

Note: [ ] shows rank out of 33 provinces.

West Java
Java Region

2017 ACI Competitiveness Index: Top-20% Strongest and Weakest Indicators

Rank	20% Strongest Indicators	Std. Score	Envmt.	Rank	20% Weakest Indicators	Std. Score	Envmt.
1	Foreign direct investment, last three year average	4.040	MS	81	Firms' application of IT	–0.626	FBMC
2	Employment in tertiary industry	3.669	FBMC	82	Net school enrolment rate (senior high)	–0.634	QLID
3	Employment in secondary industry	3.646	FBMC	83	Tertiary industry productivity	–0.638	FBMC
4	Population	3.617	QLID	84	Ease of acquiring property	–0.658	QLID
5	GRDP of secondary industry	3.370	MS	85	Openness to trade	–0.672	MS
6	Labour force	3.305	FBMC	86	Firms' equipment capacity	–0.673	FBMC
7	Employment	3.211	FBMC	87	Households with pipe water services	–0.691	QLID
8	Gross Regional Domestic Product (GRDP)	2.368	MS	88	Firms' performance	–0.947	FBMC
9	GRDP, non-oil and gas	2.362	MS	89	Gini ratio	–0.966	QLID
10	Number of bank branches/offices	2.237	FBMC	90	Non-performing loans	–1.003	FBMC
11	Tax revenue	1.933	GIS	91	Lack of corruption	–1.236	GIS
12	Government expenditure	1.849	GIS	92	Ease of dealing with banks	–1.261	FBMC
13	Employment in primary industry	1.782	FBMC	93	Unemployment rate	–1.472	FBMC
14	Government revenue	1.775	GIS	94	Student–teacher ratio (primary)	–1.629	QLID
15	Length of paved roads	1.707	QLID	95	Student–teacher ratio (junior high)	–1.694	QLID
16	Gross domestic fixed capital formation	1.698	MS	96	Student–teacher ratio (senior high)	–1.754	QLID
17	Tax revenue/Government revenue	1.603	GIS	97	Environmental quality index	–1.818	QLID
18	Minimum wage per month	1.572	FBMC	98	Population per number of bank branches/offices	–1.919	FBMC
19	Crime rate	1.551	GIS	99	Fatalities due to natural disaster	–2.485	QLID
20	Firms' innovation	1.530	FBMC	100	Population per medical worker	–3.000	QLID

Note: MS: Macroeconomic Stability; GIS: Government and Institutional Setting;
FBMC: Financial, Businesses and Manpower Conditions; QLID: Quality of Life and Infrastructure Development.

2017 ACI Competitiveness Index: *What-if* Simulation Ranking and Scores

Overall Competitiveness

	Before	After
Rank	**5**	**3**
Score	0.946	1.440

Macroeconomic Stability

	Before	After
Rank	**3**	**3**
Score	1.370	1.420

Government and Institutional Setting

	Before	After
Rank	**7**	**6**
Score	0.730	0.818

Financial, Businesses and Manpower Conditions

	Before	After
Rank	**5**	**3**
Score	0.887	1.592

Quality of Life and Infrastructure Development

	Before	After
Rank	**14**	**6**
Score	0.146	0.962

Note: Ranking and scores after simulation are derived by improving the province's top-20% weakest indicators.

West Kalimantan

Kalimantan Region

2017 ACI Competitiveness Index: Ranking and Scores

2017 Overall Competitiveness Index

21st

out of 33 provinces

std. score: –0.308

Macroeconomic Stability	Government and Institutional Setting
22nd	**16th**
std. score: –0.431	std. score: 0.178

Financial, Businesses and Manpower Conditions	Quality of Life and Infrastructure Development
9th	**29th**
std. score: 0.332	std. score: –1.100

ACI Competitiveness Index Ranking: 2013–2017

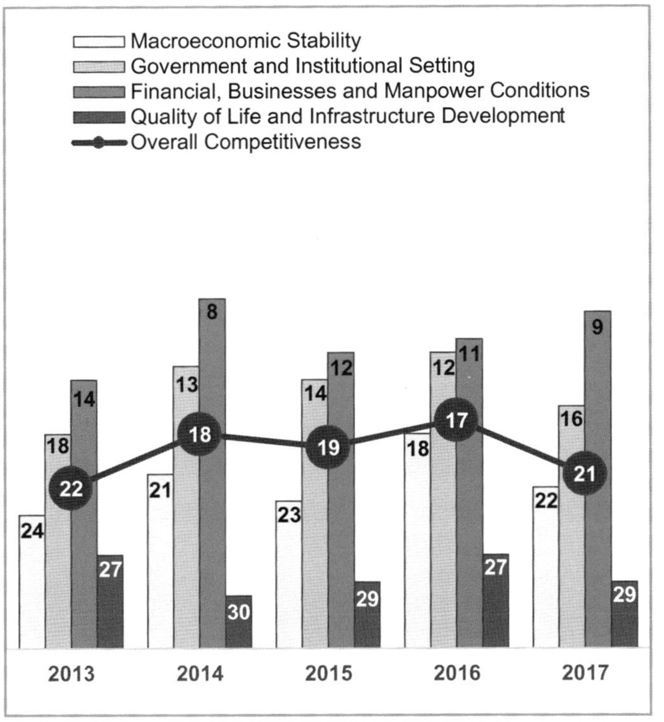

2017 ACI Competitiveness Index: Ranking and Scores by Sub-Environments

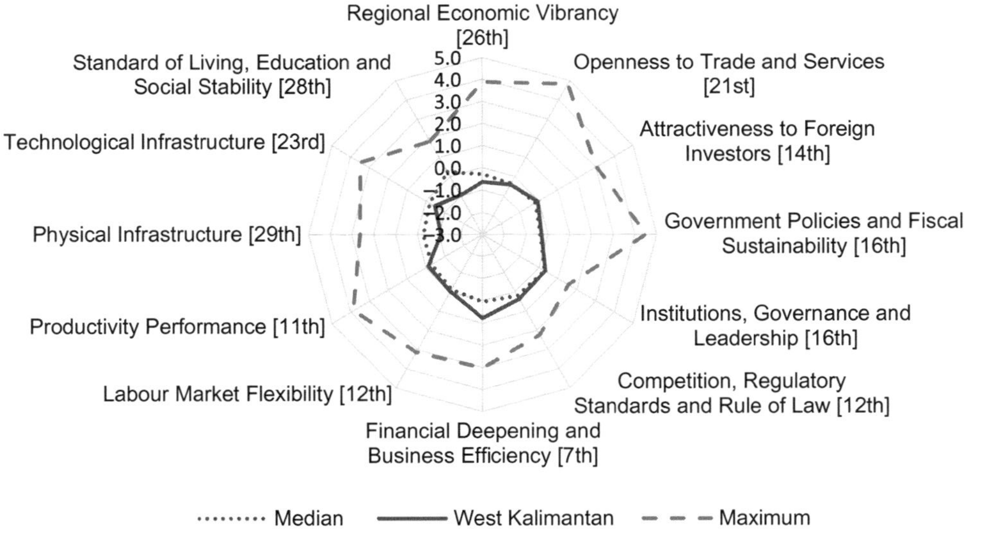

Note: [ ] shows rank out of 33 provinces.

West Kalimantan

Kalimantan Region

2017 ACI Competitiveness Index: Top-20% Strongest and Weakest Indicators

Rank	20% Strongest Indicators	Std. Score	Envmt.	Rank	20% Weakest Indicators	Std. Score	Envmt.
1	Non-performing loans per total bank loans	1.345	FBMC	81	Internet access at school	–0.485	QLID
2	Ease of dealing with banks	1.042	FBMC	82	Labour relations	–0.493	FBMC
3	Firms' performance	0.755	FBMC	83	Openness to trade	–0.506	MS
4	Student–teacher ratio (senior high)	0.719	QLID	84	Internet access at office	–0.509	QLID
5	Government efficiency	0.661	GIS	85	Primary industry productivity	–0.518	FBMC
6	Unemployment rate	0.658	FBMC	86	Student–teacher ratio (junior high)	–0.524	QLID
7	Firms' equipment capacity	0.655	FBMC	87	Laptop computer ownership	–0.552	QLID
8	Firms' application of IT	0.548	FBMC	88	Adult illiteracy rate	–0.582	QLID
9	Government progress and expectation	0.539	GIS	89	Desktop computer ownership	–0.591	QLID
10	Regulatory governance	0.526	GIS	90	Urban population	–0.667	QLID
11	Labour force participation rate	0.500	FBMC	91	Human development index	–0.738	QLID
12	Coordination of local governments	0.483	GIS	92	Households with state electricity services	–0.747	QLID
13	Firms' innovation	0.465	FBMC	93	Internet access in handphone	–0.756	QLID
14	Tertiary industry productivity	0.425	FBMC	94	Fatalities due to natural disaster	–0.764	QLID
15	Minimum wage per month	0.392	FBMC	95	Mean years of schooling	–1.195	QLID
16	Provincial governing capacity	0.384	GIS	96	Households with pipe water services	–1.215	QLID
17	Environmental quality index	0.352	QLID	97	Quality of physical infrastructure	–1.311	QLID
18	Non-performing loans	0.336	FBMC	98	Net school enrolment rate (junior high)	–1.599	QLID
19	Vibrancy of competition and collaboration	0.295	GIS	99	Inflation	–1.620	MS
20	Life expectancy at birth	0.280	QLID	100	Net school enrolment rate (senior high)	–1.695	QLID

Note: MS: Macroeconomic Stability; GIS: Government and Institutional Setting; FBMC: Financial, Businesses and Manpower Conditions; QLID: Quality of Life and Infrastructure Development.

2017 ACI Competitiveness Index: *What-if* Simulation Ranking and Scores

Overall Competitiveness	Before	After
Rank	21	15
Score	–0.308	0.019

Macroeconomic Stability	Before	After
Rank	22	17
Score	–0.431	–0.304

Government and Institutional Setting	Before	After
Rank	16	16
Score	0.178	0.178

Financial, Businesses and Manpower Conditions	Before	After
Rank	9	9
Score	0.332	0.432

Quality of Life and Infrastructure Development	Before	After
Rank	29	22
Score	–1.100	–0.243

Note: Ranking and scores after simulation are derived by improving the province's top-20% weakest indicators.

West Nusa Tenggara

Bali-Nusa Tenggara Region

2017 ACI Competitiveness Index: Ranking and Scores

2017 Overall Competitiveness Index

26th

out of 33 provinces

std. score: –0.582

Macroeconomic Stability	Government and Institutional Setting
23rd	**26th**
std. score: –0.443	std. score: –0.676

Financial, Businesses and Manpower Conditions	Quality of Life and Infrastructure Development
25th	**20th**
std. score: –0.720	std. score: –0.089

ACI Competitiveness Index Ranking: 2013–2017

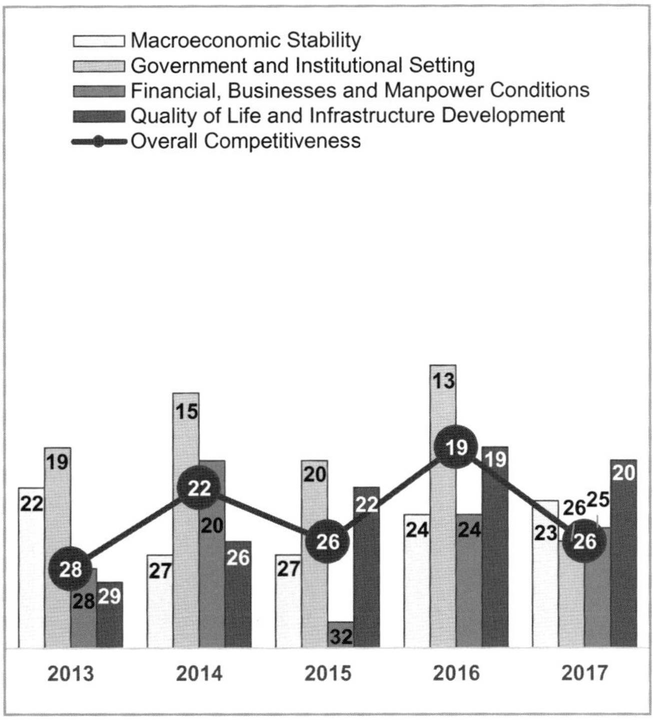

2017 ACI Competitiveness Index: Ranking and Scores by Sub-Environments

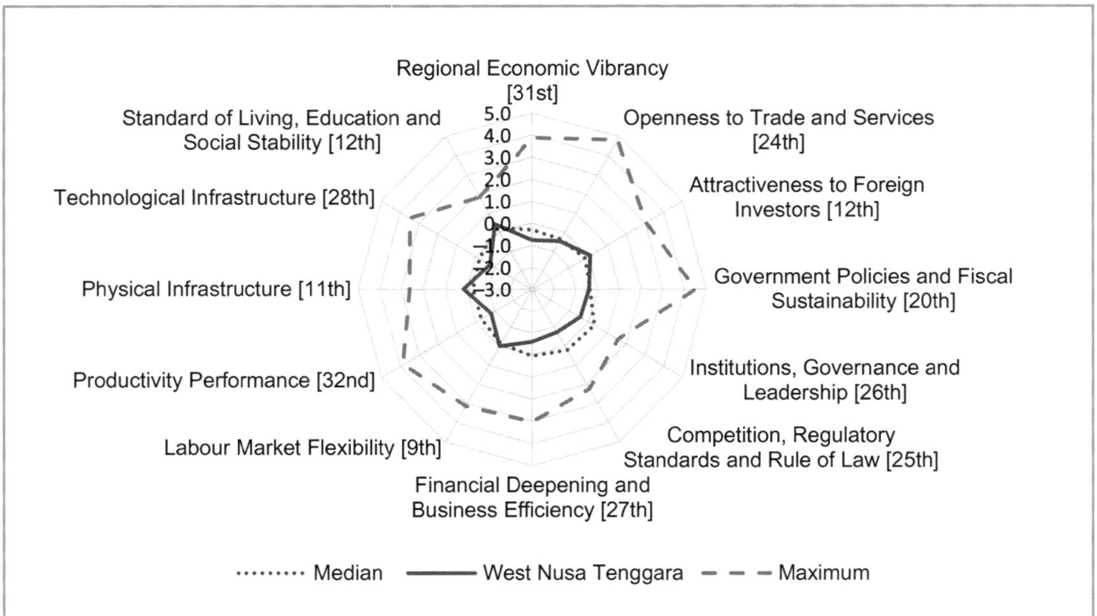

Note: [ ] shows rank out of 33 provinces.

West Nusa Tenggara
Bali-Nusa Tenggara Region

2017 ACI Competitiveness Index: Top-20% Strongest and Weakest Indicators

Rank	20% Strongest Indicators	Std. Score	Envmt.	Rank	20% Weakest Indicators	Std. Score	Envmt.
1	Student–teacher ratio (senior high)	1.872	QLID	81	Security	–0.679	GIS
2	Student–teacher ratio (junior high)	1.838	QLID	82	Inflation	–0.681	MS
3	Quality of physical infrastructure	1.201	QLID	83	Government efficiency	–0.709	GIS
4	Net school enrolment rate (junior high)	1.098	QLID	84	Overall labour productivity	–0.715	FBMC
5	Minimum wage per month	0.920	FBMC	85	Telephone ownership	–0.716	QLID
6	Investment promotion and management	0.919	MS	86	Handphone ownership	–0.725	QLID
7	Student–teacher ratio (primary)	0.865	QLID	87	GRDP per capita	–0.734	MS
8	Ease of acquiring property	0.836	QLID	88	Population per medical worker	–0.743	QLID
9	Labour relations	0.828	FBMC	89	Internet access at office	–0.813	QLID
10	Households with state electricity services	0.823	QLID	90	Rule of law	–0.860	GIS
11	Population per health facility	0.788	QLID	91	Human development index	–0.878	QLID
12	Quality of technological infrastructure	0.775	QLID	92	Internet access in handphone	–0.936	QLID
13	Households with pipe water services	0.634	QLID	93	Desktop computer ownership	–0.976	QLID
14	Net school enrolment rate (senior high)	0.628	QLID	94	Secondary industry productivity	–0.983	FBMC
15	Firms' innovation	0.612	FBMC	95	Population per number of bank branches/offices	–0.987	FBMC
16	Non-performing loans per total bank loans	0.611	FBMC	96	Laptop computer ownership	–1.074	QLID
17	Net school enrolment rate (primary)	0.518	QLID	97	Mean years of schooling	–1.081	QLID
18	Fatalities due to natural disaster	0.457	QLID	98	Firms' performance	–1.188	FBMC
19	Environmental quality index	0.450	QLID	99	Adult illiteracy rate	–1.582	QLID
20	Affordability and accessibility of goods	0.432	QLID	100	Life expectancy at birth	–1.590	QLID

Note: MS: Macroeconomic Stability; GIS: Government and Institutional Setting; FBMC: Financial, Businesses and Manpower Conditions; QLID: Quality of Life and Infrastructure Development.

2017 ACI Competitiveness Index: *What-if* Simulation Ranking and Scores

Overall Competitiveness

	Before	After
Rank	**26**	**17**
Score	–0.582	–0.193

Macroeconomic Stability	Before	After	Government and Institutional Setting	Before	After
Rank	**23**	**21**	Rank	**26**	**24**
Score	–0.443	–0.367	Score	–0.676	–0.438

Financial, Businesses and Manpower Conditions	Before	After	Quality of Life and Infrastructure Development	Before	After
Rank	**25**	**21**	Rank	**20**	**10**
Score	–0.720	–0.333	Score	–0.089	0.501

Note: Ranking and scores after simulation are derived by improving the province's top-20% weakest indicators.

West Papua
Maluku-Papua Region

2017 ACI Competitiveness Index: Ranking and Scores

2017 Overall Competitiveness Index

33rd

out of 33 provinces

std. score: –1.891

Macroeconomic Stability	Government and Institutional Setting
27th	**33rd**
std. score: –0.628	std. score: –2.788

Financial, Businesses and Manpower Conditions	Quality of Life and Infrastructure Development
33rd	**31st**
std. score: –1.295	std. score: –1.550

ACI Competitiveness Index Ranking: 2013–2017

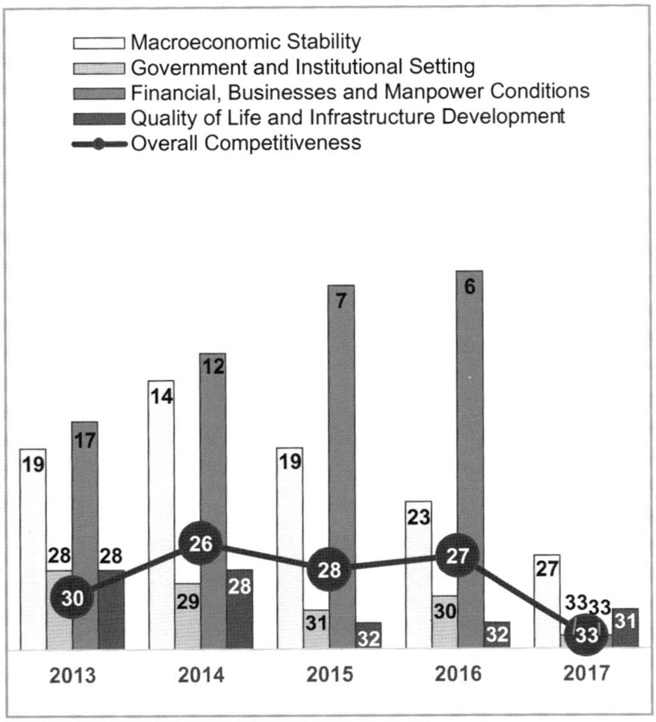

2017 ACI Competitiveness Index: Ranking and Scores by Sub-Environments

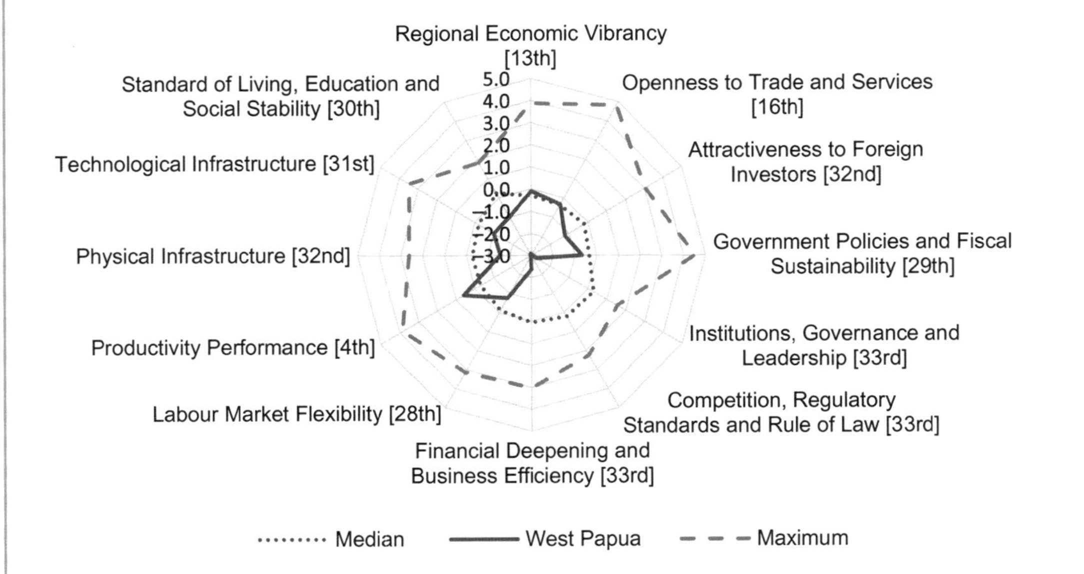

Note: [ ] shows rank out of 33 provinces.

West Papua

Maluku-Papua Region

2017 ACI Competitiveness Index: Top-20% Strongest and Weakest Indicators

Rank	20% Strongest Indicators	Std. Score	Envmt.	Rank	20% Weakest Indicators	Std. Score	Envmt.
1	Inflation	2.415	MS	81	Gini ratio	–1.784	QLID
2	Secondary industry productivity	2.385	FBMC	82	Tax revenue/Government revenue	–1.830	GIS
3	Environmental quality index	1.864	QLID	83	Ease of acquiring property	–1.875	QLID
4	Population growth	1.576	QLID	84	Quality of healthcare	–1.967	QLID
5	Population per number of bank branches/offices	1.191	FBMC	85	Regulatory governance	–1.986	GIS
6	Mean years of schooling	1.044	QLID	86	Quality of education	–2.184	QLID
7	Population per medical worker	1.020	QLID	87	Government progress and expectation	–2.239	GIS
8	Student–teacher ratio (primary)	0.966	QLID	88	Government inclusiveness and accountability	–2.377	GIS
9	Population per health facility	0.810	QLID	89	Ease of dealing with banks	–2.413	FBMC
10	Laptop computer ownership	0.613	QLID	90	Provincial governing capacity	–2.467	GIS
11	Registered motor vehicles per kilometre of paved road	0.553	QLID	91	Affordability and accessibility of goods	–2.482	QLID
12	Fatalities due to natural disaster	0.520	QLID	92	Quality of physical infrastructure	–2.595	QLID
13	Overall labour productivity	0.478	FBMC	93	Coordination of local governments	–2.709	GIS
14	GRDP per capita	0.462	MS	94	Non-performing loans per total bank loans	–2.848	FBMC
15	Non-performing loans	0.349	FBMC	95	Firms' innovation	–2.876	FBMC
16	Net school enrolment rate (senior high)	0.325	QLID	96	Security	–2.914	GIS
17	Adult illiteracy rate	0.252	QLID	97	Vibrancy of competition and collaboration	–2.982	GIS
18	Unemployment rate	0.186	FBMC	98	Rule of law	–3.061	GIS
19	Primary industry productivity	0.072	FBMC	99	Quality of technological infrastructure	–3.095	QLID
20	Desktop computer ownership	0.013	QLID	100	Firms' human resource capacity	–3.243	FBMC

Note: MS: Macroeconomic Stability; GIS: Government and Institutional Setting; FBMC: Financial, Businesses and Manpower Conditions; QLID: Quality of Life and Infrastructure Development.

2017 ACI Competitiveness Index: *What-if* Simulation Ranking and Scores

Overall Competitiveness	Before		After
Rank	33	→	25
Score	–1.891		–0.592

Macroeconomic Stability	Before		After
Rank	27	→	27
Score	–0.628		–0.628

Government and Institutional Setting	Before		After
Rank	33	→	23
Score	–2.788		–0.436

Financial, Businesses and Manpower Conditions	Before		After
Rank	33	→	19
Score	–1.295		–0.284

Quality of Life and Infrastructure Development	Before		After
Rank	31	→	28
Score	–1.550		–0.581

Note: Ranking and scores after simulation are derived by improving the province's top-20% weakest indicators.

West Sulawesi

Sulawesi Region

2017 ACI Competitiveness Index: Ranking and Scores

2017 Overall Competitiveness Index

28th

out of 33 provinces

std. score: –0.597

Macroeconomic Stability	Government and Institutional Setting
15th	9th
std. score: –0.263	std. score: 0.649
Financial, Businesses and Manpower Conditions	**Quality of Life and Infrastructure Development**
31st	30th
std. score: –1.209	std. score: –1.155

ACI Competitiveness Index Ranking: 2013–2017

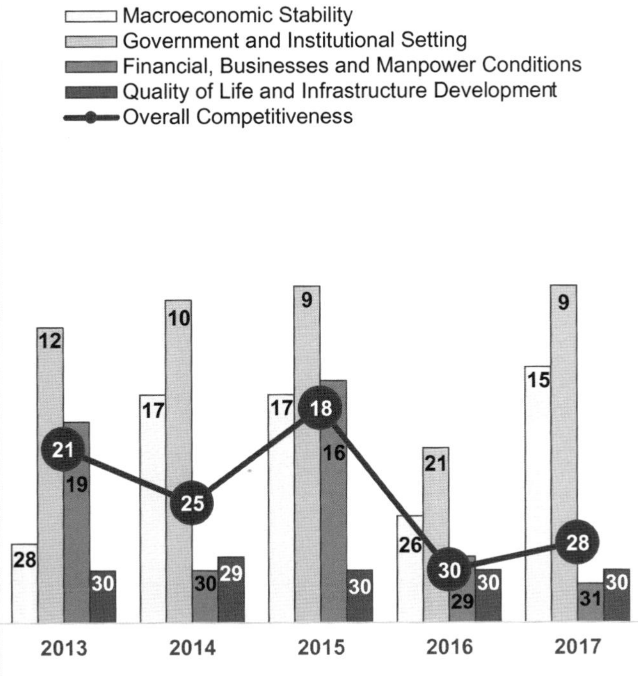

2017 ACI Competitiveness Index: Ranking and Scores by Sub-Environments

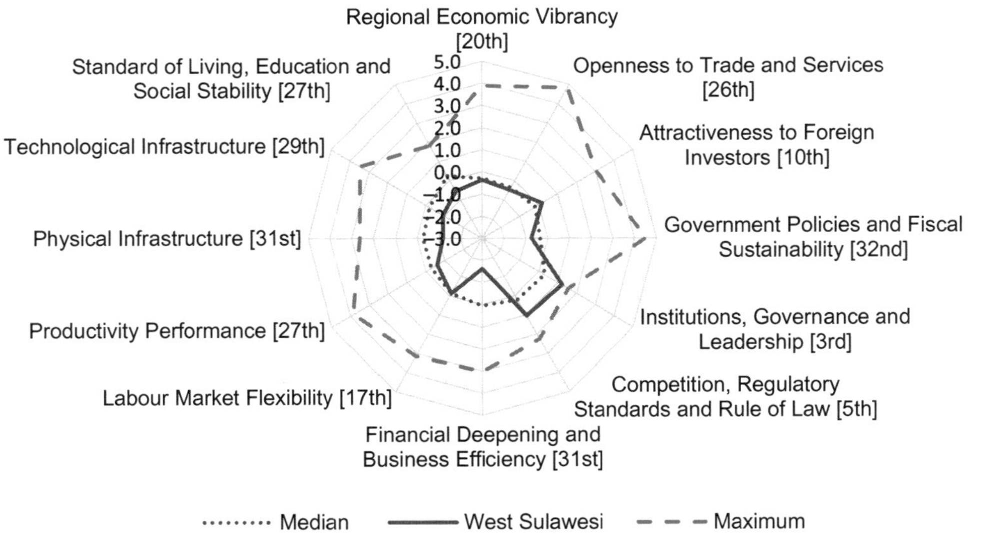

Note: [ ] shows rank out of 33 provinces.

West Sulawesi

Sulawesi Region

2017 ACI Competitiveness Index: Top-20% Strongest and Weakest Indicators

Rank	20% Strongest Indicators	Std. Score	Envmt.	Rank	20% Weakest Indicators	Std. Score	Envmt.
1	GRDP growth	2.319	MS	81	Firms' application of IT	–0.816	FBMC
2	Government efficiency	1.792	GIS	82	Non-performing loans per total bank loans	–0.843	FBMC
3	Regulatory governance	1.762	GIS	83	Internet access at home	–0.878	QLID
4	Unemployment rate	1.604	FBMC	84	Ease of acquiring property	–0.879	QLID
5	Investment promotion and management	1.543	MS	85	Internet access at office	–0.907	QLID
6	Coordination of local governments	1.426	GIS	86	Ease of dealing with banks	–0.917	FBMC
7	Provincial governing capacity	1.355	GIS	87	Internet access at school	–0.918	QLID
8	Rule of Law	1.294	GIS	88	Length of paved roads	–0.951	QLID
9	Government progress and expectation	1.128	GIS	89	Net school enrolment rate (junior high)	–0.981	QLID
10	Quality of physical infrastructure	0.756	QLID	90	Desktop computer ownership	–1.001	QLID
11	Population per health facility	0.741	QLID	91	Internet access in handphone	–1.119	QLID
12	Environmental quality index	0.724	QLID	92	Tax revenue/Government revenue	–1.122	GIS
13	Gini ratio	0.669	QLID	93	Mean years of schooling	–1.161	QLID
14	Student–teacher ratio (junior high)	0.571	QLID	94	Firms' equipment capacity	–1.191	FBMC
15	Government inclusiveness and accountability	0.532	GIS	95	Urban population	–1.196	QLID
16	Fatalities due to natural disaster	0.520	QLID	96	Firms' human resource capacity	–1.292	FBMC
17	Security	0.512	GIS	97	Human development index	–1.375	QLID
18	Population per medical worker	0.468	QLID	98	Firms' performance	–1.569	FBMC
19	Non-performing loans	0.380	FBMC	99	Households with state electricity services	–1.689	QLID
20	Registered motor vehicles per kilometre of paved road	0.356	QLID	100	Life expectancy at birth	–1.919	QLID

Note: MS: Macroeconomic Stability; GIS: Government and Institutional Setting; FBMC: Financial, Businesses and Manpower Conditions; QLID: Quality of Life and Infrastructure Development.

2017 ACI Competitiveness Index: *What-if* Simulation Ranking and Scores

Overall Competitiveness	Before		After
Rank	**28**	➡	**16**
Score	–0.597		–0.104

Macroeconomic Stability	Before		After
Rank	**15**	➡	**15**
Score	–0.263		–0.263

Government and Institutional Setting	Before		After
Rank	**9**	➡	**6**
Score	0.649		0.751

Financial, Businesses and Manpower Conditions	Before		After
Rank	**31**	➡	**24**
Score	–1.209		–0.623

Quality of Life and Infrastructure Development	Before		After
Rank	**30**	➡	**22**
Score	–1.155		–0.210

Note: Ranking and scores after simulation are derived by improving the province's top-20% weakest indicators.

West Sumatra

Sumatra Region

2017 ACI Competitiveness Index: Ranking and Scores

2017 Overall Competitiveness Index

15th

out of 33 provinces

std. score: –0.018

Macroeconomic Stability	Government and Institutional Setting
26th	**18th**
std. score: –0.547	std. score: 0.129
Financial, Businesses and Manpower Conditions	**Quality of Life and Infrastructure Development**
16th	**10th**
std. score: –0.068	std. score: 0.427

ACI Competitiveness Index Ranking: 2013–2017

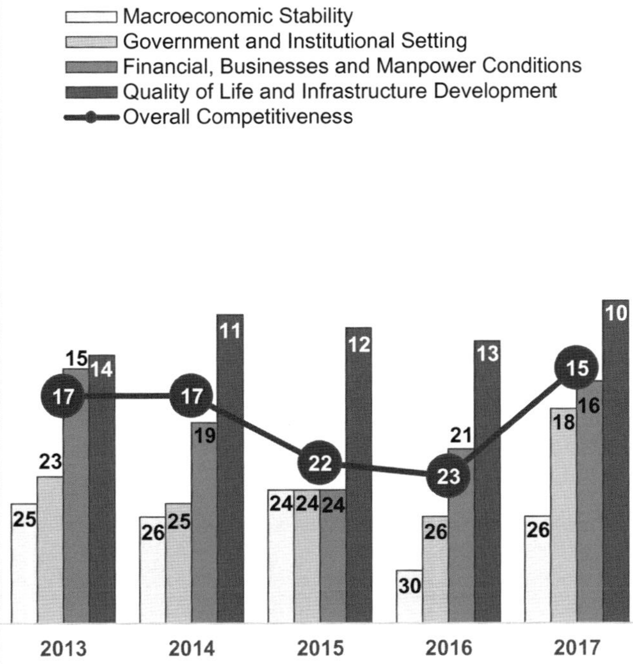

2017 ACI Competitiveness Index: Ranking and Scores by Sub-Environments

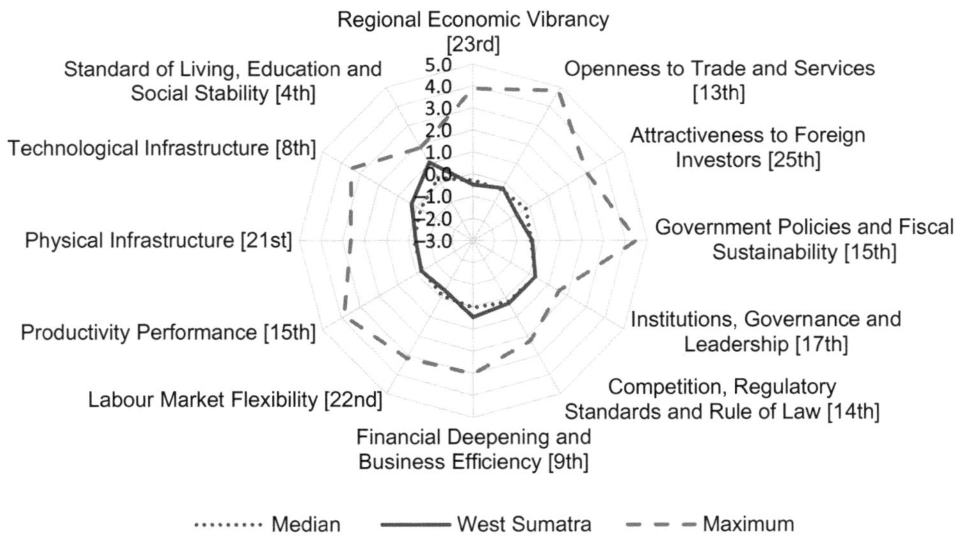

Note: [ ] shows rank out of 33 provinces.

West Sumatra

Sumatra Region

2017 ACI Competitiveness Index: Top-20% Strongest and Weakest Indicators

Rank	20% Strongest Indicators	Std. Score	Envmt.	Rank	20% Weakest Indicators	Std. Score	Envmt.
1	Student–teacher ratio (senior high)	1.286	QLID	81	Export	–0.307	MS
2	Gini ratio	1.214	QLID	82	Cargo at inter-island seaport	–0.314	QLID
3	Lack of corruption	1.193	GIS	83	Employment in secondary industry	–0.322	FBMC
4	Student–teacher ratio (junior high)	1.070	QLID	84	Gross Regional Domestic Product (GRDP)	–0.331	MS
5	Net school enrolment rate (senior high)	1.026	QLID	85	Gross domestic fixed capital formation	–0.335	MS
6	Coordination of local governments	1.016	GIS	86	Tax revenue	–0.346	GIS
7	Firms' equipment capacity	1.003	FBMC	87	Affordability and accessibility of goods	–0.363	QLID
8	Security	1.001	GIS	88	Government revenue	–0.414	GIS
9	Firms' innovation	0.851	FBMC	89	GRDP of secondary industry	–0.423	MS
10	Quality of healthcare	0.719	QLID	90	Government expenditure	–0.432	GIS
11	Quality of technological infrastructure	0.693	QLID	91	Secondary industry productivity	–0.457	FBMC
12	Population per health facility	0.670	QLID	92	Domestic direct investment, last three year average	–0.506	MS
13	Firms' human resource capacity	0.655	FBMC	93	Investment promotion and management	–0.530	MS
14	Net school enrolment rate (primary)	0.605	QLID	94	Unemployment rate	–0.532	FBMC
15	Internet access at school	0.597	QLID	95	Labour force participation rate	–0.535	FBMC
16	Firms' performance	0.583	FBMC	96	Foreign direct investment, last three year average	–0.568	MS
17	Adult illiteracy rate	0.569	QLID	97	Population growth	–0.759	QLID
18	Rule of law	0.527	GIS	98	Ease of acquiring property	–0.924	QLID
19	Households with state electricity services	0.509	QLID	99	Inflation	–1.367	MS
20	Regulatory governance	0.450	GIS	100	Crime rate	–1.681	GIS

Note: MS: Macroeconomic Stability; GIS: Government and Institutional Setting; FBMC: Financial, Businesses and Manpower Conditions; QLID: Quality of Life and Infrastructure Development.

2017 ACI Competitiveness Index: *What-if* Simulation Ranking and Scores

Overall Competitiveness	Before	After
Rank	**15**	**12**
Score	–0.018	0.281

Macroeconomic Stability	Before	After
Rank	**26**	**13**
Score	–0.547	–0.141

Government and Institutional Setting	Before	After
Rank	**18**	**14**
Score	0.129	0.362

Financial, Businesses and Manpower Conditions	Before	After
Rank	**16**	**11**
Score	–0.068	0.101

Quality of Life and Infrastructure Development	Before	After
Rank	**10**	**10**
Score	0.427	0.609

Note: Ranking and scores after simulation are derived by improving the province's top-20% weakest indicators.

Asia Competitiveness Institute - World Scientific Series

(Continued from page vi)

2016 Growth Slowdown Analysis by Income Thresholds and Annual Update of Competitiveness Analysis for 34 Greater China Economies
by Tan Khee Giap, Wang Peng & Xie Teleixi (Lee Kuan Yew School of Public Policy, NUS, Singapore)

Inaugural 2016 Ease of Doing Business Index on Attractiveness to Investors, Business Friendliness and Competitive Policies (EDB Index ABC) for 21 Sub-National Economies of India
by Tan Khee Giap, Sasidaran Gopalan, Jigyasa Sharma & Tan Kong Yam (Lee Kuan Yew School of Public Policy, NUS, Singapore)

2016 Annual Competitiveness and Growth Slowdown Analysis for Sub-National Economies of India
by Tan Khee Giap, Sasidaran Gopalan, Anuja Tandon & Tan Kong Yam (Lee Kuan Yew School of Public Policy, NUS, Singapore)

2016 Growth Slowdown Analysis, Ease of Doing Business Index, and Annual Competitiveness Studies of Indonesia's Sub-National Economies
by Tan Khee Giap, Mulya Amri, Nursyahida Ahmad & Tan Kong Yam (Lee Kuan Yew School of Public Policy, NUS, Singapore)

2016 Annual Competitiveness Analysis and Development Strategies for Indonesian Provinces
by Tan Khee Giap, Mulya Amri & Nursyahida Ahmad (Lee Kuan Yew School of Public Policy, NUS, Singapore)

2015

2015 Annual Competitiveness Analysis, Agricultural Productivity and Development Vision for ASEAN-10
by Tan Khee Giap, Nguyen Le Phuong Anh, Sasidaran Gopalan & Luu Nguyen Trieu Duong (Lee Kuan Yew School of Public Policy, NUS, Singapore)

2015 Estimation of Agricultural Productivity and Annual Update of Competitiveness Analysis for Greater China: Optimising Agricultural Productivity and Promoting Innovation Driven Growth
by Tan Khee Giap, Yuan Randong & Xie Teleixi (Lee Kuan Yew School of Public Policy, NUS, Singapore)

2015 Agricultural Total Factor Productivity and Competitiveness Analysis for States and Federal Territories and Five Regions of India: Annual Competitiveness Update and Evidence on the Agricultural Development Models for Selected Indian States
by Tan Khee Giap, Sasidaran Gopalan & Anuja Tandon (Lee Kuan Yew School of Public Policy, NUS, Singapore)

2015 Agricultural Productivity, Decentralisation, and Competitiveness Analysis for Provinces and Regions of Indonesia
by Tan Khee Giap, Nurina Merdikawati, Mulya Amri & Tan Kong Yam (Lee Kuan Yew School of Public Policy, NUS, Singapore)

2015 Annual Competitiveness Analysis and Development Strategies for Indonesian Provinces
by Tan Khee Giap, Mulya Amri, Nurina Merdikawati & Nursyahida Ahmad (Lee Kuan Yew School of Public Policy, NUS, Singapore)

2014

2014 Annual Competitiveness Ranking and Simulation Study for ASEAN-10 and Development Strategies to Enhance Asia Economic Connectivity
by Tan Khee Giap, Sangiita Yoong Wei Cher, Sasidaran Gopalan & Nguyen Le Phuong Anh (Lee Kuan Yew School of Public Policy, NUS, Singapore)

2014 Annual Provincial and Regional Competitiveness Analysis for Greater China Economies: Development Strategies under the New Normal
by Tan Khee Giap, Yuan Randong & Sangiita Yoong Wei Cher (Lee Kuan Yew School of Public Policy, NUS, Singapore)

2014 Regional Competitiveness Analysis and a Master Plan on Regional Development Strategies for India: Annual Competitiveness Update and Evidence on Economic Development Model for Selected States of India
by Tan Khee Giap, Linda Low, Kartik Rao & Tan Kong Yam (Lee Kuan Yew School of Public Policy, NUS, Singapore)

2014 Provincial and Inaugural Regional Competitiveness Analysis: Safeguarding Indonesia's Growth Momentum
by Tan Khee Giap, Nurina Merdikawati, Mulya Amri & Tan Kong Yam (Lee Kuan Yew School of Public Policy, NUS, Singapore)

2014 Annual Competitiveness Analysis and Development Strategies for Indonesian Provinces
by Tan Khee Giap, Nurina Merdikawati, Mulya Amri & Blake Harley Berger (Lee Kuan Yew School of Public Policy, NUS, Singapore)

2013

Annual Analysis of Competitiveness, Simulation Studies and Development Perspective for 34 Greater China Economies: 2000–2010
by Tan Khee Giap, Yuan Randong, Sangiita Yoong Wei Cher & Yang Mu (Lee Kuan Yew School of Public Policy, NUS, Singapore)

Annual Analysis of Competitiveness, Simulation Studies and Development Perspective for 35 States and Federal Territories of India: 2000–2010
by Tan Khee Giap, Linda Low, Tan Kong Yam & Kartik Rao (Lee Kuan Yew School of Public Policy, NUS, Singapore)

Competitiveness Analysis and Development Strategies for 33 Indonesian Provinces
by Tan Khee Giap, Mulya Amri, Linda Low & Tan Kong Yam (Lee Kuan Yew School of Public Policy, NUS, Singapore)